Economics - deals with production, preservation and distribution of wealth.

ECONOMIC HISTORY

of the

UNITED STATES

By

HOWARD R. SMITH

PROFESSOR OF ECONOMICS
THE UNIVERSITY OF GEORGIA

THE RONALD PRESS COMPANY , NEW YORK

2

Library of Congress Catalog Card Number: 55-6092

PRINTED IN THE UNITED STATES OF AMERICA

To Gwen

PREFACE

Several closely related purposes have guided the preparation of this book. First, there is the objective, common to every economics course, of helping the student acquire a better understanding of economic relationships as such and a greater facility for thinking in economic terms. Second, an economic history course enables the student to see the economic basis for and the economic consequences of the more significant events in his country's history—events he has already become acquainted with, though generally not from the standpoint of the economic factors involved. In particular, economic history should help the student understand how the economic world with which he is familiar came into being. Third, economic history is an excellent background against which to view what might appropriately be called "the historical process." Economic institutions do not arise in a vacuum, nor is the form they take accidental. Rather they grow out of interactions between various interests and the pressures these interests are able to exert, and the particular form they take at any one time can only be explained in terms of the conflicts, compromises, and alliances which have shaped them.

While in one sense all these objectives are equally important, there is a basis for claiming first importance for the purpose suggested last. An understanding of economic history includes an awareness that economic evolution is no more static in the present than in the past—that the economic institutions we know are every day changing their nature and consequently their impact on our lives. In so far as formal education is designed to help the student cope with the future, the most useful by-product of a study of history is the understanding of "the historical process" which is thereby gained. Only such an understanding can assist him in anticipating institutional changes as they occur and in interpreting these changes from the standpoint of their effect on his own well-being.

Because this objective has been given a position of high importance, this presentation purposely differs from the orthodox one. The usual procedure which carries the student from 1816 to 1860 again and again, each time examining a different area of the economy, suffers from the disadvantage that relationships among developments in more than one of these areas are either lost from sight or are at best barely visible. Yet it is only when attention is focused on a situation as a whole that the motivation and hence the behavior of various interest groups become intelligible;

and only when analysis is carried to the level of the motivation behind behavior can the resulting economic activities and institutions be understood.

Stated differently, this book is based on the assumption that the events of history are most meaningful when related as they happened, least meaningful when isolated from the dynamic situations which created them. It is, in short, a chronological rather than a topical presentation. As such it has much to offer the undergraduate student. Through this approach he can see American economic evolution in terms of the problems that arose, the way these problems were resolved, and the reason certain problems were resolved only after a long delay. He can see this process of problem solving, furthermore, relative to the context of economic conflict within which it in fact took place—the parallelogram of economic forces which bent solutions in one direction rather than another. And finally, he can see certain of these economic forces grow as others decline, and see as a result solutions which were once ignored later seized upon and successfully utilized.

It requires little argument to demonstrate that an economic history text so oriented gains pedagogically in two major ways. First, there is the fact that events related in time are related in other ways as well, and more often than not these are the significant relationships from the historical standpoint. Almost more fundamental than this, however, is the gain in student interest, that elusive factor so all-important in the achievement of real learning. To watch economic forces as they develop, coalesce, or come into violent collision, to watch in action a few of the personalities that have contributed to America's economic development, to watch economic institutions now taken for granted evolve out of the most unpromising beginnings, can scarcely help being a more fascinating experience than the study of artificially separated segments of that development.

With these premises, it seemed clear that a chronologically oriented economic history text should be written as nearly like a story as possible—highlighting from decade to decade and from year to year those aspects of the developing "plot" which were most significant during each particular period. At the same time, however, certain supplementary approaches were utilized in order to make the book more flexible for use by students with widely differing backgrounds and interests. A brief comment about each of these at the outset may be helpful.

One such approach was a short list of important dates at the beginning of each chapter. The purpose here was not to summarize the chapter, for the events discussed in the text do not coincide closely with the dates singled out at the beginning. Even less was this done on the assumption that dates in and of themselves are important. Rather, the intention was to give the student of history a better basis for integrating the economic history he is learning with the political and social history he already knows, and the student of economics a better understanding of the political ramifications of economic processes.

A second supplementary tool consists of a number of brief footnotes elaborating in simple but theoretical terms economic concepts implicit in various aspects of the "story" as it develops. Here also it is hoped that diverse interests can be simultaneously served. Thus the student already in possession of a considerable background in economics can use these notations as "bridges" leading from the historical developments under review to the fundamental economic relationships which give them a deeper meaning, whereas for the student whose economic background is less extensive they will serve primarily to make the historical account itself more readily understandable.

A third tool is a list of questions at the end of each chapter. Two kinds of questions were included. There are a number of factual questions designed to help the student test his mastery of the text material. There are also questions of a more searching nature, designed for the student who would like to think his way beyond the text. Here the emphasis is upon some of the more remote "whys" of history, the possible consequences of alternatives which were rejected, and problems related to the "philosophy" of history and historical research.

One final comment may be appropriate. It is difficult to write an economic history textbook (particularly, perhaps, one of this type) without appearing to espouse a materialistic interpretation of history. For that reason it is worth emphasizing that this appearance adheres to the task the economic historian has undertaken; it is not necessarily an indication of his point of view. And if it is suggested that only an economic determinist would undertake to write a history primarily oriented to economic relationships, it is easy to shift a part of this responsibility to the larger community by replying that only a materialistically inclined society would support an educational program in which economic history as such has a vital place. Be these things as they may, however, it is a reasonably accurate statement of this author's frame of reference that history is unintelligible to the extent that economic factors are ignored.

H. R. S.

Athens, Georgia
January, 1955

CONTENTS

PART I

The Nation Born, to 1817

PART II

The Nation Divided, 1817-1860

PART III

The Nation Rebuilt, 1860-1896

PART IV

The Nation Mature, 1896-1929

PART V

The Nation in Crisis, 1929-1954

PART I

THE NATION BORN

(To 1817)

Chapter 1

THE OLD WORLD IN THE NEW

1100–1200	The Century of the Crusades.
1447–60	Portuguese explorations under Prince Henry the Navigator.
1453	Fall of Constantinople to the Turks.
1488	Diaz (Portuguese) rounded Cape of Good Hope.
1492	Columbus' voyage in the interest of Spain.
1500	Amerigo Vespucci (Italian) gave the New World its name.
1519–21	Magellan (Spanish) sailed around the world.
1521	Cortés (Spanish) conquered Aztecs in Mexico.
1532	Pizarro (Spanish) conquered Incas in Peru.
1534	Cartier (French) explored the St. Lawrence Gulf.
1563–81	Struggle of the Dutch for independence.
1578	First venture by England in the New World.
1581	Portugal annexed by Spain.
1588	Defeat of the Spanish Armada.
1600	British East India Company chartered.
1607–24	First permanent settlements in North America by England, France, and Holland.

After the collapse of the Roman Empire, civilization in a large part of the area it had ruled fell into a very bad state of repair. Particularly was this true of Western Europe. By contrast Europe's neighbor to the southeast, Orthodox Christendom, maintained throughout the Middle Ages a much higher level of development—and the same was true of the exotic lands of Arabia, Syria, India, Japan, China, Malaya, and the tropical islands of the Far East. As would be expected under these circumstances, Europeans became economically dependent upon Eastern peoples.

The Awakening Begins. Why Europe slumbered while other lands did not may always be a partial mystery. Similarly the forces which in time awakened Europe may never be fully known. Suffice it to say that after the Norse invasions and especially after the Crusades, medieval Europe began to develop new energies and new ambitions, and that in direct proportion with this transformation Europe's demand for Oriental goods increased.

The most direct beneficiaries of this development were the merchants of Genoa, Pisa, Venice, and a number of other Italian cities. These ports, bordering on the Mediterranean and Adriatic and standing midway between Asia Minor and Western Europe, were logical entrepôts in such economic transactions and had long been in closer contact with the East than had the peoples to the north and west. Thus it was that an enhanced demand for the spices needed to preserve food against spoilage and to make it more palatable, fine textiles, dyes, perfumes, and precious stones to add variety and lend prestige to the dress of highly placed Europeans, the rare woods, fine rugs, and tapestries necessary for the furnishing and decorating of crude European dwellings, and even drugs for use by a primitive medical technology funneled profitably through the hands of the merchants standing at the Mediterranean "toll gate."

The rising nation-states to the west quickly came to realize the disadvantage to themselves of this Italian monopoly. Not only were the prices of the crude, semifinished goods exchanged for imports from the Orient relatively low, but the terms of this trade were made still more unfavorable by the profits of foreign middlemen and the transportation charges of foreign shipowners. The result was a sharply adverse balance of trade and a corresponding drain on Europe's money supply, a condition which could only be remedied by borrowing from and paying interest to Italian banking houses.[1]

Understandably western Europeans were soon seeking a more favorable basis on which to conduct their trade. The ideal solution, and the one toward which efforts were increasingly channeled, was a direct route to the East. For ambitious traders, success in this enterprise would mean wealth and prestige. To a struggling young nation it would contribute even more. On the one hand, it would be easier to retain the supply of circulating coin essential for internal development. On the other hand, the tribute received from other nations in interest, profits, and transportation charges

[1] The concept "terms of trade" refers to the prices of an economy's import goods in relation to the prices of its export goods. "Unfavorable" terms of trade means a situation in which imports are high in price while exports are relatively low-valued. The concept "balance of trade" refers to the relationship between an economy's total exports and total imports measured in monetary terms. An "adverse" or "unfavorable" (or, in the terminology preferred by economists, "passive") balance of trade means a situation in which total imports exceed total exports. The concept "balance" of payments (unlike the balance of trade, it is always zero) refers to the way in which imports in excess of exports are paid for.

would provide a source of tax revenue which could also assist in this process. Once men began to be moved by these considerations, it was only a matter of time until the Italian monopoly was destroyed.

In the shift of Europe's center of gravity from the Mediterranean to the Atlantic, it was little Portugal that led the way. Commencing shortly after 1400, her seamen began a work of discovery and expansion which did not end until she had made direct contact with the Orient around the coast of Africa and established at Lisbon what was virtually a new monopoly in Eastern goods. This achievement was the authentic beginning of the movement known to history as "The Commercial Revolution"—a movement in which European energies overflowed European boundaries and penetrated to every corner of the globe.

Close behind Portugal came Spain. Prevented from directly challenging Portugal in the East by the papal sanction already given to these acquisitions, Columbus set out from Spain to find a route to the "Indies" by sailing westward. In 1492 he made contact with the West Indies and reported that he had found the eagerly sought route. It was a bitterly disappointed Spain that discovered the truth shortly thereafter.

Still she persisted. Again certain she had succeeded when in 1520 Magellan reached the Philippine Islands by sailing around the coast of South America, she was again disappointed when the Pope awarded her only the Philippines—leaving Portugal in undisputed possession of the trade with the Orient.

Spain's frustration in the East, however, was soon surmounted by the discovery that her New World territory contained vast treasures in gold, silver, and precious stones, and an agricultural people that could be profitably exploited. With these riches at their disposal successive Spanish monarchs built an empire which was soon the envy of every other king in Europe (including the king of Portugal). So self-satisfied were the Spaniards with their imperial achievements that they neglected the underlying development of both their colonies and their own economy. For this neglect they were to pay the supreme penalty when their neighbors to the north began to flex their own muscles.

The third overseas adventurer was France. By 1530 French fishermen were beginning to exploit the "Grand Banks" fisheries of Newfoundland. Anxious to find a new route to the East, however, French sailors were soon pushing past Newfoundland, and by 1534 France was laying claim to the valley of the St. Lawrence. From this base the French gradually took possession of a huge territory in the New World, marked out roughly by the water route extending from the mouth of the St. Lawrence to the mouth of the Mississippi. In the fur resources of this region France found such a valuable asset that she too neglected the all-round development of her possessions.

The early successes of Spain and Portugal in their imperial ventures profoundly influenced the European scene. Reversing a trend centuries old, bullion began to flow into Europe. As Table 1 shows, Spain alone

TABLE 1. TREASURE FROM THE WEST

Decade	Gold	Silver
	(Millions of grams)	
1521-1530	4.9	0.1
1531-1540	14.5	86.2
1541-1550	25.0	177.6
1551-1560	42.6	303.1
1561-1570	11.5	942.9
1571-1580	9.4	1,118.6
1581-1590	12.1	2,103.0
1591-1600	19.5	2,707.6
1601-1610	11.8	2,213.6
1611-1620	8.9	2,192.3
1621-1630	3.9	2,145.3

Source: By permission from *American Treasure and the Price Revolution in Spain,* by E. J. Hamilton, p. 42. Copyright, 1934, Harvard University Press, Cambridge, Mass.

was the recipient of a stream of metal which could only be described as fabulous. Because of this inflow, or rather because of the increase in the price level which it generated, the sixteenth century is as often referred to in terms of a price revolution as a commercial one.[2] Table 2 only

TABLE 2. THE PRICE REVOLUTION IN ENGLAND

Year	Prices	Wages
1500	100	100
1650	348	189

Source: By permission from *Economic History of Europe,* by S. B. Clough and C. W. Cole, p. 129. Copyright, 1946, D. C. Heath & Co., Boston.

suggests how comprehensive this transformation must have been. It is to be remembered in this connection that during this period comparatively little bullion went *directly* to England.

Closely associated with this transfer of wealth from the New World to the Old was a fundamental development in economic philosophy. So

[2] This refers to the supply and demand analysis so indispensable to economic thinking. Speaking generally, a price will rise when demand increases relative to supply or supply decreases relative to demand, and a price will fall when demand decreases relative to supply or supply increases relative to demand. These relationships apply, moreover, whether the price is that of a commodity, a service, a factor of production (i.e., land, labor, capital, or management), or of money itself. (Note: a fall in the value of money has the same meaning as an increase in the general price level, and vice versa.)

impressed were statesmen with the benefits to be derived from empire that government policies were largely built around this objective. Known by the name of mercantilism (a name suggested by the importance at this time of merchant affairs), these policies typically included profits for national traders, a large revenue for the king, and perhaps above all an economy as nearly self-sufficient as possible.

The importance attached to a self-sufficient economy, of course, had its origin in the age-old problem of maintaining a favorable balance of payments. As a major principle of state management this philosophy no doubt outlived its usefulness before it was abandoned, but probably no single idea had so great an influence on the development of modern Europe and America. From it came the pattern of relationship between empire powers and their colonies which dominated the colonial policies of all the new nations; colonies were thought to exist solely for the benefit of the mother country. From it also came the closely related belief that one nation can gain only as another loses, a belief making mandatory the monopolization of the trade of a colony by the mother country and hence largely responsible for the bitter rivalry for colonial possessions.

England Appears on the Scene. With the rise of Spain to pre-eminence, the first phase of Europe's expansion came to an end. The second was ushered in by a conflict between Catholicism and Protestantism as Spain endeavored to prevent the spread of unorthodox religious belief.

The first act of this new drama centered around the achievement of independence from Spain by Holland. Already Dutch Protestants had become an important part of the economic life of Europe.[3] Taking advantage of Portugal's failure (as a result of lack of capital) to transport Eastern goods beyond Lisbon, the Dutch had made themselves the focal point for the distribution of Oriental goods in northern Europe.

As this struggle got under way on the Continent, the first stirrings of new life began to be apparent across the English Channel. In two important ways the British economy was being impelled by its internal development to enter competition for colonial possessions. First, a rapid expansion of wool production (the so-called "enclosure" movement) brushed aside land rights centuries old, with the result that thousands of families were forced from the land. For a time, until business was able to absorb these unemployed, the feeling was widespread that England was overpopulated and in need of a colonial outlet for her "surplus" people. Second, wool manufacturers were feeling a growing need for markets in which to

[3] Although scholars are not agreed as to why this should be so, there is no disagreement that the Protestant parts of Europe were the ones which became most actively capitalistic. The controversy arises as to whether Protestantism generated capitalism, whether capitalism generated Protestantism, or whether each contributed to the development of the other in a complex process of interaction.

sell their output. Against the background of colony monopolization, a fundamental article of faith with virtually every European statesman, the only solution to this problem semed to be to join the race for empire. And in addition to these internal factors, it must be emphasized that Englishmen did not escape the intense desire to find a "Northwest Passage" to the East or quick wealth in the form of gold and silver as in the case of Spain and the fur trade as in the case of France.

Casting about for opportunities, British statesmen saw in the struggle between Spain and Holland an excellent point of departure. For one thing, if Spain could be defeated, she would not be able to add Dutch wealth to her already formidable might, nor would Anglican England be confronted with a Catholic power just across the Channel. For another, Spanish treasure pirated on the high seas was perhaps the quickest way to wealth for a nation appearing so tardily on the scene. Through the exploits of men like John Hawkins and Francis Drake, therefore, England was able simultaneously to pursue several goals. And when Dutch independence was proclaimed in 1581, British leaders no doubt felt that an excellent beginning had been made.

Both England and Holland were now ready to join the rivalry for colonies. Both nations, moreover, were anxious to secure direct access to the Orient. Unfortunately, the Portuguese monopoly and the Spanish fleet both stood in the way.

Quite unexpectedly there occurred in quick succession two events summarily removing these barriers. First, Spain absorbed the little kingdom of Portugal, finally achieving her long-standing ambition in the East. Immediately, the erstwhile Portuguese possessions became fair game for everyone; obviously the papal decree approving Portugal's monopoly would not continue to be effective in the hands of Spain. Second, in 1588, the Spanish fleet (the "Invincible Armada"), sailing on the double mission of pacifying the Dutch and punishing England for aiding the Dutch, was disastrously defeated by a windstorm and the British navy. Both England and Holland hastened to step into this vacuum.

Nor was it only in the East that opportunities were exploited. In the opening years of the seventeenth century the first permanent settlements in North America were planted. Here the English scored first, establishing a colony at Jamestown (Virginia) in 1607. Far to the north France established herself in Quebec the following year. In 1620 the Pilgrims landed at Plymouth Rock (Massachusetts), and four years later New Amsterdam was founded by the Dutch.

An Adverse Environment. It was perhaps only to be expected that as one of the last of the new nation-states to embark upon an imperialistic career, England would have suffered initial frustrations. A listing of the difficulties the British did encounter in these early years, however, suggests that they were by no means all attributable to her delayed beginning. In the East, for example, Holland quickly carried off top honors, and England's Eastern domain was limited largely to India—a territory not then considered especially valuable. Furthermore, in her western possessions costly attempts to find treasure, oriental-type goods, or a "Northwest Passage" to the East all came to naught.

Even these facts do not give a complete picture of Britain's frustrations. Actually the only "quick" wealth found by any colonial power in North America was the fur trade. The Indian natives were superb trappers and hunters, while they had little use for the pelts in such great demand all over Europe. At the same time they soon became avidly interested in trinkets, cooking utensils, firearms, blankets, and other rudiments of the white man's superior culture. As a result profits were typically enormous. But even here the English came off only second best; although fur-bearing animals could be found in quantity almost everywhere, fur resources were most abundant in French territory along the St. Lawrence and in the area around Hudson's Bay and along the Hudson River where the Dutch had prior rights.

What all of this meant was that England would have to reap the fruits of empire in a more pedestrian fashion—through exploitation of the land, the forests, and the fisheries of the New World. To accomplish this, however, it was essential that she control the economic life of her colonies. Should she fail at this point, all would indeed be lost. Unfortunately, although it was not realized at first, efforts to achieve this result operated from the beginning under the shadow of a major handicap.[4]

The most natural point at which to begin English control over the American economy would have been the financing of settlements—and plans were laid accordingly. Notably, however, investors were typically content to rely on their ability to direct these undertakings on an absentee basis. The new settlers for their part were confronted on arrival with such harsh conditions that for years attention had to be devoted almost exclusively to eking out a bare existence. Most ironically, indeed, these representatives of a culture far higher than that of the Indian were often dependent upon the Red Man for food and other supplies, as well as some of the basic skills needed to master their new environment.

With starvation never far away and disease almost ever present, colonists understandably did not concern themselves about the capital returns

[4] This chapter (and indeed to some extent this entire book) is based upon an approach to historical development which is receiving steadily wider support among students of history. Its central tenet is not that men do not make history, for of course in the final analysis they do. Rather it emphasizes that human motivation is molded by the particular economic and social environment in which it arises, and that therefore history cannot be turned in whatever direction one chooses.

expected back in England. And, under the circumstances, it is also understandable that British investors were reluctant to throw good money after bad. Thus one cause of colonial hardship during these early years was the impossibility of maintaining a continuous flow of capital for unprofitable ventures. Finally, mutually abandoning one another, investors and colonists parted company, and capital for the development of the New World had to be secured in other ways.

England might still have kept control at this vital point if the king with his resources had promptly filled the vacuum thus created. However, here as in so many other ways the history of England was complicated by the struggle between Parliament and the Crown; the king had to husband his resources ever so carefully to avoid surrendering still more power to representatives of the people. In fact, one of the primary reasons for the encouragement of colonization by the Crown was its interest in finding new sources of revenue. But whatever the justification for the king's failure at this point, in that failure England decisively lost the first round in her battle to dominate the New World economy.

Other methods of financing settlements were soon found. Significantly, however, the most successful techniques provided little leverage for control by the British. For example, the primary need for capital was the expense of transporting settlers to the new land and equipping them with food, clothing, utensils, seed, and weapons—and many settlers were able to finance themselves.

An alternative device was the labor indenture contract. The expense of relocation was advanced by someone else in exchange for an agreement by the recipient to turn over the proceeds of his labor for a stipulated time. Although there were present here some of the ingredients of a slavery situation, the wild, new land prevented this result. On the one hand, settlers were not so determined to brave the wilderness as to be willing to sign away their entire lives. On the other hand, the scarcity of labor was so acute and the competition to secure settlers so keen that the contract period was kept within reasonable bounds. At the end of as few as three years, and rarely more than seven, the individual and his family became free agents.

Another point at which England might have kept the colonial economy under control was the distribution of land. Here, also, a serious attempt was made. The plan was simple. Ambitious Englishmen first prevailed upon the Crown to give them vast tracts of land in America. By promising to pay a revenue to the king, Britishers could then establish themselves as veritable feudal lords on New World manors, reaping profits from the toil of New World serfs. This is not to say, of course, that all proprietors intended to establish a labor slavery. William Penn, for example, utilized his grant in large part to achieve altruistic purposes. Furthermore, men like Baltimore, Berkeley, and the Duke of York would no doubt have cared for their half-slave, half-free charges as well as any medieval lord. But certain it is that private property was very far from these calculations.

These plans too went astray; the lord-serf relationship could not be implemented. After investing a large sum of money in preparing his estate for settlement, the proprietor typically found himself desperately in need of settlers. These in turn could only be secured by making liberal promises, for potential settlers were no more interested in consenting to a lifetime of serfdom than in signing a lifetime labor contract. Thus it was that much of the territory granted to would-be New World lords had to be bartered away at the outset. To be sure, quitrents were exacted; incoming settlers did not immediately secure full title to the lands thus given them. But these payments were relatively small and, what is more important, this feudal institution never became deeply rooted. As the colonial period advanced, the proprietor-tenant relationship became more and more a step in the transition to private property. With this development England lost round two of her attempt to subjugate the colonial economy.

The appearance of private enterprise in the New World was only a corollary of the rise of private property. Here again, however, the pattern of growth went counter to original expectations. Thus both Virginia and Plymouth were first organized on the basis of communal production for the profit of absentee investors. All produce was to be put into a common storehouse from which members were to take as need dictated. Whatever surplus above maintenance was produced would become the property of the company.

For several reasons this method of organizing production broke down. In the first place, the guarantee of a living and the impossibility of earning more than a living regardless of output were not favorable to maximum productivity. Furthermore, dissatisfaction arose because single men were required to help support the families of married men, and because older and more experienced hands objected to being placed on the same basis as younger men just starting out in life. Before the communal system had been in operation for long, it abruptly gave way to a system of individually organized effort.

Even the fur trade frustrated attempts at monopolization. So tempting were the rewards to be won, and so vast was the wilderness within which the valuable furs could be found, that it was impossible to prevent the ambitious from trading "on their own." Wherever furs were to be found colonial merchants, colonial representatives, and even company representatives defied monopolistic claims. Wealth earned by colonists in the fur trade did much of the work of developing the New World, and successful fur traders became an important part of the colonial aristocracy.

Words can only inadequately convey an idea of the rapidity with which the organizational pattern of New World colonization underwent a complete change. Table 3 can perhaps make the point a little more concrete.

TABLE 3. TRIAL AND ERROR

Date Founded	Colony	Type
1607	Virginia	Company
1620	Plymouth	Company
1624	New Amsterdam	Company
1629	Massachusetts	Company
1629	New Hampshire	Proprietor
1629	Maine	Proprietor
1632	Maryland	Proprietor
1635	Connecticut	*
1636	Rhode Island	*
1663	North Carolina	Proprietor
1664	New York	Proprietor
1664	New Jersey	Proprietor
1670	South Carolina	Proprietor
1681	Pennsylvania	Proprietor
1701	Delaware	Proprietor
1732	Georgia	Proprietor

* "Squatter" offshoots of Massachusetts and therefore not classifiable in these terms.

After only twenty years' experience with the company-communal type of organization, the proprietor-private enterprise approach was substituted, and not once thereafter was there a reversion to the original concept.

The Roots of Independence. Not only did the New World environment make it difficult for England to keep her American colonies in a subordinate status, but these difficulties were powerfully supplemented by a set of factors making the majority of the colonists unwilling to accept British dominance. Whether migration was for economic or religious reasons, the factor tipping the balance in favor of leaving "home" was typically a failure on the part of England to provide the opportunities coveted by her citizens.

On the economic side, the largest group of migrants consisted of people who had been jostled off the land by the enclosure movement. These unfortunates had thronged into the emerging towns where they became the responsibility of public relief, and in the existing state of Britain's manufacturing industry both townspeople and the unemployed were made unhappy by this situation. In the face of this explosive social problem, the opportunity for overseas expansion was most fortunate. The possibility of achieving a degree of independence in America understandably looked very attractive to men prevented by the power of the guilds from training themselves for the skilled trades in England.

Another group finding it advantageous to look for betterment abroad was the smaller entrepreneur. Large property owners had been able to keep pace with dynamic changes in the British economy by increasing the scale of their operations. Those less fortunate were finding themselves beset by a growing burden of taxation to provide poor-relief for those who had been pushed off the land, and were at the same time confronted with a diminishing opportunity for their own expansion. The new land offered this group the possibility of surmounting both of these obstacles to self-improvement. Similarly hemmed in were smaller traders who, running behind the competitive race in England, sought an opportunity to improve their relative position in a territory not yet exploited.

Still a third group migrated to America for economic reasons. In England in the seventeenth century land customarily passed from father to eldest son, leaving younger sons landless and faced with the necessity for making their way in the world in some other way. Yet, born and bred to desire a high material culture and a superior social status, these sons also desired to live as aristocrats. As the New World impressed itself more and more upon England's imagination, many second and third sons saw in England's empire a solution to their problem.

The religious motivation for colonization was no less significant than economic incentives, although fewer people were involved. Here was a large and vigorous group of Englishmen eager to give up Catholicism but unable to find spiritual satisfaction in Anglicanism. Given these proclivities, it is readily understandable that vigorous insistence on the creed of this national church would produce a sharp reaction.

In 1633 William Laud was made Archbishop of Canterbury, a man of strong will determined to uproot opposition to Anglicanism wherever it was to be found. Opposition there was in abundance, too, as the liberal group—the Puritans—resisted what appeared to be a reunion between England and Rome. Faced with this determined unorthodoxy, Laud's rule became so severe that Puritan congregations throughout the length and breadth of England gathered their belongings together and set out for the New World.

The consequences of this religious exodus for colony–mother country relationships were momentous. Through it there was created a resistance to absolutism in government, a fixed opposition to the union of church and state, and an antipathy toward English Anglicanism which conditioned development in America from that point forward. The fact that the Puritans were Protestants and hence more inclined to engage in capitalistic activities—activities England considered out of bounds in her colonies—

goes far to explain the rapidity with which New England and Old England came into open conflict.

Furthermore, the founding of Massachusetts was a fundamental step in American colonization as such. This colony was established not far from the earlier but never flourishing settlement at Plymouth, and overwhelmingly the steady flow of Puritans converged there. The appearance of twenty thousand like-minded people in one settlement over a period of ten years could only have resulted in the development of a large, powerful, and united colony by the standards of that day. Eventually swallowing up tiny Plymouth, the "Bay Colony" was the central focus of the economic life of the northern colonies for almost half a century. Although several other New England colonies were established concurrently with Massachusetts, their growth was for a long time overshadowed and all but dominated by that of their huge neighbor.

And finally, the rise of New England resulted in a number of significant differences between England's northern and southern colonies. Financed either by well-to-do families paying their own way, or through the pooling of the resources within a church congregation, Massachusetts was not peopled by indentured servants to as great an extent as the colonies to the south. By the same token, there was here concentrated far more potential capital and business experience than was to be found elsewhere. Not being a proprietary colony, furthermore, she did not have to fight against the vestiges of feudalism as did some of the other colonies. And while Catholicism was never the preferred religion of the majority in any colony, nowhere outside of New England was to be found such a strongly Protestant (capitalist) population. Altogether, it was most fitting that Massachusetts carried the greatest burden in the ensuing conflict between England and her American colonies—and that she was the leader in an evolution which was one day to create a great industrial nation.

Let it not be thought that because of all these factors the colonies wholly escaped domination by British capitalists, that Englishmen did not over the years reap substantial profits in the New World, or that the spirit of independence arising in the colonies had anything in common with the idea of separation from England. The mother country's economic development was greatly superior to that in America, and the colonists would scarcely have found life in America even tolerable had it not been for the availability of British goods and capital. An inevitable result was that in some respects the colonies did fall under the sway of British trade and investment, an influence which was not overcome for more than two hundred years. Perhaps, too, it was because of this fact that the idea of separating from England did not appear until the colonial period was far advanced. The independence so decisively appearing was rather an economic organization and a set of attitudes favoring assumption by colonists of control over their economic life as rapidly as economic development permitted.

It is no exaggeration to suggest that in these facts England suffered her first defeat. The issue was not yet finally decided, of course; there was yet opportunity to retrieve the situation. Obviously, however, the time would come—and soon—when England's ability to solidify her hold in the New World would be rigorously tested.

QUESTIONS FOR DISCUSSION

1. What were the economic motives behind European expansion?
2. Under what circumstances is an adverse balance of trade as serious as was assumed in western Europe at the beginning of modern times?
3. In what ways might it be said that the "price revolution" was a cause of the "commercial revolution"? Was the opposite relationship more nearly correct?
4. To what extent was it correct that one nation could gain only as another lost?
5. What were the special factors contributing to England's outward expansion?
6. Was colonial expansion as vitally necessary as leading Englishmen thought it to be?
7. To what extent is it accurate to refer to the settlement and expansion of America as a "gigantic adventure in land speculation"?
8. How did the proprietorship method of colonization differ from the company approach? Why did the latter fail?
9. What were the economic factors behind English colonization in America? The religious?
10. If the economic and religious situations in England had been more favorable, would relationships between mother country and colonies have worked out differently in the long run?

Chapter 2

SEEDS OF DISHARMONY

1607	Settlement of Jamestown.
1615	Beginning of commercial production of tobacco in Virginia.
1622	First application of mercantilist philosophy to North American colonies—tobacco.
1629	Massachusetts Bay Company chartered.
1633–40	Puritan persecution in England, and rapid expansion of the Massachusetts Bay Colony.
1640–49	Civil War in England.
1643	New England Confederation formed to resist the Indian menace.
1650, 1651	Navigation legislation aimed at Holland.
1652–54	First Anglo-Dutch War.
1660, 1663	Enumeration and Staple Acts.
1664–67	Second Anglo-Dutch War.
1672–73	Third Anglo-Dutch War.
1675–76	King Philip's War—with the Indians in New England.
1675–76	Bacon's Rebellion.
1684	Massachusetts' charter annulled.
1686–89	Dominion of New England experiment.

The test did not come immediately. The economic development of Virginia preceded that of Massachusetts, and in Virginia climatic conditions and colonial temperaments were such that conflict between New and Old World capitalists did not at once arise. In other words, England was given a breathing space before the battle with her American colonies began, a period she found useful in solidifying her position against the Dutch. An important focal point for the ensuing struggle was the growing economy of Virginia.

Economic Foundations in Virginia. Economic activity in Virginia, as in all of England's New World colonies, was predominantly agricultural.

However, an agricultural economy could not directly supply the manufactured goods which were a basic part of the colonial standard of living, and accordingly men began to seek ways of supplementing their self-sufficient agriculture. A partial solution was found in the form of household manufactures, the conversion of raw materials into crude conveniences and luxuries within the home. The further step of commercial manufacturing, production of finished goods on a larger scale for wide distribution, was slow to develop because the market was limited, capital was scarce, and the open frontier drew labor away from the more settled areas and hence made it too expensive for use in many kinds of manufacturing activity.

The wide variety of goods which could be manufactured in the home was helpful, of course, but it was only a beginning. Goods so produced were not all one might want from the standpoint of quality, and some items could not be produced satisfactorily at all in this way. Beyond this solution, therefore, the economic problem of Virginia had to be resolved along other lines.

By 1615 the basic answer was at hand. Soon after settlement began, the Indians had taught the colonists how to raise tobacco, this crop shortly becoming the great commercial staple of the South. Consisting of a few simple operations, tobacco-growing was an excellent way of utilizing both the land resources available and the inefficient labor of indentured servants. So successful was it in making use of unskilled labor that the scale of production tended to become quite large, and when indentured labor no longer furnished an adequate labor supply, a traffic in slaves from Africa was employed as a substitute. Moreover, tobacco could easily be exchanged in England for the manufactured goods demanded in America.

Not only was tobacco in great demand in England, but it was actively encouraged by the mother country as a valuable intraempire trade. It yielded a large revenue in import duties, and also relieved England of dependence upon nonempire sources for her tobacco, with the resultant loss of specie in its purchase. To the tobacco colonies in turn England was able to sell her own production at a substantial profit. Since British traders typically transported both the tobacco and the return cargo of manufactures, furthermore, England was able to earn handsome incomes from commissions, freights, and insurance. The tobacco colonies even furnished a valued outlet for surplus investment funds; a good rate of interest was virtually assured, and the principal was protected by the long arm of the British government.

Mercantilism Applied. Only one fact prevented England from being completely happy with the tobacco trade. The Dutch were actively participating in it. Using Fort Amsterdam as a base, Dutch merchants not only loaded Virginia tobacco on Dutch ships bound for continental markets, but they supplied the colonists with goods produced on the continent. British merchants who thereby lost the lucrative benefits of such a trade built around English ships and English manufactures were soon allied with a British king who thereby lost the import duties Virginia tobacco would have paid in English ports.

England was the model of caution as she moved to the attack. The first step was a regulation in 1622 requiring all tobacco exported from Virginia to be sent to England, this being only one in a long series of restrictive measures known to history as the Trade and Navigation Acts. In 1624 the control pattern was tightened by another regulation requiring all Virginia tobacco to be exported in English ships. Passed partly as an enforcement measure, to make certain the tobacco was sent to England, this law greatly favored British merchants by assuring them large freight and insurance earnings. The monopoly of the British merchants was still further strengthened in 1633-34 when all foreign traders were excluded from Virginia.

If the tobacco trade had been kept competitive, it is possible that the needs of tobacco growers would have been better served by it. As it was, of course, it was not wholly undesirable. It did make available European goods, and to that extent solved their economic problem. In fact, British regulations were themselves of some benefit to colonists as well as to English capitalists; tobacco culture in England was forbidden, and the British monopoly made credit easier to secure than would otherwise have been the case. At the same time, however, it generated an economic dependency for planters in southern colonies which became increasingly frustrating. Later, as the settled area in the South expanded, and as first rice and then indigo became important plantation staples along with tobacco, planters in Maryland, South Carolina, and Georgia were swept into the same pattern of dependence.

Such an evolution grew naturally out of the character of the tobacco trade. English merchants did not buy tobacco directly, and therefore the full risk of price changes rested with the planter. Meanwhile the merchant protected himself fully as to commissions, transport costs, and insurance since he had the planter's goods in his possession. A further economic disadvantage for the planter was his inability to supervise either the sale of his goods in England or the purchase of English goods with the proceeds. Conducive to both carelessness and fraud, this relationship produced no little friction between colonial planters and mother-country merchants.

When the price of tobacco was low, occasions arose on which there were no proceeds to use in the purchase of goods wanted from England. On such occasions British merchants would lend the planter money for his purchases abroad, secure in the protection of the British government and guaranteed by the fact of the loan the opportunity to handle the planter's crop the following year. Gradually short-term loans secured by crop liens became long-term loans secured by mortgages on land and slaves; and, with interest on past borrowings to pay, one more charge was added to those deducted by the merchant when the next crop was sold. It was not at all unusual for the factor's share of a planter's cash income to average as much as forty per cent, leaving only a little more than one-half for the payment of all costs plus whatever surplus there might be. Once in this vicious circle of increasing indebtedness, a planter could often extricate himself only with the aid of several years of good crops at good prices, a situation occurring rarely with a product having such an inelastic demand as tobacco.[1] As the years went by this pattern of economic relationships became a major source of conflict between England and her southern colonies.

Economic Foundations in Massachusetts. While the tobacco trade was fastening its grip on the southern colonies, their northern neighbors were beginning to search for a solution to a similar economic problem—the problem of using available resources in achieving an accustomed standard of living. This economy also developed as predominantly agricultural, and here too household manufactures were widely depended upon as a supplement. But these economic activities were no more adequate to the task at hand than they had been in the South. Furthermore, no agricultural staples could be found which could accomplish for northerners what tobacco had done for southern planters. No doubt the agricultural staples actually available could have been of much assistance in other circumstances, but England refused to import such items as meat and wheat, the farm commodities northern colonies were best fitted to produce. These colonies were thus forced to seek their solution in other directions as the similarity of climate and temperament between New England and Old England began to make its influence felt.

Partly because of this situation and partly because of her rocky soil, a portion of New England's economic activity was soon diverted from agriculture into other pursuits. One of the earliest of these was the fishing industry. At first dependent upon British capital for these operations, colonists lost no time transferring control to the New World. As they became more and more successful in monopolizing New England's rich fish resources, British fishermen were forced to concentrate on Newfoundland.

[1] An inelastic demand, a characteristic of most agricultural products, means that a relatively small increase in the quantity produced will result in a relatively large fall in the price. More concretely in terms of the situation under consideration here, an increase in the quantity produced will result in a decrease in the revenue received by producers.

With equal vigor the northern colonists undertook to exploit the lumber resources of the New World. Out of the world-wide interest in and expansion of trade, there had developed an almost insatiable demand for ships and the materials with which to build them. Having built the ships needed to protect the commercial independence of their fishing industry, northern colonists began to develop a world market for their vessels. So successful were they that colonial-built ships were soon sailing the seven seas under most of the flags known to the commercial world. It is worth noting that in the development of this industry American colonists were greatly aided by the Trade and Navigation Acts. England's move to exclude Dutch shipping from the colonial trade took place before she was herself able to fill the vacuum thus created. As a consequence British ships were so defined in the legislation as to include colonial-built vessels manned by colonial seamen.

Other industries were also developed by New Englanders, most notably flour milling and the maufacture of rum. The first of these utilized an important agricultural product grown within the colonies, while the second made use of a raw material imported from the sugar islands of the West Indies. Around these activities, along with shipbuilding, shipping, and fishing, New England built a complex economy far different from and far more successful than the economy built around the tobacco trade.

First, northern merchants had a tremendous advantage over their southern neighbors in that they carried most of their own goods in both the export and import trades. Thus they and not English traders received the freights and insurance earned on such business. Second, in such places as the Caribbean islands northern agents were stationed to handle the transactions of their principals in America. Northerners were thereby not only enabled to supervise the sale and purchase of goods more closely, but they rather than foreigners received the profits and commissions. Even in the European trade, business done by a New England ship captain protected the interests of Yankee traders better than the tobacco planter was protected when he loaded his produce on a British vessel. Third, the earnings of the northern colonies in the sale of ships and shipbuilding materials produced a large amount of purchasing power with which to buy European goods. Fourth, northern traders even engaged in the tobacco trade, carrying tobacco to England or to the continent.

On the other hand, the economic problem of the northern colonies was far from solved by these factors alone. In addition, an intricate pattern of "triangular" trade was necessary to enable Northerners to purchase goods from an England who refused to accept many of their goods in exchange—the need to buy in England rather than elsewhere in Europe being dictated by the English origin of most of the northern colonists, England's industrial superiority relative to the rest of Europe, and by

England's colonial regulations. Provisions, lumber, and rum were sent to the fishing settlements in Newfoundland in exchange for fish, which in turn was exchanged, in Newfoundland, for coin, bills of exchange, or

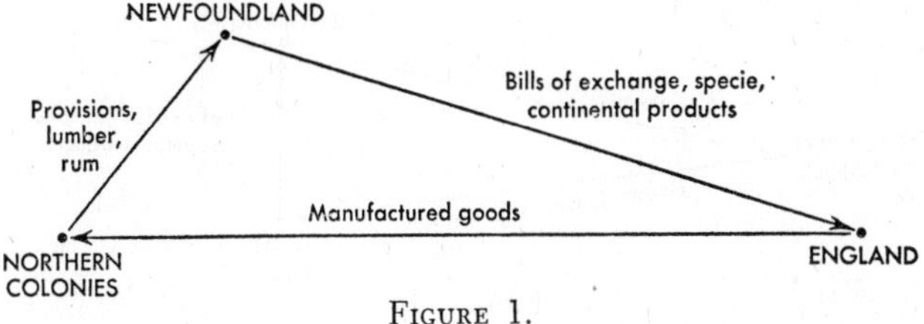

FIGURE 1.

European goods having a demand in England. Fish, furs, lumber, and rice were sent to Southern Europe in exchange for coin, bills of exchange, or southern European goods, and these were then exchanged in England

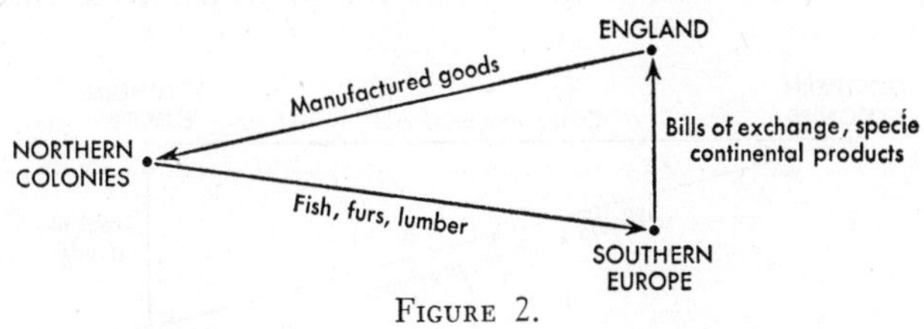

FIGURE 2.

for English goods. Ships were sent to the Portuguese and Spanish Wine Islands laden with fish, provisions, and lumber, and the wine secured in exchange was either brought into the colonies or used to purchase English goods.

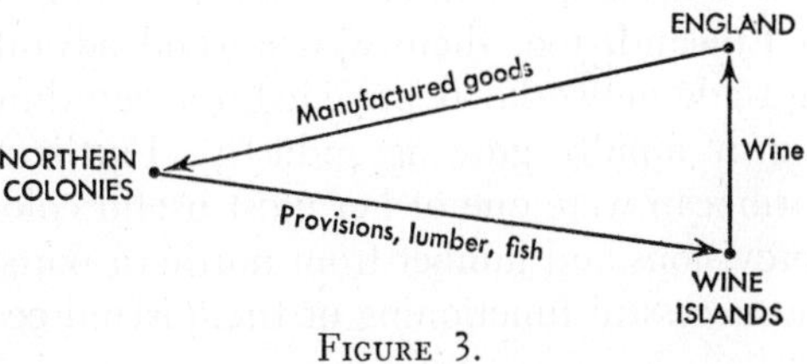

FIGURE 3.

Important though this network of trading relationships was, however, the "triangular" trade developed between the northern colonies and the Caribbean area was still more important. To the many settlements in this area the colonists sent a wide variety of goods, including livestock, lumber, and provisions, in exchange for Spanish money, bills of exchange, sugar, molasses, rum, indigo, ginger, dyewoods, and salt. In part these commodities were brought into the colonies themselves, particularly rum and molasses (the raw material for the manufacture of rum) for use in the fur trade (the Indian, it was early discovered, would part with his furs on more favorable terms under the influence of strong drink), the New England fishing industry, and the trade with Newfoundland. Most of these goods,

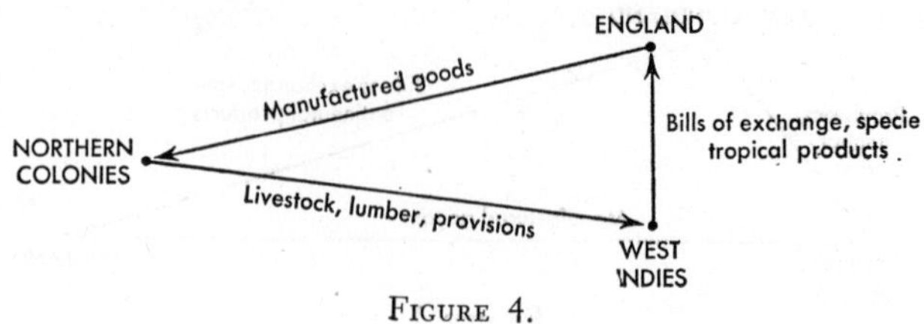

FIGURE 4.

however, were shipped to England in exchange for English goods. Another important trade centering on the West Indies used Southern Europe as a third point. Ships loaded with West Indian produce would sail for Mediterranean ports and exchange their cargo for goods available there.

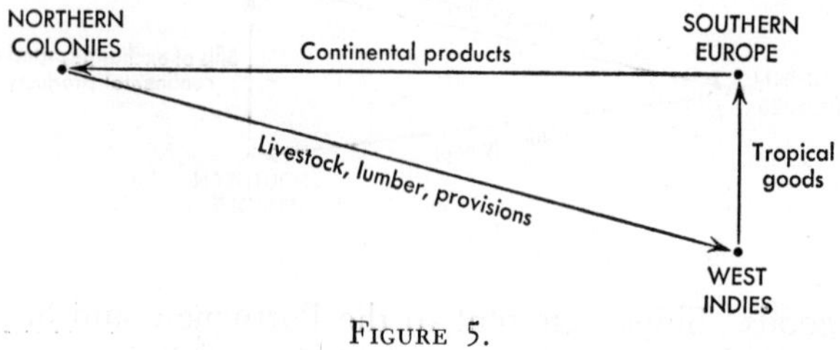

FIGURE 5.

By energetically exploiting all of these possibilities the northern colonists worked out a fairly satisfactory solution to the problem of securing European goods. To England, too, there were several advantageous features of this expanding trade network. It provided, for one thing, an important market for her own rapidly growing industry. Furthermore, her sugar islands in the Caribbean were one of her most useful colonial possessions, and supplies of provisions and lumber from northern ports were an important factor in the successful functioning of these island economies.

Mercantilism Frustrated. This account of the way in which New England colonists resolved their balance-of-payments difficulties could easily be misleading, and it is therefore of the utmost importance to emphasize again that even in these colonies the mercantile class consisted of only a tiny minority. A far larger number of people were engaged in subsistence agriculture supplemented by such crude home manufacturing processes as were essential in maintaining a tolerable standard of living. Indeed, in the early days of New England's development relatively few citizens had the money with which to buy foreign goods, much less actually to participate in commercial activities. But this "exaggeration" of the role played by the mercantile classes is justifiable nonetheless. On the one hand, in an important sense history is made by minorities rather than by majorities. On the other hand, no minority was more important in the making of early American history than the New England merchant group, for it was the particular kinds of activities in which it engaged that were such a crucial factor in the rise of friction with the mother country.

The difficulty here was that in a number of ways England was less pleased about developing relationships than in the case of the American colonies farther south. Her merchants did not receive freights, insurance, commissions, and interest as in the case of the southern trade. Moreover, against New England ships and the skill with which they were operated Britain was beginning to feel a keen competition in certain trades she would have preferred to monopolize. This was especially true of the Newfoundland trade. It was but a short step from feelings such as these to a plea for legislation giving mother-country merchants more of an advantage over their colonial counterparts.

Actually, these elements of conflict did not immediately produce an open breach between the merchants facing one another across the broad expanse of the Atlantic. Prior to 1640 the economy of New England had never been aggressive in its search for foreign exchange. Religious refugees from England, coming as they did primarily to New England, made available in the northern colonies a large quantity of English goods and also provided a steady market for New England's output. In 1640, however, there was set in motion a train of events which at one and the same time accentuated intraempire competition and prevented England from taking the firm measures British businessmen would have preferred.

One dimension of the new situation was the return of a higher level of tolerance to England. The immediate consequence was the cessation of large-scale immigration to New England, a development precipitating a painful depression there which goaded New Englanders into a competition they would have liked to avoid. It was at this point that England would have interfered had she been able. But the depression in New England coincided with (and indeed was in effect brought about by) the outbreak of civil war in England. With Puritan ships and those under the control of the Crown actively privateering against one another, New England was left free to expand almost at will and the Dutch were able to re-enter the American colonial trade. Moreover, with British industry disadvantaged by what might appropriately be called wartime inflation, and with deliveries to and from England highly uncertain, colonists eagerly welcomed Dutch ships and traders.

In 1649 one phase of England's Civil War came to an end with a victory of the Puritan merchants of London over the king. Understandably the merchants' first thought was to restore their monopoly of colonial trade. In 1650 a Puritan Parliament passed another Navigation Act prohibiting all foreign vessels from trading with England's American colonies. This measure, drastic though it was, was followed in 1651 by a law still more sweeping. By its terms foreign vessels were forbidden to participate in any of England's foreign trade.

Breathtaking in their boldness and in the self-confidence they reflected, these measures were as severe an attack on the source of Holland's power as could have been delivered. Such, of course, was their intent. Lashing out at a policy which in the end could only have resulted in the destruction of her supremacy as a sea power, Holland responded in 1652 by precipitating the so-called First Anglo-Dutch War. This phase of what was to be a twenty-five-year conflict ended indecisively but with England enjoying whatever advantage was gained. The Dutch agreed to a treaty recognizing Britain's right to regulate her trade in any way she desired.

Although this success (temporarily) removed one source of frustration for British capitalists, it did nothing to ease intraempire friction. On the contrary, the measures taken to cripple Holland's sea power continued to favor the New England economy, creating an even greater vacuum to be filled by New England shipbuilding and trade. Before steps could be taken to establish more effectively the supremacy of the mother country, Massachusetts had given her still another reason for such action.

In addition to their problem of securing European goods, all the American colonies shared another closely related problem. An exchange economy cannot operate without a medium of exchange, and the colonies could not hope to achieve their desired standard of living without developing an exchange economy.[2] They would have preferred, of course, a metallic medium. But the desperate need for more and more European goods dictated the exportation of most of the metallic money coming into the colonies, and the gap hence had to be filled by the use of commodities as money. Lumber in New Hampshire; grain, meat, and furs in the northern colonies generally; and tobacco in Virginia and Maryland, all were used as money.

This attempt to build a high level economy using commodities as money created difficulties in every colony. Inconvenient to transport and store

[2] A major key to the high per capita productivity of an industrial society is specialization, the concentration of workers on relatively small parts of the production process rather than on self-sufficient production. The obvious corollary of this fact, however, is exchange, for an individual who is striving to be non-self-sufficient must trade his "surplus" for that of someone producing items he desires to consume. Equally obvious is the importance of money in an exchange economy; without something desired primarily for its usefulness as a medium of exchange, transactions are inevitably handicapped by the problem of double coincidence—the problem of finding someone who simultaneously "has what you want and wants what you have."

and with wide variations of quality from unit to unit, such money was unsatisfactory at best. There was a strong temptation to debase the currency by offering inferior products in payment of obligations. Furthermore, it was only natural for debts to be paid when prices were low, and at such times the commodity received in payment could scarcely be sold at all. Many were the expedients adopted to remedy this defect in their economic structure; but as long as the colonies' balance-of-payments problem remained, no solution which would have been tolerated by England offered much hope of success.

England could have been of great assistance to the colonies with respect to this problem if she had so desired. The most obvious assistance, however, ran counter to prevailing European colonial policy. Colonies were supposed to provide the mother country with specie, not the other way around. In part this insistence stemmed from England's need for specie in managing her own balance of payments. In part also it reflected a fear that an effective circulating medium would assist the colonists in the creation of manufacturing industries which would then compete with her own.

In 1652, taking advantage of a disturbed political situation in England, Massachusetts erected a mint to coin money for use in the colony. Two purposes were intended to be served. First, it was felt to be a step toward uniformity in the medium of exchange. The coins of all the major nations found their way into the colonies and, "clipped" and "sweated" almost beyond recognition, created great confusion. Second, it was thought that a colonial coin containing less silver than the corresponding English coin would not be exported in exchange for English goods. The effort proved futile. The famous "pinetree" shilling coined by the Boston mint was so discriminated against in the pricing of goods that it was exported as freely as any coin in the colony. So serious did this problem become that as early as 1654 the export of home-minted coins was prohibited under pain of heavy penalties.

At one time or another all the colonies followed the example of Massachusetts, although with no greater success. This fact, however, could not save Massachusetts from having to accept most of the responsibility when at last England did begin to assert herself in the northern colonies. Certainly Massachusetts was the leader in this as well as other disapproved economic activities. In any event the Boston mint was an important cause of dissatisfaction in England; the mother country felt she could not permit her colonial charges to influence prices, the burden of debts, and the character of trade by managing their own money systems.

Independence Threatened. Action to curb the capitalist proclivities of the northern colonies, when it finally came, took the form of a tightening of the Trade and Navigation Acts. In 1660 an act was passed enumerating certain items which could not be exported to any destination other than the British Isles. The only important item produced in the American colonies included on the original list of "enumerated" items was tobacco, although numerous items (especially sugar) produced in the Caribbean area were involved. Three years later the Staple Act provided that all European imports into the colonies had to pass through one of certain designated ports in the British Isles. By these measures the British monopoly of colonial trade was greatly strengthened, the only compensating concession received by the colonies being the preference given by England to goods in the Enumeration Act received from colonial sources. The Staple Act was to assure British merchants of the business of selling to the colonies, and also by taxing foreign goods competing with British production to give English goods a price advantage to colonial purchasers. In like manner the Enumeration Act guaranteed the handling of important colonial staples by English merchants and provided an increased demand for British shipping. Both were calculated to yield a substantial customs revenue at British ports. Finally, these enactments made it safer for English capitalists to supply the colonies with goods on credit and hence provide an outlet for investment funds.

As had been intended, the new regulations were highly unsatisfactory to Massachusetts and her neighbors. For the first time England had struck directly at the economic structure they had built up. On the one hand, the Enumeration Act meant that certain products (particularly tobacco and sugar) which they had been carrying directly to southern Europe would now have the additional burden of enhanced transport costs and British taxes. On the other hand, the Staple Act would impose a similar burden on New England's continental imports. If England could arbitrarily impose such special burdens on the means by which New Englanders had solved their balance-of-payments problem, the mother country would possess the power of life and death over their economic well-being. An attempt to regulate New England's exports, for example, in the same way that southern exports were already regulated, would quickly have destroyed the New England economy.

Not only were northern merchants discomfited by the new restrictions, but Dutch traders were likewise. They were threatened with total exclusion from Britain's colonies, now one of the most valuable trades in the world. Both groups resisted the new restraints by defying them. In 1664 this defiance was rewarded when the Second Anglo-Dutch War began and England inaugurated an investigation to determine if Massachusetts should be punished for violating her charter.

England's first objective in the military encounter with the Dutch was the taking of New Amsterdam. Two purposes were simultaneously accomplished when the Dutch colony fell to the British during the first year of hostilities. On the one hand, Holland's principal base for commercial operations against the colonial trade England was reserving for herself was thereby destroyed. On the other hand, the Hudson River route to the interior and a larger share of the lucrative fur trade were thus captured. From this point forward Holland would have to be content with her Far Eastern empire.

The ease with which New Amsterdam was taken reflected several underlying factors. First and foremost, it was hemmed in on two sides by British bases, an overwhelming military disadvantage. Moreover, the Dutch settlement had never been successful. Settled primarily by alien groups (including many English colonists) because the Dutch were not a migrating people, avoided by farmers because of an attempt to carve out feudal domains on the rich, new soil, and neglected by its founding company because easy riches did not prove to be available, the will to grow and even to resist encroachment had never been strong. Finally, by now little Holland was no longer a match for her larger rival across the English Channel. When in 1667 the treaty agreement ending this phase of the rivalry between England and Holland formalized the transfer of "New York," England possessed an unbroken string of settlements between the French to the north and Spain in the territory of Florida.

Neither England nor New England was as yet seriously injured by developing intraempire relationships. On the side of England this was because colonial operations were still on a relatively small scale. On the side of the colonies two factors were involved. First, importation by way of England was only a minor hardship, while carrying goods direct to southern Europe was not basic to New England's economy. The simultaneous destruction of Dutch activity in the New World no doubt more than compensated for both of these inconveniences. Second, Massachusetts had long since fallen into the habit of believing that the laws of England did not apply to her—an attitude much encouraged by England's preoccupation with other problems (another way of stressing the relative unimportance as yet of the American colonies in Britain's scheme of things)—and her neighbors were only too happy to be also governed by this interpretation. But if both parties to this conflict were fighting essentially over a principle, the battle was not the less vital for that fact. On its outcome depended momentous consequences for the future, and as England turned from preoccupation with Holland to New World problems, leaders on both sides of the ocean well understood what was at stake.

The commission sent to investigate Massachusetts' stubborn resistance to imperial control met only hostility and tactics of obstruction. Its resultant failure only encouraged New England in her violation of the Navigation Acts. A common technique used in violating the Enumeration Act was to ship sugar and tobacco to Boston prior to their re-exportation to

European ports. By an oversight this regulation neglected to impose duties on goods shipped from one colony to the other, an oversight which also had the effect of making it possible in some instances for colonists to secure enumerated items at a lower price than Englishmen. In 1673 an act was passed remedying this defect, and a corps of customs officials was sent to New England to enforce England's trade regulations.

In the perspective of history it is apparent that this crisis in the relationship between England and Massachusetts was a case of now or never for the mother country. If Massachusetts were allowed successfully to defy Britain's laws, English rule in the northern colonies would virtually be at an end. The question was clearly whether England's first defeat in the New World was now to be turned into a major victory—or a second defeat.

Foiled Again. England's great misfortune at this point was that once again she was unable to devote full attention to the problem at hand. Two factors arose which complicated the Massachusetts adjustment. One was the outbreak of a series of internal social conflicts within the colonies. The other was an administrative blunder by England herself.

The most dramatic internal conflict arose in Virginia. Here, as in all of the other colonies, economic development had proceeded in such a way as to create large landed estates near the seacoast and to force the less successful operators to find smaller holdings for themselves on the frontier. The larger units were at least temporarily more efficient, and hence gradually those farmers with small plots lost their land. As the trend toward concentrated holdings was accentuated, the wealthy farmer was able to take advantage of his position even more because of the need of the dispossessed farmer or freedman for capital. Land was cheap and easy to acquire, but capital was essential before the land could be used effectively. Holding the small farmer's land as security, larger planters and urban merchants supplied credit to be repaid at fixed times and in fixed amounts. If the price of the debtor's output declined, he was in danger of sinking ever deeper into debt. This had the further effect of preventing him from utilizing a competitive market either for buying or selling goods; as long as his indebtedness remained, he could be forced to sell to and buy from his creditor. Out of such elements a vicious circle of dependency was developing between the colonial aristocracy and small property owners, a dependency closely resembling the relationship between southern planters and British factors.

The tobacco economy of Virginia had been fairly prosperous until the middle of the century, after which overproduction, the tightening of Britain's trade restrictions, and the ensuing Dutch wars intervened. With these developments, a protracted depression set in which squeezed the smaller farmer between the large planter and the British factor. With the government almost completely in the hands of the aristocracy (British and colonial), the debt-ridden frontier farmer had available no channels through which to make a peaceful protest. Already antagonized by hard times and a corrupt government operated on the basis of class lines, the interior farmers were roused to violence in 1675 by a destructive Indian war with which the aristocracy controlling the government refused to concern itself. This indifference, of course, is understandable; serious interference with the Indians might have diminished the flow of profits from the fur trade—profits earned in part by exchanging for furs the firearms with which the Indians were raiding the frontier.

Led by Nathaniel Bacon the aroused farmers in 1676 marched on Jamestown, seized control of the government, burned the town, and plundered the countryside. In time the rebellion was put down by the agents of the Crown and the eastern planters, and many of the insurrectionists were either hanged or despoiled of their property as an object lesson to others inclined to resist the established order. At the same time, however, the government was reformed along some of the lines demanded by the farmers.

Similar incidents took place in other colonies during the last quarter of the seventeenth century. In one sense, to be sure, these uprisings were no concern of England's. But, on the other hand, they did relate themselves to her ability to rule in the colonies, the slender thread by which her colonial policy now hung. Furthermore, in such conflicts England's interests were most often best served by allying herself with colonial aristocracies. Thus, although New England was not especially disrupted by this series of outbreaks, it was unfortunate for England's desire to enforce the Navigation Acts that a serious attempt at this time would have required a campaign against the aristocracy of Massachusetts.

England's blunder consisted of the annulment of Massachusetts' charter in 1684 and the creation in 1686 of the so-called Dominion of New England—an attempt to weld all these colonies into a single unit. Devised as a better organization technique for meeting the growing threat of France in the New World, this device may or may not have been well chosen. It is certain, however, that the new administration promptly adopted measures which made its success highly improbable to say the least. Apparently feeling that extremes were in order, officials went so far as to threaten the withdrawal of vast quantities of land from private ownership and the imposition of Anglican worship. By such steps far more resistance was created than would have arisen from an attempt merely to enforce England's trade laws.

The Dominion of New England experiment lived only three years. In 1689 it fell, a victim of intense New England hostility and the involvement of the Dominion Governor in a series of class uprisings in New York and New Jersey. Although she could scarcely admit it (possibly she even refused to believe it), England had suffered a second major defeat at the hands of the New World.

QUESTIONS FOR DISCUSSION

1. Why were southerners willing to accept a more subservient status than northerners in Britain's empire?
2. What were the economic factors responsible for the dependency of southern planters upon English merchants?
3. How were the northern colonists able to escape this pattern of developments?
4. Why was "triangular trade" such an important part of the adjustment of the northern colonies?
5. Was it just a coincidence that England's legislation did not bear as heavily on the northern colonies as on the southern ones, or were there fundamental factors involved?
6. If England had not been repeatedly occupied with other things at just the wrong times, could she have brought Massachusetts into line? How?
7. What did American colonists expect to achieve through monetary legislation? How effective were these efforts? Why did England object?
8. Why did England seem to find it easier to deal with Holland than New England? Why was Holland able to stand against England in the Far East but not in the New World?
9. Was the situation in the New World particularly conducive to concentration of wealth and income, or does the American experience indicate that such a tendency is unavoidable?

Chapter 3

THE GATHERING STORM

1689	End of the "Glorious Revolution" in England. William of Orange became king.
1689–97	King William's War (War of the League of Augsburg).
1699	Woolens Act.
1701–13	Queen Anne's War (War of the Spanish Succession).
1732	Hat Act.
1733	Molasses Act.
1741	Bubble Act extended to the colonies.

The year 1689 marked an important turning point in both American and British history. In England the line of Catholic Stuart kings came to an end, and the merchants secured an even more decisive control over their government. It is thus no coincidence that the first year of the reign of William of Orange was also the year in which the "second hundred years' war" between England and France began. In the New World an Anglo-French controversy now took the place of what had recently been an Anglo-Dutch conflict.

Challenge from France. For more than a century France had been gaining in strength and prestige. Somewhat handicapped by her failure to develop as a naval power, she had watched enthusiastically as England systematically weakened Holland. She had even taken advantage of Dutch weakness and at the same time tested her own strength by depriving Dutch merchants of a share in the trade of the French West Indies. With the Dutch no longer the dominant continental power, France was at last coming into her own. Furthermore, she was ambitious; her aim was no less than to become the most powerful empire in the world. Such ambitions could not have failed to clash with a Britain having similar aspirations.

The New World points at which the imperial plans of the two nations conflicted were several. The French had long hoped that Canada's economy would one day be able to supply lumber, work animals, and provisions to the French West Indies. Canada had consistently failed, however, to be of much assistance in this regard, while the English colonies of New England and New York seemed admirably suited to such a purpose. Accordingly French expansionism in America included the possession of these economies. While England was not completely happy with her northern colonies, she was far from ready to write them off. They were becoming too valuable in performing for England precisely the function France desired of them.

In like manner, both England and France desired to monopolize the fur trade. Still almost as profitable as ever, this trade had of late become difficult to share. The Indian by this time was highly dependent upon the traffic in furs. Preferring to consume goods produced by the white man, he had gradually lost both the skill and the tools with which he had formerly produced for his own use. Such an adjustment, of course, was only possible in so far as furs were supplied to the white man, and over the years the supply of furs had become so reduced that tribes were fighting with one another over possession of the least exhausted sources. In such a struggle European firearms were obviously the decisive factor, and the Indian was shrewd enough to play one European competitor off against another. Competition for the fur trade had, indeed, become both difficult and dangerous.

Still another point of conflict was the Newfoundland fishery. Here the French had secured control of the most advantageous locations, and had gradually built their position into what was virtually a monopoly. Rapidly losing out in the struggle for fish both in New England and Newfoundland, English businessmen were only too anxious to oust the French from Newfoundland.

None of these points of conflict in North America exceeded in importance a rivalry between France and England centering farther south. The decline of Spain was now accelerating, and each of her major rivals was striving to divert the riches of the Spanish Indies to itself. To be sure, England had long been profiting from trade with the Spanish colonies, in part legally and in part not, and could confidently expect to continue to do so as long as she had to deal only with a debilitated Spain. The recent appearance of France as an active contender for these opportunities thus created an entirely different situation.

The American colonies, especially those to the north, were far from indifferent to this battle between the giants; to them the issues at stake were even more important than in the Britain-Holland conflict. Moreover, their sympathies lay predominantly with England. While they were not altogether happy with their position in the British empire, they had every reason to believe they would be no better off in an expanded French empire. Meanwhile they could take advantage of England's preoccupation with France to further their resistance to British control.

In several ways New England and New York felt the pressure of French aspirations. Albany fur traders were actively entering into the growing competition for the fur trade and hence understood the cost of sharing an increasingly limited market. Massachusetts was discomfited by French attacks on her fishing fleet and her merchant marine. So vital were these industries to New England's well-being that she could ill afford to have them injured. And finally, all along the New England-New York frontier the French were supplying firearms to the Indians and encouraging them to harass the English settlers.

Mounting Tension. The decision of the merchant-capitalists of England to make war against their principal enemy in the New World did not mean a relaxation of regulations within the empire. On the contrary, a policy of even stricter control was inaugurated. The new policy understandably began with Massachusetts, the new charter issued to the "Bay Colony" in 1691 declaring it to be Britain's purpose to bind her colonies more closely to her. In 1694 Parliament passed a law severely curtailing the freedom of the colonies to expand toward the west. Born of the growing Indian menace associated with the fur trade generally and the war with France in particular, this legislation did little to stem the westward advance and much to alienate land-hungry frontiersmen. Two years later the famous Board of Trade was created, an agency of the British government in which the important posts were held by representatives of the merchant group.

The first fruit of the important role this group was to play in colonial policy was an act passed in 1696 requiring all colonial governors to take an oath to enforce the Navigation Acts. By the terms of the same law colonial merchants in the re-export trade were required to post bond for forfeit if goods were shipped to a foreign port, and British customs officials in the colonies were given the right to search colonial vessels for evidence of illegal trading. In 1697 a still more rigorous enforcement step was taken. Special courts were established to handle cases involving violations of British regulations, a step made necessary by the fact that colonial courts with their jury trials rarely convicted colonial merchants. This move touched off a long and bitter struggle between mother country and American colonies, a struggle waged most directly between the colonial courts and the special British courts but one which actually revolved around the most vital point in England's colonial policy.

These were harsh measures by almost any standard. But surely harsh measures were called for. The illegal trade engaged in by the northern colonists had lately come to include even piracy, and in this form was a serious menace to Britain's Oriental trade through the Red Sea and the

Indian Ocean. Although England had long encouraged piracy against the trade of Spain, she could scarcely tolerate such an activity against her own shipping. Furthermore, bad as this behavior was under ordinary circumstances, it was infinitely worse in time of war. In the swift retribution insisted upon by British merchants more than one colonial pirate lost his life, among them Captain Kidd.

King William's War, the first phase of the long struggle between France and England, came to an inconclusive end in 1697, and the business groups in England were given a brief respite in which to assess once more the situation relative to their colonial competitors. They could take no comfort in what they saw. The successful enforcement of the trade laws was producing a series of consequences most unfavorable to British interests.

For one thing, the gain of the merchants in maintaining a tight hold on colonial trade was steadily being lost in the form of diminishing colonial purchases in England. Moreover, the demand for manufactured goods in America was so great that, failing to procure what they needed in Europe, colonists might be forced to engage in manufacturing on their own.[1] If ventures in market manufacturing proved successful, the northern colonies might begin exporting such goods to tobacco planters and the West Indies. An inevitable accompaniment of this step would be control by northern merchants over the sale of southern produce, and at this point England's hold on the American economy would be in grave jeopardy.

The most distressing aspect of all of this, furthermore, was the fact that already a manufacturing future for America could be dimly discerned. On the one hand, frontier conditions were doing much to create a people anxious to take advantage of economic opportunities. On the other hand, in the vast resources available there was obviously an abundance of opportunities.

Shipbuilding, flour-milling, and brewing had long been large-scale operations producing for both the domestic and foreign markets. Gradually, too, the shortage of labor in the colonies was being overcome by means of off-season production in farm homes of such articles as nails, shingles, staves, furniture, farm tools, and casks for domestic sale and the West Indian trade. A step beyond these crude beginnings was the establishment of shops where off-season farm labor could be used to an even greater extent. From this point it was an easy evolution to neighborhood, handi-

[1] In more technical (and at the same time more concrete) terms what was involved here was the possibility that the failure to secure an adequate amount of manufactured goods abroad would cause domestic prices to rise to such an extent that even an "inefficient" manufacturing industry would be able to earn satisfactory profits. Then, once such activity began to gain momentum, the initial inefficiency might be rapidly overcome. Under ordinary circumstances investors preferred to put their money into shipping or agriculture because these activities produced larger returns.

craft industries where more or less skilled labor turned out needed goods on a full-time basis. Most communities of any size even now boasted a sawmill, a gristmill, a slaughterhouse, and a fulling mill, while larger communities might also have a shoemaker, a tailor, a cabinetmaker, a candlemaker, etc. Then as now the size of the immediately available market determined the degree of specialization.

For the most part, this steady evolution of manufacturing industries had not concerned the mother country. As yet the colonies were most acutely deficient in textile and iron products, precisely the items on which England's colonial export trade most depended. But the most farsighted British officials could see plainly that there was no reason why the advance of an ever greater degree of specialization should soon come to an end—no reason for it to stop short of embracing both iron and textile goods.

Much point was given to these foreboding thoughts when in 1699 Britain's woolen industry, still her most important economic activity, became depressed, a condition attributed to the development of wool manufactures in the colonies. No doubt the accusation was exaggerated, although the colonists were increasing the quantity and improving the quality of woolen goods produced in America. (Naturally this industry was one of the first to develop in the colonies; wool, after all, was the foundation of the entire clothing and bedding industries at that time.) In response to this threat Parliament enacted the Woolens Act of 1699 prohibiting the export of wool or wool cloth from any colony. The intent of this wording was to permit household woolen manufactures but to make commercial production impossible by limiting its market. Ironically, one of the areas in which wool manufacturing was developing was Long Island. The defeat of the Dutch had added an economy to England's possessions having economic propensities very similar to those in New England.

No Relief in Sight. Efforts to solve the critical problem of England's American colonies now merged with the outbreak of Queen Anne's War in 1701, the second phase of the conflict between France and England, and colony–mother-country relationships were not thereby improved. Whereas in King William's War New Englanders had demonstrated their lack of loyalty to England by engaging in piracy against her, New Yorkers now signified their disloyalty by negotiating a neutrality agreement with French Canada. Albany fur traders had discovered what would happen to their business as a result of military activities in their area. By this act New Yorkers also indicated the weakness of their feeling of solidarity with New England, for this refusal to participate threw the burden of defending the northern frontier all the more upon her neighbor to the north.

When next England was able to turn to problems of imperial administration she found herself confronted, not with a single major difficulty, but with two. The balance-of-payments problem of the northern colonies was still unsolved, and the money question had arisen again in a particularly critical form. So critical was this issue, in fact, that to it she gave first consideration.

During the latter part of the seventeenth century the need of the colonists for metallic money had become so desperate that they had again taken matters into their own hands—this time by enacting laws increasing the value of coins circulating within the colonies. In the North the principal purpose was to increase the money supply by attracting money which circulated at a lower value elsewhere. Tobacco planters, on the other hand, were primarily motivated by a desire to reduce the burden of their debts. However, the most difficult aspect of the situation was that as the legislation of one colony was nullified by that of others, the first was forced to legislate a still higher value in order to attract the wanted metal, and colonies which would otherwise not have taken action at all were forced in self-defense to follow suit.

At first England was not especially concerned with the money manipulations of the northern colonies, for she did not derive revenue from them and had little capital invested there. She was vitally concerned, though, with money legislation in the tobacco colonies. Enactments to debase both the revenue received by the Crown and the principal of debts owed to British merchants were unthinkable. Accordingly England invalidated most of the southern legislation.

Immediately the tobacco colonies complained that the freedom to legislate money values retained in the North drew away their coin into the trading areas of Boston, New York, and Philadelphia. While it can legitimately be doubted if money regulations of this kind were ever very successful, these complaints did prod Britain into still stronger measures. She could ill afford to be responsible for increasing the supply of money in the North, indicative as such a result would be that Southerners were buying goods in America rather than England, and in 1704 she decreed maximum values for the major coins in an effort to bring about uniformity.

Turning from the money issue to the balance-of-payments problem in New England, England next took her first and almost her only constructive step. The Board of Trade proposed a bounty for the production of naval stores in the colonies. Heretofore England had been buying naval stores from Europe, using precious specie for this purpose. If such goods could be produced in New England, New Jersey, and New York, her own limited supply of specie would be conserved and the northern colonists would have the purchasing power necessary to buy English goods without engaging in activities viewed as undesirable by Britain's colonial policy. It was only a necessary precaution to place pitch, resin, tar, turpentine, ship timber, masts, and hemp on the list of enumerated items (along with rice, the newly developed and extremely important plantation crop of South Carolina). This would assure that the expensive bounty underwritten in England would not be misused.

It is to England's credit that she did try to find an acceptable solution to this problem, although these efforts did come too late to be of much assistance and would have been inadequate even if successful. Unfortunately, her well-intentioned plans went far astray. Despite her sincere efforts the naval stores industry could not be rooted in the northern economy, where it was opposed to the industries already developed there. When a law passed in 1710 to reserve certain trees on ungranted lands in the northern colonies was almost openly defied, England was forced to abandon the venture. The sequel was the ironical fact that the naval stores industry soon became an important economic activity in the pine forests of the Carolinas.

During the latter part of Queen Anne's War the northern colonies secured a considerable amount of British purchasing power in the form of money sent from England to finance the conflict. As long as these resources were available their money problem was much abated. But when the war ended in 1713 it was as compelling as ever. Britain was no doubt somewhat consoled for this fact by the terms of the Treaty of Utrecht. To her went Newfoundland, Acadia, most of the Hudson Bay area, and important monopoly rights in the slave trade of the Spanish Indies. However, France was not yet dislodged from the New World; in Canada and Louisiana she was as strong as ever.

The Complication of Dynamics. England's naval stores experiment indicates that she might have succeeded in solving her most pressing colonial problem. Given time, in other words, a more or less satisfactory solution might have been found. Time, however, was the resource least available. The growth of America was producing a situation too dynamic and changing to be dealt with between military encounters with a major European enemy. Before she was prepared to deal with one status quo another had arrived presenting the underlying problem in a still more acute form.

The dynamic factor now permeating the colonial scene was a new wave of immigration. Europe's economic, social, and religious environment continued in a variety of ways to favor migrations to the New World. Destructive wars between ambitious nations striving for commercial or religious dominance, the concentration of control over productive resources in the hands of a relatively few landholders and businessmen, restrictive legislation governing economic and religious behavior—all played their part in making the New World appealing. There one might escape war, poverty, and persecution; there one might find peace, security, religious freedom, cheap land, and high wages.

No longer did England supply the bulk of the incoming immigrants. The new settlers were German peasants and Protestants despoiled by a succession of devastating wars and victimized by a determined attempt to enforce Catholic uniformity; French Huguenots exposed to one of the most severe periods of persecution in the annals of modern history; Scotch-Irish farmers who had become so efficient as competitors of English landlords and manufacturers that Parliament had destroyed their industries by legislation; and unemployed Swiss artisans who had fallen prey to an economic transformation which had not yet worked itself out. The appearance of these different peoples began the process of racial amalgamation which has been such an important part of America's history.

The new arrivals did not distribute themselves evenly throughout the settled regions of the new land. In New England the scarcity of good farm land, the system of land distribution through the town fathers, the Indian menace on the frontier, and religious intolerance combined to keep this area overwhelmingly English. New York was scarcely more popular as a result of her Indian problem, remnants of medieval feudalism, and barriers to expansion in the form of the Catskill and Adirondack mountains. Virginia and Maryland were at this point primarily in the market for slaves to add to their labor supply, and the Carolinas were also still wrestling with the problems associated with feudal land rights.

By a process of trial and error, Philadelphia became the point of entrance for a majority of the new immigrants. Here an excellent port, religious toleration, an abundance of fertile farm land, the freedom of the frontier from Indian wars, and opportunities for employment in the coastal region made Pennsylvania the recipient of a steady stream of immigrants. Largely as a result of this fact Philadelphia rose to a position of prominence equal to that of Boston and New York, and Pennsylvania and the backcountry areas on the southern frontier assumed an economic significance equal to that of New England or the tobacco south. Included in this new exodus from Europe to America were the ancestors of Jefferson Davis, Abraham Lincoln, and John C. Calhoun.

The consequences of this stream of settlers were as profound as those arising from the earlier migration of English colonists. Pushing westward to the frontier, making their way southward by way of river valleys to settle in the piedmont and hilly regions of Maryland, the Carolinas, and Virginia, as well as in western Pennsylvania, America's growing population sharpened the conflict between England and France. It became evident that English expansion could not long continue unless French positions began to give way.

Eighteenth-century expansion also accentuated the conflict between rich and poor, in part by increasing the numbers of the poor but in part too by strengthening the position of the rich. On the one side, the democratic movement was given greater support by the fact that the new arrivals, as soon as they had completed their indenture, typically acquired land and hence the right to vote. On the other side, aristocracy gained through the operation of the indenture system itself, as well as by the improvement in general business opportunities resulting from an increased population. The indenture contract was profitable enough in a high wage economy to permit the creditor to earn a money surplus during its life. This surplus then made it possible for him to lend money to the laborer when the latter emerged from indenture without the capital needed to make a start on his own. The debt thus incurred in turn provided a lever for compelling the debtor to turn his produce over to his creditor immediately after harvest when prices were at their lowest point in the seasonal cycle. Such relationships provided many a merchant-capitalist with great wealth, and at the same time contributed to the nation's heritage of poor, debtor farmers.

The new immigration even intensified the conflict between England and the American colonists. For one thing, it provided an increased labor supply on the basis of which industries could be developed on a larger scale. As this was accomplished such activities as shipbuilding, fishing, shipping, and the fur trade became more competitive with British aspirations, and capital accumulations resulting from this development made possible an even greater expansion. Still more important, however, the development of the backcountry in the South and in the middle colonies increased the surplus of grains and livestock above domestic needs. This surplus northern merchants increasingly sought to dispose of in ways contrary to the interests of British merchants. When England responded in perhaps the only way possible in a mercantilist world, the crisis between her and America inevitably deepened. Indeed the period between 1713 and the next outbreak of fighting with France was filled with one incident after another, all reflecting attempts by various elements in the colonies to shake off the bonds within which they felt restrained.

Internal Stress and Strain. One such incident occurred in South Carolina, an incident typical of a number of others in which colonists came into conflict with absentee proprietors. This group, in South Carolina as elsewhere, was by now primarily interested in selling land at a price as high as possible with little or no concern for the welfare of settlers. When planters and colonial speculators sought more land and a vigorous policy of defense against the Indians as rice cultivation became an economic activity of commanding importance, the proprietors were for the most part indifferent. Defense was too expensive, and land sold today might rise in value tomorrow. The resulting planter dissatisfaction readily gained the support of the smaller farmer and the Charlestown fur trader. Lesser landholders were equally interested in an adequate defense and in the lands proprietors were holding for speculative purposes. Fur merchants, beginning to feel the effects of French competition, were primarily in need of the support of a strong government.

At this point, as earlier, England's colonial policy could not avoid becoming implicated in such issues. On the one hand, her principal rice colony had to be kept out of the hands of both France and Spain, and therefore defense of the southern frontier was vital. This need was all the more urgent, too, because of South Carolina's importance in the fur trade and her function as a buffer state between the more important tobacco trade and hostile foreigners. On the other hand, the Navigation Acts needed to be enforced and the proprietors had been especially ineffective in this work. Under the circumstances it was not difficult for the colonists to secure the assistance of England in overthrowing the proprietors.

In 1719 the long threatened revolt became a reality. Angered by the proprietors' neglect of the colony in such matters as the administration of justice and the provision of educational facilities, colonists became particularly incensed by a proprietary ruling restricting the surveying and granting of additional lands. Marching on Charlestown in a body, they seized control of the government, elected a legislative assembly, took charge of the colony in the name of the king, and invited the Crown to assume control. This the Crown did with such alacrity as to further a suspicion that the revolutionary movement had actually been fomented by English officials.

TABLE 4. MOTHER ENGLAND TAKES OVER

Colony	Original Charter Revoked in	Primary Factor
Virginia	1624	Failure of company-type organization
New Hampshire	1680	Difficulties involving proprietors
Massachusetts	1684	Defiance of British rule
New York	1688	Difficulties involving proprietors
Maryland	1691 [a]	Difficulties involving proprietors
New Jersey	1702	Difficulties involving proprietors
South Carolina	1721	Difficulties involving proprietors
North Carolina	1729	Difficulties involving proprietors
Georgia	1752	Difficulties involving proprietors
Pennsylvania	1776	Revolution
Delaware	1776	Revolution
Maryland	1776	Revolution
Connecticut	1776	Revolution
Rhode Island	1776	Revolution

[a] Restored in 1715.

South Carolina was not the first colony to be taken over by the Crown at least in part because of mother-country dissatisfaction with proprietary rule. Neither was it the last. Gradually England was forced to assume control over most of her North American colonies, and only four out of the entire list went through the whole of the colonial period without losing their original charters to the British king. It perhaps tells us much about the character of William Penn that "his" colony was one of these four, the only major colony in this category.

Trouble to the South. While several colonies were acting out the drama of the struggle over land distribution, another conflict was intensifying. The tobacco and rice economies, held in the grip of Britain's trade restrictions and ravaged by a series of depressions, were becoming hopelessly burdened by debt. Moreover, the loss of control by the planter over his economic destiny was generating an allied evil—a progressive soil exhaustion resulting from the failure to practice sound farm-management principles.[2] One consequence of this was a growing competition between the older producing regions and newer areas.

Various expedients had been tried for the purpose of securing relief. At first the introduction of Negro slavery had promised some improvement. But slave labor was extremely inefficient, the price of slaves had steadily risen, and, worst of all, slave labor required a capital outlay which drew even tighter the planter's encirclement by debt. Slowly some modification in the situation was being achieved by diversifying farm production, thus reducing the plantation's dependence upon a single crop. But the problem nonetheless continued.

Understandably southerners began to think in terms of legislation as a way to relieve their distress. They tried, for example, to introduce a duty on the import of slaves for the protection of older producing areas against the newer settlements. The curtailment of production was another expedient appealed to. A petition was drafted requesting a reduction in the tobacco duty in England. There were even attempts to reduce the burden of debt by legal means.

It was no use. Measures seeking to curtail production failed because a wide enough voluntary cooperation could not be secured and because intercolonial enforcement was impossible without England's help. More specifically, Maryland and Virginia could never agree on how to proceed, and in the absence of almost complete coverage restriction programs invariably broke down because complying planters were penalized in favor

[2] The use of the term "sound" at this point must not be interpreted too literally. Intelligent use of resources in any economy requires that scarce (and hence expensive) resources be husbanded very carefully, while abundant (and hence cheap) resources may be used with much less caution. Throughout most of America's history land was the most abundant resource available, and until the western frontier gave out this factor of production was available in almost unlimited quantities. The phenomenon of "wasting" land resources was to be a fixed feature of American economic life for many years.

of the "chiseler." Furthermore, England actively opposed all such legislation, for her profits from the slave trade, an expanding tobacco production, existing marketing practices, and import duty revenues gave her a strong interest in maintaining the status quo. Although in 1730 she did relax the Enumeration Act slightly on sugar and rice, permitting exportation to Southern Europe, she stood for the most part firmly against relief measures. In order to prevent the colonists from levying import duties on slaves, England in 1731 forbade colonial governors to sign any bills so written, and in 1732 she put her full weight behind the collection of debts owed British merchants by a law making lands and slaves forfeit in the event of failure to pay debts. The same year a new American colony was chartered, the colony of Georgia, having as one of its major purposes providing a buffer area between the claims of European rivals and the increasingly important plantation economy in South Carolina. The distress of the southern planter was not to be relieved if Britain could possibly prevent it. And apparently she could.

More Trouble to the North. Colonial conflicts involving proprietors and southern planters gave England comparatively little trouble. In the one case she took over the troubled colony herself, and in the other she simply used the economic and political power at her disposal to resist undesirable adjustments. Two other kinds of conflicts, however, she did find difficult to cope with. One was her chronic feud with the northern colonists; the other was the struggle between the colonial aristocracy and the backcountry farmer.

The economy of the northern colonies had not altered its basic structure materially since the seventeenth-century crisis had been temporarily bridged by war. The same balance-of-payments problem necessitated the same complex, triangular pattern of trading relationships. Several features in the underlying situation, on the other hand, had altered sufficiently to change somewhat the focus of the conflict between colonial and English merchants. For one thing, northern industry was growing rapidly. Thus England's task of keeping this economy within bounds was becoming more formidable. Second, the appearance of the traffic in slaves had altered the relationship between the colonies and the West Indies.

The slave trade, as colonial ships and merchants began to assume an important role in it, was handled as follows. Ships loaded with rum and trinkets were dispatched to Africa and there exchanged for slaves. These were then taken to the West Indies where goods marketable in England were purchased, or perhaps the molasses out of which more rum could be produced in the colonies for another voyage. Unfortunately, the British West Indies were languishing under the high costs resulting from British restrictions and heavy duties on sugar, while the French West Indies were flourishing under a promotional and much freer trade policy. As the production of grain and livestock in the colonies increased, the British West Indies became unable either to absorb the American surplus or to keep pace with the colonial demand for molasses. At the same time, this trade

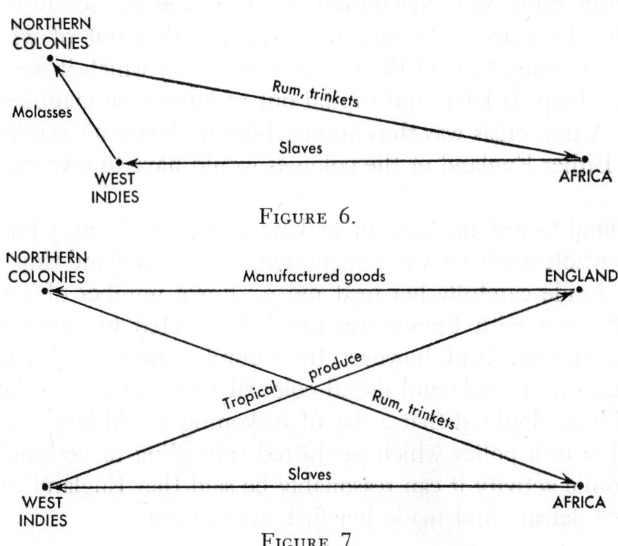

FIGURE 6.

FIGURE 7.

was greatly desired both by French interests in the Caribbean and by France. The French empire could not supply the islands with provisions, and the French brandy and wine interests would not permit the importation of rum into France.

What was England to do? Any serious attempt to check this trade would certainly divert northern capital into manufacturing. Even as it was she had found it necessary in 1732 to forbid the exportation of hats from any colony, another attempt to prevent the development of large-scale manufacturing. (Located as they were so close to the source of supply of the raw material from which so many hats were then made—the skin of the beaver—the colonists had a distinct advantage over England in this industry.) Simultaneously English sugar interests in the West Indies were clamoring for relief from an unequal competition with France, assisted as this rival was by trade with the American colonies. Even British merchants in England had much at stake in the form of credits to debtor-planters on the islands and a fleet earning large returns on Britain's trade in the Caribbean.

Although in the circumstances it could be no real solution, England proceeded to do the only thing possible for a colonial power imbued with the mercantilist tradition. She took steps in 1733 to sacrifice the interests of the northern colonies to the interests of sugar planters and English merchant-investors.

The device was a substantial duty on foreign sugar, molasses, and rum imported into any English colony, a step raising the issue of England's relationship to her northern American colonies more sharply than ever before. Rum particularly was one of the bases of the New England fishery, the fur trade, trade with Newfoundland, as well as the recently developed slave trade. Free access to rum (and the molasses out of which it was made) was a cornerstone of the northern economy which it could not give up and still keep its labor and capital out of large-scale manufacturing enterprises. A new crisis was thus approaching in America's economic development. Either England or the colonies would have to give up important interests.

The colonists lost no time in making their intentions known. Smuggling on a wholesale basis was inaugurated, and an England thus defied was forced to decide carefully her next move. For a number of reasons—and of these the war with France was one—she elected to close her eyes to what was going on. Still, however, the wounds remained, the sugar industry's distress on one side and illegal colonial trading on the other, and no one could have doubted that a day of reckoning would have to come. In the adoption of a policy which permitted smuggling to become a respectable economic activity it can reasonably be said that England suffered her third major defeat—and made her first major error.

The Money Problem Again. A second reason why England decided not to force a showdown with the northern colonies over the molasses question was because still another long standing controversy in the colonies was approaching crisis proportions. The seventeenth-century attempts of the colonists to solve their money problems had not been successful. No more successful had been England's attempt to legislate uniformity in the money circulating in these economies, for most colonies had freely ignored the British proclamation and there was no satisfactory way in which such laws could be enforced.

Although Britain had long since given up that battle as hopeless, the money issue was now arising in other and, from her point of view, more vicious forms. In particular, the colonists had discovered paper money and the wonders which could be performed by its use. Not only could the money circulating in the colonies be supplemented in this way, but debtor-farmers could reduce the burden of their debts and raise the prices of their produce by the simple expedient of printing paper money. No wonder colony after colony had succumbed to the habit-forming practice of emitting bills of exchange.[3]

[3] The issuance of paper money, whether indirectly through banks or by governments directly, was a continuing source of conflict between various interests on the colonial scene because significant changes in the money supply can influence the distribution of the goods and services by changing the general level of prices. A significant increase in

At first paper money was issued in anticipation of taxes in the course of financing the first phases of the Anglo-French War. After Queen Anne's War, however, farmers were faced with the problem of finding a security other than taxes on the basis of which new issues could be put into circulation. Their solution was the creation of colonial land banks. With the farmer's land as security, these banks could loan money to farmers and thus reduce their economic dependence upon merchant-creditors, and it was even argued that the colony itself could be operated on the interest received from these loans in lieu of taxes.

For the colonial aristocracy this device represented a grave threat. Much of its economic position was the result of its financial hold over the farmer—a hold which the farmer was now trying to lodge with the colonial government instead. As they moved to oppose the new departure, colonial aristocrats were soon joined by the British government. English creditors could no more afford to have the burden of colonial debt tampered with than could colonial creditors. In such a context rigorous enforcement of the Molasses Act seemed scarcely feasible. This was all the more the case because the most critical battle over the land bank question arose in Massachusetts.

Massachusetts had issued bills of exchange perhaps more freely than any other colony; there private as well as public institutions were being created. In 1733, however, England called a halt and gave the colony a limited period of years in which to retire the private-bank notes in circulation. Farmers all over the colony were appalled at the thought of the consequences for debts and prices which would result and determined to stand fast. In 1740 a land bank was created whose issues were at least to compensate for the withdrawal of earlier emissions. Immediately the merchants banded together in refusing to accept the newly issued money. A mass uprising of farmers in 1741 to force acceptance was put down with the aid of His Majesty's Government in Massachusetts, and in the same year Parliament passed an act outlawing all private banking operations.

This turn of events threatened every one of the thousand or so subscribers with ruin. And since many were actually insolvent anyway, those who had resources were all the more exposed to legal action. For their part, the merchants were determined to ruin as many subscribers as possible. Many of the land bankers were in fact ruined, and most of them were troubled by lawsuits for some twenty years. Few actions taken by England during the colonial period did more to generate ill-feeling against her than this action in 1741. It is worth noting, for example, that one of

---

the money supply tends to shift real income from creditors to debtors by lowering the value of money, while the opposite change tends to make creditors better off at the expense of debtors by raising the value of money. It is basic to an understanding of American economic history that farmers have typically been debtors.

the directors of this ill-fated land bank was one Samuel Adams, father of another Samuel Adams even more important in America's history.

Clearly the situation between England and her colonies was going from bad to worse. An uncertain truce highlighted by British tolerance of economic activities proscribed by English laws could not be permanent. Perhaps the outbreak of still a third phase of the struggle between Spain, France, and England was a welcome relief from the mounting tension.

QUESTIONS FOR DISCUSSION

1. How fundamental was the conflict between England and France in America?
2. What steps did England take after 1689 to enforce the trade and navigation legislation more effectively?
3. Why did England's attempt to develop a naval stores industry in the northern colonies fail? Was the growth of this industry in the southern colonies a gain for the mother country?
4. Might England have accomplished more in preventing competitive manufacturing from developing in the colonies if she had forbidden local industries instead of acting only against large-scale manufacturing enterprises?
5. What were the reasons for the continuing flow of immigrants to the New World? Where were they coming from during this period and where did they settle?
6. Would the southern colonists have achieved significant results by way of economic legislation if England had not constantly intervened?
7. What was the relationship between the balance-of-payments problem in the colonies and monetary difficulties there?
8. In what ways did the New World situation generate conflict within the colonies having nothing to do with relationships between the colonies and England?
9. If the Puritans had congregated in Virginia rather than Massachusetts would American history have been significantly different?

Chapter 4

TWO WORLDS IN CONFLICT

1740–48	King George's War (War of the Austrian Succession).
1750	Iron Act.
1751	Currency Act.
1754	Albany Congress.
1754–63	French and Indian War (Seven Years' War).
1763	Land Proclamation.
1764	Currency Act.
	Sugar Act.
1765	Stamp Act.
1767	Townshend Acts.
1770	Boston Massacre.
1773	Boston Tea Party.
1774	First Continental Congress.
1775	Fighting began at Lexington and Concord.
1776	Declaration of Independence.

King George's War was both short and unsatisfactory. Made necessary in the first place by the failure of the Peace of Utrecht to effect a permanent settlement in the New World, the new conflict fell even wider of this goal. In Newfoundland and Nova Scotia, France refused to stop trying to dominate a fishing and lumbering industry she had legally made over to England. Concessions made by Spain at the end of Queen Anne's War had only whetted the appetite of British mercantile interests, and Spain's empire continued to be one of the prizes at stake. And in the vast interior of North America the two giants still battled one another over the fur trade and the tremendous land resources available there. Plainly both England and France had decided upon an all-or-nothing stand.

Prelude to Conflict. The actual fighting was as uneventful as the outcome was temporary, and perhaps the most important event of the period was the beginning of indigo production in South Carolina—a product in great demand in the dye industry for its deep and delicate blue color. Production of indigo had lately declined in the West Indies, and simultaneously South Carolina's soil and climate were found to be suitable for its growth. One factor which was especially important to this new development was the rapid increase in slavery throughout the South (and with respect to this factor indigo was perhaps as much cause as effect), for indigo was produced by means of a fermentation process so disagreeable that only slave labor could yield the large profits planters earned during the first years of the new crop. England's eagerness to establish the new industry, as well as the financial weakness of South Carolina as a colony, was indicated by the generous bounty accorded producers that was paid for out of the British Treasury.

Mother-country relationships with the northern colonies, as usual, were much less pleasant. Soon reconciled to the wholesale smuggling of molasses in defiance of the Molasses Act, British capitalists did not propose to countenance the development of manufacturing as well—especially iron manufacturing. Yet there was a powerful incentive for colonial manufacturing to move in this direction, for the cost of importing heavy and bulky but indispensable iron tools was very great. For years the question of colonial manufacture of iron had been debated in England, although never conclusively, since two important interests involved could not come to an agreement. The interests most concerned with the making of pig iron—ironmasters, mineowners, and forest magnates (because charcoal was then used in the smelting process)—insisted on the suppression of the entire industry. Iron manufacturers, however, most interested in a supply of cheap pig iron, wanted the high quality colonial metal to be imported duty free and colonial fabrication suppressed. In 1750 the latter group won out; the importation of pig and bar iron was freed of duties, and the expansion of iron manufactures was forbidden.

Simultaneously the money issue again became prominent, not in Massachusetts this time but in nearby Rhode Island. From its earliest colonial days this colony had perhaps exemplified the spirit of democracy more than any other, no doubt a direct heritage of the spirit of its great founder—Roger Williams. A basic outlet for democratic tendencies throughout the colonial era had always been cheap money, and it was therefore most appropriate that little Rhode Island now led the other colonies down the inflation road. With direct franchise control over both the governor and the legislature, farmers here had created no less than nine land banks.

Rhode Island was not the only offender. During King George's War most of the New England colonies had issued paper money to offset the scarcity of coin. The resulting depreciation had been so destructive of property values that colonial and British merchants appealed to Parliament for assistance, and before this issue was finally settled creditors all over New England had become almost desperate.

On the other hand, however, the struggle in Rhode Island was the most acute. The governor tried to intervene with a veto, but the democracy successfully frustrated this move. Meanwhile Parliament had at first refused to accept authority in the matter on the ground that Rhode Island's bills were not legal tender, although the pressure of popular sentiment was so great that they became for all practical purposes fully lawful currency. Creditors next sought to exclude debtors from the legislative assembly by raising the property qualifications for voting, but this step was nullified by the increase in property values resulting from currency inflation.

In 1751 Parliament acted. With a single stroke land banks and paper money in all of New England were prohibited. As the Iron Act of the previous year had created ill will in the colonial aristocracy, so now did the Currency Act intensify the antagonism of rural debtors.

These events, however, were simply evidences of "normality." Of a very different order was the steadily worsening relationship between the English-speaking peoples and those Indians most essential to the colonial stake in the fur trade. Traditionally friendly to the English, the Iroquois were becoming restive as the colonists infringed more and more ruthlessly on lands they considered their own. With the Indians beginning to abandon the British cause in favor of France, and with another phase of hostilities with France already pending, the situation on the New York frontier had become quite dangerous by the end of 1753. Although this situation was not directly related to colony–mother-country affairs, the organization of colonists formed to deal with the Indian menace contributed much to the success with which they were able to combine a few years later for an altogether different purpose.

More specifically, the colonies were provided with an unusually favorable opportunity for intercolonial cooperation—a situation appearing rarely in the colonial experience. Economically the several colonies had needed goods produced in Europe rather than in other colonies, and hence their closest ties were abroad. Furthermore, intercolonial integration was no more possible than it was necessary. On the one hand, so superior were water transportation facilities to those for land carriage that it cost less to ship a ton of iron across the Atlantic Ocean than the seventy miles between Lancaster and Philadelphia. For this reason settlements had been located to give the colonists the easiest possible access to the ocean while minimizing their need for land carriage. On the other hand, the east coast of North America, although favored with an excellent waterway system, is possessed of rivers running predominantly east and west rather than north and south. Therefore they were of little value in cementing the colonies together. Late in the colonial period Benjamin Franklin in a letter to Burke discussed frankly the impossibility of colonial union.

In 1754, at the instigation of the Board of Trade, there was held a general colonial congress for the purpose of securing additional support from the Indians. Representatives from all the New England colonies, New York, Pennsylvania, and Maryland met the Iroquois in Albany. Little was accomplished at this gathering, and its failure was only in small part due to the absence of Virginia—now by far the largest landholder among the colonies and hence the most important colony from the point of view of the French and Indian problem. But a beginning was made toward colonial unity. In the French and Indian War now about to begin, giant forward strides were taken in this same direction.

However, intercolonial cooperation was not the same thing as cooperation with England, and the one was decidedly not promoted by the other. Although the colonies did successfully combine forces in carrying on some phases of their own war effort, the fighting was also accompanied by such a flagrant disregard of England's interests on the part of the colonies as to give the mother country cause for considerable uneasiness.

In the first place, the colonies shamelessly continued during the war their commerce with the French West Indies, a trade much of which was illegal even in time of peace. Not only did such trade furnish provisions more or less directly to French military and naval personnel, but exports to France made that much more difficult the acquisition of supplies by British forces. And so determined were colonial merchants not to alter their trading relationships that they became exceedingly angry when England made use of the so-called "writs of assistance" (general search warrants enabling customs officials to enter ships or houses for the purpose of locating contraband goods) in the enforcement process. Such general warrants were essential, however, because special warrants required that the name of the informer be made public, and New England especially had developed a powerful sentiment against men who informed on Yankee smugglers.

In the second place, the colonies were anything but cooperative in helping to finance their struggle. On the assumption that the defeat of France was as important to the colonies as to England it seemed only reasonable to expect them to assume some of this burden. Yet colonial assemblies used every device to minimize their contribution and even to delay the assistance grudgingly given. In two ways in particular did colonial tactics annoy Britons. On the one hand, England's emergency was used to wrest concessions from the imperial administration as the price of military grants which the mother country felt should have been gladly supplied. On the other hand, the war economy touched off perhaps the most extreme wave of paper money issuance the New World had yet seen. England was placed in the uncomfortable position of being forced to acquiesce in a practice she abhorred or to give up the military aid available from this depreciating currency. Virginia, the worst offender, even refused all aid after her ambitions had been satisfied by the conquest of Canada. It is understandable why embittered British creditors determined to insist upon a rigid anti-paper-money policy as soon as the war emergency was over.

Amid the stresses and strains of war the underlying significance of all this was largely lost. The fact was, however, that the colonies were becoming actively defiant of English rule. Toward the end of the conflict there occurred two events which, perhaps more than any others, furnished a key to the New World developments of the next quarter of a century.

The first concerned the writs of assistance. With the law on which these were based coming up for renewal in Massachusetts, Boston merchants decided to make a court fight against them. James Otis was employed as the merchants' attorney. Already famous as a defender of colonial smugglers, Otis in this case is often said to have reached the pinnacle of his career. Basing his brief upon the proposition that British subjects, including colonists, possessed fundamental rights which even Parliament could not impair, he crystallized public indignation against the writs and simultaneously set in motion the constitutional debate which was to wax hotter and hotter as the Revolution approached. No doubt partly because James Otis lost his case it was not realized how serious was the challenge he had thrown down to Parliament and to England.

Virginia and paper money provided the context for the other prophetic event. In Virginia the issuance of an excessive quantity of paper currency bore mute testimony to the plight of tidewater tobacco planters caught in the grip of Britain's colonial policy. For many years the Anglican clergy of Virginia had been paid in tobacco, a mode of payment which seemed overly expensive as the issuance of paper money pushed the price of tobacco higher and higher. Early in the war this situation was remedied by a Virginia statute permitting payment in money at a fixed rate for each pound of tobacco due. Supported by British merchant creditors, the clergy objected, and as a result the law was disallowed in England. Among the suits for damages to recover the balance in tobacco still owing, one case has a special importance. Patrick Henry, then a very young attorney, conducted the defense for one parish being sued and made an effective verbal attack on the royal disallowance. Patrick Henry also lost his case, but in the award of damages of one penny a Virginia court laid down another open challenge to Britain's imperial rule.

England Tightens Her Grip. Separated from these two events by the entire width of the Atlantic Ocean, another event was taking place which was to have momentous consequences for the world's history as the implications of American defiance worked themselves out. In 1760 George III was crowned king of England. Ambitious and strong willed, Britain's new king was determined to govern as well as reign. If he could possibly avoid it, his kingship was not to be a continuation of the habit of subservience to Parliament into which British kings had lately fallen. Perhaps a group of rebellious colonies would make an excellent point at which to begin.

The defeat of the French proved to be relatively easy. With one million settlers in the New World as compared with only one hundred thousand French subjects, the resources available to England were a decisive factor. It proved to be unfortunate for the French that they had not developed themselves in America on a settled agricultural basis as had the English, and that they did not have an ocean and a difficult mountain range keeping their colonial population relatively compact. Even the fact that the English type of agricultural economy had put the Indians largely on the side of the French was not a sufficient compensation for these disadvantages. The Treaty of Paris in 1763 awarded to England the territory held by France east of the Mississippi River and Canada (which after long deliberation England finally decided to take rather than Guadalupe, a tiny sugar island in the French West Indies). From Spain Britain received Florida, and to Spain France gave New Orleans and her territory west of the Mississippi River. At long last England's New World struggle with her European rivals was virtually ended.

The expulsion of France from America altered drastically relationships within the British Empire. No longer did England need to act cautiously in order not to antagonize colonial allies in a foreign war. Moreover, the conquest of Canada and the Ohio Valley brought England face to face with a new task of government; a policy had to be developed governing expansion into the western part of America. And these factors were in addition to the deep-seated tension within the empire as revealed and accentuated during the war.

It was thus in no spirit of retribution that England turned immediately after the war to the task of establishing a long-range program for western expansion. Britain was guided as she had long been by the needs of her merchant capitalists, and for several reasons she was inclined to feel that colonial expansion to the west should not be encouraged. Settlement west of the mountain barrier was no longer necessary as a defense measure, and such expansion did not seem to promise much as far as British merchants were concerned. In the undeveloped state of transportation, production on the other side of the Applachians could not readily be exported to England and hence exchanged for British manufactures. Furthermore, the westward movement threatened British investments in the older tobacco areas, and debts owing Britons in this area should be collected before Virginia and Maryland planters were ruined. Merchants interested in the fur trade, too, urged against rapid western settlement because the advance

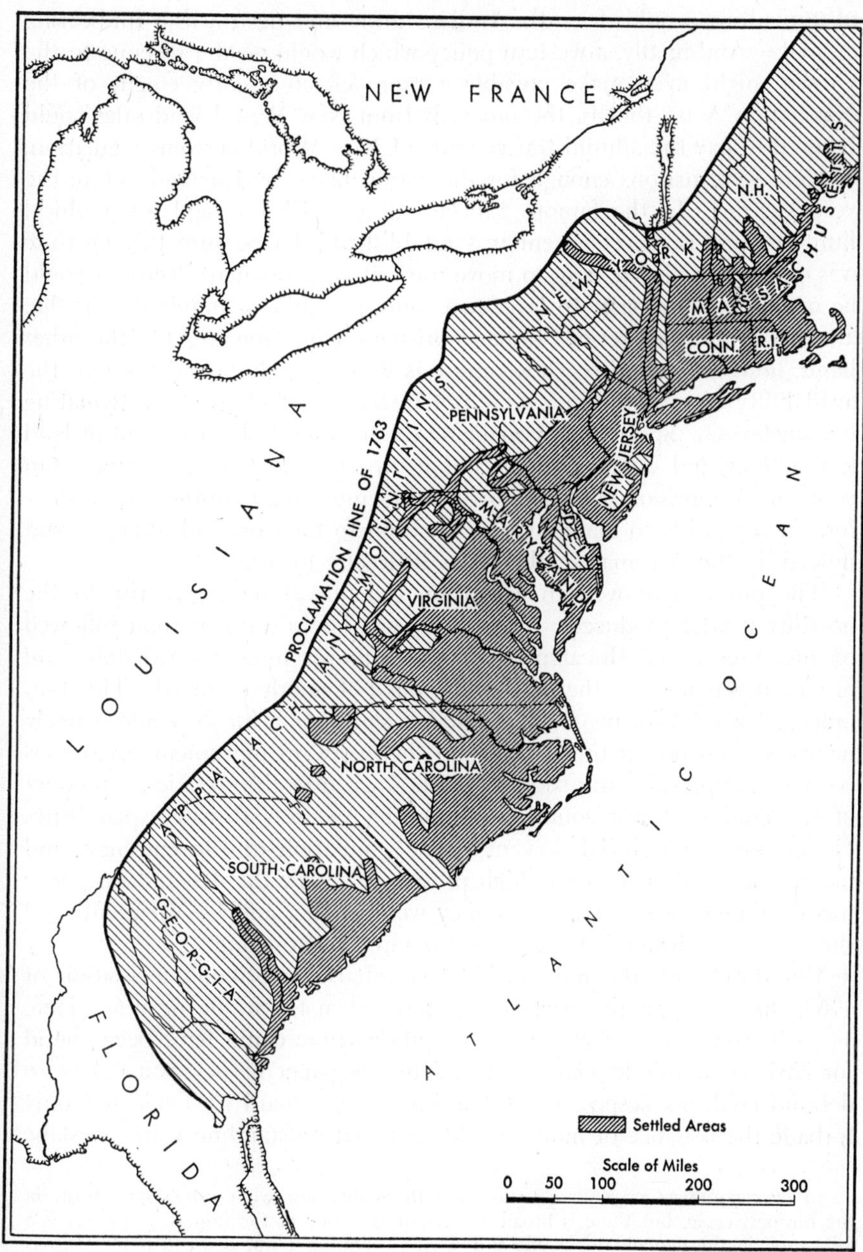

FIGURE 8. Barrier to the West

of agriculture would drive the Indians away and destroy the fur-bearing animals. And finally, a western policy which would yield a revenue to the Crown might even make possible a more effective enforcement of the Navigation Acts—that is, the proceeds from New World land sales could be used to pay the administrative costs of New World customs regulation.

Here were reasons enough for the action taken by England before the year was out. In the famous Proclamation of 1763 a rigid geographical limit to western development was established. To be sure this measure was only adopted as a stopgap move until more permanent decisions could be made, and the haste to lay down some preliminary standards was due almost entirely to a serious Indian uprising on the frontier. On the other hand, however, colonists whose interests were strongly bound up with the availability of western lands were not inclined to look at the extenuating circumstances. Speculators visualizing the fortunes to be made out of land transactions and debtor-farmers looking to the West as an escape from economic oppression could see in Britain's move only another attempt by foreign capitalists to manipulate a situation to their own advantage. And indeed, in the last analysis there was little else to see.

The problem of western expansion did not at once give rise to the hostility it later produced. In part this was because it was soon followed by measures which threatened colonial interests more immediately, and in part it was because the new policy was but poorly enforced. This last, indeed, was most fortunate from Britain's standpoint, for she could scarcely have chosen a poorer time to restrain the westward movement. A serious economic depression was soon to settle down over the colonies, a product of the ending of war conditions.[1] During the war British expenditures (including a substantial flow of specie), inflation of the currency, and privateering had generated a high prosperity. Now the demand for goods was declining, issues of paper money were smaller and less frequent, and the field for privateering activities was rapidly narrowing.

But if colonists did not quickly take offense at Britain's legislation of 1763, the same was not true of the steps taken the following year. Here again it would seem that a more propitious time could have been found for basic economic legislation. Condemning paper money as a device to defraud creditors (especially British ones), the Board of Trade not only forbade the issuance of more but decreed that outstanding issues must be

[1] Few economists are willing to assert with finality just what causes downturns in the business cycle, but there is broad agreement that one of the important factors is a falling off in the demand for goods and services. During a war demand is for obvious reasons greatly enhanced, and the ensuing depression is a rough measure of the extent to which new demands arise as offsets to those which disappear after the war. Put differently, a postwar depression in a private enterprise economy roughly measures the difficulty encountered in shifting the focus of an economy from government sponsored demand to a more normal basis.

retired on schedule. There was perhaps a little vindictiveness here, although this was a long-standing English policy. Not even notes issued by the Bank of England were legal tender; why should colonial governments be allowed greater powers? The Currency Act of 1764, in other words, extended to all the colonies the earlier prohibition directed at New England, and depressed farmers facing the prospect of an early contraction of the money supply were still further alienated.

The middle of an economic depression was scarcely the time, either, to place added burdens on such trade as was available. Yet in 1764 Parliament began the enactment of a series of momentous statutes designed to raise a revenue for the British treasury. The Indian uprising of the preceding year had demonstrated that large expenditures would be needed for frontier defense, while the behavior of colonists in the recent war had made it evident that they could not in their present state of disorganization defend their own frontier. Accordingly a decision was made to use British regulars for this purpose but to finance the cost at least in part by taxing the colonies.

The first of these new revenue measures, the Sugar Act, was intended primarily to secure a revenue by collecting a duty from the import of foreign molasses—along with a number of other foreign items such as sugar, coffee, silks, and wines. Already, of course, such a duty was technically in existence, but as a result of widespread evasion almost no revenue had been forthcoming. The new program, therefore, was designed to collect a tax reduced by one-half. Northern traders were thus again confronted with essentially the same situation as after the original passage of the Molasses Act; they were to be forced to give up one of the foundation stones of their economy for the benefit of inefficient West Indian sugar producers and British investors. Moreover, this same enactment contained another blow to northern business interests. Important northern products such as iron and lumber were enumerated; henceforth they would have to be shipped only to England, at least in the first instance.

In two other and more subtle ways the Sugar Act was intended to benefit English businessmen. First, it removed most of the drawbacks (repayments of a proportion of duties paid) on goods exported to the colonies by way of English ports. As a result these goods were increased in price relative to goods of British origin. Second, the new duties on imports included a number of items produced by foreigners in competition with British manufactures. Again the English products were given an artificial advantage. And, to make more certain that the colonists did not step into this manufactured goods vacuum, England inaugurated a series of additional bounties to further the production in America of certain raw materials needed by British manufacturers.

A Sharp Reaction. England's colonial legislation of 1764 marked in two respects a major departure from earlier policy. True she had always treated colonial interests as expendable, and certainly no change was visible at this point. A careful analysis of previous legislation and its effect on the colonies, however, reveals a most significant fact; at no major point had it been seriously restrictive as far as the northern economy was concerned. The laws had often enough contained the ingredients of real restriction, but for one reason or another enforcement had always been sufficiently lax to keep these consequences at a minimum. Even legislation against the development of commercial maufacturing had never been particularly painful. America was a high wage economy, skilled labor was scarce, land was abundant and hence cheap, and profits from agricultural and mercantile activities were very attractive. Under such circumstances the desire of colonists to enter the manufacturing field had never been particularly strong. And finally, the enumeration legislation which bore so heavily on the southern tobacco planter had not been employed against northern merchants.

Put differently, the Sugar Act for the first time forced American capitalists to weigh the advantages of membership in the empire against the disadvantages. Heretofore British and American merchants had in effect stood together against the underprivileged groups in America who thought in such uncapitalistic terms as paper money and relief from debts. Now England had deeply outraged the merchant aristocracy, and among northern capitalists the calculation of net advantage began at once.

Northerners were not inclined to minimize the value to them of the empire. Protection by the British navy, privileged access to empire markets, the ready availability of British capital, and British assistance in controversies with other powers were benefits of high importance. Perhaps in part because they had never before been forced to think in such terms, northerners had not yet begun to visualize themselves as being able to stand alone. From this point forward, however, such thoughts were bound to occur with increasing frequency.

In one other important way the new policy was a break with the past. Prior to this the burdens placed on the colonial economy had been only for the purpose of regulation. Now, burdens were being instituted for the avowed purpose of raising a revenue. A colonial environment thoroughly imbued with mercantilism would scarcely have raised questions of principle regarding regulation, but taxation—especially, perhaps, "taxation without representation"—was another matter.

The passage of the Sugar Act might well have failed to rouse emotions to fever pitch if it had not been followed in 1765 by the notorious Stamp Act. This measure was another revenue-producing device, placing a stamp tax on newspapers, bonds, notes, commercial bills, legal documents, insurance policies, almanacs, advertisements, leases, pamphlets, and so forth. Now, indeed, American indignation was given full vent. Anger and protest combined to produce a succession of violent acts which for a time threatened law and order. Only with some difficulty was resentment finally channeled into more constructive action.

It is not too much to say that in these attempts to collect a revenue in the colonies England made her second major error, and this despite the fact that the levies imposed were eminently reasonable. Nor did the error consist merely of the burdens placed upon trade, substantial though these were. Not only did these measures add to the cost of doing business, a business already in the throes of economic depression, but the taxes were to be paid in specie and would thus threaten still more a money situation already made difficult by the currency enactment. Furthermore, the sums paid into the British Treasury by colonists would be expended via contracts to English merchants which would even more give mother-country competitors an economic advantage.

No, the issue went deeper than this. By these acts, and especially the Stamp Act, England united the several groups in the colonies against her (in addition to alienating newspaper publishers and lawyers, two of the most vocal groups in any society). The northern aristocracy was pushed into an unwelcome alliance with its "unnatural friends," the southern aristocracy, and with its "natural enemies," the back-country and urban democracy.

Merchants and planters were both, to be sure, aristocracies, and hence possessed in common a feeling of self-satisfied superiority over the average citizen. One, however, was a merchant aristocracy, while the other held its position on the basis of land. From the standpoint of the quarrel with England, northern merchants were essentially concerned about restrictions on opportunities to make profits, while the great resentment among southern planters was the burden of debts. The planter aristocracy would have liked nothing better than an adjustment relieving it of this load, an idea which could not be other than abhorrent to northern merchants. Now, with the passage of the Stamp Act, these "unnatural friends" became allied together in the first major movement of resistance to British rule.

Neither the Sugar Act nor the Stamp Act as such bore with any appreciable weight on the lower classes. Why, then, did they rise up against the mother country? It is widely said that their interest was in freedom, independence from the government of an "alien" ruler. More specifically, it is often urged that the motives of the aristocracy were largely economic, while those of the democracy were primarily political. Such an explanation will hardly do. The democracy had its economic interests, also, and if it stressed the constitutional arguments, the principal reason was that such an approach best suited the furthering of those interests. On the other hand, if merchants avoided the constitutional question, their reason was that along this road lay an alliance with the anticapitalist debtor who had little respect for the "rights" on which aristocratic institutions rested.

Throughout colonial history the back-country democracy had felt the heavy hand of British rule as severely as any group, and nowhere more severely than in Britain's stand on paper money. On the other side, however, this group had on occasion been favored by England where the local aristocracy had resisted pleas for defense and more land. But such favors had been all too few at best, and with the inauguration of restrictive land and monetary policies England had become essentially an obstacle to be overcome. To these frontiersmen whose habit of self-reliance made them reluctant to confess a need for any government, it was not so much "taxation without representation" as taxation which was objected to.

Even the rising class of artisans and laborers in the cities felt abused. Not only did they blame the depression on Britain's economic legislation (a charge not wholly unjustified), but American workers were already beginning to lay stress on the availability of land and credit as a refuge from economic oppression in the towns. And it had not escaped notice by this group that English businessmen ran successfully to Parliament in opposition to any colonial industry which threatened their profits. No wonder farmers and workers were the first to think in terms of independence, and no wonder the colonial aristocracy considered them "natural enemies."

From Defiance to Rebellion. There were some misgivings even in England as to whether the new imperial firmness in America could achieve the objectives sought. During most of their history England's American colonies had been relatively unimportant, and in consequence they had more often than not been neglected in favor of other of Britain's far-flung interests. The question now sharply raised was whether a policy of neglect could be retrieved by sterner measures as the colonies in the New World assumed a new importance in Britain's imperial plans, and it was not necessary to wait long for an answer.

In the first American reaction to Britain's new policy—the wave of violence—merchants played little part. When this reaction had begun to spend itself, however, northern merchants helped direct aroused energies into more constructive channels. On the assumption that petitions such as the one prepared by the Stamp Act Congress would avail nothing, a plan was drawn up to cease importing goods from England until the Stamp Act was repealed. Surprisingly successful (although in part because it caught British business interests at a time when trade was already depressed), nonimportation galvanized British merchants into a determined protest to Parliament. One of the obvious consequences of this policy if long continued would so clearly have been to give further impetus to colonial industry. In 1766 this protest bore fruit and the Stamp Act was repealed. Simultaneously the Sugar Act was modified by reducing the molasses duty to a nominal sum and abolishing the discrimination against foreign molasses.

Rejoicing in the colonies at this turn of events was matched by a stiffening of attitude in England. In 1767 a new British Chancellor of the Exchequer, Charles Townshend, made a new attempt to relieve the heavy burden of taxation in England by increasing the revenue received from the colonists. Much had been made during the Stamp Act controversy of a distinction between external and internal taxes, and the conclusion seemed to have been that the colonists would accept the former but not the latter. In conformity with these preferences duties were laid on a number of goods imported from England.

It became quickly apparent that the new taxes would be accepted no more readily than their predecessor. Again the colonial merchants resorted to nonimportation to compel England to back down. A second victory was not to be so easily won, however. For one thing, those merchants who traded primarily with England were not especially concerned about the Townshend Acts. It was the smuggling, free-trading merchants (such as John Hancock) who had reason to fear a corps of customs officials in every American port. As a result of this internal conflict it was more than a year before nonimportation became fully effective. Moreover, whereas the first such endeavor had caught the British economy at a weak point in the trade cycle, the repeat effort was handicapped by expanding trade conditions abroad. Thus British merchants were slower to respond.

Added to these difficulties was another important factor. Scarcely had nonimportation commenced to pinch the British economy than many of its most ardent enthusiasts within the colonial merchant group began to withdraw their support. In the larger urban centers the revolt against established authority was visibly producing political self-consciousness in the artisan-mechanic class. Never treated with respect or consideration by the colonial representatives of Britain's ruling class, and living in the shadow of the prosperity of America's wealthy, this group was quick to respond to what appeared to be an opportunity to get rid of one set of oppressors. The anticapitalist attitudes of these people, particularly if they became allied with the debtor-farmer group, might conceivably produce a social revolution if the aristocracy persisted in teaching them bad habits. Feeling that it would be far better to put up with the inconveniences of the British colonial system than to risk losing its power at home, the merchant class decided to leave well enough alone—to retreat before it was too late.

It was already too late. The genie could not be put back into the bottle. Although in 1770 most of the Townshend duties were repealed (because British businessmen felt the taxation of British imports to be bad economics, and particularly so to the extent that they stimulated the expansion of colonial manufacturing), the unrest of the urban poorer classes was not quieted. In fact the repeal of the protested duties, although apparently not at all coerced, served to exaggerate their feeling of their own growing importance. With the aid of the political genius of Samuel Adams the revolutionary fervor remained alive, feeding at first on aroused hopes but sustained also on incidents such as the so-called Boston Massacre.

Who were these artisan-mechanics who had suddenly become such a potent force in American history? Broadly speaking, they were the embryo beginnings of the working class which an industrial society inevitably produces. The specialization of function (division of labor) in the industrial East and the agricultural South created a need for clothing, food, tools, and luxuries produced by still other specialized persons, and increasingly this need was being met by domestic production rather than imports. One evidence of this development was the fact that by now almost 5 per cent of the entire population lived in cities containing more than 2,500 persons. Of these the most important were Boston, New York, Philadelphia, Baltimore, Richmond, and Charleston—these coastal cities containing most of the urban residents of the colonies. In short, there had even now commenced an evolution which was not to come to an end until these colonies had become the greatest industrial nation in the world—and indeed not even then.

The overwhelming majority of the residents of cities were laborers, most of whom were producing goods for sale which had earlier been produced primarily in homes for home use. Artisan shopkeepers, artisans-journeymen-apprentices in such industries as printing, smithworking, and baking, laborers in gristmills, sawmills, and the brewing, distilling, and meat-packing industries, workers in the building trades (especially shipbuilding), and seamen—all these and others were included in the urban uprising against British rule. Perhaps for the first time northern industrialists were beginning to appreciate the fact that the development of their economy in the direction they desired was to bring with it certain undesirable domestic consequences as well as a major clash with England. What this meant, of course, was that even if the mother-country dispute were favorably settled there would still be forces within which would have to be contended with. For the moment, however, merchants were too preoccupied with their immediate dilemma to concern themselves with the long-run consequences of an exchange economy.

The Last Straw. Colonial aristocrats were no doubt deeply reinforced in their resolve to quiet the populace when in 1770 and 1771 conflict with the mother country was temporarily replaced by still another phase of the long-standing conflict between the tidewater area and the frontier. For years incoming settlers on the North Carolina frontier had been fighting against the claims of eastern speculator-capitalists. Forced either to be satisfied with the poorest lands or pay extravagant prices for the better, these farmers had fallen into the same debt nexus which had enslaved so many of their back-country fellows. Moreover North Carolina's tax system bore most heavily on them, a situation which could not be remedied as long as the coastal residents controlled the government. Driven to desperate measures by the depression, the "Regulators" resorted to violence in order to secure some control for themselves. On May 16, 1771, an army financed by the eastern aristocracy finally brought the rebellious farmers to heel in a pitched and bloody battle. Well might eastern merchants reflect on the dangers of a society in which the masses had lost their respect for constituted authority.

The return of prosperity by 1771 and a temporary lull in objectionable mother-country legislation might easily have defeated even the genius of Samuel Adams, for the urban worker was extremely weak without the support of the merchant group. But in 1773 Britain made a move which forced the merchants to bury their dread of the mob and participate in yet a third resistance movement.

Britain's East India Company was on the verge of bankruptcy in 1773, a condition brought about by a combination of depression, mismanagement, and corruption. Appealing to Parliament for help, the company was liberally rewarded by a new set of regulations governing its distribution of tea in America. Henceforth the company need not auction off its tea in Britain, but instead might handle its own sales and without paying the tax normally assessed at British ports.

There was a certain ironic appropriateness in these new arrangements for selling East India tea in America. Of all the Townshend taxes only the import duty on tea had been retained, and the resultant impetus given illegal importation of tea had been partly responsible for the company's financial distress. With seventeen million pounds of tea on its hands the company was now authorized to by-pass all middlemen and sell tea in America at a price even lower than the stocks of illegal Dutch tea on hand in America could be sold. No wonder merchants engaged in illicit traffic in tea were quick to take up the cudgels of opposition.[2]

[2] This was not because the East India Company could perform middleman services cheaper than established dealers. In addition to a tax advantage, the new regulations meant that the company was no longer forced to sell to existing operators at "distress" prices, thus allowing these concerns to profit from its difficulties. The tables, in other words, were turned by permitting the company to offset inventory losses with whatever portion of the current rate of middleman returns it could secure through its own distributive efficiency.

Merchant opposition, on the other hand, was not limited to those engaged in smuggling. The East India Company could now undersell even legitimate traders and at the same time avoid paying commissions to regular American dealers. Even more important there was a basic principle involved in these developments which was most disquieting to colonial capitalists. If England could legislate a monopoly of the tea business, why not of other or even of all businesses? If Parliament could protect the East India Company from bankruptcy at the expense of the colonies, why not other concerns? Possibly membership in the British Empire was not worth its cost after all.

Once more the merchants, the urban worker group, and debtor-farmers united in opposition. Although there were popular demonstrations bordering on violence, for the most part resistance was orderly. In Charleston a shipment of East India Company tea was locked securely in a warehouse. In Philadelphia and New York ships bearing tea were sent back to England still loaded with tea. In Boston, however, negotiations between colonial leaders (chief among these being Samuel Adams) and empire officials broke down, and at the historic Boston Tea Party the tea loaded on three ships was emptied into the harbor.

Again the merchant class withdrew from active involvement. The destruction of private property had no place in their program, and this act of revolution made them recoil sharply. Even when Parliament passed the so-called "Intolerable Acts," measures to punish Bostonians by taking away almost every right and privilege for which the colonists had been fighting, the merchants were reluctant to stand with the crowd.

Shortly after the passage of these disciplinary measures, England's temporary land policy in America was replaced by a permanent one. In 1774 the Quebec Act was passed, and the colonists could see in even sharper perspective what it meant to be a part of Britain's colonial empire. Under the terms of this law the quitrent exaction on lands granted in the future was to be double the rate then prevailing in Virginia, no further gifts of land were to be made, and all sales were to be by auction to the highest bidder. At one stroke the free availability of western lands was destroyed for speculators and settlers alike, and the claims of colonies to certain of the lands to the west were extinguished. This policy, however, applied only to land west of the colonies. Elsewhere a much more liberal land policy was declared. In Nova Scotia, Canada, and Florida large tracts of land were given to British merchants, squires, and soldiers. These areas, notably, were within easier reach of England's manufactures, and were not apt to produce goods competitive with industries in which Englishmen had an important vested interest. Finally Britain's new policy sought to direct the fur trade to Montreal away from colonial traders in the east and the Spanish at New Orleans. Here was mercantilism in as pure a form as was ever achieved.

Even in the face of this new assault, the merchant class still endeavored to remain aloof. It was unable to do so for long. Revolutionary fervor had risen to such a high pitch that the merchants had to decide whether to join the radicals or oppose them. Most merchants chose to act with their countrymen, although with misgivings and often only with the idea of restraining the extremists. Under the guidance and enforcement of the Continental Association—the First Continental Congress—a new non-importation program was inaugurated, this time accompanied by a program of withholding vitally needed goods from the British West Indies. So powerful were the forces now arrayed against British rule that these economic sanctions were more effective than any yet applied. British commerce with the colonies ceased almost completely at many ports, and British merchants and manufacturers were quick to feel the pinch.

In vain now did English businessmen protest to the British government that steps should be taken to conciliate the rebellious colonists. The king and the ministry would have none of it. From their point of view it was precisely England's effort to conciliate and compromise which had brought affairs to their present state. By this time, moreover, the attempt of George III to establish rule by the king in England had reached such an advanced stage that English businessmen were no longer wielding the influence in government circles they had once enjoyed.

As sentiment in England hardened against all measures hinting of retreat, sentiment in the colonies hardened against even a return to the status quo ante. The tide of independence, heretofore kept well beneath the surface (if for no other reasons than because such ideas were treasonous), was now rapidly rising. Then, in 1775, the "shot heard round the world" was fired, and the following year the Declaration of Independence was defiantly framed. The last phase of the American Revolution was under way.

QUESTIONS FOR DISCUSSION

1. What was the nature of the conflict in England over iron production in the colonies?
2. How democratic was the paper money policy followed in the colonies during these years?
3. How did the colonists "sabotage" England's war effort between 1756 and 1763? Was this deliberate?
4. Why did the various elements in the colonies protest against Britain's tax program after 1763?

5. Was the monetary policy adopted by England during this period really injurious to economic interests in America?

6. As of 1763 could England have adopted any program of legislation which would not have aroused intense opposition without completely abrogating her governmental responsibilities? Could any policy have been adopted at any time which would have avoided the Revolution?

7. What was the nature of the freedom for which Americans were fighting in the struggle with England? Was it really freedom that was wanted?

8. To what extent were the upper classes in America "forced" to join the independence movement?

9. Why is it reasonable to think of the fighting after 1775 as the *last* phase of the American Revolution? What was the first phase?

Chapter 5

FROM CRISIS TO CRISIS

1777	Articles of Confederation adopted by Congress.
1778	Lowest point in the fortunes of the colonies.
	Franco-American alliance.
1779	Spain entered the war against England.
1780	Mutiny in General Washington's army.
1781	Robert Morris (a conservative) made Superintendent of Finance.
	Articles of Confederation ratified.
	Bank of North America chartered.
	Cornwallis defeated at Yorktown.
1782	Fall of the ruling ministry in England.
1783	Peace of Paris.
1784	The China trade opened.
1785	Attempt to negotiate a commercial treaty with England.
	Basic land ordinance.
	Boundary difficulties with Spain.
	Trough of the postwar depression reached.
1786–87	Shays' Rebellion.

If the attention and energy of the colonists could have been devoted wholeheartedly to the military conflict with Britain, the New World would no doubt have made a better showing than it did. Unfortunately, however, two other conflicts had simultaneously to be fought out at home, with the result that the battle for "home rule" was waged without the singleness of purpose such an important endeavor ideally required. As it was, success resulted primarily because for the first time in many years most of England's European neighbors sided against her.

The Revolution at Home. The first of these internal conflicts in point of time was the battle between radicals and conservatives for control of the machinery of government. Always the radical democrats (small farmers, small traders, artisans, and laborers) had sought to increase their share of power, while conservatives (larger traders, planters, speculators, and manufacturers) had endeavored to keep the influence of such groups to a minimum. Now, with England's authority at least temporarily destroyed, a power vacuum was created which each group wished to fill from its own ranks.

It is a mistake to suppose that this conflict was a side issue to the main business of the revolution. On the contrary, it was with many people the very center of the broader problem. Radicals did not raise objection merely to the management of affairs in the interest of British capitalists; their resistance was aimed at the management of affairs in the interest of any capitalists. As it has been well said, the revolution was fought not simply for home rule but to determine who was to rule at home. Much of the misunderstanding which often arises at this point no doubt stems from the interpretation of the phrase, "Taxation without representation is tyranny," as an essentially political slogan. When its deeper economic implications are understood, confusion largely disappears. Tyranny as thus defined means placing on one group the economic burden of supporting a government which is first and foremost interested in furthering the interests of some other group. To the radical democrats of 1776 it made no difference whether this other group consisted of Englishmen or Americans.

This battle opened with a struggle for control of the new state governments. Here the hand of the radicals was greatly strengthened by the trade depression which swept over the land as England made effective war on American commerce and as the radical-sponsored cessation of trade with Britain became fully operative. Radical efforts were still further aided by the momentum which the resistance movement had achieved under their leadership. But despite these advantages they were far from completely successful. Once the die was cast in the conflict with England, the ranks of the aristocracy strongly tended to close against the "rabble." In all, about half of the states—Pennsylvania, North Carolina, Delaware, Georgia, Rhode Island and Connecticut—developed what might be called democratic constitutions. The remainder adopted constitutions distinctly aristocratic in tone.

Limited though this radical victory was, it nevertheless made possible a much greater one. Not only were state governments necessary, but the withdrawal of British authority, coupled with the problems of war, made some kind of a central government imperative. However, democrats felt that such a government should be the loosest kind of an arrangement, subsidiary in virtually all respects to the states. England, the model of a strong central government in their minds, had most frequently used her authority for the benefit of the upper classes—a result radicals proposed to avoid if possible. Conservatives had almost opposite views on this subject. Thinking of mother-country control as an ideal to be copied rather than a pitfall to be shunned, men of property believed in a central government with power greater than that possessed by the states in matters involving property rights.

The issue was quickly resolved. Although the committee appointed by the Continental Congress to draw up a plan of union brought in a conservative document, the state rights majority was able to force a major revision. The Articles of Confederation as finally approved provided for a government without an executive or a judiciary, without power to levy taxes, without power to pass any law in conflict with a state law, and requiring the approval of the delegations of nine states for the exercise of what powers it did possess. A government was established, in short, which lacked the power to govern. Such a government was now given the responsibility of mobilizing the economy for a major war effort.

Even after the Articles document was approved by Congress, it had still to run the gantlet of state acceptance. Here a delay of several years arose during which time the new government carried on its assigned functions without legal basis. The delay arose out of a controversy over the ownership of western land. Some states had laid claim to large tracts of this land, certain of these claims overlapping one another, while some states had no claims at all. To the landless states the situation seemed grossly unfair. With the proceeds from the sale of western land their neighbors could largely escape both state and national taxation, while they struggled against the handicap of this double burden. Little Maryland, neighbor to the state with by far the largest western claims (Virginia), refused to consent to the Articles until these western claims were turned over to the central government.

The second internal conflict was the one-sided contest between Patriot and Tory. Even after the decision for independence was made the Patriot group found itself confronted with a large number of friends and neighbors who remained loyal to the king and waited anxiously for the heavy hand of the royal discipline to fall on their associates. Civil strife between these two groups appeared almost immediately, and as the war progressed the intensity of this struggle grew apace. As the Patriot majority became more and more overwhelming, the lot of Loyalists became progressively more difficult. They were subjected to double or even treble taxes, compelled to pay obligations in specie, assessed unusually heavy fines for small and even imaginary transgressions of the law, openly despoiled of their real or other property, and excluded from office and professional positions. As early as 1777 the Congress went so far as to recommend that all Loyalist estates be confiscated.

Who were the men and women willing to undergo such hardships rather than desert their king? They were landed proprietors and royal

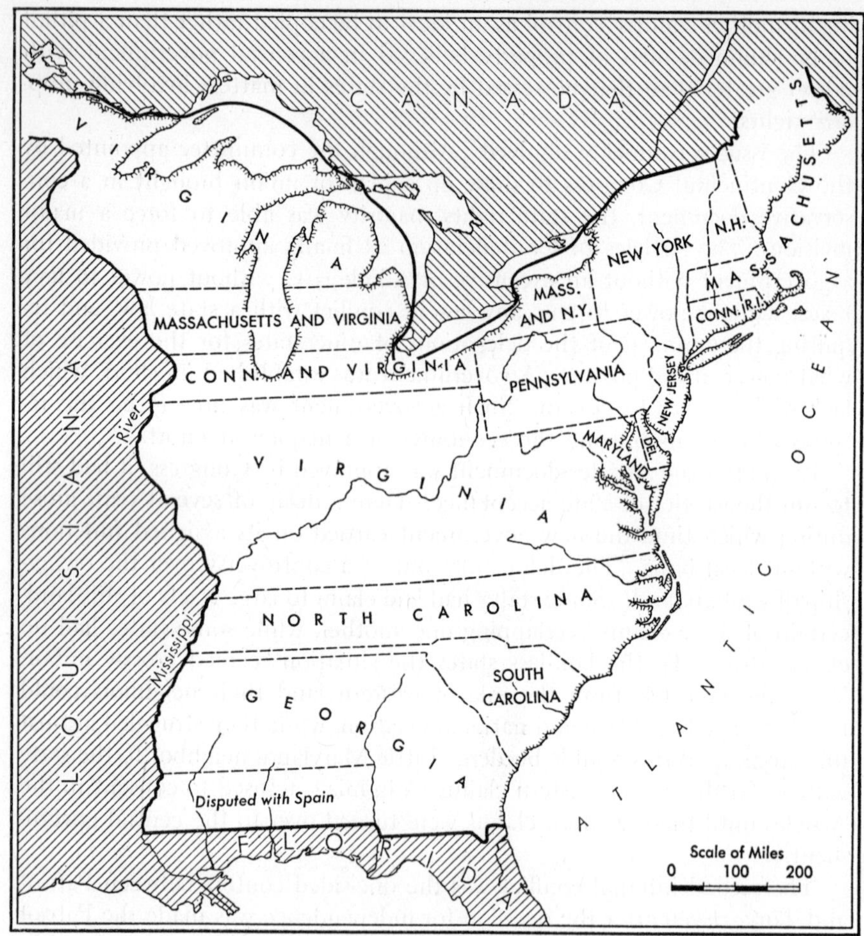

FIGURE 9. Obstacle to Unity

officials whose income depended upon the continuance of British rule. They were back-country southerners whose antagonism toward the tide-water aristocrats had become so intense that the enemies of their enemies were automatically accepted as friends. They were producers of naval stores and indigo to whom the disappearance of British authority meant the cessation of generous bounties. They were merchants and planters whose economic relationships fitted into British regulations without friction. In short, just as the Patriots had an economic stake in altering the status quo, the Loyalists had an economic stake in its maintenance.

Closely related to this civil war was an even more decisive attack on the vestiges of Old World institutions. The states, for example, quickly took possession in their own name of the ungranted lands within their borders. Patriots also ceased to pay quitrents, a step preliminary to the abolishment of these payments altogether by state legislation. In their place was substituted a tax paid into the treasury of the state. Primogeniture and entail, the passage of land to the eldest son and prohibitions against transferring property out of the family, two other lingering remnants of feudal Europe, were also abolished by legislative action. The Anglican Church was disestablished in the southern colonies, and even the institution of slavery felt the impact of this revolution as several states prohibited the importation of slaves and the Continental Congress went on record in disapproval. With this wholesale eradication of institutions which had never entirely found a place in America, the New World completed the work begun more than one hundred and fifty years earlier when England suffered her first defeat.

The primary gainers from civil war and the upheaval in land ownership were without doubt the smaller operators. Often, of course, those most able to buy the lands thus put on the market were men who already held large plots. Equally often small holdings were soon lost and concentrated again through the activities of the more shrewd and unscrupulous members of society, and corruption frequently found its way into the disposition of state-held lands. But a sincere effort was made, especially in the states most completely controlled by the democrats, to use state holdings as an opportunity to democratize land ownership. This effort, plus the great assistance this cause received from the abolishment of primogeniture and entail, did much to weaken the economic prop supporting America's traditional landed aristocracy.

It is not to be inferred from all this that the "have nots" made war on the "haves" during the American Revolution. Rather the situation was that the Loyalist group was primarily made up of individuals in the "have" category, while it was the "have not" group within Patriot ranks which was most anxious to despoil internal enemies. As between "haves" and "have nots" inside the Patriot group there was not a perfect harmony, although enough of a basis for wartime cooperation was found. Most Americans at this time were property holders, and since small holders aspired to become large holders the institution of private property as such was not threatened. Moreover, men of means as well as men without means could find a great deal of protection within a government of limited powers. Finally small property holders were dependent upon the wealthy for credit on one side of the production process and markets on the other, while most conservatives were dependent upon laborers and customers in the carrying on of their businesses.

Incompetence in War. Upon this foundation of mutual dependence, but handicapped by the intensity of the conflict within, the way of government preferred by the radicals was given its first great test—the waging of an important war effort. The most persistent problem encountered was the securing of sufficient supplies—provisions, clothing, and weapons—to wage the conflict effectively, and the irony of this situation was the fact that the nation on whom America had most depended for manufactured goods was the very nation with whom the war was being fought. As England proceeded to close colonial ports to world trade as far as she was able, a trying scarcity of goods not produced at home was quickly felt.

This sudden dearth of goods was not as great a shock to the economy as it would have been without the earlier experience with the nonimportation agreements. Already the American economy had twice been forced to adjust to a sharply reduced flow of goods from abroad. On both occasions the increased demand had generated a rise in prices sufficient to stimulate a marked expansion of domestic production—both household and for the market.

Both of these earlier occasions, however, produced an interval of deprivation too short to alter significantly the basic fact that the colonial economy was not yet bent in a manufacturing direction. Over such a short period there was little encouragement for manufacturing requiring a large capital investment, and where little capital was involved the reversion to preinterruption conditions had not been long delayed.

Conditions were different when war broke out in earnest. Now the country was faced with a longer interval of reduced external trade. In addition, the economy was confronted with the tremendous rise in demand which always accompanies a war and which still further stimulated the development of manufactures. Also, a large amount of capital was now made available for this purpose by the declining opportunities in the field of trade as the British blockade became increasingly successful. Perhaps the only factor unfavorable to manufacturing growth was an inadequate labor supply. Always scarce in the colonies at best, especially in the skilled categories, it became even scarcer as a result of the manpower required for the army and the exodus of a number of skilled workers accompanying the persecution of Loyalists.

Despite a rapid increase in manufacturing activity, there was a real and painful shortage of goods during the first years of the conflict, a shortage particularly reflected in the privations suffered by Washington's army during the difficult winter of 1777-78 at Valley Forge. After this crisis had been safely passed, the supply of necessary goods was ample though never abundant. The greater availability of goods in the later years of the conflict, however, is not to be explained solely by the expansion of manufacturing. On the one hand, foreign nations increasingly assisted the colonies as a subtle way of inconveniencing England. On the other hand, American traders were never wholly inactive, and much of the decline in legitimate trading activity was compensated by the growth of a huge American fleet of privateers. So active and successful were American privateers that British prizes captured by Americans were perhaps as numerous as American prizes taken by the English. Furthermore, so profitable was the business of privateering that the great New England fishing industry almost disappeared during the war.

Although in terms of the output of goods the American economy functioned adequately during the Revolution, little credit for this performance can be given to the government except to say that it did not seriously hamper the necessary economic adjustments. A much more significant test of the effectiveness of the government was its success in distributing such goods as were available. How well did the government insisted upon by the democrats function with respect to this problem?

Stating the matter bluntly, it did not function at all well. In the absence of a centralized organization for the buying of military supplies, the "central" government often found itself competing with the several state governments, and where such choices had to be made it was typical for the Continental Army to go without rather than the states. A major consequence of this failure was the fact that far too many people carried on their lives and work "as usual" despite the life-and-death struggle going on around them, a struggle already characterized by a good deal more outright indifference than history books have led us to believe.

The story was exactly the same when it came to financing the war, another aspect of the task of distributing available goods. Forbidden to tax, the Congress could only requisition funds and goods from the states. The states in turn, governed by the urgency of their own needs, their antipathy toward the "central" government, and the general hostility of the people to taxes in general, could meet these requisitions or not as they chose. The result was a wholesale delinquency in making available the aid requested, long delays in transmitting such aid as was made available, and a gross inadequacy in the level of taxation imposed. A part of this deficiency was made good by domestic borrowing, but by no means enough to place the financing of the war on a sound footing.

In these circumstances the money necessary for carrying on the fighting was obtained in the only way possible—the issuance of paper money. From the very beginning of the conflict both the Congress and the states issued vast quantities of unredeemable currency. The more such money was issued, of course, the more it depreciated, and the more it depreciated the more had to be issued to secure the desired result of wresting goods from rival purchasers. With prices rising higher and higher, earnest attempts were made to keep them within reasonable limits through price control legislation. But it was not to be. As long as the vicious circle of paper money issuance continued, the currency thus thrown into the channels of trade could not be prevented from depreciating. And so the cycle went on, making life more and more difficult for everyone except currency speculators. It can be said conservatively that the variety of moneys in use and the steady though unpredictable fluctuations in their value made much more difficult the economic adjustments occasioned by the war. Furthermore, the refusal openly to tax in support of the war effort resulted in an inequitable, disguised taxation in the form of money depreciation.

Toward the end of the war, methods of finance did greatly improve. Paper-money issuance both by the "central" government and the states ceased, and collections from the states became more substantial. But at the same time it is doubtful if improvement along these lines could have been achieved had there not occurred another basic change in the underlying situation—the securing of foreign loans and the resultant increase in the amount of coin available. In the early years of the war other nations had felt they could not afford to aid the rebellious colonies because England's superior resources seemed to give her such an overwhelming advantage. By the beginning of 1778, however, France had decided it was safe to stand openly against England, and the aid she gave the cause of independence was considerable. Later both Spain and Holland joined the fight against England, although the assistance received from these sources was less important than that given by France. The aid given by Holland and France especially often took the form of specie loans and thus immensely eased the always difficult money situation.

November, 1779, saw 38½ paper dollars exchanging for one silver dollar, with most of the nation's specie being hoarded rather than risked in the market place. Simultaneously the winter of 1779-80 turned into a period of even greater hardship for the army than the experience at Valley Forge, as citizens hesitated to exchange goods which were appreciating in value for money which was depreciating in value. Plainly something had to be done. In July, 1780, the Bank of Pennsylvania was organized in the hope that some relief could be provided by better monetary manage-

TABLE 5. MONEY, MONEY EVERYWHERE

Date	Paper Money Issued by the Continental Congress	Number of Paper Dollars Having Same Value as One Specie Dollar
1775	$ 6,000,000	
1776	19,000,000	
1777	13,000,000	
1778	63,000,000	
1779	140,000,000	
January 14, 1779		8
February 3, 1779		10
April 2, 1779		17
May 5, 1779		24
June 4, 1779		20
September 17, 1779		24
October 14, 1779		30
November 17, 1779		38½

Source: By permission from *Financial History of the United States* (9th ed.), by Davis R. Dewey, pp. 36 and 39. Copyright, 1924, by Longmans, Green & Co., Inc., New York.

ment. As an experiment this endeavor was no doubt helpful. But it did not make use of the fundamental principle of specie economy—that is, the idea that a given amount of specie can do more "money work" if it is concentrated in a few places and used as reserves rather than circulating [1]—and hence did not really assist with the underlying problem. In December, 1781, this experiment was carried further in the creation of the Bank of North America. Made possible by an opportune shipment of metal from France, this bank did operate on the basis of specie concentration and was therefore able to help in the financing of the war by loaning money to the government. However, with the nation's money system already far from any semblance of a specie standard, even at best a small island of better financial management amid a sea of chaos could not greatly improve the situation.

Neither the aid given by foreign nations nor the creation of the Bank of North America were achievements for which the Confederation govern-

[1] Where a commodity such as gold or silver is widely accepted as money, but where citizens also recognize the greater convenience of "folding" money, an effective banking system can keep in circulation without inflation a substantially greater amount of paper currency than there is specie "backing." The factor making the difference here is *credit*, the confidence citizens have in their money system which makes them willing to transact business with a paper money thus indirectly but still closely tied to commodity money. Paper money such as was issued in large quantities during the Revolutionary War had inflationary tendencies primarily because it was unredeemable—that is, the tie with commodity money was wholly broken. It is possible but much less likely for commodity money to increase sufficiently to generate inflation.

ment could take credit. Foreign aid was motivated by hostility to Britain rather than friendship for America, while the banking innovation was prompted by sheer desperation as the Continental currency sank in value to a one-thousand-to-one ratio with silver dollars and virtually ceased to circulate. Prompted by the same desperation, another step was also attempted in 1781—an even more courageous innovation which might have gone far to answer the critical need. Seeking to extend its powers under the Articles of Confederation, the Continental Congress asked the states for permission to levy a 5 per cent import duty. Immediately an angry discussion began as people everywhere hotly demanded why, if taxes were to be levied by a power outside their own state, was there opposition to the Stamp Act or the tea duties in the first place? Most of the states finally assented to the levy, although some by the barest of majorities. Democratic Rhode Island, however, flatly refused on the ground that her integrity as a state would be jeopardized by the presence on her soil of "federal" tax collectors. Since unanimous consent was necessary for the desired extension of authority, the duty could not be imposed.

By 1783 there was an even more urgent reason for trying desperate measures. Unable to pay the army, and fearful of what the soldiers might do if they remained mobilized but unpaid, Congress disbanded the army even before the treaty of peace was signed and before the British evacuated New York. At the same time, and in part with the idea of partial payment for army personnel, Congress renewed its request for permission to levy a 5 per cent import tax. Again most of the states gave their consent, although in some cases subject to extremely hampering conditions. Again, however, unanimous consent was not secured when New York this time stood on her rights and refused to approve. Americans were still unable to see in the Continental Congress anything other than the authority of England in a different but still easily recognizable guise.

Incompetence in Peace. The financial situation of the Confederation government was to become much worse before it improved (for example, the time was to come when the government was even to default on interest payments), but in an entirely different way the year 1783 marks a basic turning point in American history. War with the mother country ended and in England a vigorous segment of the politically influential group insisted on a peace calling for extremely generous terms. The capture of American markets by the business interests of other countries had become a threatening possibility to Englishmen in the habit of dominating those markets. Moreover, many Whigs had been reading Adam Smith's *Wealth of Nations* and were becoming convinced that profitable trading relationships were not necessarily dependent upon political control. As Britain's struggle against virtually all the nations of western Europe increased still further the burden of her national debt, with the rebels across the sea still as far from defeat as ever, the idea of peace on the basis of American independence became more and more appealing.

Even in detail the peace terms were far more liberal than Americans had any reason to expect on the basis of the effectiveness with which the war had been waged. The Mississippi River was agreed upon as the western boundary, slaves carried from the South during the war were to be returned or payment was to be made, New England fishermen were accorded rights in the Newfoundland fisheries almost as great as those possessed before the war, no restitution to Loyalists had to be promised, and the Floridas were returned to Spain. Almost the only concessions made to England were a commitment not to put legal obstacles in the way of reimbursements to English creditors for debts contracted before the war—a procedure dictated in any event by common honesty—and the granting to British ships of free use of the Mississippi River. Surely no more favorable foundation would have been wanted on which to build a new nation.

However, the fundamental question still remained. Could the government which had been so inadequate in time of war be more successful in combating the problems of peace? Could a loose federation of states, a "league of friendship," take full advantage of the treaty terms negotiated by John Jay, Benjamin Franklin, and John Adams? Could the new nation disentangle itself from the heritage of incompetence built up in earlier years?

The answer was not long in coming. No sooner had the treaty been approved on both sides of the ocean than the impossibility of carrying out its terms in America became evident. When Congress recommended to the states that persecution of Loyalists cease, the request was met with a storm of indignation. In part because Loyalist persecution was now completely safe and perhaps in part simply because England and the Continental Congress were protesting, hostility against the Loyalist group appeared with renewed intensity. Although the peace negotiators had carefully avoided committing the nation to anything more than this recommendation by Congress regarding the Loyalists, such a striking demonstration of the absence of loyalty to the "central" government did not generate respect and friendship abroad, particularly in an England feeling a heavy responsibility for the Loyalists thus mistreated.

While England could not charge treaty violation in this treatment accorded Loyalists, she was soon given this opportunity in the complete failure of the nation to make arrangements for the payment of British creditors. Instead, all sorts of obstacles were placed in the way of these collections, not, to be sure, by the Congress, but by the states, over whom Congress had almost no control. No doubt already anxious to recoup her lost fortunes in the New World, England promptly took advantage of this situation by refusing to withdraw her troops from the posts she still held on the American frontier. When American merchants sought to develop the fur trade in the territory their nation had "acquired," they found British merchants using these military outposts as a lever to engross a large share of the business for themselves. At the same time England made no move to compensate American citizens for the slaves carried away during the conflict, a behavior fully appropriate in view of the fact that a large share of the uncollected debts were owed by southerners.

But the problem of treaty enforcement was only the beginning of difficulty. In addition the new nation had to face the task of rebuilding an economy dislocated by a major war effort. It was not that war had brought widespread destruction to the American economy. On the contrary, apart from the ruin of the New England fisheries, the using up of capital, and the loss of the thousands of slaves carried away from the South by the British, the economy had suffered little damage. Certain readjustments were necessary, however. Capital losses had to be made good, privateers had to be integrated into the economy in some other way, and the impetus given manufacturing by the war had to be brought into conformity with peacetime conditions.

These realignments would have been painful enough under any circumstances. Their accomplishment, however, was made doubly difficult by the fact of independence. Since America was no longer in the British colonial system, England immediately began to treat her as a foreign nation. The markets of England, thus, were closed to American whale oil, a heavy blow to the incentive to rebuild the New England whale fisheries, and a long list of American products was either excluded from empire ports or severely discriminated against. Similarly, southern planters were no longer accorded "empire preference" in the British market, and British bounties and subsidies were discontinued. Indigo promptly became a minor crop on the American scene, the rice and tobacco economies suffered for years from the price weakness resulting from these altered conditions, and even wheat and meat producers in the northern colonies felt the pinch of the nation's new position in the world. American-built ships were no longer freely admitted to British registry, and American fishermen were denied privileges along the coast of Canada they had long enjoyed. Still worse, as England withdrew from the responsibility she had always assumed for protecting American commerce, the Barbary pirates were quick to seize the new opportunity for plunder, and a once valuable trade with the Mediterranean was sharply curtailed. And finally, in what was the cruelest deprivation of all, the supremely important trade with the West Indies was greatly reduced as both England and France changed their previous policy toward America. While this new attitude and policy was understandable enough from England's standpoint, it did complicate

America's transition to peace. The old problem of how to earn enough foreign exchange to purchase the goods people desired to buy in England reappeared with great force.

Some of these reconversion difficulties could have been dealt with more readily than they were if American trade could promptly have shifted to non-English relationships, and to some extent such a transition was made. A profitable trade was springing up with the Continent, and a significant trade with China, the Baltic area, and the Near East had its beginning at this time. However, for a number of reasons this shift was not made on a scale broad enough to be really helpful. English and American traders, accustomed to one another's ways of doing business, continued long-established trading connections. Furthermore, with the balance of trade heavily against them, American businessmen were only too happy to accept the more liberal credit terms offered by British traders than could be secured in other countries. Unfortunately, also, with England already on the threshold of a technological development which was soon to give her an unchallenged world supremacy in the field of manufacturing, English goods were cheaper than those available elsewhere. Thus, desirable as a shift away from England would have been from the standpoint of America's balance of payments, this method of escaping England's adverse regulations proved to be impossible.

Real though these difficulties were, it would nonetheless be unreasonable to criticize the American government because they arose. There is a limit to what can be done for an economy via government, and the inconveniences which now beset the new nation were a natural consequence of the turmoil in international relations. Perhaps there was only one thing the government might have done to help, and the test of its effectiveness is whether this one thing was or was not done well.

The most to be said in its favor is that Congress did its best. In 1784 a request was made for authority to pass a navigation act to prohibit exports or imports in ships belonging to or navigated by subjects of any power with whom the United States did not have a treaty of commerce. This power would have placed in the hands of the "central" government a weapon with which a more favorable relationship with England might have been coerced.

The merchants of Massachusetts in general and Boston in particular enthusiastically welcomed this show of strength. Elsewhere, however, the request met with a reception varying from indifference to outright hostility. Southern planters especially were afraid the authority would be used primarily for the benefit of northern commerce. And, what was even more frustrating, this power the states refused to give Congress they refused also to use themselves in sufficient unison to accomplish the desired objective, and Massachusetts quickly recognized that a law passed by her alone would simply drive commerce to other ports.

The Challenge of Independence. Depression resulting from unfavorable legislation abroad was next intensified by the deflationary forces which almost invariably follow a war period. Immediately after the war the country held large quantities of specie sent here as loans from France, Spain, and Holland, and for financing the British army. At the same time there existed in America a great deficit of European goods because of the wartime interruption of commerce, while across the ocean and especially in England goods had accumulated on merchants' shelves for the same reason. These three economic facts now combined to produce a situation which took from the country in a few short months most of its circulating specie in exchange for far more foreign goods than America could pay for with her own exports.

The consequence can only be described as a tragedy, particularly for the infant manufactures the war had brought into existence. As prices plunged downward with the fall in demand brought about by the cessation of war and the outflow of specie, and as English merchants slashed prices even lower in order to reduce their inventories and recapture American markets, young manufacturing establishments found themselves in an almost desperate position. They had arisen to fill a vital need when the country faced a grave emergency. It did not seem fair to them that they should be sacrificed the moment cheaper goods were once more available.

Statesmen did not think it fair, either. Men whose ideals and attitudes inclined them emphatically in the direction of free trade suddenly became conscious of America's need to develop herself as a manufacturing nation. If the United States was not always to be a raw-material-producing nation with all the disadvantages accompanying such a status, she would have to become less dependent upon foreigners for manufactured goods. And, since Europe and especially England had at the moment a decided advantage in this kind of production, the only way for the United States to develop would be by protecting her infant industries.

The crying need was for tariff duties to prevent American manufactures from total eclipse in the face of the depression temporarily ravaging the economy. In view of the helplessness of the "central" government, the problem could be met only by state action. As the economy became enveloped in a painful deflation, state after state enacted tariffs designed to protect its own industries. By the time economic skies began to clear, every state possessing any considerable manufacturing activity had come to the rescue of these firms. For the first time, perhaps, a decisive action had been taken by the new nation, an action in which, significantly, the Confederation government took no part.

It was in the midst of postwar depression, too, that America sought to mend her commercial relationships with other nations. Striking at the problem of America's commerce at its foundations, John Adams went to England in 1785 to negotiate a comercial treaty. He found the people with whom he had to deal pleasant but adamant. Some there were in England, and influential men too, who advised a policy of concession for Britain. These counsels fell on deaf ears, however, as the majority insisted that England would receive the lion's share of American trade without making concessions. Unfortunately, it was true, and nothing John Adams could say produced the slightest softening of attitude. Moreover, America's poor economic relationships with France stemmed to a large extent from the preference in the United States for doing business with England.

Meanwhile, relationships with Spain had assumed a most threatening character. By the treaty with England, Florida had been returned to Spain, but America had been granted title to a large area in what was then called West Florida to which Spain also laid claim. Now, in order to enforce her claims, she was proposing to close the mouth of the Mississippi to American comerce. While this was an action Spain had every right to take, holding as she did the territory on both sides of the river at its mouth, it nonetheless posed a grave problem for the United States.

For two decades settlers had been streaming through the passes in the Appalachian Mountains to come to rest in the region now known as Kentucky and Tennessee, and by 1785 this territory was filling up at a very rapid rate. These settlers, however, were no more able to satisfy their demand for the goods of an advanced civilization than the original settlers on the Atlantic seaboard. To secure such goods westerners could hardly use the extremely poor inland transportation facilities across the mountains; the more obvious procedure was to utilize the facilities afforded by the Mississippi River. However, as long as Spain chose she could thwart this solution, and it was clearly evident that unless westerners were assisted by the United States in securing the use of these facilities, they could not be expected to cast their lot with the new government. Already, in fact, Spain was beginning to negotiate with them.

In 1786, Ambassador John Jay reported to Congress that Spain would sign a commercial treaty if the United States would agree not to press for use of the Mississippi River for a period of twenty-five years. A long and angry debate ensued. The southern states insisted on rejection of Spain's terms, for it was citizens from those states who were locating on the new frontier. Northern states, and especially New England, were anxious to conclude negotiations with Spain. Their interest was in a commercial treaty and they understandably cared little for the Southwest.

With the agrarian West threatening "secession" if its demands were not met, and with New England threatening to leave the union if they were, the nation was forced to choose between trading concessions in South America and navigation rights on the lower Mississippi. Anticipating by a few years the temporary loss of control over the American economy by the agrarians, concessions in South America were selected, although the resultant treaty was never ratified by the required number of states (nine). Neither the West nor New England seceded, but the problem of the West and its need for efficient transportation facilities was only beginning.

A New Crisis. While the government which was not really a government was demonstrating its incapacity in so many ways, men of conservative temper who had bitterly opposed that government in the first place were uneasily watching the approach of a new crisis in America's affairs. During the war these men had been given little reason to regret their association with the radicals. Business had been good and new opportunities had generally been found to replace those destroyed by the war. Now, however, the situation was different. The new government was obviously unable to protect their interests in international relationships, and as the depression deepened they became more and more convinced that their interests were being sacrificed at home as well. Responding to hard times just as they had always before, debtor-farmers were now insisting on paper money issues as well as other devices for lessening the burden of their debts. With the currency already in hopeless confusion, the prospect of never being able to restore a semblance of order and uniformity—a prerequisite for the development of the capitalistic economy conservatives desired to promote—was indeed frightening. Equally unpleasant were the immediate economic consequences of new issues of paper money. Although its issuance was motivated by the postwar shortage of specie, the first result of printing-press money was to drive such specie as was still in the country out of circulation.[2] Without specie, trade could not flourish in the latter part of the eighteenth century; although coins were notoriously "sweated" and "clipped," they were still the nearest approach to a uniform currency available.

While not every state succumbed to the temptation to issue paper money (another way of saying that in some states the conservatives were in control), a cheap-money group did become powerful in every state. Moreover, even where the sound-money interests were able to resist tampering with the currency the threat still remained; the debt-ridden agrar-

[2] This phenomenon demonstrates the operation of what is known in economics as Gresham's Law. A money that is worth more as money than as a commodity will be used as money, while a money that is worth more as a commodity than as money will be hoarded. In other words, "bad money drives out good."

ians, frustrated by their inability to legislate their favorite panacea, openly defied law and order in their desperation.

The two types of situations were excellently illustrated by Rhode Island and Massachusetts. Democratic Rhode Island had been one of the first states to give in to the paper-money solution to depression difficulties. Almost always extreme in her democracy, Rhode Island had even passed laws making her paper money legal tender. So critical had this situation become that shops were closed and many farmers refused to bring their crops to market. (The farmer who could not take the proceeds from the sale of goods to a creditor before it depreciated, in other words, was also apt to be the loser from an inflationary monetary policy.) When a harried merchant challenged the legal tender law in the courts and was awarded the decision, agrarians in 1786 promptly exercised their franchise rights to alter the personnel of the state's courts.

Conservative Massachusetts avoided this sequence of events. In firm control of the governmental machinery, her aristocracy resisted all pressure to lighten debt burdens. Then this success turned hollow in their hands when frustrated farmers not only prevented by force the normal operation of the court system in the foreclosing of mortgages, but also took up arms in an attempt to seize the entire government of the state. When Daniel Shays' poorly organized but determined army sought to capture the federal arsenal at Springfield, more favorably situated citizens throughout the entire nation were filled with alarm.

Historical scholarship is now urging us not to believe that "the critical period" was really as "critical" as it is commonly supposed to have been, although it is universally acknowledged to have been difficult. It is asserted rather that the nation could not in any event have avoided an exceedingly trying period as it endeavored to implement its newly found independence in a postwar depression environment, and that from the standpoint of the operation of the economy rather than political organization there was much less cause for concern. Certainly in support of these contentions it can be emphasized that economic recovery was hearteningly steady, that most foreign nations soon began to soften their attitude toward the new nation, and that for the majority of people engaged in farming or other local pursuits it must have seemed that there was nothing substantially wrong. Most Americans in truth had little visible need for the kind of government which the Articles of Confederation was not.

Here indeed is the real key to an understanding of the "critical period in American history." It was a "critical period" primarily for the conservative and wealthier groups, and perhaps this is reason enough to discard the traditional "critical" interpretation. Before this is done, however, several facts need to be carefully weighed. First, the unrest of the aristocrats was sufficiently general that a much altered philosophy of government was put into operation—a feat which would have been impossible if only "aristocratic" interests had supported the change. Second, the government thus created was soon so widely accepted that even when an opportunity was later afforded, farmer interests made little effort to return to the Articles philosophy. Third, the America that exists today could not have come into being under the government which presided over the Revolutionary War.

However, whether these considerations do or do not rescue a view of the period prior to 1787 long regarded as acceptable, one thing is clear. From the standpoint of the developments which took place *after* 1787, the appropriate frame of reference is surely the men who were most active in guiding history's next steps. In February, 1787, as Shays and his fellow rebels were pursued and shot down by forces financed by Boston merchants, the business classes could only have believed that the Articles of Confederation government was bankrupt in every way. To men whose economic well-being depended upon international relationships and internal stability, a government whose credit was almost worthless and which was unable to win the respect of a single important world power was little less than disastrous. To men whose economic activity knew no state boundaries, a government unable to establish rules and regulations where more than one state was involved could only be considered a bitter deprivation. Furthermore, the situation was ridiculous because America was obviously a land of great resources which needed only to be developed. In short, it was clearly apparent that the time had come for conservatives, men who wanted nothing so much as the opportunity to develop these resources, to put forth strenuous efforts in their own behalf.

QUESTIONS FOR DISCUSSION

1. What were the principal differences between the "two revolutions"? Who achieved what in the internal revolution? Who suffered the greatest losses?
2. Was there any alternative to the issuance of large quantities of paper money during the war?
3. Who bore the burden of the Revolutionary War in America? To what extent was this burden postponed until after the war by borrowing?
4. What were the major problems confronting the nation after it secured its independence? Which of these problems were most closely associated with independence as such, and which were primarily an aftermath of the war?
5. How did England expect to profit from the actions she took relative to the colonies after the war?

6. How convincing was the case for a tariff to protect war-born infant industries?
7. Would this period of postwar adjustment and transition to independence have been significantly easier if a "strong" government had been functioning?
8. What was to be gained by issuing paper money during the postwar depression, and who would reap these benefits?
9. Was the "critical period" really critical?

Chapter 6

BUILDING A FOUNDATION

1787	Constitutional Convention.
	Northwest Ordinance.
1788	Constitution ratified.
1789	First presidential election and first Congress convened.
1789–92	"Hamiltonian System" enacted.
1793	War broke out in Europe.
1794	"Whiskey Rebellion."
1795	Controversy over Jay's Treaty.
	Pinckney's Treaty with Spain.
1796	John Adams elected President.
1798	Alien and Sedition Acts.
1798–1800	Undeclared naval war with France.

Making the Constitution. In one way only did the government under the Articles make a positive contribution to the development of America. By 1787 the flow of settlers to the West had become so rapid that a set of principles was required specifying relationships between the "parent" states and the new settlements. Justly called one of the most important documents in American history, the Northwest Ordinance set forth the basic principles to be followed. Every aspect of this measure can be traced directly to its roots in the American experience (including the fact that the immediate occasion for its passage was the intense lobbying activities of men who wished to engage in land speculation in this area). The new territories were to become states, not colonies, land was to be widely distributed and not restricted in its passage from father to child, private property was to be protected, slavery was prohibited, and every citizen was guaranteed certain fundamental rights. So thoroughly American was this legislation that the principles it outlined were closely followed in all of the land legislation required as America expanded westward to the Pacific Ocean. With this problem, at least, the makers of the Constitution did not need to concern themselves.

It was altogether fitting that the poorer elements of the population were not represented in the group of distinguished men who gathered in Philadelphia in May, 1787, to revise the Articles of Confederation. The nation's debtors, frontiersmen, and urban laborers had been given their chance and had failed. Governmental autonomy within each state would have been appropriate to the conditions prevailing in medieval Europe. But times had changed; the development of strong nations had been made possible only by abandoning small-area particularism. England, France, and Spain had grown strong through the unification of small, autonomous units into a centralized whole. Germany and Italy were still weak because they were as yet unable to rise above the medieval type of social organization.

At the same time it is most fortunate that the Constitutional Convention came when it did rather than two or three years earlier. The problems to which answers were sought in Philadelphia were difficult ones, and able men held widely divergent views concerning their solution. Only the harrowing experiences of the preceding months made it possible for these men to stay with their task all through that hot summer in the face of discouraging disagreements. As it was, even with the powerful cement of a common distress, not all of the original fifty-five members stayed through to the end. A number gradually drifted away as it became evident that the outcome of these labors could not possibly conform with their views, some of those who left setting about immediately to organize an opposition against the day when a revised Articles of Confederation would be put to a vote of the people.

Probably there were many among those present in Philadelphia who from the outset had their tongues in their cheeks when they referred to "revising" the Articles. Certainly the finished document had little in common with such a purpose. At every point where particularity in the old government had interfered with the broad growth of trading relationships, the new instrument took an opposite stand. The result was a scheme of governmental organization flatly denying the most basic premise underlying the Articles.

For example, the Constitution provided that the central government rather than state governments was to have final jurisdiction in all matters relating to commerce. Similarly the states were prohibited from levying duties or imposing any other restrictions on imports. In these ways was eliminated the basis for a state sovereignty which had already produced friction between the states and which in time would have resulted in the kind of situation which Europe today finds so debilitating.

Furthermore, the right of levying import duties denied to the states was specifically granted to the national government. Here was provided both a source of revenue for the central government and a basis for the uniformity of action never achieved under the Confederation. Export duties were prohibited, a provision insisted upon by southerners who feared that taxes on the export of their great staples would place on them an undue share of the tax burden. The taxing power of the new government was limited in another way, too, at the insistence of southerners; it was provided that direct taxes could be assessed against the states only in proportion to population, an assurance that land wealth would not be excessively taxed. In counting population, moreover, a slave was to be counted as only three-fifths of a person (although this ratio was applied to representation in the lower house as well as to direct taxation).

Slavery as an institution was not outlawed in the Constitution, although the sentiment for such a prohibition was strong. Even Virginia's representatives would no doubt have assented to a stronger stand than was actually taken, for in the raising of tobacco the value of slave labor had become highly dubious. However, at the insistence primarily of rice farmers in Georgia and South Carolina, a provision was added stating that the importation of slaves was not to be prohibited for a period of twenty years. In this interestingly negative way the Constitution carried still further the growing hostility to an institution which seemed at the time to be ill suited to the American environment.

One other set of provisions was of vital importance in the context of the time within which the Constitution was written. The conservatives assembled at Philadelphia would hardly have overlooked the problem of paper money. First and foremost they wanted uniformity in the money system, and hence control over the supply of money was given to the central government. While a proposal to give Congress power to issue paper money was defeated, this power was not expressly forbidden to Congress as it was to the states. In addition, the credit of the new government was provided for by giving it a firm taxing power and by stipulating that all obligations entered into by the Continental Congress were to be honored.

By September, 1787, the document had been completed. Its creative work done, the Convention adjourned; and its members set their minds and energies to the task of securing ratification.

All well understood it was to be no easy task. The dilution of state sovereignty, the prohibition of paper money, and the placing of a strong taxing power in the hands of the federal government were matters to which men still reacting against years of British rule would not readily consent. Fortunately, however, the men who wrote the Constitution were not unskilled in the art of persuasion, and acceptance was voted in state after state until the required nine had ratified. All the states even then did not "consent." Little Rhode Island at first elected to stay outside the new union, but was forced to think better of the idea when faced with the prospect of a tariff barrier erected against her. Moreover, too much credit should not be given either to the propaganda efforts of the conservatives or to the inherent logic of the proposals they were making. Thousands upon thousands of American citizens were still disfranchised, and those citizens who did not have the vote were especially apt to be opponents of the Constitution. Of a similar mind, frequently, were enfranchised, back-country farmers who for one reason or another found it difficult to cast the vote which was theirs. As a result, pro-Constitution representatives were often sent to the various state ratifying conventions rather than opponents. It is interesting to reflect, in other words, that this document, which proved in time to be the vehicle for the creation of a great democracy, was perhaps saved from defeat by the absence of democracy. And the paradox is broadened when it is remembered that the creation of a democracy was the farthest thing from the minds of the Constitution's framers.

An Economic Program Emerges. The American Constitution was as fortunate in the economic environment in which it was launched as the Articles of Confederation had been unfortunate. Instead of the problems of war and depression, the nation was now favored with a long period of peace and prosperity. Thus, although there were economic problems to be resolved, the context for the making of decisions was rapidly improving. By the time of Washington's inauguration the worst consequences of the postwar depression had disappeared except in the South, and the country was eagerly looking forward to the long delayed fruits of independence.

In these economic developments the radicals were unquestionably dealt a serious blow. On the one hand, the postwar depression had so solidified their enemies that the Constitution document had in fact been approved. On the other hand, economic conditions had become better just in time to take much of the force from the arguments of the Constitution's opponents. But, having lost the contest at the polls, they did not propose to let the victory stand by default. They began at once to make plans to carry their fight into the halls of the new Congress.

Motivated more by necessity than a desire for harmony, Congress took up as its first piece of legislation a measure which generated comparatively little controversy—a duty on imports. No other method of raising the revenue so badly needed by the new government seemed feasible, and there was never any question about major reliance on the tariff for this purpose. In the northern states much of the revenue received was already based on import duties, and since the states were forced to give up this source of revenue, the central government could either avail itself of these same duties or endeavor to tap tax resources the states would also need to utilize. Faced with this choice, the obvious step was agreed to by all.

There was, however, some controversy over whether the duties were to be protective or not. Manufacturing interests took it for granted that they were, although there was opposition to this view. New England traders, for example, insisted on free trade in the interest of the merchant marine, while many farmers expressed concern that protective duties would raise the price of farming tools. Even James Madison, who had little feeling on the question of protection as such, urged the passage of a horizontal 5 per cent duty because such a measure could be passed more quickly and hence begin producing revenue for the government at an earlier date.

There was also criticism leveled against the merchant class by the "common" folk because of the use made of the tariff debate for private profit. In anticipation of the imposition of duties, importers gave particularly large orders to foreign concerns. The seven weeks of debate then gave these orders time to be filled before the law actually went into effect. And finally, when the goods arrived duty-free and the new duties were in effect, these same goods were priced to consumers as though they had paid the full duty. Great was the outcry at a practice said to have cost the new government one and one-half million badly needed dollars.

In the end the protectionists won out. The tragedy which had befallen America's infant manufactures after the Revolution was still too fresh in men's minds to permit the nonprotectionist outlook to dominate. Shortly after the tariff was enacted it was followed by other measures designed to give American ships a competitive advantage in the carrying trade of the United States. A 10 per cent reduction in the tariff was allowed on goods imported in American ships, and a tonnage duty on incoming ships was levied discriminating sharply against ships built and owned abroad. Not for nothing had the makers of America grown up under the tutelage of British mercantilism.

Agrarian Versus Capitalist. Shortly after these measures were enacted Alexander Hamilton took up his duties as the nation's first Secretary of the Treasury. A man of strong aristocratic inclinations, Hamilton was a staunch friend of the mercantile, financial, and manufacturing interests. All his superb talents he devoted to the accomplishment of two closely related objectives. First, he desired to encourage the development of American capitalism. Second, he wished to guarantee the continuation of the new government by giving the capitalistic interests a stake in its existence. As Hamilton labored to achieve these purposes, at times none too subtly, the anger and opposition of the agrarian radicals were often roused to fever pitch.

The first item on the Hamiltonian agenda was funding the national debt. No one could have objected to the establishment of a sound national credit, and few doubted the necessity of funding both the foreign and domestic debts. But when Hamilton demanded funding the domestic portion of the debt at par to present holders, the agrarians quickly challenged his proposal. It was common knowledge that many purchasers at par had disposed of their holdings at a fraction of their cost when the credit of the Confederation government had collapsed. Moreover, speculators had scoured the countryside in search of securities to buy at low prices immediately after it began to be whispered about that funding at par was a possibility.

Hamilton's arguments for his proposal were reasonable enough, starting with his major premise. For one thing it would be impossible to distinguish between original and other holders with the accuracy required for full justice, and it would not do to give original holders anything less than par. Furthermore, funding the debt at par would establish the credit of the government without any of the questions which would be raised if the basis used were below par. And finally, a larger government debt would increase by that much the nation's fund of liquid capital and hence its capacity to develop its resources.[1]

The radicals, led by Madison, were not convinced. To them it seemed only a device to throw an added burden upon land and labor for the benefit of the business groups. Since capital could not be created out of nothing by government fiat, the answer must be that this augmented capital would be built out of taxation. In the state of economic thinking then prevailing the doctrine that taxation always comes to rest ultimately on the land was widely held, and with a tax system built almost exclusively around customs duties this judgment was reasonably accurate. Honest and sincere agrarians could not justify by any thinking understandable by them the taxation of the industrious farmer for the support of the "indolent" creditor.

Acrimonious though this part of the debate was, it became still more bitter when Hamilton proposed to fund the debts of the several states as an obligation of the national government. Again the arguments in favor were well thought out. Most of these debts had been incurred in the course of the Revolution, and since this was a struggle for the good of all, it was only fair that all should collectively assume the burden. Again, however, the agrarians did not fail to note that still more fluid capital was

[1] Capital, as the economist views it, consists of goods which have been produced for the purpose of increasing the economy's capacity to produce other goods. In an exchange economy, however, an important process must take place before capital can be accumulated. Money income must be saved rather than spent. Where, as is so often the case in a modern economy, the people who save are not identical with the people who invest, paper claims to assets are given to savers in exchange for the use of their money for a time. Such claims may be in the form of bank deposits, corporate securities, government bonds, real estate mortgages, and so forth. These claims are often broadly referred to as "liquid capital," although they are not always and necessarily liquid, nor are all liquid assets equally "liquid."

to be built up at agriculture's expense, and that still more "indolent" creditors were to be kept in luxury at the expense of the poor, hard-working farmer. Besides, some states had already paid the bulk of their debts and could see no reason why they should be taxed again for the benefit of their less thrifty neighbors.

The agrarians were defeated at every point in this battle; on August 4, 1790, the Funding Act was passed without agrarian alterations. Even the continental currency was redeemed, and although the redemption ratio was only one hundred to one, substantial speculative profits were made out of this arrangement as well.

The Issue of Centralization. More and more frustrated at the turn events were taking, agrarians resolved to battle even harder against Hamilton's next proposal—the creation of a national bank. Here was a measure which seemed to the nation's farmers to be even more clearly class legislation than its predecessors. It was not, of course, that banks were a bad thing in themselves, but they had a tendency to work in the interest of those who controlled them—and a national bank would be apt to be out of reach of agrarian banking needs. The farmer's idea of a satisfactory bank was one which made available large quantities of paper money to help him expand and keep his debts under control. The capitalist's notion of how a banking system should operate placed too much emphasis upon a "sound" currency to suit the farmer, and the capitalist's "sound" currency seemed to mean a money supply manipulated in such a way that debts could not be repaid. Furthermore, a national bank with a monopoly of the handling of public funds would all the more be in a position to affect adversely the operation of the farmer's state banks, the banks over which the agrarians did have control. And besides, the proposed bank was unconstitutional.

Men of substance and capitalist inclinations were no more given pause by opposition to the bank than by criticism of earlier fiscal measures. They were too much concerned about America's underlying monetary needs (as these were interpreted by them) to give heed to the pratings of ignorant farmers. Only a national bank could remedy the country's chronic shortage of specie and serve as an adequate fiscal agent for the government. More than this, the new independence was giving rise to an increased exchange of goods within the nation, and hence currency uniformity was an especially important objective of the bank's proponents, while the constitutional argument could be met in part by emphasizing that the need for a uniform currency was precisely the reason states had been forbidden to issue paper money. Even the lesson of history could be urged in support of the bank. Every modern nation, especially Great Britain, was far advanced in the practice of banking, and the great cities of America—Philadelphia, New York, Boston, and Baltimore—already had banks in their respective areas.

Understandably, these arguments were not convincing to agrarians. They could only feel that it was adding insult to injury to use the need for local institutions as an argument for centralization, or to suggest England's experience as a model for the United States to follow. After all, the United States had come to exist in the first place only as a result of resistance to the centralization implicit in government of the English type. And the argument that a central bank could be justified under the implied powers granted the federal government in the Constitution proved to agrarians only how far the capitalists had been perverted by central-government heresies.

This battle ended exactly as had its predecessors. In February, 1791, the First Bank of the United States was chartered, and the sequel to this event did nothing to quiet agrarian fears. Almost simultaneously with the chartering of the bank a group of businessmen were creating a private organization (the ancestor of the New York Stock Exchange) which would make it easy for shares of stock to be bought and sold and which would therefore still further promote the accumulation of liquid capital. At the moment there were few securities available for exchange—only governments, including private subscriptions to the First Bank of the United States. But so enthusiastic were investors over the economic outlook and the turn events were taking on the political front that a wave of speculation in the newly issued bank stock shortly precipitated the nation's first financial panic. Clearly there were problems associated with the capital liquidity found so desirable in other respects.

One other major defeat was suffered by the agrarian group as the Constitution was transformed in these early years from a document into a living institution. Hamilton strongly recommended the passage of an excise tax on distilled spirits, and indeed in 1791 it was evident that all the government's expenses could not be met unless additional revenue was derived from some source. When this proposal was placed before Congress, southern and Pennsylvania farmers especially were more indignant than they had yet been. Thousands of farmers manufactured whiskey from home-grown grain in small backwoods stills, much of which was shipped to the seaboard cities. To those farmers whose production was subjected to this added burden, it seemed that the federal government was taxing their already inadequate transportation facilities. Their grain was too bulky relative to its value to bear the haul to the city as grain. As whiskey, however, their surplus could be disposed of expeditiously.

All the animosity which had earlier gone into opposition to the Stamp Act was now focused on the first internal taxation attempted by the new government. On March 3, 1791, the agrarians lost the battle when President Washington signed this measure into law. But the Hamiltonian victory was by no means complete. Probably no action did more than the whiskey tax to arouse opposition to the Federalists.

Although Alexander Hamilton's support was not an essential element in the nation's decision to enact a protective tariff, the able and active Secretary of the Treasury was given an opportunity to express approval. Asked by Congress to prepare a report on the nation's finances, Hamilton presented his famous *Report on Manufactures*—the classic American defense of protection. More than anything this paper illustrates the close connection between revenue and protection in America's early history. The occasion for new tax legislation at the time was wholly fiscal. General St. Clair had just suffered a disastrous defeat at the hands of the northwest Indians, and additional funds were needed for frontier defense. Yet it was this need which prompted Alexander Hamilton to discourse at length on the desirability of tariff protection. Submitted in December, 1791, this document provided much of the basis for the revenue legislation of March, 1792, at which time some twenty of Hamilton's specific recommendations were followed.

With the passage in 1792 of the nation's first currency act the initial Federalist program for ending financial chaos was concluded. A uniform currency was established based on a bimetallic standard of gold and silver. Unlike Hamilton's other measures, however, this work came to virtually nothing. Gold was undervalued at the mint by a fifteen-to-one ratio with silver, and hence almost no gold was coined. (Gresham's Law is no respecter of *intentions.*) In turn, silver dollars were typically exported to the West Indies in exchange for Spanish silver dollars having a slightly higher silver content; apparently the brightness of the American dollars made them more desirable to the natives. These Spanish coins were then converted into bullion and presented to the mint for coinage. Not until much later did the nation have a satisfactory metallic coinage system, and until then the principal circulating medium continued to be paper (that is, bank) money.

Elements of Prosperity. Despite the violent opposition aroused by every part of their program, the Federalists had built well. The credit of the new nation was now established, and the fund of circulating capital was greatly improved. The country was thus in a far better position to carry on the work of capitalistic development than it had been five years previously. Moreover, this development did go rapidly forward. But it would be a mistake to attribute the high prosperity which now set in wholly to the Federalist achievement. For in quick succession three events occurred which contributed much to that prosperity, and which in other ways as well were fraught with immense consequences for the future.

In 1793 the last phase of the long struggle between France and England broke out. America quickly proclaimed neutrality and set about the task of taking over much of the trade of the belligerents. The result was a dramatic increase in shipping activity and shipbuilding, and an unprecedented demand for American foodstuffs and raw materials. So profitable did agriculture and shipping become at the expense of the warring nations that capital investments once again avoided manufacturing, which activity consequently languished.

It was in 1793 also that Eli Whitney invented the cotton gin, one of the most significant technological advances in the nation's history. Long staple cotton had for some years been produced in the American South in small quantities. The seeds adhered loosely to its longer fiber and hence could be easily removed by a simple roller gin. Short staple cotton, however, was not a paying proposition because the seeds were tightly held in the shorter fibers and therefore had to be removed by hand.

Ever since the Revolution southern agriculture had been depressed. Tobacco and rice had lost their privileged position in the markets of England, bounties on indigo and naval stores had been discontinued, and the lands on which tobacco had been grown for many years were nearing exhaustion. Prosperity in the South was almost visibly awaiting a change in its pattern of production, and it was well known that the contemporary technological revolution in England would provide a tremendous market for the cotton so easily produced in the United States if only the problem of cleaning short staple cotton in a high wage country could be solved.[2] Eli Whitney's cotton gin proved to be the answer, and an economically depressed South began to share in the prosperity the rest of the nation was enjoying.

Without question this development marked out a pattern of growth and expansion for the South very different from that which would otherwise have taken place. Slowly but surely one-crop agriculture and slavery had both been losing their hold, and in the process the great difference between the South and the rest of the nation seemed likely to disappear. The almost insatiable demand in Europe and America for the cheap cotton which could be produced in the South now sharply reversed these trends. In a few years the South was embarked on a cotton career which in almost every detail was to duplicate its experience with tobacco—and the climax this time was to be even more tragic.

[2] Trade takes place between regions (or nations) because a region can profit from concentrating on producing for export goods requiring for their production relatively large quantities of the resources most readily available there (and hence most inexpensive), and importing in exchange goods which if produced at home would require relatively large quantities of the resources least readily available there (and hence most expensive).

In 1794 the economy was given still another impetus when the Lancaster-Philadelphia Turnpike was completed. Until now land transportation had consisted of stump-filled, rut-ridden clearings barely wide enough for a single vehicle. Even the so-called "plank" roads were not greatly superior to unimproved dirt "highways." Now, however, with the development of a much better type of road constructed of broken stone overlaid with gravel, it became possible to provide for the nation's growing transportation needs in a far more adequate way. The cost of carriage over these new roads fell to one-half or one-third of the cost incurred over alternative routes, and thus goods could be profitably sold over a much wider area. Still more important, the new turnpikes drew sufficient traffic to make them of interest to private capital, thus obviating the need for the full assumption of responsibility by either the state or federal government.

To be sure, the new toll roads were not feasible except over the most widely traveled routes, and they were in addition seldom considered anything other than feeder lines to ocean or river carriage. To be sure also, the farm-to-market roads, though of the poorest quality, continued to be of great importance to the economy. But a beginning had been made toward linking the several parts of the country together more effectively, a beginning of American interest in man-made transportation facilities which has never disappeared. Ushering in a movement which has been called "the turnpike era," the Lancaster-Philadelphia Turnpike was followed by a virtual craze for road-building which was not to end until thousands of miles of "first-class" highways had been built.

There were dark spots on the horizon, of course, a sufficient number to keep the antagonism between capitalists and agrarians alive and vigorous. For example, in 1794 frontier resistance to the tax on whiskey gave way to open rebellion. Pennsylvania farmers, settlers from Scotland and Ireland who had brought the habit of whiskey-making and whiskey-drinking with them, refused to pay the tax and organized themselves in opposition. They would give a lesson in economics to an Alexander Hamilton who thought whiskey to be simply a luxury.

Hamilton welcomed this encounter as an opportunity to demonstrate the power of the Union. Urging Washington to send troops to the scene of the uprising, he even accompanied the expedition which put down the rebellion. There was little bloodshed and the poorly armed Pennsylvania farmers were quickly dispersed. But these back-country agrarians were now more ready than ever to join the opposition party Thomas Jefferson was patiently putting together. So too were many of their countrymen who saw in this display of force a new attempt by central government capitalists to "enslave" the agrarian class.

International Complications. Material for agrarian tempers to feed upon was also provided by developments in the field of international relations. No sooner had war broken out between France and England than the former threw open the trade with her West Indian colonies, a move designed to prevent the isolation of these colonies and to bring about a breach between England and America. England promptly announced that she would not permit Americans to give economic assistance to her enemy. This threat of retaliation by the "Queen of the Seas" almost paralyzed American shipping, although only briefly, and the state of mind of the mercantile areas of the nation was most gloomy.

Table 6 shows the fluctuations of the international trade sector of the economy during the period of Federalist control. The significant fact about these fluctuations was that the entire economy was so obviously dependent upon the state of trade. In what could easily have become a major setback for the new nation, consequently, there was reason enough for statesmen being somewhat alarmed. The "privilege" of being the principal neutral carrier in a world at war, in short, was already proving to have certain drawbacks.

TABLE 6. THE FRUITS OF NEUTRALITY

Year	Domestic Exports	Re-exports	Domestic Imports
		(Millions of dollars)	
1790	19.7	0.5	22.5
1794	26.5	6.5	28.1
1795	39.5	8.5	61.3
1800	31.8	39.1	52.1

Source: Bureau of the Census, *Historical Statistics of the United States, 1789-1945*, p. 245.

Jefferson as Secretary of State and Madison in the House took advantage of this situation to recommend trade restrictions against England. New Englanders were aghast. American trade with England made up by far the largest share of American imports and much of her exports. Northern Federalists did not want central government protection of their interests at such a cost. Especially did they not want a war with their best customer. Their solution was to secure a treaty opening the West Indian trade. Against this background John Jay was sent to England.

Even before negotiations began, England agreed to permit trade between the Islands and America, prohibiting only direct trade between the Islands and France. Long before negotiations had been concluded Yankee traders had developed a vast re-export trade by which goods were brought from the French West Indies to United States ports and then reshipped to

France. Such trade did not violate the letter of British regulations if it did the spirit, and for a number of years England did not see fit to challenge this adjustment.

Late in 1794 the Jay treaty was signed in England, the first commercial agreement the new nation had succeeded in securing with England, a document much less satisfactory from the standpoint of this country than had been anticipated when Jay left. Ships of not more than seventy tons could engage in the West Indian trade, all British ships could trade with the United States, our own ships were not to carry molasses, sugar, cotton, coffee, or cocoa to any place except points in the United States, and steps were to be taken to secure payment to British creditors of pre-Revolutionary debts.

These were harsh terms which the nation's erstwhile mother was insisting upon. Awarding to England almost complete trade freedom, they accorded to the United States only the right to send our smallest vessels to the West Indies—and even then restricting the goods which could be carried from these islands to Europe. No wonder the commercial classes were unhappy when news of the treaty reached the United States.

Rule by Businessmen Challenged. But if the commercial classes were unhappy, the agrarians were furious. After all, the commercial groups had achieved some advantages, small though these were. The interests of the agrarians, on the other hand, had been sacrificed at virtually every point, particularly the interests of the southern states. First, the Jay treaty was completely silent on the matter of England's returning the slaves she had carried off during the Revolution. Yet the new treaty was to set in motion an administrative mechanism which was to force payment of pre-Revolution debts, a burden that would fall primarily on the shoulders of southerners. (The treaty itself was not discriminatory, of course, but most northern merchants had long since made a virtue of necessity and paid their English debts in order to secure additional credit.) Moreover, as a result of the postwar depression in the American tobacco and rice economies, southern planters were even less able to pay these debts than at the time they fell due. And finally, this burden of debt repayment to be borne by the South was in large part for the purpose of securing England's withdrawal from the western frontier for the advantage of northern land speculators and fur traders.

As if all this were not enough, the treaty even committed the United States to refrain from shipping cotton to Europe, the new staple which was the basis of the South's prosperity. (The fact that Jay was probably unaware of the invention of the cotton gin was entirely beside the point as far as southern hostility to his treaty was concerned.) And finally, ever since the French Revolution the Republicans had strongly sympathized with the new French government and hoped to improve economic relations with that country. It seemed certain that the Jay treaty would make such overtures much more difficult.

The defenders of America's rapidly growing capitalism ably supported the treaty in the bitter contest over ratification. It was emphasized that England's trade was indispensable to the prosperity of the United States—that her place could not be taken by France. Emphasis was also placed upon the large amount of credit which American traders were allowed in Britain, it being insisted that a young economy is peculiarly dependent upon the availability of outside capital.

Still secure in their control over the government, the Federalists succeeded in achieving ratification, although certain provisions could not be retained—the most notable of these being the clause pertaining to the export of cotton. The agrarians were but little mollified when news was received of a new treaty with Spain giving this country the "right of deposit" at New Orleans. This meant that cargo floated down the Mississippi could be loaded on ocean-going vessels without paying Spanish duties. The West was jubilant, a mood much enhanced when American arms achieved a resounding victory over the Indians in the Northwest and thereby won for America a fuller opportunity to expand into most of the so-called Ohio Territory.

Far overshadowing these favorable developments, however, was a rapidly worsening situation in Europe, where the gravest fears of anti-Federalists were being realized with a vengeance. France had indeed taken offense at the Jay treaty and proceeded to make war on American commerce. And by a most unfortunate coincidence a business depression affecting primarily the commercial and financial interests of the North now complicated international relationships still further.

Almost inevitably businessmen began applying pressure to precipitate war with France. This was precisely the result agrarians had feared when they had earlier sought to defeat the new relationship with England, and they could hardly be blamed for becoming alarmed. Moreover, it is understandable that their alarm turned into a new anger when the impending war with France resulted in not only an increase in taxation for the purpose of building the nation's defenses, but in addition a new departure in taxation which once again seemed to bear most heavily on them. The new device was the nation's first direct tax, levied in 1798 on houses, land, and slaves. To the great majority of farmers whose assets were almost exclusively in these forms, as compared with merchants whose capital typically took other forms, this act seemed to be the grossest sort of discrimination. It was exasperating in the extreme to be thus burdened as the direct result of a policy they had sought to prevent.

America in 1798 was an overwhelmingly agrarian economy. In every state in the Union most people still made their living directly from the land. The capitalistic interests could not long have held the government against the agrarians under any circumstances, and developments during the preceding decade had gone far to convince farmers throughout the nation that their interests would be protected only if they controlled the government. Slowly but thoroughly Thomas Jefferson had been organizing these interests into a force capable of taking over. Most fortuitously for this cause, however, the Federalists now made their biggest blunder to date, virtually guaranteeing Republican success in the next election. In 1798 they passed the alien, sedition, and naturalization laws, which far overreached acceptable bounds in dealing with criticism of the government. This Federalist attack on free speech was met by the Virginia and Kentucky Resolutions (written respectively by Jefferson and Madison), the mature expression of the state-rights, strict-construction philosophy on which the agrarian program was to be built. And when the people went to the polls in 1800, these political documents produced a rich harvest.

QUESTIONS FOR DISCUSSION

1. What were the major provisions of the Constitution, and how were they related to the problems the nation had been confronted with in the years immediately preceding?
2. Was the creation of a stronger central government inevitable? What would have been the consequences to America of the failure to create such a government?
3. What were the major items in the Federalist program? What specific difficulties of businessmen were to be solved by each one?
4. How valid were Hamilton's beliefs about the creation of liquid capital in the interest of business development? If Hamilton was right, were the agrarians wrong?
5. Of what assistance could the First Bank of the United States have been in bringing about a uniform currency as long as state-chartered banks were in existence?
6. Why did Pennsylvania and southern farmers object to the excise tax on whiskey so violently?
7. In what ways were international trading activity and domestic prosperity related?
8. Why was a minority group such as businessmen were at this time able to maintain control over the government as long as it did?

Chapter 7

THE STRUCTURE THREATENED

1801	Anti-Federalists secured control over the government—Thomas Jefferson, President.
1803	Louisiana Purchase.
1801–05	Tripolitan War.
1806	Tension with England and France.
1807–09	Embargo Act.
1808	James Madison elected President.
1809	Non-Intercourse Act.
1810	Annexation of West Florida.
1811	"War Hawks" in command of Congress.
	Battle of Tippecanoe Creek.
	First Bank of the United States refused a new charter.
1812	War declared against Great Britain.

Most reluctantly did the business interests relinquish control over the government on March 4, 1801, for they felt they had fulfilled every reasonable expectation in their stewardship. Inheriting a nation bankrupt in almost every respect, they had restored it to health and prosperity. The credit of the new government was now excellent, and the new nation was beginning to be respected abroad. It could speak with authority to and for its own people; it could take action in its own interest without destructive delays. Most important of all from the businessman's point of view, the outgoing Federalists had developed a climate within which business enterprise could operate more effectively.

Agrarians in Command. It was not merely their loss of power, either, that gave them concern. The other side of loss of power for Federalists was its assumption by the agrarian interests. What would these radicals do now that they were once more in charge of affairs? The capitalist minority could only wait and see, and it is easily understandable that this waiting was done somewhat anxiously.

On their side the agrarian anti-Federalists were confronted with the same set of questions in reverse. They had resisted the adoption of the

Federalist program because they sincerely felt that the measures enacted were opposed to their best interests. With power now in their own hands they could reinforce those interests as rapidly as the solidarity of their own organization would permit. What kind of a program should they try to put into operation?

Clearly nothing could be done about the funding of the debt--i.e., unless the agrarians wanted to take responsibility for plunging the nation again into bankruptcy. This the Republicans had no intention of doing; they too could appreciate the value to the nation of a good credit rating. By the same token they did not propose to advance the cause of a central government without adequate taxing power. Here, also, they had learned their lesson well.

Even within these limitations, however, there were some steps which could be taken in the fields of taxation and the public debt. The debt itself could be reduced, and the annual interest burden thus lessened. Such a move would be a reversal of Hamilton's idea of a perpetual debt, but this reflected only the difference in thinking between agrarians and capitalists on the matters of liquid capital and public creditors. Albert Gallatin, the new Secretary of the Treasury, shared the view of other prominent agrarians that at base the tax and debt burden rested on the land and hence should be reduced. These men, starting from this premise, were not swayed either by the argument about the nation's capital structure or by the insistence on a need for a permanent group of bondholders.

If the first item on Gallatin's agenda was debt reduction, the second was tax reduction. Here two special problems had to be resolved. To a degree, debt and tax reduction were antithetical, for the debt could be paid only by means of the nation's tax resources. Gallatin did not take an all-or-nothing stand on this question, however. He determined that both goals must be accomplished and that the degree of accomplishment in either area would have to be tempered by the need in the other. It speaks volumes for Gallatin's ability and persistence that in a little over a decade the national debt was reduced by more than 30 per cent despite the

TABLE 7. ALBERT GALLATIN VERSUS ALEXANDER HAMILTON

Year	Total Revenues	Internal Taxes	Total Expenditures	National Debt
		(Millions of dollars)		
1792	3.7	0.2	5.1	77.2
1801	12.9	1.0	9.4	83.0
1811	14.4	—	8.1	48.0

Source: Bureau of the Census, *Historical Statistics of the United States, 1789-1945*, pp. 298, 301, and 306.

elimination of internal taxation. Another factor making this result possible, of course, was the enlarged customs revenue produced by America's role as a neutral carrier in a world at war.

The second question had to do with the kinds of tax reductions which should be made. In principle the agrarian interests did not approve of import duties. Such taxes, they felt, tended to build up a relatively less productive financial, mercantile, and manufacturing segment of the economy at the expense of the more productive agricultural segment. But at the same time, and for similar reasons, agrarians had a deep-seated aversion to internal taxation—especially after the whiskey excise episode. Which taxes were to stay and which to go?

Almost immediately the Republicans made their choice in favor of retaining the import duties. Several factors entered into this decision. First, they objected to internal taxes more strenuously than to protection. Second, some agrarian interests specifically desired protection for their own products. Third, the experience of the nation during and after the Revolution had made a deep impression even on the leaders of farm groups. Too great a dependence on other nations for manufactured goods was clearly not a healthy thing.

The last major item which Gallatin wished to achieve was a reduction in the executive machinery, the patronage of the federal government. Centralization had always been one of the chief objects of agrarian fears, and the Federalists had gone out of their way to build up the government at this point. Here again, however, the remedy was to be found largely in the reduction of the debt and the amount of money made available to the government.

The Republicans set to work at once to bring about the indicated reforms, the first and most basic step being the introduction of rigid economies in government expenditures. Realizing that little could be done by way of reducing outlays for civil purposes, attention was concentrated primarily on the military establishment which the Federalists had been preparing for the war with France. This war, fortunately, had not become as serious as it had once threatened to do. So successful were these efforts that it was possible to repeal all the internal revenue levies almost immediately, and a few years later the duty on salt was withdrawn as well.

Centralization Continues. Even more would have been accomplished if circumstances had been more favorable. In addition, the Jeffersonians would have made a much better record with respect to their doctrine of strict construction of the Constitution if the turn of events had been more accommodating. The first unfavorable development was a brief cessation of hostilities in Europe. This resulted in a falling off of business activity and a reduction in the customs revenue by several millions of dollars, although this interlude lasted only a year, and business quickly responded to the renewal of active fighting.

In 1802 the issue of admitting Ohio into the Union came up. This territory now had the required number of inhabitants, it had organized a government for itself, and had otherwise met the general requirements for admission. With an eye on the federal budget Gallatin suggested to Congress that the federal government continue to administer and receive revenue from the unclaimed lands within the state's boundaries. Partly to make this idea palatable to westerners, and partly because he believed these other provisions to be desirable in themselves, Gallatin also suggested that 10 per cent of the proceeds from public land sales within the state be used for the purpose of building improved roads connecting the Ohio River with the navigable waterways emptying into the Atlantic, and strongly supported a provision in the nation's basic land legislation calling for the granting of one section in every township for the use of schools.

Congress was less liberal than Gallatin's recommendation. The grant of land for use in building schools was reduced by more than one half, while the fund for the building of roads was reduced to 5 per cent. But Ohio accepted the proposal, and a pattern was thus set which was followed from this point forward. It was an excellent precedent. A splendid start was thus made toward the creation of America's public school system, and the foundation was laid for the first great internal improvement at the expense of the national government. On the other hand, though, it was a strange performance for men who had insisted that the Constitution was not to be interpreted liberally.

Both the nation's finances and the constitutional doctrine of the agrarians were strained again in 1803 when Louisiana and the problem of navigation on the Mississippi once more became important. In one of those international "deals" for which this period in history is famous, Spain had ceded Louisiana back to France. Simultaneously Spain withdrew the hard-won right of "deposit" at New Orleans. Immediately the entire western country was again in an uproar.

Strong measures had to be taken, and quickly, or the United States would be thrown into an alliance with England which the Republican agrarians did not want. Louisiana in the hands of a weak Spain was one thing; the threat of a powerful France as a border neighbor was another. Accordingly, negotiations were begun for the purchase of Louisiana. Only one obstacle stood in the way of speedily terminating this transaction; neither party had the legal right to act. Napoleon had promised Spain he would not alienate Louisiana, while the strict-constructionist agrarians could find no authority whatever in the Constitution for going ahead. However, statesmen are often forced to be practical above all, and neither

Americans nor Frenchmen overly concerned themselves with the niceties of legal interpretation. The sale was concluded, America adding in the process some $15 million to her financial needs and one more nail in the coffin of eighteenth-century strict construction. It was a most fortuitous event. Important to America's development far beyond the imagination of men then living, Louisiana could probably never again have been acquired so painlessly. As only one indication of its value to America, never again was her right to the free use of the Mississippi River seriously questioned.

The next blow which befell Gallatin's plans to reduce the debt and the nation's tax burden appeared in the form of a war with the Tripolitan pirates. Tripoli had taken full advantage of America's weakness and her preoccupation with more pressing matters to exact tribute as the price of trading in the Mediterranean area, and when the Republicans reduced naval expenditures the pirates were given every reason for believing America would continue to be an easy target.

They were soon disillusioned. A decision was made to pay no more tribute, even though such a decision clearly implied war. Perhaps America's leaders felt it would be cheaper that way in the long run. Furthermore, men like Jefferson, Madison, and Gallatin were realistic enough to understand that a war must be waged seriously or not at all. The result was a strenuous campaign which reached its peak in 1803 and speedily thereafter produced victory.

The Tripolitan war, however, also produced something else. Early in 1804 it became necessary to raise additional revenue to help defray its cost. Despite its commitment to the cause of tax reduction, the administration was now forced to request an increase in the tax burden. Reluctantly Gallatin recommended, not internal taxes, for the Republican pledge on this point was almost inviolable, but an increase in customs duties. To soften this blow to the prestige of the party the receipts from the increased levies were earmarked "The Mediterranean Fund"—to emphasize their emergency character and to make easier their repeal when the special need was past. When the time came to repeal them, however, it seemed more appropriate to do away with the salt duty instead, and the general customs increase remained.

In one other major way did the Republicans forsake the strict-construction ground on which they had made their stand. By 1806 the high cost of efficient land transportation, the need for a land interconnection between East and West, and the success of the turnpikes rapidly springing up in various parts of the country had led to a renewal of agitation for federal support. Albert Gallatin was a willing listener to such agitation. Already he had been instrumental in using the admission of Ohio as a step in that direction, and on this foundation Congress now expressed a desire to build further. A turnpike was authorized to be built westward from Cumberland, Maryland. Funds from the sale of public lands were to be used in its construction, and when finally completed the Cumberland Road—or "National Pike," as it was more frequently called—stretched all the way to Vandalia, Illinois. Even before it was completed, however, it furnished one of the principal avenues of commerce between East and West.

Many intense constitutional battles were fought out over the Cumberland Road before it was finished and, as things turned out, the role of the federal government was not to be as great as originally anticipated. But it was not the fault of Albert Gallatin. Shortly after the National Pike was first authorized he enunciated a broad plan of internal improvements—both roads and canals—to be undertaken at the expense of the federal government. Reflecting the intense desire of many for closer contact with the West, Gallatin broadly justified this program on the ground that in a new country, where capital and labor were scare, it was not appropriate to leave the development of transportation facilities to private initiative. Put differently, the example of the Lancaster-Philadelphia Turnpike was proving to be misleading. Private capital invested in improved roads was not returning the expected dividends, and in the less populous sections of the country it was not even building roads.

Disunity Proceeds Apace. As the historical differences between Federalists and Republicans began to give way in the face of the realities of life in the early nineteenth century, harmony was not so visibly making its appearance in other respects. During this period, the conflict between North and South over slavery had its definitive beginnings. Simultaneously there arose a bitter struggle between New Englanders and most of the rest of the country over international relationships.

Scarcely had Jefferson been inaugurated than southerners sought to secure federal legislation designed to prevent southern slaves from escaping into nonslave territory. Already the influence of the cotton gin on the institution of slavery was being felt, and cotton planters were seeking to strengthen the legal foundation on which it rested. They soon learned to their sorrow, however, that the Anti-Federalist party was not united on this issue. The proposed measure was defeated by a narrow margin when northern Republicans voted against it, even though southern Federalists voted for it.

As the time suggested in the Constitution for forbidding the importation of Negroes approached, there arose a sentiment in favor of implementing the constitutional provision by legislation. This sentiment, furthermore, was enhanced by an action by South Carolina repealing a law prohibiting slave imports. Year by year this controversy lingered just beneath the surface until in 1807 a federal law was passed prohibiting the importation of slaves. In connection with its passage two events stand out. During the debates John Randolph of Virginia predicted that if the Union broke apart, the line of cleavage would be between free and slave states. Equally prophetic was the vote on the bill itself. Once again party alignments gave way before sectional interests, although President Jefferson did support the measure.

It was approximately at this point that the efforts of the agrarians to fix upon the nation the principles for which they stood came to a reluctant end, victims of growing tension in international affairs. England and France were steadily becoming more serious in their endeavors to destroy one another's trade, the United States feeling this conflict with particular severity. Goods this country customarily exported to European markets became increasingly hard to market with regularity and at satisfactory prices after the high cost of insurance or actual losses were deducted, and as the war went on, England became increasingly defiant of the United States in her assumption of the right to take (impress) American seamen for use on British vessels, men whom she claimed were really Englishmen.

Neither England nor France, perhaps, was guilty of viciousness in the treatment accorded America. Both nations were engaged in the serious business of fighting a major war, and economic warfare has always been an accepted way of carrying the fight to the enemy. Both were often inconsistent, to be sure, and it was this inconsistency and uncertainty which made up a large part of the frustration felt by Americans. Opinions have always differed, for example, on the issue of the impressment of American seamen, and no doubt this will always be the case. One fact, however, is vital to an understanding of this issue. Because of the almost insatiable demand for labor in America, the several states had established citizenship requirements on an extremely liberal basis. At the same time America's high wages furnished a powerful incentive to foreigners to "adopt" the new country as their own. Whether or not the American merchant marine contained a large number of men who had not gone through the motions of renouncing British citizenship, it did contain a large number who had so recently been British subjects as to justify England in raising the question.

By the end of 1807 much of America had become aroused to a point of high excitement by the continued impact of the war abroad, an excitement much enhanced by an attack on an American vessel by a British ship. Seeking a method of retaliation short of a war the nation did not yet want, and remembering the success of the restrictions used against England in the years prior to the Revolution, Jefferson's administration in December declared an embargo against the departure of any ship bound for a foreign port.

Many exaggerated accounts of the results of America's restrictive policy have been given. It is certain that grass did not grow on the wharves of Boston, but it is true that the policy was more damaging to American interests than to the interests of those it was intended to injure. As indicated in Table 8, domestic exports fell more than 80 per cent, re-exports

TABLE 8. THE FRUITS OF RESTRICTIONISM

Year	Domestic Exports	Re-exports	Domestic Imports
		(Millions of dollars)	
1801	46.4	46.6	64.7
1807	48.7	59.6	78.9
1808	9.4	13.0	44.0
1811	45.3	16.0	37.4

Source: Bureau of the Census, *Historical Statistics of the United States, 1789-1945*, p. 245.

more than 75 per cent, and domestic imports almost 50 per cent—all in a single year. It is equally certain that American restrictionism was one of the factors which several years later brought England to the point of willingness to negotiate a peace with the United States and also a more favorable commercial treaty. However, the most important fact about America's restrictive policy is that its burden fell most heavily on the commercial classes. As a result of this fact, a remarkable reversal of attitudes on the part of the major economic groups in the country now developed.

When the Constitution had first been put into operation, it was the business classes who insisted upon the need for a liberal interpretation in favor of the power of the central government. Led by Albert Gallatin, agrarians had gradually but perceptibly relaxed their opposition to this view, and their change of position had been so convincing that the distinction between Federalist and anti-Federalist promised to disappear completely. Now, with the passage of legislation greatly reducing the legitimate profits to be derived from trade and commerce, the mercantile interests, the most influential segment of the business community, were no longer sure that the central government's power should be interpreted as loosely as they had once insisted. Throughout the entire period of restrictive legislation this newly discovered strict constructionism became an increasingly important value with the commercial classes. Thus have the constitutional principles of Americans always been governed by the interests for which they stood.

War Comes Closer. The international situation rapidly went from bad to worse, and as early as 1810 there was already talk of war. At first there was some question as to whether the United States should go to war with

England or France. Certainly an excellent case could be made for hostilities against France, as Federalists never tired of pointing out. She had ignored American rights as consistently as had England, and had as ruthlessly interfered with American commerce. Furthermore, New England merchants felt that their views should be given much weight, since they were bearing the burden of commercial restrictions to a greater extent than any other group.

Other counsels prevailed, however, and for reasons which today appear both reasonable and adequate. First, it was urged that the nation's merchants were too biased to give good advice on the question at hand. The skill and determination with which Americans had engaged in trade outlawed by the warring nations, and the success with which they had shifted many of their vessels into privateering activities, had given them a vested interest in the status quo rather than a superior judgment as to whether or not it should be altered. Put differently, the merchants' views could easily be disposed of at the outset on the ground that their holders were motivated by considerations of private advantage instead of the welfare of the nation as a whole.

Second, when the situation was viewed from the standpoint of the long-range interests of the United States as an independent nation, the matter took on a very different character, and from such a standpoint there could

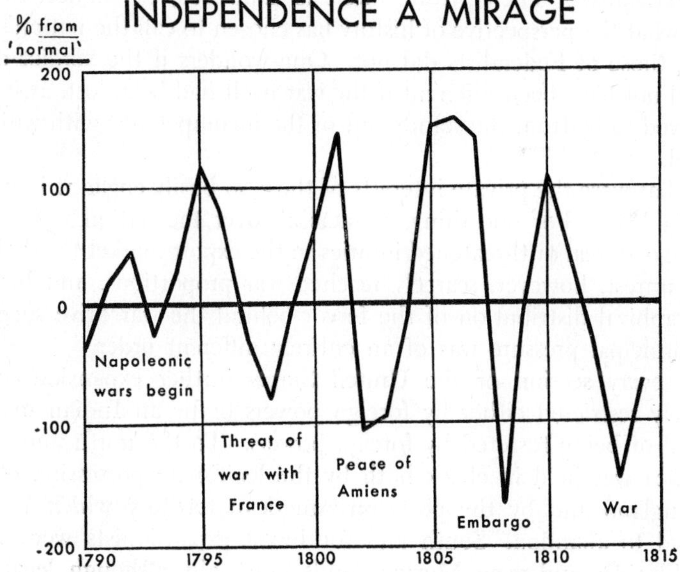

FIGURE 10. BUSINESS CONDITIONS, 1789-1814.

be no question who America's adversary should be. True, England was no more guilty than France of using America's merchant marine as a pawn in her far-flung activities. But England had a navy powerful enough to enforce her orders-in-council, while France was almost helpless once she had promulgated her decrees. The fact that England chose for many years to permit American ships to engage in a profitable trade which could have been closed to them, while reason enough for Federalists to prefer war with France, was precisely why many argued vehemently for war with England; it was humiliating to have one's prosperity dependent upon the whim of another nation. Furthermore, it was not France but England who had the right to use the Mississippi River and who had military posts on the American frontier. In short, although nominally independent, the United States was still virtually a member of Britain's colonial empire. It is no casual use of words which refers to the war soon to be fought with England as America's "second war for independence."

This argument, the one actually used by those who pushed the United States none too gently into war, sounded highly convincing at the time it was used to hasten the beginning of actual hostilities, and even today it readily justifies to Americans the war that resulted. It is inaccurate in the context of its time, however, because it proves too much. The war enthusiasts of 1811 were no less concerned with their own interests than were the Federalists. Their private interests happened, by chance, to coincide with what the perspective of history has chosen to call the nation's interest, while those of Federalists did not. One wonders if the verdict of history would not have been different if the war itself had been lost, as it certainly deserved to be from the standpoint of the incompetence with which it was waged.

What were the private interests of those so busily engaged in promoting war in 1811? For one thing, farmers all over the nation were becoming restive over real or threatened injuries to the export market for their staples. This unrest, however, scarcely reached war proportions, and besides, the geographical distribution of the fervor behind the war drive suggests that the principal pressure was of an entirely different order.

In every section of the United States further expansion was being severely restricted either by foreign powers or by an Indian menace suspected of being fostered by foreign powers. To the north and northwest America was held in check both by the legitimate possession of Canada by England and by the posts on American territory which Britain still refused to abandon. South and southwest expansionists were eying the two Floridas and even Mexico, lands nominally although legally in the hands of Spain. America's urge to fight, and to fight against England rather than France, was motivated by that insatiable land hunger which has made up such an important part of her history. The resistance to

England's commercial restrictions, the motive so freely applauded by the perspective of history, was in large part a pretext.

If there is any doubt about this conclusion it can readily be dispelled by glancing at a map of the United States as it existed in 1811. The Congress that assembled for the first time early in that year contained a group of young men, the so-called "War Hawks," whose great work in 1811 was insisting upon war between England and the United States. It has been shown that when the home counties of these men are located on a map almost all of them lived near foreign soil or facing dangerous Indian tribes. Behind this frontier the sentiment in favor of war tapered off sharply, reaching something approaching zero in coastal, Federalist areas. Apart from the impetus given to war by these frontiersmen, this fact is significant for another reason as well. It clearly demonstrated that the United States was now one generation removed from the Revolution. Western America was coming into its own.

The year 1811 was an eventful one in America's history. Filled primarily with talk of and preparations for war against England, it did contain other features which, although not unrelated to the impending hostilities, mark it as an important one in its own right. In 1811, for example, America occupied West Florida and thus validated a claim which had been in dispute ever since the Louisiana Purchase. The claim itself was shadowy, but Spain's imperial weakness plus the steady influx of Americans into the area ultimately gave it enough substance to permit its exercise with only a minor show of force.

It was in 1811, too, that William Henry Harrison won lasting fame by his great victory over the Indians at Tippecanoe. That the British in the Northwest did foster hostility to America among the Indians, there can be no doubt. But that the campaign ending with the Battle of Tippecanoe was totally unprovoked is equally certain. However, the Indians were getting in the way of the unceasing westward movement once more, and again drastic steps were necessary. Perhaps nothing is as indicative of the expansionist state of mind in the United States as the use of this unprovoked attack on the Indians of the Northwest in promoting a war with England on the ground that she was inciting the Indians against the United States. As the push toward war became more and more intense, no propaganda weapon proved more useful than the memory of Tippecanoe Creek. (The value of this memory in promoting the war probably rested as much on the fact that American arms had won a substantial victory as on the "incitement" argument typically used.)

Although frontier Americans to the north and to the south were equally interested in expansion, the year 1811 demonstrated that in other ways unity was still not the order of the day. A bill was passed by the House providing for one representative in the House for each thirty-seven thousand inhabitants, a bill occasioned by the need to reapportion representation on the basis of the Third Census. In the Senate the House bill was amended to substitute the figure of thirty-five thousand, and a major battle between North and South was precipitated.

This major controversy over an issue which seems on the surface to be trifling is readily explained. The Senate amendment would have left the nine northern states with an unrepresented, fractional population of eighty-two thousand, while the eight southern states would have had more than twice as many in this category. Furthermore, by the terms of the Senate amendment the northern states stood to gain nine Representatives to the South's two. For the first time the North and the South opposed one another on an issue in which slavery was not directly involved. As southern Federalists supported the House bill and northern Republicans voted for the Senate version, and as the Senate amendment won the day, there were some who remembered John Randolph's earlier prediction.

A new controversy between North and South might have postponed indefinitely a war whose major purpose was to clear the way for further expansion. Certainly the South would not have been willing to see the North grow larger at its expense, and vice versa. But the sectional strife within did not call a halt to war talk and preparations because a successful war with England would serve both sections; not only was Spain weak but she was at the moment allied with England. On the other hand, however, one of the reasons for the blundering way in which the war was carried on both in Canada and in Florida may well have been a reluctance in each section to help its rival advance too rapidly relative to its own progress.

The "Bank" Destroyed. In one other important way did disunity appear in 1811. When the Republicans had taken over the government they had made no move against the First Bank of the United States, although they had earlier objected to it. No change of opinion as to the evils of a strong bank attached to the central government was responsible for this failure to act. Rather it had become apparent that the bank actually created was not really a centralizing agency at all. Whereas agrarians had feared for the future of state banks in competition with the national bank, the First Bank of the United States had not prevented a rapid development of state banks. When the national bank was originally chartered, only three state banks were in operation; by 1811 this number had grown to eighty-eight. Far from hampering the operation of state banks, it had even on occasion helped certain of them out of financial difficulties. Still more important, most of the money in circulation consisted of the notes issued by state banks.

It would appear, therefore, that the failure most requiring explanation is not so much that of the agrarians in not making war on the Bank of the United States as that of the capitalists in not taking advantage of an excellent opportunity to erect a monetary system more suitable to their own inclinations. Certainly they were aware of the problem. The financial clauses in the Constitution clearly demonstrated their desire to take responsibility for the money supply out of the hands of the states. Perhaps they expected more help from the working of the United States Mint than in fact developed. Perhaps they refrained from going as far as they would have liked because of the much stronger agrarian opposition which would have been aroused. Perhaps there was not enough understanding of bank operations to permit the accomplishment of capitalist ends when the nation was first founded. Whatever the reason for the failure of the Hamiltonians, the fact remains that the monetary situation had not really been changed appreciably either by the Constitution or by more than ten years of Federalist control.

Agrarians were naturally not displeased by the failure of capitalist interests to give the nation a strong central bank. They watched with satisfaction as state banks grew in number and size, not even dismayed when the nation's money supply became almost as chaotic as in the days following the Revolution. Specie was poorly distributed, concentrated in the cities and the older areas, and as a result the newer areas and the smaller communities were forced to do their banking with an inadequate supply. In such situations overissue of bank notes was a chronic condition—a state of affairs aggravated by the tendency to organize banks where the available business would not support a banking venture, to sell bank stock on credit, and to issue notes secured by long-term loans—and the connection between circulating paper and its commodity security was correspondingly weak.[1] Even banks in larger, well-developed areas were often managed so poorly as to share the difficulties suffered by their frontier and local counterparts.

Most of these banking difficulties centered around the failure of the young economic community to practice a few elementary principles of banking. In the early nineteenth century a bank could perform the function of economizing specie, but it could not make it possible to dispense with specie. As long as a bank's notes enjoyed the confidence of those

[1] "Overissue" of bank notes means to lend money in this form in such quantities that specie redemption either cannot be maintained or is thought by noteholders generally to be in doubt. The basic criterion as to whether notes have been overissued and the extent of overissuance is the purchasing power differential between specie as money and bank notes as money. The greater the discount on notes, the greater is the excess of their number in circulation. One of the problems which perennially arises where a "fractional reserve" banking system is in use is how to prevent too much money from being put into circulation.

using them, they would circulate while metal lay idle in the bank's vaults. Under these circumstances there seemed to be no limit to the quantity of notes which could safely be issued. Trouble developed because there arose occasions on which public confidence waned, a condition which overissue helped bring about, and at such times the specie lying idle in the vaults became of the greatest importance. Until American bankers and statesmen learned with greater accuracy the limits within which the public would accept notes in lieu of specie, little basic improvement in the banking system could be expected.

All in all the existing situation was not a wholesome one. It was not merely that the federal government had not exercised its authority in this field. In addition the states persistently refused to exercise their powers to bring about improvement. The largest number of banks was located in New England, where a veritable banking craze had recently terminated in a bank stock panic, but even here Massachusetts was the only state in which governmental controls had seriously endeavored to deal with the situation. These controls had no doubt done some good, and the first Bank of the United States had exercised a little restraint, but when its charter expired in 1811 it is only fair to say that banking was essentially uncontrolled. Even worse, bank charters were typically granted by a special act of the state legislature, and these acts were often the result of direct or indirect fraud.

To renew or not to renew was the pressing question facing the administration. Finding the bank extremely useful in handling the national government's finances—as a depository for government funds, as an agent helpful in transferring funds for the government from one place to another, and as a source of funds borrowed by the government—Gallatin recommended and worked hard for renewal. Other agrarians were not yet convinced. The old constitutional argument was used to the utmost, and to it was now added the charge that the bank was largely owned by foreign creditors (a charge accurate enough as far as it went, although foreign investors were allowed no share in control). Added to these arguments was the further fact that a number of Republicans at this point could be counted on to vote against renewal if only because Gallatin favored renewal. To such a state had Republican unity come by 1811.

Nonetheless, enough Republicans did favor renewal to have won out in the voting if only the business interests had been united against the bank's destruction—if they had, in short, taken the same stand they had taken twenty years earlier. But times had changed in the intervening period. Since the inauguration of the restrictive system against the major European belligerents, many Federalists had come over to the strict-construction position so lately held by a majority of the agrarians. Banking legislation, furthermore, provided many a businessman with an excellent reason for maintaining this new stand. Since the chartering of the First Bank of the United States capitalists in every state of the Union had acquired a vested interest in state banking, an activity which stood to be enhanced if the business now being done by the national bank had to be taken care of in some other way. Especially in New England, where state banking had enjoyed its greatest growth, capitalists now joined agrarians to defeat the drive for renewal. The struggle of the nation for a more uniform monetary system had again ended in failure.

It was a most unfortunate time to take such a step. On June 18, 1812, a land-hungry but badly divided nation declared war on another nation so occupied with other matters as to be unable to give her full attention to the American conflict. This, at least, was fortunate.

QUESTIONS FOR DISCUSSION

1. What were the main features of Gallatin's financial program?
2. Was it impossible to reduce government centralization, or did the agrarians really not value this objective very highly?
3. Why has the provision of road transportation facilities always been a responsibility of government rather than private enterprise?
4. What was the economic basis of the dispute over the impressment of American seamen?
5. Why was a policy of trade restriction a less powerful weapon than it had been forty years earlier? What more effective steps might Jefferson have taken?
6. In the context of its own times, how convincing was the case for going to war with France rather than England?
7. Why were Americans so anxious to expand their territory as to be willing to fight a major war in 1812?
8. In terms of a peacetime economy how much and what was lost in the failure to renew the charter of the First Bank of the United States?

Chapter 8

NATIONHOOD AT LAST

1812	New England disaffection.
1813	British blockade made effective.
1814	War Embargo against England.
	Washington burned by British.
	Hartford Convention.
1815	Peace of Ghent ratified.
	Unsatisfactory commercial treaty negotiated with England
1816	Second United States Bank chartered.
	Tariff of 1816.
1817	Madison vetoed Calhoun's internal improvements legislation.

By the time the War of 1812 broke out agrarian leaders had accomplished two things of major significance with respect to the nation's finances. They had materially reduced the national debt, and they had placed the federal government on a tax base consisting almost entirely of duties on goods imported from foreign countries. As the nation now embarked upon an expensive war adventure the first of these accomplishments stood it in good stead. The second was to hang like a millstone around its neck.

Problems of War Finance. Actually even before war came the dependence upon customs revenue had given cause for concern. Thus, the restrictive policy adopted to force the belligerents to recognize our rights on the high seas had reduced the government's revenue by approximately one-half. At first little attention was given to this ominous fact because the nation had been running a substantial Treasury surplus for a number of years. However, Albert Gallatin was too conscientious not to think seriously about the future as relationships with England grew steadily worse. In consequence he promulgated a plan of war finance to be put into operation in case war did come. Ably prepared, as was everything to which he gave his energies, this plan was most significant for its one major omission. Under no circumstances, Gallatin declared, would he insist on internal taxes.

This attitude the Secretary of the Treasury retained until the very eve of hostilities. Congress was easily persuaded to adopt the policy urged by Gallatin—to finance the war when it came mainly by borrowing; increases in taxes always put the representatives of the people under severe pressure. But when Congress refused to recharter the United States Bank, thus destroying one of the primary sources of the government's borrowed funds, the Secretary did demand internal taxes. In the absence of actual fighting Congress did not feel inclined to take such a step, and a loan was negotiated instead. Coupled with the extent to which the agrarians had allowed the military establishment to deteriorate from lack of appropriations, all this was a poor financial basis on which to build a major war effort.

The declaration of war instantly galvanized Congress into more decisive action. To supply the government with the goods it most urgently needed, Treasury notes were issued in anticipation of tax revenues, a decision accompanied by much controversy in Congress. Opponents insisted it was the first step toward paper money, depreciation, and impaired credit, while proponents argued that these notes bore no resemblance to the continental currency issued by a government without taxing powers and hence without the sound credit now enjoyed by the government. As it turned out Treasury-note opponents were correct, although had certain other circumstances been more favorable the result might have been different.

Immediately, also, Congress acted to increase existing duties by 100 per cent. This was a part of Gallatin's earlier program, but it proved to be of little actual assistance. Although the decline in customs revenue was fortunately much less drastic, in a period of two years American imports declined by 80 per cent while exports fell almost 90 per cent. By February, 1813, pressing needs which could not be filled by existing taxation forced resort to another large loan and another issue of Treasury notes in anticipation of taxes Congress persistently refused to legislate. When the February loan was opened for subscription it was evident that the predictions of the opponents of Treasury notes were already coming true. The subscription books had to be opened twice, and in the end bids below par had to be accepted.[1] Furthermore, this issue might never have been sold

[1] The poorer the credit of a debtor, the greater is the risk taken by the borrower of non or partial repayment. In turn, the greater the risk the higher the rate of interest which will be demanded by the creditor in compensation. When a fixed-interest security (such as a government bond) sells for less than the amount the borrower must repay (par), this means that the rate of interest demanded by lenders is greater than the fixed rate of interest paid by the security. The greater the "discount," furthermore, the greater is the creditor's estimate of the risk he is taking.

at all if John Jacob Astor, America's fur king and a personal friend of Albert Gallatin, had not formed a syndicate with two Philadelphia bankers to rescue the government.

In a sense the administration had only itself to blame for these difficulties into which the government had already fallen. But when the statistics of this loan were tabulated and its results summarized geographically, it was obvious that the cause was not alone the negligence of the nation's leaders. Subscriptions in all of the states east of New York combined amounted to only 3 per cent of the total, and to less than 8 per cent of that subscribed in Philadelphia alone. New England, with the largest share of the nation's wealth and the nation's most highly developed banking and capital facilities, was refusing to help the government in a time of great need.

No one, of course, would have raised a question about New England's failure to do her part if it had resulted from economic impoverishment brought about by the war. After all, the impact of the war on the American economy was substantial, and in many respects it was adverse. Goods customarily purchased abroad increased greatly in price, as did goods (such as flour) ordinarily transported from one part of the economy to the other by water but which had now to be carried by land at much greater cost. These price increases, moreover, were in addition to a substantial increase in the general price level resulting from inflationary methods of war finance. On the other hand, the prices of goods customarily exported fell, and those whose incomes were derived from exports hence suffered a double injury. Especially in the South in general and Virginia in particular was the effect of the war unfavorable. Largely dependent upon three export staples—tobacco, rice, and cotton—these states were almost prostrated by the tight British blockade. In Virginia, where exploited tobacco soil was already beginning to rebel against long continued abuse, conditions were even more serious than in the rest of the South.

Yet, despite these conditions, Virginia subscribed almost as much to the February, 1813, loan as the state of Massachusetts, while the City of Charleston, South Carolina, contributed more than Massachusetts. Was New England, then, devastated by the war to an even greater extent than the South? Were American restrictions and the British blockade so effective as to render New England unable to contribute to the war effort? Not at all. On the contrary, the war which was impoverishing much of the rest of the country was actually enriching New England. Until almost the end of the war the blockade by means of which England sealed American ports from New York southward was carefully kept from closing New England ports, and New England was carrying on a thriving commerce with the enemy. Not only, in short, was New England refusing to place her financial resources at the disposal of the government, but she was doing her best to see that the British army in Canada was well fed. Her failure to respond to the call for funds was the result of her resistance to a war she thought should never have been fought.

These were hard facts for the young nation, and men who had assumed that the war would never extend beyond a campaign or two in Canada and the Floridas were forced to find some other way of raising desperately needed money. In July and August a Congress called into special session by the President levied a direct tax and excise taxes, although the excises were absurdly low and neither tax was to yield revenue until the following year. Simultaneously another loan was offered for subscription; again bond sales were possible only at a substantial discount.

TABLE 9. WAR WITHOUT TAXATION

Year	Total Government Revenues	Customs Revenue	Internal Revenue	Deficit
		(Millions of dollars)		
1812	9.8	9.0	–	10.4
1813	14.3	13.2	–	17.3
1814	11.2	6.0	1.7	23.5
1815	15.7	7.3	4.7	17.0

Source: Bureau of the Census, *Historical Statistics of the United States, 1789-1945,* p. 298.

The nation's financial situation became steadily darker. Earlier in 1814 another large sum in Treasury notes was issued and the largest loan to date had to be floated. Before this loan was disposed of some subscriptions had been accepted in state bank notes worth only 65 per cent in specie. Moreover, successive issues of Treasury notes were beginning to behave more and more like outright paper money. It was approximately at this point in the war's financing that the nation's leaders began especially to regret the scuttling of the United States Bank.

But an even worse disaster was in store. New England's trade and manufacturing activities made available to the other states many goods which would otherwise have been difficult to procure. However, the New England market could absorb only a fraction of the staples by means of which these other states normally purchased the goods they needed. The result was that specie was gradually withdrawn from the banks in the southern and middle states into New England banks. Finally, in August, 1814, all the banks outside of New England were forced to suspend specie payments. From that point forward the government had to accept taxes or loan proceeds in whatever money was available, and with the expansion of state banking activities following the demise of the United States Bank a currency chaos was unavoidable. Again the loss of the United States Bank was keenly felt.

The new crisis was met with new loans, increases in internal taxes, and more Treasury notes. Thereafter the outlook steadily brightened, an improvement occasioned primarily by the signing of a peace treaty with England. It was not a moment too soon. The government was so near bankruptcy that a single important adverse development might have completed the process. Morever, leading New England Federalists were holding formal discussions to decide what amendments would have to be added to the Constitution (amendments limiting the power of the central government) in order to make it worth New England's while to stay in the Union. Probably the nation was as near disaster toward the end of 1814 as at any time during or immediately following the Revolution.

A Favorable Settlement. The Treaty of Ghent was signed December 24, 1814, an excellent candidate for the distinction of being the strangest document in the history of international relationships. Of the impressment of American seamen and restrictions on American commerce, ostensibly the reason the war had been entered into in the first place, there was no mention. Even more amazing, there were no clauses dealing with the question of America's westward expansion, the more fundamental reason behind the war. Every question for which the war had been fought was simply left to the arbitrament of time, a most favorable arbiter as far as America was concerned. Even more important, the end of the Napoleonic Wars ushered in a period in which the reasons for restrictions on America's commerce largely disappeared, a fact marking a tremendous gain for the United States which her participation in the war had done nothing to bring about.

Negative though these treaty results were, they were extremely favorable for a nation which had fought a war most incompetently and was almost bankrupt. They were even more favorable, moreover, when considered in the light of a controversy arising during the negotiation process which very nearly brought America's commissioners to blows with one another. Henry Clay, speaking for the West, wanted to insist on denying England the right to navigate the Mississippi River. John Quincy Adams was most concerned about New England's right to fish along the coast of British America. Neither Clay nor Adams, furthermore, was at all interested in the concession most demanded by the constituents of the other, and it was fully understood that England would not give in on both of these issues. Only the patient and good-humored diplomacy of Albert Gallatin kept enough harmony within American ranks to permit suggesting to Britain a treaty draft omitting all mention of either of these vital issues, and the final treaty followed the American suggestion.

Why under such unfavorable circumstances was it possible for the United States to secure terms so favorable? For one thing, it must be remembered that England's war was not with the United States alone. She was simultaneously fighting Napoleon, a much more formidable opponent, and this phase of her struggle with France had now been actively prosecuted for more than twenty years. Debt-ridden, heavily taxed, and weary of war, Great Britain wanted peace. Put differently, given the primitive state of America's economy, it was likely that the United States could continue to fight even though bankrupt; it was much less likely that the ministry in control of England's government could survive another substantial increase in taxes.

In the second place, England over the preceding ten years had made a startling discovery. The enactment of the original embargo law under Jefferson had precipitated a sharp stock-market decline in England, a decline indicating that America was more important to England's economy than she had been prepared to admit. As America's restrictive policy had continued in force against England this unpleasant truth became more and more evident. British manufactures were piling up on producers' shelves, and business was languishing in the absence of one of its principal markets. Moreover, and this fact was even more compelling, the cessation of American imports from England was visibly prompting the expansion of manufactures in America. Many British manufacturers were rapidly coming to the view that this nonsense of war against America had best be promptly stopped before America's manufacturing development had gone to far.

The war over, America turned promptly to the problems of peace. In a sense it was the same America that had so recently been engaged in fighting against England. Yet, on looking closer, it was easy to distinguish an important difference. The earlier America had been shot through with violent controversies; the new America was highly unified. The old America had stood in such a close relationship with Europe as to give rise to the suspicion that it was still a part of England's colonial empire; by 1815 the new outlook in America promised the development in fact of the independence claimed in theory more than thirty years before. And, most important of all, whereas America had become accustomed to looking primarily toward its past in the East and Europe, now the most customary view was to be the nation's future in the West. In a few short years, it seemed, America had grown up.

As energies shifted from the requirements of war to the requirements of peace, the first need was obviously to begin settling some of the issues between the United States and Great Britain which the treaty had not settled. A first, but short, step in this direction was the signing of a commercial treaty on July 3, 1815. This document provided for reciprocal liberty of commerce between the territories of the United States and the territories of Great Britain in Europe and Asia, and prohibited discriminatory duties or other restrictions by either party. Unquestionably a great gain for the United States as compared with prewar conditions, this settlement still did not resolve the most important issue as far as America was concerned. Each nation was left with the right to legislate concerning its own West Indian trade as it saw fit.

Another Experiment in Central Banking. With the war behind it, the nation could also take steps to improve its financial situation. More particularly, the agrarians could now return to the financial road they were traveling when the war had derailed their plans. The national debt had grown astronomically during the war, and their view was still that the best debt would be the lowest possible one. Moreover, with foreign trade no longer held to a minimum by hostilities and by the actions of other nations, conditions appeared to be favorable for doing away with internal revenue taxes once more. Accordingly, legislation was drawn up abolishing these levies.

Far more pressing than the question of taxes and the national debt, however, was the prevailing disorder in the nation's currency system. Even before the war ended, agitation had begun for a new United States Bank. The motivation behind this move had been the need felt for a fiscal agency to assist the government in its financial crisis. After the war, an even more basic need was visible. Many of the nation's banks were still not redeeming their notes in specie and as a result various currencies were in use, all of them with varying rates of depreciation and most having only a local circulation.

There were two ways in which the currency problem could be viewed. On the one hand, the nation could not tolerate for long such a complete lack of uniformity in its circulating medium. The government could not accept as tax receipts 90 per cent money in Rhode Island and 70 per cent money in Georgia. No more could the government accept a situation in which tax receipts from New York could not be spent in South Carolina, and it was highly coincidental for the government's spendings in a state to be equal to its receipts in that state. From a broader standpoint it was unhealthy in the extreme for American imports to come to Philadelphia and Baltimore primarily because currency there was more debased (and hence prices higher) than in Boston. And, finally, the nation's rapidly developing internal trade could not help suffering from this situation.

On the other hand, emphasis could be placed upon the constitutional aspects of the matter. The Constitution had specifically forbidden the states to issue paper money, and yet states were freely chartering banks to do what the states were forbidden to do. In only five years the number of state banks had increased from less than one hundred to almost two hundred and fifty, and state bank notes in circulation had increased more than in proportion. Providing no uniformity of value from one note to the other or even universality of acceptance, these arrangements could not by any stretch of the imagination be said to be fulfilling constitutional responsibilities.

The obvious remedy was the creation of another United States Bank. Serving as a fiscal agent for the government, such an institution could also contribute to the need for a uniform currency. Not only could it issue its own notes but it could take steps to bring other banks to a specie basis by refusing to accept notes from institutions not redeeming in specie and by sending for redemption notes held out to the public as redeemable. Resistance to the proposed bank was much the same as that which had destroyed the earlier national bank. Many agrarians could not see their way clear to support such a centralizing institution despite the clearly demonstrated need. (As always, however, the Constitution was only the superficial factor involved. More fundamentally, the difficulty was that a central bank might limit the usefulness of state banks in providing farmers with an abundant money supply.) Interests actively involved in the state banking business were also opposed, because this remedy would eat heavily into their profits. The discipline of specie redemption would make it necessary to reduce note circulation (i.e., loans) and hence interest receipts would be diminished.

However, the opposition forces were not as powerful in 1816 as they had been earlier. In 1811 there had been no crisis to put pressure on legislators. Five years earlier, moreover, there had not existed the spirit of national unity which had emerged from the "second war for independence." In addition, the economic development of the nation had been so rapid that in a few short years the inconvenience of a currency that was not uniform had grown appreciably greater; a smaller and smaller proportion of the nation's economic transactions were taking place outside the exchange nexus. And finally, there were important business leaders—of whom John Jacob Astor was one—who felt that a national bank would bring about a rise in the market value of the government securities they held. On April 10, 1816, the Second Bank of the United States was chartered, and the drive for a uniform currency was greatly strengthened by requiring the payment of money to the government in specie or in bank notes redeemable in specie.

Infant Manufactures Again. From the standpoint of America's manufacturing industries the second conflict with England had been in many respects analogous with the first. By partially closing the shipping and agriculture industries to the continued investment of labor and capital, and by raising the domestic price of manufactured goods, restrictive measures had improved profit possibilities in manufacturing sufficiently to attract large investments. Each time, moreover, the period of voluntary restraint was followed by outright war, during which the level of restriction became much greater and during which also the nation's need for manufactured goods rose to crisis proportions. Each such experience, in other words, stimulated a rapid development in manufacturing activity. Table 10 gives one indication of how inviting to manufacturing was the economic context surrounding the "second war of independence."

TABLE 10. ENCOURAGEMENT FOR MANUFACTURING

Year	Wholesale Price Index (1926 = 100)
1808	93.9
1809	98.7
1810	107.7
1811	104.9
1812	106.3
1813	123.6
1814	154.6

Source: Bureau of the Census, *Historical Statistics of the United States, 1789-1945*, p. 234.

On the other hand, however, there was one important difference between the two periods. The Revolutionary War had seen an increase primarily in manufacturing in the home and in small plants, not in factory production. At that time the industrial revolution was none too far advanced even in England, let alone in the United States. Factory output had to await the basic inventions making large-scale production cheaper than small-scale, and for a few years England successfully prohibited the export from England of the technological advances giving her an advantage over other nations.

In the quarter of a century following the Revolution these conditions began gradually to change. Basic secrets relating to manufacturing technology filtered out of England, this policy of secrecy being almost completely nullified when emigrants from England to America came with the design and construction details of basic innovations firmly fixed in their memories, although American dependence upon European technological advances was to continue for many years. The improvement of transportation as the turnpike era advanced broadened the market for domestic goods and in this way also improved the environment for production on a larger scale. Slowly but surely the prerequisites for America's modern factories were springing into existence. Thus, whereas the "first war for independence" had stimulated manufacturing, the second marked the definitive beginning in this country of what has ever since been called "the factory system"—production on a large scale with a large number of workers gathered under a single roof and using mechanical power.

It is not to be supposed that factory production was destined to win a quick victory over its rivals—household manufacture and nonfactory production for sale. Rather the battle was to be a long and bitter one, and as long as the nation's internal transportation system consisted primarily of turnpikes and rivers the greatest disadvantage was felt by large-scale, factory organizations. The factory was not in fact to be an important element in the economy for another twenty-five years—and not for still another quarter of a century was this country to be able to compete with western Europe on even terms. But a foundation was being laid, and this wartime development did much to set the stage for another fierce battle over the tariff.

While the war was still in progress a dramatic demonstration had been given of the transformation taking place in America. When, as one phase of America's policy of economic restrictionism against England, a nonimportation law had been passed, one Elisha Potter representing the shipping interests of Rhode Island had vehemently opposed its passage. In the middle of the war, in order to bring a greater support for the war effort from New Englanders, John C. Calhoun especially had sought to secure the repeal of nonimportation. Now, however, as vehemently as he had earlier denounced the bill's passage, Potter opposed its repeal. War and restrictionism had driven Providence and Pawtucket into manufacturing, and the repeal of nonimportation would threaten this adjustment.

The problem confronting the constituents of Elisha Potter was also confronting many another American. In any number of communities capital which had gone into manufacturing in order to meet the country's emergency needs and which had been enticed into this activity by the restrictive conditions of war was now faced with the prospect of the sudden disappearance of its protective umbrella. And what made the situation doubly serious was the fact that investment in factory production is *fixed investment* to a much greater extent than is the case with nonfactory manufactures; once invested, such capital cannot readily disentangle itself and go elsewhere. Everywhere men with capital sunk in manufacturing facilities began clamoring for special protection by the government. English manufacturers had urged the conclusion of Britain's war with the United States before it was too late. Unfortunately for them, it was already too late.

The problem of American manufacturers would have been difficult enough in any event. Two circumstances, however, made it especially acute. With the advantage of a longer background of capitalistic economic development, England possessed a superiority over America which would have enabled her to drive many American manufacturers out of business in a free and open market. In England the industrial revolution had decisively begun, and no matter how rapidly technological secrets filtered to the United States, there was bound to be a lag. Capital was more readily available in England, she had a larger market available for her output, her labor was cheaper, and the development of such institutions as a capital market and a uniform currency had progressed there much farther than in this country.

Protection Versus Revenue. The other circumstance had to do with America's tariff policy. At the outbreak of war tariff duties had been doubled, and these war rates were scheduled to be eliminated one year after the end of the war. This meant that unless some change in legislation were enacted, the expected deluge of imports would be assisted by a lowering of the nation's import barriers. Few manufacturers could contemplate such a development without deep anxiety.

Neither could most of America's leading statesmen, and the agrarians now took the lead in preventing a fall in tariff duties to the prewar rates. President Madison, as he submitted the peace treaty to Congress for ratification, took notice of the tremendous increase in manufactures and recommended their preservation and promotion. Secretary of the Treasury Dallas drew up a report in which he too urged the enactment of a duty level which would be adequately protective. Even that arch-agrarian Thomas Jefferson gave it as his considered judgment that manufacturers were now absolutely essential to the nation's independence. Lowndes and Calhoun from South Carolina enthusiastically supported the principle of protection, while Henry Clay was already one of its stanchest advocates. For thirty-odd years the nation had seen its interests buffeted and tossed about on the tides of international relationships, and Americans had typically grown weary of this economic helplessness.

Sentiment favoring protection to manufacturers was by no means unanimous. Daniel Webster, the outstanding spokesman for those business interests in New England still primarily commercial, made a vigorous plea against a policy of unfree trade which would destroy an industry so vital to the past and future development of the country. Many agrarians, too, were still opposed to protecting manufacturers at the expense of the nation's farmers, although the new tariff received broad support from every section of the country.

These two groups combined, however, made up only a vigorous minority when the time came to vote on a tariff adjustment. By 1816 the anticipated flood of imports was already clearly visible, rising in that year from a wartime low of $13 million to an amount more than ten times that figure.

As a result debate on the tariff took place in an atmosphere charged with the distress of the nation's manufacturing industry. Under these circumstances opposition had to be presented in slightly muffled tones, and manufacturers would have had a clear field if the situation had not been complicated by an issue which perhaps should have been considered separately.

For a very fundamental reason, however, this could not be done. It was a fixed agrarian principle to collect no more in taxes than was essential for running the government, and, of course, for scaling down the national debt. Since the several interests in the nation were agreed that customs revenue was to be the primary income of the government, it proved to be impossible to consider these issues separately. Unfortunately for the aspirations of the manufacturers, the deluge of imports threatening to engulf their infant plants was also bringing with it a stream of revenue larger than had ever before been available. In 1816 the customs receipts alone would have met all the government's expenses with $5 million left over to apply on the national debt. This intrusion of the revenue question into what would otherwise have been a clear-cut issue produced one of the outstanding paradoxes in American history.

TABLE 11. TAXATION WITHOUT WAR

Year	Customs Revenue	Deficit − / Surplus +
	(Millions of dollars)	
1815	7.3	−17.0
1816	36.3	+17.0

Source: Bureau of the Census, *Historical Statistics of the United States, 1789-1945*, p. 298.

The alternatives confronting the nation were to continue the war rates, return them to the prewar level, or enact a tariff schedule somewhere in between. So strong was protectionist sentiment that a return to prewar rates was never seriously considered. But as between the other two possibilities protectionists could not agree because the revenue situation constantly intervened. As a result "free traders" were able to unite with proponents of revenue reduction to enact a schedule of duties higher than the prewar rates but lower than the levels in effect during the war. In other words, the high tide of protectionist sentiment flowing through the nation in 1816, as the result of a strange set of circumstances, produced a tariff measure which, far from raising the duty level industry had already found inadequate, lowered the level of protection in the face of as intense foreign competition as the nation had ever faced.

American mythology has it that the tariff of 1816 was a protectionist measure enacted under the impetus of America's newly found nationhood.

This is only half right at best. Certainly it was enacted by men sincerely professing protectionist sentiments. Certainly also it was intended to be protectionist legislation. But that in the context of its time it was *not* protectionist, there can be no doubt. In the face of an import level causing much discomfort to American manufacturing concerns, men who sincerely claimed to be protectionists did in fact reduce the tariff. Only by raising duties to a level high enough to choke off both imports and revenue could the inconsistent requirements of increased protection and decreased revenue have been met in 1816.[2] Such a step, so well understood in later stages of the tariff controversy, was not a part of men's thinking at this time.

Internal Improvements. One other great problem arose while the nation was still under the influence of postwar nationalism. The recent war had demonstrated more clearly than ever before the grave lack of adequate transportation facilities. On the one hand, this inadequacy had been a great handicap in the moving of troops from one point to the other, and hence the argument of national defense was now added to other arguments in favor of prompt and vigorous action in this field. On the other hand, America's decisive "second declaration of independence" implied turning her back on Europe and attending to her own development. Such a development required, and virtually everyone understood this fact, integrating the West with the seaboard areas. Here was another basic reason for expanding and improving the nation's transportation facilities.

Late in December, 1816, John C. Calhoun presented to the House a bill outlining a program of internal improvements for which the national government was to be responsible. In broad detail this proposal differed in no important way from that outlined earlier by Gallatin, still placing primary emphasis upon arterial turnpike connections between major centers and sections of the country. A nationalist still, and soon to be Secretary of War in Monroe's Cabinet, Calhoun began his supporting arguments with the unquestioned need for better communication in the interest of the nation's defense. From here, however, he branched out into the general requirements of the Union as a union. "Whatever impedes the intercourse of the extremes with this, the centre of the republic, weakens the union. The more enlarged the sphere of commercial circulation . . . the more strongly are we bound together—the more inseparable are our destinies."

[2] The American tariff of that day, serving simultaneously as it did the interests of both revenue and protection, was an economic anomaly at best. Under a broad range of circumstances these two things operate at cross purposes with one another. The more successful a duty is in producing revenue, the more ineffective is it in keeping foreign goods out of the country. Conversely, the more successful a duty is in restricting imports, the more ineffective it is in producing a revenue.

Without question the outstanding fact about Calhoun's position on this issue was his grasp of the essential conditions necessary for the development of an industrial civilization. Industrialism requires the exploitation of the machine, and the machine can profitably be used only on a large-scale production basis and hence only if there is available a large market which can be inexpensively reached. England had begun to make her way along the road to industrialization by the use of sea lanes which could be used at no cost. America would have to make her way along this road by developing internal transportation facilities at great cost. It is indeed ironical that the man who in 1816 understood better than almost anyone else the kind of future America was destined to have, and who in 1816 bent every effort to promote America's industrial growth, was to become the most brilliant leader of southern agrarianism in its resistance to a future so plainly marked out.

Opposition to Calhoun's proposal was primarily based on constitutional grounds; although without greatly impairing the usefulness of the bill, enough of the constitutional objections were overcome to secure its passage. On the final vote, however, New England's representatives voted almost solidly against it. Federalists had not yet become reconciled to centralization after their recent experience with trade restrictions. In addition, New England was already possessed of good roads, and thus had less to gain from East-West transportation than any other section. (And, of course, these facts were not unrelated to the constitutional stand of New Englanders). The South was divided almost evenly, although voting against the bill by a small margin. Western representatives voted in favor, but even western agrarians were far from unanimous in their support.

As in the case of the tariff, the strongest support came from New York and Pennsylvania. Businessmen in New York City, Philadelphia, and Pittsburgh were not slow to grasp the meaning for them of improved economic relationships within the country. New York stood to gain primarily by the opening up of the West. Pennsylvania also sought internal unity as a state, for she was divided by the difficult Alleghenies. In addition, Philadelphia would very much have liked to see the construction at federal expense of a canal connecting her with the South.

The passage of the internal improvements bill by a Republican administration marked the high point reached by postwar nationalism. Federalists were now thoroughly discredited and were never again to put a presidential candidate in the field. The recent war had welded the nation together as had no other event in its history. For a moment it seemed that historical animosities had disappeared in the flush of victory and real independence. But it was only the calm before the storm. That the underlying conflicts dividing Americans one from the other were only being held in abeyance was forcefully demonstrated on March 3, 1817. On his last day in office, President Madison vetoed the internal improvements measure.

QUESTIONS FOR DISCUSSION

1. What is the difference between an issue of paper money and a bond issue? Why is paper money an undesirable way to raise funds, and why despite this fact was it done?
2. How did the government's war financing contribute to the suspension of specie payments? In what ways did suspension make financing the war more difficult?
3. Why did the hardships of the War of 1812 fall disproportionately on the South?
4. Was the War of 1812 worth its cost? What were its costs and its achievements?
5. Why was England so anxious to bring hostilities with the United States to an end?
6. Was a United States Bank more or less necessary in 1816 than in 1791?
7. Was a protective tariff more or less necessary in 1816 than in 1791? Why were steps not taken at this point to break the connection between the government's revenues and the tariff?
8. What are the relationships between technology, factory development, and transportation?

PART II

THE NATION DIVIDED

(1817–1860)

Chapter 9

THE BREACH OPENS

1817	James Monroe became President.
	"Era of Good Feeling" began.
1818	First Seminole War.
1819	"Panic of 1819."
	East Florida acquired.
	McCulloch v. Maryland.
1820	Missouri Compromise.
	Defeat of a general tariff increase.
	African slave trade declared to be piracy.

Depression in Industry. In the period immediately following the war the American economy was peculiarly out of joint. Although manufacturing enterprises were severely depressed, agriculture for the most part enjoyed a high prosperity. Just as there was in America an accumulated demand for European exports, so was there in Europe an abnormal demand for American exports. As a result the large influx of manufactured imports into this country was matched by an equally great volume of agricultural exports. Moreover, what would in any event have been a prosperous period for American agriculture was made doubly so by a succession of short grain crops abroad and by a speculative boom in the Liverpool cotton market.

No only was agriculture prosperous while manufacturing was depressed, but it was the farmer's good fortune which contributed as much as anything else to the difficulties confronting manufacturing operations. Some of the imports now causing so much consternation in America could have been financed by foreign credits and by draining the country of specie. But these sources would by no means have supported such a huge volume of imports without the funds currently being earned by a swollen export trade. And the most trying aspect of the entire situation as far as the nation's infant manufactures were concerned was the fact that, apart from the failure of the country's statesmen to enact a protective tariff, European manufacturers were to a considerable extent successful in evading the duties which were in effect.

In three ways British exporters were able to nullify tariff protection. First, they developed the practice of dealing simultaneously with two agents in this country. To one agent they would send the goods together with an invoice declaring arbitrary prices far below the real worth of the goods. To the other would be sent a "true" invoice. The first agent would pay duties on the basis of the low values declared, then turn the goods over to his colleague for distribution. Second, the practice of selling goods at auction became widespread, a technique enabling the British seller to meet whatever competition he found. If the result was occasionally the sale of goods at a "loss," foreign manufacturers could still easily rationalize such transactions on the ground that out-of-pocket costs were covered and that these temporary "losses" might help to destroy America's newly developed manufacturing industry and hence clear the field for the future.[1] Third, America's tariff laws permitted duties to be paid on credit, and English merchants were thus enabled to delay payment until their goods were sold.

The commercial segment of the economy was as slow to regain its health after the war as manufacturing. American traders had hoped that the West Indies trade would be thrown open to them, and they were greatly disappointed when England enacted legislation putting non-British traders at a disadvantage. For example, England still held to her policy of allowing only an enumerated list of goods to come into her colonies. In addition, American ships were prohibited from entering British West Indian or North American ports and were hence denied access to the lucrative triangular trade with the West Indies.

This was a heavy blow to the nation's carrying trade, one felt to be doubly severe because in the general treaty with England the United States had already given up discriminatory duties against British imports. Within two years after the end of the war a substantial proportion of America's ship tonnage was threatened with ruin, and of course this loss was felt equally severely by America's shipbuilding industry. The new nationalism in America promptly responded with a navigation act of its own, limiting the importation of West Indian goods to American vessels or ships belonging to West Indian merchants. Simultaneously American ships were given a monopoly of the valuable coasting trade in the United States,

[1] Economists often divide production costs into two categories—"overhead" or fixed costs, and "out-of-pocket" or variable costs. The first refers to costs such as rent, depreciation, interest on borrowed capital, and salaries of executives. Such expenses are relatively fixed in total amount rather than closely related to the volume of output. The second refers to wages or outlays for raw materials, costs which vary in total amount roughly in proportion to the quantity of goods produced. Sales at a price in excess of out-of-pocket costs do result in a "loss" from the standpoint of full costs, but since overhead costs have been incurred anyway there is in another sense no loss involved at all. Sales of goods in a foreign market at a lower price than domestically are often referred to as "dumping."

and these enactments were soon followed by a third, excluding from American ports all British ships arriving from a colony legally closed to American vessels. If Americans could not profit from the rich, triangular trade they could at least see to it that Englishmen did not. During the next two years British tonnage entering American ports fell almost 80 per cent.

In the sparring which both accompanied and followed these skirmishes, several unsettled issues between the two nations were resolved. A commission was appointed to decide upon the compensation due America for the slaves carried off during the Revolution. Gradually it came to be taken for granted that England was not to have navigation rights on the Mississippi River, and a clear-cut division of territory was thus marked out for English and American fur traders as this activity moved steadily westward. After much negotiation New England fishermen were granted limited though substantial fishing rights in British America and the northern boundary of the Louisiana Purchase was fixed at the forty-ninth parallel. But the principal controversy remained unsettled, and as a result the shipping industry did not regain its position of importance in the economy.

Currency Inflation. While manufacturing and trade were still depressed, the farmer's prosperity received its first setback. Here, too, one of the principal factors was the emergence of peacetime international relations. The relative costs of grain production were such that continental sources continued for many years to enjoy a competitive advantage over the American product, and only in times of unusually high prices did grain from this country invade European markets on a large scale. Moreover, the British enacted a Corn Law which put American grain at an even greater disadvantage in the British market, and discriminated against American grain in the West Indies. A typical mercantilist performance, designed on the one hand to protect English farmers from foreign competition and on the other to give England's other colonies (especially Canada) an advantage over nonempire nations, this legislation helped further to depress the American grain economy. As grain crops in Europe improved and America's grain exports ceased to bring famine prices, only the cotton economy was still prosperous.

No doubt America as a nation would not have regretted so much missing the postwar prosperity if she had thereby missed as well the postwar depression. No such good fortune was available, however. Once again the nation's monetary system got completely out of hand, issuing ultimately in the most serious economic crisis the nation had yet seen. And the major irony of this new monetary failure was the part played in it by the Second United States Bank.

The immediate task of the bank had been to bring about the resumption of specie payments, for both Treasury and bank officials clearly understood that legislation alone was not enough. A law demanding the payment of revenues to the government in specie-redeemable notes might have no other effect than making it impossible for the government to collect taxes if the cooperation of the state banks could not be secured. Furthermore, the state banks could easily make life miserable for the bank by forcing it to redeem its own notes in specie if specie payment could not be made general shortly after the new bank began to operate.

After repeated negotiations an agreement was finally worked out. Most unfavorable to the bank (so completely was the nation's money system in the grip of the state banks, despite constitutional provisions to the contrary), this agreement demanded the making of large loans by the bank before collections could be made from the state banks. At the same time the bank was prevented from demanding specie from the state banks even though it had to make itself liable to specie calls from them. By agreeing to these harsh terms the bank did lay the foundation for the return to specie payments which thus far the Treasury had failed to achieve —perhaps the major accomplishment of the bank during its entire career.

Even with such an unpromising beginning, however, conservative operations could still have prevailed for the longer run if the bank's managers had been so inclined. This, however, was far from the case. Committed by the agreement with the state banks to a greater volume of discounts than would have been wise in the uncertain condition of business generally, the bank immediately proceeded to extend its credit even farther than was called for in the agreement. Apparently the men in charge took more seriously their responsibility to stockholders than to the nation's monetary mechanism. No attempt was made to fix limits to expansion in the various branch offices, and in many instances the branch directors seem to have had no conception of the relationship between specie and bank notes required by sound banking practices. Moreover, the perils of ignorance were magnified by the fact that the country's economic transactions invariably showed a balance of trade in favor of the East and against the South and West. Thus notes issued in western or southern branches were typically presented for redemption in branches in the East. Without a check on their own credit extension, overexpansion in the South and West kept eastern branches under such a continuous pressure that they were all but destroyed.

Mismanagement bordering on criminal incompetence was in numerous instances liberally mixed with outright fraud. When the bank was established, the country was in the midst of a reckless speculation of which dealings in bank stocks was an important feature. No sooner had the bank's stock appeared on the market than there was a scramble for voting control and, what was far worse, intrigues to manipulate the price of the bank's stock for speculative profit. In this process much of the bank's specie capital was never paid in; instead the bank issued credit secured by the first instalment in order to furnish stockholders with the means whereby to meet the second instalment.

It was in Baltimore that both mismanagement and fraud reached their height. Here a group of four men, two of them officers in the Baltimore branch, borrowed from the bank in order to manipulate the stock. Security for these loans was the bank's own stock—accepted at 25 per cent above par for this purpose. When this shameless fraud was at last exposed, these four men owed the Baltimore bank almost $1½ million which they were unable to make good.

This laxness by the management of the United States Bank was a happy development for state banks. Their primary objection to a federal rival had always been the fear of a conservative banking policy. But when the bank's methods turned out to be so completely supplementary to their own, they continued with a will a process of expansion already far advanced. Although the country was theoretically on a specie basis after early 1817, there was in fact never a time during the bank's early years when metallic money did not command a premium. One of the drains on the bank's resources was its constant purchase of specie at a premium in order to redeem notes at par, and a proximate cause of the postwar panic was the ultimate inability of the bank to secure specie with which to continue meeting its obligations.

Speculation and Expansion. A prosperity limited essentially to agriculture and especially to the southern economy, and a rapid expansion of the nation's currency, were by no means unrelated phenomena. Bank speculation could absorb some of the new money being placed into circulation. The more important basis, however, was an active and excited speculation in land and slaves as America resumed after the war the westward movement temporarily interrupted by international complications and difficulties with the Indians. Within this development as it progressed could be seen several of the most important aspects of the next fifty years in American history.

Of primary importance in this connection was the dramatic growth of cotton culture as the dominant economic activity in the South. And, inseparable from this dramatic change, was the new lease on life thereby given to the institution of slavery.

To be sure, there was no inherent connection between cotton and slavery, as the experience of the South since the Civil War so clearly demonstrates. These two things would certainly never have become closely associated with one another if the rudiments of the institution had not already been present. But given the moral, legal, and physical basis which did exist, there were several understandable reasons why southerners proceeded to build on those foundations.

The production of cotton (and this was perhaps even more true in the case of rice and sugar cane) consisted of a relatively small number of simple operations which could readily be mastered by unskilled labor. Even the few, simple tools required could easily be managed by ignorant, uneducated Negroes. Morever, cotton requires the expenditure of labor over a larger fraction of the year than almost any other important crop, and as a consequence the amount of idle time paid for under the slave system was held to a minimum. This was all the more true, too, because approximately twice as much labor was needed at harvest time than at any other stage in the production process, and this special requirement could be met by using slave women and children. And finally, since crops such as cotton, sugar, and rice required one laborer for every three to ten acres as compared with thirty or more acres for such crops as corn or wheat, the supervision needed could be more effectively applied than with most other crops.

Fully as significant as the rebirth of slavery was the shift in the economic center of gravity within the South from the tidewater tobacco area to the later developed coastal region of Georgia and South Carolina. While the "Virginia Dynasty" Presidents—Jefferson, Madison, and Monroe—were dying in poverty as worn-out tobacco land refused longer to support Virginia's dominance in the South, the South's new leaders became Calhoun, Hayne, Lowndes, and Cheves of South Carolina, and Crawford, Cobb, and Forsyth of Georgia. The importance of this development is illustrated by the fact that at the peak of the postwar cotton prosperity, exports from Georgia and South Carolina amounted to one-third of total exports from the United States.

Not only was the center of gravity of the South shifting from tobacco to cotton, however, but the center of gravity of cotton production was also unstable. Already states not included in the original thirteen were producing half as much cotton as the states which had participated in the Revolution, and in a few years Alabama and Mississippi would be producing more cotton than South Carolina and Georgia. This, in fact, was the heart of the westward movement with which much of the nation was now so thoroughly preoccupied

The dynamics of this new westward movement is itself interesting, continuous as it was with America's earlier development. From the very beginning of colonial settlement in the South the larger planters had lived near the sea and the small farmers in the interior. Taking advantage of their prior arrival, furthermore, the coastal planters had early concentrated political power in their own hands. In this way the slave economy avoided the taxes and other burdens which might have been levied upon it for the

TABLE 12. ECONOMIC TRANSFORMATION IN THE SOUTH

State and Area	1791	1801	1811	1821
		(Cotton crop in millions of pounds)		
South Carolina	1.5	20.0	40.0	50.0
Georgia	.5	10.0	20.0	45.0
Virginia		5.0	8.0	12.0
North Carolina		4.0	7.0	10.0
Total, Old South	2.0	39.0	75.0	117.0
Tennessee		1.0	3.0	20.0
Louisiana			2.0	10.0
Mississippi				10.0
Alabama				20.0
Total, New South		1.0	5.0	60.0
Grand Total	2.0	40.0	80.0	177.0

Source: By permission from *Rise of the New West, 1819-1829,* by Frederick J. Turner, p. 47. Copyright, 1906, Harper & Bros., New York.

benefit of a frontier democracy seeking better education, more transportation facilities, or protection from Indian raids. Gradually the pressure from the frontier became so great that concessions had to be made to the residents of interior counties, although such concessions tended to follow rather than precede the expansion of slavery into these counties. Thus political power remained in the hands of slaveowners, and where the economic interests of free farmers and plantation operators came into conflict, it was the yeoman interest which typically gave way.

Here was one reason why the vanguard of the new westward movement was filled with free farmers seeking a land in which, with men of their own outlook, they could carve out an existence more appropriate to their needs. Combined with this factor were certain economic influences. The institution of slavery could only function successfully with large land holdings; whatever advantages slaves possessed as a labor force, these were only available where a relatively small number of whites supervised the labor of a relatively large number of blacks. In consequence, planters became obsessed with the need to expand their operations, an obsession which kept land values high in plantation territory. The smaller farmer was often unable to resist the offers made for his plot of land, or to buy more land in the vicinity when economic conditions made it impossible for him to meet his mortgage payments. Rather it semed more logical for him to find cheaper land somewhere else, land which he could borrow the money to purchase without having to face the competition of an expansionist slaveowner.

But by no means all of the western migrants were free farmers. Many a slaveowner pushed onward himself, taking his slaves with him. Into the area known then as the Territory of Missouri, many new residents were slaveowners. Even in the southern part of such states as Illinois and Indiana slave importation was not uncommon, although here the Northwest Ordinance imposed a legal barrier which could be surmounted only by the indentured servant fiction. The above figures on the growth of cotton production in the West are indication enough that the westward movement was in large part a shift in the center of gravity of slavery.

On the other hand, however, plantations were forced to remain close to good transportation facilities, and were hence almost limited to the coast or the vicinity of a navigable waterway. Behind such areas there were vast tracts of land more suitable to the largely subsistence farming done by the smaller operator. There was, in other words, plenty of land for all, and in terms of numbers the bulk of those now trekking westward were nonslaveowners.

There were two reasons why most of the westward expansion now under way was taking place from the South. One was the high prosperity of the cotton economy. Probably the more important factor, however, was the superiority of the transportation facilities connecting South with West as compared with those connecting East with West. Just as the preceding wave of expansion had taken advantage of the terrain through the Cumberland Gap into Kentucky and Tennessee, so now was a new wave taking advantage of the Mississippi and other rivers emptying into the Gulf of Mexico.

Possibly the transportation advantage of the South as compared with the North would have been decisive even apart from the appearance and immediate success of the steamboat. But with the steamboat becoming widely available at just this moment, the South's advantage was overwhelming. Previously the Mississippi River had been essentially a one-way transportation facility. Its use involved constructing a flatboat at some point up the river, loading it with goods destined for New Orleans, and selling it for little or nothing after its work was finished—all this then culminating in a long trek upstream on foot by the men who manned it. A vessel equipped with power to make the return trip, to say nothing of the greater speed of carriage now possible, made the Mississippi waterway many times more valuable to westerners than before. In fact, whereas this new technology was important in every part of the nation, it was virtually indispensable wherever water transportation had to contend with a formidable current.

Throughout America's history one of the central facts, and one to which Americans point with the greatest show of pride, has been the rapid spread of an American civilization from the Atlantic to the Pacific. Yet it is all too common to be severely critical of the operations of the Second Bank of the United States and the state banks without properly recognizing the part these institutions played in making the westward movement possible. Few farmers, be they slaveowners or yeomen, were able to purchase land with their own resources. It was the creation of bank credit which made it possible for the larger planters to bid up the price of small holdings and thus tempt the small operator to sell. It was no less paper money which made it possible for the displaced easterner to purchase cheaper lands in the West. A government policy retiring the wartime Treasury notes and returning to a full specie basis in the face of an extremely limited supply of specie would have generated a deflationary environment drastically limiting the westward expansion.

Panic and Deflation. However, be all that as it may, the fact remains that the United States was caught up after Ghent in a gigantic land boom, a boom encouraged by the government's policy of selling the public domain on credit and financed in large part by an institution acting as the right arm of the government in financial matters. Such a boom could not last forever. In 1818 the bubble burst, victim of a financial and industrial crisis in England. Foreign loans in this country ceased to expand, and British creditors began demanding payment. As large quantities of specie moved out of the country the overextended banking system could not long stand the strain.

The effect of the panic on the economy of the South was immediate and drastic. The price of American cotton in the Liverpool market began first to waver and then to break. Before the end of the year it had fallen from 30 cents a pound to 24 cents, and when the news reached America early in 1819, cotton dropped in price from 32 cents to 26 cents in a single day. When at last the decline halted, the New Orleans price was less than 15 cents. With the price of cotton went also land prices. In a six-month period many land values fell more than 50 per cent. The strain of these disasters on the over-all economy was so great that the general price level edged sharply downward, and by the end of the year every segment of the economy was deeply involved in what has since been termed "The Panic of 1819."

Even before the full force of the panic was felt the Second Bank of the United States, and indeed the nation's entire banking structure, was in difficulty. The bank's assets, particularly in its southern and western branches, consisted in large part of real estate loans, and it was clear even to the bank's incompetent administrators that the nonliquidity and inflated values represented by such loans made the institution highly vulnerable to economic deflation.[2] In consequence, efforts were made to contract the circulation sufficiently to maintain specie payments despite a fall in land prices, but such efforts proved to be completely futile in the South and West where the greatest need for contraction lay. Instead they struck an almost mortal blow at the eastern branches which were already both weaker in terms of the banking system and sounder with respect to specie coverage. When the bank in some desperation turned to the state banks to make collections, these institutions were as often as not forced to declare their insolvency.

For a moment the great bank itself stood on the edge of bankruptcy. To these troubles were now added a public wrath activated by the attempts at retrenchment. Many people had long felt that this institution was opposed to the public interest, and such an opinion was thus easy to confirm. Especially were state banks and debtors whose loans had been foreclosed in the abortive contraction angry at the inconvenience caused them by the bank. While much of this rise of popular feeling was misplaced since the bank did not in any sense "cause" the panic, the popular instinct was correct enough in sensing that it should have remained in a position to help when the pinch came rather than accentuating the decline through frantic efforts to save itself.

Public indignation rapidly reached Congress, and a move to destroy the bank by legislation was almost successful. Instead, however, an investigation was authorized which charged the bank's management with ignorance while "whitewashing" it of charges of fraud. Immediately the bank's stock fell below par while its president hastily resigned.

From this point forward the financial situation grew steadily darker. Langdon Cheves was made president of the bank, and his undoubted talents were devoted to saving the bank from total ruin. A stringent contraction order went out to the western and southern branches, and the inconvenience felt earlier turned into the keenest distress. The bank looked to the local banks for remittances, local banks foreclosed on debtor-farmers and then were forced to close their own doors, and the entire banking system abandoned all pretense of a specie basis.

The anger of the populace now knew no bounds, for in the debacle of wholesale foreclosures the bank took into its possession vast amounts of real estate. At one point, for example, it owned a large part of Cincinnati,

[2] From a certain standpoint, a period of deflation can appropriately be thought of as an attempt by an economy to liquidate its assets—i.e., convert them into cash. Of course this is impossible in a modern economy, since these assets consist in the last analysis of natural and human resources and the existing stock of capital, and in consequence an attempt to achieve this result generates a sharp decline in asset values. Stated differently, in these circumstances sellers of assets abound while buyers are few. The focal point of this part of the process of deflation is the commercial banking system, and for this reason it is of the utmost importance that banks remain relatively more liquid than other segments of the economy.

its holdings including coffeehouses, hotels, residences, warehouses, stables, and iron foundries, as well as thousands of acres of good farm land in the area. Dispossessed owners, refusing to acknowledge their own recklessness, held the bank responsible, and politicians were given an issue which was to prove useful for many years. As Thomas Hart Benton of Missouri expressed the sentiment of Westerners: "All the flourishing cities of the West are mortgaged to this money power. They may be devoured by it at any moment. They are in the jaws of the monster! A lump of butter in the mouth of a dog! One gulp, one swallow, and all is gone." The spirit of the agrarians who thirty years before had opposed the chartering of the First Bank of the United States was clearly arising again.

In 1819 the bank was saved in more ways than one. Not only was it determined in that year that the bank would remain in operation even if the nation did go off specie, but simultaneously arch-Federalist John Marshall, Chief Justice of the United States Supreme Court, rendered a classic decision which rescued the bank from legal destruction by the states and hence held open the banking area as a legitimate function of the national government.

From the beginning state governments had resented the existence of a federal competitor. Maryland, Tennessee, Georgia, North Carolina, Kentucky, and Ohio had early expressed their displeasure by means of a tax on the bank in so far as it operated within these states. The bank opposed these levies, arguing that as an instrumentality of the federal government it could not be taxed by the states, and the ensuing litigation ultimately reached the Supreme Court. Ironically, it was the Maryland case which appeared on John Marshall's calendar first, and hence the historic pronouncement in McCulloch v. Maryland involved the very bank in which outright fraud had been most pronounced. Although fraud was not at issue, it is probable that popular unrest against the bank was greatly enhanced by a decision favoring the bank in a case in which the plaintiff (the bank's cashier) had made off with almost $500,000 worth of the bank's assets. In stern and uncompromising language Marshall declared that states may not use their taxing power to frustrate an attempt by the federal government to exercise its constitutional powers.

The settling of this issue in this way was well timed. Legislatures in several other states were only awaiting the outcome of the McCulloch case to levy special taxes of their own against the bank. Had the opposite decision been rendered the days of the United States Bank would have been numbered. If this had occurred, the banking history of the United States would no doubt have been substantially different.

The Missouri Compromise. As a decision freeing the nation's central bank from state intereference, McCulloch v. Maryland was a serious enough blow to southerners and westerners. But it was perhaps even more disturbing, especially to southerners, when considered from the standpoint of the old issue of state rights. In the enthusiasm of postwar nationalism this issue had lain dormant and would perhaps not now have been revived had the bank alone been at stake. Unfortunately, however, as deep depression settled over the country the problem of the bank merged with another problem which had not arisen since before the war. In this broader context the issue of state rights took on a more intense meaning.

Missouri was seeking admission into the union as a state. As yet the admission of a new state had not created a major stir, and this one might not have done so either if James Tallmadge of New York had not proposed an amendment to the Missouri Enabling Bill prohibiting slavery in the new state. When the House by a strictly sectional vote approved this amendment, southern agrarians suddenly realized their grave peril within the Union.

The industrial East was rapidly outstripping the slave South in population, and in 1819 representation in the House was already adverse to the South's interest on any matter producing a strictly sectional vote. That southerners had not earlier awakened to the fact that an industrial economy tends to develop a substantially larger population, and hence representation, than an agrarian one is no doubt due in large part to the security they had felt under a succession of southern presidents. The South had not yet lost the presidency, to be sure, but the nation was visibly restive under the "Virginia Dynasty." With the House already lost and control over the executive branch of the government threatened, southerners understandably were much concerned about their position in the Senate.

More by chance than design the admission of states had proceeded in such a way as to keep a very close balance between slave and nonslave strength in the Senate. In 1819 each group was represented in that body by twenty votes. However, the admission of Missouri without slavery

TABLE 13. A PRECARIOUS BALANCE OF POWER

Free	Slave
New Hampshire	Delaware
Massachusetts	Maryland
Connecticut	Virginia
Rhode Island	North Carolina
New York	South Carolina
New Jersey	Georgia
Pennsylvania	Kentucky (1792)
Vermont (1791)	Tennessee (1796)
Ohio (1803)	Louisiana (1812)
Indiana (1816)	Mississippi (1817)
Illinois (1818)	Alabama (1819)

would tip the balance, possible once and for all, against the South, particularly since Maine was also applying for admission. There was, of course, no possibility of Maine's ever becoming a slave state.

The danger to the South was twofold. First, if the central government possessed the power to exclude slaves from Missouri, might it not also one day assume the power to abolish slavery in the present slave states, or at least take away the three-fifths representation for slaves now enjoyed by the South? Furthermore, success in the Missouri abolition would not merely establish the right to tamper with the South's institutions, but it would also give the central government the power to do so at the same time.

Before the Missouri issue was settled, southerners were given an even greater assurance that the battle was worth fighting. General Andrew Jackson, admittedly far exceeding any instructions his superiors were willing to confess having given him, occupied East Florida, to the delight of many of his countrymen, the consternation of those in charge of America's foreign policy, and the dismay of a Spain too weak to interfere. But if Jackson's superiors denied authorizing his action, they carefully refrained from repudiating it. Thus the nation's land hunger was fed in 1819 by the addition of another substantial piece of territory, and another potential slave state was brought within easy reach.

The legislation by means of which the North-South representation was kept even by the admission of Missouri as a slave state and Maine as a free one is most frequently referred to as the "Missouri Compromise" and attributed to Henry Clay. While the term "compromise" is appropriate enough, the idea was no more Henry Clay's than that of a half a dozen other men. It was such an obvious solution. At the same time Henry Clay did perhaps express what was involved more bluntly than anyone else. Said he, "equality is equality, and if it is right to make the restriction of slavery the condition of the admission of Missouri, it is equally just to make the admission of Missouri the condition of that of Maine." What this assertion lacked in logic was more than compensated by the clarity with which it set forth the terms the antislavery forces would have to meet to secure Maine's admission. After a bitter debate the terms were met, although with the added proviso that slavery be prohibited in all the Louisiana Purchase above Mason and Dixon's Line except Missouri.

Sectionalism Emerges. Thomas Jefferson, among others, understood the meaning of the Missouri struggle. He called it "a fire bell in the night," and suggested that it signaled the ultimate dissolution of the union. John Quincy Adams also understood what had taken place, and his understanding was not significantly different from that of Jefferson. There was, perhaps, one difference. Jefferson was saddened by the thought of dissolution; Adams already felt that that a union half slave and half free would be better off dissolved.

But if the leading statesmen of the day understood the rift arising, they probably did not yet know the issue which was first to threaten the expected dissolution. Almost immediately after the Compromise measure became law, this too was vaguely understood. The part of the iceberg first visible above the water line was to be the tariff.

Most protectionists had been keenly disappointed with the postwar tariff adjustment, and many of the nation's leaders had quickly recognized the mistake which had been made. Now, assisted by the depressed condition of business generally, the imminence of a government deficit for the year 1820, and the active support of workers in manufacturing industries, protectionists brought to Congress a plea for a comprehensive increase in duties.

The schedule of increased duties met with no difficulty in the House, where the greater populousness of eastern states was decisive. In the Senate, however, it was lost—by a single vote. Both the House vote and that in the Senate were rigidly sectional, with the slave states overwhelmingly opposed. So completely had sectionalism invaded the tariff issue that southerners who four years earlier had supported protection now cast their votes in opposition. And although Missouri was not yet a voting state, southerners must have felt well rewarded for the trouble they had taken in that contest.

Why was it that sectionalism was now so decisively replacing America's recently achieved and hard won unity? It was because the longer range consequences of the South's new identification with cotton and slavery were only now becoming fully apparent, and because at no point was this so evident as in connection with the tariff. A cotton South could only live by exporting, and if other nations chose to retaliate against America's tariff policy it would be the South that would suffer most.[3] Already England, the market for the largest proportion of America's exports, had passed measures restricting the inflow of American goods, and this trend promised to become general throughout Europe. Furthermore, not only would a protective tariff injure the South by limiting the market for her exports, but it would at the same time raise the price of the manufactured goods she purchased.

---

[3] Although mediated by a complex monetary mechanism, exchange is a process in which goods are traded for other goods. In international trade this means that imports must normally be paid for with exports or the promise of future exports. This fact was the economic foundation for the South's fear that the restriction of imports would bring about a curtailment of exports as well.

Even after the second war with England many had still taken it for granted that the South's growth would be parallel to that of the rest of the nation, a not unreasonable expectation in view of the fact that the third Census had reported a very sizable manufacturing activity being carried on in the South. With such a development in mind, the first steps had been taken to outlaw the slave trade. By 1820, however, it was understood by all not only that slave imports had not ceased but that it would be virtually impossible to stop them. Thus, although "slaving" was made piracy after 1820, it is extremely revealing that no one was ever hanged for this crime until the very eve of the Civil War. (Equally revealing is the fact that slave-trade "pirates" were rarely southerners.) In short, the South had to come to a parting of the ways with the rest of the country.

QUESTIONS FOR DISCUSSION

1. Why was prosperity uneven after the War of 1812?
2. How did English exporters evade this country's protective legislation?
3. How nearly did the nation's monetary system in 1818 correspond to what was required by the Constitution?
4. What was the connection between "cheap" money and westward expansion during this period?
5. Why was the South expanding more rapidly than the North at this time?
6. What factors were responsible for the shift in the center of gravity of cotton production?
7. To what extent was public policy responsible for the "Panic of 1819"?
8. Was the Second Bank of the United States worth saving in 1820?
9. Was a national bank "constitutional" in 1816? Were state banks?

Chapter 10

THE "AMERICAN SYSTEM"

1820	Basic changes made in public land policy.
1821	Property qualifications for voting abolished in New York.
1823	Monroe Doctrine proclaimed.
1824	"American System" Tariff.
	Gibbons v. Ogden.
	John Quincy Adams elected President.
	"Suffolk System" inaugurated.
1825	Erie Canal completed.
1826	Coalition against Adams formed.
1828	"Tariff of Abominations."

The Impact of Depression. The depression from which the nation was suffering in 1820 fell with uneven force on the several branches of manufacturing industry. Household production, no doubt the most important segment at the moment, probably profited from the cataclysm at least in the sense that the shift to industries of a commercial type was drastically retarded. Producing goods for the market depended first and foremost upon farmer purchasing power, and this was the major casualty of the economic decline. Farmers were simply forced to continue (or resume) producing many items for themselves or go without them.

Even in the area of commercial manufacturing the impact of depression was not uniform. Its destructive force was least seriously felt by the nation's factories (still the least important branch), although the major reason was that the flood of postwar imports and the failure of efforts at protection had already almost prostrated so many of these concerns. That this activity had not wholly disappeared before the onset of depression is, in fact, primarily to be explained in terms of the rapid advance of a technology appropriate to factory output.

Prior to the depression the principal commercial rivals of the factories—operators of the small neighborhood industries and merchant-capitalists who distributed raw materials to laborers working in their own homes—

had profited at the expense of the factories. Because of their much smaller capital requirements the decline in demand struck them less forcefully at first; a larger proportion of the burden could be shifted to workers. Conservative capital suppliers were apt to be prejudiced against factory organization anyway, and the appearance of numerous failures seemed ample vindication of this bias.

Later, when depression added its force to that of excessive imports, these operations were also severely depressed, thus destroying most of this temporary advantage. As a consequence, when better times began to appear the factory was able to continue its forward march on something like even terms with its rivals. Meanwhile the depression was producing its natural fruit wherever commercial manufacturing was to be found. For the first time in America's history depression unemployment became a difficult problem; the urban soup kitchen made its first appearance on the New World scene.

However, industrialization was still in its infancy in America, and the number of unemployed was not great by the standards of later times. The larger problem, and not only because a larger number of people was involved, was the relationship between debtors and creditors in agricultural communities.

Overexpansion during the preceding prosperity had resulted in a precarious situation for the nation's farmers. Not only had speculation in land become a fever with professional gamblers and investors, but farmers themselves had freely engaged in the practice. As long as there remained virgin land in large quantities in the United States it was not profitable to expend large amounts of labor and capital on land. The better procedure was to crop the land heavily until the newness had worn off and then begin again on another plot. But since a second move to the West was not inviting to most men, the thing to do seemed rather to buy more land than could be tilled as an insurance against the day when the land tilled would be unable to compete with newer lands farther on.

With most of this buying done on credit, it was only natural that deflation would bring with it wholesale foreclosures. So deep-rooted was the desire for ownership in young America that the prospect of being wiped out generated a great deal of tension between debtor-farmers and the legal machinery which would dispossess them. As a result, there was reenacted a sequence of events which had taken place on many another occasion in America's earlier history—a process by which debtors sought and obtained relief from the demands of legitimate (if sometimes ruthless) creditors.

The situation in Kentucky was illustrative, if not entirely typical, of developments in a number of frontier states. During the preceding prosperity Kentucky had chartered a "litter" of forty banks, a number far greater than could be justified in such an undeveloped region. When the panic struck and the Bank of the United States began to retrench, every one of these banks was forced to close its doors. The Kentucky legislature promptly repealed their charters and incorporated in their place the Bank of the Commonwealth of Kentucky, a concern having no stockholders and whose officers were selected by the legislature and paid by the state. One of its major functions was the issuance of notes, and indeed the only real capital invested in the bank consisted of $7,000 with which to buy material and plates for the printing of paper money. Assigning notes to counties on the basis of taxable property, this bank was nothing more than a land bank of precisely the sort that had relieved debtors of their burdens in colonial days.

This use of the state's treasury as a land bank was not the only way in which debtors passed legislation primarily benefiting themselves. The Kentucky legislature next passed a law providing a moratorium of one year on all debts, and if the creditors should refuse to accept notes of the Bank of the Commonwealth of Kentucky in payment the moratorium was to be extended for a second year. Another law prohibited the sale of land in the satisfaction of a debt at a price lower than three-fourths of its value as determined by a board of neighbors. Since neighbors were typically debtors also, the land values so arrived at were usually most generous.

These measures naturally precipitated a bitter struggle between debtors and creditors for control over the government. Thus at one point the Kentucky court of appeals declared the relief laws to be unconstitutional. Immediately the legislature passed a law abolishing this court and establishing another in its place. This act too was declared unconstitutional by the "old" court, and for many months the conflict raged between "new court" and "old court" advocates. Finally the "old court" group won out, but not until the worst of the depression was long past and the laws declared unconstitutional had consequently performed their function. Certainly as one result of this legislation in Kentucky and such other states as Tennessee, Missouri, Ohio, and Illinois, property did not become as concentrated in a few hands as would otherwise have been the case.

If Kentucky furnished the extreme in one respect, Ohio did in another. Defying John Marshall and McCulloch v. Maryland, Ohio officials staged an armed robbery of the Ohio branch of the United States Bank, collecting by force the tax the Supreme Court had declared to be unconstitutional. At the same time the state's legislature virtually outlawed the bank by withdrawing from it the protection of the state's laws. Time and another Supreme Court decision were required completely to establish the bank's right to exist.

A New Land Policy. In all these relief activities the national government played little part. An unsuccessful attempt was made to pass a national bankruptcy law, but the sentiment against federal action in this field was too strong. As a result only one important step was taken by the federal government, and it is to be explained as much by nondepression factors as in terms of the postwar deflation. From the beginning of the nation, it had been assumed that the public domain would be a major financial asset to the government. At the same time legislation governing the distribution of the public domain had been framed in part from the standpoint of the needs of the land speculator. Experimentation along

Table 14. In Search of a Policy

Year	Minimum Quantity in Acres	Minimum Price per Acre	Terms
1785	640	$1.00	Cash
1796	640	$2.00	One half cash; balance in one year
1800	320	$2.00	One fourth in cash; balance in four years
1804	160	$2.00	No change
1820	80	$1.25	Cash
1832	40	$1.25	Cash

these lines had resulted in the law currently in effect—a law permitting purchases on credit, fixing the price at $2.00 per acre, and establishing 160 acres as the minimum amount which could be purchased.

For a number of years westerners had been protesting against this policy, insisting that the primary objective should be the needs of the settler. As yet, however, this agitation had not achieved notable results, although the minimum number of acres to be sold as a unit had been progressively reduced. Now, assisted by the aftermath of a painful depression, the West was able to win a substantial victory. With the debt owing the government for land sales at the unprecedented figure of $22 million, this question was presented to the government in such a way as to require decisive action.

Because of the existing situation, the nation's leaders in Washington really had little choice. The alternatives were to liberalize the land laws or begin to foreclose on those settlers whose payments were in arrears. No one in a position of real responsibility would have suggested foreclosure, and so a major revision of the nation's land laws was undertaken. The minimum price was reduced to $1.25 per acre, the minimum holding was reduced to 80 acres, and only cash sales were allowed. The result was that a settler could purchase a small farm for as little as $100.00. In addition, a law was passed allowing delinquent purchasers to apply past payments on a portion of the land originally bargained for, letting the remaining land revert to the public domain. By these laws the nation embarked upon a new policy, and at the same time made a significant contribution toward relieving the distress which followed the postwar speculation and panic. Along with the relief laws passed by the several states, this legislation was indispensable in helping the country maintain the expansion gains of preceding years.

Feuding with England. In the very midst of the depression the commercial feud between America and England was renewed with even greater vigor. On May 15, 1820, Congress passed a law prohibiting the entrance into American ports of British vessels from any point in Britain's Western Hemisphere colonies and importation of any goods from those places except goods produced within and exported directly from the exporting region. So complete was this prohibition against British vessels that goods could not even be shipped from such places as Canada, Newfoundland, or the West Indies to England and re-exported to America.

At this point in the conflict the restrictions imposed by the United States were substantially more stringent than Britain's. In her regulations regarding both British North America and the British West Indies, England had designated certain free ports through which American ships might trade with her possessions. To be sure, this had been done out of consideration for the West Indian planter and the desire to build a thriving entrepôt business in certain New World ports rather than friendship to America. Nonetheless, the fact remained that Britain had stopped well short of outright prohibition.

Obviously the new nation was feeling very powerful indeed. And well she might, too, for circumstances were running strongly in her favor. While British shipping interests had reason to and did urge further retaliation, there were two reasons why such a course was out of the question.

First, stronger measures would have completed the ruin of the West Indian economy. Already discriminatory legislation had been enacted against many American exports to these islands, a policy adopted for the purpose of giving to Canada a competitive advantage in supplying this market. The unfortunate fact was, however, that Canada could not adequately supply the West Indies, and further discrimination would therefore injure Britain's West Indian interests more than those of the United States. Furthermore, the restrictions imposed by Britain and now reciprocated by the United States placed an artificial burden upon the exports of the West Indies and hence still further threatened the profits of sugar planters and British investors. Here again the compounding of restrictions would do the greatest injury to England's interests.

Figure 11 illustrates the extent to which restrictions and counter-restrictions had been carried. America's 1820 law prohibited Alternative I, an alternative allowed by England in order to give Nova Scotia and New Brunswick a profitable entrepôt trade. Alternative II still remained, but

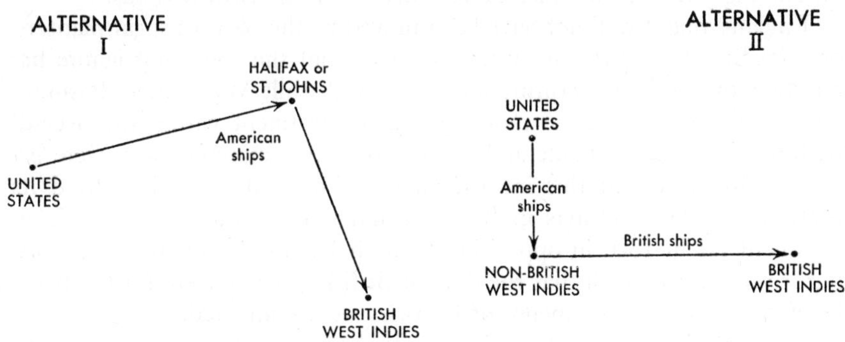

FIGURE 11.

even here, while the total shipping costs were less than in Alternative I, to the advantage of American exports if not American ships, the indirectness of the haul and the additional transfer of lading added significantly both to the cost of American exports in the British colonies and to the cost of West Indies' exports in the United States.

The second basic factor was the attitude of British manufacturers. As England rapidly became an industrial nation it was increasingly evident that to make the most of the opportunities now available to her, freer trade was an absolute necessity. Successful manufacturing must be done on a large scale. Large-scale operations, however, require a large market—and the British islands, even combined with Britain's colonial empire, scarcely provided what would for this purpose be called a large market. For the most part the empire areas were poorly developed and could not buy English manufactures in large quantities. Few places, in fact, offered a market for such goods as fine as the United States. Painful though the admission must have been, British manufacturers were forced to concede that anyone who wished prosperity for England's manufacturing industry must also wish prosperity for the United States.

It was against a background of such thoughts as these that English factory owners began to observe a decided falling off of British exports to America. In part, of course, this was due to a normal tapering off of the postwar trade boom and, more recently, to the American depression. But there was just as clearly another factor at work as well. The destruction by England's Navigation Laws of America's part in the triangular trade with Europe by way of the West Indies limited greatly the earnings available to the American merchant marine, earnings which would have been spent primarily for English manufactures.[1] In addition, discriminations against American goods in the West Indies together with her own duties against certain American products in England still further reduced the purchasing power with which Americans could buy British goods.

England might well not have been moved by the pleas of sugar planters, or even British investors in sugar properties, but she could not ignore her rapidly growing manufacturing interests. And while West Indies businessmen would have urged no more than a readjustment within the over-all pattern of England's Trade and Navigation Laws, manufacturers were beginning to insist that this intricate network of controls had outlived its usefulness. Manufacturers in Britain could not, of course, carry such an argument far in 1820 in opposition to both landlords and ship operators, but it was clear enough that the days of British restrictionism for the benefit of ships and at the expense of factories were numbered.

The question of which nation could hold out the longer was soon answered. In 1820 Lord Liverpool, speaking to the House of Lords (and obviously speaking for British industrialists), emphasized how important the American market was to the British economy and stated that England's policy should be concerned primarily with America's tariff legislation rather than with her navigation enactments. Two years later Britain opened up the direct West Indian trade to American vessels, although the discriminatory legislation against American goods was retained.

But the new nation was not to be so easily pacified. Less than a year after this conciliatory British enactment, America passed a law providing that British vessels trading with the West Indies would be treated in the United States exactly like American vessels in so far as American vessels trading with these ports were treated exactly like British vessels in these ports.

The demand was breathtaking in its audacity. America was holding out for no less than the elimination of all empire discriminations against American ships. Of course it was impossible. It was one thing for England to relax the Navigation Laws in the interest of the British economy; it was another to repeal them in the interest of a foreign economy. England was not so desperate as to be ready for so far-reaching a step as this.

The "American System." Americans did not flinch from the implications of this refusal. If, as Lord Liverpool had said, American tariffs were the thing to be feared, a higher level of protection was obviously the best

[1] Where economic transactions take place between citizens of different countries, goods or services are typically paid for with the money (in the form of what is called foreign exchange) of the buying country. Such money can, in the last analysis, be used only to buy goods or services in the country whose money it is. This is another way of viewing the fact that imports and exports are closely related to one another.

way to tighten the screws. Moreover, by the same token that England was now orienting policy more toward manufacturers than the shipping industry, so too was the United States. Here was an even better reason for trying once again to rectify recent tariff defeats.

This was much more easily said than done, however. The South had already served notice that support for higher duties could not be counted on in that area. Still worse, the reasoning by means of which the South had made this determination applied also with considerable force to western grain and meat producers. If a truly protective tariff were to be passed, this destructive southern "propaganda" would have to be vigorously combated.

The "counter-propaganda" device hit upon was a pattern of ideas termed by Henry Clay, its originator, the "American System"—this very terminology indicating clearly the propaganda purpose to be achieved. Whereas southerners were insisting that a high tariff would destroy foreign markets, Clay turned this argument around by asserting that adequate protection would create domestic markets. Eastern cities would thereby be turned into manufacturing centers and eastern farmers into factory employees, while factories as users of raw materials and laborers as consumers would soon relieve the West of any need to depend upon foreigners for the sale of their goods. Furthermore, an adequate duty level would even bring into the Treasury enough revenue to build the transportation facilities needed to carry western surpluses to eastern cities.

The bait was very tempting, and farmers threatened with adverse trade restrictions abroad were in the end unable to resist. With support for their program assured, manufacturers lost no time in framing their answer to Lord Liverpool and British industrialism. The prologue consisted of the Monroe Doctrine, written by John Quincy Adams as Secretary of State and announced to the world by President Monroe on December 2, 1823. Although this document was not at base a statement of tariff policy, one of its more significant paragraphs referred to "the encouragement which ought to be given to our manufacturers" and to the need for "additional protection to those articles we are prepared to manufacture, or which are more immediately connected with the defense and independence of the country."

The main event was next staged. This was the Tariff of 1824, a measure substantially raising duties all along the line. To be sure, protectionists did not get the level of protection they considered necessary, one reason being that southern resistance was powerfully fortified by a new argument —that a *protective* tariff was unconstitutional. At the same time, however, there is no exaggeration in saying that this law was the nearest thing to a victory manufacturers had achieved since the recent war with England.

Two sequels to the Tariff of 1824 are also worth noting. First, in order that there would be no misunderstanding about what the United States had in mind, Americans put in office a national administration fully committed to the line American policy was now taking. The new President was the author of the Monroe Doctrine—John Quincy Adams. In turn Adams selected as his Secretary of State none other than the author of the "American System"—Henry Clay.

The second sequel might appropriately be called the domestic corollary of a policy of protection. The United States possessed a huge internal market for manufactures—a market large enough to support most of the advances then taking place in the direction of large-scale production. Put differently, the free *internal* trade guaranteed by the Constitution was the American manufacturer's substitute for free external trade. If advantage were to be taken of this guarantee, however, it was necessary that the internal market be kept *open*. Massachusetts manufacturers had to be just as free to sell goods in New York as New York or Pennsylvania manufacturers. In 1824, in the celebrated case of Gibbons v. Ogden, John Marshall was given an opportunity to strike a resounding blow for this important freedom.

For some years the steamboat had been slowly revolutionizing American transportation. On the Hudson, the Mississippi, in the coasting trade, and at many other points, haulage time had been reduced by more than 50 per cent and costs lessened approximately in proportion. However, by means of America's patent laws, an exclusive right to navigate the waters of New York was given to Fulton and Livingston by that state's government, and Louisiana had accorded these men similar rights in her waters.

The original New York rights had been passed on to a man named Ogden who sought to prevent a man named Gibbons from operating a boat on the Hudson River between New York City and New Jersey. Gibbons maintained that the New York grant was prejudicial to interstate commerce and hence unconstitutional. Using words which have perhaps never been exceeded for comprehensiveness in the definition of interstate commerce, Marshall upheld the "interloper," striking down as he did so the New York and Louisiana laws. "The power of Congress, then, comprehends navigation within the limits of every state in the Union, so far as that navigation may be, in any manner, connected with 'commerce with foreign nations, or among the several States, or with the Indian tribes'."

Better Banking in Boston. The "American System" never became a reality. Highly effective as a tariff argument, the several elements in Clay's proposal could never be put together into a program of national action. The nation was too firmly set against national centralization of power. It was not merely the cotton South, either, that was primarily responsible for this development. Certain business interests also took this stand as, first in banking and then in domestic transportation, giant strides were taken toward a more favorable adjustment with a minimum of federal assistance.

In the banking field some credit must be given to the Second United States Bank. After its narrow escape during the depression, this institution behaved in an altogether different manner and hence served the nation in a much more wholesome way. Its third president, Nicholas Biddle of Philadelphia (Langdon Cheves having resigned because his policies were too conservative to suit the bank's stockholders), was a well-trained student of banking and monetary affairs. Under his direction the bank issued notes acceptable at par throughout the nation, provided an elastic element in the currency supply by making a large volume of loans on short term paper to meet seasonal needs, and gave the nation an effective clearing arrangement. So well managed was this bank, in fact, that the notes of many state banks circulated at par side by side with the bank's notes. Since the bank had regular dealings with many such banks, the simple discipline of sending notes to the issuer to be redeemed in specie could easily coerce a colleague into maintaining adequate reserves. A demand for redemption of notes in specie might necessitate the calling in of four or five times as many dollars worth of loans.

Unfortunately for the nation's circulating medium, however, the United States Bank did not have regular dealings with all banks, and therefore not all state bank notes circulated at par. This situation the business interests found most undesirable. A currency that is not uniform in its purchasing power is one of the most serious deficiencies an exchange system can have from the standpoint of carrying on modern business activities. Certainly a rising industrialism would not long tolerate a disorderly circulating medium, and the only real question was whether delinquent banks were to be disciplined by the federal government or otherwise. And as long as the South and West retained their hatred for federal banks, there was little likelihood of a national control more substantial than that provided by "Biddle's bank."

Just as in colonial days it had typically been Boston that had taken the lead in monetary matters, so now was it Boston that first assumed the responsibility for developing a more adequate banking system. Specialization had been carried further for a longer period of time in Massachusetts generally and Boston in particular than anywhere else in the country, and necessity is often a contributory factor in invention. As New England's chief commercial and financial center, Boston carried on business relationships throughout a wide area. Bank notes from towns in this hinterland were constantly making their appearance, in part as payment for purchases made in Boston and in part as payment for commercial paper or other kinds of loans. But whereas the notes of Boston banks circulated at par, notes from out of town typically circulated at a discount the magnitude of which varying with the difficulty of sending them home for redemption.

The banks of Boston were given by their commanding position an excellent opportunity to work out disciplinary arrangements relative to out-of-town correspondents. In addition, they had an excellent incentive because the notes circulating at a discount had largely replaced their own notes. At one point it was estimated that, although Boston banks had more than half of New England's banking capital, the circulation of Boston bank notes amounted to less than 5 per cent of total circulation.

In 1824 the Suffolk Bank took the lead in developing a more stringent control. Joining hands with five other major banking institutions, the Suffolk management agreed to handle all notes received from outside banks. Such of these banks as would retain a permanent deposit with the Suffolk Bank were to be rewarded by having their notes received at par. Banks refusing to come into this clearing system were to be disciplined by having their notes returned. For many banks in the outlying regions this eventuality would have been so disastrous that they were compelled either to participate or to manage their affairs in such a way as to maintain their ability to redeem their notes.

The "Suffolk System" constituted a great advance in the practice of banking in the United States. To a remarkable extent the discount on state bank notes disappeared in New England, even outside the immediate range of Suffolk influence. This increase in par circulation served further to reduce the circulation of specie; and as the demand for specie for this purpose declined, reserves were strengthened—thus making possible a more adequate but still sound note circulation. In view of these important achievements, it is interesting, if somewhat ironical, that the "Suffolk System" failed to accomplish the purpose for which it was created. Boston businessmen had already taken the first step beyond the use of notes in their financial transactions. Deposit currency, the use of checks, was proving to be far more satisfactory, and therefore putting the banking practices of the area on a sounder basis did not significantly increase the note circulation of Boston banks. However, the use of the deposits of a multitude of country banks proved sufficiently profitable to allow the innovation to continue, and hence the gain for the nation's money and banking system was retained. Equally important, the achievement of more effective banking practices in New England did much to reduce the pressures working toward bank centralization—particularly since the rudiments of a similar solution were slowly being worked out in such centers of business activity as Philadelphia, New York, and New Orleans.

New York Forges to the Front. While the business East was solving banking and currency problems at the local level, pressures toward centralization in transportation were also meeting with difficulties. This time the drama was acted out in New York. At the moment little more than an episode in the century-old struggle for supremacy between the major Atlantic ports, New York now took what can readily be distinguished by the perspective of history as a decisive step. Within a few years she had commenced to outdistance her rivals beyond any fear of being overtaken.

New York was exceedingly well situated for a successful commercial development. Founded by the nation which then led the world in shipping, and founded specifically as a trading center, New York had from the beginning made good use of her hundreds of miles of natural harbor and the Hudson River connection with the interior. She did not, of course, spring immediately into a position of leadership. Boston had the advantage of a much earlier development, while Philadelphia had enjoyed far more than her share of the eighteenth-century immigration. The three cities had grown together, first one claiming the lead and then another as America passed through the major economic changes accompanying revolution and independence.

The "second war for independence" particularly had produced major consequences for this competition between America's North Atlantic cities. By tightly blockading most of the nation's coastline while leaving New England's ports open to full scale operations, England had given Boston a substantial advantage. This could conceivably have been decisive if after the war England had not quickly put New York once more in the lead by making that city the scene of the largest share of the "dumping" engaged in by her manufacturers and merchants. In several ways New Yorkers now took a step which helped their city retain and even enlarge this advantage relative to its competitors.

First, English traders had thought seriously at one point about shifting the destination of their postwar exports to a market less inundated by foreign goods. But in the very middle of this deluge of imports the state's legislature had passed a measure reducing taxes on auction sales and requiring final sale of all goods put up for auction. In one sense this legislation was adverse to the interests of foreign sellers, for the law prevented the withdrawal of goods in case the bidding ran low, and it was especially hard on domestic manufacturers. The more important result, however, was to make the New York market a more dependable one for hinterland dealers shopping for goods which could be sold in their localities at a profit.

Second, an action producing similar consequences was the establishment in the same year of the nation's first regular freight service between the United States and Europe. Sailing between New York and Liverpool, this pioneer "Black Ball" line, as it was called, helped still further to attract merchants seeking foreign goods. The intense need of the economy for imported goods made it certain that the nation's greatest import center would at least have the opportunity of becoming equally significant as a wholesale center (a causal relationship which of course worked both ways). Since New Yorkers were always alive to such opportunities they quickly made use of their facilities in building their city in this direction.

Third, development as a wholesale center carries with it the opportunity of becoming a financial center as well. Retailers typically possess limited capital, and it is to the interest of the wholesaler to help his customers handle as many goods as possible. Moreover, there is a strong tendency for retailers to take their business to the wholesaler who grants the most generous credit terms. New York merchants in turn, of course, relied heavily on credit abroad in their own transactions, although one of the reasons was the domestic demand for the capital available to them in financing their own customers. New Yorkers proved to be equal to these requirements, and the center of the American money market soon came to be New York. One symbol of this status was the establishment shortly after the Treaty of Ghent of the New York Stock and Exchange Board. Although this step was essentially only a formalization of the earlier informal arrangement by which securities were bought and sold, it nonetheless marked a basic advance by New York toward financial dominance and by the nation toward a more adequate financial system to accompany its growing industrialization.

All these evidences of the energy and imagination of New York merchants, however, did not take care of one vitally important aspect of the city's growth needs. Incoming goods had to be disposed of over an area large in proportion to the volume of goods to be distributed, and, by the same token, the export goods furnishing the purchasing power with which imports could be bought had to be collected over an area equally large. Both of these activities necessitated easy transportation access to a large hinterland. Where could New York develop a hinterland equal to her ambitions? The region traversed by the Hudson River between Long Island and Albany would scarcely suffice, and a hinterland which could be reached only by means of land transportation was no solution in the first quarter of the nineteenth century. Furthermore, along the coast of the Atlantic New York's hinterland quickly merged with Boston's to the north and Philadelphia's to the south.

A part of the solution to this problem New York found in relationships with the cotton South, another example of the ingenuity of New York traders. Strange though this relationship now seems, the facts remain that New York ships carried cotton some two hundred miles out of its way in its journey to Europe, and that a large portion of the South's foreign imports were received by way of New York. Thereby an eastbound cargo was provided for the ships bringing English goods to America, and simultaneously a market for the goods thus brought in. No doubt the passivity of southerners, their stubborn clinging to a purely agrarian way of life, was also a factor in this situation, although it is to the credit of New Yorkers that this trade passed by Philadelphia in both directions.

The Erie Canal. Even with the southern trade, however, New York's hinterland would never have sufficed to make it the nation's leading city. A fact understood by almost all practical businessmen in the 1820's was that the city which first successfully tapped the resources of the West would be the victor in the competitive struggle between the eastern ports. In New York State the man whose understanding at this point was most liberally intermingled with the imagination and faith necessary to act boldly was Governor DeWitt Clinton. Irked by the failure of the federal government to finance the development of a water route taking advantage of the highly favorable topography between Albany and Buffalo, and unhappy over the success of New Orleans in relating itself profitably to the western grain and meat economy, Clinton and others began to dream of a canal built by local capital.

Of course such a project met intense opposition. And it was not merely the opposition of vested interests, nor even the revolutionary nature of the idea of canal-building. Actually transportation by means of canals was no new thing in American thinking. Rather the most difficult opposition was prompted by the very prodigiousness of the project. To date the largest canal in the nation was twenty-eight miles long. Governor Clinton was proposing to build a canal more than three hundred and fifty miles long, much of this distance traversing an almost unsettled wilderness.

Owing a great deal to the vision and unceasing efforts of Clinton himself, legislation looking toward just this achievement was finally passed. Immediately successful even beyond Clinton's fondest hopes, tolls received on the earliest sections completed contributed much to financing the remaining work. On October 25, 1825, some eight years after it was begun, "Clinton's Ditch" was finished and vessels could sail from New York to Buffalo. With the addition of Lake Erie this new waterway quickly became one of the finest internal transportation systems in the world.

The completion and immediate success of the Erie Canal marked an important turning point in America's transportation development. By now it was apparent to all that the turnpikes afforded no solution to America's basic transportation problem. Not only was private capital abandoning this field, but land transportation was so expensive even over these roads that men had never ceased to concern themselves with alternatives. The best evidence of this failure of the turnpikes is the fact that the position of Baltimore among the Atlantic seaboard cities had not significantly improved as a result of the building of the "National Pike." Now, once again, there was reason for feeling confident that the transportation problem had been resolved—that canals could achieve for the economy what the turnpikes had not. The Erie Canal was no feeder line to existing transportation facilities. Here was a basic arterial connection between East and West which could compete on more or less even terms with the Mississippi River. Freight charges between New York and Buffalo fell by 90 per cent, and even with these reduced rates the canal returned its cost to the state within ten years.

The consequences of this forward step were not long in getting under way. Immediately there was precipitated a veritable orgy of canal building throughout the country which, by the time it had spent itself, had contributed much to the capacity of the nation to care for its transportaion needs. In one sense, of course, this mania was motivated by the nation's undeniable need for better transportation. More specifically, however, the primary motivation was the desire of America's principal cities to maintain or advance their position relative to rivals. For example, New York endeavored to consolidate the gains of the Erie Canal by constructing a series of branches within the state and in Ohio to consolidate the hinterland available to New York merchants. In Maryland the principal project was the Chesapeake and Ohio Canal, an undertaking designed to provide a navigable waterway in the Potomac River valley as far as Cumberland. Ultimately successful in accomplishing this purpose, this project did not put Baltimore into serious competition with New York. On the one hand its completion was too long delayed, while on the other hand it did not in any event succeed in making contact with the trans-Allegheny region. This after all was the real secret of New York's success.

TABLE 15. FOLLOWING NEW YORK'S EXAMPLE

State	1830	1840	1850
		(Number of miles of canals)	
Pennsylvania	230	954	954
New York	546	640	803
Ohio	245	744	792
Virginia	–	216	216
Indiana	–	150	214
New Jersey	20	142	142
Maryland	10	136	136
Illinois	–	–	100
Massachusetts	74	89	89
All states	1,277	3,326	3,698

Source: By permission from *The Transportation Revolution,* by G. R. Taylor, p. 79. Copyright, 1951, Rinehart & Co., Inc., New York.

Philadelphia made a better showing than Baltimore in this respect. At great cost Pennsylvania developed a transportation contact between Philadelphia and Pittsburgh. The tragedy of these efforts, their failure to put Philadelphia on an equal footing with New York, lay in the impossibility of traversing the intervening mountains by means of a waterway. Instead a facility was constructed which combined two stretches of waterway with two stretches of railway and required three transfers of lading en route. Pennsylvania deserves credit for a gallant attempt, and she did succeed in welding together western and eastern Pennsylvania, but a complex facility of this sort obviously could not compete effectively with the all-water route between New York and Cleveland. All too many Philadelphia merchants and manufacturers found it cheaper to ship goods to and secure goods from the West by way of New York.

Although the Erie Canal, like the Lancaster-Philadelphia Turnpike before it, was misleading in the optimistic conclusions men drew from it, certain major economic changes can be broadly associated with its opening. Never again, for example, was New York's commercial supremacy to be seriously challenged. Furthermore, new opportunities were opened up for expansion in the Northwest in the form of a more rapid emigration from the Northeast, a dynamic development creating graver adjustment problems in the Northeast than this area had yet known. More rapidly than ever before eastern farm lands lost their ability to compete with the West in the production of grain and meat, and eastern farmers were still further harassed by a painful rise in land values in the vicinity of urbanized areas. Pressed in these ways farmers began more and more to substitute an intensive type of farming for the extensive agriculture earlier practiced,[2] and displaced farm families and farmer's sons and daughters began to find their way more rapidly into factory work or the other economic activities fast growing up in eastern communities. The result was a more rapid industrialization and urbanization in the East providing an expanding market for the dairy products and truck crops being turned out by the "new" agriculture.

Massachusetts Recants. Although the construction of the Erie Canal with state funds sealed the doom of a policy of internal improvements at

2 "Intensive agriculture" refers to a type of farming in which relatively more labor and/or capital are employed per unit of land than in the case of what is called "extensive agriculture." Thus dairying is an intensive use of land, while wheat production in the United States is extensive. Where land is relatively scarce (expensive), it will be used intensively; where it is relatively abundant (cheap), it will be used extensively. In other words, the very fact that land was increasing in value in the East was one of the important factors compelling its use on a more intensive basis. On the other hand, it was largely the expansion of urban centers which brought about the increase in the value of outlying land. In this complex way do economic forces interact with one another as industrialization evolves.

federal government expense, the "American System" was vigorous enough to secure the passage of one more increase in the level of manufacturing protection. This was the "Tariff of Abominations," this epithet resulting from the series of weird political machinations (authored largely by Martin Van Buren of New York, Andrew Jackson's campaign manager) associated with its passage. As John Randolph caustically expressed the situation, the tariff of 1828 referred to the manufacture of nothing except a President of the United States. Mr. Randolph did exaggerate a little, however; this was the highest duty level enacted prior to the Civil War.

But the significance of the "Tariff of Abominations" for American history does not lie in either of these facts. Its most important aspect was rather the support it received from Massachusetts. Four years earlier Daniel Webster, eloquently championing the commercial point of view, had powerfully opposed the tariff measure then before Congress. Now, just as eloquently, he defended the principle of protection. Webster's own explanation of this change of front was that the nation had made a basic choice between manufacturing and commercial enterprises, and that Massachusetts was simply adjusting to the implications of that decision. Put differently, Webster was saying that his constituents had changed their occupation—and consequently their minds.

There was much truth in this account of what was happening; the economy of New England was indeed undergoing a transformation of precisely this sort. One by one the greatest merchants of the day were abandoning the field in which their fortunes had been made, and the nation's shipping industry was never again to enjoy the status of a major economic pursuit.

TABLE 16. MANUFACTURING SPURTS FORWARD

Census Year	Total Population (Millions)	Per Cent Urban	Per Cent of Private Production Income Created by Manufacturing *
1800	5.3	6.1	4.9
1810	7.2	7.3	6.1
1820	9.6	7.2	7.5
1830	12.9	8.8	10.3
1840	17.1	10.8	10.3
1850	23.2	15.3	12.5
1860	31.4	19.8	12.1

* Data for the year preceding census year. In addition, these data make no allowance for fluctuations in the business cycle.

Source: Bureau of the Census, *Historical Statistics of the United States, 1789-1945*, pp. 14 and 25.

However, this change in orientation was by no means all to be explained by American stubbornness regarding the West Indian trade and the new tariff policy. A secularly falling price level, for example, severely damaged the import business because of the long time lag between the purchase of goods and their sale. Another factor was a competition in oriental goods so severe that western tea markets were ruinously glutted. In the Hawaiian Islands, moreover, a prohibitive tax on sandalwood virtually destroyed this trade, and the fur trade was similarly losing ground as the source of supply moved farther inland and as silk began to replace beaver in the hats worn by Europe's upper classes. Perhaps, in short, shipping was suffering the effects of a particularly vigorous economic dynamics.

But whatever the cause of this transformation, America's persistence in her new policy of tariff restrictionism wrenched relationships with England even more painfully. An angry reaction in Parliament first prohibited America from engaging in trade with any British colony, a reaction met in Congress by the closing of American ports to British vessels arriving from any point in the Western Hemisphere. Later it became evident to both nations that they were spiting primarily themselves, and with this realization a full reciprocity policy was inaugurated. On this side of the water this meant that apart from the coastwise trade other nations' ships were treated in American ports just as American ships in foreign ports. Ironically, when vessels of the United States were again allowed in British West Indies ports these islands were a relatively unimportant part of America's trade. Commercial decline there, the rise of a tariff-protected sugar industry in Louisiana, a new trade with Spanish Cuba, and a rapidly expanding commerce with Europe and the Orient—all these factors were beginning to dwarf what had once been this country's most important trading relationship.

It is not given to one generation to judge the way a preceding generation solved the problems with which it was confronted. Despite this fact, however, much criticism has been leveled against American leaders for carrying the nation down the road to protectionism rather than in the direction of free trade. In view of this criticism it may be worth while to comment upon several factors which, if they are not fully extenuating, are at least too often ignored.

First, there is no denying that this period was a difficult one in the industrialization of this country. English manufacturers had sought by every means at their command to drive American manufacturing enterprises to the wall, working toward this end with much success, and scarcely had this threat begun to diminish than the enterprises which were still standing had been subjected to a severe deflation. When, in the face of these disasters, manufacturing industries had endeavored to secure protection against the worst hazards of this trying period, they were unable to elicit anything but the most grudging response. Not until 1828 did these industries achieve a level of protection approximating that considered necessary. To be sure, today, with the perspective of more than one hundred years of history, it is apparent that protection was not a major factor in America's industrial growth. But the men who had to face the trials of the 1820's did not have this advantage.

Second, while it is true that America was restricting international trade, it is a gross exaggeration to suggest that she was pursuing a policy of unfree trade. When progress in domestic transportation is taken into account, together with the care with which internal trade was kept unrestricted, a good case can be made for the proposition that American trade was growing progressively more free.

QUESTIONS FOR DISCUSSION

1. Why did the West want a liberal land policy? What does this mean? Did the country as a whole stand to gain or lose from such a policy?
2. What were the economic issues at stake in the controversy between England and the United States? What advantages did each contestant possess?
3. Was the western farmer's acceptance of the "American System" reasonable, or were the farmer's leaders just not thinking straight?
4. How necessary to the development of the country was this trend toward more protection from foreign-produced goods?
5. How were banks in urban centers able to put pressure on banks in smaller communities? Why did they want to?
6. What were the principal elements in the economic successes now being achieved by New York?
7. How did the Erie Canal and the "Suffolk System" contribute to the defeat of centralization of functions in the hands of the federal government?
8. Why was cheap transportation for western products deemed so important? Was too much emphasis placed upon this need?
9. What is the special sense in which the term "free trade" is used here when protectionist United States is referred to as a "free-trade nation?"

Chapter 11

A NEW REVOLUTION

1828	Andrew Jackson elected President.
	Workingmen's Party organized in Philadelphia.
	South Carolina *Exposition and Protest.*
1829	"Kitchen Cabinet" and "Spoils System."
	Workingmen's Party organized in New York.
1830	Webster-Hayne debate.

It would be just as accurate (if not more so) to insist that America was inaugurating a protective tariff policy because she was becoming a manufacturing nation as to say that she was becoming a manufacturing nation as a result of her newly adopted protective tariff. But, whichever the causal relationship emphasized, the fact remained that the United States was becoming steadily more industrialized. Inevitably this development was accompanied by important consequences for many people, and equally inevitably those most affected reacted sharply against changes which seemed opposed to their best interests.

Rise of a Working Class. In one sense central to the changes taking place was a rapidly growing specialization of function, although this development was possibly more a resultant of the over-all evolution than a causal factor. Whereas the "merchant" capitalism of colonial America had been one in which the entrepreneur had performed a wide variety of functions for himself, the new capitalism was to be one in which the major entrepreneurial activities were to be broken apart. Thus, as the nineteenth century advanced, transportation, finance, marketing, and production were more and more separated from one another, each becoming the responsibility of enterprisers specializing in a single type of activity. No longer were great merchants to invest primarily their own capital, ship their own goods in their own vessels, and provide their own insurance services.

Two economic facts provided the basis for this transformation in economic organization. One was the long period of steadily falling prices after the Napoleonic wars which made profit-making much more hazardous on the older "Jack-of-all-trades" basis. The other was the growth in size and complexity of efficient business operations. With the use of more capital and production for a wider market, increasing specialization was simply a condition of staying in the competitive running. Except in the smaller communities and in types of operations inherently geared to small-scale output, the "Jack-of-all-trades" was too apt to be master of none and hence soon working for someone else.

This specialization of function had perhaps its most adverse consequences for the rising urban proletariat. An early important step in industrialization had been the appearance of skilled workers manufacturing by hand the goods needed by the larger community. At first goods were produced on order for customers usually known personally by at least the master craftsman, and these masters thus combined in their own persons an entrepreneurial and a labor function. As the market broadened with the improvement of technology and transportation facilities, however, custom work declined in importance. The result was that the dominant role came more and more to be played by a merchant-capitalist who functioned essentially as an intermediary, buying from a diverse group of suppliers and in turn selling finished goods to his own customers. This arrangement destroyed the close, personal relationship between worker and customer, and at the same time put the various shops within a single market area into active competition with one another. The price of survival in these circumstances was for the master craftsman to become an "employer" in the modern sense of that term, striving to hold his head above the current by means of greater output from his "employees" and even by depressing wages.

It was these changes in industrial organization, changes which had been long in the making but which developed with an accentuated intensity in the 1820's, that produced the beginnings of the American labor movement. Buffeted about by an economic transformation he did not fully comprehend, and threatened with declining real wages, a lowered status in the community, and periods of painful unemployment, the worker was faced with extremely difficult problems of adjustment. Furthermore, dependent upon others for many of his tools, the materials with which he worked, his workplace, and even the right to work, his capacity for self-help was limited indeed. Understandably, therefore, one of the first steps taken in this direction was organization.

By no means all types of workers participated in this new movement. Broadly speaking, and entirely logically, the dissatisfied and hence restless workers were those laborers who were being most painfully separated from customary relationships with society, customer, and employer. Other worker groups (and indeed groups containing the majority of all workers) remained relatively inert.

For example, many semiskilled laborers were at the moment working in their own homes with materials and tools furnished by merchant-capitalists. Partly because they did not gather in a central workplace to do their work, and partly because they were often not dependent upon wages for the largest share of their income, these workers either were unable or saw no particular need to organize. Only as the workplace became differentiated from the home was a labor organization able to speak for the working group.

Factory workers were inactive for different reasons. For one thing they were still too few in number to be a significant force. But, in addition, the way in which these organizations typically evolved in these early years prevented them from becoming aggressive relative to their employers. Located typically where water power was available and other facilities were not, factory promoter-owners were often forced to develop their industries from scratch. This meant, for example, the provision of homes for employees and retail outlets through which the various goods needed by the community could be secured. Thus a "company town" situation tended to develop and with it an employer-employee paternalism not deliberately sought by employers. Once created, however, this paternalism could be (and was) used in a number of different ways, varying from the careful regulation of the moral life of factory girls by puritannical New Englanders (a regulation explained in part by the fact that New England farmers would not permit their daughters to engage in this activity unless such precautions were taken) to the grossest form of economic exploitation such as was often found in the semifeudal organization of Pennsylvania iron factories. Moreover, this situation was not apt to be overlooked by enterprising employers faced with the beginnings of labor self-consciousness.

For another reason, too, factory workers did not take part in early labor organizations. Most of these laborers consisted of women and children—individuals not responsible for the full support of a family. (On the one hand most men possessed a skill paying substantially higher wages than unskilled factory labor could expect, and on the other hand men were still too independent of mind to make good factory workers.) Hence, they felt less economic pressure to organize. Furthermore, a large proportion of these early factory workers consisted of individuals who had been directly or indirectly forced off eastern farms by the expansion of agriculture farther west. These folk were apt to view the opportunity to work in a factory in a favorable light, whereas craftsmen looked upon a wage-earning status as a distinct drop in the economic hierarchy.

The Labor Movement Begins. Beginning early in American history there are records of concerted action by laborers designed to achieve higher wages, shorter hours, or some improvement in working conditions. After the second war with England, however, such episodes occurred with greater frequency, and especially so after the worst years of the postwar depression had passed. Yet, despite this greater frequency of concerted action, labor organizations continued to be put together primarily for the specific occasion at hand, being disbanded as soon as this purpose had either been achieved or abandoned.

There were two major reasons why more permanent associations did not arise in America earlier than they did. For one thing, the courts of the nation persistently declared labor organizations to be "conspiracies" in restraint of trade and therefore illegal. Even more important was the prevailing attitude of workingmen. Overwhelmingly laborers refused to acknowledge that their lives were committed to the labor class. Instead they persisted in believing that work as a laborer was only one phase of the march upward in the social economic scale guaranteed by the American dream. A permanent organization to protect oneself in a temporary situation seemed a questionable strategy.

This attitude was for many years to retard the development of a real labor movement, although gradually a different sentiment arose as it became evident that industrialization had come to stay. During the 1820's, however, skilled workers in the so-called hand and neighborhood industries were induced by an extraordinary set of circumstances to embark on a special kind of organizational activity.

Table 17. Pressure on the Worker

Year	Wholesale Price Index (1926 = 100)
1814	154.6
1819	89.7
1824	71.1
1829	67.6
1834	65.6

Source: Bureau of the Census, *Historical Statistics of the United States, 1789-1945,* p. 234.

In the first place, this decade was an important part of a full quarter of a century characterized by a falling general price level. On the one side this trend was favorable to labor in so far as constant money wages were thereby converted into rising real wages. But on the other side falling prices did much to accentuate the competition which was pushing the craftsman into the status of wage earner, and therefore falling prices were as apt as not to be met with a wage level falling even more rapidly.

Second, as western states had come into the union, the overwhelming preponderance of frontier farmers making up their population had resulted in the inclusion of universal male suffrage in their constitutions, and eastern states had been virtually compelled to meet this competition of the western states for population. One by one eastern states had extended the vote to a wider and wider group, a concession begrudgingly given against the opposition of eastern conservatives. By the late 1820's, by the time Andrew Jackson's campaign for the presidency began to gain momentum, most laborers possessed the right to vote. Determined to use their new power to improve their economic position, laborers in most large eastern cities began to organize for political action. It is often said that the American labor movement began in Philadelphia when several trades joined forces in an organization called the "Mechanics Union of Trade Associations." Soon thereafter a similar organization was functioning in a number of other cities.

The keynote of the political program launched by laborers in 1828 was the concept of "equal citizenship." Stating the issue as essentially between the underprivileged poor and an aristocracy which had usurped the government for its own advantage (rather than between employees and employers as such), laborers sought to alter the conditions preventing them from rising out of the laboring class. Several specific grievances were to be alleviated. In some states, for example, a compulsory militia system worked a hardship on the poor. The penalty for failure to serve was a fine or imprisonment, and wealthy eligibles could easily purchase freedom from duty. Imprisonment for debt was also common in those days. In most places, too, there was no protection to the workingman whose wages went unpaid in the event of an employer's bankruptcy. The rule was rather share and share alike with the concern's other creditors.

Important though these grievances were, however, two others were even more important. The issue occupying most of the foreground of this labor agitation was education. Men and women of low economic status then as now felt that "equal citizenship" demanded an equality of opportunity which could be effectuated only by means of a free school system provided at public expense. The education system of that day was indeed deplorable, at least by the standards of modern democracy. Public schools were not unknown, but so great was the social stigma attached to their use that many families who could not afford to send their children to private schools preferred to have them out of school rather than face the community's scorn by asking for "charity."

At a time when public schools are taken for granted, it is difficult to recapture the bitterness of the battle fought over this issue. It is still easy, however, to understand the resistance of conservative groups. America was a much more aristocratic society in those days than now; many persons sincerely felt that the "lower classes" were born to serve, and that the idea of equal education was therefore nonsense. In those days it was even possible publicly to utter and defend such views without being considered "antisocial." Given such a sentiment it is understandable that many wealthy men would feel the cost of providing free education to the sons of workers, a cost which would be borne primarily by them, to be a waste of resources. And in some cases perhaps the sentiment of disapproval even grew out of a contemplation of the resultant tax burden. But this too is understandable. In any event, one of the important tasks of the public school movement was to combat these ideas held by conservatives *through* public education.

The other major issue had to do with the nation's monetary system. Focusing attention on the special legislation by which banks were then chartered, a process lending itself to corruption and favoritism, laborers complained that banks operated as a major agency for their enslavement. On the one hand, a paper money was issued for circulation which by its deterioration defrauded the laborer of a portion of his wages. On the other hand, by extending credit to the employer and not to the employee, banks helped perpetuate the position of the employer at the expense of the employee. The apparent alignment of banks as chartered monopolies, merchants as unchartered monopolists, and the legislatures which granted the banks their monopolies could only be interpreted by the unsophisticated mind of the worker as a conspiracy to prevent him from attaining his "rightful" place in society. How, for example, could the worker become an entrepreneur with the cards thus stacked against him? In this way began a worker concern for the monetary institutions of his society which was not to disappear for many years.

At the moment it could not be said that this new labor movement was particularly successful. Perhaps this was partly due to the fact that it was a political effort rather than an economic one; there are some who insist that the labor movement in America became an important social force more slowly than elsewhere primarily because American workers were tempted by their possession of the franchise to expend their energies on political campaigns rather than in economic contests with employers. Perhaps, too, this failure was in part a result of the naïve misunderstanding of laborers regarding the nature of the rising industrial economy, a misunderstanding excellently demonstrated by their attitude on the money question. But both of these facts were in turn related to labor's failure, as yet, to accept its new status in economic society. And it is important to remember not only that labor was exceedingly weak from the standpoint of sheer numbers but that economic pressure against employers is not a promising activity during a depression when jobs are scarce.

Suffice it to say that labor was rarely able to elect its candidates, and that even when it did labor incumbents were often unable to accomplish much against the opposition of conservative majorities. However, in the larger perspective of history it is clear that this episode in labor's development marks the beginning of a major trend in American evolution. To these small origins in and after 1828 can be traced the abolition of debtor's prisons and compulsory militia service, the beginning of a series of mechanic's lien laws (which was one day to include every state in the Union), and the rise of a free public school system which is today the marvel of the world.

More immediately the achievement of labor lay in the part it played in the "Jacksonian Revolution." No doubt feeling more of an aversion to the governing administration than a fondness for the Jacksonians, laborers supported the western candidate and thus contributed something to the large margin by which he won. Moreover, this fact was so obvious as to give conservatives reason for grave misgivings about the future of "their" country. For their part Andrew Jackson and Martin Van Buren, although they would certainly have been victorious in the national election without labor's support, did not neglect their laborer friends when they did hold the reins of power.

Specialization and the Farmer. Not only laborers but farmers as well were feeling adversely the consequences of the greater specialization accompanying advancing industrialization. Self-sufficient agriculture has its special disadvantages, the most basic of these being its low per capita productivity, but the transition from self-sufficiency to specialization carries with it a disadvantage against which a higher per capita productivity must be carefully balanced. He who produces specialized agricultural products for a market and uses the proceeds to buy the goods he needs for his own use thereby puts himself at the mercy of a price system over which he has almost no control. Put differently, specialization breaks the close connection between the farmer's output and his economic well-being. And as the producer of goods especially sensitive to changes in demand conditions, and as a debtor, the farmer was particularly vulnerable to the downward drift of the price level.[1]

Among the farmers on the American scene none was thrown as completely into dependence on the outside economy as the one-crop southern

[1] On the one hand because the demand for agricultural products is inelastic, an increase in output may easily result not only in a reduced price but in a reduced real income for farmers. On the other hand because the supply of agricultural products is also inelastic, a fall in demand will be reflected primarily in price reductions rather than in output curtailment. The converse is also true—in both cases.

farmer. A single crop, little of which is consumed locally, is the quintessence of dependence; a fall in the price of cotton, or tobacco, or rice, or sugar, and an entire year's net income was gone. Two or three years of low prices and a planter's chances of ever again being solvent might be severely damaged, for the planter's costs were essentially embedded in the capital sunk in lands and slaves and hence did not vary with the price of his product. In short, one-crop specialization was found to be as undesirable in the nineteenth-century South as in the seventeenth- and eighteenth-century South. Unfortunately, as in the earlier period, this discovery was not made in the cotton economy until many planters were so deeply implicated that retrenchment was almost impossible.

The gradual process by which this came about was no new thing to the southern economy. Commercially passive, southerners let New Yorkers handle their imports and exports, carrying both two hundred miles out of their natural way. Then, putting their own capital into the fixed form of land and slaves, cotton planters were forced to borrow the working capital necessary to plant and harvest their crop. As collateral the next crop was pledged, with the result that this crop when ready was turned over to the creditor who, assuming virtually no risk because he did not take title to the goods, deducted interest, freight, insurance, storage, and a commission. The proceeds, if any, went to the planter, and all too rarely was there enough to avoid borrowing on next season's crop. So complete did the control of the factor over the planter become that oftentimes the crop pledge was stated as a minimum number of bales of cotton with a penalty for failure, this practice accentuating the planter's risk of inclement weather conditions and also encouraging overproduction.

The West was far less caught in the web of debt and dependence than the South, but these farmers too were rapidly falling under the sway of industry. By 1828 the postwar depression in the West as well as the South was already ten years old with no relief in sight. When the American people went to the polls in 1828 to choose between a western farmer and a New England aristocrat for the presidency, farmers the country over had no difficulty making up their minds. Of the New England aristocrat they had had enough. And when Andrew Jackson was elected President by an overwhelming vote, men of "property and principle" were given another reason for shuddering when they thought about the future of "their" country.

The Search for New Allies. The "Jacksonian Revolution" marked an event of major importance in America's economic development. One of the important factors involved, of course, was the reappearance of the laborer as a power on the national scene for the first time since the Revolution—and this time his influence was not to be eclipsed in the sequel.

Far more significant, however, was the fact that once again the nation's farmers were revolting against the policies of the business interests.

There were a number of reasons why the tariff union between western farmers and eastern businessmen was so soon falling to pieces. Chief among these, perhaps, was the fact that a new issue was rising to the forefront in the West's scale of values. What she now wanted more than anything else was a more liberal land policy—the abandonment of the continuing reliance on the revenue importance of the public domain and more of a recognition of the interests of the men who were braving the frontier to develop the country. Not only were the West's eastern allies doing nothing to promote such a policy, but they were even doing their best to sabotage it. Simultaneously with the passage of the tariff measure in 1828, a policy the West had generously supported, a bill presented by Senator Benton providing for gradually reducing the price of such public lands as did not sell at the original price was defeated by a close vote in which the East voted almost unanimously in the negative. Had two more southerners voted for the bill, it would have passed.

It was no accident, either, this opposition by easterners to a cheap land policy. Manufacturers were clearly supporting a high price policy deliberately. Not only was protection from foreign competition necessary for the development of industrial production, but so also was an ample labor supply. A cheap land policy, they feared, would have the effect of draining away the eastern labor supply into agricultural endeavors on the frontier. In addition, eastern landholders felt that any encouragement to emigration must have the effect of reducing property values farther east. Moreover, these fears were not wholly groundless. It was a notorious fact that Americans had traditionally shown much more eagerness for land ownership on the frontier than for urban employment. In this connection it could be pointed out that in the preceding twenty years real per capita income had fallen 20 per cent, a development widely (if largely erroneously) attributed to the westward migration of capital. Thus it was that few voices were lifted in the manufacturing states in favor of cheaper land—except that of the laborer whose voice was too weak to be heard.

This alone would have been basis enough for westerners reassessing their relationships. But there were also other factors involved which were equally compelling. The alliance with the business interests had been motivated by a desire for domestic markets for staple surpluses, including internal improvements by means of which these surpluses could be economically transported to market. Now, for a variety of reasons, there no longer seemed to be so close a connection between a protective tariff and the West's economic well-being.

First, progress in the internal improvement field made this need far less desperate than it had once been. Second, the international economic outlook was no longer as dark as it had been a half-dozen years earlier. While the United States was still not a prime source of foodstuffs for Europe, the special discriminations against this country were disappearing and there seemed good reason for believing that this would continue to be the case. Third, the rapid development of manufacturing in the East was indeed making urban workers out of eastern farmers, thus reducing their production and increasing their consumption of western-type goods—and Henry Clay's "American System" scarcely deserved the credit.

But if these developments explain why the West was now abandoning the East, they do not make it clear why southerners were beginning to flirt with the West. The fact was that the cotton economy was still expanding more rapidly than the grain and meat economy with the result that the South's capacity for absorbing western surpluses had proved unexpectedly great.

The westward movement of cotton production and the perfection of the steamboat had indeed worked out fortunately for both the western and the southern economies. Southerners were inclined to specialize in the production of cotton, thus having need of the meat, wheat, furniture, implements, and the like produced in the West. In turn westerners found the cotton plantations to be an excellent outlet for their surpluses. While droves of cattle and hogs were frequently driven from western farms to the Atlantic Coast, far more western meat was sent to southern destinations over the Ohio and Mississippi Rivers. It was, of course, necessary to cure the meat sent southward lest it spoil on the still slow journey down the river, and therefore most of the meat exports to the South consisted of pork. Likewise the wheat shipped to cotton plantations was most frequently in the form of flour. But these requirements further aided the western economy by helping it give effect to a distinct manufacturing bent of its own. By 1828 Cincinnati was already so important as a pork-processing center that no westerner misunderstood what city was meant when the name "Porkopolis" was used. St. Louis and Louisville had also become thriving river cities.

Although the West and the South were both exploring the possibility of a mutually profitable alliance, the question of the basis on which it could rest had still to be decided. The several alternatives are roughly set forth in Table 18. Neither section could be satisfied with a program excluding the policy it considered to be most important. At the same time each would have to give up a policy also considered desirable if its ally was to be satisfied in its Number One demand. Thus the South would have to give up its insistence on expensive land, making itself vulnerable to the possibility that the government's revenue needs would one day require a higher tariff than could otherwise be justified. Likewise the West would have to give up whatever expectations it might still have of

TABLE 18. A SEARCH FOR NEW ALLIES

Policy	West	South	East
Most important	Cheap land	Low tariff	High tariff
Next in importance ..	Internal improvements	No internal improvements	Expensive land
Least important	High tariff	Expensive land	Internal improvements

retaining a high tariff. Fortunately the policy to be given up in each case was the one held to be least important by the section making the sacrifice. By contrast, for the East now to ally itself with either the West or the South would require some section to give up a policy higher on its scale of values, only another way of saying that the interests of the two agricultural areas were closer together than the interests of agricultural and business sections.

A Coalition in the Making. The South took the first step toward a realignment of forces—by expressing its opposition to the tariff in a more dramatic way than ever before. The legislature of South Carolina, several months prior to the passage of the "Tariff of Abominations," had acted to draw up an exposition of grievances and a protest against the tariff. This document was intended to set forth simultaneously the injury done to the South by the tariff and the unconstitutionality of the policy of protection. Appropriately, John C. Calhoun undertook the preparation of this document; as the outstanding statesman of the South and a veteran of almost twenty years on the national scene, he was especially fitted for such a task. Meanwhile, when the tariff act became law, great mass meetings were held in South Carolina at which it was freely compared with the Stamp Act, and a similar sentiment was visible although to a lesser extent in Georgia.

Late in 1828, the South Carolina legislature met to consider what was to be done about the tariff. Much of these deliberations was devoted to the *Exposition and Protest*, and all were agreed that Calhoun had made an excellent statement. Constitution-wise he took the ground earlier taken by Jefferson and Madison in the Virginia and Kentucky Resolutions. America's government was one in which the national agency possessed only limited powers, and the promotion of industry was not one of these. Since the states had entered into the compact with the understanding that only the enumerated powers would in fact be exercized by the federal government, it followed that any state was free to consider itself not bound by an action which the federal government could not legitimately take. Calhoun did not recommend nullification in 1828, although there were extremists in South Carolina who did. His only thought, as yet, was to establish the right of a state to nullify acts of the federal government.

As always, however, the constitutional argument was essentially a cloak behind which specific interests were more or less camouflaged. So had it been when New England had talked of secession in Hartford some fifteen years earlier; so was it now as South Carolina asserted the right of southern states to refuse to abide by protective tariff legislation. Nor did John C. Calhoun ignore the economic factors behind the tariff agitation. Frankly, if passionately, he analyzed the consequences of protection for the producers of cotton. The attempt by manufacturers to monopolize the home market could only have the effect of ruining staple producers forced to rely on a world market. And against the argument that the underlying cause of the South's difficulties was overproduction, Calhoun had two things to say. First, if this were true manufacturers should improve their situation by reducing their output rather than by asking for a subsidy at the expense of the taxpayer. Second, the South could not improve its position by reducing output because other producing areas through the world would only increase theirs.

But the South Carolina *Exposition* can only suffer by being summarized. In Calhoun's own words:

> We would be compelled to abandon the cultivation of three fourths of what we now raise, and receive for the residue, whatever the manufacturers, who would then have their policy consummated by the entire possession of our market, might choose to give. Forced to abandon our ancient and favorite pursuit, to which our soil, climate, habits and peculiar labor are adapted, at an immense sacrifice of property, we would be compelled, without capital, experience, or skill, and with a population untried in such pursuits, to attempt to become the rivals instead of the customers of the manufacturing States. The result is not doubtful. If they, by a superior capital and skill, should keep down successful competition on our part, we would be doomed to toil at our unprofitable agriculture,—selling at the prices which a single and very limited market might give. But, on the contrary, if our necessity should triumph over their capital and skill,—if, instead of raw cotton, we should ship to the manufacturing States cotton yarn and cotton goods, the thoughtful must see that it would inevitably bring about a state of things which could not long continue. Those who now make war on our gains, would then make it on our labor.

Few men in 1828 had such a clear grasp of the nature of the conflict between farm and factory or the close relationship between this conflict and the tariff.

There is no difficulty in understanding why it was a southern rather than a western state which first declared open war on the nation's factories. The commercialization of agriculture had been carried much farther in the South than in the West, and therefore southerners had a keener appreciation of the painful adjustments required by such a status. What is less clear is why South Carolina took the lead in this protest rather than Virginia or Alabama. A part of the answer no doubt is the fact that John C. Calhoun was born and raised in South Carolina rather than in Virginia or Alabama. Precisely because the man who understood the South's problem most thoroughly came from South Carolina, it was given to that state to guide her neighbors.

However, historical relationships are seldom as clear cut as this would suggest. Why, for example, did the South's outstanding statesman arise in South Carolina? Table 19 is at least suggestive in this connection. Not

TABLE 19. TIME MARCHES ON

State	1821	1826	1834
	(Cotton production in millions of pounds)		
South Carolina	50.0	70.0	65.5
Georgia	45.0	75.0	75.0
Virginia	12.0	25.0	10.0
North Carolina	10.0	10.0	9.5
Total, Old South	117.0	180.0	160.0
Tennessee	20.0	45.0	45.0
Louisiana	10.0	38.0	62.0
Mississippi	10.0	20.0	85.0
Alabama	20.0	45.0	85.0
Florida		2.0	20.0
Total, New South	60.0	150.0	297.0
Grand Total	177.0	330.0	457.0

Source: By permission from *Rise of the New West, 1819-1829*, by Frederick J. Turner, p. 47. Copyright, 1906, Harper & Bros., New York.

only was the entire South suffering from a chronic general depression, but the old cotton South was suffering in addition from a painful competition with the new cotton South. In a period of eight years the output of the new producing areas increased almost 100 per cent while the production of the older areas declined more than 10 per cent. While three states in the western cotton region were increasing output by more than forty million pounds each, production in South Carolina fell by almost five million pounds. Year after year of soil mining as distinguished from what is today called scientific farming was placing the old South at a disadvantage in competition with soils less mistreated.

If the South led the way in inviting a coalition between the great agricultural regions of the country, the West was not slow to respond in kind. The *Exposition* was published in December, 1828. In the same month Governor Ninian Edwards of Illinois, a state having neither slaves nor cotton, in an address to the Illinois legislature, asserted the constitutional right of the western states to the land within their borders. Like Calhoun, Edwards was stating the major grievance of his section in constitutional terms. Like Calhoun, too, he minced no words about the economic foundation on which the grievance actually rested. "We are gratified," said the Governor, "that the discussion of the graduation bill has led the able Representatives of the Western States to examine into the pretext under which they have been made to pay tribute, to the last shilling in their purses." Other prominent westerners in both cotton and noncotton states were simultaneously taking a similar position. It was no coincidence that Ninian Edwards and John C. Calhoun had long been political friends.

The "Great Debate." An opportunity to strengthen the bond between West and South was soon offered by action of the manufacturing states themselves. On December 17, 1829, Hunt of Vermont proposed a bill distributing the proceeds of the sale of public lands to the states. Two purposes would be served by such legislation as far as eastern conservatives were concerned. Against the desires of the West, it would assist in keeping the land price high and it would imply ownership of the public lands by the national government. Against the policy preferred by the South, it would take away the land revenue as a deterrent to higher duties. Twelve days later, Foot of Connecticut suggested halting the survey and sale of new lands.

Either of these proposals would have inflamed a westerner. Both of them, coming as they did so close together, could scarcely have provoked a reaction more restrained than the one which followed. Senator Benton opened the debate with an attack on the factory system and the tariff-public land policies which supported it. The tariff, he said, stimulated the production of manufactures in the East and thus prevented emigration by keeping wages high; the public land policy accomplished the same end more directly. As Benton summarized the situation: "A most complex scheme of injustice, which taxes the South to injure the West, to pauperize the poor of the North." A clearer invitation for the South to join hands with the West could not have been issued.

The invitation was immediately accepted. Senator Hayne announced with equal directness the terms under which the South would support the West's position. After the federal government was out of debt the western lands should be sold to the states within which they lay for a nominal sum. That the West would reciprocate by supporting a move for tariff reduction was clearly implied, although it was not mentioned.

Hayne's speech was delivered on January 19, 1830, the opening phase of what has since been known as the "Webster-Hayne" debate. Eastern protectionists saw at once the danger to their way of life and could not afford to let it grow unchallenged. No more fitting champion could they have found than Daniel Webster, the New Englander so recently converted from the free trade cause. On January 20 he made his justly famous "First Reply to Hayne." It was in no real sense a reply to Hayne, or to anyone else. What Webster chose to do, and what he did do superbly, was to change the subject, discussing instead the constitutional theories in the South Carolina *Exposition* which Hayne obviously believed. The rest of the "Great Debate" was occupied with this discussion—Hayne defending state rights, Webster the doctrine of national sovereignty. Never, perhaps, has either position been more ably defended, especially the union side of the controversy. Few Americans today can fail to feel a thrill of emotion at the words with which Webster concluded his "Second Reply to Hayne" —"Liberty *and* union, now and forever, one and inseparable." With these words one of the most dramatic episodes in American history reached its climax.

There were two major reasons for Webster's strategy. First, he singled out Hayne for attack rather than Benton because easterners felt it would be easier to work out a new coalition with the West than with the South. Second, there was so much of truth in what Benton had said that a campaign of denial did not seem indicated. A better way to take the West away from the South seemed to be to associate the South's position with "treason" to the Union. No less than a stroke of genius on the part of one of America's greatest statesmen, it was not the fault of Daniel Webster that as a strategy it was not successful.

Daniel Webster was wrong, Calhoun and Hayne right, regarding the historical origin of America's government. But Daniel Webster was right, Calhoun and Hayne wrong, as far as the nation's future was concerned. When the sequel to the events of 1830 was written three years later, it was evident that the nation would stand with Massachusetts' interpretation of the Constitution rather than South Carolina's. Perhaps it was at this point that the Civil War became inevitable—if it ever did.

QUESTIONS FOR DISCUSSION

1. What were the economic roots of the labor movement?
2. Why did the factory become prominent first in textile and iron manufacturing?
3. Would it have been possible for industrialization in America to have taken place without creating a large group of poverty-stricken, helpless, and bewildered workers?
4. How reasonable was labor's first program of action in terms of the problems workers were facing?

5. What are the economic consequences of depression for farmers? Why does one-crop specialization create particularly difficult problems from this standpoint?

6. On what foundations was a new coalition between western and southern farmers to be built?

7. Did the West exaggerate the importance to it of a cheap land policy? Did the South exaggerate the cost to it of manufacturing protection?

8. Was Webster "fair" in his campaign to prevent a South-West coalition? Would any other strategy have been more successful?

Chapter 12

THE BREACH WIDENS

1830	Maysville Road veto.
	Reciprocity achieved for British West Indies trade.
1831	Jackson's break with Calhoun.
1832	Moderate tariff reduction.
	Bank recharter bill vetoed.
	Jackson overwhelmingly re-elected.
	South Carolina's Ordinance of Nullification.
	Jackson's Nullification Proclamation.
1833	Compromise Tariff.
1833–34	Deposits removed from the Second Bank of the United States.
	"Biddle's Panic."
	Rise of the Whig Party.
1836	Texas secured independence from Mexico.

Little came of the South-West alliance in 1830, although in voting on Benton's graduation proposal southern and western Senators did team up against the East. The same combination of forces also operated in the House, but here the manufacturing East wielded a substantially greater power and the measure was consequently lost. Before another opportunity was presented to enact land legislation favorable to the West, the alliance itself was severely shaken by the reappearance of the tariff as a major issue; and before either of these issues had been settled, the underlying situation had become even more complicated by the intrusion once again of the banking question.

Public Lands and the Tariff. The tariff issue, when it next arose, was not essentially a contest over protection. For the past half-dozen years the Treasury had been running a surplus of about $8 million annually, and in the past fourteen years almost $100 million had been applied against the national debt. Soon the debt would be extinguished, and since it would be unthinkable for the government to accumulate a surplus, steps would have to be taken to reduce the government's income. With the major part of the government's income derived from import duties, it was inevitable that a contest over protection would be thereby precipitated.

In January, 1832, the manufacturing interests presented their solution—the repeal of all duties on noncompetitive goods and an increase in other duties large enough to reduce the flow of revenue. Appropriately enough it was Henry Clay who threw down the challenge. A few days later the antiprotectionists responded. Hayne proposed an amendment to reduce the tariff to a purely revenue basis as soon as the debt was paid. Moderate in tone, this amendment even provided for the gradual reduction of the most highly protective duties to avoid shock to the economy.

The issue could not have been more directly joined. Protectionists wished to destroy the historic "tariff-for-revenue-and-protection" by substituting in its place a "tariff-for-protection-only." Antiprotectionists also wanted to change from the approach of the past, but their idea was a "tariff-for-revenue-only." More sharply than ever before, protectionists and antiprotectionists were now to fight this issue through to a definitive decision.

There was no objective need for the reappearance now of the bank issue, for the charter of the Second Bank of the United States had yet four more years to run. However, Nicholas Biddle had become nervous over the future of "his" bank under the Jacksonians and was easily induced to apply thus prematurely for renewal. Henry Clay had his own reasons for urging this course of action on Biddle. A presidential election was in the offing and Clay sincerely believed that with the bank as an issue his position would be greatly strengthened. In February, 1832, the bank recharter bill was introduced into a Congress already seething over the tariff and land questions.

On March 22 both Clay's and Hayne's resolutions on the tariff were referred to the Senate Committee on Manufactures, and with them a proposal to reduce the price of the public lands and to cede them to the states. The result of obvious cooperation between South and West, this move was especially intended to embarrass the chairman of this committee—Henry Clay. If he supported the eastern position on the public lands, he could scarcely avoid antagonizing the West; if he abandoned the eastern position on this issue, his manufacturing friends would be alienated. In either case his chances of being the next president would be seriously threatened.

Political genius that he was, Clay worked himself out of this difficult situation in a masterful way by taking the most neutral ground it was possible to take. Separating the land issue from the tariff, he proposed distributing the proceeds of the public land sales to the several states on the basis of their federal ratio. This proposal did not give up anything essential from the ideas held by business interests, but at the same time it offered something more than a gesture in the direction of the West.

Fully as significant as his proposal was Clay's reasoning. To begin with there could be no sound argument for reducing the price of the public lands unless the present price were unfairly high, and the rapidity with which new lands were in fact being taken up was an excellent indication that such was not the case. The principal western states were increasing in population three times as rapidly as the states which had no public lands. Furthermore, the greatest number of emigrants at the moment was coming from Ohio, Kentucky, and Tennessee, and a reduction in the price of unsettled lands would reduce the value of lands already settled and denude these western states of population. Finally, ceding the land to the western states might result in unfortunate consequences. States would compete for settlers by reducing the price, a result unfair to the older states. At the same time a debtor relationship would be created between the new states and the central government which might one day strain the Constitution.

Meanwhile a tariff bill was slowly wending its way through the legislative process. This bill was far different from the measure Clay had originally suggested, although it conceded nothing as far as the principle of protection was concerned. Duties on a number of noncompetitive items were to be reduced to zero, but duties on competitive manufactures were to be reduced rather than raised. In short, it was a compromise measure of a sort, a fact which produced many votes in its favor by traditional antiprotectionists.

Even more important were the consequences of this maneuver for the coalition of southerners with westerners. Only one western vote was cast against the new tariff, and the South quickly responded by supporting Clay's distribution proposal in the Senate. The South-West alliance on the tariff and the public lands was indeed having a difficult time amid the confused circumstances under which these issues were now arising.

The Challenge of Nullification. It was at this point that the controversy over both of these questions disappeared temporarily in the heat of a presidential campaign fought out over the issue of the United States Bank. By 1832 much of the hostility the bank had aroused during its early years had been half forgotten and the recharter measure passed both Houses of Congress with little difficulty. But, latent though it was, this hostility still lingered on, waiting only to be activated by the skill of an Andrew Jackson, a Martin Van Buren, and a Thomas Hart Benton. At Jackson's and Benton's back were the western and southern debtors who had been most severely squeezed by the panic precipitated by the "monster." At Van Buren's back were the banking interests of New York and the "hard money" labor group throughout the East. For his part, Henry Clay had apparently forgotten how bitterly resented in much of the West he had become as a result of his identification with the "Bank" and with creditors generally as against agrarian debtors.

If Clay desired to make an issue of the bank's recharter, Jackson could see no reason for withdrawing from such a contest. On July 10 he vetoed the recharter measure. In the ensuing campaign no other issue became important, and in early November Henry Clay discovered how badly he had miscalculated. So overwhelming was Jackson's victory that he stood at the pinnacle of his popularity throughout the bitter tariff struggle now about to begin. It is interesting to reflect that if the charter issue had come up at the time of its scheduled expiration, when farmers were experiencing rising rather than falling prices, recharter would probably have been approved without incident.

On November 24 South Carolina, despairing of ever achieving tariff relief by less drastic means, passed her historic Ordinance of Nullification. This document declared the tariff laws in force to be unconstitutional, and prohibited duty collection under them in the state. Sentiment in South Carolina was not unanimous in this action, the crisis bringing to the fore a large and capable minority of "Unionist" leaders. This strong core of opposition in South Carolina itself, plus the failure of other southern states to join the cause advanced by their neighbor, provided Jackson with much of the support he needed in the stand he was to take.

It is somewhat surprising that other southern states did not join with South Carolina. There was almost as much reason for Georgia, say, to take a strong stand against the tariff as South Carolina. By 1832, moreover, an impressive case could be made for the proposition that the tariff was really responsible for the South's distress. During the five years preceding Henry Clay's "American System" tariff, the price of cotton had averaged almost 9½ pence per pound in Liverpool. Under America's first really protective tariff, and the first tariff strongly opposed by the South,

TABLE 20. FOUNDATION FOR REBELLION

Period	Price of Cotton in Liverpool
	(Average price in pence)
1819-1823	9.48
1824-1828	7.05
1829-1833	6.25
1834-1838	7.68

Adapted from: M. B. Hammond, *The Cotton Industry* (New York: The Macmillan Co., 1897), App. I.

the Liverpool price fell almost 25 per cent. Under the "Tariff of Abominations" the price fell another 10 per cent while the price increased 25 per cent under the tariff reductions enacted during Jackson's administration. Certainly, from an economic standpoint, the relationship between the price of cotton and the tariff was not as close as these figures would indicate, the principal factor being rather the secularly falling price level, but such data were convincing in documenting the unquestionable fact that the tariff burden did fall most heavily on the South.

On December 4 Jackson's annual message was presented to Congress. The tone was most conciliatory on the tariff issue. Bare mention was made of the action taken by South Carolina; apparently the President was not yet prepared to deal with it as he intended. Six days later, however, he was ready. On December 10 he gave to the world his own famous Nullification Proclamation. Challenging the constitutional interpretation on which the South Carolina stand rested, he announced that the nation's laws would be enforced. This announcement was followed by a request for special powers in the event the laws were disobeyed.

Simultaneously another measure was started on its way through the legislative process. This was a bill to adjust the tariff, and the "Compromise Tariff" and the "Force Bill" began what was to be a hotly contested race to see which measure would be passed first. The new tariff proposal, presented by Henry Clay, called for a gradual reduction of all duties to an across-the-board level of 20 per cent over a period of nine years. With little difficulty it was passed, the South voting strongly in favor, New England and the Middle States strongly opposed, and the West moderately in favor. Although some of this western support was no doubt the result of Clay's stature in his own section, the "Compromise Tariff" may appropriately be thought of as the first significant achievement of the South-West coalition.

Clay's willingness to sponsor a tariff reduction measure at this point reflects several underlying factors. To his tariff friends he could argue that under the American Constitution one legislature could not really bind the hands of another, and that concessions were necessary in the circumstances to save the *principle* of protection. Even more he could insist that his distribution measure was an integral part of the compromise financial program.

The "Compromise Tariff" and the "Force Bill" were both signed by the President on March 2, 1833—the former indicating the success of nullification on a short term basis, and the latter indicating the longer term failure of the South Carolina conception of a union of federated states. During the remainder of the year much of Congress' deliberations centered on the land issue. With the South following Clay's lead since it had gotten tariff relief through him (even though the distribution approach could hardly fail to work against the South in the long run), Clay's proposal was approved in both Houses of Congress. Then, much to Clay's disappointment and the relief of southerners, Jackson returned it with a veto.

Jackson Versus Biddle. Before the public land question again became a major issue, however, economic conditions throughout the country had changed so markedly that its consideration took place within a greatly altered context. The depression which had persisted during the decade of the 1820's gave way to prosperity, the Liverpool price of cotton in 1833 rising to a level 50 per cent higher than at the depression trough. For several years thereafter the nation enjoyed an intense period of growth and expansion.

Only one development marred the prosperity era following 1833. About the middle of the year Jackson began removing the government's deposits from the United States Bank. While the government did not technically remove its deposits, it did pay bills by means of deposits already made without making new deposits. Thus the result was the same, and gradually the government's deposits in "Biddle's" bank became zero while the government's deposits in certain state banks grew in proportion. The banks actually selected for this purpose were called by Jackson's enemies "pet banks," although they were apparently carefully selected (at least at first) and just as carefully governed by certain special restrictions designed to safeguard the government's resources.

As soon as Jackson's intent became unmistakable, Biddle took steps to contract the bank's outstanding credit preparatory to losing its principal customer. This of course necessitated calling in loans both to other banks and to business firms, and as always a major effort of this sort in a credit economy had a chain of consequences extending far from its source. The bank's customers in turn were forced to call on their debtors for payment, and a brief, nationwide panic was thus precipitated. Wages and prices fell, unemployment increased, the interest rate rose, and most bank notes began to circulate at a substantial discount. Even in the face of panic, however, Biddle continued his policy of contraction until July, 1834.

In Biddle's defense it can be emphasized that it really was highly uncertain just how an impetuous and implacable Andrew Jackson would carry out his intention of destroying the bank, and that ordinary prudence dictated preparing for the worst. But, on the other hand, there is reason for believing that Biddle's action was in part motivated by a desire to bring pressure to bear on the President to reverse his action on the bank's charter. As Biddle himself expressed it in a letter: "This worthy President thinks that because he has scalped Indians and imprisoned Judges, he is to have his way with the Bank. He is mistaken—and he may as well send at once and engage lodgings in Arabia."

But Biddle underestimated the mettle of his opponent, just as Clay had earlier underestimated the popular temper against the bank. When delegations went to the President, as Biddle had intended they should, to ask for relief from the financial distress sweeping over the land, Jackson would reply: "Come not to me, sir!—Go to the monster." And as time passed more and more people did turn against the "monster" until the net effect of Biddle's policy was to bring even more of the voting population to the view that the bank possessed too much power. Perhaps this was really why Biddle reversed his policy in mid-1834.

The battle still goes on as to whether Jackson served his country well by destroying the Second Bank of the United States. Hamiltonians insist that the result was an economic catastrophe, that an institution capable of bringing some order into the nation's financial system was a major necessity. Jeffersonians, on the other hand, urge that the bank was not a truly national bank in the sense that its administrators were responsible to the people but that its charter granted immense power to a small group of men. At the same time "Biddle's bank" was not a central bank within the modern meaning of that term, although it could and did perform some of the services of a central bank.[1] Since both of these views have merit, the verdict must perhaps be rendered in terms of the contribution the bank actually made to the economy. Here, however, an imponderable intervenes. If the issue is resolved in terms of the way the bank functioned at its best, the answer must clearly be adverse to Andrew Jackson. But if the test is to be the functioning of the bank at its worst, Nicholas Biddle and Henry Clay just as clearly come off second best.

One thing at least can be said. Several administration commitments were discharged by the destruction of the United States Bank. State banking interests, especially those in New York, were given a greater opportunity for expansion. The money-hungry South and West (especially the latter) were relieved of the restrictions imposed by the national bank against overissue, and eastern laborers were given what they thought was a "harder" circulating medium. Since, however, all these purposes could not be simultaneously served, it is no doubt legitimate that the desires of the agrarian West and South were met rather than those of the still tiny body of laborers.

New Progress in Transportation. With the ending of "Biddle's panic" prosperity began in earnest, a prosperity greatly aided by the relaxation of

[1] A central bank performs as one of its major functions the provision of a reservoir of credit which in ordinary circumstances is not used and can therefore be drawn upon in times of difficulty. In order to perform this function satisfactorily, it is generally understood that a central bank should not directly participate in the creation of ordinary commercial credit (i.e., it should not make loans directly to business firms). At this crucial point, the Second Bank of the United States bore no resemblance to a central bank.

the conservative influence in money and banking circles which Biddle had unquestionably provided. As money became easier, however, a normal and natural prosperity was converted into a dubious speculative fever which could have only one conclusion. But while the boom lasted much was accomplished that represented fundamental achievements in the nation's economic development.

For one thing this period saw the definitive beginning of the railroad as a part of America's transportation network. The railroad was not yet, to be sure, an important part of that network. Neither railroad technology nor American manufacturing were far enough advanced to push this development forward as rapidly as was later to be the case; not until this country became independent of England in both technology and the manufacture of locomotives did the railroad begin to compete effectively with other modes of transportation.

However, there was an even more basic reason why the railroad's development was initially slow. The nation was still in the grip of the craze to build canals, and until this mania spent itself no other medium of transportation could take the center of the stage. This fact affected the early fortunes of the railroad in two ways. First, the prevailing belief was that this medium would be primarily useful as a supplement to transportation by water—as a connecting link between waterways or between waterways and their hinterlands. Second, railway promoters and the capital behind the early railroads were typically more concerned with the water transportation business, and hence did not vigorously promote the new transportation. It is significant that the Baltimore and Ohio, one of the few early railroads built without any such orientation behind it, was the nation's first common carrier by rail.

To those who today take the railroad for granted in its present form, the beliefs and problems associated with its early development seem almost incomprehensible. There was, for example, the belief that the principal use of the railroad would be the transportation of passengers since such a high speed as five miles per hour would be most important for this kind of traffic. Another major issue was whether the railroads were to be public highways over which anyone might run his own vehicles, as was the practice with canals and turnpike. This procedure commended itself especially in those instances in which the state took a prominent part in building the railroad, although when actual operations began such a conception proved quickly impossible regardless of financial and other construction arrangements.

Indicative of the uses made of railroads during their early years, all the major Atlantic ports from Savannah to New York hastened to build lines westward to tap the adjacent hinterlands. Feeder lines were built from centers on the Great Lakes and on such rivers as the Illinois, the Ohio, and the Tennessee. The Pennsylvania Portage System contained two railroad links over difficult terrain which would not accommodate a canal. Whereever there were water transportation facilities in the middle 1830's men were thinking of making these more effective by means of rail extensions and interconnections.

Still, however, developments in the field of railroad transportation were only a part of the country's more general interest in improving its transportation in whatever ways possible. This period, in fact, saw the culmination of the internal improvement fever generated by the completion of the Erie Canal. Where canals were feasible, as in Ohio, New York, and Pennsylvania especially, the emphasis was on artificial waterways. Always roads were a part of the transportation extension actually under way. And where a railroad could effectively supplement water facilities, natural or otherwise, time and funds were expended on railroads. Everywhere states were burdening themselves with debt in order to improve their transportation facilities.

The reason for this burden of debt was simple enough. As far as road building was concerned, this activity had more and more become a government responsibility. And as for canals, there had never been any question of private responsibility for the securing of capital. The cost of any worth-while project was simply too great. As a result virtually all canals received support from state governments (although both local governments and the federal government also gave assistance) in one form or another. This support extended all the way from the use of the state's credit in borrowing money, through government construction and private operation, to government construction and operation. Perhaps the most interesting type of aid given was the occasional granting of banking privileges to transportation companies.

Internal Improvements and Speculation. No doubt Pennsylvania and New York had accumulated the largest debts in number of dollars. In each case the figure was well in excess of $10 million. Both states, moreover, had a great deal to show for these outlays. Pennsylvania, with nine hundred miles of canals and five hundred miles of railroads, had more canal miles and more railroad miles than any other state, as well as more than one-fourth of the nation's canal mileage and almost one-sixth of the total railroad miles. New York had somewhat fewer miles in both railroads and canals, but the economic value of her properties was substantially greater and her debt was consequently less burdensome.

In the South expenditures for internal improvements were smaller, although when measured against population, resources, or results achieved they were actually larger. Virginia contracted an indebtedness in excess of $6 million, while Maryland's exceeded this amount by one-third. Georgia in a single year authorized a loan of $1½ million to construct a railroad connection with the Tennessee River. Only in such states as North Carolina and Alabama were extensive expenditures in this field not made, and the reason was poverty much more than lack of enthusiasm.

It was in the West, however, that extravagance in transportation development reached its peak. Illinois and Indiana expended funds totaling almost as much as Pennsylvania and New York combined, despite their much more limited economic basis for such expenditure, and most of these funds were borrowed. Missouri and Michigan, relative to their population and resources, were equally extended. Of the major western states the most conservative of all was Ohio, but even here a sum of $8 million was spent on transportation facilities. And of Ohio it could at least be said that a great deal was achieved; in canal miles she ranked second in the nation. Most of these western projects were canals and roads rather than railroads, and many were technically feasible and ultimately economically useful projects. But unfortunately these projects were too many and too soon in terms of the stage of development then reached by the western economy. And the same was true, if to a lesser degree, in the southern states. The result was a burden of debt which in the end could not be paid.

Where did the capital come from to finance these mammoth undertakings? First, much foreign capital was attracted to the United States by the boom being experienced in Europe as well as in this country. Imports exceeded exports on the average by more than $20 million a year, and instead of withdrawing the balance in specie (which would quickly have

TABLE 21. EXPANSION BY BORROWING

	1830	1836
	(Millions of dollars)	
Merchandise exports	58.5	106.6
Merchandise imports	49.6	168.8
Silver imports (+) or exports (−)	+6.6	+2.4
Gold imports (+) or exports (−)	−0.6	+6.6

Source: Bureau of the Census, *Historical Statistics of the United States, 1789-1945*, p. 245.

put an end to America's speculative fever) foreigners instead shipped specie to the United States at a rate of several million dollars a year. In part this capital was finding its way directly into the new railroad industry, but in the main it was invested in the securities of states and municipalities, thus indirectly contributing to the overbuilding of this country's transportation facilities.

Second, aided by the flow of capital from abroad (and in part as only another way of looking at this fact), capital in America was transferred on a large scale from agriculture to transportation. At this time the United States rarely imported more than small quantities of foodstuffs. Yet during the prosperity of the middle 1830's imports of flour and grain averaged $6 million annually. In one year alone American exports of these products fell by $1 million while imports increased by $4½ million. (These developments were, it is true, accentuated by an especially severe attack of the Hessian wheat fly during this period, but historical scholarship has been unwilling to attribute this phenomenon entirely to American crop shortages.) This situation, of course, was only to be expected as long as high wages were being paid for construction work on projects which would never be able to pay even operating expenses.

These observations have to do only with the source of the *real* capital going into internal improvements. Equally important, and in some respects more so, was the financing of this speculative activity. A vast structure of credit was being built up by means of an unprecedented expansion of the nation's banking facilities. In the absence of any real restraint banks could be and were created out of virtually nothing. Specie, for example, would be paid into a bank in accordance with the terms of a loosely written state law, and when the charter had been officially granted it would be removed. The bank would then proceed to issue notes on the basis of little or no actual specie reserve.

In Michigan, the state having perhaps the most grandiose program of internal improvements, forty-nine banks were authorized during a single year with the privilege of issuing more than $4 million of bank notes based on almost no metallic reserve. Other southern and western states differed from Michigan only in degree, and throughout the country as a whole the

TABLE 22. PROSPERITY BY INFLATION

Year	Number of Banks	Capital	Circulation	Loans
			(Millions of dollars)	
1830	329	110.1	48.4	159.8
1834	506	200.0	94.8	324.1
1835	704	231.3	103.7	365.2
1836	713	251.9	140.3	457.5
1837	788	290.8	149.2	525.1

Source: Bureau of the Census, *Historical Statistics of the United States, 1789-1945*, pp. 263 and 265.

extent of overexpansion in construction activities correlated very closely with bank overexpansion. The number of banks increased well over 100 per cent, banking capital more than 150 per cent, and note circulation and loans more than 200 per cent—all in a period of seven years. Not for nothing has this period been named the "wildcat banking period." Moreover, "wildcat" here does not merely refer to the "wild" expansion which took place. Rather it means that the secret of the expansion going on was the establishment of banks in places so remote that only a wildcat could get to them to redeem notes in specie.

The expansion of bank credit, however, not only made possible speculative construction projects. It also contributed to another wave of land speculation, paralleling although far exceeding the similar experience of twenty years before. Every class in the population and every section of the country contributed to this phase of the economic life of the period. Real estate values in eastern cities rose rapidly, the value of cotton land in the South more than doubled in a period of a few years, and public sales of western lands increased from 5 million acres to 20 million acres in only two years.

Not only did the availability of bank credit contribute to speculation in land, but there was a reverse relationship. The more of the public domain that was sold the greater were the federal government's deposits in the "pet" banks. As these deposits grew they in turn furnished the basis for a still further expansion of bank credit and in this way made possible more speculation. Thus a vicious circle was set in motion by which speculation and bank overexpansion mutually reinforced one another.[2] This vicious circle even contributed to overexpansion in the internal improvements field because the higher the price of land within a state, and hence the value of its taxable property, the more was it encouraged to expand its indebtedness.

Expansion and Prosperity. Again, however, it is essential to emphasize that all this had its good side. Economic overexpansion and similar judgments are largely a retrospective evaluation; to most of the people living through such a period, a speculative boom is difficult to distinguish from mere prosperity. So it was in the 1830's and, just as many projects for transportation improvement proved of great value to the country, so too did an active interest in public lands bring about an accelerated rate of settlement in the West. And whereas expansion had earlier taken place most rapidly in the South, now it was most pronounced in the Upper Mississippi Valley. With this territory made more accessible by the development of transportation improvements, settlers eagerly sought the fertile, level land thus made available. As shown in Table 23, the popula-

[2] The term "speculation" can be broadly defined as buying and selling with the expectation of profiting from short-term changes in prices. In the case at hand, purchases of land were financed by bank credit. The availability of this expansible purchasing power helped push land prices up, thus inviting more speculators into the field. In turn, higher land prices and an increasing number of purchasers drew out even more bank credit and pushed prices still higher—and so on and on.

TABLE 23. GROWTH OF THE NEW NORTHWEST

Year	Population in			
	Ohio	Indiana	Illinois	Michigan
1820	581,295	147,178	55,162	8,765
1840	1,519,467	685,866	476,183	212,267

Source: Bureau of the Census, *Fourth and Sixth Censuses of Population.*

tion of Ohio tripled in a period of twenty years, while Indiana's more than quadrupled, Illinois' increased eight times, and Michigan grew from a few thousand to one-fifth of a million.

The filling in of the new Northwest greatly increased the agricultural surplus produced in that area. Interestingly enough, however, the route over which the new settlers traveled to their new homes was not the route over which these surpluses were sent to market. To be sure, much wheat and flour did find its way to the East as the transport cost between Buffalo and New York fell. But the Mississippi River still carried the bulk of this produce to New Orleans, and that city continued for a time to be a threatening rival to New York's position as the nation's Number One exporting center. The major effect of the improved facilities to the East was the maintenance of New Orleans prices at a higher level than would otherwise have been possible. A lesser result, but one destined to be of more permanent significance, was the emergence of certain lake points as important cities—points such as Chicago, Toledo, and Cleveland, where a waterway connected with one of the lakes.

The new westward expansion also had the inevitable result of advancing the "frontier" farther to the west. Now well past the Mississippi River barrier, energetic traders were developing a thriving business through Santa Fe with territory held by Mexico, as well as with frontier outposts as far west as California. Not large in total volume, this trade was nonetheless important for several reasons. It destroyed the last hope of the Indian for a permanent frontier against the white man by dispelling the myth of an impassable American desert. In addition the Santa Fe trade exposed for all to see the weakness of the Mexican hold on the Southwest, and established a friendly relationship between that territory and the United States. Already Americans were beginning to settle in these areas—and to look at Texas with covetous eyes. As so often in history the establishment of a trading relationship and the beginning of actual settlements were only precursors to more drastic moves. Thus it is not wholly a coincidence that Texas achieved a long-sought independence from Mexican rule in 1836.

No segment of the economy failed to enjoy the prosperity accompanying the speculative boom of the middle 1830's. One of the most solid achievements, one of those least marred by overextension, was the growth of manufacturing. On every front—woolens, shoes, cottons, leather, glass, flour milling, iron, and many others—production for sale continued to make gains in its war against household production. Moreover, progress in manufacturing was now beginning to take on a visible momentum which allowed this branch of the economy largely to free itself from the laborious struggle which had characterized its growth to this point.

The economic basis for this new momentum was also visible. Several separate developments, each one significant in its own right, were beginning to interrelate with one another in a cumulative fashion. Thus large-scale production is essentially geared to the size of available power units. These had typically been small because the wooden water wheel was itself relatively fragile. As the wooden wheel began to be replaced by an iron one the scale of output could be greatly increased. In turn, however, the wider use of iron was closely related to the use of coal rather than charcoal as the basic fuel, while the new anthracite-tidewater canals had contributed much toward making this improved fuel more generally accessible. So important was this complex of developments, in fact, that these canals were the only major ones constructed with virtually no public assistance. Iron was also the basis of a thriving young machine-tool industry, without which the epoch-making idea of interchangeable parts—one of the principal foundations on which modern industry rests—could never have been translated into reality.

TABLE 24. PRESSURE ON THE WORKER

Year	Cost of Living (1913 = 100)
1834	51
1835	60
1836	68
1837	72

Source: Bureau of the Census, *Historical Statistics of the United States, 1789-1945*, p. 235.

As manufacturing concerns multiplied in number and grew in size, more and more laborers fell under the domination of the industrial system. Unsuccessful in politics, incited to action by the threat to their real wages implicit in rising prices, and given their opportunity by the general prosperity, workers shifted from political to direct economic action. On the one hand, most of the important trades organized themselves for applying economic pressure against employers on a city-wide basis, this kind of organization having become indispensable now that workers within a sizable urban area had come into competition with one another. On the other hand, in a number of cities intertrade organizations were also formed for the purpose of seeking common goals on a broader front (for example, the ten-hour day). This period even saw the organization of the first national labor group—the National Trades Union—although economic conditions were not yet favorable for this kind of organization and in consequence it did not last long. The best indication of the success of these militant endeavors was the fact that aroused laborers soon found themselves confronted by counterassociations of disturbed employers.

With these developments the American labor movement took its first major step toward a "fighting" career. Simultaneously labor leaders learned to their sorrow that this kind of career was to be a tremendously difficult one. For one thing employers with the entire labor market to choose from and in possession of the facilities without which effective production could not be carried on had such a bargaining advantage over the individual worker that only a tightly organized labor group could cope with them successfully. Not until workers became thoroughly convinced that their future was inescapably linked with a wage-earning status could such organizations be formed on a significant enough scale to make a real difference in the lives of workers generally.

In the second place, and closely related to the employer's bargaining superiority, success along this road requires that workers without property must create for themselves certain "rights" which in a nation of farmers had traditionally "belonged" to "property." This transfer of rights was itself understandably considered revolutionary enough in a land made up essentially of private property owners, to say nothing of the semirevolutionary techniques used by laborers in accomplishing this goal. Given the bargaining power disadvantage of the worker and the public storm created by labor's first attempts to move in this direction, it is not to be wondered that the infant labor movement did not immediately conclude that its important gains would have to come by way of this approach.

Speculation and prosperity would themselves have altered substantially the context within which the major problems of the day had to be resolved. Unfortunately, before much progress had been made toward resolving them within this context, inflation gave way to deflation and depression. At the same time, however, the heritage of the boom did contribute to the difficulties encountered when once more these problems rose to the surface.

QUESTIONS FOR DISCUSSION

1. What would have been the consequences for the country of the success of the nullification challenge? Why did it fail?

2. Was Jackson or Biddle the more nearly right about the value to the country of the Second Bank of the United States?

3. What is speculation? What are the relationships between speculation and prosperity?

4. How did land speculation contribute to the internal improvement program of this period?

5. Where was the capital secured which went into internal improvement projects? What is the difference between credit and capital?

6. Did the expansion of the banking system in the 1830's contribute to capital formation, or do banks only add to an economy's outstanding credit?

7. How was international trade interrelated with the prosperity of this decade?

8. Is it "fair" for laborers through organization to exercise power over "private" property?

Chapter 13

GROWING PAINS

1836 "Deposit Act" passed.
"Specie Circular" issued.
1837 Martin Van Buren became President.
Prosperity ended in panic.
Abolitionist controversy in Congress.
1838 "Specie Circular" repealed.
1839 Depression deepened.
1840 Independent Treasury created.
1841 John Tyler became President at the death of William Henry Harrison.
Independent Treasury Act repealed.
Pre-emption Act.
1842 Tariff increased.

The Problem of the Government's Surplus. The most fundamental problem brought about by prosperity was one never before encountered and one never to be encountered again in so acute form. The government was receiving more money than it knew what to do with. Whereas the tariff adjustment had been made largely because the revenue was excessive, an expanding level of imports had kept the decline in customs receipts to a much lower figure than had been anticipated. Even more important, however, speculation in the public lands was bringing into the Treasury a stream of revenue which in 1836 exceeded the customs—the only time in the nation's history when this was the case. With the national debt now completely extinguished, a surplus was rapidly accumulating in the Treasury.

Inevitably the controversy over the disposition of the public lands merged with the problem of this accumulating surplus. The public lands, after all, were the source of the difficulty. Moreover, the nature of the problem was such as to give particular weight to the solution offered by the West, altered though this solution was as a result of the speculative boom. Graduation was still insisted upon, but a new demand was also appearing. What the West now wanted was the restriction of land sales

TABLE 25. TOO MUCH MONEY

Year	Customs Receipts	Public Land Revenues	Surplus
		(Millions of dollars)	
1830	21.9	2.3	9.7
1831	24.2	3.2	13.3
1832	28.5	2.6	14.6
1833	29.0	4.0	10.9
1834	16.2	4.9	3.2
1835	19.4	14.8	17.9
1836	23.4	24.9	20.0

Source: Bureau of the Census, *Historical Statistics of the United States, 1789-1945*, p. 297.

to actual settlers. The recent experience with speculators buying large quantities of government land at the government's fixed price, and then reselling it to settlers at values inflated by real estate speculation, had been most annoying to the West.

Measures curbing speculation were not well received in the East, although easterners were still willing to see the public lands reduced in importance as a source of government revenue. But in the view of eastern manufacturers and property owners, a lower price was not the way to achieve this end, and hence Henry Clay's distribution proposal still won favor in that section of the country.

The sympathies of the South were all with the West as far as land speculation was concerned, although southerners could not afford to see the public lands made permanently less important among the government's revenue assets. At the same time, however, southerners admitted the necessity of doing something about the growing and sharply inflationary surplus in the "pet" banks. Accordingly, as still a third solution to the problem at hand, Calhoun suggested "depositing" the *accumulated* surplus with the states. The result of this move would be to provide needy states with capital for use in completing their internal improvement programs more rapidly than would otherwise be possible, while still leaving the public land revenues intact over the longer run as against the day when the compromise tariff would expire.

The Calhoun proposal gained friends outside the region in which it originated more readily than either of the other alternatives. To westerners it had the advantage of providing funds to assist them in their expansion plans, while at the same time it was not permanent legislation as Clay's distribution bill would have been. Easterners were somewhat less interested at this point in transportation projects, but they too could appreciate the fact that Calhoun's measure did not prevent them from later achieving their own objectives on a more permanent basis. On June 23, 1836, the "deposit" bill was signed by the President, and controversy over the problem of the government surplus abruptly ceased.

Prosperity Comes to an End. The controversy over the land question, however, did not. While there was nothing more Congress could do for the moment, Andrew Jackson was not satisfied. Neither was Martin Van Buren. Motivated by his western upbringing and a consequent dislike of speculation (especially paper money speculation), Jackson sympathized with the western desire to restrict public land sales to settlers. Motivated by the strong support he had always received from eastern laborers and by labor opposition to the use of state bank notes as money, Van Buren desired to see the use of metallic money increased in the nation's circulating medium. On July 11 an important step was taken which helped to achieve both of these objectives. By executive decree Jackson issued the so-called "Specie Circular" requiring that payment for the public lands must henceforth be in gold or silver.

As Andrew Jackson by destroying the restraining influence of the United States Bank had earlier accentuated the speculative boom, so now did Andrew Jackson contribute to the end of prosperity by the "Specie Circular." By reducing the acceptability of bank notes in money transactions, the President's order increased the demand for specie. But since specie is much more efficiently used when concentrated in banks as reserves for note and deposit money, one consequence of bringing more specie into circulation was the calling in of loans. Specie was still far too scarce to permit its widespread use as *circulating* money.

While the money market was tightening as a result of the "Specie Circular," the machinery for giving effect to the "deposit" act was generating similar tendencies. Government funds deposited in state banks variously located throughout the country had to be paid out to the states on the basis of the federal ratio. Although this meant that some sections of the country would achieve a net gain in banking assets, certain other sections were forced still further to retrench. The "deposit" measure, in fact, was one reason why depression struck first in the East and only later in the South and West.

One other factor contributed to the conjuncture of circumstances now bringing an end to American prosperity. England had also been enjoying a period of speculative prosperity, a prosperity devoted largely to railroad construction. This period of rapid capital formation was accompanied, just as in the United States, by an expansion of banking facilities to the point where specie coverage had stretched very thin. While this process was still going on the American Congress had enacted a coinage law altering the ratio of silver to gold from fifteen-to-one to sixteen-to-one, a move to correct the previous undervaluation of gold at the American mint. Unfortunately for America's bimetallic monetary system and England's unstable equilibrium, the new ratio overvalued gold at the American mint. The result was a change in the par of exchange between pounds and dollars favoring the exportation of gold from England in exchange for American goods or securities.

Toward the end of 1836 the Bank of England found itself forced to raise its discount rate and to refuse bills drawn on many of the newly created English banks. In November the Irish banking system was kept afloat only by shipping two million pounds sterling in gold from the Bank of England, and in March, 1837, three Anglo-American concerns were unable to meet their obligations. A chain of events was thus set in motion in England generating a scramble for specie in the United States and compelling New York financial houses to call on southern planters for payment. Neither of these expedients was successful. Much of America's specie was flowing over the Appalachians for use in buying land, and cotton planters were unable to make the payments called for as a result of a decline in the price of cotton.

Deflationary factors of this sort are not necessarily fundamental to the onset of a serious depression such as was now threatening the nation. As long as the flow of investment continues, the economy can remain active and full employment can continue.[1] It is only when outlets for investment begin to seem less attractive and the rate of capital formation falls off that retrenchment is enforced throughout the economy. To be sure, it is possible for monetary factors alone to precipitate a decline in the rate of investment, but this sequence of events is rarely true to life and it seems definitely not to have been the case in 1837. In both the United States and England the rate of canal, road, and railroad building was already tapering off before the more purely monetary factors intervened. The industrializing world was simply endeavoring to develop along certain lines at a rate more rapid than could be sustained.

This falling off of investment was not an auspicious environment within which to launch deflationary forces such as the "Specie Circular" and the "deposit" of the surplus. In March, 1837, the pressure was severely enough felt in New Orleans to produce near-panic conditions there. By May a similar pressure was building up in New York, and on May 10 New York banks suspended specie payments. Almost any other city in the country

[1] It is now generally agreed among economists (this is a part of what has come to be called "Keynesian" economics) that the most crucial factor in the ups and downs of economic activity is the rate of investment. If the desire to create new capital for use in the production process falls without a corresponding increase in the desire to spend current income for consumption purposes, unemployment must appear. One of the sets of circumstances under which this is apt to happen, moreover, is a situation in which investment has been expanded to what might be called a temporary saturation point.

could have suspended without generating financial panic throughout the country. Within ten days most of the banks of the country had followed suit, and America was once again on a paper standard consisting of depreciated state bank notes.

This breakdown of the nation's monetary system was soon followed by a paralysis of general business activity. Foreign trade was drastically curtailed, factories began to close their doors, businesses failed by the score, and laborers by the thousands walked the streets in search of work. Understandably the impact was felt most painfully in the East, for here the growth of the interdependence which is a part of the industrialization process had been carried furthest. In the South and West good crops kept these sections of the country in a fair economic condition (despite low prices) for the time being.

Throughout the remainder of 1837 and into 1838 business stagnation continued. One factor especially seemed to prevent New York from moving off dead center. With the suspension of specie payments coins had disappeared from circulation, their place being taken by bank notes of small denomination. But since state laws did not permit New York banks to issue such bills, the notes circulating in New York were from outside the state—often the notes of unknown or even bankrupt institutions. A monetary environment less conducive to business expansion could scarcely be imagined. In February, 1838, this situation was greatly improved by legislation lifting New York's ban on small denomination paper.

Shortly thereafter another step was taken which helped pave the way for an improvement in the financial situation in New York. To this point bank charters everywhere had been granted by special acts of state legislatures. Public criticism had long been directed against this procedure on the ground that valuable privileges were thus given to individuals on a monopoly basis. Furthermore, this granting of special charters was often accompanied by fraud and/or corruption. Only the onset of depression, however, developed sufficient force behind an alternative procedure to see it enacted into legislation. Now, providing a model which was soon to be adopted by state after state, New York took steps (in the words of Governor Marcy) to "open the business of banking to a full and free competition under such general restrictions and regulations as are necessary to insure to the public at large a sound currency." This opening up of the banking field plus the steps simultaneously taken to safeguard note issues seemed to raise the morale of New York business to a significant extent.

Meanwhile, the economy was receiving a boost from another source. Largely through the initiative of Nicholas Biddle, now head of a major Pennsylvania-chartered institution, an arrangement was worked out whereby the losses of eastern banks on cotton paper could be minimized. The price of cotton had fallen so low that even possession of cotton did not save banks from heavy losses. Biddle's plan was to keep American cotton off the world market until the price improved. Accordingly an agency of Biddle's new bank was set up in England to handle the financial transactions at that end. Extremely successful at first, the plan was soon carried to the point where Biddle and his bank were exercising a significant control over the cotton market and reaping large profits—on paper.

The combined effect of these and other favorable factors was to touch off another wave of speculation. Business and especially banking confidence improved so markedly that specie payments were resumed in the spring of 1838, assisted by the overwhelming repeal on May 30 of the ill-fated "Specie Circular." Speculative internal improvement ventures, an activity which had received a severe setback during the panic months, again went forward, as did bank expansion—despite a large number of bank failures the preceding year. And although the flow of foreign capital to this country had also been checked by the onset of depression, America's quick "recovery" opened up these channels once more and the flow began anew.

Unfortunately it was all a mirage. The economic readjustment required on this occasion was not to be accomplished so quickly. In 1839 commodity prices declined once more, another flurry of bank and other failures occurred, foreign trade declined still further, and unemployment again rose. Toward the end of the year the banks south and west of New York suspended specie payments for the second time, and one of the most noteworthy incidents associated with this phase of the depression rapidly enveloping the nation was the failure of Biddle's bank and its disappearance from the American scene. From this point until the depression had spent itself, every section of the nation felt its baneful influence, agricultural West and South no less than industrial East. Moreover, its duration was not destined to be short.

Old Problems in a New Setting. It was this context of panic and depression which furnished the background for another economic battle between the sections as long unsettled issues once again came to the surface. As always, proponents of the various interests sought to turn a new situation to their own advantage, and soon Senator Benton was urging a policy of graduating the price of the public lands on President Van Buren—as a way of increasing the government's revenue. This was not mere chicanery, either, despite the fact that graduation had so recently been held to be a way of *reducing* the income of the government. In 1839 it was not at all unreasonable to suggest that under the impact of depression enough people would take advantage of a reduction in the price of the public lands actually to increase Treasury income from that source.

Henry Clay's solution to the land problem was also presented from an altered vantage point. To date the western states had been so successful in financing their improvement programs by means of bank credit and foreign capital that distribution of the proceeds of public land sales had not been especially appealing. Now, however, these sources of capital were becoming less abundant at just the moment that funds were desperately needed to finish projects already under way. Even some of the southern states were vulnerable to an appeal to support distribution stated in terms of their own keen desire to complete important transportation projects. But, unfortunately for Clay's presidential ambitions, the distribution approach was dead—although only for the moment. To suggest giving the government's tax resources to the states in the face of a mounting federal deficit would scarcely have been considered statesmanlike.

Benton's argument supporting graduation may have had some influence on Van Buren's thinking. Another factor, however, was a much more important reason for the administration's adopting the West's program at this point. The nation's laborers, once again thrown by economic depression into the political arena, were currently making several insistent demands, demands the President was striving desperately to meet.

Actually, there was reason enough for an administration motivated by the interests of the working man to support the West's land program on its merits. As early as the 1820's labor leaders had begun to take a strong stand on the matter of making the public domain freely available to the "poor," and during the 1830's this idea grew in importance in labor circles. The National Trades Union went on record as favoring the disposition of the public lands in such a way that every citizen would have "a just claim to an equitable portion thereof, a location upon which being the only just title thereto." Another labor leader deplored "the practice of reserving the public lands for the benefit of speculators and wild beasts, while thousands of God's children have not where to lay their heads." Still a third took an even more radical position: "We have proposed, and do propose that the public lands should no longer be sold, but that any man, unpossessed of land, should be allowed to take possession of a certain portion of the unappropriated domain for the purpose of cultivation."

That Van Buren did not, however, adopt a liberal land program on its merits is equally apparent. The reason was that another demand was at the moment more important to the worker, and the administration's land policy clearly reflected this weighting of issues.

For many years the urban laborer had been rising up against monopolies in general and banks in particular. At first the chief complaints had been the monopoly, class-privilege aspects of banking, and the fact that labor was often forced to accept wage payments in depreciated state bank notes. More recently two new objections had been added—a prosperity complaint against the erosion of the worker's standard of living as a result of rising prices, and, with the coming of depression, an outcry against a widespread unemployment which could be attributed with some logic to the malfunctioning of banks. New York's "free banking" law was one phase of this reaction, but laborers also desired a more substantial achievement. Their aim was federal legislation reducing the importance of state bank notes in the nation's currency. No doubt labor leaders thought they had succeeded when the "Specie Circular" was issued, but with its repeal it was clear that the task had to be accomplished all over again.

Van Buren's response to this demand was a measure popularly called the subtreasury system, a proposal to divorce the operations of the government completely from the banks. Since neither a national bank such as the nation had twice experimented with nor the use of state banks as depositories would accomplish the desired end, the solution indicated seemed to be some procedure whereby the government handled its own funds without using the banks as intermediaries and thus providing a basis for artificially expanding the money supply. Such a procedure in turn would provide a foundation for a larger use of coin in monetary transactions, a carrying further of the program the "Specie Circular" had begun.

Unfortunately, Van Buren's proposal could not be passed on a direct appeal for support, and one of the principal centers of opposition was the West. The western farmer might abhor the idea of a national bank, but he was no enemy of banks. At the same time, when he was asked to choose between a liberal land policy and government funds in state banks he quickly chose the former. Thus it was that the administration supported the West on land legislation while westerners supported the subtreasury.

The South also was prepared to support the subtreasury proposal. Southerners, too, were agrarians, but agrarians of a very different stripe from westerners. Here an insistence on state rights was still an extremely important point, and many southern leaders would go to some lengths to defend this interpretation of the Constitution. Already the South had seen centralization in the form of a national bank and in the form of selected "pet" banks fail. More important, by 1839 southerners were becoming sensitive over their economic dependence on the North. At the same time it was obvious how disparate the banking resources of the South and the North were, and it seemed logical to conclude that this disparity in bank capital was causally related to the more general dependence. If the government's deposited funds were distributed in the same way as private banking capital—and there was no reason why they should be distributed any more favorably to the interests of the South—the result would be to accentuate the superiority of the industrial East. An arrangement separating the government from banking might throw each region onto its own resources and thus give the South a better opportunity to develop a more balanced economy. No doubt there was much wishful thinking here, but it is equally certain that these considerations won many a vote for the subtreasury.

In this preoccupation with the South's economic "vassalage" to the North, southern leaders were unquestionably nearer the heart of the South's difficulty than when attention was directed to the tariff. This is not because the tariff issue was unimportant; it was never that. Rather two other factors were primarily involved. On the one hand, so easy is it to blame others instead of one's self when misfortunes arise that there existed an unwholesome tendency for southerners to overemphasize the tariff. On the other hand, even if the tariff were as important as many South Carolinians believed, the fact still remained that the burden fell on the South as heavily as it did primarily because of her exclusively agrarian economy.

Even so, however, an emphasis on banking was still a far cry from the most crucial point at issue. The South might well have studied more carefully the lesson taught by the experience of New England. When protective tariff legislation had continued to be enacted over her opposition, she had forthwith developed an economy which could share in the fruits of such a policy. To be sure, the South was not thinking seriously at this time of developing a manufacturing economy, but the same principle applied to another aspect of economic "vassalage" with which many southerners were actively concerned. That was the South's trade with Europe. Here was an obvious drain on the South's economy, a leakage of wealth which could be stopped only by determined action. But, since the South was unwilling to perform such services for herself, it was futile to suggest surface remedies such as banking legislation.

Not only were southerners willing to go along with the worker on banking legislation, but they were even ready to accept the western view of a desirable land policy. It was not that the South was any more anxious to reduce the government's land revenue than it had ever been. The contrary was more nearly true. But the compromise tariff was due to expire shortly and protection would once again be an important issue. Before the West could be expected to support lower duties, the South must bend its efforts toward helping the West achieve the policies it most wanted.

This formidable combination of western farmers, southern farmers, and eastern laborers succeeded in getting both an "Independent Treasury" measure and a graduation bill through the Senate. Both items, however, were defeated in the House where the eastern business interests were more strongly represented. This was the way matters stood as another presidential campaign got under way in late 1839, and as two other factors intervened to complicate the controversies in which the nation's leaders were now engaged.

The Independent Treasury. The first of these complicating factors had to do with a significant change in public land thinking in the West. Although graduation continued to be desirable to westerners, still another demand was beginning to rival it in importance. As the frontier pushed westward it frequently happened that the settler moved in ahead of the surveyor and set up an "illegal" occupance. Later, when the land was sold by the government to another settler or a speculator, ugly difficulties arose between "good faith" purchasers and men who had sunk their labor and a little capital into permanent improvements but who were only "trespassers" as far as the law was concerned. The rise in the price of land together with active speculation in land had raised this problem to acute proportions. As a solution the West was now asking for "pre-emption," legislation giving the actual settler first chance to buy the land he occupied on the same terms as any other first purchaser. Actually for some years "retrospective" pre-emption had been granted on a temporary basis for the benefit of those settlers actually caught in this unpleasant situation. The demand for *permanent* pre-emption, therefore, meant something else. It meant that the settler would be given a real advantage over the speculator in unsurveyed territory as far as selecting the best land was concerned. He could take his choice without fear of later difficulties.

The second complication was an outgrowth of the depression rather than the preceding prosperity. With business depressed and land values well below their inflation peaks, many states found themselves unable to meet the foreign obligations they had incurred. Most of these states being western, here was another important key to those issues involving the land question. In its financial embarrassment relative to outside creditors the nation could perhaps legitimately consider Clay's erstwhile distribution proposal. Distributed funds, implicitly earmarked for debt payment, would seem to have a claim on the country's financial resources second only to the need of the central government itself. The business interests eagerly grasped at this straw. Not only was it to their advantage that the credit rating of Americans remain good, but this still seemed the surest road to a higher tariff at the end of the compromise period.

The interest of the businessman in the precarious financial position of the states first appeared in connection with the presidential campaign—and in a most unfortunate way. On October 18, 1839, Baring Brothers of England issued a circular declaring that the completion of the elaborate internal improvement network in the United States would require a more substantial credit foundation than was available, and that a national pledge would make it possible for capital to be raised in any part of Europe. When Whig leaders, speaking for the business interests, began to talk openly of federal assumption of state debts or the use of the proceeds of public land sales for this purpose, a cry of foreign interventionism was promptly raised. The Whigs immediately denied foreign influence, but were henceforth forced to work toward this end by indirection—by way of Clay's timeworn distribution proposal.

Because of the many complexities involved, it was not until 1840 that Van Buren was able to deliver on his labor promises, although the achievements of that year must have gone far toward justifying labor's faith in its New York champion. By an executive order it was decreed that all work under government contract was henceforth to be organized on the basis of a ten-hour day. For a number of years labor had been pressuring private employers to make ten hours the standard day's work, and with some little success, and more recently the government as an employer had been placed under a similar pressure. While the President's order, even though it did stipulate that the day's pay was not to be reduced with the hours, was not all that was desired—leaving as it did much to the discretion of the employing agency—it was as much as a President of the United States could do with his power alone. And the federal government as a whole was not notably prolabor at this point.

In 1840 also the Independent Treasury bill finally succeeded in passing the House, a victory all the more sweet to laborers because of the bitter opposition of the business interests—especially Nicholas Biddle, Henry Clay, and Daniel Webster. When the bill was signed by the President on July 4 many a laborer must have felt that its passage signaled an emancipation from "serfdom" scarcely less far-reaching than another Declaration of Independence sixty-four years earlier.

It is common for evolution to halt at intervals between advances. On the other hand it is rare for an evolution to take a long step backward. Certainly, however, progress toward an effective money and banking system did in the Independent Treasury System take a backward step as long as could readily be imagined. It contributed nothing either to the search for a more uniform currency or the need for greater financial stability. On the contrary, it directly threatened the circulating medium by forcing the nation to rely more heavily on metal in the face of a specie shortage, and at the same time subjected the economy to arbitrary currency withdrawals and additions as the government's revenue now exceeded and now fell short of its revenues.

Henry Clay's Frustration. By mid-1840 it was time once again to select candidates for the presidency. For obvious reasons Whig (the party of the business interests) attention was focused primarily on the problem of attracting western votes. Webster was, of course, out of the question because of his close connection with eastern manufacturers. Clay's Kentucky residence was in his favor, but he was so closely identified with the distribution measure which the West opposed that he could not be considered.

Instead William Henry Harrison, the hero of Tippecanoe, was nominated and represented as possessing liberal views on the land question. This fact plus the depression with which Van Buren's administration was now identified won for Harrison a sweeping victory at the polls.

In view of the Whig success in the West, it might have been thought that the party's strength would at least have been thrown behind a pre-emption measure. But Henry Clay had different ideas, and the fact that he was not the party's standard bearer did not mean that he was not the party's leader. This few people doubted, least of all Henry Clay, and the Kentuckian promptly laid out the legislative program "his" party was to enact. On the land question Clay chose to assume that the election had been a referendum on distribution.

There can be little question that Clay's efforts would have been successful if the fates had not dealt him a particularly underhanded blow. In making the intersectional appeal for votes that is necessary to win the American presidency, the Whigs had put up John Tyler of Virginia as their candidate for Vice-President. Tyler was a strong states-righter as well as a southerner, but one who had become alienated from Andrew Jackson in the nullification controversy and never returned to Democratic ranks. Tyler's following was large enough to make it worth the while of the business interests to reward him, and on March 4, 1841, he was in consequence sworn in as the nation's choice for the presidency should anything happen to William Henry Harrison. When Harrison died one month after his inauguration, "His Accidency" became President, much to the chagrin of Clay and many of his colleagues.

The first item on Clay's agenda was quickly achieved. On June 4, 1841, the Independent Treasury Act was repealed. The objective here was to destroy the mechanism by means of which the government handled its funds, defective though this mechanism undoubtedly was, so that opposition to Clay's next item, a new national bank, would be minimized.

Congressional action on Clay's bank bill gave a foretaste of what was to come. Although the bill was passed with little difficulty, it was apparent that the Tyler Whigs had already abandoned Clay's program. It could not, therefore, have surprised anyone very much when Tyler vetoed the bank bill on constitutional grounds. In the Senate the veto could not be overridden.

Meanwhile action had commenced on a land bill. Clay's basic proposal was a bonus of 10 per cent of the proceeds of land sales plus five hundred thousand acres of land to each western state, the rest of the proceeds to be distributed to all the states on the basis of the federal ratio. Despite the bonus this measure could not be passed without a great deal more "sweetening." To satisfy southern Whigs a proviso had to be added whereby distribution would cease whenever the duty level rose above the

20 per cent maximum specified in the compromise. For westerners two other measures were necessary to assure passage. The first was permanent pre-emption. The second was a national bankruptcy act.

It is ironical that both of these measures thrown in to satisfy the West were of greater importance for America's history than the distribution measure purchased by them. Pre-emption became a permanent part of the country's land policy to the great inconvenience of eastern speculators. The Federal Bankruptcy Act was in all probability an even greater inconvenience, even though it was repealed five years later. By its terms some $500 million in debts owed to a million or so creditors were wiped out or greatly reduced.

The distribution measure was signed by the President on August 26, 1841, Tyler taking pains to observe that his acceptance of it relied on the provision whereby distribution should cease if the compromise tariff was violated. Shortly thereafter a second bank bill was presented to the President. This measure too was vetoed, Tyler maintaining (and correctly) that the changes made to satisfy his constitutional objections were superficial and not substantive. The fact was that agrarian America would not accept the bank wanted by industrial America if it could help it. And apparently it could as long as Tyler was in the White House. Although the second bank veto precipitated a crisis in Whig circles and Tyler was read out of the party, Clay and his followers did have to bear with the fact that John Tyler was still President.

The next matter to which Clay directed the attention of Congress was the problem of the government's revenue. For several years the Treasury had been running a deficit, and the government was even now operating on the basis of loans which met with considerable resistance abroad as a result of the failure of several states to pay their foreign creditors. No one questioned the necessity for raising additional revenue; no one, furthermore, seriously doubted that this must be done primarily by raising the tariff. The controversy was to arise in connection with distribution. Could the tariff be increased and distribution still be retained?

Henry Clay was determined that this be done. His strategy was delay. Fortified by an interpretation of existing tariff laws which held that no customs revenue could be collected after June 30, 1842, unless another revenue measure were passed, Congress waited until almost the end of June before presenting Tyler with a revenue bill. It was essentially a trial balloon. The last reduction under the compromise, scheduled to take effect June 30, was postponed until August 1, and distribution was to continue. If Tyler would approve a measure involving a *small* abrogation of the compromise, and agree to a continuation of distribution at the same time, Clay would have his foot firmly in the door.

TABLE 26. NOT ENOUGH MONEY

Year	Customs Receipts	Public Land Revenues	Surplus (+) Deficit (−)
		(Millions of dollars)	
1836	23.4	24.9	+20.0
1837	11.2	6.8	−12.3
1838	16.2	3.1	− 7.6
1839	23.1	7.1	+ 4.5
1840	13.5	3.3	− 4.8
1841	14.5	1.4	− 9.7
1842	18.2	1.3	− 5.2
1843	7.0	0.9	− 3.6
1844	26.2	2.1	+ 7.0

Source: Bureau of the Census, *Historical Statistics of the United States, 1789-1945*, p. 297.

As it turned out, however, John Tyler would not. Maintaining that existing revenue laws continued in force until superseded, Tyler vetoed the "little tariff." In early August the Whigs defiantly placed a second tariff measure before the President, a general increase also calling for the continuance of distribution. This bill too was returned with a veto. Swallowing their wrath and their pride the Whigs now sent the tariff measure to Tyler again, shorn of the distribution provision. Because of the condition of the Treasury, Tyler signed it. Henry Clay's cherished distribution scheme was once and for all laid to rest.

With the failure of distribution the last hope of federal aid to defaulting states faded. Already, moreover, some of the states had unequivocally signified their intention not to pay. A combination of circumstances was probably responsible for this repudiation. Agrarians broadly identified the depression with the banks, and everywhere men had seen banks fail and not repay outstanding liabilities. Furthermore, the federal government and most of the states had passed legislation forgiving debts and otherwise lessening the burden of debtor-creditor relationships. While banks and governments condoned and even encouraged nonrepayment as between neighbors, foreign creditors could not hope to collect.

John Tyler's four years in the White House excellently illustrate how weak the business interests in the United States still were. Their first real achievement of national power in some twenty years, it was their misfortune that they were unable to achieve it without the assistance of economic interests alien to their own. Of course, their achievements would have been much greater if Harrison had lived, but it is only additional evidence of their weakness that they were unable to make their bid for power with one of their own leaders rather than a man whose only claim to public popularity was a thirty-year-old victory over the Indians at Tippecanoe Creek.

QUESTIONS FOR DISCUSSION

1. What was the problem of the surplus? Why did different groups see it so differently?
2. How did the "Specie Circular" and the "Deposit" Act contribute to the outbreak of panic?
3. What factors outside the United States contributed to the "Panic of 1837"?
4. Could the "Panic of 1837" have been avoided? Would the nation have been better off if this episode had not occurred?
5. Why is it easier to secure economic reforms in periods of depression than in periods of prosperity?
6. How did depression alter the views of the various economic interests toward the land question?
7. Who gained by the creation of the Independent Treasury? In what ways?
8. Did the economy of the nation gain or suffer from Henry Clay's failure to enact his program into law?

Chapter 14

THE FRUITS OF DEPRESSION

1842	Improved bank legislation in Louisiana.
	Dorr Rebellion.
	Commonwealth v. Hunt.
1843	Beginning of political nativism.
1844	James K. Polk elected President.
1845	Texas annexed.
	"Manifest Destiny" phrase originated.
1846	Mexican War began.
	Oregon boundary settled.
	Walker tariff.
	Independent Treasury restored.

Whether or not it is true that depressions are not unmixed evils, it is certainly true that they are eventful periods. The decline in business is not necessarily, of course, wholly responsible for the changes which take place; often long-standing problems simply stand out in sharper focus during such times. But, be that as it may, the economic depression associated with John Tyler's four years in the White House brought a multitude of significant developments in its wake, some of which permanently altered the structure of the American economy.

Better Banking in New York and Louisiana. One of the most dynamic areas was the field of banking, where states as well as the nation were endeavoring to find a solution to pressing problems. As the nation developed more and more of an exchange economy, the need for an adequate banking system was acknowledged by virtually everyone. Metallic money, however useful in retaining public confidence in paper circulation, was too inconvenient (as well as too scarce) to serve the country's currency needs effectively. Yet, on the other hand, the nation had not yet learned to use a paper system in such a way as to prevent money panics and inflations from convulsing the economy at intervals. Admittedly, of course, a search for liquidity in a highly developed exchange economy is bound to produce painful consequences, and the problem was, therefore, how to cushion the system against shocks of a less comprehensive nature.

The first major attempt to solve this problem had been the Suffolk System. However, this solution had been slow to expand beyond such places as Boston and New York, and by now it was plain that improvements in banking practices on a more general basis would have to be brought about by governmental action. Bank overextension was too profitable, in the absence of strong penalties, for self-restraint to be very successful. Moreover, with the failure of centralization, it was evident that state action would be required.

Shortly after the Suffolk System was established in New England, New York had tried another expedient. This innovation called for a contribution by every bank of 3 per cent of its capital into a protective fund administered by the State Treasurer. Designed to protect depositors and noteholders of failing institutions, such a step had some merit. But it did not strike at the root of the problem, which was to keep bank failures from occurring rather than to avoid the worst consequences of failure.

When the "free banking" law was passed, an attempt had been made to remedy this defect. Every bank was required to deposit with the state comptroller United States bonds, state bonds, or real estate mortgages in exchange for which an equal amount of bank notes could be issued. Furthermore, every bank was required to redeem notes in specie on demand. These provisions were widely copied by other states and later became the model in some respects for a *national* banking system. Immediately, however, it was of less assistance in New York than it might have been because a bank could obviously be no sounder than the security deposited with the state. Not until this part of the law was revised to permit the deposit only of Federal and New York bonds did it really serve the purpose for which it was intended.

In other respects, too, the "free banking" movement was not all net gain. Without rigorous standards governing the establishment of banks, it was still possible for banks which the economy did not need to be organized by men who knew nothing about banking. Thus Michigan's early experience with "free banking" ended in disaster, although the problem here was as much the failure to enforce the specie provisions of the law as imperfections in the law itself.

Another approach to the banking problems was the state-owned bank. Experience with these institutions indicated once again that the important factor was not the institutional arrangements made but the principles followed in operating the institutions created. Indiana's state bank was conservatively administered and highly successful. Mississippi, on the other hand, created a state bank which was speculatively financed and which consequently failed to survive the panic.

Two further steps were taken in 1842, a landmark year in the history of American banking. One was the decision of New York to use the safety fund to protect only noteholders rather than depositors *and* noteholders. Two considerations were apparently involved. First, the fund had given out in the recent depression and there was good reason for trying to avoid a repetition of this unfortunate episode. Second, if a choice had to be made between noteholders and depositors, as was apparently the case, the depositor rather than the noteholder should be sacrificed. Noteholders had very little choice as to whether or not they would use bank notes, whereas depositors still had a fairly free choice whether they would or would not become bank creditors. Put differently, the idea was that protection was required not so much for the people doing business with a bank as for the major function performed by the banking system—that of supplying the community with a medium of exchange.

The second 1842 development, and much the more important one, was a new banking law in Louisiana. Spurred into action by the failure of a land bank, a new departure in government regulation was inaugurated. A 100 per cent reserve against public liabilities was required, of which one-third was to be in specie and two-thirds in ninety-day commercial paper. In addition banks were forbidden to pay out any notes except their own, and under a rigid system of supervision interbank obligations had to be cleared each week. So stringent was this regulation that, although the Louisiana law was technically a "free-banking" law, only a few banks of importance were chartered.

The small number of banks chartered in Louisiana, however, was not the most important reason for the success of this innovation. For the first time the emphasis in control was placed upon reserves against *total* liabilities, rather than against bank notes only as heretofore. Similarly the requirement that two-thirds of a bank's reserves had to be commercial paper was an insistence upon elasticity hitherto unknown in banking regulation.[1] The backing of notes by ninety-day paper rather than long-term bonds and real estate loans related bank operations much more closely to the state of business; contraction or expansion in the underlying economy could more easily be accompanied by contraction or expansion in note circulation without paralyzing panics or runaway inflations.

[1] "Elasticity" in monetary arrangements can best be understood in terms of what is called the "quantity theory of money." Thus it is emphasized that an increase or a decrease in the volume of money in circulation *relative to the volume of business being transacted* must inevitably be accompanied by an increase or a decrease in the price level. Relating money in circulation to deposit money has seemed by many to be an ideal way of permitting an increase in money where necessitated by business expansion and at the same time avoiding an increase great enough to disturb price relationships. The difference between this approach and the use of securities and mortgages for this purpose is especially worthy of note.

Too much credit, of course, should not be given to Louisiana, nor too much criticism to the rest of the country for not quickly following suit. It is especially to be noted that New Orleans was the center of a thriving export trade, receiving every week large quantities of gold and silver from Latin America, and that in consequence so rigid a specie-reserve requirement would scarcely have been practical in other places. Furthermore, in an agricultural economy the principal capital requirement is for the purchase of real estate, and therefore in most of the country the available security for bank notes was still predominantly illiquid long-term mortgages rather than the more liquid ninety-day commercial paper. In short, the significance of this achievement would seem to lie essentially in the fact that in Louisiana, to an extent perhaps greater than anywhere else, political power was vested in those most desirous of a "sound" banking system.

Put differently, in all these attempts to improve the country's banking system there can be seen at work a significant fact. Speaking generally, where the economy was farthest advanced the most progressive steps were being taken in the field of banking. Conversely, where frontier conditions were most prominent, bank operations were most speculative and unrestricted. In New England, New York, and New Orleans—three highly developed industrial communities—elements of America's present banking system were beginning to appear. Michigan and Mississippi, on the other hand, were still managing their banking affairs with the utmost recklessness. Obviously the nation still had much growing up to do before it would be ready for conservative banking practices on a nationwide basis.

A New Labor Movement. Another extremely dynamic area of the economy was the world of labor, where panic and the ensuing depression were dealing the rising trade unions an almost mortal blow. With hundreds of thousands of workers out of work, the unemployed for a time estimated at almost one-third of the urban labor force, industrial organizations could accomplish little for workers and were hence largely abandoned. Only a part of this failure was directly attributable to the depression, however, for counterassociations of employers were beginning to be very effective. It was at approximately this point that the lockout and blacklisting (shutting workers out of a plant and circulating a list of union workers among employers in an area) became important employer weapons against militant groups of workers, and a sizable and growing stream of immigrants provided employers with still another effective weapon against workers who did not "know their place." But at the same time the condition of the economy provided an excellent environment in which employers' associations might work. Wage cuts of up to 50 per cent were forced on the workers, and with hungry, anxious men eager for any opportunity to work little could be done by way of defense.

This temporary eclipse of trade unions, however, did not mean a cessation of activity oriented to the worker's well-being. On the contrary labor leaders were if anything more than ever busily engaged in advancing the cause of the mass of workers against one of the major evils of industrial society. The way these men went about this task during the depression of the 1840's makes one of the most interesting chapters in labor history.

Heretofore labor activity had been overwhelmingly dominated by workers in the skilled trades. The vast majority of operatives in the early factories had been women and children from nearby farms who had no intention of doing factory work for any long period of time, and appeals to join unions were therefore rarely heeded. Gradually, though, a more permanent factory labor force had begun to emerge, consisting in substantial part of men whose only income was their weekly wage and whose future was inescapably linked with a continuance of that situation. While it is far from true that the labor movement was now dominated by this group, it is true that the first unmistakable stirrings of active unrest by factory workers were now plainly visible, and that the labor program with which the new labor movement now challenged the depression was one factory laborers found highly congenial to their needs.

Fifteen years earlier labor's response to depression had been a protest against a society organized in such a way that laborers had an inadequate opportunity to rise higher in the social scale. Workers in the 1840's were not taking so unrealistic a view of their careers. Reconciled to a life of labor, these men were primarily concerned with improving the environment within which that life was to be spent—although this phase of the labor movement did adopt a highly unrealistic view of what might be done to improve the worker's environment.

The fact about the new industrial society growing up about them which was especially disturbing was the idleness of workers and productive facilities at the same time that men and women were in want. This surely must have seemed to laborers the quintessence of loss of control over their own economic destiny.

Not unnaturally in this situation the laborer began to focus his attention upon a very prominent symbol of his loss of position in the community. Large-scale manufacturing necessitates the use of tools, buildings, and machinery which it is neither practicable nor possible for the worker to own. Already landless, in other words, workers were becoming even more propertyless in a society in which property ownership was exceedingly important. Could anything be more obvious than that a restoration to labor of ownership of the tools of production would on the one hand restore to labor its lost power and prestige and on the other hand make it possible for the wheels of industry to be put into motion once more?

TABLE 27. A DECADE OF UNREST

Year	Wholesale Price Index (1926 = 100)
1839	83.5
1840	71.1
1841	70.5
1842	65.7
1843	61.8
1844	62.1
1845	62.6
1846	64.8
1847	64.9
1848	61.8
1849	60.1

Source: Bureau of the Census, *Historical Statistics of the United States, 1789-1945*, p. 234.

What the laborer now began to dream about and work toward was a social system in which the "people" would again own the instruments of production. Such a "cooperative" society, if participated in enthusiastically by everyone, would bring a world of freedom, harmony, and peace to replace oppression, conflict, and war.

One of the leaders of this new "utopianism" (or "communitarianism," as these ideas are sometimes called) was Robert Owen, a "free-lance" reformer from the British Isles (born in Wales) who came to the United States because he felt Europe was too infused with its feudal past to be successful in the "new industrialism." Owen's idea was a community in which private property as such would not exist, but in which every member would share in the fruits of production to the extent of his needs. A greater equality in property ownership, thus, was to be restored by abolishing property ownership altogether.

Perhaps no scheme for altering the basic foundations of society has ever received such an enthusiastic hearing, and all the more so because Owen's first attempt to root his ideas on the American scene followed close behind a successful Owenite experiment in industrial democracy in New Lanark, Scotland. Coming to the United States during the depression following the "second war for independence," Owen's major venture in this country was his famous "New Harmony" (Indiana) project. This innovation soon succumbed to the realities of the New World, however, and Owen himself returned to England saddened and disillusioned.

The failure of "New Harmony" was followed in the late 1820's and the 1830's by the establishment of other Owenite communities, all of which likewise failed. By the early 1840's this movement had subsided, its place being taken by another also of European origin—Fourierism, named after

Charles Fourier, whose American disciples sought to introduce another version of industrial utopia into the United States. The underlying premise of Fourierism was that in actual society the worker received a smaller share of the product of industry than his contribution warranted. To remedy this situation, Fourier proposed that industrial activity be carried on in "phalanxes" of only a few hundred persons each and that distribution be organized on a "community" basis. Although less sweeping in its implications than Owen's approach, this procedure too would have altered significantly the structure of ownership of private property by substantially modifying the distribution of the real income produced by such property.

Fourier societies attracted thousands of enthusiasts from all walks of life before they too failed, leaving barely a trace. Again an uncongenial environment destroyed sincere and high-principled ideas as to how the benefits of industrialization might be enjoyed without its evils. Many specific factors contributed to the decline of particular communities, but the most important single factor was unquestionably the failure to attract capital. The development of industrialization on any basis required a large investment, and most men who had capital to invest were not willing to commit it except on private enterprise terms. American industrialization was thus forced to make its way without the leavening influence of reformist ideas.

Another solution to this same problem was the idea of forming producer and consumer cooperatives—yet a third technique for restoring workers to the property-owning class *as workers*. Here, too, little was accomplished, except a temporary amelioration of conditions for a few. For this failure two additional factors were responsible. One was that cooperatives were too frequently based on the ill-considered belief that middlemen either performed no useful function or were grossly overpaid for what they did contribute to the productive process. Partly as a consequence of this belief there was a persistent failure to put into the task of organizing cooperatives the intelligence, effort, and capital necessary if the employer or distributor were really to be dispensed with. In other words, cooperation was in its way just as utopian as Owenism or Fourierism.

Not all labor's efforts at self-improvement, however, went into visionary schemes for transforming society. Some attention was still devoted to bringing about practical improvements in the existing situation, although for the most part this effort had to be made on the political front since the depression had so nearly destroyed the "fighting" unions. In Rhode Island, for example, the state most noted for its democracy in colonial days, the franchise still remained in the hands of property owners. Voteless laborers, now a sizable group in one of the most highly industrialized states in the union, hotly resented this discrimination. Peaceful efforts having failed, in 1842 an armed uprising took place in behalf of a more liberal constitution. Although the uprising did not succeed as an attempt to bring about change by force of arms, "Dorr's Rebellion" did directly contribute to the framing of a new constitution which improved labor's franchise status.

In 1842 there also occurred another event of importance to labor, in some respects the most important of the entire decade. Prior to this time one of the basic weapons used by employers against employees had been a court action charging criminal conspiracy. Not all such suits had been won by employers, although they were a threat to the existence of any militant labor organization. As long as this situation existed, the advantage in bargaining was all on the side of the employer.

The year 1842 saw a suit charging criminal conspiracy against a group of employees carried to the Supreme Court of Massachusetts. In the famous case known as Commonwealth *v.* Hunt, Chief Justice Shaw speaking for the majority declared that an association of workers is not illegal unless "its powers are abused," and that therefore the mere fact of combination was not sufficient evidence of actual conspiracy. Of course, a decision by the Supreme Court of Massachusetts was not binding elsewhere, and even in Massachusetts criminal conspiracy cases were still won on occasion by employers. At the same time, however, this event did clearly mark the beginning of the end of one major disadvantage against which labor had been forced to fight. Nonproperty rights for labor unions had won a resounding victory.

Progress in Railroad Building. In still a third way were the depressed 1840's characterized by dynamic economic developments. Prior to the panic the railroad had been in a clearly experimental stage of its growth. However, with the appearance of a drastically altered economic situation, men were given an opportunity to make a fresh appraisal of the nation's transportation development. The resulting analysis was exceedingly favorable to the railroad relative to its major rivals.

For one thing, there could no longer be any doubt that the canal, with exceptions, was destined to be only a feeder to other transportation media, whereas it was already evident that the railroad offered far greater possibilities. Thus after the debacle of avid prosperity building, depression bankruptcies, uncompleted projects, and the repudiation of state debts, there was no resumption of general interest in and state aid for roads and canals. The general interest was now in the railroad even though panic and depression had dried up most of the government funds available even for this purpose, and thus the new medium of transportation was for the first time launched on an independent career of its own. Greatly aided by the simultaneous development of the telegraph, the railroad was to enjoy a half-century at the very center of the nation's zeal for improved transportation facilities. Never again was the nation's interest in artificial waterways to be so great as it had lately been; not until the coming of the automobile was the nation's interest in road building to reach the intensity now giving way to interest in railroads.

The rise of the railroad to an independent status was by no means an unmixed blessing. No longer supplementary to canal and turnpike lines, it became their competitor. Large investments in these alternative facilities had been made by both governments and private individuals, and a quick success by the railroad would destroy the capital thus irretrievably sunk. Furthermore, because canal supporters were already well intrenched in the seats of power while the railroad was new, much of the advantage in the ensuing struggle lay with the established interests.

The obstacles placed in the way of the railroad were numerous and difficult to combat. In New York the Utica and Schenectady Railroad was for many years prohibited from carrying freight, and for an even longer period tolls equivalent to those charged by canals were assessed against all traffic on railroads paralleling and within thirty miles of a canal. The Pennsylvania Railroad was required to pay a special tonnage tax in order more nearly to equalize competition with adjacent canals. In New Jersey the Camden and Amboy Railroad was forced to bring to completion a canal project which was to be its direct competitor. Frequently the issuance of railway charters was delayed or otherwise harassed by rival interests including innkeepers, stage coach drivers, and even the farmers served by rival facilities.

These delaying and obstructing tactics were not the only adverse factor in railway development, either. An equally important barrier was the difficulty of securing capital. America had always been plagued by capital scarcity, but this problem was greatly enhanced during the period of railway construction. On the one hand, the rapid expansion of manufacturing with the expensive machinery and other facilities required for this purpose provided keen competition for such capital as was available. On the other hand, railroad building was itself an extremely expensive process. Not only was a permanent and fairly level way necessary, but in addition costly equipment had to be provided for the actual hauling process.

Moreover, there were special problems associated with financing the railroads. American development had always relied heavily on European capital. European capital, however, was now busily engaged in industrializing Europe and there was consequently little incentive to undertake speculative ventures in the United States. This reluctance, too, was accentuated by the fact that European financiers had recently gotten their fingers burnt badly in connection with American investments. Local capital was no less reluctant; alternative investments more often than not offered such a secure return that there was little reason for investors to tie their fortunes to ventures as speculative as railroads still were. When to these factors are added the intense public and private opposition to the railroad and the depression itself, it is understandable why investment in these enterprises was limited primarily to enthusiasts.

The difficulty of securing capital was in turn complicated by the fact that it was cumulative in its consequences. Projects were often commenced with inadequate funds and hence not completed. New railroad concerns frequently began operations with an inadequate amount of working capital in the face of meager revenues. When these facts often resulted in failures and hence capital losses, the investing public was still further deterred from committing funds.

That the railroad did surmount these difficulties, emerging at the end of this decade much stronger than at the beginning, is an indication of the vision, persistence, and energy of early railway promoters and the vital need of the nation for better transportation. During this period almost all the important centers of population were linked with one another by rail, and most major market centers and their respective hinterlands were connected by these same bands of iron. Some building was even taking place between market centers and isolated communities in the vicinity of the frontier, although here was where the highest proportion of failures and uncompleted projects was to be found.

More than enterprise and need, however, were responsible for the progress being made in this field. Another factor was the rise of the business corporation. Incorporation meant limited liability, the avoidance by investors, in case of failure, of losses greater than their committed investments. By contrast with the law of partnerships, providing that owners could be held liable for the concern's liabilities without regard to actual investment, this development was of great assistance in attracting capital into industries requiring a large capital. Indeed the industrial structure with which we are today familiar would have been impossible without an organizational device allowing limited liability in some form.

The corporate device was not easily made available for a railroad industry controlled by private investors and promoters. Up to this point American practice, following England's lead in this as in many other ways, had treated incorporation as a privilege rather than a right. More than this, legislatures had typically been reluctant to grant this privilege to concerns interested primarily in private profit. As a result only a limited number of charters had been granted, and these predominantly in such semipublic fields as turnpikes, bridges, canals, docks, water supply, fire fighting, banking, and insurance. Given the hostility to the railroad stemming from government investments in transportation, the corporate form of organization could have been of only slight assistance in the attraction of capital as long as a special legislative act was required for every incorporation.

As the economy grew and the forces behind industrialization became stronger, promoters in a number of fields began to apply pressure in the direction of general incorporation laws, based on the view that this form of organization should be a right rather than a privilege. Agrarian and urban "radicals" were coming to this same position, too, on the ground that special charters were conducive to industrial monopoly. Gradually, first in the field of banking but spreading to other fields, this point of view prevailed, and in the 1840's general incorporation statutes became the rule. Few industrial devices have had such profound consequences for economic evolution in any country. The stage was thus set for an unprecedented industrial growth.

A New Expansionism. One other major dynamic development accompanied the depression of the early 1840's. International relations again became prominent in the nation's affairs, and slavery became once more an open issue in America's economic and political life. Furthermore, these two facts were closely related. Slavery and international relations crossed paths in Texas, and for several years both were burning issues on the American scene.

The trouble began with the mutual desire of Texas and the United States to get together; complications arose in connection with reactions in Mexico and England. Mexico's objection was not so much that she hoped to regain Texas as a part of her own territory as that she was reluctant to see her aggressive neighbor strengthened by the acquisition of a huge and valuable territory so near her own border. An independent (and hence a buffer) Texas would have suited her much better.

England's interest in Texas had to do primarily with slavery. For some time Great Britain had been emancipating slaves throughout the empire, and it was becoming evident that her tropical possessions could not easily compete with slave-produced goods in the United States. Her preference, therefore, in the Texas dispute, was also for a state which would act as a buffer against the expansion of American slavery and which would at the same time provide a beginning in the direction of abolition. The fact that Texas was in the direct line of slavery's advance was too obvious to be missed. Indeed, it was so obvious that it was bordering on the naïve for either Mexico or England to entertain thoughts of slowing this advance.

However, England's interest in a free Texas was not the only reason slavery became inextricably involved with the rapidly approaching Mexican War. Abolitionism in the United States was beginning to take on the characteristics of a moral crusade. In the House of Representatives old John Quincy Adams attacked the institution of slavery at every opportunity, and hence interpreted every move made by the South as an attempt to maintain and extend slavery. As early as the middle of 1843 he had denounced America's interest in Texas as a conspiracy of the slaveholders, simultaneously announcing that the annexation of Texas would ultimately mean dissolution of the Union. This prediction came perilously near fulfillment, but few paid any attention to it at the time, for Adams was by now a very crabbed old man.

There were reasons enough for Adams' suspicions. The first law of human existence was then, as now, self-preservation, and southerners were beginning to adopt a defensive attitude regarding their "peculiar" institution. No better evidence of this could be wanted than a paper prepared by John C. Calhoun, Secretary of State during a part of the negotiations relative to Texas. This document was an impassioned defense of slavery transmitted officially to England as a state paper. Not intended for publication, this document broadly confirmed New England suspicions when it did come to light.

Moreover, there was a solid basis underlying the South's interest in acquiring Texas. Settled primarily by southerners, many of whom had taken their slaves with them, Texas unquestionably would be a slave territory. As such it would provide in time a support for the political strength of the slave states, a support they would one day surely need.

Nor was this the only basis for southern agitation favoring annexation. Economic considerations were equally compelling. Slavery was such an inefficient form of labor that only large-scale, extensive cultivation was compatible with it. Put differently, the plantation system was reasonably profitable only where the land produced well without crop rotation, soil conservation practices, or investment in fertilizers. Where the land had to be treated as an exhaustible resource, slavery inevitably began to disappear. Thus cotton planters were always searching for new, unmined soil as the lands in use began to show signs of exhaustion. A territory possessing as many desirable features as Texas was well worth fighting for in the middle of the 1840's.

Obviously, of course, only a minority of cotton planters would actually move to a new territory opening up. Why, then, was annexation sentiment so widespread throughout the South? The reason is that slaveowners in declining areas also had much to gain from an extension of the area in which slavery was practiced. A decline in the profitableness of slavery in a region would have resulted in a painful reduction in the value of slaves in the absence of a favorable market somewhere else. New cotton lands made it possible for regions in which the plantation system was losing ground to get rid of slaves no longer needed without heavy capital losses. This was the economic foundation for the slave trade against which the wrath of the abolitionists was so bitterly directed but which was at the same time a completely natural outgrowth of the conditions producing it. Given these conditions, the general interest throughout the South in Texas becomes immediately understandable.

It would be misleading to assume that the South was careless in its handling of available soil resources while northern farmers were conservationist in their outlook. On the contrary, throughout the entire country land was the expendable resource, and men took no more care of it than was absolutely necessary, Whatever difference there was between the two sections of the country existed only in degree, and the difference in degree was not all attributable to slavery. Soil mining in the South began before it did in the West. It is possible, too, that on the whole northern lands possessed a greater reserve of plant food than did southern soil, and some even insist that the southern climate is more debilitating for soil resources.

It would be misleading, also, to conclude that the South alone was interested in expansion at this juncture in American history. Much evidence points to the opposite conclusion. For example, in the preliminaries leading up to the presidential campaign of 1844, a public statement by Martin Van Buren opposing annexation cost him so much support in both North and South that he could not be nominated on the Democratic ticket. Furthermore, the Democratic slogan on the expansion issue did not embrace Texas alone but included also Oregon where for some time furs and fertile lands had been attracting eager settlers, and it was in connection with the question of Oregon that the cry of "Fifty-four forty or fight" brought further grave international complications with England.

In other words, as expansionism thirty-two years earlier had been a *general* "disease" in America, so was it in 1844. The westward movement —"Manifest Destiny," as it was coming to be called—had always been an integral part of the American dream, and it was to continue to be a driving force in American history until the Pacific Ocean was reached. The frontier had always been regarded as a haven for those who had fallen on evil days in the more settled regions, and in this depression era the thoughts of bankrupt farmers and unemployed laborers especially turned in this direction. It is not without significance that land reform was now changing its status in labor's creed from a minor to a major item. It is not without significance either that the appearance of this new wave of expansionism coincided with an extremely low level of agricultural prices; on January 1, 1845, the New York price of cotton was the lowest in the nation's history. And finally, in the South as well as the North there arose a determined (although minority) opposition to war with Mexico. All in all it is difficult to escape the conclusion that territorial acquisitions in the Southwest would have taken place about when they did even if slavery had not been involved.

The Walker Tariff. Territorial expansion was not the only issue in the presidential canvass. Also prominent was the tariff. The expansionist

South wanted a revenue tariff, while the expansionist East wanted protection. Thus in order to keep the expansionist groups from splitting apart it was necessary for Polk to be put on both sides of the tariff question. Since Polk was himself a Tennessean and hence presumed to have southern ideals, the campaign ticket was balanced by nominating for the vice-presidency George M. Dallas from protectionist Pennsylvania. In addition, Polk made public a letter carefully worded so that it could be interpreted as protectionist in the East and antiprotectionist in the South. The value of these precautions was clearly demonstrated when Polk won Pennsylvania's electoral votes by the narrow margin of six thousand popular votes.

On the first day of March, 1845, a few days before Polk's inauguration, Texas was annexed and diplomatic relations with Mexico began a deterioration which was to lead to war. The United States was almost eager for it to begin, much more eager than would have been the case if only a defense of annexation had been at stake. What was really involved, however, was that with Texas already taken for granted, Americans—and none more enthusiastically than James K. Polk—were already casting covetous eyes at California. Simultaneously, and indeed intensified by the annexation itself, the cry of "Fifty-four forty or fight" became a fixed objective for a large number of American citizens.

Within the Democratic party plans were going forward with respect to the legislative program to be enacted. The most important arrangements being made included the strengthening of the coalition between South and West. In exchange for southern support in securing federal funds for internal improvements and a graduated price for the public lands, the West pledged itself to help the South secure a revenue tariff. When on December 3, therefore, Secretary of the Treasury Walker from Mississippi presented his report on the tariff, the stage seemed set for a prompt enactment of the measures agreed upon. Walker's recommendation was not a free-trade suggestion, although it did call for an appreciable reduction of protection. Almost as classic a presentation on the tariff as Hamilton's *Report on Manufactures*, this document outlined a tariff program designed to vary the tariff according to the relative elasticities of demand for the several kinds of goods imported. Those goods having the most inelastic demand were to bear the highest duty rates; those goods having the most elastic demand were to be placed on the free list.[2] Thus, within the framework of the government's revenue needs, the Walker Tariff was intended

[2] A good with an inelastic demand will return to the Treasury relatively high tax revenues without burdening consumers heavily by forcing them to stop buying it. On the other hand, taxes on a good having an elastic demand will significantly reduce purchases and thereby produce little revenue for the government. More concretely, an excise tax program built along the lines of the Walker Tariff takes advantage of the fact that there are some things consumers are much more determined to buy than they are other items.

to reduce protection as much as it was possible to do under the circumstances.

The legislative mill did not run smoothly, however, for two complications intervened. In the first place, the tariff bill became intricately entwined with the Oregon issue. England had for some time been gradually freeing her trade from mercantilist restrictions, and had recently been confronted with a situation making outright repeal of her Corn Laws virtually a certainty. The potato crop in Ireland, the potato being the basic food of the Irish, had recently been destroyed by a virile fungus disease, and restrictions on the importation of food could not be maintained for long in the face of starvation in the British Isles.

While from one point of view England's action was simply a recognition of her dependence on food raised in other parts of the world, it is understandable that she would at the same time want the tariffs of other nations to be as low as possible. Since the United States had maneuvered herself into a vulnerable position on the Oregon controversy, concessions in Oregon in exchange for a lower American tariff seemed to be a promising basis on which to conduct negotiations. For her part, the United States saw an opportunity to exchange concessions of her own in Oregon for a relaxation of British import restrictions. In this way, the nation saved its prestige in the Oregon dispute by an action it was already scheduled to take in any event. The compromise agreed to in Oregon was the forty-ninth parallel.

In the vote on the Walker Tariff the West fulfilled its part of the bargain made with the South. The South in turn endeavored in good faith to deliver on its part of the agreement. A bill was presented to improve navigation on the Mississippi River System, this being the only major internal improvement Calhoun could square with his constitutional scruples. Another measure was introduced graduating the price of the public lands. In the House Calhoun's internal improvement measure was dropped and in its place was substituted a "pork-barrel" bill which would have been of little real value to the West. When this measure was given to President Polk, he kept it, unsigned, until he also had in his possession the tariff bill and a measure restoring the Independent Treasury System. Only then did he veto the internal improvement bill. Immediately thereafter the House tabled the graduation proposal.

Meanwhile war with Mexico had begun. As the economy received the stimulus inevitably accompanying even a small military endeavor, the long depression began to lift. Commodity prices improved, the tempo of business quickened, and workers returned to their jobs. But if the war with Mexico helped bring relief from economic distress, it also brought about other changes which were to have an even more profound effect on the American economy. For example, it brought California into the center of public attention.

QUESTIONS FOR DISCUSSION

1. What important banking innovations were inaugurated at this time?
2. Why was note elasticity considered so important for the nation's monetary system? Does note elasticity automatically contribute to note safety?
3. What was the central feature of labor's program during the 1840's to reorganize society on a more desirable basis? Why did these efforts so consistently fail?
4. In what ways did public policy put artificial obstacles in the path of railroad development? How were the railroads able to surmount these obstacles?
5. How were proponents of incorporation as a *right* able to prevail over those preferring to retain incorporation as a *privilege?*
6. Why was it so difficult to secure an adequate supply of capital for railroad building? How did the use of the corporate form of business enterprise help solve this problem?
7. What were the interconnections between slavery and the difficulty with Mexico?
8. If the North had not been interested in expansion when the Texas-California issues arose, what would have been the consequences for later American history?
9. Given the legality of slavery, is the buying and selling of slaves of a different character from transactions involving wheat, cotton, or automobiles?

Chapter 15

THE UNION UNDER PRESSURE

1846 "Wilmot Proviso" first presented.
1847 Calhoun's resolutions denying the federal government any right to legislate concerning slavery.
1848 Discovery of gold in California.
Treaty of peace with Mexico.
Zachary Taylor elected President.
1849 "Address of the Southern Delegates" listing acts of "aggression" by the North against the South.
1850 Clay's Compromise approved.
Nashville Convention presenting the South's position on the Compromise and southern rights.
First railroad land grants.
Millard Fillmore became President at the death of Taylor.

If the annexation of Texas and the ensuing Mexican War did not wholly grow out of the slavery issue, the same could not be said of the aftermath of these events. Furthermore, if the nation's economic system began to function more satisfactorily with the onset of war, the same was not true of the economic alignments making up the administration of James K. Polk. Almost immediately this coalition began to crumble, and the focus of tension was primarily the issue of slavery expansion.

The Issue Joined. The Walker Tariff was signed into law July 30, 1846. It was less than a month later that David Wilmot of Pennsylvania offered an amendment to a war appropriation bill calling for the exclusion of slavery in any territories acquired as a result of the conflict with Mexico. The wording of Wilmot's famous "proviso" was deliberately copied from the Northwest Ordinance to take advantage of the sanction time had given that document, and throughout the North it was immediately given enthusiastic support. In the South, on the contrary, it was received with alarm and indignation. More than ever sensitive where their "peculiar" institution was concerned, southerners felt insulted at what was in many respects justifiably interpreted as an unprovoked attack on their way of life.

The immediate consequence of these reactions was that sectional lines began to form more threateningly than at any time since the Missouri Compromise. Northerners defended their point of view on the ground that no injustice would be done to southerners who could migrate freely to the West without their slaves, while if slaves were permitted, northern white labor would be injured, since self-respecting workers could not live in a slave environment. Southerners denied this charge (and the suggestion that southerners migrate to the West without their slaves did indicate how unrealistic many northerners were on the subject of slavery), and insisted further that they too were contributing blood and treasure to the nation's war effort. It seemed to them legitimate to ask what justice resided in a proposal to deny them a share in the fruits of whatever victory was achieved.

Wilmot's measure did not win the approval of Congress, and the sectional stir it created died away without seriously damaging existing intersectional alignments. However, the prominence this proposal enjoyed for a brief period did raise certain questions in men's minds, the answers to which explained much about the tension now so obviously mounting. Why, for example, did northerners consider it so important to prohibit slavery in a territory most thinking men agreed was not suitable for slavery? Why, on the other hand, did southerners vehemently defend their right to expand into an area which again seemed unsuited to their way of life?

On the side of the North, several considerations undoubtedly played a part. For one thing, many northerners were disgruntled about the outcome of the Oregon controversy. Polk had campaigned on a platform of all Texas for the South and all Oregon for the North. Then the administration had settled for only a part of Oregon, while all Texas had been annexed and a war undertaken to acquire still more territory with a southern latitude. Moreover, Wilmot was from Polk's own party, representing the state which had narrowly cast its electoral votes for Polk on the strength of a tariff stand later repudiated. Thus there was perhaps a little of sheer pique in the northern attitude.

The Ways of Revolution. However, such narrow emotions rarely produce a mass reaction as powerful as that aroused by the "Wilmot Proviso" in the northern states. In addition, it must be remembered that America was living through an age of revolution, a revolution affecting simultaneously every major part of the western world. In England this revolution could be seen in the form of a general movement for slave emancipation throughout the empire, in a broadening of the franchise to include the new middle class (manufacturer-employers), in the Factory Acts designed to curb the growth of monopoly power and the exploitation of England's human resources, and in the repeal of the Corn Laws. On the Continent revolution was taking the form of an uprising against feudal institutions, the destruction of hereditary privileges, the freeing of the bourgeoisie from mercantilist restrictions, and socialist thinking and organization designed to improve the industrial worker's lot in life. Everywhere men were analyzing institutions and the functions of government from the standpoint of the idea that society exists for the benefit of *all* the people.

Revolutionary thinking was just as pronounced in America as in Europe. There was, for example, the Dorr Rebellion, the antirent agitation of Hudson Valley farmers against remnants of feudalism in New York, the espousal of utopianism and cooperationism by the labor movement, prohibitionism, an agitation for fuller rights for women, outcries against pauperism, and pleas for reforms in penal institutions, insane asylums, and education. Indeed, a reformer in America in the 1840's could literally take his pick of causes.

As important as any other reform issue, however, and steadily gaining in importance, was the cause of abolition. To many it seemed that Negro slavery was the greatest single defect of America, an outrageous betrayal of the American dream. Taking their stand on the Declaration of Independence and arguing that America must take the responsibility for leading the world to higher ethical standards, abolitionists attacked the southern slaveowner as an outstanding example of aristocracy and privilege. It was only natural for "Proviso" proponents to ask defiantly why the United States had spilled blood in Texas and Mexico. Was it only to extend the area of human bondage?

But it is naïve to think that a reform movement such as abolitionism would ever have become a potent force if it had not served practical interests as well as ideal ones. Thus reformism, both at home and abroad, was designed to achieve specific objectives, and in general the larger the groups seeking to benefit by a given reform the more successful was that reform likely to be. In the case of American slavery only one group was as yet taking a strong stand. That was American labor. For the moment the western farmer and eastern business interests were too profitably related to the South to join this company, and it was essentially for this reason that the "Wilmot Proviso" failed.

By 1846 the labor movement was beginning to shake off the depression-oriented utopianism in which it had been caught. Indicative of this return to practicality was the launching on a nationwide basis of a new drive to reduce the working day to ten hours. Pursued by means of collective bargaining and legislation this project absorbed much of labor's energies for the next dozen years. To be sure these efforts were accompanied by many disheartening reverses, including the fact that it was easier to secure the passage of laws in state legislatures than to bring about their enforcement. But the disappointment of these failures was more than counterbalanced by achievements, and when this movement came to an end, the ten-hour day was standard in most places.

At first labor had not concerned itself with the issue of slavery. It saw no particular connection between the Negro's situation and its own, and there lurked a widespread fear that the Negro if freed would come to the cities and lower the wage level. Besides, in the early days of American industrialization it was not easy to distinguish wage slavery from chattel slavery, and northern laborers felt they had their hands full fighting their own battles. Not until abolitionists themselves espoused the cause of the free laborer did labor concern itself with Negro slavery. Gradually laborers came to feel that, precisely because there was so little difference between forms of slavery, their cause was one with that of the Negro. By 1846 they were becoming alerted to the danger of the *spread* of slavery, and the "Wilmot Proviso" was an instrument designed to prevent such a development. It was no accident that David Wilmot had already distinguished himself as a fighter for the rights of labor, hard money, and the abolition of imprisonment for debt.

The Ways of the South. What of the South? Why were southerners so quickly and violently aroused by the "Wilmot Proviso"? There is, of course, the obvious fact that the South was a typical agrarian aristocracy, at the pinnacle of which stood the large planter and his many slaves. With slave ownership and the accompanying pattern of land ownership widely accepted as symbols of success, it is not surprising that the institution of slavery did not lack defenders.

It has been pointed out, and with an overtone of half-disguised amazement, that nonslaveowners often defended slavery more vigorously than their more successful neighbors. Actually there is nothing in the least astonishing about such a phenomenon. Conservatism always takes the form of a defense of established and accepted avenues to success as well as the alternative form of a defense of actual success. In the case of slavery, for example, agitation for reopening the external slave trade typically came from slaveless whites. The ambitious in a society defining success in these terms would naturally seek to broaden their own opportunities.

However, what is somewhat surprising about the pre-Civil War South is that many slaveless whites defended slavery even after it began to be doubted that the South had achieved an effective way of organizing its economy. The fact is that slavery was rarely profitable. For a short time, until fertile soils were either exhausted or washed down southern hillsides, a few large operators would accumulate wealth. Then the center of gravity of cotton production would move westward, leaving worn-out land on which smaller operators could eke out only a bare existence. Much of the profits which were made, moreover, really represented the general rise in land and slave values as the country grew, plus the low standard of living which was the lot of the slave.

Why, after these facts became widely understood, did the slaveless majority still uphold the cause of slavery? Two factors stand out. First, it was easy to "prove" that northern tariffs, factors, bankers, and shipowners were really responsible for the South's poverty—that northern wealth was essentially parasitic. At the moment, thus, it could be demonstrated that the price of cotton had steadily fallen under Clay's new tariff. Moreover, was it not because of "Yankee meddling" that the external slave trade had been virtually closed and the price of slaves pushed so high that only a few could afford them?

Second, and probably by far the more important, there was the existence of the Negro himself. There were states in which the Negro population exceeded the white (and of these the case of South Carolina especially stands out), and in several others the two populations were almost equal. Certain areas in these latter states, too, contained more blacks than whites. A result of these facts was that a large majority of southerners had developed a great dread of the possibility of the Negro being freed from the iron control in which he was held, and occasional slave insurrections did nothing to allay this fear. Large planters no doubt feared for their lives as well as their economic well-being, for a few whites in one dwelling on a large plantation surrounded by Negro houses would be at the mercy of a slave uprising. Most, however, were probably more concerned with the economic competition for a livelihood which would result if the Negro were freed. Probably a majority of southerners, by the time of the Civil War, would have voted to free the Negro if by some miracle he would then have disappeared. Sharing with northerners (who unashamedly discriminated against the Negro in all walks of life) a feeling that the colored race was inferior to the white, southerners did not believe Negroes should be permitted to take bread from their own mouths.

Put differently, the South's reaction to the "Wilmot Proviso" was essentially defensive. All over the South there was arising a paralyzing fear that if the federal government were given legislative power over the extension of slavery, it would be only a matter of time until Congress would turn

TABLE 28. THE BALANCE OF POWER DESTROYED

Free	Slave
Michigan (1837)	Arkansas (1836)
Iowa (1846)	Texas (1845)
Wisconsin (1848)	Florida (1845)
California (1850)	
Minnesota (1858)	
Oregon (1859)	

millions of Negroes loose among their erstwhile masters. Such thoughts, furthermore, were made even more paralyzing by the fact that the now certain admission of California as a free state would place the slave South at a numerical disadvantage in the Senate for the first time since that issue became important.

Planters and Merchants. Early in 1848 the worst fears of opponents of slavery extension were fully confirmed. By the terms of the treaty of peace with Mexico that country agreed to give up all claims to Texas, California, and a vast territory in between. Immediately Wilmot's proposal became again a vital issue. The nation was suddenly possessed of a great new area which would one day require legislative organization. When that day came, the slavery issue would once again be fiercely raised.

However, while no one minimized the reality of the new focus of the slavery controversy there was a tendency to minimize its immediacy. After all, California was far distant, New Mexico was not especially desirable, and Texas was already a slave state. There seemed to be no reason why sectional and partisan forces should not thresh this question about for years before a decision would be compelled. But a reason did exist, nonetheless. Even before the treaty with Mexico was completed rich gold deposits had been discovered in the valley of the Sacramento. As the news spread throughout the territory, men by the thousands dropped whatever they were doing to join the hunt. Vessels arriving in San Francisco were deserted by their crews and left stranded in the harbor. Wages for the most unskilled labor skyrocketed, so difficult was it to secure workers for the ordinary tasks of the economy. Within six months some ten thousand persons were located in the vicinity of the first finds.

Inevitably the news spread eastward. As excited and often exaggerated stories of the richness of the California finds passed from person to person and from place to place, men and women by the tens of thousands made ready to seek their fortune in the Far West. In an incredibly short time the Spanish and Santa Fe Trails were crowded with gold seekers as was the long sea lane between New York and the Pacific Coast. Moreover, as the news spread beyond America, gold seekers from Europe, Asia, and South America set out for the new Eldorado. In this process what would have been a slow trickle of settlers to California became instead a flood. The result was a boom development of the economy of California. San Francisco became a city almost overnight, land values rose 1,000 per cent, and the rate of interest rose to more than 50 per cent a year.

While the foundation for a major problem was thus being laid in the Sacramento River Valley, Americans "back east" were preparing to elect another president, and it was most fitting that a chief contender was a hero of the war which had once again raised the issue of slavery and slave states to a position of commanding importance. This, however, was not the only reason the Whig mantle fell on Zachary Taylor in 1848. Taylor was a southern slaveowner—a Louisiana sugar planter—and through him northern business interests were endeavoring to make an intersectional appeal for support which would secure for them control of the government. A successful intersectional appeal could at this point be made only by keeping the slavery question from becoming an open issue.

Actually, as long as the slavery issue was not prominent, the larger planters and businessmen got along well together. Each group was an elite in its own community, and both possessed, therefore, a common bond in the form of a feeling of superiority over the other groups with which they lived. More than this, the two groups were closely related to one another in the functioning of the nation's economy. Southern cotton was increasingly finding a market in northern textile mills, and when it did not it was most frequently carried to European destinations in northern ships. Northern manufacturers in turn supplied northern plantations with many of the manufactured goods on which southern agriculture depended, while manufactured goods coming to the South from European factories more often than not came in northern ships. Northern banks even performed many of the functions required in the handling of both the South's imports and exports.

To be sure, both planters and merchants had occasional misgivings about the company they were keeping. On such matters as protection, central banking, and federally financed internal improvements a wide gulf separated these two interests. Furthermore, in the South protests against economic "vassalage" were steadily growing more vigorous, while in the North businessmen had been among the first to express opposition to the expansion of slavery. But on both sides there were extenuating factors which, until years later, made these two groups reasonably content with one another.

On the side of the South, for example, it is understandable that slave aristocrats, men who had achieved success in the existing social and economic system, would not be especially indignant about paying interest, freight charges, insurance fees, and commissions to "Yankee" middlemen. In addition, attempts at economic emancipation almost invariably failed, and for this reason the southern aristocracy typically left it for the more radical groups to do the protesting while they made the most of their own opportunities. As to public policy differences, the important fact was that as long as the economy of the East continued to be closely integrated with that of the South businessmen would be forced to temper their inclinations accordingly.

On the side of the North, the rationalization process was very similar. Although both at the time of the "Missouri Compromise" and on the occasion of the struggle over the annexation of Texas businessmen had opposed the extention of slavery, it had soon become apparent that this position was not a sound one. For one thing, it would not do to take a strong stand against slavery while employers' associations were doing everything in their power to keep northern laborers as docile as southern slaves. For another, it would not do to antagonize the South to the point of losing the political support of the planter aristocracy. And both of these considerations were entirely apart from the obvious fact that the business done in the South was essential to their economic well-being. A number of reasons, therefore, suggested that it was still the better part of wisdom for northern merchants to cast their lot with the South.

The Issue Compromised. The candidacy of a southern slaveowner on the ticket of the businessmen's party was successful in attaining its immediate objective—keeping the Whig Party from breaking to pieces over slavery. But the "free-soil" split in the ranks of its rival was the best evidence of the impossibility of keeping slavery in the background. And although the Whigs reaped a rich harvest from this split, in another way it was most ominous. It was an unmistakable warning that the new Whig administration would have to face squarely the slavery issue. No seer was required to predict that this necessity could easily prove fatal to the alliance between southern planters and northern merchants.

Long before Taylor was inaugurated the "free-soil" battle began in the form of a contest over the speakership in the House. Almost immediately thereafter a new "Wilmot Proviso" measure was introduced and bitterly debated. No action was taken, and businessmen in northern cities hoped against hope that the agitation would die away. They were not afraid of southern attempts to emancipate the South from northern domination; all this was now understood to be mostly smoke and little fire. What they were afraid of was being branded as abolitionists to such an extent that "Boston," "Providence," or "New York" printed on a box of merchandise would arouse southern hostility. Even more did they fear the movement for secession which they knew was now just under the surface.

These hopes of businessmen, however, were dashed by the hopes of the tens of thousands of "forty-niners" who braved the elements and the Indians in the search for California gold. As soon as Congress again convened the bitter struggle began anew, and by now tempers were at white heat. By early 1850 the debate was at its highest pitch. So intense had the situation become that both sides were beginning to stress the need for compromise if the Union were not to be dashed to pieces, and on January 29 Henry Clay stepped into the breach with a proposal calling for a retreat by both sides. California was to be admitted without restriction, New Mexico was to be organized as a territory without any reference to slavery (on the express ground that slavery was not apt to flourish there), slavery was not to be abolished in the District of Columbia although the slave trade in the nation's capital was to be discontinued, and a more effective fugitive slave law was to be enacted. What these terms meant was that an end had been reached in the organization of slave states, but that the federal government would help maintain the free interchange of slaves between the several parts of the South.[1]

As is typically the case with compromises, the Compromise of 1850 did not please everyone. Extremists in the North charged that it granted too much to the South. Southerners maintained that too much of a concession was made to the northern viewpoint. Calhoun, arising from what proved to be his deathbed, sat in the Senate while a colleague read his views on Clay's compromise. They were as usual incisive, but they were negative. The South, said Calhoun, could not safely stay in the Union unless the federal government would renounce all authority concerning where slavery could or could not be extended. His remarks proved to be more prophetic than effective, for the sentiment favoring compromise had proceeded too far to be deterred even by John C. Calhoun.

Shortly after Calhoun's speech was read, Daniel Webster made his great speech supporting Clay's proposal. Although not perhaps decisive in assuring passage of the measure, Webster's speech no doubt did make many feel better about its provisions. For this reason if for no other the "Seventh-of-March" speech is deservedly classed among the nation's most brilliant orations. Daniel Webster too was prophetic. Said he, "There can be no such thing as a peaceable secession." Because he believed this to be true, his speech was a magnificent defense of the Union. History does no injustice to the facts when it places Webster among the most ardent proponents of the *United* States of America.

By the same token, however, it does no injustice to the facts to assert that if the voice was that of Daniel Webster the thoughts were those of northern businessmen. And if anyone were inclined to doubt this relationship, a brief glimpse at the "Boston Associates" should readily dispel them. The corporate device not only permitted the accumulation of large sums of capital for particular enterprises, but by decentralizing ownership to many and scattered portfolios it made possible the concentration of control as well because voting control could usually be secured with much less than an investment of 51 per cent of the common stock. By 1850 a group of

[1] In an exchange economy the value of an economic good is determined primarily by the interplay of supply and demand factors. For these factors to perform this function effectively, however, it is necessary that there exist a market in which they can come to a fairly sharp focus. Had the internal slave market been outlawed, one result would have been to increase the cost of slaves (and hence the cost of producing cotton) in shortage areas, while at the same time the value of slaves would have significantly fallen in surplus areas.

fifteen Boston families (calling itself the "Associates") had utilized these possibilities to such an extent that it controlled one-fifth of the nation's cotton-textile manufacturing capacity and approximately the same proportion of New England's banking resources, insurance capital, and railroad mileage. No group worked so zealously for Daniel Webster's political career, and probably no small group on the entire American scene had such a powerful voice in American politics.

Historians tell us, and there is no reason to dispute their judgment, that the Union almost collapsed in 1850. That it did not, that the nation was given a few years of reprieve to try to solve its problems without violence, is surely owing largely to the stand taken by northern business interests. No group during and after 1850 worked more earnestly to make the compromise settlement permanent. For example, a list of "abolitionist" merchants was compiled by northern merchants and distributed to southern traders, an economic pressure which proved extremely effective in quieting antislavery agitation.

At the same time, however, it is misleading to suggest (as is so often done) that this zeal was motivated by sheer love for the Union. Also involved were profits from the North's trade with the South. Not only did Daniel Webster in particular and businessmen in general love the Union, but they had good reason for doing so. It is therefore an oversimplification to conclude that Webster was a Unionist in 1850 while Calhoun was anti-Unionist. Both men believed in and worked for the values with which their lives had been associated; it so happened that these values were not the same, and that it was Webster's values which in 1850 demanded that the Union be kept intact. It is too easy to forget that thirty-five years earlier John C. Calhoun had been a far more ardent Unionist than Daniel Webster.

The Issue Unresolved. The efforts of businessmen were not the only reason, however, and perhaps not the most important reason, that the Compromise of 1850 was for a time accepted as permanent. Almost simultaneously with the legislative achievement a mild postwar depression was supplanted by prosperity—that great salve for all sorts of wounds. Citizens of both the North and the South turned away from controversy to enjoy a higher level of economic well-being than they had enjoyed in more than a decade. Paradoxically, although it was the thousands of settlers moving West which did so much to generate the mid-century threat to the Union, it was at the same time the resultant eastward flow of western gold which contributed a great deal toward easing the tension thus created.

Unfortunately, even though this was the last reprieve the nation was to be given, prosperity was not enough. No solution to America's sectional controversy could have been permanent which did not transfer a significant proportion of the South's working population from the less productive agricultural pursuits to the more productive secondary and tertiary industries. And in this all-important area virtually nothing was accomplished.

For this failure no single factor was responsible. It is especially true that certain factors emphasized in the South were quite superficial. For example, the South's complaint that it did not possess an adequate amount of capital for an industrial development almost wholly missed the point. On the one hand, a lack of capital was as much a result as an explanation of failure to industrialize. On the other hand, the South was no more short of capital than the North had been at the beginning of industrialization there. The real test on this point was what was actually done with such capital as was available. What the shortage-of-capital argument really meant was that those southerners who possessed capital were precisely those who most profited from the cotton economy at its best.

Here, indeed, lay one essential part of the difficulty. What the South (and hence the nation) was up against was a state of mind—a cultural outlook which rejected the way of life in the North and endeavored by every means at its command to prevent that way of life from interpenetrating its own. And although this state of mind was not entirely generated by the existence of slavery, it was powerfully conditioned thereby.

This relationship was especially visible in the noncotton economic activities undertaken by the South. Overwhelmingly these tended to be of the sort slave labor could engage in when work in the cotton fields was slack. The raising of corn, plantation gardening, livestock raising, and simple industrial pursuits, all demonstrated the strength of this tendency. It is true, as many have emphasized, that the South was not as dependent on cotton as history books often lead us to believe. But at the same time it is also true that nonstaple pursuits were not allowed seriously to compete with staple production.

In the field of industrial production, moreover, there were additional evidences. Many southerners were explicit in their expression of fears about the incompatibility of industrialization and slavery, and the possibility of a free Negro population could not seriously be entertained. By the same token, many southerners believed that industrialization would create a white wage-earning class which would be abolitionist in sentiment. These anxieties were in turn supported by the fact that in southern cities Negroes did have a tendency to become "free," and that white labor in northern cities was becoming vigorously abolitionist.

But these fears were not the only barrier to southern industrialization. Another key factor had to do with sheer economic disabilities. Although it was true that the nation's tax burden fell most heavily on the South while expenditures for internal improvements were disproportionately spent outside the South, these considerations were trivial by comparison with another handicap under which the South labored.

To promote its own industrial progress the North had secured a substantial and helpful protective tariff. No such aid was possible for the South as against her keenest competition in the industrial states. The Constitution, coupled with such interpretations as Gibbons v. Ogden, had seen to that. It is small wonder that secession sentiment began to grow from this point forward. "Yankee" dominance seemed to be inescapable within the Union whether the South elected to industrialize or not.

Prosperity Takes Command. The new prosperity now gaining momentum was especially active in the field of railroad building. No longer forced to fight its way against the opposition of many vested interests, the railroad was now receiving general support from the nation's investors. Moreover, American railway construction was beginning to receive helpful support from foreign investors. With the demonstration of the value of the railroad on the European scene came an appreciation of its possibilities in America, and as the rate of interest here once again rose above that in Europe, investors were willing to forget the repudiation of state debts. Capital was even available in substantial quantities from communities along the rights of way of the emerging railroads. Realizing the value of railroads to their future development, communities would vie with one another to see which could give the approaching railroad the greater inducement.

There were other reasons, too, why capital was becoming increasingly available. One was the growing interest in the West, naturally accentuated by the rapid development of California. Another was the competition between seaboard cities for more traffic. Just as the success of the Erie Canal had touched off a sharp competition between New York, Philadelphia, and Baltimore, so now did the demonstration of the value of the railroad. The initial advantage in this new competition went to Baltimore and Maryland. So quickly had the Baltimore and Ohio Railroad been brought into operation that the parallel canal facility—the Chesapeake and Ohio Canal—never carried as great a coal tonnage as did the railroad.

New York was slower to respond because her canal was successful, and indeed for a time the Erie Canal enabled New York successfully to maintain her position as against Baltimore. Time demonstrated this to be insufficient, however, and a railroad was built paralleling the canal all the way to Buffalo, New York again taking advantage of her possession of the only "water-level" route from the Atlantic to the Midwest. Later the Erie Railroad was built connecting New York City with the West by still another route, and creating a sharp competition with the New York

Central—a competition which gave New York's port an even greater advantage over its rivals. Pennsylvania was even slower to get under way with serious railroad building, a rather surprising fact in view of the inferiority of her water facilities. But when she did begin, she moved so swiftly and built so well that the Pennsylvania Railroad managed to maintain for Philadelphia her lead over Baltimore.

Boston was not so directly involved in this competitive race, for she could scarcely have been an important contender for trade with the West in any event. Her field lay rather in New England, and her problem was to retain this hinterland for herself. Realizing that railroad development was the key to success in such an endeavor, Massachusetts set about the task of supplying herself with railway connections. So effectively did she achieve this end that at an early date her territory was girded with rail lines, and Boston was thus able to maintain her dominant position in New England and her relative position among the other seaboard cities.

Still a third reason why capital was becoming more readily available for railroad construction was the policy of federal land grants established in 1850. In that year Stephen A. Douglas of Illinois sought a grant of land for the Illinois Central Railroad as a rail link between West and South. Southern support for the project was secured by linking it with the Mobile & Ohio Railroad, a project long cherished by southerners, and by wording the grant in such a way that the transfer was made first to the states of Illinois, Mississippi, and Alabama, and from them to the railroad. By 1850 it was obvious that private enterprise would advance in this important field very slowly (because of the tremendous capital requirements) unless government aid were forthcoming, and land grants seemed to offer the best opportunity for government aid without government interference.

Grants of land assisted railway building in a number of ways. Materials useful in actual construction, especially lumber, were made available without charge. Land actually used by the railway cost it nothing. The practice of donating alternate sections of land along the entire right of way gave the railroad the opportunity of selling land which its own development would make attractive to settlers, thus not only creating a demand for the land and hence a source of capital in the form of land sales but also providing for the generation of the traffic. Moreover, in order to make certain that the new lines received full benefit from these gifts, the government followed a policy of doubling the price at which it sold the retained sections. Land-grant railroads, however, did have to pay a price for these benefits. They had to agree to transport government property and personnel at reduced rates, a concession which was in time to more than reimburse the government for the land sales thus foregone.

Not all the government aid given the railroads came from the federal government, either. Many states purchased railroad bonds, or at least guaranteed their sale. Some state construction also continued, particularly in the South and West, despite the unfortunate earlier experiences with roads and canals; but almost invariably such projects soon reverted to private hands. In other instances, again especially in the South and West, banking privileges were granted to railroads to help these projects secure the necessary capital. Much money was lost by state governments in these ways, especially when state construction was involved, and railway banking companies added their share to the nation's banking difficulties. But railroads did get built.

The accompanying table shows the accelerated progress of railway building in the 1850's. Prior to 1850 only nine thousand miles of railroad existed in the entire country. In ten years this number had increased more than 250 per cent, and an investment of only $300 million had grown into a $1 billion industry.

TABLE 29. A NEW AGE DAWNING

Year	Miles of Railroad	Investment
1830	25	$ 2,000,000
1840	2,800	80,000,000
1850	9,000	300,000,000
1860	31,000	1,000,000,000

Source: Bureau of the Census, *Historical Statistics of the United States, 1789-1945*, p. 200.

In its railroad progress the nation had much to be proud of. Yet, when one looked closely at this achievement, a major defect was apparent. It was passing the South by. Of the nine thousand miles of railroad in the country in 1850, scarcely two thousand miles were in the slave states. Furthermore, the rapidly expanding lines in the East were built to the West rather than to the South. Even the Illinois Central, although receiving the first of the federal land grants, proceeded too slowly to provide a West-South rail connection. Not for ten years was this line continuous from Chicago to New Orleans, while several rail lines plus the Great Lakes connected East with West.

The period of the 1850's was the golden era of the river steamboat. Never had the Mississippi carried so much freight; never had she floated such large vessels. It must have seemed to many southerners that expensive railroads were entirely beside the point when such a splendid transportation facility was already available. When southerners and westerners were making the agreements which led to the passage of the Walker Tariff, the internal improvement measure most prominently included was improvement of the Mississippi River. How pathetic this seems in retrospect! Such an emphasis was outdated in two major ways. For the South the anachronism consisted of an exaggeration of the importance of river transportation in the face of the appearance of the new mode of transportation. For the West it consisted of an exaggeration of the importance of the river as compared with the magnificent possibilities of the Great Lakes, where the clearing away of a few miles of obstructions on the St. Marys River would open a waterway from Minnesota to the Atlantic Ocean.

To be sure, the Great Lakes had not been completely neglected by the West, nor had the federal government been wholly inactive on this front. And, as the sequel was abundantly to demonstrate a few years later, it was not entirely the fault of westerners that progress here was as slow as it was. At the same time, however, it is equally clear that, dollar for dollar, expenditures on the Great Lakes would further the cause of improved transportation at this point more rapidly than expenditures on the Mississippi River —and that westerners as well as southerners were slow to realize this fact.

The day of the river was past; the day of the slave South was rapidly passing—although in the 1850's few men understood these things clearly. Moreover, in the perspective of history it is apparent that the decline in the importance of the Mississippi and the fall of slavery were closely related phenomena.

QUESTIONS FOR DISCUSSION

1. Why did revolutionary thinking become important in every part of the Western world at almost the same time, and why were the objects of revolution so similar in widely separated locations?
2. What was the attitude of the various economic interests toward the "Wilmot Proviso"?
3. Why did southerners who did not possess slaves defend slavery so vigorously?
4. What was the relationship between the discovery of gold in California and the issue of sectionalism?
5. How did businessmen and planters rationalize political cooperation with one another despite their differences?
6. Why was the Compromise of 1850 not permanent?
7. Was the inability of the South to protect her infant industries by tariffs one of the "causes" of the Civil War?
8. Who were the principal beneficiaries of the federal government's land grant policy—settlers or railroad promoters and investors?

Chapter 16

THE UNION COLLAPSES

1852	*Uncle Tom's Cabin* first published.
	Franklin Pierce elected President.
1853	Gadsden Purchase.
1854	Reopening of Japan.
	Kansas-Nebraska Act.
	Republican Party organized.
	"Know-Nothing" Party formed.
1855	"Popular sovereignty" tested in Kansas.
1856	"Bleeding Kansas."
	James Buchanan elected President.
1857	Tariff reduced.
	Dred Scott decision.

The South's backwardness in the field of railroad building was not wholly due to an outmoded outlook on economic affairs. Several of the South's most influential citizens were active railroad promoters, and indeed the Charleston and Hamburg Railroad once boasted of being the nation's second common carrier by rail and the longest railroad in the world under a single management. Charlestonians long dreamed of a connection with Louisville and Cincinnati, and had this project born fruit the South would have had a firm root in the Northwest. But the depressed 1840's and the deaths of Abraham Blanding and Robert Y. Hayne (the most ardent proponents of this project) brought it to an untimely end, and the coming of Civil War saw no significant contact between Charleston and the Ohio River.

Rather this weakness was due to the same factors that had made her what she was in so many other ways. Her low density of population, especially white population, and her very nearly static economy, promised less traffic and hence profits than other parts of the country. In the absence of a diversified agriculture, moreover, a large proportion of this traffic was destined for some southern port, and such products as cotton and tobacco typically originated on waterways open to traffic twelve months in the

TABLE 30. LAG IN THE SOUTH

States Having an 1850 Railroad Mileage in Excess of 300	Mileage	
	Free States	Slave States
New York	1409	
Massachusetts	1042	
Pennsylvania	900	
Georgia		666
Ohio	590	
New Hampshire	471	
Connecticut	436	
Vermont	366	
Michigan	349	
Virginia		341
New Jersey	332	
Maryland		315

Source: By permission from *The Transportation Revolution,* by G. R. Taylor, p. 79. Copyright, 1951, Rinehart & Co., Inc., New York.

year. Finally, southern capital was primarily absorbed by the steadily increasing price of slaves and land.

Railroad to the Pacific? Still the South refused to give up its dreams. Not only were plans continually forming for the building of southern railroads, but a route to the Pacific was as enthusiastically desired by southerners as by northerners. With the annexation of Texas and the acquisition of California, this project had become an important national issue.

There was little basis for such a hope on the part of southerners. While railroad stems were pushing across the Mississippi River in a half-dozen places farther north, the South Atlantic area had scarcely made contact with the Mississippi, much less crossed it. Thus the South was forced to be content with nursing her hope and utilizing her powers to prevent the Pacific railroad from being undertaken elsewhere.

In this defensive posture conditions strongly favored the South. On the one hand, the most likely rival route was a central one starting at Chicago and traversing the area then known as Kansas and Nebraska Territories. But as yet no territorial government had been established there, and until this was done there could be no serious discussion of a railroad over this route. On the other hand, it was obvious that federal government aid would be necessary for such a project. This meant Congressional action, and the South was well situated to prevent legislation she felt to be against her best interest. Not only did southern planters possess minority control over their own state governments, but they were rapidly establishing a minority control over the federal government as well.

In 1853 the South was given an opportunity to do more than defend her Pacific railroad claims against northern ambitions. Franklin Pierce of New Hampshire was President, a so-called "northern man with southern principles," and Jefferson Davis of Mississippi was Secretary of War. A War Department survey indicated that a southern route—extending from Memphis to San Diego—would ideally require access to territory still owned by Mexico, and in December, 1853, the "Gadsden Purchase" transferred this land to the United States. Meanwhile Congress had received a bill proposing that the federal government guarantee $30 million for the construction of a Pacific railroad, a bill enthusiastically supported by southerners and certain New York interests.

The developing situation contained a grave threat to the central route preferred by Stephen A. Douglas and his colleagues in the Northwest. Yet there was no possibility of suggesting the alternative location, for the Kansas-Nebraska territory would have to be organized first. As Chairman of the Senate Committee on Territories, however, Douglas could at least bring in a bill providing for the necessary organization—thus paving the way for the desired railroad action. Herein, however, lay the difficulty. No measure for organizing Kansas and Nebraska could receive Congressional approval without running the gantlet of the slavery controversy. At the same time no bill which did not deal generously with the South would be signed by the President. Facing this issue squarely, the "Little Giant" brought in a bill which would allow citizens of the area to decide by majority vote whether they would or would not permit slavery in their midst.

Douglas' famous "Kansas-Nebraska Bill" was exceedingly bold—if not foolhardy. Much of the territory in question lay north of the area the Missouri Compromise had said was to be forever free. What Douglas was demanding therefore, was the "repeal" of the Missouri Compromise—the opening of westward expansion to the slave economy.

At this stage in historical research it would be naïve to suggest that Douglas was motivated primarily by considerations relating to a Pacific railroad. It would likewise be naïve, however, to explain this step without reference to the railroad issue. After due emphasis is given to the role of impulse in the "Little Giant's" momentous proposal, to his own presidential ambitions, to the weak and strife-ridden nature of Pierce's administration, to Douglas' profound belief in the doctrine of "popular sovereignty," and to his enthusiasm for the West and its development, the conclusion is forced that railroad development in the West was one of the important factors involved.

Douglas well knew his measure would create a storm; there is some reason for believing he was not prepared for the hurricane actually aroused. Fighter that he was, he determined to see the issue through to the finish;

and this he did, setting in motion a train of events leading directly to secession and to the frustration of his own hopes for attaining the presidency.

Western Farmers Rebel. The first consequence in point of time was the formation of the Republican party. Douglas' bill was introduced into the Senate on January 4, 1854. Less than two months later a public meeting was held in Ripon, Wisconsin, to consider the national political situation. The outcome was the passage of a resolution declaring that if the pending bill were passed, a new political party would have to be formed, based solely on opposition to the extension of slavery. Here also the new party was given its name; it was to be called "Republican" because its principles would be taken directly from the Declaration of Independence. On March 3 the Kansas-Nebraska Bill passed the Senate and an equally bitter debate in the House began; on May 9 thirty members of the House of Representatives held a private meeting at which it was emphatically agreed again that a new party was necessary. President Pierce signed the measure into law May 30. Early in July the first elements of an actual party organization took form in Jackson, Michigan.

Why was it that emotions were so quickly and deeply aroused by the appearance of Douglas' suggestion? Why was this new reaction so much more violent than that temporarily quieted by Clay's compromise? Why, finally, was adverse sentiment so much more powerful in the Midwest on this occasion than formerly? There are several answers to these questions, and it is difficult to give priority to any one of them. Most of them, however, take reference from the economic situation then confronting agriculture in the Northwest and labor in the East.

The Northwest in the middle 1850's was prosperous and growing rapidly. Ohio was already one of the ranking states in the Union in population, while Illinois, Iowa, and Michigan all had populations comparing favorably with Massachusetts and New Jersey. The growth of population, moreover, was supplemented from the standpoint of economic development by the fact that the lands of the upper Mississippi Valley were unbelievably rich in soil fertility. The corn, wheat, and meat which supplied the nation's consumers with much of their food and its ports with a portion of their export goods were appearing in ever larger quantities.

Growth of population and soil fertility were still further supplemented, moreover, by striking developments in agricultural technology. Factory equipment was rapidly replacing inferior hand-made tools. Reapers, threshing machines, plows, mowers, drills, rakes—all these were helping to make the farm ever more productive and increasing the surplus of agricultural goods seeking an outlet in world markets. Progress in improving plant types for better quality products and higher yields was generating similar results. Even meat production was growing in efficiency as advances in scientific stock-breeding developed better meat-producing animals, and as medical science began to take seriously the conquest of livestock diseases.

Not only western agriculture, but other western industries as well, were developing rapidly. Meat slaughtering was growing in importance, as was also flour milling, and these industries were key factors in the rise of such new cities as Chicago and Milwaukee. Manufacture of farm implements and miscellaneous other items used by farmers began in western rather than eastern manufacturing centers. A number of other secondary and tertiary industries likewise grew up in support of the increasing commercialization of western agriculture. The result was a circle of mutually interrelated developments leading to an ever greater degree of industrialization. Improved methods of production led to greater agricultural surpluses; greater surpluses led to the release of agricultural workers to other pursuits; the availability of urban workers made possible still more expansion of factory output and hence even larger surpluses.

Where was the Northwest to dispose of its surpluses, down the Mississippi River or over the shiny new railroads to the East? The popular belief has it that because the East built railroads and the South did not, the West began to send its goods eastward rather than southward. Certainly this was a factor. But the important point is that there existed a complex of factors favoring the one set of economic relationships rather than the other.

In the first place, the close relationship which had grown up between West and South had been made possible by the rapid growth of the southern economy. Now, however, the West was growing much more rapidly than the South. Since the industrial East was also growing rapidly, western surpluses were more necessary in New York than in New Orleans. Now that eastern agriculture had relinquished to the West the task of raising the nation's food staples, itself turning to truck farming or dairying or even sending its sons and daughters to work in eastern factories, the eastern population had become dependent upon the staple production of the West. By the same token, of course, and stating the same relationships in reverse, westerners were dependent upon the East for a long list of manufactured goods they were not producing for themselves. In brief the new East-West transportation facilities were not used because they existed; rather they existed because they were needed.

Similar considerations governed where surpluses for export were involved. The principal foreign markets were in Europe, and a route through New York was the shortest way to that market. To be sure, if New York merchants had been listless while New Orleans businessmen had been aggressive, much midwestern grain and meat might have gone to Europe by way of New Orleans. The fact of the matter was, however, that the situation was precisely the opposite. A people who would pay to have others haul their own goods to Europe over a circuitous route would scarcely be aggressive in engrossing the trade of another area. Besides, carrying on a large-scale export business would have required large capital outlays, and the South no more had capital for these facilities than for railway development.

It is tempting to be too harsh on the South in judgments of this sort. The fact remains, however, that the South was out of step with the rest of the economy. Apart from a few progressive spots, innovation in the South was rare and its way made difficult by conservative interests, in striking contrast to the spirit of invention and discovery characterizing the rest of the nation—including western agriculture. Furthermore, these differences tended to be perpetuated because the flow of settlers to the West was now predominantly from the Northeast, and because the environment in the South was so inhospitable to the "Yankee" outlook.

Why was the South so stubborn about her economic development? Why was she unwilling to introduce mechanization even into agriculture as the Northwest was so rapidly doing? Of course, a complex of interrelated factors was involved here, but one item in particular is worthy of note. Capital formation in America, the discovery of mechanical ways of doing tasks which would otherwise have to be done by hand, has resulted in large part from the fact that labor in the United States has always been scarce and therefore expensive. Put differently, the rapid development of technology in this country has been related to a never-ceasing struggle to economize in the utilization of labor, a scarce factor of production. In the South, however, this incentive was almost wholly absent. The existence of the Negro, and especially the standard of living he "enjoyed," gave to the South a cheap supply of labor. This fact set the South apart from the rest of the nation in a way which could hardly have been more fundamental, and because this difference was so basic it was not to disappear for a considerable time.

In short, when the Kansas-Nebraska Bill raised the slavery issue once again it was met by a situation already undergoing profound changes resulting from economic dynamics. The industrial East and the agricultural West, because their economies did complement one another well, inevitably began to ally themselves in common political causes. An agricultural area adapting itself willingly and rapidly to industrialization was allying itself with its industrial partner against an agricultural region which steadfastly refused to adapt itself to the emerging industrial pattern.

This fact, however, is only a general explanation of the new alignments now forming. More specifically, why did many westerners fight so bitterly against Douglas' bill? Why was the Republican party born of this opposition in the very midst of the wheat, corn, hog, and cattle country?

Westward expansion was a fundamental article of faith with the midwestern farmer. Furthermore, the yeoman farmer was as unable to visualize a satisfactory life different from the one he was then living as was the slaveowner. His comparative indifference to the slavery issue to this point, and hence his willingness to ally himself with the slaveowner, had been due to the protection he felt within the framework of the Missouri Compromise. As long as his own expansion opportunities were guaranteed he was not inclined to protest the expansion of slavery. But with the repeal of the Missouri Compromise it appeared that his opportunities were to be sacrificed to the interests of the slaveholder.

This fundamental fact can be stated more pointedly. The western farmer's idea of an acceptable land policy had become by this time a *free* "homestead" of 160 acres for any settler willing to live on it and develop it. Slavery, however, demanded a large area for successful operations. It required no high-level mathematical computation to calculate how many free settlers would be prevented from securing a "homestead" by every plantation of, say, 1,000 acres created out of western territory. As one student of this period has expressed it, the western farmer was not so much opposed to slavery as he was impressed by the fact that slavery and farms of 160 acres were not compatible.

Long before 1854 was over, furthermore, westerners were given concrete evidence that southerners did intend to sacrifice their western friends to their own interests. A rivers and harbors bill, designed to assist especially the West with its transportation problem (including basic improvements on the Great Lakes), was vetoed by President Pierce. With southerners the dominant force in Pierce's administration, it was easy to interpret this action as a dog-in-the-manger stand by the South. In 1854 also the Graduation Act was finally passed, reducing the price of western lands on the basis of the passage of time, but a homestead measure was defeated by the negative votes of southerners. Obviously slaveowners also fully understood that a slave economy could not be built on 160-acre farms.

Eastern Workers Rebel. It was not alone farmers who rose up against the Kansas-Nebraska Act. Laborers also protested bitterly against it. And the motivation behind this opposition was no less obvious and no less compelling than in the case of farmers.

Labor unionism in the 1850's, although it was continuous with predecessor labor efforts, could boast substantial progress. More adequate financial provision was being made for the work of organization through systematic collection of dues and the accumulation of strike funds. Collective bargaining was becoming a more integral part of the labor movement, and the standard collective bargaining unit was everywhere tending to become the entire trade within a single city. Moreover, the growth of production for a wider and wider market, the consequence of the cumulative and interrelated development of railroad transportation and the factory, was bringing about such an intense competition between workers on an even wider basis that in a number of fields national labor unions were being organized. So firmly had "fighting" labor organizations become rooted in the American economy that never again—despite future panics and depressions—was this thread completely lost. Although workers were not wholly avoiding political action, and while labor utopianism in America was not yet a thing of the past, labor leadership had decided that the fight for nonproperty rights was to go on.

This advance in the importance, breadth, and effectiveness of collective bargaining could with some truth be termed the most important development in the labor field to date. On the other hand, however, it is necessary to add that it was much more defensive in character than offensive. The flow of gold from California had, naturally, affected prices, and labor organizations were constantly spurred on by the steady upward climb of the cost of living.[1] Such times are invariably difficult for the working man because wages tend to lag behind the rise in prices. In the 1850's there took place an unprecedented wave of strikes as labor sought to minimize this lag.

For two reasons the fight was almost hopeless. First, the development of transportation, manufacturing technology, and the corporate form of business organization all combined to strengthen the bargaining power of the employer. Not only was the number of employers relatively reduced, a fact contributing to the ease with which employer organizations could be formed and to a greater "waiting power" for the employer as compared with workers, but in addition the greater mobility of both goods and men (particularly the latter) was bringing more and more workers into effective competition with one another. Moreover, and equally damaging to the worker's position, the large production unit was bringing about a visible weakening of the personal relationship between employer and employee and hence a lessening of the social pressure against exploitation. Already the corporation was beginning to be referred to as "soulless," and a large part of the feeling implied by this term was the difficulty workers had in securing what they considered justice from it.

The second factor was a rising flood of immigration. While America had continued to be a destination for a substantial number of immigrants every year, several factors had recently combined to convert this steady

[1] An expansion in the amount of gold available to the economy would not necessarily have contributed to a rise in prices apart from the prior existence of prosperity. The important point here is that with a paper circulation based on fractional specie reserves, the quantity theory of money functions with a powerful multiplier effect. A small increase in bank holdings of specie can become a large increase in circulating money and hence in purchasing power.

flow into a veritable torrent. The Irish potato famine, revolutionary upheavals in Europe, agricultural depression in Germany, and the lure of gold motivated more newcomers than were regularly coming to America. Increasing from a rate of less than one hundred thousand per year ten years earlier, the influx climbed to almost five hundred thousand in 1854. In the six years ending with 1854 the total number of immigrants was more than two million.

TABLE 31. PRESSURE ON THE WORKER

Year	Immigration	Retail Price Index
	(Thousands)	(1913=100)
1849	300	51
1850	315	54
1851	409	60
1852	397	60
1853	401	64
1854	460	64
1855	230	67

Source: Bureau of the Census, *Historical Statistics of the United States, 1789-1945*, pp. 37 and 235.

Obviously no such influx of new people could be absorbed into the economy without important consequences. Partly because the newcomers were representatives of an alien culture and hence had adjustment difficulties at best, partly because they were typically almost penniless when they arrived, partly because "Yankee sharpers" did their best to "fleece" them, and partly because European governments often deliberately sent their undesirables to America, immigrants frequently became public charges. Even though the country was enjoying prosperity, the resultant tax burden understandably generated a certain amount of grumbling.

For a number of other reasons, too, various groups objected to this "invasion" by foreigners. Southerners, for example, protested because many of the newcomers established themselves on western lands, thus limiting expansion opportunities for slaveholders. Northern businessmen were alarmed, not so much by the influx of people (indeed, they were actively employing agents to search foreign lands for cheap labor), as by the influx of European ideas, which they felt might make the urban labor force more difficult to manage. The high place in the American labor movement achieved by many European immigrants was evidence that such misgivings were warranted.

But it was the laborer himself who had the most reason to object. Coming to this country accustomed to a lower standard of living than that enjoyed by Americans, the immigrant tended to compete with native laborers in terms of his own standard of living rather than the one prevailing in the new environment. Here was the most important reason workers were finding it difficult to keep pace with the rising price level. As long as every boat arrival was bringing contenders for urban jobs, collective bargaining and strikes could scarcely be effective.

Because the price level was rising in the 1850's and because labor was not particularly successful in coping with this fact, the labor movement was now a fertile field for the growth of a new utopianism. This time the emphasis was upon the possibility of laborers becoming entrepreneurs (farmers) by the simple expedient of taking up a portion of the vast public domain. Given this emphasis, free western "homesteads" came to be an article of faith with eastern laborers as well as with western farmers. It was not so much that members of the eastern labor force expected to make the western journey themselves, but it was reasonable to suppose that enough of the immigrants would be drained off into agriculture to permit a raising of urban wage levels. Laborers had no more difficulty than farmers in calculating how many surplus workers would not be able to find a frontier opportunity if the western public domain were opened to slaveholders. The elimination of "wage slavery" thus became so intimately related to the problem of negro slavery that the Kansas-Nebraska Act succeeded in achieving the almost impossible task of uniting farmers and laborers behind a common economic program.

A Defeat for Slavery. It would be too much to say that the powerful resistance to slavery now arising was motivated solely by economic considerations. A substantial element of moral indignation was undoubtedly present. But it is not too much to say that this element would never have created the Republican party, kept it together in the trying years after 1854, and later actually precipitated the Civil War. Too few ordinary human beings can become ethically outraged over wrongs geographically far distant. A sustained opposition to personal injuries concretely present is much more easily accomplished. But whatever the complex of factors involved, the event itself was ominous. Thomas Jefferson had said that if the division between economic interests ever coincided with a geographical line the Union could not endure. If conditions did not soon improve enough to reduce the pressure producing the new sectional organization, Jefferson's reputation as a prophet might soon be tested.

There was little chance of a lessening of the pressure. The second consequence of the Kansas-Nebraska Act was the battle for Kansas, and as long as Kansas continued to "bleed" Republican sentiment remained strong. In 1854 this territory was almost empty of people, and so when an act was passed awarding it to whichever side built up the larger number of representatives, what was more natural than for a competition to develop in the settling of this territory? Proslavery and "free soil" groups set up a drive for funds and made broad appeals for people willing to settle in Kansas. It is only natural under the circumstances that these two kinds of settlers, playing for "keeps" as they were, would often come into open conflict. Especially at election time would tempers flare and guns roar as citizens of nearby Missouri "invaded" Kansas in order to cast illegal votes for slavery. Even these irregularities are readily understandable. A free Kansas would have meant a Missouri surrounded on three sides by free and hence hostile states.

The form taken by the battle for Kansas was not at all what Stephen A. Douglas had in mind when he advanced his concept of "popular sovereignty." Rather, his view was that for slavery to exist anywhere it must have the good will of the community. He was right in this, and because he was right there was never any real chance of slavery's securing a legitimate majority in Kansas. Capital is notoriously timid, not flowing freely where there exists danger of confiscation or destruction. Few slaveowners would have been willing in any event to risk the capital invested in slaves north of the Missouri Compromise line. This result was doubly certain when the "free soil" sentiment became thoroughly aroused over the Kansas issue. Many southerners were willing to slip over the Missouri border long enough to cast a vote (or fire a bullet) for slavery. But to move to Kansas with valuable property under these circumstances was quite another thing. In short, the issue was already decided when Douglas presented his bill; it was unfortunate that blood had to be shed which could not really help decide the issue.

Prosperity and Recession. As the first stages of civil war were being fought out in Kansas the nation's economy was enjoying a splendid prosperity. In international trade the decade of the 1850's was marked by a high level of exports and an even higher level of imports. On the export side the principal factors were the industrialization of Europe, a succession of excellent crops, the Irish famine, revolutionary upheavals on the Continent, the repeal of the British Corn Laws, and the Crimean War. The

TABLE 32. PROSPERITY BY FOREIGN TRADE

	1849	1857
	(Thousands of dollars)	
Merchandise exports	131.7	278.9
Merchandise imports	132.6	333.5
Silver imports (+) or exports (−)	−0.8	+1.9
Gold imports (+) or exports (−)	+2.1	−58.6

Source: Bureau of the Census, *Historical Statistics of the United States, 1789-1945,* pp. 244-45.

import level was primarily influenced by such factors as the industrial superiority of England, America's huge exports providing an abundance of purchasing power abroad, the influx of gold from the West creating still more foreign purchasing power, and the country's great need for foreign capital. Special factors also contributing to a flourishing international trade were the discovery of gold in Australia, a significant expansion of trade with the Orient (including the "opening" of Japan by Admiral Perry), and an especially favorable reciprocity treaty with Canada.

Closely related to this boom in international trade was a corresponding upsurge of activity for the American merchant marine. This was the "clipper ship" era, the period in which these small, fast, beautiful, wind-driven, wooden vessels reached the peak of their development. Carrying American and foreign goods to and from virtually every port in the world, these ships created effective competition for every type of vessel and for the merchant marine of every other nation.

At home the major economic development was unquestionably the advance of industrialization. Conditions could scarcely have been more propitious. On the one hand, foreign capital was flowing into the country in unprecedented amounts at a time when capital was more necessary to the country's development than ever before. The greatest need was undoubtedly in the railroad field, but the development of the railroad also intensified the nation's other capital problems. With the improvement of communication between East and West, and with the impetus the railroad was giving to the growth of the factory, much capital was absorbed in western agriculture and in manufacturing. Without the flow of European capital, therefore, the economic expansion of the 1850's would have been impossible.

On the other hand, conditions were extremely favorable to domestic capital accumulation. Rising prices and the lag between price rises and the cost of living, which labor was finding so painful, were prime sources of new capital—made even more fruitful, moreover, by the influx of immigrants which successfully frustrated labor's attempt to narrow this gap. With large domestic capital accumulations, plus an abundant supply of foreign capital, the simultaneous advance of several capital-using industries was less limited than would otherwise have been the case. Thus the fact that the 1850's saw, as one student has expressed the situation, American labor degraded to the lowest level in all of America's history did have its other side.

Given such favorable conditions, it is not surprising that manufacturing grew by leaps and bounds. The appearance of the corporation as an important form of manufacturing enterprise contributed much to the channeling of capital to the nation's factories. Large crops and good prices for agricultural products, furthermore, supplied them with the necessary raw materials and simultaneously gave farmers the purchasing power with which to buy factory-made goods. At the same time a burgeoning technology provided an ever larger number of profitable manufacturing outlets, while the expansion of the railway net widened the market for factory output, thus still further supporting investments in manufacturing. Conversely, there were numerous instances in which factories were organized in more or less out-of-the-way places by railroad capital for the primary purpose of guaranteeing the investment in the railroad. In short, although transportation, agriculture, and manufacturing were actively competing with one another for the available capital, all three were interlocked in a development in which each contributed to the prosperity of the others. As far as manufacturing was concerned it is especially worthy of note that during this period the factory at long last won a clear-cut victory over household and neighborhood production. From this point forward there was no question that America's manufacturing future belonged to the factory.

To be sure, there were a few problems associated with the economic advance of this period, although some of them were not then recognized as such. For example, in 1854 a brief money panic inconvenienced the money market, with minor repercussions throughout the economy. An evidence that all was not well with America's banking and currency system, this episode was soon swallowed up in a further burst of prosperity and speculation. Given other circumstances this setback might have served as a warning of larger difficulties ahead, but in the exuberant confidence of this decade it scarcely made an impression. Instead a period of sustained although moderate land speculation set in which boosted the economy to even greater heights.

In 1854 also, and in part brought about by the decline in business activity of that year, there developed a flurry of cutthroat competition between major railroads serving the eastern seaboard—the New York Central, the Erie, the Baltimore and Ohio, and the Pennsylvania. With its large investment of sunk capital the railroad is an excellent example of a decreasing cost industry. An increased output spread over high fixed costs means lower per unit costs. Conversely it is profitable within limits to quote prices below full cost if the prices charged leave something above out-of-pocket expenses to apply on fixed costs. Cutthroat competition means the charging of less than full cost on so much business that fixed costs are not covered. The nation's first real glimpse of this phenomenon so peculiar to a highly developed industrial economy was the 1854 "rate war" between the nation's major railroads.

Here too was no large economic problem—for the moment. Certainly this railroad rivalry was no obstacle to the country's prosperity. But it also could have served as a warning of problems ahead which were one day to become chronic as industrialization rose to a higher stage of development. For the people directly involved there seemed to be only one way to avoid ruinous competition in the railroad business. This was to come to an agreement on the matter of rates (and it is scarcely necessary to add that railway men in the 1850's did not hesitate). Unfortunately, however, such agreements mean monopoly, and this is a matter with respect to which the public must take a decisive stand. In view of the fact that one of the central problems of the last half of the century was the kind of stand which should be taken in such situations (both inside and outside the railroad field), it is significant that the definitive beginning of this problem occurred at this time.

Of a very different order was the problem of the nation's merchant marine. Here the difficulty was that the high prosperity currently being enjoyed, though real, was essentially false. As the scale of industrial production increased and the size of the typical cargo increased in proportion, the small size of the "clipper" ceased to be an advantage. When that time came the wind-driven vessel lost its speed superiority, because the speed of the "clipper" was largely a function of its lines and hence its size. Simultaneously iron began to replace wood as the basic material in shipbuilding, a development taking from the United States most of her advantage in this field. Even in the coasting trade the ship was now losing much of its pre-eminence to the expanding railway net, a fact which was rapidly completing New York's victory over New Orleans as an export center. In short, even while men were insisting that a new and greater age was dawning for American ships, fundamental changes were taking place which were to produce an altogether different sequel. Actually, the American merchant marine was enjoying its last peacetime prosperity.

One other dark spot appeared in the economy. It was the manufacture of woolens. Here was the only important segment of the manufacturing industry not participating in the general prosperity. The blame for this condition was most frequently placed on the Walker Tariff which had reduced the duty on woolens along with almost everything else. Moreover, there was still a substantial tariff on raw wool, and unfortunately for the wool manufacturing industry the country's dependence upon imported raw materials was steadily increasing. Whether or not New England wool manufacturers were correct in attributing their plight to the tariff, it was clearly enough true that a reduction in the duty on raw wool would be helpful. This fact plus the desire of southerners for another reduction in the tariff set the stage for a renewal of the chronic controversy over this issue.

The political situation was extremely favorable for the legislation soon to be enacted. President Pierce was a New Englander and the administration he headed was dominated by southerners. On the other hand, the center of the country's wool production was now in Ohio. There was thus no obstacle to a tariff revision which would simultaneously satisfy both southerners and New Englanders. Accordingly a measure was drawn up reducing protection on most items but giving a substantial boon to wool manufacturers by a reduction in wool duties greater than the reduction in the woolen schedules. At the same time cotton textile production, another major New England industry, was shielded from the reduction by lifting its output to a higher rated class. The vote on passage indicated unmistakably what was happening. New Englanders and southerners voted for the measure; westerners and middle staters voted against it.

The Tariff of 1857 was not the last victory won by the South in these trying times, but there were to be few more. Just prior to the passage of the tariff the Democrats had met the Republicans in the first presidential contest since the new party was formed. The results were most revealing—and foreboding. Although the Democrats won the victory, the Republican party clearly emerged as a major party. Not yet victorious, the Republicans were plainly not far from the door of power. If the Democrats should ever lose their unity, there was no doubt that a Republican would be elected President.

During the next twelve months there occurred two events which were in time to complete the work of turning the nation over to sectionalism. The first was the Dred Scott decision, a pronouncement by the Supreme Court to the effect that Congress did not have constitutional authority to legislate concerning slavery. A logical sequel to the Kansas-Nebraska Act, this event greatly intensified northern opposition to slavery. The second was the bitter rupture between Douglas and the Buchanan administration. When the new President sought to "bribe" Kansas into accepting a slave constitution, the staunch defender of the doctrine of popular sovereignty was forced to withdraw his support. With this action the last vestiges of the once powerful South-West alliance were dissolved, although this had been clearly foreshadowed by the Tariff of 1857. Without its western wing the Democratic party was helpless.

All that remained was for another presidential election to make official what had already taken place. The Union was no more.

QUESTIONS FOR DISCUSSION

1. Why was it important to the various regions whether the first transcontinental railroad was located to the north or to the south?
2. What was the connection between the Kansas-Nebraska Act and the formation of the Republican party?

3. Did the "repeal" of the Missouri Compromise "cause" the Civil War? Would there have been no Civil War if there had been no public domain?

4. How were the grain and meat economy of the West and the industrial economy of the East interrelated?

5. How did immigration make this period a more difficult one for workers? What was the economic basis of this rapid influx of foreigners?

6. How realistic was the eastern laborer's insistence that an open frontier would assist him in his battle against the cost of living?

7. To what extent was the "Battle for Kansas" a political rather than an economic controversy? How can the line between these two things be drawn?

8. Could the United States have had a period of prosperity without a high level of foreign trade? Could the nation have had a high level of foreign trade without at the same time having prosperity?

9. Why did economic recession precipitate cutthroat competition in the railroad industry?

Chapter 17

TWO CULTURES IN CONFLICT

1857 Prosperity gave way to panic.
1858 Douglas and Lecompton.
Lincoln's "House Divided" speech.
Lincoln-Douglas debates.
Economy at its lowest point.
1859 John Brown's raid.
Southern Commercial Convention at Vicksburg recommended reopening of the African slave trade.
1860 Threats of secession.
"Black" Republicans secured control over the government.

History Repeats Itself. American prosperity during the 1850's was less wild and unrestrained than in the 1830's. At the same time, however, there were present the same factors of rapid expansion and ultimate overextension which had characterized earlier American prosperities.

For example, land speculation continued to be prominent. In the South the rising price of slaves put unceasing pressure on the cotton economy to abandon deteriorating soil and move westward. In the Northwest land speculation was promoted less by necessity than by sheer good times, although there were several other factors promoting activity in western lands. The Graduation Act reducing the price of unsold lands stimulated not only the sale of land but also the purchase of larger quantities than would otherwise have been the case. California continued to lure settlers by the thousands, and the discovery of gold and silver in the Denver ("Pike's Peak or Bust") area promoted settlement in that region. Especially, perhaps, was the western march of railroad building related to land purchase and sale. Extension of lines across the Missouri River and across Minnesota made economically valuable land which would not have been attractive under other circumstances, and the government's land grant policy in aid of western railroad building gave railroad companies a substantial incentive to promote both colonization and speculation. Even the frantic haste to settle Kansas contributed its share to speculation.

But not all speculation was on this occasion carried on in land. In addition, corporate securities and commodities furnished other outlets. As the corporate form of doing business gained momentum, New York emerged as the nation's central market for stocks and bonds, and "Wall Street" (often used as a synonym for the New York Stock Exchange) became the scene of intense activity in prosperity years. To legitimate and necessary trading in securities was being added the first large-scale attempts at market manipulation, a development creating many speculative opportunities. Railroad securities, moreover, were often inherently speculative because of the "overbuilding" of lines into territory not yet sufficiently developed to yield a net income and the effects of financially disastrous rate wars. Throughout this period banks and insurance companies for the first time became heavily implicated in the structure of credit, with banks not only holding large quantities of securities in their own portfolios but also liberally extending credit to brokers and traders.

Speculation in commodities was not carried as far as speculation in securities, in part because institutional facilities were less adequate. Whereas in 1857 formal trading in securities had existed for forty years, the Chicago Board of Trade had only nine years to its credit. Similar in function to the New York Stock Exchange, and logically located in the heart of the grain country, the Board of Trade was a place at which grains could always be bought and sold. Useful as an institution for (among other things) smoothing out seasonal price fluctuations and hence distributing commodity consumption more evenly throughout the year, [1] such central markets also provide opportunities for speculation. Although the market mechanism for exchanging other commodities was not as far advanced as in the case of grain, speculation in such commodities as sugar, cotton, and wheat was sufficiently widespread to occasion critical editorial comment.

Not all America's prosperity, of course, is to be explained by speculation. Real factors such as the growth of the West, factory expansion, and railroad building were the foundation on which the boom ultimately rested. But when to the needs of real capital formation was added the widespread use of funds for speculative purposes, it is understandable that the strain on a poorly developed monetary system might at some point become too great.

[1] Speculative transactions in a commodity (that is, buying and selling for future delivery) make it much easier for such a good to be purchased at harvest time when prices are low and held until supplies would otherwise be short and prices are consequently more favorable. The result is that prices are strengthened at the seasonal low point, and correspondingly weakened at other times. And to whatever extent prices throughout the year are stabilized, so too is consumption.

Monetary Vulnerability. Actually the nation's money and credit structure was vulnerable at several points. In the first place, it was highly centralized in a few great commercial centers, which, because of the immense importance of foreign trade to America and the later development of the American interior, were primarily the great coastal ports of New York, New Orleans, Boston, Philadelphia, Baltimore, and San Francisco. These centers were in turn overwhelmingly dominated by New York. The six ports accounted for well over 90 per cent of all imports and exports, while New York's share was greater than that of the other five combined and well over twice as great as that of its nearest rival (New Orleans). Furthermore, it has been estimated that more than 90 per cent of all domestic manufactures was distributed from New York, Boston, and Philadelphia. While both the American export market and domestic trade were financed by a complex credit edifice built on the banking system of the eastern port cities in general and the New York money market in particular, the soundness of the exchange mechanism in the interior was inseparable from conditions in the eastern money market.

In the second place, this relationship operated also in reverse. The products of the interior were sold only at certain seasons, and as a result credits for the South and West tended to be large in the late fall and early spring. In fact, during the fall, gold was often shipped from New York to New Orleans to handle the seasonal peak of the cotton movement. When heavy grain credits coincided with a shipment of specie southward, the strain on the New York money market might become severe. Moreover, it was in the summer that gold was most apt to flow from New York to foreign centers in payment for imports purchased in anticipation of a fall demand arising from the sale of seasonal agricultural produce. If such an outflow of gold coincided with a loss of gold to the interior, the pressure on New York would be great indeed. Because, finally, quarterly payments of many kinds—that is, rents, interest, dividends, fees, premiums—frequently fell due in August, that month was a critical one for the nation's financial structure.

In the third place, the functioning of the nation's monetary mechanism was dependent upon economic conditions in the interior in another important way. Because the internal balance of payments normally favored New York, notes issued by interior banks were constantly flowing eastward. Since it was too expensive to send all these notes home for redemption, while it was at the same time of the utmost importance that as a part of the circulating medium they pass at face value, a substitute program was necessary. In Boston the technique hit upon had been the "Suffolk System," and in New York a similar program was inaugurated. Country banks maintaining deposits in New York were not subject to having their notes returned for redemption, and since New York paid 4 per cent interest on these deposits (for use in the call-loan market particularly for security trading) there was a strong inducement to cooperate in this program.

These country bank deposits provided an extremely volatile element in the assets of the city banks. Since country banks rarely had an adequate supply of specie, they were typically allowed to issue notes on the basis of security holdings. In addition, agricultural mortgages were apt to represent a substantial part of country bank assets. The consequence of these facts was that a deposit by a country bank in a city bank was often the principal *liquid* asset the former possessed. In a period of declining security and/or land values, therefore, country banks were apt to withdraw their city deposits. Because of the close connection between these deposits and the stock market, a still further decline in security values might be precipitated and a vicious circle of deflation set in motion.[2]

A fourth vulnerability of the nation's money and credit system arose out of still another facet of America's financial organization. The country's banking system was in fact a curiously dual affair. Country banks, serving an agricultural clientele, were primarily concerned with the historic function of banks—the supplying of a medium of exchange. City banks were no longer so concerned with this function, doing much of their business on a deposit basis. But, although the practice of these banks was already following modern lines in this respect, city bankers still tended to apply criteria for monetary management derived from the older type of banking operation. Rather than insisting on an ample specie reserve against deposits, they still watched most carefully the ratio of specie to circulating notes. Many bankers were to learn that the new type of banking operation required new standards for safe practice, and in the ensuing panic that lesson was learned in the hardest possible way. Only in Louisiana were the new criteria being applied in a thoroughgoing manner (and when panic came Louisiana banks did not suspend specie payments), but unfortunately it was in New York that the greatest need for understanding existed.

The "Panic of 1857." Had conditions in the 1850's been different, the monetary difficulties of the United States might have arisen solely out of these vulnerabilities. As events worked themselves out, however, the impetus seems to have come largely from another and in some respects an even more basic vulnerability of the financial system—the dependence of the American economy upon the British money market. Internal factors

[2] A seasonal outflow of specie from New York, for example, might start such a vicious circle. Call loans would be called in, forcing security holders to reduce portfolios. Security prices would then fall, at which point country banks might be forced to retrench by withdrawing deposits in city banks. For each dollar of reserves thus removed from use as a "central" bank reserve, credit outstanding might well have to be reduced by several dollars. This development would put still greater pressure on security and land values, and the deflationary spiral would then be ready for its second turn.

thus were primarily influential in reinforcing the blow when it fell and providing the vicious circle which carried the process of deflation to extremely painful lengths.

The continued importance of foreign capital in America is fully understandable in terms of the scarcity of such resources relative to the capital needs of a rich and rapidly devoloping economy. It is likewise understandable that the principal source of foreign capital was England, in view of the fact that Great Britain and her empire bought about one-half of all American exports and provided an equal proportion of total American imports. English capital financed most of America's import and export trade with England, and much of her trade with other countries was also financed by British capitalists. In addition, funds used in the New York money market often came from the British Isles, and English investors continued to purchase American corporate securities. Obviously, with so many interconnections between the two financial structures, a tightening of conditions in London could easily have significant repercussions in the United States.

The tightening which eventually did take place was in part an outgrowth of prosperity conditions and in part the result of special factors. One of these special factors was the outpouring of gold from California and Australia. All over Europe the market ratio between gold and silver was upset, and silver in silver standard countries began to disappear into private hoards. Instead of the new gold representing a net increase in specie support for the world's money, therefore, it had the opposite effect.

Another factor leading to a dilution of the specie foundation of Europe's money was the Crimean War. The fighting in the Near East required large expenditures, much of which had to be transferred in metal. More indirectly this encounter increased the importance to Western Europe of the Far East, an interest which entailed a further drain on specie reserves. Still more indirectly it contributed to the financial weakening of an already overextended France, who responded by "raiding" the gold resources of the Bank of England.

All these special factors, combined with the monetary expansion of a high prosperity, had produced by the mid-point of the decade a situation in which the Bank of England was forced to follow a policy of cautious retrenchment. Gradually the discount rate on prime commercial paper rose to 7 and 8 per cent. The availability of so high a return with virtually no risk left little incentive for the purchase of speculative securities in the United States. As the Bank of England rate rose, therefore, one result was a withdrawal of British funds from America, and a weakening of security prices. The depreciation in these assets in turn put a corresponding pressure on the money mechanism undergirding the American financial structure. At some point this weakness would have to come to terms with the increasing need for capital to support the rapid economic growth in this country.

By mid-1857 the financial situation had reached what was recognized by many as a saturation point. During the early summer, however, with the balance of payments favoring New York, no crisis developed. Then, in August, as foreign and interior needs began to make the usual seasonal demands on New York funds, the strain became too great. On the morning of August 24 the New York branch of the Ohio Life Insurance and Trust Company was forced to declare itself bankrupt. Almost instantly panic gripped the New York money market and swiftly spread to other vital points. The inevitable vicious circle of deflation now took command, and for two months the economy of the nation was virtually prostrate. Panic was then followed by the inevitable depression; the optimism of earlier years gave way to a mood of dark foreboding, which, mingled with the tension on the political scene, created an environment in which nerves were taut and tempers set on edge.

Impact in the South. A major economic holocaust such as the "Panic of 1857" could not have taken place without vital consequences for sectional interrelationships. The late summer of 1857 saw southerners planning to harvest abundant crops for sale at extremely high world prices. Shortly after the harvest began, however, it developed that cotton bills drawn on New York could not be discounted with the usual facility, and prices sagged dangerously, A little later it became known that cotton bills could scarcely be sold at any price, and the bottom literally fell out of the cotton market.

Nothing, perhaps, could have done more to solidify the southern view that the South's economic difficulties were primarily the fault of the industrial East. Here was tangible evidence of economic "vassalage" more plain than anything provided by the tariff controversy, and more painfully convincing than any of the statistics used in the argument for diversification of industry or direct trade with Europe. Coming at this particular juncture in the conflict between the sections, moreover, the panic suggested strongly that any success achieved by the South in emulating the North would result only in converting the southern economy into the weak and hollow structure the North was now demonstrating itself to be.[3] And when to the failure of the machinery for marketing cotton during the

[3] This was an exaggeration, of course, but the basic fact could not be gainsaid. The truth is that a financial panic is an attempt on the part of an economy's members to liquidate their assets—to transform noncash resources into cash—whereas it is obvious that in an industrial economy real resources cannot be so converted. If there were no other reason, furthermore, fractional reserve banking would adequately explain this impossibility. The wholesale economic distress associated with panics is the consequence of this attempt to do the impossible; an economy in the throes of such a convulsion is indeed weak and hollow.

1857-58 selling season was added the fact that the South suffered less severely from the depression than either the East or the West, even more fuel was added to the fire of southern discontent.

The readiness of southerners to belittle the importance of the Union to them was clearly demonstrated by the response given Raymond Kettell's book, *Southern Wealth and Northern Profits.* Intended as a "Union" document, this work was a detailed calculation of the value of union to the northern economy. It purported to demonstrate that a large proportion of the capital accumulated in the North was the result of a siphoning off of southern wealth. Kettell maintained that because of this fact a rupture in the Union would fall more heavily on the North rather than the South, and that therefore the North would be well advised not unnecessarily to agitate the slavery question. As dubious as was the reasoning on which these conclusions were based, it is not surprising that northerners did not take it seriously. What is much more significant is that it became a widely quoted secession document as southerners chose to emphasize the South's losses from union rather than the North's gains.

Another consequence of depression significantly affecting the attitude of the South toward the North was the failure of a number of southern industrial enterprises. Inevitably every such failure was pointed to by secessionists as evidence that the South could not develop an industrial economy in the face of the North's overwhelming advantages, advantages the South could not overcome as long as it remained in the Union. Furthermore,

TABLE 33. THE MEASURE OF DEFEAT

Industry in 1860	South	North
Establishments	31,365	109,068
Capital invested *	167.9	842.0
Cost of raw material *	167.1	864.5
Persons employed	189,532	1,131,614
Cost of labor *	51.6	327.3
Value of products *	291.4	1,594.5

* Millions of dollars.

Source: By permission from *Economic History of the South,* by Emory Q. Hawk, pp. 311 and 414. Copyright, 1934, Prentice-Hall, Inc., New York.

it was apparent that even in agriculture the South was making no progress toward diversification; the per capita output of every crop except cotton was either decreasing or at most remaining constant. In the face of such overwhelming evidence that cotton *was* king, and growing more regal with every passing year, it is not surprising that more and more southerners began defending enthusiastically (if defensively) the notion that cotton *should be* king.

It was during the depression following the "Panic of 1857," too, that southern opposition to slavery in the South reached its peak. For long it had been emphasized that only a minority of southern whites actually benefited from the institution of slavery. In all no more than three hundred sixty thousand whites owned any slaves, and of these a large number owned only one. In addition, it was easy to demonstrate that the slave-cotton economy was not providing expanding opportunities for whites to the same extent as the northern economy. For example, it was well understood that immigrants seeking improved economic opportunities carefully avoided the South. It could also be demonstrated that fifty years of cotton culture had transformed the population of South Carolina from one containing a majority of whites to one containing a majority of blacks, and that the largest share of the white population was in the "poor white" category.

Reflecting these attitudes, there now appeared one of the classic pieces of literature of the entire slavery controversy—Hinton Helper's *The Impending Crisis: How to Meet It.* An attack on slavery by a southerner, and specifically pleading the cause of the "poor white," this volume defended the thesis that a handful of southern whites was maintaining a majority of their white brethren in as vicious a state of subjection as the Negro slave. Full of imperfections—both errors of fact and weaknesses in analysis—Helper's work nonetheless was a powerful statement, one which would easily have convinced anyone inclined to believe its basic premise. Furthermore, this appeal could hardly have been better timed. To the normal woes of the smaller operator were now added the evils of a severe depression. If the spark of revolution could be kindled at all, such a work at such a time would surely have started a flame.

Actually it did nothing of the sort; its influence was as perverse as that of Kettell's work. Aimed at inciting southerners to rise up against the slaveholding aristocracy, it was destined to be used mainly in northern abolitionist circles where the ideas it contained, its statistics, and the fact that it was written by a southerner were put to active use. Only in the border states—those with relatively declining Negro populations—did any substantial movement of opposition to the vested aristocracy arise. And it is, of course, significant in this connection that Helper himself was from North Carolina. In the "deep" South agitations such as these could not take root.

The reason is, in retrospect at least, obvious. Exactly the same factors which were giving impetus to secession prevented slaveless southerners from breaking with their own elite. If the South's economic difficulties were the result of northern "exploitation," revolution would not help. From this standpoint it was a handicap to Helper's cause that his book coincided with depression. Moreover, if the North did intend to free the slave, with all the undesirable economic and social consequences expected to flow from that contingency, here was a basis for joining hands with the aristocracy rather than overthrowing it. No better evidence of the intellectual bankruptcy of Helper himself could be found than the fact that his remedy was deportation of the Negro (to Africa), a solution which all thinking men agreed was impractical. Precisely because there was no solution to the problem of "getting rid" of the Negro, there could be no strong southern sentiment favoring "getting rid" of the institution of slavery. Rather, when the time for decision ultimately came it was the non-slaveholders who took the lead.

As the South's attitudes crystallized against abolitionism, southerners more and more found common ground in the extension of slavery. Thus, in the late 1850's, the sentiment in favor of reviving the slave trade became strong, and the illicit traffic in slaves (carried on especially by New Yorkers) showed a marked increase. At first this agitation was a prosperity oriented attempt to "democratize" the institution in the face of steadily rising slave prices. Later other considerations became paramount. Thus as the battle for Kansas became obviously a victory for the North, the importation of slaves seemed more than ever necessary. It was clearly the surplus population of the North in the form of European immigration which was making a free Kansas possible. Since white immigration avoided the South, the only way southerners could compete with the North in the culture struggle was by making Negro "immigration" legal. Moreover, if the fates had written that the South's principal activity was to be the raising of cotton, few southerners doubted that slavery was the only basis on which economic opportunities in the South could be expanded. Few southerners doubted either that cotton production would have to be expanded if the United States' position supplying the world's textile mills was to be maintained. And if that were lost, the South's economic position would be desperate indeed.

Powerful as were the reasons for agitating a revival of the slave trade, however, this solution was never upheld by a majority of southerners. On the one hand, such agitation was so bitterly opposed in the North that the South's well-being in the Union semed to demand that it be kept beneath the surface. On the other hand, threatening to reopen the external slave trade would seriously have damaged relations between the "border" states and the states of the "deep" South. The good will of these states was of the utmost importance to the cotton economy whether it continued to be a part of the Union or not. And doubtless many southerners who resented the presence of the Negro did not want to see a larger Negro population. This state of affairs was pathetically indicative of the South's dilemma. Committed to the extension of slavery, southerners were unable to unite in support of a program essential to achieving that end.

Impact in the North. But it was not only in the South that depression generated feelings intensifying sectional hostility. In the North both farmers and laborers were experiencing difficulties making them even more certain that the spread of slavery must be curbed.

For example, the depression winter of 1857-58 saw as intense a period of social misery as the country had ever experienced. There were more workers in the nation now, more men and women whose sole source of livelihood was a job which could be taken from them without notice. Half of the textile workers of the country were idle. In addition, lumbermen in Wisconsin and Michigan, New England fishermen and sailors, St. Louis factory hands, and Pennsylvania iron workers demanded from society a sustenance they would have been delighted to earn but which a malfunctioning society would not permit them to earn. Even those workers fortunate enough to remain employed were forced to accept repeated wage cuts as employers took advantage of their own increased bargaining power. So sharp was the reversal of the fortunes of laboring men in America that immigration came virtually to a standstill and thousands of new arrivals hastened homeward.

In the face of these new conditions, trade union activity was once more threatened with extinction, although this time worker solidarity was by no means destroyed. So limited in value were these organizations that labor turned once more to political self-help. And while various projects occupied labor's political attention locally, the most important achievement of this new drive was to be its success on the national front. That success was to be nothing less than a major share in the destruction of chattel slavery in America.

There were several reasons why an attack on southern slaveholders became a major preoccupation with labor. For one thing, there was in the North a kindred feeling for white laborers in the South. The slavocracy had unmistakably indicated that it would use its control over a slave labor supply to the fullest extent in preventing the growth of a labor movement in "Dixie," and labor leaders (probably correctly) concluded that one of the main reasons industry was not developing in the South was that the southern aristocracy feared such an evolution would promote the rise of cities in which their control over labor would be less complete than on the plantation.

However, it is to be doubted that class sympathy for unknown white laborers in the South explains any but a minor part of labor's drive against slavery. Still less were northern workers concerned about the welfare of Negro workers in the South, although some moral abolitionism was undoubtedly present. In the dark depression days following the panic, northern laborers had more immediate concerns. Unemployed workers and other workers virtually at the mercy of employers were more than ever eager to see the wide open spaces of the West made freely available to the nation's "surplus" labor supply. Administration talk of annexing Cuba and southern agitation for reopening the slave trade, together with the attempt to make Kansas a slave state by fair means or foul, made eastern laborers certain that free land could be made available only if the slave power were destroyed.

This motive, however, was only a continuation of the earlier resistance of labor to the Kansas-Nebraska Act, although it was no doubt accentuated by the depression. In addition, laborers had now an altogether different reason for resisting the advance of slavery. While endeavoring to protect themselves from ruinous competition with Negro labor in America, workers did not become insensitive to the need to protect themselves from a competition with the cheap labor of the Old World considered equally ruinous. When panic and depression threw thousands of workers out of their jobs, it was only natural that the labor movement would weigh the pros and cons of protection from the flow of foreign imports more thoughtfully than ever before. As a result organized labor became strongly protectionist and hence uncompromisingly opposed to southern proponents of revenue tariffs.

Farmers were not faced with outright distress to the same extent as labor; they stood closer to the ultimate source of the nation's well-being and could therefore fall back on their own resources with greater effectiveness. But farmers the country over indignantly laid the blame for the depression on money "manipulations" in Boston, New York, and Philadelphia, and thousands of western settlers resented losing their land to eastern mortgage holders. When eastern-owned railroads persistently refused to reduce freight charges in the face of depression and short crops, farmers in the Middle West began to listen to radical remedies for their distress. Wherever there were farmers in large numbers there was excited, enthusiastic, and often belligerent talk of the need to make the public lands of the West more readily available.

Here was a major policy item which labor and the farmer still clearly shared. Laborers were not particularly concerned with the freight rate on wheat, and many farmers would perhaps have preferred a lower tariff to a higher one. But the dream of free homesteads in the West was common to both groups, and both were agreed on several things about that dream. First, it was being threatened by the slavocracy. Second, it was being threatened by the government's policy of throwing public lands open to eastern monopoly by grants to states, railroad grants, and the bidding in of large tracts by speculators. Third, the eastern business interests and the slavocracy were closely cooperating with one another in an effort to keep the public domain out of the hands of the average citizen. This pattern of convictions proved sufficiently concrete and basic to keep the fortunes of the Republican party at a high ebb.

Prelude to Secession. Judgments such as these did not do injustice, either, to eastern business groups. Although, to be sure, some business interests revised their allegiances as worker influence began actively to support tariff protection, on the whole businessmen continued to press for measures designed to keep the Union together at almost any cost. When the first shadows of depression began to fall, indeed, eastern merchants were all the more eager to conciliate the South because that section of the country was the one most nearly able to pursue a business-as-usual policy. Thus, as Republican efforts to secure control of the government gained momentum, northern businessmen denounced "Black" Republicanism and its purely sectional appeal almost as vigorously as southern secessionists.

If southerners felt that the development of an exclusively sectional party furnished them with a justification for the hostility they felt, northern laborers and farmers were soon given a still greater incentive for the stand they were taking. In January, 1859, a bill providing government aid to a Pacific railroad by way of a northern route was resoundingly defeated in the Senate, and the project of a railway connecting eastern United States with California was once more shelved. Shortly thereafter Buchanan vetoed a measure which would have granted public lands to the states for use in establishing colleges of agriculture and the mechanic arts; southerners especially found fault with this proposal both on constitutional grounds and because the grants were to be made in proportion to Congressional representation. This development was quickly followed by a second Buchanan veto. Here the victim was a bill to make more easily navigable the difficult waters connecting Lakes Huron and Erie, a project which would have been a great boon to lake transportation for western farmers. Simultaneously a bill to raise the level of the tariff failed of enactment, although on this occasion the northwestern farmer did vote with the South.

These 1859 reverses at the hands of southerners were almost identically repeated in 1860. First, another measure to increase the tariff failed to pass the Senate despite the critical condition of the government's finances since the panic. Next, still another measure to improve navigation on the St. Clair River was vetoed by the President on the ground that even such an obvious interstate commerce matter should be the responsibility of state governments. In May another vote was taken on a Pacific railroad with an eastern terminus north of Mason and Dixon's line, and again the proposal met defeat. Finally, in what was the cruelest blow of all, a compromise homestead measure passed both Houses of Congress, receiving southern support partially because it contained little in the way of real homestead provisions and partially in anticipation of the forthcoming presidential veto. It was this conflict between the southern demand for slavery expansion and the northern demand for homesteads that prompted one northerner to assert that the fundamental question now before the country was whether the "niggerless" were to have "niggers" or whether the landless were to have land.

The deadlock in Congress at this point exactly mirrored the issue between the sections. Southerners could not accede to the broad powers for the federal government implied in banking, tariff, homestead, and internal improvement legislation without appearing to concede the right of Congress to legislate concerning their way of life. Northerners, on the other hand, were seeking to achieve a way of life which required the exercise of precisely these powers by the central government. The issue thus was not slavery as such although slavery was an almost perfect symbol of the conflict. The South could not feel at home in the Union until the Union accepted its culture, a culture the most representative item of which was Negro slavery, and in the face of growing antislavery sentiment outside the South it was apparent that the South's culture would be accepted in the North only on the basis of coercion. Therefore the South's most pressing need was enough expansion of slave territory to enable her to protect herself within America's constitutional system. On the side of the North the need was to grow strong enough to override southern opposition, a condition rapidly coming to pass in any event. Part of the northern strategy, in consequence, was resisting slavery expansion, an attitude which could only result in a redoubling of southern efforts—which efforts in turn made all the more important to the North the containment of the slave power.

In mid-1860 the most tense presidential campaign in the history of the country got under way. A party asking for no votes south of Mason and Dixon's line faced a party so strife-ridden that it did not even expect victory. The situation looked dark indeed for the South. Many years before the slave power had lost control of the House of Representatives. More recently it had lost control of the Senate. Now the presidency too was slipping from its grasp, a fact which seemed all the more threatening because of the Republican candidate's statement that a nation divided against itself could not stand—that America could not go on half-slave and half-free. In vain later did Lincoln insist that he had not meant this statement to be interpreted as an abolitionist utterance; rather it had been intended as an observation in the field of historical evolutionism. But in the emotionally charged atmosphere in which these historic events were occurring it is not at all surprising that southerners misunderstood. And later, when southerners were called upon to make their fateful decision, these words by Abraham Lincoln contributed as much as any one factor to the transformation of secessionist sentiment from a minority to a majority view.

QUESTIONS FOR DISCUSSION

1. Why did prosperity and speculation so frequently go together in America's early history? Is this still a characteristic of the American economy?
2. In what ways was the American banking system weak at this time? Why had these weaknesses been allowed to become so serious?
3. If the country's banking system had not been as vulnerable as it was, would the "Panic of 1857" still have occurred?
4. What were the interconnections between international economic relationships and the onset of a new panic and depression?
5. How did the economic downturn affect the developing conflict between the sections?
6. To what extent did the South draw correct conclusions from this panic and depression experience?
7. Why is the South's attitude toward the African slave trade appropriately called a "dilemma"?
8. Was the worker's support of protective tariffs at this time wise or foolish? Is there any difference between immigration and imports from the standpoint of labor's economic well-being?
9. In what ways did the South stand against policies considered important in other parts of the country?
10. Could the issue between the sections have been resolved in any way other than by violence? Was the Civil War, in other words, inevitable, as many have maintained?

PART III

THE NATION REBUILT

(1860-1896)

Chapter 18

STRUGGLE FOR SUPREMACY

1860	Secession.
1861	Morrill Tariff.
	Fort Sumter fired upon; Civil War began.
1862	Homestead Act.
	Pacific Railroad Act.
	Morrill Land Grant Act.
1863	Emancipation Proclamation.
	Turning point in the war fortunes of the combatants.
	National Banking Act.
1864	Labor contracts for immigrants authorized.
	Beginning of "Presidential Reconstruction."

Prelude to War. Even with Lincoln's victory virtually certain, southerners did not give up their cause. An important tie between North and South remained in the close relationship between the cotton economy and northern businessmen, and southern leaders made good use of this asset. No effort was spared in convincing eastern merchants that a rupture between the sections would be disastrous to business profits. This effort, moreover, became almost a "reign of terror" when northern creditors were informed that a Republican victory would mean an end to debt payments by southern debtors.

It was no empty threat, as any informed industrialist knew. The fifty-year delay in the collection of southern debts by British merchants after the Revolution was all the evidence necessary. As a result northern businessmen responded magnificently to the call for action. To be sure, some were attracted by the tariff plank in the Republican platform, and by no means a majority supported the southern candidate. But a majority did oppose "Black" Republicanism in general and Abraham Lincoln in particular, and so effective were these political efforts of New York businessmen that the "Empire City" gave a majority of its votes to Republican opponents.

The value of this support for the southern cause was not destroyed by Lincoln's election, either. Since it would be eastern businessmen who would be called upon to finance a shooting war, as long as such a strong bond existed between the industrial East and the cotton South the federal government could scarcely afford to take an uncompromising stand. The memory of federalist behavior in the "second war for independence" yet lingered in the minds of American statesmen. Thus when the news of Lincoln's election precipitated a stock market panic, and especially when Lincoln refused as President-elect to take a conciliatory stand toward the South with a view to relieving distress in the business community, administration support in eastern financial circles was anything but assured.

Unfortunately, however, this relationship between the sections rapidly became artificial. On the one hand, northern support for the South's position could not indefinitely have been coerced by holding over the heads of businessmen even $250 million in unpaid debts. On the other hand, the southern threats themselves in time bore their natural fruit when northern merchants refused further credit to southern purchasers. And when many southern debtors refused to respond to appeals for remittances in the face of the postelection business crisis (caused in part by the withdrawal of eastern deposits by southern banks), relations became badly strained.

One last northern attempt was made to heal the wounds from which the Union was suffering. On December 15, 1860, a large group of New York businessmen, many of them prominent, met to draw up a program of concessions to the South in the interest of reconciliation. Called a "Friendly Appeal," this document suggested substantial compromises. But, partly because the business interests were by now such a small minority in their zeal to keep the South in the Union, and partly because the wheels of secession had already progressed too far, these efforts were "too little and too late." On December 20 South Carolina took the fateful step of secession.

Almost instantly the attitude of the eastern business community underwent a marked change. A firm policy with reference to South Carolina was urged, although efforts to conciliate the other southern states were continued. The tool most effectively used in helping Buchanan take a strong stand with respect to South Carolina was the Treasury's desperate need for funds. Panic and depression had resulted in a chronic deficit, and southern intransigency had successfully prevented raising the tariff. By the end of 1860 the government had been brought to a position where a loan had to be floated, and the first attempt to sell subscriptions to a new loan failed to raise the desired funds. Howell Cobb of Georgia was then Secretary of the Treasury, and the Cabinet contained other southerners and men of like sympathies. Financial leaders made it clear that until Buchanan reconstructed his administration on a "sounder" basis it would be difficult for the government to raise money. After a reorganization of the Cabinet the financial situation became much easier.

Shortly after South Carolina's secession six other states followed her lead, and an independent government was formed. Having decided that safety inside the Union was no longer possible, the South had gone on to conclude that it might never again be as strong relative to the North as at that moment. Immediately the stand of northern businessmen became even more firm. Not only did they now have nothing to gain and everything to lose by further conciliation, but the new Confederate government was beginning to formulate an economic policy which seriously threatened northern interests at several key points.

A number of considerations were uppermost in the minds of southern leaders as they met to formulate some guiding principles. They did not deliberately alienate their friends in the East, although they did of course put their own interests first. Thus they had to think in terms of relationships not only with the East but also with the states in the upper Mississippi Valley, the border states, and between different southern interests themselves. For example, the Confederacy's tariff and navigation policy brought into focus a complex web of conflicts. Free trade, the policy the South had most consistently supported in the past, offered several advantages. Direct trade with Europe might thereby be stimulated, navigation of the Mississippi River would be settled in such a way that the Northwest might well remain friendly to the new "nation," and the important business of exporting staple agricultural products would not be injured.

On the other hand, however, there were certain agricultural and mining industries and embryo manufacturing interests which were desirous of protection, particularly from competitive activities in the North. Furthermore, free trade was undesirable precisely because northerners would (with reason) object to it so vigorously. Such a policy would give the South a substantial advantage in trading with Europe and the Northwest. In the third place, it was argued that a protectionist policy would make it possible for the border states to take over the function of providing the staple states with manufactured goods.

Another difficult point to be settled was the question of the external slave trade. Here also the policies decided upon bore all the marks of the conflict context within which they were determined. The African slave trade was expressly forbidden, and the importation of slaves from Union states was likewise—both of these decisions aimed at attracting the border states into the Confederacy. A revenue tariff was enacted, but in order to keep the level of protection low an export duty on cotton was also levied—and this measure was also expected to have an incidental value in protecting a domestic textile manufacturing industry. The navigation of the Mississippi was made free, and even the South's coastwise traffic was opened to all nations.

Confederate compromises designed to win the allegiance of the upper South were not directly successful, for union sentiment there was stronger than disunion sentiment. But the economic legislation enacted had an indirect effect which operated powerfully in the opposite direction. With the Confederate government collecting duties substantially lower than the North, eastern industry was placed in a difficult situation. Secession was one thing, even peaceful secession, but a commercial war against the economic position of eastern port cities was another thing. Acceptance by northern businessmen of the idea of peaceful separation promptly disappeared and full business support for the government's efforts to maintain the Union by force was available. In turn the government's efforts to coerce the states of the lower South turned the tide of public opinion in much of the upper South (the so-called "middle border") in favor of secession.

The pattern of secession and nonsecession among the southern states is shown in Figure 12. A variety of factors entered into the decisions made, and narrow calculations of economic advantage could scarcely be said to have been the decisive factor. Rather the states whose antecedents and culture were most thoroughly southern—those nearest the deep South—went with the Confederacy, while the state with the fewest southern elements in their culture—those nearest the free states—stayed in the Union. It is noteworthy, for instance, that Missouri was a slave state only to the extent of a narrow belt of counties in its very center, and that the Virginia counties which broke away to form West Virginia were virtually without slaves. It was as though the United States contained two fundamentally different cultures, each of which became progressively weaker as one moved away from its heart. Indeed, this is perhaps as useful a way as any to think of the lineup of states as economic warfare gave way to bloody civil war.

Economic Strength of the Combatants. The resources of the two combatants as they began to mobilize for the great struggle were pitifully unequal. Only nine million people resided in the Confederate states, more than one-third of these being Negro slaves, while the Union states had a population of twenty-two million. Property resources North and South were similarly divided; of an estimated $16 billion in all, the Confederacy claimed not more than $6 billion, and of this amount $2 billion represented the value of the South's slaves. The South possessed practically no shipping, less than 20 per cent of the nation's manufacturing plant, and scarcely one-third of the railway mileage. Still worse, her dependence for manufac-

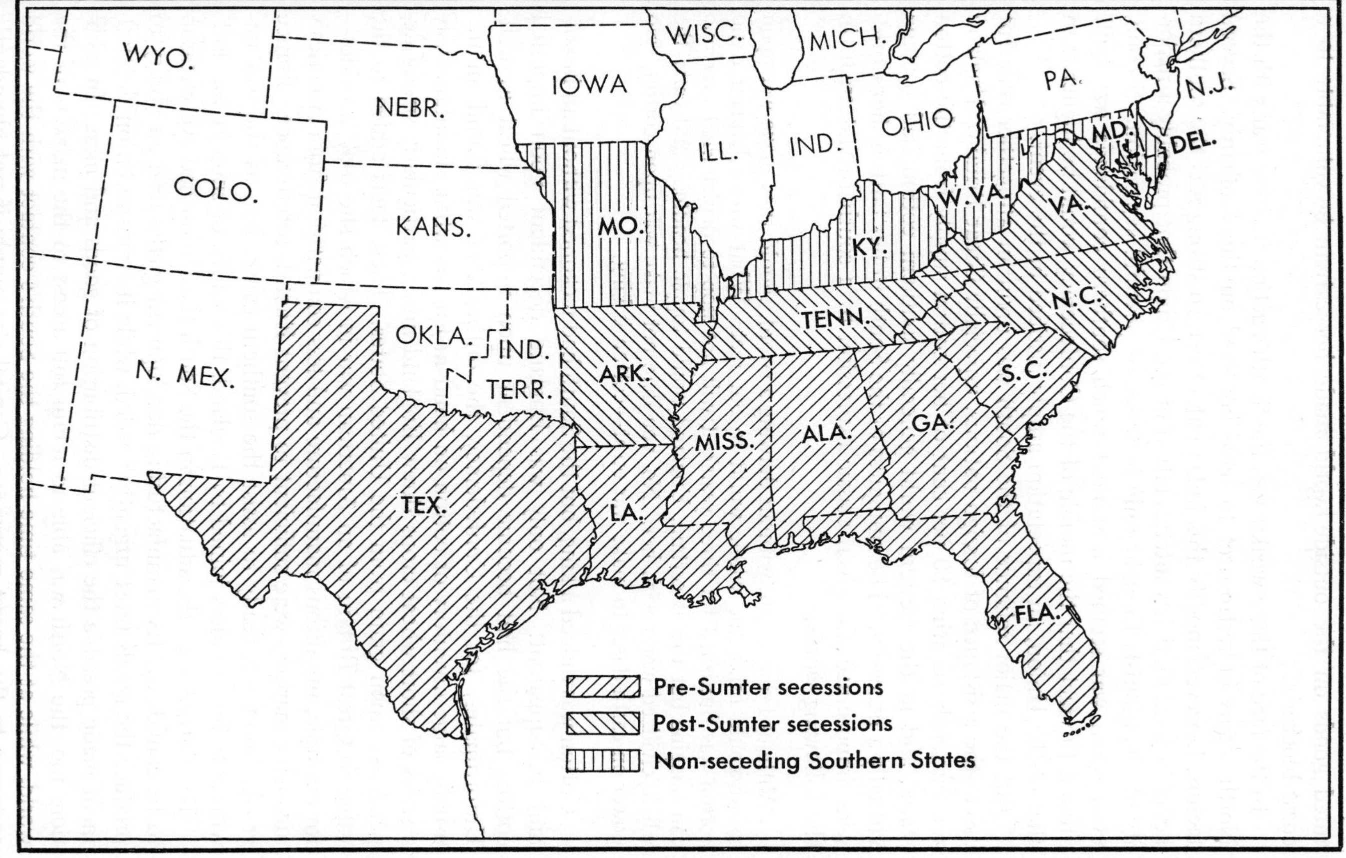

FIGURE 12. Choosing Up Sides.

tured goods on the outside world made her extremely vulnerable to a coast blockade.

In the face of these weaknesses the South's action inviting war with the North seems in restrospect to have bordered on the foolhardy. Several factors, however, modify this judgment. First, so strong was the southern belief in its state-rights interpretation of the Union that probably a majority of secessionists thought only in terms of peaceful separation. Second, even when war seemed imminent much southern confidence was built around the fact that the morale of the Confederacy would be higher than that of the Union, an expectation amply justified in the event.

But the major reliance of the South was upon an altogether different asset—the assistance of foreign nations, especially Great Britain. England was currently securing 80 per cent of her cotton supply from the cotton states, and in the western world generally southern cotton had become virtually a necessity. The smugness of the South in her faith in her world-wide importance was given classic expression by a southern statesman in the following words:

> Without firing a gun, without drawing a sword, should they make war upon us we could bring the whole world to our feet. What would happen if no cotton was furnished for three years? I will not stop to depict what everyone can imagine but this is certain; England would topple headlong and carry the whole civilized world with her. No, you dare not make war upon cotton. No power on earth dares to make war on it—cotton is king.

Cotton was indeed a king, but the South had reckoned without an important heir-apparent. Not only was England dependent upon imported cotton, but she had become dependent upon imported wheat as well. Unfortunately for the Confederacy, the outbreak of war found an unusually large inventory of cotton on hand in Europe while simultaneously a series of short wheat crops threw England into a particularly strong dependency upon grain from the United States. These facts added to the value to Great Britain of an American war in which she took no sides—for example, munitions manufacture and less competition from America's merchant marine—were sufficient to prevent English interference. France at one point was ready to assist the southern cause, but, as she was unwilling to do so unless joined by England, this source of support was lost.

By contrast with the situation in the South the Union had every reason to be confident. Its manufacturing development guaranteed an ability to produce the goods most urgently needed, while its transportation development made possible the efficient distribution of goods and men. In addition, too, the North was able to retain full access to the markets of the world, while at the same time holding the South's contact with the world economy to the barest minimum. Capital was amply if not abundantly available, and it was thus even possible to raise a large army without altering the outflow of goods by the rapid introduction of laborsaving machinery.

Despite these advantages, the North's situation was not all that might have been desired. The postelection depression proved to be more serious than its political origin had led people to anticipate. Repudiation of southern debts and the "repatriation" of southern banking capital touched off a vicious circle of credit retrenchment precipitating a more pronounced succession of business failures than the panic of three years earlier. Particularly hard hit was the western banking community. Partly because here relations with the South were more basic and partly because western banking was still largely of the "wildcat" variety, the crisis pulled under a large proportion of the bank enterprises in this area.

This was not an auspicious environment in which to launch a major war effort, and particularly did it not make easy the kind of tax program such a war effort required. The "lame-duck" Congress which assembled in Washington after Lincoln's election had made some inroads on the financial problem. But the Morrill Tariff, passed in the Senate after the Senators from the seven states first to secede had abandoned their positions, was far more of an instrument for increasing protection than for remedying a critical financial situation. As a result of this preoccupation, and because foreign trade suffered greatly from the secession depression and the outbreak of war, it was hardly adequate to the government's needs before war broke out, to say nothing of the greatly accentuated needs occasioned by the military endeavor.

Financial Mismanagement in the North. There was perhaps little the government could have done about the economic crisis, and indeed this difficulty was soon remedied by the outbreak of war. Much could have been done, on the other hand, to bring the government's finances more into line with the growing need. This would have meant firm action, however, and no one was yet willing to take a strong stand on this issue. The reason was overconfidence, the most fundamental obstacle the North encountered in its entire mobilization program. Because of its obvious resource superiority, northern leaders typically took it for granted that the war would be over in three months. This expectation coupled with the high morale characterizing the Confederacy's effort was probably one of the important reasons why the conflict actually dragged on four long and bloody years.

Starting from an erroneous premise, war financing proceeded on a logical enough basis. Since time is required to set in motion an increase in taxes, the first step was the floating of a series of loans. And because long-term loans could not be sold except at extremely high rates of interest, so low had the credit of the government fallen, a heavy reliance was placed on short-term securities. As a consequence throughout the entire war period the government's financial program was complicated by the necessity of refunding short-term obligations simultaneously with the raising of new funds.

This was only the beginning of difficulties. Even after it became apparent that the war was not to be short, a realistic tax program was not inaugurated. A beginning was made in August by the enactment of a direct tax, an income tax, and increased duties on coffee, tea, sugar, etc. But since Secretary of the Treasury Chase was not sympathetic with the nontariff taxes, no steps were taken at first to put them into effect. In December many duties were raised still higher, but the falling off of foreign trade made customs levies too frail a financial reed to be of much assistance. Obviously so much reliance on borrowing rather than taxation could not have failed to put the nation's money and credit mechanism under a severe strain.

Fiscal unrealism was next compounded by Treasury mismanagement. Under the Independent Treasury System the government's payments were carried on entirely in specie and largely apart from the banking system. Along with the first tax enactments, however, Congress authorized a departure from these restrictions, permitting the Secretary of the Treasury to deposit government funds in specie-paying banks. The banks naturally assumed that with this authority the Secretary would keep the proceeds of borrowings on deposit for use by the banking system while drawing on them by check.

But Salmon P. Chase had different views. Essentially a hard-money man, he insisted on withdrawing the proceeds of a $150 million loan in three equal installments in specie. The banks, with only $63 million in specie, were understandably perturbed by the pressure this procedure placed upon them, a pressure increased still further by the continued Treasury issue of short-term notes payable in specie on demand. The only hope for the banking system was that specie would be redeposited as it was paid out by the government. But with the news filled with military reverses and the government embarked upon a program of inflationary financing, much gold went into private hoards instead. There could be but one result, and on December 30, 1861, specie payments were suspended by the banks, the government following suit the next day. So early in the conflict, thus, the government was forced to carry on its affairs without the assistance of an effective monetary system.

No doubt the government's tax policy would have brought about an abandonment of specie payments at some point in any event. But with the disappearance of gold from many of the channels of ordinary trade, special facilities had to be organized by means of which gold could be secured for those transactions in which its use was still required—the payment of international obligations, customs duties, and interest on government bonds. On January 13, 1862, a special gold market was established in New York in which gold could be bought and sold for paper money. From this point until long after the end of the war the country was greatly inconvenienced by the existence of two moneys—paper and gold—which were constantly changing in value relative to each other.[1]

The most serious immediate consequence of the loss of gold for ordinary circulation was the disordered state of the circulating medium which resulted. Closely related to this difficulty was a disruption of the nation's money markets, making it almost impossible for the government to borrow needed funds. Obviously the confusion in the currency and the Treasury's embarrassment demanded a remedy, and soon. For a time there was talk of establishing a new national bank for these purposes. Time was of the essence, however, and this approach seemed too time consuming. Moreover, opposition from vested banking interests was so strong that national banking legislation could not have been passed at this time in any case. There seemed to be no alternative except the issuance of paper money and on February 25, 1862 the first of a series of three issues of fiat money (the famous "Greenbacks") was authorized and made legal tender for all money uses except the payment of the customs and interest on government securities. With the completion of this "comedy of errors" the North's financial program reached its darkest point, a bare twelve months after the outbreak of hostilities.

It is easy, as well as customary, to be harsh with Mr. Chase and his program of war financing. However, it is worth emphasizing that the difficulties he faced were extremely great. As a British editorial expressed it: "The hundredth part of Mr. Chase's embarrassments would tax Mr. Gladstone's ingenuity to the utmost, and set the [British] public mind in a ferment of excitement." Furthermore, it is to be remembered that after this succession of "blunders" (which did not, in the last analysis, prevent the securing of the money needed to wage the contest) the government's financial policy became steadily more sound. And this, of course, is only another way of saying that when it became fully understood that the war was to be a long one, more appropriate measures were taken.

Economic Gains. Before this stage in the financing of the war in the North was reached, however, certain other matters had to be attended to. The war, after all, was not an end in itself. It was rather a way of achieving specific purposes, among these being certain economic policies the

[1] Actually the most convenient way of thinking about these developments is to consider gold as a commodity whose value was constantly fluctuating in terms of money. On this analogy the new gold market can appropriately be thought of as a commodity market much like that for wheat or cotton. This analogy is particularly apt, too, because for obvious reasons many transactions in gold had to be on a "futures" basis (that is, of a speculative nature).

voting power of the South had consistently blocked. Little time was wasted in taking advantage of the South's absence. In May, 1862, the long-desired Homestead Act was passed; henceforth any settler could secure one hundred sixty acres of ungranted land simply by cultivating it and residing on it for five years. In July the first step was taken to provide government aid in the building of a Pacific railroad by way of a northern route, this legislation ushering in a second period of land grants—primarily in the Far West. July also saw the passage of the Morrill Land Grant Act giving every state thirty thousand acres of public land for each senator and representative in Congress to help establish agricultural and mechanical colleges.

Even the tariff was not neglected, and indeed legislation in this field was perhaps the most generous of all. In July, 1862, the first comprehensive tax measure was enacted, a measure seeking to secure tax revenue from virtually every economic activity. Then, in order to maintain the margin of

TABLE 34. AN ALTERED TAX STRUCTURE

Year	Customs Receipts	Internal Revenue	Other Receipts	Deficit
		(Millions of dollars)		
1860	53.2	–	2.9	7.1
1861	39.6	–	1.9	25.0
1862	49.1	–	2.9	422.8
1863	69.1	37.6	6.0	602.0
1864	102.3	119.2	52.6	600.7
1865	84.9	209.5	39.3	963.8

Source: Bureau of the Census, *Historical Statistics of the United States, 1789-1945*, p. 297.

tariff protection contained in the Morrill Tariff, manufacturers were given what was almost a blanket privilege to suggest to Congress what compensating duties would be necessary to offset these internal taxes. In principle this step was sound enough. But in the interest of time and as a result of the absence of southern opposition, no close supervision was given to the fixing of offsetting duties and errors were made in the direction of overcompensation far more often than in the opposite direction. Furthermore, this entire process was repeated two years later when internal taxes were again increased. The over-all result of these comprehensive tax measures was a tax structure far different from any the nation had ever had, one in which tariff duties were higher than ever before but in which customs revenues were overshadowed by other sources of income.

The slavery issue could not be dealt with as directly or as promptly as these other matters. Many Republican leaders, most notably, for example,

Abraham Lincoln, had insisted that they were not abolitionists, and Union policies were largely shaped to prove this contention. Yet the issue could not in the end be handled in a neutral manner. Negroes were constantly seeking refuge in Union-held territory, and Union arms were continually securing territory populated in part by slaves. Some Union officials declared such persons to be free without further ado, but just as frequently these orders were countermanded at higher levels. The reason for this ambivalence was plain enough. On the one hand, to free the slaves on principle would alienate the slave states attached to the Union cause. On the other hand, to take no stand on this vital question was to give the appearance of fighting a war without a purpose.

Finally the issue could be evaded no longer. Recognizing slaves as an asset to the southern economy, emancipation was declared to be the Union policy with respect to all states and persons participating in the "rebellion." Lincoln's Emancipation Proclamation took this position, admittedly framed as a weapon of economic warfare. The hold of the Union on the loyalties of Delaware, Maryland, Kentucky, Missouri, and Tennessee was still too loose to risk emancipation as such.

But emancipation according to the exigencies of war could not for long satisfy the needs of the day. It was too vulnerable a position, this freeing slaves where the government's jurisdiction was weakest and maintaining the institution intact where the government actually exercised authority. As the war went on, emancipation became more and more a northern war aim, the apex of antislavery sentiment being reached when, shortly after the war, "rebel" states were compelled to ratify an amendment to the Constitution abolishing slavery while they were at the same time declared to be insufficiently "reconstructed" to be admitted to full membership in the "new" Union.

The economic well-being of northerners was not advanced only by legislation, either. In addition, the stimulus of war created a high prosperity. War-inflated demand for manufactured goods stimulated this branch of the economy to unprecedented levels. Not only were large quantities of goods needed by a buyer to whom price was not important, but the steady rise in prices generated by inflationary war financing was an additional highly favorable factor. Especially benefited was the manufacture of woolen goods; the government paid unheard-of prices for anything that looked like wool cloth. Only the cotton manufacturing industry suffered a decline in output, although prewar stocks, illicit trade with the South, war goods captured in Confederate territory, and high prices made possible continuous profits. Even the government's financial difficulties provided large returns to those with capital to invest. Bonds carrying a high rate of interest were sold at low prices in order to compensate holders for the risk of loss, and after the war all issues were retired on schedule at par or higher. When to the legitimate profits of industry are added the profits resulting from selling "shoddy" goods to the government and the fact that the government did not exercise precautions with respect to the prices it was charged, it is understandable why the number of millionaires increased many times over.

Agriculture prospered no less than industry. Favorable weather conditions, the introduction of laborsaving machinery, and the westward migration accentuated by the passage of the Homestead Act and the search for precious metals maintained a level of production even larger than during the prewar years, the most extreme example being the output of wool. This product increased in quantity 250 per cent as Ohio sheep growers endeavored to keep pace with the increased demand of wool manufacturers. The source of much of the labor supply making possible this accomplishment was a new influx of European immigrants seeking to take advantage of America's prosperity and her liberal land legislation. Outlets for an expanded production were provided by the war demand, a steady increase in the nation's population, the return of general prosperity, an increase in the proportion of the population engaged in nonagricultural pursuits, and the limited wheat crops harvested in England in the early years of the war, while the inflationary war financing being indulged in by the government assured the sale of farm products at high and steadily rising prices. To be sure, many farmers did spend their gains by buying a mortgage on a farm, and to be sure many of these mortgages were foreclosed after the war, but the wartime prosperity was no less real for this fact.

Financial Management Improves. By late 1863 the North's war finance program was beginning to improve. One of the ways in which this was accomplished was by lowering the ratio of loans to taxes—by taxing citizens

TABLE 35. WAR WITHOUT TAXATION

Year	Ratio of Loans to Taxes
1861-62	8.52 to 1
1862-63	5.51 to 1
1863-64	3.38 to 1
1864-65	2.95 to 1

Source: By permission from *Financial History of the United States,* by Davis R. Dewey, p. 299. Copyright, 1924, Longmans, Green & Co., New York.

on a more realistic basis. During the first year of the war only a little more than 10 per cent of the government's income was derived from taxes, whereas in the last year this percentage had increased to 25. By means of this improved program of taxation, inflation could be combated more effectively; fewer dollars were artificially added to those already bidding up the prices of goods in short supply.

A second step was closely related to the new tax program. Lessening the financial pressure on the Treasury and thus reducing its need to inflate the currency made it easier to float long-term securities. As a consequence it was possible substantially to reduce the ratio of short-term to long-term securities. Whereas some three-fourths of the loan financing during the first half of the war took the form of short-term obligations, this proportion fell to one-half in the last two years. A second important factor making this achievement possible was an unprecedented "grass roots" bond campaign conducted by Jay Cooke and Company, the first important attempt in this country to market securities in large numbers outside the financial sections of large cities.

Far more important than these measures, however, especially for the longer future, was the creation of the country's first genuinely *national* banking system. Actually, under the Independent Treasury, not only did the country not have a national banking system, but it was scarcely possessed of a banking *system* at all. It is true that during a period given to extravagance in banking, the "sterilization" of government funds by the use of nonbank depositories did have certain advantages. But at the same time successive Secretaries of the Treasury had interpreted this part of the Independent Treasury law very liberally, and early in the Civil War it had been expressly repealed. One of the main reasons it had proved to be impossible to "live with" this provision was because the withdrawal of funds from the stream of circulation frequently threatened monetary stringency at times of high seasonal demand for funds. In short, effective monetary management was impossible within the framework of the Independent Treasury System.

Despite this fact, however, when the business interests (along with western farmers and eastern laborers) had set about the task of enacting legislation long frustrated by the slavocracy, no fundamental changes had been made in the banking field. One of the principal reasons was the fifty-year-old conflict between banking and nonbanking business interests, the former being primarily concerned about maintaining profits at a high level and the latter most interested in achieving uniformity and stability in the circulating medium. It was only as a result of the serious financial difficulties of the government during the war that these two sets of interests were able to get together on a new approach.

Herein lies the irony of the National Banking Act. Made possible by the need to relieve a desperate financial situation, it in fact ameliorated little. A measure which could not have secured approval in time of peace, this enactment was to provide the most important element in the nation's banking system for half a century of peacetime economic development.

In two ways the new legislation was intended to help in financing the war. The law provided for national bank notes to be issued by such banks as joined the national system, these notes to be secured by federal bonds. Not only would the new national bank notes thus become a *uniform* national currency, but at the same time the issuance of this currency would require the new national banks to purchase large quanties of government securities.

The reason the expected results were not forthcoming was that there was too little incentive for a bank to exchange its state charter for a federal one—in view of the fact that federal regulations and restrictions were typically more stringent than those applied by the states. It was not until a 10 per cent tax was placed on state bank notes that the national system began to enroll a large number of banks, and by then the war was virtually over. Thus, although this innovation did not significantly affect the nation's wartime finances, by the time the war came to an end the nation

TABLE 36. A NATIONAL BANKING SYSTEM

Year	Number of Banks		Total Assets	
	National	State	National	State
			(Millions of dollars)	
1863	66	1,466	16.8	1,191.8
1865	1,294	349	1,126.5	231.0
1868	1,640	247	1,572.2	163.5

Source: Bureau of the Census, *Historical Statistics of the United States, 1789-1945*, pp. 264-65.

had achieved for the first time in its history a really uniform currency—although the law did provide that national bank notes could not be used in payment of customs duties or in paying interest on the government debt.

Relating bank notes to securities held was one of the central provisions of New York's banking legislation, the new law passing up at this point Louisiana's successful experience in relating liabilities to commercial paper. But the new law did borrow from Louisiana's legislation (as well as the prewar panic experience) by requiring reserves to be held against deposit liabilities as well as note liabilities.[2] Recognition was also given to the semicentral banking role played by banks in the larger cities, especially

[2] Although it is true that an economy can not in fact "liquidate" itself, it is still considered essential to keep illiquidity within some bounds. Put differently, from the standpoint of banking, although the "cash" reserve against claims is only fractional, it is still essential to prevent the fraction from becoming too small. If the pyramiding of claims were allowed to go on unchecked, it is possible that a point would be reached at which any small shock to the system would precipitate a crisis. Since claims were beginning to be created extensively in the form of deposits, this fact had to be recognized in arriving at the proper fraction.

New York, by allowing banks in smaller communities to keep a portion of their own reserves in the larger banks and by requiring the larger banks to maintain a greater reserve against their deposits. This last, however, did not go far toward correcting the evil of "pyramiding" bank reserves which the recent panic had highlighted, an evil which could be corrected only through the agency of a genuine central bank.

One other episode in the financial operations of the Union government is worth recounting, although it is perhaps more amusing than significant. Convinced that inflation was being produced primarily by speculation in gold (thus ignoring the part the Treasury and the state banks were playing in this phenomenon), Chase persuaded Congress to prohibit short sales of gold. This interference with what had become an essential economic activity contributed still more to the fall in the price of paper money relative to gold. In thirteen days the gold price of paper fell from 51 to 35 cents, and in July, 1864, less than three weeks after its passage, the prohibition was hastily repealed.

Labor and the War. Although war prosperity created good times for many groups in the northern economy, including the fact that the Union was able to put into the field the best cared-for army the world had ever seen, it is not to be supposed that all groups were equally fortunate. The urban middle class, for example—professional people such as teachers, ministers, lawyers, clerks—went through the war with incomes relatively fixed in the face of rapidly rising prices. Another group also suffered from the economic dislocations caused by the war. For the urban laborer, in fact, there were so many adverse factors as to make him suspect a deliberate conspiracy to prevent a fair distribution of the fruits of the economic process. The most basic complaint of the worker was the lag between rising prices and increases in wages. As shown in Table 37, the five years of war saw a rise in the index level of prices of well over 100 per cent while the index of wages paid increased less than 50 per cent.

TABLE 37. THE BURDEN OF WAR

Year	Prices	Money Wages
1860	100.0	100.0
1865	216.8	143.1

Source: By permission from *Financial History of the United States,* by Davis R. Dewey, p. 294. Copyright, 1924, Longmans, Green & Co., New York.

Their standard of living being steadily ground away, laborers naturally sought to protect themselves. Jobs were plentiful enough in the war prosperity to make possible a successful effort at concerted action; and in addition to prosperity, army enlistments made labor even more scarce. The resulting organization work was helpful as far as it was able to go; many permanent gains were registered during the period. Of these by far the most important was the development of national labor unions on a more extensive scale than ever before.

There were several reasons why labor union progress especially took this form during the 1860's. The first and most important had to do with improvements in transportation. Whereas up to this point the railroad had brought workers into competition with one another primarily by making the individual worker more mobile, now a much more formidable competition was being promoted by the new medium. When stoves manufactured in Albany and Detroit began to compete with one another in the St. Louis market, the problem of wages and working conditions over the entire producing area became a matter of great importance to every iron molder. Such conditions were beginning to prevail in a number of fields.

A second factor, and one almost as fundamental, was an accelerated progress in the introduction of machinery. This development promoted division of labor on a scale hitherto unknown, with the result that established trades were broken up or gravely threatened, skilled craftsmen being put into active competition with unskilled laborers. Here again only a national organization could meet this threat, not of course by stopping the technological revolution under way but by protecting established interests against its most painful consequences.

However, perhaps even more important than labor's progress during this period was the fact that workers were still unable to achieve gains nearly as rapidly as an adverse economic environment was destroying them. Moreover, the inflated money supply was not the only reason for this failure. Another was the increase in foreign immigration, a wartime threat to the laboring class of unusual severity for a very special reason. In July, 1864, Congress enacted a law ("An Act to Encourage Immigration") legalizing the signing of labor contracts between employers and immigrant workers, contracts making one year's wages a *quid pro quo* for passage to the United States. A more effective strike-breaking weapon could not easily be imagined, and it is not to be supposed that employers were reluctant to take advantage of such an opportunity.

Still another reason for labor's failure to maintain its economic position was an accentuated drive by employers to organize themselves against labor's efforts. The lockout and blacklist techniques were utilized as never before in labor's short history, and an embryo type of "yellow dog" contract was also employed (a pledge by laborers not to join a union). It would be futile to speculate whether national employers' organizations caused or resulted from national employees' organizations. Probably each arose in response to the other in the sort of mutually interactive evolution which characterizes much social development. Suffice it to say that employers' organizations on a national scale did begin to emerge during this period and that they were used with a high degree of effectiveness. Added to the superior influence of employers on the policies of government, all these devices combined made it impossible for any but the most favored workers to maintain their economic position.

Even in basic wartime legislation the laborer had reason for believing he was being discriminated against. Wartime immigration regulations were of course one case in point. Another was a system of conscription permitting exemption on payment of a substantial money fee (or hiring a substitute). Here was obviously class legislation, even though the government did need revenue almost as badly as it needed men. And, finally, it did not escape labor's notice that the bulk of the tax burden levied during the war was coming to rest on the defenseless consumer.

All in all, it is difficult to escape the conclusion that the major part of the cost of the Civil War in the North was borne by the laboring classes. This conclusion, to be sure, should occasion no surprise, for it is invariably the weakest group within a society to whom burdens are shifted. It has been said that labor more than any other group stood to gain in the long run through the destruction of slavery. If this be so, it is perhaps fitting that labor bear most of the cost. On the other hand, this is not why labor did pay the largest price. The laborer in the America of 1865 was not a "forgotten man"; he had as yet scarcely been recognized in the first instance.

QUESTIONS FOR DISCUSSION

1. What finally turned northern businessmen against the South?
2. Could the Confederacy have developed an economic policy which would have served its needs reasonably well but which would not have antagonized eastern business interests?
3. What were the principal "blunders" committed by the North in the early months of the war?
4. Why is it that a nation can badly mismanage its finances during a war but at the same time build a reasonably effective war effort?
5. What economic groups gained most from the economic legislation passed during the war?
6. Why was it not possible to free the slaves in America by compensating their owners, as was done in England?
7. Was financial management in the North adequate by the end of the war? What would a reasonable ratio between taxes and loans have been?
8. How was the National Banking Act intended to aid the northern war effort? Why was it not effective for this purpose?
9. What experiences in the preceding years contributed to the National Banking Act?

Chapter 19

RECONSTRUCTION AND INDUSTRIALISM

1864 Sherman's "march to the sea."
1865 Lee's surrender at Appomattox.
Lincoln assassinated; Andrew Johnson became President.
1866 First attempt to retire the greenbacks failed.
"Radical Reconstruction" begun.
"Radical" victory at the polls.
1867 Wool and Woolens Act.
Alaska purchased.
1868 Impeachment of Johnson; acquitted with only a single vote to spare.
Ulysses S. Grant elected President; helped swing the balance against paying bond interest in greenbacks.

Foundation for an Industrial Economy. It is often said that the Civil War marks a distinct "watershed" in America's economic development—that before the war the United States was an agrarian economy while afterward it was an industrial economy. However, if one focuses attention on manufacturing activity in relation to agricultural activity, no such conclusion can be reached. True, manufacturing had long been steadily growing relative to agriculture, and obviously an evolution of this kind must reach a point at which the two change places in comparative importance. Yet, speaking statistically, this did not happen during the Civil War; not for another twenty-five years was manufacturing quantitatively superior to agriculture in either output or employment.

Actually the most that can be said about the Civil War from this standpoint is that wartime prosperity gave industrialization the kind of impetus associated with every one of the periods of prosperity the nation had enjoyed. It could almost be said that the Civil War marked the end of a period of relatively slow and the beginning of a much more rapid development, although the decade prior to the pre-Civil War panic is an equally good candidate for this distinction. The wartime growth of manufacturing perhaps did exceed any such growth the country had yet experienced, but at the same time there were segments of the economy that did not fare well. Railroad construction was almost at a standstill, cotton manufacturing was relatively depressed, and the merchant marine suffered a severe decline as hundreds of vessels transferred to the British flag to avoid the hazards of war commerce. Thus, taken all in all, the development of the economy during the Civil War seems best described as a cyclical high point in a secular upward trend.

It does not follow that it is incorrect to think of the Civil War as an important turning point in the advance of America's industrial society. When attention is directed away from economic growth to the process of making economic decisions, the situation appears in an altogether different light. From this standpoint there exists an excellent basis for considering the Civil War the real beginning of the United States as an industrial nation.

For many years prior to the outbreak of sectional strife, the economic policies followed had been those most desired by agrarians. Whether because the South and West were able to agree on the policies to be inaugurated, or because the South was able to frustrate the wishes of both West and East, industrialists could only rarely make their influence strongly felt. Nowhere was this pattern of relationships more clear than in connection with banking and the tariff on the one hand and land policy on the other. It is no coincidence that a great conflict, foreshadowed by a cessation of cooperation between the agrarian sections of the economy and precipitated by the fall from power of one of these groups, was accompanied by such legislation as the wartime tariffs, a new land policy, and a national banking system. This legislation was highly symbolic of the new age now dawning. The American Civil War ushered in a long era within which economic policy was overwhelmingly dictated by the industrial groups.

Devastation in the South. It would be an exaggeration to claim that the Civil War alone was responsible for this development. There is, however, a substantial basis for crediting a part of it to the war. And in so far as the new pattern of relationships was brought about by the war, the first phase was the disastrous defeat suffered by the South.

The military defeat itself is not surprising, of course. Once the full power of the northern adversary was mobilized, no other outcome was possible. Far more important, however, than military defeat was the fact that in this process the South was devastated.

The central difficulty was a specialization in agricultural products, and a corresponding neglect of the facilities for producing the sinews of war. Understandably, in these circumstances, the South waged a strenuous campaign to keep open enough channels of distribution to enable her to import the items most needed. Without shipping, however, and without the means of acquiring either a merchant or a naval fleet, such a campaign was doomed to failure. Some trade slipped through the blockade, some

TABLE 38. THE DEATH OF KING COTTON

Year	Cotton Exports From New Orleans
	(Thousands of bales)
1859-60	2,235
1860-61	1,849
1861-62	39
1862-63	22
1863-64	131
1864-65	271

Source: Hammond, *The Cotton Industry*, p. 263.

exchange in the early years of the war was carried on with Mexico, and there was even an illicit trade between the belligerents (many southern planters preferring to take their chances with northern greenbacks rather than accept almost worthless Confederate money or risk government confiscation). But the goods made available in these ways were only a trickle compared with the flow necessary to sustain a war economy.

This failure placed the South in an impossible situation—desperately needing to begin producing goods customarily secured by importing. Without an industrial foundation, however—including such things as skilled labor, equipment, and a general atmosphere conducive to this kind of activity—the South's economy could not be made adequately self-sufficient in the few years actually available. To be sure, the South did become virtually self-sufficient during the war, but it was a self-sufficiency based upon the low standard of living of a barter system rather than that ordinarily associated with a modern economy.

Even such goods as were made available could not be used to best advantage because of a deficiency in transportation facilities. Developed for the purpose of transporting goods from the interior to the coast, the existing rail network was inadequate to the task of carrying men and materials between various parts of the South. Moreover, whereas these railroads were already poorly constructed, poorly equipped, and poorly maintained, it now became still more difficult to secure maintenance items and equipment replacements—even if the manpower needed had been available. Long before the end of the war most railroads were unable to perform at all except for the carrying of a limited amount of government freight.

The sum total of the handicaps under which the Confederacy labored was almost exactly mirrored in the financing of the war in the South. Partly because of an insistence on state rights, partly because of inadequate fiscal machinery, partly because of the war-created poverty, and partly because of the usual unwillingness of a government to impose adequate war taxes, little success was achieved by taxation in securing the needed purchasing power. Failing in this, recourse was had to borrowing. However, so lacking was capital, and so disorganized were the region's finances as a result of the derangement of trade, that this resource too fell far short of bringing in the needed funds. The only remaining alternative was the issuance of paper money. This was done on a tremendous scale with the

TABLE 39. THE ESSENCE OF FUTILITY

Confederate Revenue, 1861-65	Amount
	(Millions of dollars)
Tax receipts	122.5
Other current revenues	125.9
Borrowings:	
Non-paper money	602.9
Paper money	1,360.0

Source: By permission from *Economic History of the South*, by Emory Q. Hawk, p. 414. Copyright, 1934, Prentice-Hall, Inc., New York.

inevitable result. Prices skyrocketed, despoiling almost everyone through whose hands the inflated money passed. Then still more paper money had to be put into circulation to take care of the government's needs, until finally the premium on specie compared with paper money reached more than 6,000 per cent. Ordinary exchange relationships became so disturbed by the day-to-day uncertainty as to the value of the principal medium of exchange that for this reason if for no other southerners would have been forced to adopt a barter basis for carrying on their economic affairs.

The connection between the South's economic disabilities and her ultimate collapse was direct and cumulative. Before the war ended the military ages for conscription had become seventeen at the lower limit and fifty at the upper, and virtually all white males between these ages were actually in the army. With the most efficient labor withdrawn from productive work, it was not even possible to husband what resources were available. When it is remembered that on a relatively small number of the white males now in the armed forces had rested most of the responsibility for supervising the unskilled labor of the southern economy, the full consequences of their absence can be more fully appreciated.

Farm buildings, fences, livestock population, and land were dissipated by neglect, abuse, and the sheer incapacity of those left behind to care for them properly. Banks were inundated by the flood of paper money. Insurance companies lost a great proportion of their capital by investing funds in a government destined to become completely bankrupt. Most factories were forced to close their doors, victims of the labor shortage, the unavailability of replacement parts, or the destruction of a war fought on domestic soil. Mines all over the South were abandoned for lack of labor, machinery, and a market, standing at war's end filled with water and all but ruined. Everywhere shops had been boarded up because of lack of capital with which to lay in a stock of goods, inability to secure goods, or a shortage of sales personnel.

Never in the history of the United States has a war required such heavy sacrifices as the Civil War brought to the South. Never has an American war left such complete disorganization in its wake. Whereas in the North the war burden fell primarily on two small groups, in the South a heavy burden fell on almost everyone. No important group, including the Negro, escaped a share in the carnage.

The Problem of Reconstruction. In turn, the South's devastation provided the context within which the drama of reconstruction was acted out. Some of this problem was simply the existence of such a mass of destruction that men scarcely knew where to begin the task of taking up their peacetime lives once more. Closely associated with the physical aspects of reconstruction, however, were its emotional overtones. There could have been no avoiding the bitterness of defeat in any event, and such feelings were made even more intense by a succession of episodes, of which Sherman's "march to the sea" was only one. On the part of the South's aristocracy particularly there was a feeling of paralyzing uncertainty. With the majority of the South's plantations, including some of her finest, already so heavily mortgaged that their owners were in danger of losing their homes, the talk of confiscation by the northern conqueror was a painful prospect. In all walks of life there prevailed a deep anxiety for the future, an anxiety made doubly severe in the case of the many families now missing one of their most important members.

All this would have created enough of a problem of reconstruction at best. Unfortunately this herculean task was gravely complicated by the fact that the South's central institution, Negro slavery, had been shattered as a result of the military defeat. In this way $2 billion worth of capital was destroyed, a substantial fraction of the South's total capital. The Negroes themselves, untrained and undisciplined for work on their own responsibility, were literally overnight put upon their own resources while much of the land they had once tilled was idle for want of hands. All too often Negro workers identified freedom with the right to do nothing, and the roads were for a time filled with wandering Negroes exercising this freedom to the utmost. In some cases, too, freedmen migrations were caused by the deliberate action of planters fearing confiscation of their property for distribution to ex-slaves. Both whites and blacks, in short, mutually distrusted one another, a fact which contributed nothing to the making of the necessary adjustments.

The first step, of course, was to restore the land to productive use. But with labor short, and seed, implements, and livestock often almost unavailable, rapid progress was not to be expected. This in and of itself would have been no tragedy. A crop such as cotton has an inelastic demand and hence producers frequently receive more money from a smaller crop than a larger one. Indeed one of the weaknesses of the prewar cotton economy was chronic overproduction. However, during the immediate postwar years accumulated stores of cotton which could not be sold during the conflict were thrown on the market. This fact, plus the impetus given by the war to rival cotton-producing areas and the postwar depression, resulted in extremely low prices in spite of a pathetically small output. Many whites and more Negroes were utterly destitute, undernourishment and disease taking their terrible toll. In the first four postwar years the Freedmen's Bureau, a federal relief agency set up to assist the South in its reconstruction efforts, issued twenty-one million meals—fifteen million to Negroes.

Fortunately, the South's economy was predominantly rural, a type of economy possessing more effective self-healing powers than an industrial economy similarly devastated. And since an economy cannot long function far below its capacities, a new institutional basis for southern agriculture began to develop. After a system based on renting land and paying wages in cash had failed (because cash was not readily available and Negroes typically did not work well under their own management), the immediately successful "share" method of operation began to emerge. Under this system the owner furnished the tenant with tools and animal power in exchange for a fixed share of the crop at harvest time. This arrangement did have disadvantages, among these being the fastening of the prewar crop mortgage system on the economy more firmly than ever before—and this in turn accentuating the South's too exclusive devotion to cotton. After the Civil War the cultivation of corn almost disappeared from the cotton belt. Ultimately, moreover, this method of operation probably outlived its usefulness.

Other factors also entered into the reorientation of southern agriculture. Concentration in property ownership and the accompanying aristocratic social structure were powerfully shaken. The coming of more favorable cotton prices coupled with low land values encouraged thousands to break into the landowning class, although less land redistribution took place than is commonly supposed. (For example, prewar creditors and "carpetbaggers" often accumulated large estates in the postwar South, and not every prewar aristocrat lost his property.) Moreover, nothing substantial was done to put land into colored hands. Great plantation owners were often happy to be relieved of the responsibility of property they could not secure labor to work effectively. Another adjustment producing similar results was westward migration. With disaster imminent, thousands of southern farmers made their way to Texas and Arkansas. Here cheap and fertile soils and a large expanse of grassland provided opportunities extending all the way from cotton growing through mixed farming to stock raising.

Favorable developments in agriculture in turn provided the foundation for a more general rebuilding of the South. As more land was restored to productive efficiency, a larger proportion of the population could be released for secondary activities. Mines could be drained and worked, factories made ready to turn out badly needed goods, banks reopened to restore the money mechanism, shops manned in order more effectively to distribute the goods now becoming available, and professional persons could once again make their normal contribution to the life of society.

Victory by Delay. So successfully did the work of reconstruction proceed (it has always been a striking historical fact how quickly the physical-economic devastation of war is in fact restored) that there seemed to be no serious obstacle to the early recovery by the South of her old place in the "new" Union. But this calculation reckoned without the temper of the rising industrialism. Whereas moderates like Andrew Johnson (perhaps moderate primarily because their sympathies were essentially agrarian) sought to restore the South speedily to full Union status, such men were ruthlessly swept aside. Then, taking advantage of the fact that the South was already a defeated "enemy," the industrial interests proceeded to use every device at their command to delay the recognition of "reconstructed" states. With this development was ushered in the second phase of the process by which the Civil War assisted in converting the United States from an agrarian to an industrial society.

It is easy to understand the motivation prompting this strategy of delay. For decades either the South or an agrarian coalition had been the chief stumbling-block in the way of the development of economic policies demanded by the industrial East. Moreover, not only were the southern states to be returned to a status of equality with other states, but when they did return they would have even more power than before since the destruction of slavery had simultaneously destroyed the three-fifths limitation on southern representation. It was even reasonable to anticipate that an embittered South would use her power in an even more reactionary way than before the war.

Fully as obvious as the motivation was the wisdom of a strategy of postponing the inevitable. Here was no place for the philosophy of "ultimately, why not now." The longer the period of time required to "reconstruct" the South, the longer would business interests enjoy an exaggerated policy-making influence, and a few years of peacetime legislation unhampered by southern prejudices might be very valuable. At the same time, of course, it would not have done to use any but the most subtle approach. A campaign oriented directly toward the economic policies desired might quickly have united other groups in opposition. The only logical approach seemed to be to keep alive by every means available the hate and abolition-idealism which had accompanied the war. Then, under cover of this screen, the situation could be maneuvered in such a way that the South herself would appear to be delaying her own return to the Union.

An episode will illustrate the subtle way in which legitimate reconstruction measures were inseparably combined with delaying tactics. One of the first major pieces of reconstruction legislation to receive Congressional approval was the Fourteenth Amendment to the Constitution, the central purpose of which was to help with the process of guaranteeing the Negro full citizenship status in the reconstructed Union. In brief the history of this legislation is as follows: after much debate and substantial compromise it was passed by Congress, the "rebel" states not participating. Submitted to the states for ratification before the states of the South had had fastened upon them the infamous "reconstruction" governments, it did not receive enough affirmative votes to be declared in force. Later, after northern-dominated governments were in charge of political machinery in the South, enough states approved for it to become a part of the fundamental law of the land.

In addition to clauses directly related to the Negro, the Fourteenth Amendment contained several other sections. One called upon southerners to renounce any claim to compensation for their slaves or to reimbursement on account of the Confederate debt. These renunciations, of course, were not calculated to make southerners happy, but on the other hand few southern leaders could seriously object to such provisions as a part of the "war settlement." Certainly such terms for a defeated "enemy" were the very minimum northerners could be expected to agree to. In this connection it must be remembered that the war had often been accompanied by inconvenience and suffering for northerners as well as southerners. Any other arrangement as to these points would have imposed a part of the South's war cost on the North or relieved the South of some part of its share in the Union debt burden. Either of these alternatives would have been ridiculous on its face.

Another provision denied the franchise to "all persons who voluntarily adhered to the late insurrection, giving it aid and comfort." Here was a clause which looked straightforward enough when not examined closely. All it purported to do was to prevent "traitors" to their government from securing control over the postwar South. It was only on the second look that its real significance became apparent. What it really meant was that virtually the entire class of people to which the South had always looked for leadership must be repudiated as a condition of re-entry into the Union. Not content with establishing equality between two races which had always lived together in an owner-slave relationship, the conqueror here was endeavoring to reverse the situation by making the erstwhile slave group into a new "master" class. As a consequence of this approach, as an extreme example, a state government was established in South Carolina consisting of more than 50 per cent Negroes.

Two consequences could confidently have been expected to flow from an attempt such as this—and both did. First, few self-respecting southerners would voluntarily accept these terms, involving as they did no less than a repudiation of the very basis on which the South's society was built. This rejection could then be pointed to as conclusive proof that the South was still bent on the evil designs which had brought the nation to bloody conflict in the first place. When because of this refusal the Confederate States were not readmitted to the Union, public sentiment was not aroused against northerners for "refusing" them admission.

The second consequence followed directly from the first. The refusal of the defeated "enemy" to agree to "reasonable" terms could only be met by military rule. This involved further delay, and even after rule by the conqueror was established, a period of time was required for the new government to agree to the conditions laid down. And it was even possible to use such time to create some elements at least of a ruling group that would live on after military rule ceased, continuing policies established by the conqueror until natural social processes brought about a different equilibrium. In the drama of southern reconstruction, where time was of the essence, all of these ways in which it could be bought were of high importance.

However, it is still a third part of the Fourteenth Amendment which is for present purposes most significant. This is the so-called "equal protection of the laws" and "due process" clauses forbidding a state to "deny to any person within its jurisdiction the equal protection of the laws," or to "deprive any person of life, liberty, or property, without due process of law." The first of these clauses was no more than a necessary precaution against a racial discrimination nullifying the work of emancipation, a precaution which for many years was perhaps honored more in the breach than in the observance, while the second simply wrote into the Constitution a prohibition against the state governments which was already operative against the federal government.

On the other hand, however, when the "due process" clause is examined more carefully, certain facts about it stand out. First, it seems strangely out of place, for it added nothing to the protection of the Negro or even the "war settlement" in general. But, second, when this wording is analyzed in terms of basic economic developments then taking place, this anomaly begins to take on real significance. And, finally, when it is recalled that the amendment was presented as a "package" to be accepted or rejected as a whole, the intent of the procedure becomes still more suspect. The attention of everyone was to be centered on the problem of the unfortunate Negro while at the same time a special protection for the vigorous and not at all unfortunate corporation was to be given constitutional sanction.

With the advance of technology, production was more and more coming to depend upon ever more complex machinery. This meant that more capital was required to install the requisite equipment and that an ever larger ouput was essential to profitable operations. In consequence an increasing number of concerns was outgrowing state boundaries, looking for interstate markets. Such concerns, with their large outlay for fixed and highly specialized capital, were virtually at the mercy of any adverse circumstance which would render these facilities unprofitable.[1] One of the greatest of such hazards was the threat of the exercise of state police power in the public interest. By taxation or regulatory enactments a state legislature could virtually destroy an immense outlay of capital at a single stroke. The effect of the Fourteenth Amendment, thus, was no less than to establish a constitutional prohibition against the exercise of police power by a state. And we have it from the pen of one of those who originally framed this enactment that this was precisely what it was intended to do. With some justice the passage of the Fourteenth Amendment can be referred to as the definitive beginning of American laissez faire.

It is only fair to observe in passing that historians of this period are not agreed as to the origins of the "due process" clause. Thus there are those who insist that this terminology was in fact intended as a part of the Negro's protection, and the written record of the deliberations of the group that wrote the Fourteenth Amendment is offered in evidence on this point. Unfortunately, this evidence is too negative to be very helpful; its principal contribution is that there is nothing in the written account which supports the thesis that there was an intent to write special protections for private property. Furthermore, it is surely not cynical to suggest

[1] "Specialized capital" is capital that can be effectively used in the production process in one way only. Thus a railroad locomotive can be effectively used in the economy only for the purpose of hauling railroad cars. If anything interferes with the use of capital in the way it was meant to be used when liquid capital was first converted into the fixed form, the owner is apt to suffer an almost complete loss.

that considerations of this sort would hardly have been included in the written record in any event. And while the principal evidence on the other side admittedly consists of the fact that protection for interstate corporations was so consistent with the totality of the Congressional reconstruction program, it is at least reasonable to suggest that a slight presumption exists in favor of that view. Perhaps, in other words, the answer will never be definitely known. All that is certain, and with respect to this there can be no question, is the historical use that has been made of this part of the Constitution; *the Supreme Court has consistently interpreted the "due process" clause as though the intent had been to protect property rather than the colored race.* For present purposes, this is the important point.

It is unnecessary to emphasize that there were other motives entering into "radical reconstructionism" after the Civil War. There was a certain amount of genuine idealism, although the relative weakness of this force is attested by the fact that little of a constructive nature was attempted in the Negro's behalf. Many who had suffered during the war, moreover, were no doubt happy to have an opportunity to vent a little of their vindictive wrath. But in the press of postwar problems these sentiments would quickly have died away if they had not been carefully kept alive by the "Radicals." It seems clear, in short, that the only real beneficiaries of delay in the reconstruction process were those economic interests which had traditionally favored economic policies the South had opposed. Of these interests the business community obviously had the most to gain.

The Uses of Power. This being the case it is especially appropriate to ask how much the heartbreaking delay of reconstruction actually achieved. It is of course impossible to say with accuracy. At the same time it does seem clear that much of the desired result would have been achieved anyway. The agrarian West and the urban laborer had their own reasons for not joining hands with southern agrarians. Land policy and tariff protection were still important matters, too important to risk sabotage through an alliance with the South. Furthermore, the South would have been weak for a long period of time in any event as a result of the wholesale destruction of her old pattern of life. This fact alone would have given the East a breathing space to use in further cementing the West to its own economy, especially by investing capital in that area. Given these facts, who can say how much southern isolation was contributed by reconstruction policies? All that can be said for certain is that the business interests emerged from the Civil War in secure control of the Republican party, and that in the succeeding seventy years the Democratic party held full control over the federal government for only eight years.

With the stage set for an exercise of power in their own behalf, the business interests lost no time in utilizing this advantage. The key issues in the immediate postwar period were money and taxation, and conflicts of interest immediately arose. Businessmen were anxious to restore the country to a stable, specie basis as quickly as possible, for currency confusion made it more difficult to carry on most business activities. On the other hand, farmers were at the moment especially interested in an abundance of circulating medium. They had accumulated large debts under the stimulus of high wartime prices, and a shrinking currency would be disastrous. (Perhaps this was one reason the creditor East wanted to return to specie.)

The taxation question was then as always the problem of who was to pay the taxes. Businessmen preferred that the burden rest on the consumer, or at least the agricultural producer. This, indeed, was the foundation on which America's tax structure had always rested. Farmers, however, insisted that business had now reached a sufficient maturity in the economy to enable it to shoulder some of this load. During the war a long step had been taken in this direction, and the problem of the business interests was to alter the wartime structure of taxation in their own favor.

In 1865 the first steps were taken in connection with both of these issues. March saw the appointment of a Congressional committee to study the revenue question, and while this body was at work attention was directed to the currency. In December Congress pledged itself to withdraw the greenbacks from circulation, a step which had been taken for granted at the time they were authorized. By the terms of the Funding Act of April 12, 1866, Secretary of the Treasury McCulloch was required to retire $10 million worth of greenbacks immediately and up to $4 million worth each month thereafter.

At this point efforts to solve the currency question met their first defeat. The initial contraction ran afoul of a money panic in England, a short grain crop in the West, and the primary postwar recession in this country, with the result that the Secretary was put under pressure not to retire notes as rapidly as the law allowed. Some of this pressure arose from an attitude holding deflation responsible for the contraction itself; another part arose out of feeling that a period of liquidation was no time to contract the currency. Even businessmen were not eager to see maximum contraction under existing conditions.

A downturn in business conditions, however, was not the only reason the business community did not insist on a prompt solution to the money question. Another reason was that it did not suit the purposes of the industrial East to ride heavily over the wishes of their agricultural colleagues. The support of the western farmer was indispensable to the dominance of the Republican party, and farmer support had to be purchased with something more substantial than assertions of friendship. Furthermore, the important issue was taxation, and businessmen were willing to make concessions on the money question, at least temporarily, if they could have their way on the matter of the tax burden.

The report of the tax revision committee was duly made to the House Committee on Ways and Means. Its major emphasis was the need to revise and lower the complex and overlapping structure of internal taxes inherited from the war, although it also contained passages which could be interpreted as recommending a reduction in import duties. Such a move was eminently logical. The wartime duties had been enacted only to offset internal taxation; no one had so much as intimated that they were to be permanent.

However, the "logical" approach did not accord with the thinking of eastern business interests. A tax on imports was the tax par excellence as far as they were concerned. Not only did it bear most heavily on consumption (with a substantial secondary incidence on agricultural production), but it served the additional function of placing foreign-produced manufactures at a competitive disadvantage relative to domestic production. Far better to raise the tariff than lower it. In accordance with this thinking two bills were started on their way through Congress. One proposed to reduce internal revenue taxation; the other called for an increase in tariff schedules. The former was quickly passed, but opposition to the tariff "adjustment" was so strong that it had to be tabled until after the fall elections in 1866.

The forces standing for tariff reduction—primarily the agricultural interests of the Midwest—almost won a major victory; for when the Senate reconvened, the tariff measure presented to that body was not the upward revision earlier tabled but a genuine attempt at reduction. Passing the Senate by a substantial margin, it could readily have secured a majority in the House as well. But as a revenue measure originating in the Senate rather than the House, a two-thirds vote had to be secured before it could be put before the House. This extraordinary majority could not be secured and the measure consequently died. Thus it was the protectionists who won the victory, because under the circumstances to reduce internal taxes without reducing the tariff was equivalent to a significant increase in protection.

However, the battle was not over, and no sooner was the general tariff measure abandoned than the business interests endeavored to achieve their purposes in other ways. In March, 1867, a campaign was launched to do away with the income tax, the only progressive element in the federal government's entire tax structure. This move, too, failed, but a step toward that end was taken; the exemption was substantially raised. In 1867 also Alaska was purchased from Russia at a cost of a little more than $7 million. To be sure, this purchase price has proved to be a great bargain in terms of the fishing and mineral resources available there. But protectionists were as always seeking ways to spend surplus revenues derived from "necessary" tariffs, and a $7 million expenditure was helpful from this standpoint as well.

The big 1867 achievement was the Wool and Woolens Act. When the general tariff measure died, the wool and woolens portions—with schedules worked out in cooperation between wool growers and woolens manufacturers—were presented as a separate measure. Both branches of this industry had tremendously expanded during the war and the setting in of postwar adjustments was putting a corresponding pressure upon them. Now, whereas the western farmer had fought strenuously against general increases, it was largely western support which pushed this special legislation to a successful conclusion. With the passage of this act the foundation was laid on which the American tariff structure was to be built for almost three-fourths of a century.

In 1868 it was the money question which occupied the center of the national stage. Early in that year the authority given the Secretary of the Treasury to retire greenbacks was repealed, and pressure immediately appeared to force the retired notes back into circulation. At the same time a new focus of controversy arose. Ever since the suspension of specie payments the government had persisted in paying interest on government bonds in gold even though much of the legislation creating debt authority had not so specified. With greenbacks still circulating at a large discount relative to gold, this seemed a gross injustice to many. Whereas the majority of citizens received their incomes in deflated currency, the wealthy received theirs in gold at a handsome premium. As the presidential campaign of 1868 began to get under way, agitation mounted for the payment of bond interest in greenbacks.

It was not merely the farmer, either, who supported such agitation. Organized labor took a similar stand. Laborers no less than farmers felt that there was an elementary principle of justice involved in the paying of bond interest in coin. Six per cent interest in gold on bonds purchased with greenbacks worth 40 per cent of face value in gold was equivalent to 15 per cent interest on the greenback investment. The platform for the Democratic party called for "one currency" for all the country's citizens, and laborers were included in the listing of the kinds of citizens specifically meant. Farmers and laborers combined, however, were unable to outvote business interests already beginning to wield the power of the agricultural South as well as their own.

This economic legislation provided the basic elements out of which the fiscal policy of the nation was constructed in the years following the Civil War. Year by year internal taxation was reduced until almost nothing remained of these levies except taxes on such things as liquor and tobacco. Ultimately even the income tax was completely eliminated. Meanwhile tariff increases were enacted on one item after another, the most notable increases being on copper, salt, and steel plates, while from time to time duties were reduced on imports which were not competitive with American production. Thus slowly but surely taxation was brought back to a consumption basis, with primary reliance on customs duties, while the tariff was being oriented more and more to a purely protective basis.

TABLE 40. FINANCIAL READJUSTMENT

Year	Customs Revenue	Other Revenues	Total Revenue
		(Millions of dollars)	
1866	179.0	379.0	558.0
1867	176.4	314.2	490.6
1868	164.4	241.2	405.6
1869	180.0	190.9	370.9
1870	194.5	216.8	411.3
1871	206.3	177.0	383.3
1872	216.4	157.7	374.1

Source: Bureau of the Census, *Historical Statistics of the United States, 1789-1945*, p. 297.

Several key figures will make these trends stand out in sharper relief. In the first postwar year customs revenue was barely one-third of total revenue and internal taxes amounted to more than 40 per cent. Six years later customs revenue was some 60 per cent of total revenue and producer-income taxes had fallen virtually to zero. Put differently, over a period of time in which customs revenue rose by one-fifth, other revenues fell by almost 60 per cent. The national government's fiscal policy was not yet an important factor with respect to such matters as income distribution and capital formation, but in so far as it was, the scale was rapidly being tilted in the direction of income concentration and capital accumulation.[2] As such it was a policy excellently suited to dramatic industrial expansion, and the event was not to disappoint this promise. But at the same time it was not a policy which could be expected to develop unopposed in America's dynamic society. And it did not.

[2] Speaking generally, the greater the income received by a given income recipient, the greater will be the volume of saving from that income. Since without saving there can be no investment, it follows that up to a certain point at least the more income is concentrated in the process of its distribution the more rapid will be the rate of capital accumulation. Economists refer to this phenomenon as an increase in the "propensity to save" (a decrease in the "propensity to consume").

QUESTIONS FOR DISCUSSION

1. What is an industrial society? How did the Civil War contribute to the development of such a society in the United States?

2. In what ways was the South's economy ill-suited for a war against the North?

3. Why is postwar rebuilding more easily accomplished than the original development of the economy ravaged by war? Why does an agricultural economy recuperate more rapidly after devastation than an industrial economy?

4. How was reconstruction in the South complicated by the abolition of slavery? Did this step decrease the quantity of any of the factors of production available in the South?

5. Why did the South not become an industrial society after the Civil War? If the Negro had by some miracle disappeared in 1865, would the South have been more likely to have become industrialized?

6. What were the major elements in the "victory by delay" strategy adopted by the "Radicals" after "Presidential Reconstruction" was overthrown?

7. How essential was something like the "due process" clause to the growth of modern America?

8. How essential was a regressive tax structure at this stage in the country's economic growth?

Chapter 20

FARMERS UNDER PRESSURE

1869 Union-Pacific–Central Pacific Railroad completed.
Jay Gould's attempt to corner the gold market.
1870 First Congressional legislation against the Ku Klux Klan.
"Grange" becoming a formidable organization.

It would be misleading to suppose that success on the political front was solely or even largely responsible for the dramatic growth of the industrial sector of the economy after the Civil War. On the one hand, economic evolution over half a century had been preparing the nation for just such an advance. And, on the other hand, if any one factor were given credit for the phenomenal development now taking place it would have to be the progress of technology. Never in all previous history had the advance of knowledge proceeded so rapidly. Never before had a society so widely accepted the scientific point of view, or made so many resources available for its furtherance. Never had science been harnessed to the task of providing ever more abundantly for man's wants on such a scale—both by substituting mineral for animal energy and by discovering valuable, new

TABLE 41. INDUSTRIAL TRANSFORMATION

Census Year	Total Population (Millions)	Per Cent Urban	Manufacturing Income as Per Cent of Total Income [1]
1860	31.4	19.8	12.1
1870	39.8	25.7	15.9
1880	50.2	28.2	14.5
1890	62.9	35.1	21.1
1900	76.0	39.7	19.6

[1] Data for the year preceding census year. In addition, these data make no allowance for fluctuations in the business cycle.

Source: Bureau of the Census, *Historical Statistics of the United States, 1789-1945,* pp. 14 and 25.

resources. Not without reason is the period following the Civil War referred to as "America's industrial revolution."

The dynamic nature of this period can be especially seen in the manufacturing and railroad industries. Profits in these fields were often enormous, and when reinvested for expansion purposes huge profits could also be earned on an augmented capital. In a period of ten years the nation built a railroad from the Missouri River to the Pacific Ocean, doubled its railway mileage, doubled its investment in manufacturing facilities, and broke virtually every production record in every industry. Confronted on every hand with evidence of the emergence of a new age, men could not doubt that America's last great agricultural era was over.

The New Society. Certain specific aspects of the transformation taking place are especially deserving of emphasis. First, the new age was to be the age of "big" business. By installing improved machinery and inaugurating employee division of labor, costs could be lowered and profits increased. Vertical expansion by certain kinds of firms (the inclusion under a single management of more than one stage in the production process) was similarly promoted. The greater complexity of production by means of the new technology often made necessary close coordination between interdependent processes or production schedules, a coordination best accomplished by bringing them under a common management. Furthermore, tendencies toward larger-scale operations were cumulative because they in turn made it possible to utilize hitherto unusable by-products, engage more actively in research, and reduce marketing costs. And finally, this entire development was made possible by the greatly expanded use of the corporate device.

Second, the new age was also to be the "age of steel." By this is not meant merely that steel replaced iron, although that change was fundamental. What is meant is rather that the new period was dominated by "heavy" industries using steel in large quantities. Most specifically, what was involved was the reduction in the price of this metal sufficient to enable it to become a *basic* raw material. Before the Civil War steel was so costly that it could be used only in the making of razor blades, fine cutlery, watch springs, and the highest quality tools, while iron was so brittle that it could not have provided the basis for a "heavy" industry in the modern sense even if it had been cheap enough.

Shortly before the Civil War an Englishman named Bessemer and an American named Kelly invented the so-called Bessemer process of steelmaking. Soon thereafter this technique was supplemented by the open-hearth process (which was one day almost to supplant the Bessemer method), and within ten years after the Civil War a great new industry centered at Pittsburgh had increased this country's output from 3 thousand to 400 thousand tons per year. Five years later the United States was turning out nearly one million tons annually, and already her independence of English production was clearly foreshadowed. Significantly, steel technology made virtually inevitable large-scale output. The vertical coordination of blast furnace, converter, steel furnace, and finishing operations in a single plant makes it possible to avoid the heat loss entailed when pig iron or steel ingots are cooled for shipping purposes.

In the third place, the new age was to see the development of the West carried forward with an energy and an enthusiasm hitherto lacking. Until now the West had primarily attracted the farmer, except as secondary and tertiary industries followed the frontier line. Beyond the prairie country, however, and this included most of the undeveloped West, available resources were such as could best be exploited in an "industrial" rather than an "agricultural" fashion—on a large scale and with the aid of large amounts of eastern capital. In this category were mining, lumbering, and ranching. These were the years of the "cowboy" and the "cattle drive," years in which thousands of herds of cattle from the Great Plains were driven to the nearest railroad—the length of the drive gradually decreasing as the rail network expanded. Earlier the pioneering farmer had paved the way for eastern capital; now the two were pioneering the West side by side. Earlier, too, the West had been "attacked" only from the East; now there were two frontiers as men sought to conquer these great open spaces (the "last frontier") from Pacific Coast "strongholds" as well as from the East. As a result the frontier as a geographical entity was completely destroyed before the end of the century.

In part because of the interest of eastern capital in the West, the age now dawning was in an important sense the age of the railroad. The major obstacle to the exploitation of western wealth was distance, and distance could now be overcome most economically by means of railroads. On May 10, 1869, men all over the nation felt a thrill of exultation when the telegraph flashed the news that the last spike had been driven in the Union Pacific-Central Pacific link with California. And this was only the

TABLE 42. MASTERING A CONTINENT

Year	Railroad Mileage
1860	30,626
1870	52,922
1880	93,262
1890	166,703
1900	193,346
1910	240,293

Source: Bureau of the Census, *Historical Statistics of the United States, 1789-1945*, pp. 200 and 202.

beginning. Thousands upon thousands of railway miles were constructed in the feverish haste to make the West more accessible—a haste in which the millions of buffaloes ranging on western grasslands were destroyed so rapidly that buffalo hides became practically worthless, and in which the Indian was to become only a little less extinct than the buffalo he could not live without. This extension of the railroad into the West was, indeed, the real secret of the rapid conquest of America's vast frontier.

For another reason also the new age can appropriately be referred to as a railway age. Not only was the railroad pioneering in the West, but much progress was also being made toward rounding out the rail network in the East. By now the fact that the railroad was to be primarily useful for long, intersectional hauls was becoming evident. As a result the older concept of many short lines rather than a smaller number of longer ones was now outmoded. Among other things this meant that the different gauges which had characterized railroad building in the past would have to give way to a uniformity making unnecessary frequent and costly transfers of lading. Thus, in the railway field as well as in manufacturing, larger-scale operations seemed to be indicated. With this development men naturally began to envisage vast railway empires ruled by themselves, and in a period when the "impossible" was commonplace such dreams were soon translated into reality.

As still another characteristic of the era now opening, a full development of the railroad made possible geographical specialization to a degree never before attained. One field in which this was especially true was meat packing. As the railroad moved into the cattle country and cattle began to populate the grass regions of the West, a great development in the slaughtering industry took place in the Middle West—a development centering primarily in Chicago but secondarily in such places as Milwaukee, Kansas City, and St. Louis. It is significant in this connection that the Union Stockyards project in Chicago, one of the decisive factors in Chicago's pre-eminence, resulted from the cooperative endeavors of nine railroads. When to the expansion of the rail network in general was added the innovation of the refrigerator car, the meat packing industry in the East could not withstand the competition thus brought into the field. Just as the westward movement of the center of gravity of agriculture had earlier forced painful adjustments in eastern agriculture, so now a westward shift in the center of gravity of industry was forcing a painful adjustment in eastern industry.

However, not only was the victor in this economic transition the West as against the East, but the small butcher was rapidly destroyed in favor of the larger operator. With the development of a more and more minute division of labor plus the discovery of uses for many of the in-

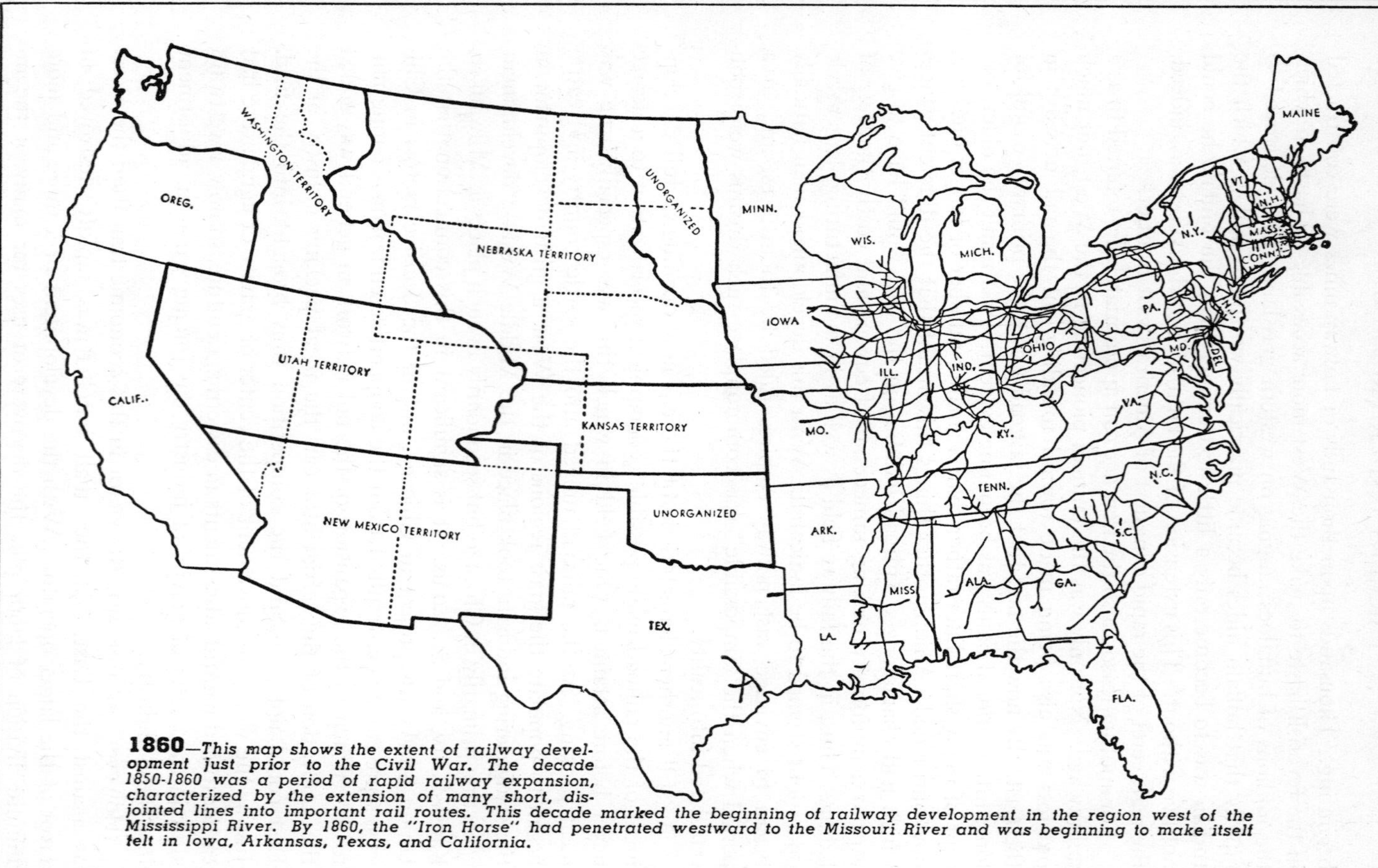

1860—*This map shows the extent of railway development just prior to the Civil War. The decade 1850-1860 was a period of rapid railway expansion, characterized by the extension of many short, disjointed lines into important rail routes. This decade marked the beginning of railway development in the region west of the Mississippi River. By 1860, the "Iron Horse" had penetrated westward to the Missouri River and was beginning to make itself felt in Iowa, Arkansas, Texas, and California.*

1890—*The period from 1880 to 1890 was one of rapid expansion. More than 70,300 miles of new lines were opened in that decade, bringing the total network up to 163,597 miles. By 1890, several trunk line railroads extended to the Pacific. In thirty years from 1860 to 1890, the total mileage of the region west of the Mississippi River increased from 2,175 to 72,389, and the population of that area increased fourfold.*

FIGURE 13-B. The Railway Net in 1890. (Courtesy Association of American Railroads) dustry's by-products, there was no longer economic justification for the small butcher even in the major centers of the industry.

Flour milling also illustrates these same tendencies. The opening of the West on the one hand brought about a shift in the center of gravity of this industry to the West—primarily to Minneapolis and secondarily to St. Louis and Chicago—and on the other hand placed the small operator at an overwhelming disadvantage.

Another way in which the economy might be characterized takes reference from the brand-new oil industry. Here a new product exploited by means of new processes became in an incredibly short time the foundation of a basic industry. First commercially important as a result of drilling in Pennsylvania just before the Civil War, oil so took the economy by storm that by the end of the war a speculative mania in oil stocks accompanied every new "strike." Boom towns appeared to live out their numbered days in wild extravagance only to die a lingering death after the bountiful flow began to taper off.

Initially the major problem of this industry was transportation. The inventive and aggressive spirit of the times soon solved this problem, however, by the development of oil freight cars and pipelines, and soon a great refining industry had sprung up which summarily destroyed the whale-fishing industry. Here again an advanced technology and the availability of valuable by-products made the economical unit of production large, and small operators were quickly crowded out. At the same time production was concentrated at a few points—Cleveland, New York, Pittsburgh, and Philadelphia, in the order of their relative importance.

Last but by no means least, this period of American economic history can be characterized in terms of the men who made it. There was Andrew Carnegie who pioneered his way to fame and fortune in the steel industry, "Commodore" Vanderbilt who originally put together the New York Central Railroad, Philip D. Armour and Gustavus F. Swift who transformed America's meat packing industry into an activity of international importance, Charles A. Pillsbury who played an important part in the development of the new flour milling industry, and the unforgettable John D. Rockefeller who more than anyone else built the new oil industry into one of major importance. Whether it was the age that produced these men or these men who produced their own age (and no doubt both are correct) is unimportant. What is important is that neither can be thought of apart from the other without injury to both.

In only one area of the economy was the new economy not making its way rapidly forward. That was in the South. Apart from cotton textile manufacturing, the South's major manufacturing activity in pre-Civil War days, the rise of Birmingham as a steel center, and the further development of southern railroads, life went on much as it always had in the ex-Confederate states. One explanation for this is the preoccupation of southerners with the problems of reconstruction. Another is the anti-industrial sentiment in the South, which had contributed greatly to the onset of Civil War and which had if anything been intensified by the war. Still a third is the fact that the South could not develop along industrial lines without eastern capital, and eastern capital was largely absorbed in developing the West. But with the exception of this one region the American economy presented an unbroken spectacle of unprecedented industrial expansion.

Its Ugly Side. The new society coming into being, however, did have its other side. Just as this was an age of great development, it was an age of great temptation. Expansion more often than not depended upon the exploitation of resources possessed by the public, or the exercise of privileges which only the public authority could grant, or the following of practices which only organized society as a whole could prevent or modify. For these reasons industrial leadership found it helpful if not indispensable to establish a close enough liaison with government to secure the necessary exploitation rights, privileges, or immunities. A situation more made to order for corruption could hardly be imagined, for the fabulous growth in the nation's income furnished not only an incentive but the material means by which such activities could flourish.

A few examples will illustrate this other side of the post-Civil War expansion. In Albany it was common knowledge that votes in the legislature were as freely bought and sold as groceries in a grocery store, and some legislators even engaged in a vicious form of blackmail by threatening to propose damaging bills and accepting cash as a reward for refraining. These conditions, furthermore, were the rule rather than the exception. Corporation influence in state and city politics, an influence shrewdly managed by men such as "Boss" Tweed in New York and Matthew Quay in Pennsylvania, was almost complete. This influence was also rooted deeply in national politics, in part directly and in part as a result of the election of United States Senators by state legislatures. In Kansas a legislator named York once rose, pale and trembling, to lay on the speaker's desk the $7,000 he had been paid for his vote for a certain man for United States Senator.

It was in Washington in fact that the grandest projects for "legal larceny" were worked out. Railroad lobbyists spent money with a lavish hand. For years an arrangement between most of the large distilleries and government officials was agreed upon that permitted a large share of the distilled spirits produced in the country to escape taxation. "Unofficial" tax evasion also flourished, protected by an elaborate network of blackmailers who chose to collect a larger reward from the evader for not informing rather than a smaller one from the government for informing. In these and other ways the national government as well as state and local governments furnished a part of the setting against which the "moral collapse" of the nation took place.

A more detailed view of the way in which big business and government cooperated in some of the most flagrant abuses of the time will more adequately explain the revulsion of popular feling which was in time to rise up against the nation's corporations and the men behind them. The Union Pacific Railroad promoters awarded themselves (in the name of a construction company called the *Crédit Mobilier*) the contract for building and equipping most of this road, with the result that the cash proceeds of the sale of the land grant from the government and the liberal purchase of bonds by the government in large part accrued to promoters rather than the railroad for which they were intended. And in order to make certain that Congress did not interfere, as it might very well have done in view of the government's stake in this project and the importance to the country of having a well-built railroad to California, *Crédit Mobilier* shares on liberal terms were distributed to a number of Representatives and Senators.

Another episode involved the stock market and such titans of finance as Vanderbilt, Jay Gould, Daniel Drew, and Jim Fisk. It began, if complicated events can be said to have a clear-cut beginning, with a commercial rivalry between Vanderbilt's New York Central and Drew's Erie so bitter and so costly to the New York Central that the "Commodore" resolved to secure a strong enough control over the Erie to bring this uncomfortable expense to an end. His technique was to buy up a controlling interest in the Erie on the stock exchange. But he had not accurately anticipated the greedy ruthlessness of Gould, Fisk, and Drew. From their vantage point in control of the legal machinery of the corporation, his opponents printed some $10 million of (100 per cent watered) shares which were thrown on the market at the cost of weakening still further the already shaky credit of a great, if unfortunate, railroad.

The sequel to this episode is equally revealing. Vanderbilt sought through "his" New York judge to secure an injunction against this outrageous abuse of power by corporate officials. This challenge was met by a counterinjunction issued by a judge "belonging" to Vanderbilt's opponents. As a further precaution the Erie Railroad set up temporary headquarters in a New Jersey hotel, while the New York state legislature was induced to authorize the stock issue recently put on the market. In the battle for votes in Albany, incidentally, one legislator accepted $75,000 (although the going rate was only $15,000 per vote) from Vanderbilt and $100,000 from Gould. The man's vote went to Gould.

Another major scandal involved some of the same men but centered primarily on the New York money market. The Drew-Fisk-Gould combination, in preparing for this next "adventure," first sold heavily in the stock market on the "short" side; that is, they sold large quantities of stock which they did not have.[1] Then they went to banks in New York and withdrew *in cash* an amount of money substantially in excess of $10 million. This precipitated a sharp contraction in the money market, one of the most immediate consequences of which was the calling in of large amounts in brokers' loans. The liquidation of stocks to enable payment of called loans brought about a panic decline in share prices. At these lower levels the combine was able to fulfill its "short" contracts and make a handsome profit.

But unquestionably the most brazen manipulation in this age of brazen manipulations was Jay Gould's attempted corner of the gold market. No other money-making scheme touched so directly the relationship between the public and its basic institutions, involving as it did both the country's medium of exchange and the official family of President Grant.

The Gold Exchange was still operating, for the nation had not yet returned to a specie basis. To supply the nation's legitimate day-to-day gold needs, the gold market contained some $100 million worth of specie. In addition the United States Treasury held upward of $20 million as a reserve against its needs. What Gould set out to do was to buy enough of the market's supply to force up the price of gold. Obviously it was essential to keep the government's holdings out of the market, and the danger of government selling was a real one in view of the close relationship between the gold market and the financial operations of the Treasury.

The strategy was an intensive propaganda campaign designed to convince Grant that the public interest made it imperative that the government not part with any of its gold holdings in the fall of 1869. This was accomplished in part by the more or less legitimate use of ordinary media of communication such as newspapers and financial journals, and in part through the use of substantial amounts of bribe money placed in the hands of Grant intimates. Even the President himself was lavishly entertained on several occasions as the "education" campaign developed.

It is to Grant's credit that he never unequivocally committed himself. At the same time it is an indication of the character of the man that he did allow himself to be used indirectly by unscrupulous men whose de-

[1] In speculating, that is, buying and selling with the expectation of profiting from short-term price changes, the existence of a futures market makes it possible to make profits no matter which way the market goes—provided only one guesses correctly which way it is going. On a rising market, the proper procedure is to buy in order to sell later at a higher price. When the market is falling, however, it is necessary to sell first, buying later at the expected lower price. But for this to work out, it is essential that the stock (or whatever) originally sold be stock not already owned.

signs he was not astute enough to penetrate. Actually, Grant was an excellent chief executive for this period in America's history. Few men were so easily impressed with wealth and the men who were able to flaunt it. Nor was this any surprise to those anxious to see him elected to the presidency. What the business interests were looking for in a Washington administration was, as one phrase-maker expressed it, men who would not steal but who would not interfere with those who did. Ulysses S. Grant was, in these terms, an ideal choice.

Gould's plan carried almost, but not quite, to perfection. In the early fall he began his purchase program. Higher and higher went the price of gold as the grand scheme unfolded. With painful slowness it began to dawn on the Treasury Department what was going on, and that high government officials were deeply implicated. After several days of hurried and half-frightened conferences it was decided that the government should break the corner with its own gold supply. The day the government's gold hit the Exchange has ever since been known as "Black Friday" because of the large number of innocents who were irretrievably ruined in the crash.

Perhaps the moral of this story should be that Jay Gould was one of those who went down. However, the story does not read that way. Learning in advance what the government was planning to do, he induced Fisk and his brokers to buy gold heavily (although he did not divulge to his "business friend" all that was involved.) This provided a market prop which enabled Gould to get out from under his purchases at a profit, while Fisk and his group were taking huge paper losses. Then Gould, with the spirit of "honor" said always to prevail among thieves, used his influence to help the Fisk group repudiate its commitments and hence avoid real losses.

History has been unqualified in its condemnation of the seamy side of this "gilded age," although explanations are not lacking. It is pointed out, for example, that time is required for a society to regain its moral perspective after engaging in bloody warfare. Another emphasis is the fact that the birth of a new social order is almost necessarily accompanied by a temporary blurring of accepted standards of behavior.

Valuable though these explanations are, at least one more is required to round out the picture. This period exhibits laissez faire in its purest form. It was for this that the business interests had worked in seeking to keep the agrarian South out of the Union for a time. With labor not yet a powerful interest group, and with industrialism rapidly altering the agrarian character of such states as Ohio, Indiana, and Illinois, who was there to interfere? Laissez faire in its European origins was a class philosophy intended to destroy *past* regulations which had ceased to perform a useful function. Laissez faire in America was a class philosophy intended to prevent *present* regulations which society might feel would serve a useful function. Obviously in its extreme form such a philosophy could not dominate the nation for long, and it did not. It is not wholly a coincidence that the most glaring excesses of the "gilded age" began to disappear immediately after the South re-entered the Union under its own leadership, and that laissez faire lingered on to almost exactly the extent that business interests dominated the instruments of policy-making.

Apart from explanations, too, there are certain other aspects of this period which deserve to be mentioned. First, the standard of morality which was flourishing is readily understandable in terms of the problems confronting America in the last half of the nineteenth century. Riches such as few had ever realistically dreamed of stretched out before men to be developed. Here was no static society demanding a pattern of closely restricted statuses and narrowly defined behavior. Here was rather a dynamic society presenting its members with such an abundance of opportunities that a large degree of unhampered freedom to experiment seemed desirable. Put a little differently, America's economic margin above subsistence was so wide, and the readjustment opportunities for casualties were so great, that much flexibility could be permitted without damage. It was a standard of behavior which would be intolerable in a more highly urbanized society and one not expanding so rapidly, but for the moment it served a useful purpose.

Second, and more concretely, there is another dimension to scandals such as the one accompanying the building of the Union Pacific Railroad—and most railroad building during this period resulted in similar incidents. With minor exceptions the important transcontinental railroad stems were constructed before enough traffic existed to justify their cost. The same was true of much construction in the East. Obviously private enterprise could not be expected to undertake such activities unless a source of profit were found outside ordinary business channels. Insisting as it did on free enterprise the nation was virtually forced to permit a certain amount of "leakage" of funds, although perhaps no harm would have been done if the country's development had not proceeded quite so rapidly. This cost, in other words, must not be viewed apart from the context of the importance the nation attached to railroad expansion. Just as before the Civil War excesses in the field of banking had to be measured against the value of westward expansion, so after the war did excesses in the railroad field have to be judged by the same standard.

Challenge from the West. It was most fitting that it was the farmer who threw down the first challenge to America's postwar laissez faire. On the one hand, no other group was powerful enough to make the attempt. More important, on the other hand, the farmer had grown accustomed to wielding the reins of power, and understandably felt inconvenienced now that this was no longer the case.

At the same time, it was not the success of the business interests in giving effect to their ideas about fiscal policy which was responsible for the middle western farmer's rebellion against eastern industrialism. In fact it was not even the publicity given to the sordid details of government and corporate corruption which galvanized the agricultural West into action. Both of these factors were too remote to motivate the traditionally individualistic farmer to organize in opposition. However, these two general grievances did lend fuel to the farmer's anger once it was aroused by more specific factors. Whether or not "Commodore" Vanderbilt ever actually said, "The public be damned," is not certain. But as some of the practices of men such as Gould, Fisk and Drew became common knowledge it was unimportant; to the simple and hard-working farmer actions are far more apt to be read and interpreted than words.

What were the specific factors which aroused the ire of the western farmer? More specifically and more important, why did the farmer's wrath rise up against the railroad and related services? Why did the "farmer's friend," the agency without which the tremendous development of the West would have been impossible, bear the brunt of the first phase of what is frequently referred to as "the revolt of the farmer"?

One fact which should be kept in mind in this connection is the semi-frontier condition of much of this territory. Work was hard and long, and few comforts were available. It was in this area, moreover, that troubles with the Indian developed once again as the white man overran lands to which he had given the red man full title. Here, too, prairie fires, blizzards, droughts, and locusts were a constant peril to crops, animals, and men alike. The Middle West, to be sure, was on the threshold of a remarkable development which was to ease somewhat the burden of men of the soil, but at the moment these men were dominated by the difficult environment in which they actually lived. Since men facing the hardships of life on the fringes of "civilization" are apt to have a poor understanding of a more highly developed culture, some of the farmer's battle against the railroad may be put down to simple ignorance. Thus the very presence in their midst of the representatives of absentee corporate owners with their silk hats, frock coats, white gloves, polished canes, and patent-leather boots created such a contrast that many farmers were alienated for this reason alone.

Much more important as a factor goading the farmer into rebellion was the postwar recession which ravaged the wheat areas more seriously than any other part of the economy. By the end of 1869 the prices of wheat and flour had fallen more than 50 per cent. For the next several

TABLE 43. PRESSURE ON THE FARMER

Year	Index of Farm Prices (1860 = 100)
1866	185.6
1867	181.9
1868	179.1
1869	163.9
1870	130.6
1871	127.6
1872	124.3
1873	119.5

Source: Bureau of the Census, *Historical Statistics of the United States, 1789-1945*, p. 234.

years, furthermore, they remained low. The tremendous expansion of wheat acreage made possible by the coming of the railroad (a development also taking place in Russia and South America), the expansion in wheat output induced by the war, and the importation of the "gradual reduction" method of flour milling (making possible the manufacture of a quality flour from spring wheat as well as winter wheat), were more than the postwar wheat price structure could stand.

Chronic low prices in the face of mortgages contracted when prices were much higher meant a change in economic well-being for tens of thousands of farmers from relative prosperity to a situation in which each half-year was spent in anxious wondering if the next semiannual installment could be met—an anxiety greatly accentuated by the knowledge that creditors (often Easterners and almost always supported by eastern capital) would make little or no allowance for the permanent improvements added to the land. Given these conditions the obvious prosperity of eastern-owned corporations, especially railroads, could only heighten such conflicts as should develop on other grounds.

TABLE 44. THE FRONTIER AND FOREIGN TRADE

Period	Percentage of United States Exports Consisting of Crude Foodstuffs
1851-1860	6.6
1876-1880	23.9

Source: *Statistical Abstract of the United States, 1941*, p. 533.

It is not without interest that the western farmer was himself partially responsible for his plight. Much of the intensive push into the West was motivated, not by a rational calculation of economic advantage on the basis of supply and demand conditions, but by a desire to live an independent existence. As a result (and the widespread employment of the new factory-built farm machinery only made matters worse), production outran world demand and the farmer suffered in proportion. The very debts he had contracted to achieve independence became a boomerang plunging him into one of the most painful kinds of dependence known to man—economic inflexibility in an interdependent world. As expressed by one student, the United States after the Civil War made available to the world the most fabulous "bargain counter" in agricultural products the world has ever seen.

However, whatever the causal factors, these were circumstances under which American farmers had in the past placed emphasis upon inflation as a remedy. And on this occasion too, attention was not wholly directed into other channels. But the farmer had just finished winning something of a victory on that front in the repeal of the law to retire the greenbacks, and the difficulty of achieving even so small a concession seemed to mean that this door was closed for the time being.

Besides, a nearer scapegoat was at hand. In the complex interrelationships between the farmer and the agencies responsible for distributing the farmer's products, the farmer found a number of reasons for grave dissatisfaction. Thus, for a brief but important period the chief focus of the farmer's anger was the railroad and the railroad-associated warehouse.

The railroad had indeed been responsible for the building of the West. Although some settlers had pushed beyond the frontier ahead of the railroad, it was soon found that without an effective means of transportation to haul surplus products to market, frontier life was almost intolerable. Many farmers actually mortgaged their farms in order to help the railroad get its start, and many rural frontier communities made substantial stock pledges designed to put the oncoming railroad nearer to their needs. Farmer-dominated state governments were also generous in this regard, while farmers without number at first took great pride in the assistance given the railroad by their national government.

Not only did the farmer help the railroad come into the West, but the railroad did much to help the farmer do the same. With huge quantities of land to use as a lure, railroad promoters searched both eastern United States and Europe for prospective settlers and in numerous ways made resettlement on the frontier easier than would otherwise have been possible. They laid out town sites, surveyed land and marked off farm sites, furnished free transportation, made limited amounts of capital available, and made arrangements for settlement in groups rather than individually. These "colonization" efforts, of course, were not philanthropic activities; success meant cash from the sale of land and traffic to pay operating expenses.

In short, it was not that the farmer did not appreciate the value of the railroad to his economic well-being, or the efforts of the railroad in his behalf. Had these been the only factors involved there would have been no conflict between the farmer and the railroad. The conflict arose from deeper causes, one of the most fundamental being a basic incompatibility between railroad land grants and the Homestead Act.

The land grant program called for the awarding of a minimum of ten square miles of land to the railroad for each mile of track. In practice this meant reserving alternate sections for the railroad in a strip of territory ten miles on each side of the line. A number of the land grant acts reserved alternate sections in an even wider strip, and in extreme cases the strip had to be broadened to as much as sixty miles on each side of the railroad to allow adequate compensation for tracts already held within the reserved area.

The difficulty was this. In order to make the land grant of the greatest immediate value to the railroad (and after all the point of the grants was to get railroads built), the government withheld its sections until the railroad land had been taken up. Even then for a number of years only 80 acres could be secured rather than the customary 160. The result was that the settler had to choose between taking up free land ten to fifty miles from the railroad or paying the railroad's price for railroad-owned land —a price made artificially high by the government's decision to withhold its land from occupation. While it is not easy to see how else the land grant program could have been administered, it is at the same time not difficult to understand the resentment felt by western farmers.

Freight rates were another bone of contention. It is the nature of a railroad to be monopolistic over large sections of its line. The expense of building a railroad is so great that it would be prohibitively wasteful from society's point of view to provide full-length competition. At the same time, it is the nature of a railroad to be a highly fixed-cost enterprise; that is, there is a wide margin between the level of rates which will pay out-of-pocket costs and the level required to pay full costs. A consequence is that railroad rate making is based upon "what the traffic will bear"; rates tend to be higher in the absence of competition than where competition prevails. Thus a competitive rate may well be little higher than out-of-pocket costs, while a noncompetitive rate may be at full cost or even more.

Now under the best of circumstances a farmer is apt to feel ill-treated in the freight rates he is charged. This is so because his products are bulky relative to their value and hence expensive to transport. But a farmer faced with falling prices and mortgage payments is even more apt to feel overcharged, a feeling accentuated by the little then known about watered railroad stock.[2]

For these reasons the western farmer's attack on freight rates must be interpreted with caution. At the same time, however, several facts were glaringly in evidence. First, it often cost one bushel of grain to transport another one, and the cost of shipping wheat from Chicago to Liverpool was often less than the freight rate from some Dakota areas to Minneapolis. Furthermore, freight rates did not appreciably fall when the prices of the goods farmers sold fell drastically. Second, differences in rates from one locality to another and as between large and small shippers were flagrantly obvious. Third, the sharp differences in rates west of the Mississippi River as compared with east of it, and west of the Missouri River as compared with east of it, were considered just as obviously to be violations of acceptable morality. Furthermore, in neither case was it of concern to the farmer whether the higher rate was the result of charging a price calculated to yield a monopoly profit, or the unremunerative level to which rates had been driven at competitive points, or the smaller volume of traffic available over western lines. Fourth, the activity of railroads in influencing governments by bribery, stock sales at less than market prices, and free passes was accepted as further proof of the indifference of the railroad to the plight of the ordinary citizen.

Still another major grievance focused on the commercial warehouse. At first few warehouses were available and grain was piled on the ground near the railroad to be hauled when the railroad could furnish cars. As a remedy for this situation railroads often went into the warehouse business, at which point the difficulty became the refusal of a railroad to haul wheat from a rival elevator (or the addition of an elevator charge even though an independent warehouse had actually been used). Then, too, virtually all warehousemen had their own system of grading, and all too often the grade given was lower than that assigned by the central elevator. When to all these hazards was added high storage charges (in part in order to "coerce" the farmer into selling his product at once when the price was at its seasonal low), there was certainly reason enough for substantial farmer dissatisfaction.

Even in a large wheat center such as Chicago the situation was little better. At one time Chicago had fourteen elevators owned by thirty

[2] A fact which is frequently not understood about "what-the-traffic-will-bear" pricing is that the lower rate does not necessarily make other rates higher. If the lower rate contributes something to overhead, and if the traffic would be lost to a competitor if the lower price were not quoted, this kind of discrimination may even help keep rates down. Similarly the relationship between watered stock (securities issued which do not result in a corresponding increase in the assets of the firm) and freight rates is easily misunderstood. Prices for freight services will tend to be low if competition is keen, and high if there is little competition, but the capitalization of the railroad company is not a price-determining factor.

persons and nine firms which at some point handled nearly all the marketed grain from a half dozen states and charged a scale of prices agreed upon in advance. It was in Chicago too that the most important futures market for wheat was located. Although the operations of the wheat pit no doubt served a beneficial purpose over the long pull, it gave the farmer much reason for still more distrust. On the one hand, not understanding its complexities, he could easily convince himself that it was another machination of the corporate world for his exploitation. On the other hand, its operations were subject to speculative manipulations which rarely benefited the farmer and often worked to his disadvantage.

It was not only the wheat farmer who had complaints, either. Farther west and to the south was the huge area devoted to livestock raising, the "rancher's frontier," where the slaughter of the buffalo had cleared the way for the substitution of a domesticated counterpart. Here there were special grievances against the land laws then in force. Cattle raising is an *extensive* economic activity—one requiring a much larger area for successful operation than crop farming. (And even when, later, the "farmer's frontier" overran much of the rancher's domain, inadequate moisture continued to make a larger farm necessary for the support of a family.) The unit, however, for free homesteading was 160 acres—too small a plot for success in an extensive operation. As a result the rancher-frontiersman was compelled to try to make a living on too little land, or to go into debt to buy more, or to "poach" on unclaimed or forest reserve land. Whichever alternative he selected he was apt—in a period of declining prices—to find himself at the mercy of some eastern capitalist or a government surveyor (all too often allied with an eastern capitalist or, what was almost worse, a homesteader).

These farmers, moreover, had special grievances against the railroads, too. Because his product was a living animal (and a large proportion of the corn grown in the Middle West was marketed in this form) transportation was if anything a more vital matter to the cattle farmer than to the grain farmer. Inadequate cars, crowding, and careless shipping practices reduced both the quantity and quality of the farmer's product with a consequent reduction in its value. This, moreover, was added to the problem of high freight rates, and oftentimes farmers not too distant from a packing center would elect to drive their stock to market rather than pay the freight and entrust animals to the care of the railroad. Once in the marketplace other hazards were encountered. For example, there continued to be a close relationship between western railroads and the Union Stockyards.

By the early 1870's farmers throughout the West had had enough. The main instrument by means of which their resentment was being made effective was an organization called the Patrons of Husbandry, or more popularly the "Grange." Originally this agency had been formed for the purpose of broadening the social and cultural horizon of the individualistic farmer through a greater mingling with his own kind. On this basis, however, it had achieved little, and only after the farmer became hemmed in by the world price for his product on the one side and the industrial East on the other did this movement begin to spread and grow. Now, in cooperation with independent farmers' clubs working for the same objectives, it mobilized its full resources behind a drive to secure a greater measure of justice from the nation's railroads and middlemen. Farmers as well as other nonindustrial interests were unquestionably on the defensive, and this situation was not soon to change, but it had already been determined that they were not to be passive.

QUESTIONS FOR DISCUSSION

1. What were the principal characteristics of the new industrial society?
2. Why was eastern capital not as vigorously used in developing the South as the West?
3. Do men make history or does history make men? How correct would it be to say that prior to the Civil War America's most important citizens were statesmen whereas after the Civil War they were industrialists?
4. Was the "ugly side" of the new society a natural accompaniment of the rapid development of the American economy?
5. Of what benefit was it to capitalists to issue watered stock? If benefits were actually derived, was the stock really "watered"? What effect did watered stock have upon labor?
6. What was the essence of the conflict between the farmer and the railroads?
7. Was there any more satisfactory solution to the conflict between the railroad land grant policy and the Homestead Act than the one actually arrived at?
8. How could it be determined whether or not the freight rates charged western farmers were unreasonably high?

Chapter 21

A LIMITED VICTORY

1871 Civil service reform agitation.
Railroad land grants ended.
"Tweed Ring" exposé.
1872 *Crédit Mobilier* scandal first came to light.
"Liberal" Republican movement defeated.
1873 "Crime of '73"—silver dollar left off the list of coins to be minted.
"Panic of 1873."
1874 Windom Committee report.
1875 Resumption Act passed.
Whiskey Ring broken.
1876 Sixth World's Fair held in Philadelphia.
America's only disputed presidential election.
Munn v. Illinois.
1877 Rutherford B. Hayes, Republican reform candidate, declared President.
End of "Black Reconstruction."

Another Tax Defeat. As farmers began to prepare their attack against the railroads, the business interests were feeling increased pressure from another quarter. The industrial boom was accompanied by a high level of international trade and, as foreign capital continued to flow into America and as America's gold mines continued to turn out a sizable stream of the yellow metal each year, imports were regularly substantially above exports. The result was a lavish yield from the customs duties inherited from the war. With the government's revenue far exceeding its needs, including debt retirement, taxpayers were insisting upon a reduction of their burden.

There seemed to be no way out; a tax reduction would have to be made. On the other hand, however, alternative ways of bringing this about were available. Representatives of the business interests set to work examining them to see which one best suited their purposes. A way out was soon found. Since much of the demand was for lower taxes rather than reduced protection, why not isolate the antiprotectionists by lowering nonprotective duties?

It was a hazardous undertaking. The antiprotectionists were primarily midwest farmers, and the Republican party still depended on their support. Possibly, however, it was felt that the farmer could be appeased in some other way, and the decision was made to proceed. Accordingly a bill was introduced raising the duty on some protected items and greatly reducing many purely revenue duties—that is, those on tea, coffee, sugar, and the like—and some of these items were even put on the free list. (A sugar duty was not a purely revenue item, of course, but in 1870 few Republicans would have conceded that Louisiana's interest in protection was an important consideration.) As expected, the western farmer did raise strenuous objection but the bill was passed nonetheless, and on July 14, 1870, President Grant signed it into law.

Did the farmer receive his concession? If one is not careful in his choice of words, the answer is "yes." In 1870 the House of Representatives passed a resolution pledging the cessation of railroad land grants. The following year, however, 20 million more acres were granted before the pledge was made good. Railroad land grants were ended, but a clearer case of locking the stable door too late could not be found.

In this frustration of the farmer, a pattern of behavior was exhibited which was to be many times repeated in the ensuing decades as businessmen won victory after victory over the opposition of nonbusiness interests. Not only farmers but laborers as well often desired policies industrialists could not approve. Where farmers and laborers were able to agree on policy issues, business was forced to give way. But wherever there was not concurrence between farmer and laborer, the business interests found themselves in a splendid balance-of-power position. Here was another basic reason why the business interests were able to dictate economic policy after the Civil War.

In the case at hand the fact was that the laborer did not take the same view of tariffs as many farmers. At this time, just as when the Republican party had first been put together in part by laborers, workers saw eye to eye with manufacturers on the matter of reserving the American market for Americans. The worker attitude on this issue can be seen most clearly in the Congressional career of William D. Kelley of Pennsylvania ("Pig Iron" Kelley, as he was more popularly known). Speaking for the working classes in general and steel workers in particular, Kelley was one of the most ardent protectionists that could be found. A measure reducing the cost of the workingman's breakfast was, to a man like "Pig Iron" Kelley, a far different thing from a measure making it easier for foreign workers to compete with Americans.

Blood was next drawn by the farmer, although the scene now shifted to faraway Illinois. In 1870 the "Granger Movement" achieved its first major success in the form of a constitutional amendment giving to that state legislature power to regulate various aspects of railway and warehouse operations. This hard-won success was promptly followed in 1871 by a law fixing maximum charges for railroads and warehousemen, outlawing discrimination, and creating a special commission to enforce its provisions. Accepted as a model for similar laws in states farther west, it was soon followed by others.

By 1872 the scene of battle had once again moved back to the nation's capital. The government's surplus continued to accumulate more rapidly than could be justified to tax-conscious citizens, and once again pressure for reduction appeared. So successful had the earlier strategy been in diverting tax-reduction sentiment away from tariff reduction that it was decided to try for a repeat performance. This time, however, a new twist was added. The Civil War income tax still lingered on, a constitutional test having failed to dislodge it. As a part of what was to become the general tax revision of 1872, the income tax was repealed.

TABLE 45. TOO MUCH MONEY

Year	Federal Government Surplus (Millions of dollars)
1866	37.2
1867	133.1
1868	28.3
1869	48.1
1870	101.6
1871	91.1
1872	96.6

Source: Bureau of the Census, *Historical Statistics of the United States, 1789-1945*, p. 297.

The other major part of this revision was to be the complete elimination of the duties on tea and coffee; from the standpoint of the government's financial needs it would perhaps have been necessary to go no further. But 1872 was a presidential election year in the United States and governing administrations in this country have a way of being more attentive to public demands at such a time. As this particular campaign developed, there was even more than the usual reason for incumbents to proceed with their ears close to the ground. Angered and insulted by the revelations of graft and corruption now reaching the general public in full force, and blaming the Grant regime for a large part of this state of affairs, a substantial element in the Republican party was endeavoring to break away in order to promote the cause of reform. Already "Liberal" Republicans had chalked up impressive victories in several state elections.

Since tariff moderation was a part of the reform program of this splinter group, it did not seem a propitious time for protectionists to be obdurate on the matter of the tariff. The spirit of concession now evinced appeared in the form of a bill proposing a horizontal 10 per cent reduction on most protected items. However, how little of real concession this proposal contained is indicated by two special facts. First, the reason the reduction was suggested in this form—and a more unscientific way of framing a tariff measure could scarcely have been devised—was that such an adjustment would be the easiest kind to reverse. Second, another measure was simultaneously passed repealing the duty on tea and coffee, one more step toward a tariff-for-protection-only.

The irony of this maneuvering appeared in the sequel. As it turned out any reduction at all in the tariff proved to be unnecessary, for when the "Liberal" Republicans met in Cincinnati to nominate a candidate for the presidency, a quirk of politics intervened and Horace Greeley was named. As a reform candidate in general Greeley was at least no worse than others who might have been chosen. But on tariff reform he was impossible. Rarely has the American scene produced his equal for avid protectionism, and long before the election the forces of antiprotectionism were hopelessly scattered. Perhaps this was one reason why Grant was renominated rather than a rival reform candidate, and no doubt it goes far to explain Grant's overwhelming victory.

Labor Utopianism Again. There was another reason, too, why Republicans did not need to give heed to reformers in 1872. The structure of American politics is such that it tends strongly to produce two-party government. Third, fourth, and fifth parties, although each may hope to become a major party, are in any one election little more than protest organizations and can safely be ignored by the major groups. In 1872 labor chose to work independently of the major parties, and hence did not wield significant influence. Furthermore, laborites still further weakened their position through a disagreement among themselves as to what their program should be. The result was one of the more interesting episodes in what has since been called "the greenback period" in the history of the American labor movement.

Since the war, labor had been engaged in three basic kinds of activities. One of these, and perhaps the most important from the standpoint of the longer future, was trade union work as such. In the years immediately following the war, for example, some sixteen national unions had been formed, almost as many as were functioning at the end of the war. This progress, plus a rapid growth in the membership of already existing national unions, was sufficiently great that a large proportion of the organized workers of the nation were enrolled in a national organization.

Supplementing the growth of local and national unions, a body was formed for the purpose of pursuing labor's common goals, and when the postwar recession made trade union work difficult the National Labor Union became a powerful group. It devoted its attention to a number of objectives, among them an improvement in the position of women in industry and the organization of Negro workers. These goals were especially indicated because of the obvious need to destroy such means of undercutting existing or desired wage scales.

More important than these objectives, however, was that of coping constructively with the problem of postwar unemployment. Two major solutions were suggested, and both were vigorously prosecuted. One was the eight-hour day; the other was cooperation. In a short time cooperative experiments had been established in virtually every important trade in the economy.

By 1872 short-run needs were less compelling as a result of the return of prosperity, and workers had consequently changed their program. Thus the eight-hour day, although still important, was no longer motivated primarily by a desire to increase employment—or even to convert higher real wages into leisure. Rather this drive had been transformed into a program for the achievement of an increase in real wages in the first instance. Originated by a Boston machinist named Ira Steward, this unique conception of the relationship between hours and wages became virtually an official theory of the labor movement. In brief it insisted that the level of wages is determined largely by labor's standard of living since a worker would not work for any length of time for a wage which necessitated a lowering of his accustomed level of life. If workers had more leisure they would expand their wants and one way or another would insist on higher earnings. In turn employers would be able to pay higher wages because higher labor costs would force them to be more efficient. As appropriately expressed in a couplet much used by the speechmakers of the day:

> Whether you work by the piece or work by the day,
> Decreasing the hours increases the pay.

Not only was the eight-hour day an important project with labor leaders, but to a considerable extent they elected to achieve it through political action. Especially is it worth noting in this connection that, whereas thirty-five years earlier success in achieving the ten-hour day from private employers was used as a lever to secure federal legislation, now the federal and state governments were to be used as a starting point. In all some eighty eight-hour leagues were formed representing workers in every state having a significant amount of industrial employment. In the field of state legislation, little was achieved. Laws were often passed, but just as frequently no substantial enforcement provisions were included, and even more often a longer work week was permitted if specified in a labor contract. However, with federal legislation making the eight-hour day the standard for government work, the movement was more successful—although it was forty years before the eight-hour principle was extended to government contract work by private employers.

Not only the eight-hour movement but also the idea of cooperation had basically changed its nature. Once again, just as twenty years earlier, labor was insisting that only through producer cooperatives would the worker ever be able to secure his rightful place in society. In turn this decision had transformed labor's postwar concern over the money issue into a drive closely resembling the money aspect of the labor utopianism of forty years before. The fact was that labor's new venture into the field of cooperation had collapsed—the various concerns meeting with almost insuperable obstacles. But instead of attributing this failure to its real sources—misunderstanding of the functions performed by the producer, especially the middleman, and an inadequate understanding of business operations—labor placed the responsibility on the excessive cost of hiring money, which in turn was assumed to be due to the credit monopoly possessed by bankers and middlemen.

The philosophy behind labor's new money interest was, in short, even more bizarre than that associated with the eight-hour movement. Greenbacks were to be made freely exchangeable for low interest government bonds, and vice versa, with the result that workers would always have available credit at a low rate of interest. With low cost funds available cooperative ventures would not be at the mercy of money monopolists, and workers could make their escape from the toils of private enterprise capitalism. Not since the 1840's had organized labor been so far from down-to-earth realities.

For this new program of utopianism, labor paid a substantial price in 1872. On the one hand, there was division within the ranks of organized labor as to whether the major effort was to be launched on the political or the industrial front. Significantly, the national unions had by now largely abandoned the political approach. On the other hand, a split developed within the ranks of the political enthusiasts as to whether the main emphasis was to be on the eight-hour program or "greenbackism." When this issue, at a convention to nominate a labor candidate for the presidency, could not be resolved and the "greenbackers" alone stayed to complete the business of the convention, the rout of the National Labor Union was complete.

Depression Replaces Reform. The re-election of Grant meant a postponement of reform for at least four years, a fact farmers and laborers would have been able to accept with more equanimity if the status quo had remained unchanged in other ways as well. But such good fortune was not to be. Six months after Grant was inaugurated the nation was plunged into a money panic of disaster proportions, a panic followed by a half-dozen years of as dark depression as the nation had yet experienced. In consequence the nonbusiness interests were confronted not only with the problems which had disturbed them during prosperity but also with new difficulties produced by the business downturn.

It would not be argued, of course, that depression came *because* Grant was re-elected. In fact, few economists would make serious argument in defense of any particular cause of an economic downturn. Certain facts about this period do stand out, however, and any description of the elements entering into the "Panic of 1873" must come to terms with them.

For example, it is to be remembered that the depression of the 1870's was set in a world economy context no less than all the other depressions the nation had weathered. In this connection, it is an important fact that the western world had been for the preceding twenty years engaged in a series of wars which altered the structure of the world economy in ways that could not have been permanent. When the day of reckoning came, adjustments were impossible without deflation in some sectors, and in an industrial, exchange society deflation is apt to spread far beyond its point of origin.

In the second place, certain developments in the field of transportation and communication had generated an economic situation bound sooner or later to result in deflationary pressure. The completion of the Suez Canal shortened the voyage between London and Calcutta from more than six months to one month—a fact which for a time rendered surplus much of the world's shipbuilding capacity. Moreover, the perfection of telegraphic communication made it no longer necessary to hold such large inventories of Far Eastern goods in Indian warehouses.

Other external factors also played a part. In Europe as well as in the United States there were under way feverish railroad building campaigns. In other countries, too, just as in this country, speculation was mingled with actual construction. Especially in Germany was this true; the rapidity with which the French paid off the Franco-Prussian War indemnity had made capital so abundant that the interest rate on bank loans fell to 1 per cent. Mileage increases were proceeding at a rate which could not indefinitely be sustained, and it was obviously only a matter of time until the failure of speculative ventures to produce profits would result in the drying up of capital and the laying off of workers.

These characteristics of the underlying economic situation can be readily illustrated by one aspect of the experience of the United States. In the eight years since the Civil War railroad mileage had risen from thirty-five thousand to seventy thousand. Still more striking, two-thirds of this increase was in the relatively undeveloped West. The most that could be expected from these roads was the distribution of a certain amount of capital as promoter rewards; most of them could not earn dividends until the territory traversed was more intensively developed. Even if all American railroads had paid regular dividends the pace of construction would one day have had to taper off. When expected dividends did not materialize, this day was hastened, particularly when the absence of dividends coincided with new and startling announcements of stock watering, corruption, and defalcation. In the year preceding the panic less than one-third of America's three hundred fifty railroad companies paid any dividends at all.

The relationship between the onset of depression and the nation's capital formation process can be constructively viewed from another vantage point. A fiscal policy assessing taxes largely against the lower income groups and yielding a large government surplus for debt reduction is highly deflationary. By concentrating income, it contributes to the accumulation of savings and hence real investment. Such a policy has its uses during a boom period in that it limits consumption and thus reduces one of the major bases for the familiar inflationary consumption-investment spiral. However, by limiting consumption such a policy has consequences apt to be less salutary when the boom reaches its peak. Only consumption can make boom-accumulated capital profitable, and of course this is the primary reason for its accumulation in a free enterprise economy. When capital formation reaches a level at which it cannot be supported by existing consumption, the rate of formation must decline.[1] This process is apt to be the first stage in a painful period of liquidation.

Even the brand-new national banking system contributed to business instability. While it did achieve substantial advances over the money and banking structure it replaced, it still possessed grave shortcomings from the standpoint of economic equilibrium. Thus note circulation was not "elastic"; it did not expand and contract with the needs of business. In times of prosperity, when the needs of business were greatest, banks tended to sell the government bonds on which national bank note circula-

[1] Another way of saying this is to emphasize that investment and consumption are to a considerable extent complementary rather than competitive. Investment cannot be profitable unless the goods produced by new capital can be sold to consumers at a remunerative price, while an economy with any propensity to save at all is dependent upon a corresponding flow of investment if consumption levels are to remain high. For a limited period an economy can apparently get along with a relatively high propensity to save and invest. There comes a time, however, when the capital structure thus created can be supported only by a distribution of income which favors a higher propensity to consume.

tion rested because they could put their funds more profitably into other assets. Conversely, when the economy was depressed, bank funds tended to return to the government bond market even though a diminished note circulation would have been adequate. Instead of possessing the kind of elasticity desired, in other words, the national banking system was "perversely elastic."

Other aspects of this inelasticity were equally serious. Thus the farmer's special need for funds in the fall and in the spring could not be well met by a circulation related to government securities. Worse still, the new system encouraged the movement of funds to New York because out-of-town banks were allowed to count as a part of their reserves money thus used. Since both the depository and the depositing banks could count the same funds as reserves, reserves were pyramided and hence not as mobile as would have been desirable. When the money demand of the farming community reached one of its seasonal peaks, the pressure on the New York call money market would often become severe, threatening the speculative commitments made at off-peak times. September, 1873, saw this pressure become so great as to break the delicate thread holding the financial structure together.

In retrospect (as always) it is easy to see that deflationary pressure had been building up for some time. Nowhere was this more clear than in international economic relations. America's postwar prices were very inviting to foreign exporters, and imports therefore held at a high level. On the other hand, American exports were limited by domestic costs, by the weakness of the world price of wheat, and by the debilitated condition of the cotton economy. These factors in turn were accentuated by the fact that the American economy at this time was characterized by what economists call a high propensity to import. By this is meant that as long as the United States was dependent upon foreign nations for manufactured goods, prosperity normally resulted in a greater increase in imports than in exports.

The resultant unfavorable balance of trade was made still more unfavorable by a heavy annual charge for the service of foreign-held American securities. For a time payments were readily made by selling additional securities abroad. But as speculation began to run its course throughout the western world, and as foreign investors became suspicious of America's financial structure, foreign security holders commenced unloading their portfolios. When, as was eventually certain to happen, the annual specie drain to other countries became substantial, the close relationship between specie and the American monetary system could only mean irresistible pressure on the nation's exchange system.

The most dramatic incident associated with the "Panic of 1873" was the failure of Jay Cooke and Company. Indeed, while this failure was not the

TABLE 46. PROSPERITY BY FOREIGN TRADE

Year	Excess of Imports Over Exports—Merchandise	Excess of Exports Over Imports—Gold and Silver
	(Millions of dollars)	
1866	86.0	75.3
1867	101.3	38.8
1868	75.5	79.6
1869	131.4	37.3
1870	43.2	31.7
1871	77.4	77.2
1872	182.4	66.1

Source: Bureau of the Census, *Historical Statistics of the United States, 1789-1945,* p. 244.

first important one to take place, for special reasons it was the event which precipitated the crisis. Jay Cooke was a name as familiar in American finance as that of Jay Gould, although in an entirely different way. Noted for its conservative, if shrewd, business methods, this company engaged primarily in the banking business. To it, for example, had been entrusted the task of conducting a "grass roots" campaign selling government bonds during the Civil War when the government's credit was at its lowest point—an activity which earned for Cooke the sobriquet "financier of the Civil War."

The unhappy fate which befell Cooke's firm is especially illustrative of the economic situation characterizing the post-Civil War period. To Jay Cooke and Company was given the task of selling bonds for the Northern Pacific Railroad. However, carried away by the speculative fever of the times, the firm took the tragic step of exchanging its banker function for a promotional one. It became heavily committed to an enterprise unable to pay immediate returns, and these assets consequently became "frozen." When the money pinch came, Jay Cooke and Company was too illiquid to make the adjustment. So completely was this firm identified in the public mind with the best in American financial operations that a policeman in Philadelphia arrested a newsboy for crying Jay Cooke's failure in advertising his papers.

If the re-election of Grant made the cause of reform more remote, the onset of depression tremendously increased the demand for relief by both farmers and workers. Already depressed farmers were subjected to still lower prices, and debts became even more burdensome. As railroad construction came to a halt, as approximately half of the capacity of the steel industry was closed down, and as these primary factors induced retrenchment throughout the entire economy, unemployment mounted to unprecedented levels and wages fell sharply. And not only did business retrench frantically in order to meet the threat of declining demand, but even with this protection thousands of business firms could not meet their obligations and in this process the circle of deflation spread even wider. In most large cities bread lines were organized, local taxation was increased to provide funds with which to care for hardship cases, and private charitable organizations were strained to the utmost.

Monetary Reform Fails. Naturally, first endeavors were aimed at self-help. Under the depression stimulus the Grange flourished as never before, reaching the peak of its effectiveness in the middle of the 1870's. A large share of the activity of this organization during this period was the establishment of cooperatives to help the farmer escape the clutches of "vicious" middlemen, the first adventure by farmers into the cooperative field. Beginning at once to pool their buying power, farmers early conceived the idea of dispensing with the middleman's "take" entirely. In the field of machinery purchases where the greatest successes were registered, surprising economies were achieved. Threatened with this new competition, moreover, private operators often cut their own prices—although usually only for the purpose of destroying the cooperative interloper. The most ambitious (as well as the most disastrous) attempts at cooperation were in the *manufacture* of farm implements. Here the step proposed was too advanced for either the farmer's business understanding or the available capital, and these enterprises invariably failed.

It is difficult to say how much was achieved by the farmers' cooperative efforts in the 1870's. Certainly farm leaders did learn some of the facts of economic life which they had only imperfectly understood before. As labor leaders had already learned, if not as thoroughly as they were soon to do, it is possible to do away with the middleman but not the function he performs. There was also gain in the fact that one more step was taken to break the hard crust of agricultural individualism, an individualism obviously outmoded in an age of corporate specialization. But perhaps the most important success was the launching of Montgomery Ward & Company. Originated specifically to deal with the local granges, Montgomery Ward was a mail-order concern which on a private enterprise basis did eliminate middleman profit to the extent that local dealers over a wide area were compelled to consult the "catalogue" before they made up their own prices.

Laborers were much less fortunate than farmers. Not only is unemployment a greater hardship than low farm prices, but the laborer's capacity for self-help was thereby weakened. Striking was largely a wasted effort and the opportunity offered employers to make war on labor was so fully utilized that a number of the recently organized national unions were virtually destroyed. In their place, the worker found himself turning again to cooperatives and to secret labor organizations. However, activities such as these were not able to accomplish much for the worker during this period of depression.

In addition to these techniques, and perhaps primarily because they were inadequate, both workers and farmers turned also to political action. For a number of reasons the focus of these political endeavors was the money question. First, the most potent workers' organization was still the "greenback" remnant. Second, the panic had appeared essentially in the form of a money crisis, and the first frenzied public policy acts had been aimed directly at the currency derangement. Thus the Treasury moved quickly to put some of its specie holdings into more general use by buying its own bonds, while the New York Stock Exchange closed its doors to keep panic from spreading unduly through the stock market, and the New York Clearing House issued $10 million in clearinghouse certificates for use in settling interbank balances. Third, and in some respects most important, the farmer had for some time quietly been accumulating certain grievances of his own against the nation's monetary arrangements.

For example, the allocation of national bank notes on the basis of population and existing banking facilities, as required by law, had produced some rather unfortunate results for the farmer. Whereas the state of Rhode Island was allotted more than $75 of notes on a per capita basis, Arkansas' allocation was only 13 cents. Likewise, Connecticut had been allotted more notes than Michigan, Iowa, Minnesota, Kansas, Missouri, Kentucky, and Tennessee combined. While no case could be made for equal distribution on either a population or a state basis, it did seem that a more equitable allocation could have been devised. Because of this fact, however, greenbacks were the only real bank reserves available in the West, and every additional dollar's worth of greenbacks meant that several dollars could be loaned by the banking system.

Beyond this obvious discrimination, furthermore, the farmer operated under other money handicaps. The period following the Civil War saw the rapid development of "checkbook" money supplementing notes. Paradoxically, however, this innovation was replacing bank notes precisely where these were most abundant, in the more densely populated commercial centers, while it was making its slowest advances in thinly populated agricultural areas where circulating money was already most scarce.

Third, the burden of the farmer's debt seemed also closely related to the operation of the banking system. Of course interest rates would have been high in the West in any event because the risk was great and facilities were few. But farmers could with some justification insist that facilities were artificially limited by the East's banking legislation. For example, the National Banking Act prohibited the creation of national banks in places smaller than six thousand persons, and virtually prohibited real-estate loans by national banks.

Finally, the paper money issued during the war had been for use by the North alone. When the South re-entered the Union existing currency had to be painfully diluted, especially in agricultural areas where "check-book" money was not prevalent. In other words, as far as the Mid-West was concerned the mere fact that the Union was restored was a deflationary fact of significant proportions. Here again this was doubly significant because greenbacks were the only effective bank reserves.

Things had not been so for the farmer in pre-Civil War days. Then banking and monetary policy had been made by the agricultural interests, and it is no doubt true that the debtor-oriented policy followed promoted agricultural expansion at the expense of the industrial community. The farmer was now learning to his sorrow what it meant to have monetary and banking policy in the hands of creditor easterners. Understandably he was not inclined to accept the new situation on the basis of a turn-about-is-fair-play philosophy. Supported now by the "greenback" sentiment in labor's ranks, farmers prepared for another fight on the money issue.

The battle opened early in 1874. On his own initiative the Secretary of the Treasury had already reissued the greenbacks earlier retired. This, however, only whetted the appetite of inflationists, and in April Congress passed a bill to raise the amount of the greenbacks and the national bank notes to $400 million each. Then, with this small victory almost within their grasp, the inflationists were frustrated by a stinging Grant veto. In June the conservatives broadened their victory by placing a ceiling on the greenbacks at the number then outstanding.

Time out from the money controversy was taken in 1874 when a Senate Committee headed by William Windom of Minnesota brought in the famous Windom Committee report. The subject was the railroad, and the major preoccupation of this group was how the federal government might assist in keeping railroad behavior within bounds. One suggestion was the provision of water competition at federal government expense. Another was the creation of a government agency similar to the commissions created by state laws to eliminate discrimination and stock-watering. Still another was a government railroad to furnish a competitive rail route to the eastern seaboard. It had not escaped the attention of legislators representing farm constituencies that railroads invariably lowered rates where they encountered water competition, that slowly but surely the railroad was winning out in the transportation battle against water routes (except on the ocean and the Great Lakes), and that many land grant charters already contained restrictive provisions of one sort or another. No action was taken on the committee's report.

In 1875 the money problem was again foremost in the public mind, and it was in this year that the conservatives achieved their great success. A "lame-duck" Congress, meeting after many incumbent Republicans had been repudiated at the polls, passed the so-called Resumption Act. By the terms of this measure greenbacks were to be made exchangeable at par for gold at the end of four years. As a compromise it was also provided that the greenbacks were not to be retired in the process of resuming specie payments, and the legislation limiting the number of national bank notes and governing their distribution was repealed. For the moment, but only for the moment, currency expansionists were on the defensive.

The year 1875 also saw victory for the conservatives on the tax issue. Taking advantage of the depression decline in government revenue the same "lame-duck" Congress also repealed the earlier 10 per cent reduction in the tariff. Simultaneously a reciprocity treaty was concluded with Hawaii whereby Hawaiian sugar was to enter the United States free of duty. To be sure, one of the things involved in this action was Hawaii's threat to establish closer economic relationships with Britain, but here was another clear-cut case in which Louisiana interests were held to be expendable in favor of the interests of eastern investors in Hawaii and American sugar manufacturers. Here was also a subtle way of undermining the arguments of the antiprotectionists. The less customs revenue the government received, the less basis for suggesting a "tax" reduction.

The Farmer Vindicated. Farmers and laborers could take little comfort in compromises achieved on the money question. They were not at all substantial; indeed, they were scarcely even sincere. But the first postwar decade was not to end without achievements for these interests. The election of 1876, for example, came in the midst of one of the worst series of disclosures of corruption and incompetence in high places which had ever shamed a nation. Forced by circumstances to take the defensive on this issue, the Republicans nominated a genuine reform candidate—Rutherford B. Hayes. Even with this candid Republican confession of guilt, however, the Democrats were unable to win. "Solid" Republican strength was still too strong. Thus, although it was evident that the party in power did not intend to concede anything that was not absolutely necessary, it was heartening to see a recognition of some needs along this line.

Moreover, an even greater victory was in store for the farmer. A number of cases involving the Granger laws regulating railroads and warehouses had been slowly wending their way to the Supreme Court. In the term of court which began to sit shortly after Hayes was elected these cases were heard, and soon thereafter the Court's decisions were rendered. The leading case was one involving Chicago warehousemen who had refused to be bound by the Illinois law fixing maximum charges. In Munn v.

Illinois, Chief Justice Waite delivered one of the most important and far-reaching judgments ever handed down by the United States Supreme Court. This decision, together with the decisions rendered in the companion railroad cases, in every important particular sweepingly upheld the right of the Granger states to impose restrictions on their "favorite enemies."

The regulated companies, through their attorneys, made a number of contentions any one of which would, if upheld, have destroyed the validity of the Granger legislation. It was maintained first that the concerns in question were private and hence not subject to public control. Second, the charters awarded to these companies had said nothing about a reserved right of the state to regulate rates in the public interest. Third, the business in question was one primarily involving interstate commerce and thus not within the regulatory jurisdiction of Illinois. And finally, even if the laws were valid the rates fixed were so low as to threaten outright confiscation of property.

Using language which could not have been misinterpreted, the Court made answer to each of these contentions. When, said the Court, a property owner devotes his property to a public use it ceases to have the same rights as fully private property, and the transporting and storing of the major means of livelihood for an entire community is the sort of economic activity which from time immemorial has been held to be dedicated to the public interest. Silence on the subject of regulation on the part of the charter signified only that conditions had fundamentally changed since the charters were granted, and in no uncertain terms the Court asserted that the police power of a state could not be vitiated by economic dynamics. Admitting that interstate commerce was involved, it was held that until the federal government acted to curb abuses the states might do so. And finally, the Court informed the regulated concerns that the place to remedy confiscation was at the polls and not in the courts.

The "Granger Cases" are a distinct landmark in the evolution of the modern American economy. Ever since, the courts have held that there is a class of economic activities which is to be left in private hands as far as it is possible to do so, but which at the same time is to be supervised in so far as is necessary in the public interest. Almost every state in the union has since created a regulatory commission to exercise restrictive powers over its own "public utilities." To be sure much development work was necessary before state commissions became effective protectors of the consumer interest. To be sure also the Court later felt compelled to retract some of the things it said in these cases. But on the basic principle there was no retreat, and on this there was ample foundation on which to build further.

Munn v. Illinois was not only an unqualified vindication of the farmer's position; it was also conclusive evidence that Republican "reconstruction" was about over. Chief Justice Waite's decision was a major defeat for the conception of economic centralization which the business interests had written into the Constitution under the guise of reconstruction legislation. Of course, the Fourteenth Amendment protection to property rights was not demolished; it was yet to prove highly serviceable in precisely the way that had originally been intended. The very fact that this *exception* to the general rule was implemented made it possible to apply the *rule* even more rigorously. But a deep channel had been cut through which state restraints could be smuggled into the corporate world.

There were other evidences of the end of the "reconstruction" period, too. Although the "bloody shirt" was waved by the Republicans from one end of the land to the other, the Democratic candidate for president received more popular votes than his Republican rival and very nearly received more electoral votes as well. And early in 1877, as one of the first actions of the new administration, President Hayes removed the federal troops from the South.

QUESTIONS FOR DISCUSSION

1. What were the politico-economic bases of the strategy adopted with regard to the tariff in 1870?
2. Which of labor's solutions to its own difficulties was most nearly based upon reality? Which was the least realistic?
3. How did the national banking system contribute to the economic downturn?
4. How did international economic relations contribute to the economic downturn?
5. Why did farmers and laborers turn to money as the key to a solution of their problems?
6. How effective would an increase in the supply of money have been in remedying the farmer's problems? The laborer's problems?
7. Why did conservatives work so hard to prevent changes in the money supply?
8. What was involved in the resumption of specie payments? Why was there so much controversy over this step?
9. Was the victory agriculture won over the railroad a good substitute for the failure to achieve monetary changes?

Chapter 22

WORKERS UNDER PRESSURE

1877 Labor unrest; violence in the railroad industry.
1878 Bland-Allison Act.
Hayes' battle against the spoilsmen in New York.
Terence V. Powderly elected Mayor of Scranton, Pennsylvania.
1879 First Standard Oil Trust arrangements put into operation.

Although Munn v. Illinois was a fundamental factor in America's longer range economic development, it was not a significant victory for farmers in the 1870's. Well illustrating the ebbs and flows in the affairs of men, the next few years were to witness the demise of virtually every trace of the Granger legislation.

There were several reasons for this turn of events. For one thing the depression and technological advance had done much to bring about the lower freight rates farmers had demanded, while the economic downturn had placed the railroad industry in such an unfortunate financial plight that restrictive regulations aimed against it seemed beside the point. Then, too, much of this legislation had been so badly drawn as to give rise to great difficulties and even outright injustice in the process of enforcement. When to these facts are added the skill with which the railroads evaded the spirit of the law and the unprecedented political activity in which they engaged to secure modifications, it is easy to understand why this first major attempt to make the large corporation responsive to the popular will did not produce permanent results.

Labor's Challenge to Society. But if the Granger laws were soon swept away, it is also true that the farmer was not the focus of social unrest during the latter part of this decade to the extent that he had been ten years earlier. This role now shifted to the laborer. Year by year he sank deeper into debt as long as he could get credit, and into misery when he was considered no longer a good business risk. As labor's position became more distressed, evidences of deep social disturbance mounted. Labor demonstrations were held demanding relief, not relief administered on the basis of charity but as a right possessed by the worker and a duty of society. Many workers responded to the frustration of continued unemployment by becoming wanderers, and where these congregated in more or less stable groups they often became defiant of established authority and embittered against the society which had robbed them of their livelihood. A formidable socialist movement developed, offering workers an opportunity to challenge the entire foundation of America's industrial society.

Law-abiding (and well-fed) citizens were appalled at this show of temper—frightened by this hint of revolution—and in many cases even mild resistance was met with brute force. In Fall River, Massachusetts, textile workers on strike against a second 10 per cent wage reduction and marching to the City Hall to demand bread for their children were prevented from carrying out their purpose. Later, starved into submission, they were forced to return to work at the reduced rates and to sign "yellow-dog" contracts. Moreover, all workers who had in any way exercised leadership in connection with the strike were not only refused re-employment but were "blacklisted" by all other Fall River employers. The inevitable result was the total destruction of most of the unions involved, the last bulwark between the laborer and what he could in the circumstances only feel was an alien society.

A similar incident took place in connection with the mining of anthracite coal. From the very beginning of this industry the ownership of coal deposits and transportation facilities had tended to concentrate in the same hands, and with the coming of the railroad the owner of both tended to be a railroad company. In the case at issue the railroad involved was the Philadelphia and Reading, whose monopoly over transportation facilities from the Mahoning and Schuylkill coal fields had put it in a position to dictate wage policy to independent operators. Since the road's president (F. B. Gowen) was one of the most avid labor haters of the day, he hastened to take advantage of the opportunity offered by depression. A drastic wage decrease was proposed, not so much as a way to reduce costs and hence meet the depression more effectively as to goad the workers into a strike, and when the strike did materialize Gowen spent $4 million of the company's money to break the strike and destroy the union.

It is not surprising that out of this situation an organization such as the "Molly Maguires" should arise. This group, speaking for the anthracite coal miner, operated essentially on the basis of violence and intimidation. Forced into secrecy by the simple fact that overt organization activity meant loss of employment, these men had taken the next step toward outlawry. At the same time, so skillfully did they operate that they attained an important influence in Pennsylvania politics before being crushed with the aid of the Pinkerton detective agency. No doubt the "Molly Maguires" deserve the opprobrium in which history holds them, but it is worth emphasizing the provocations which led to their behavior and the fact that students of this period are steadily becoming more certain that some of the crimes attributed to this group were actually committed by the paid agents of employers.

But such encounters as these between employees and employers were only warmups for the big event which was to follow. In June and July, 1877, a second 10 per cent wage reduction was announced on the Pennsylvania, Baltimore and Ohio, and New York Central railroads. At once the laborers affected were aflame with indignation. Long since the organizations behind which these workers had once rallied had been dispersed by depression and the concerted action of employers, and without this steadying influence it is not surprising that the worker reaction was a violent one. Led as often as not by members of America's new "tramp society," resistance quickly took the only path left open.

The first challenge was laid down in Martinsburg, West Virginia, on July 17. Cessation of work quickly spread to other points along the Baltimore and Ohio line, and in some places the strikers secured physical control over the situation. In Baltimore all freight trains stopped running, and when two companies of militia were about to be dispatched to Cumberland a mob prevented their departure. This situation, mild though it was, remained out of hand until federal troops arrived.

In Pittsburgh, on property owned by the Pennsylvania Railroad, the dispute took a more serious turn. There the labor conflict was aggravated by a popular resentment against the railroad on account of its alleged discriminations against the city. So pronounced was this feeling that the Pittsburgh militia joined the strikers in resisting the company, and when troops arrived from Philadelphia a pitched battle was fought in which twenty persons were killed. The mob was now thoroughly aroused, turning on the soldiers with such fury that they were forced to take refuge in a roundhouse. In the ensuing battle the railway yards were fired, the blaze doing some $5 million worth of damage before wearing itself out. Finally a semblance of order was restored, but not until the conflict had degenerated into a mob drunkenness and pillage which had no direct connection with the labor conflict.

Before this strike fury spent itself it had spread to the Erie Railroad, and there were labor disturbances as far west as San Francisco, although no other uprising was as tragically threatening to the foundations of organized society as that in Pittsburgh. In every particular the strikes failed to accomplish their purposes, and labor was forced to sink back into one of the worst disasters ever experienced by American labor. With unemployment at its approximate peak for the decade, the cold of northern winters was now added to the undernourishment from which workers' families were already suffering. The spring of 1878 saw Terence V. Powderly, one of the outstanding labor leaders of the day, elected mayor of Scranton, Pennsylvania.

While depression strikes and especially depression violence did not accomplish their intended aims, they were not without influence. On the contrary, it would scarcely be an exaggeration to suggest that no event in a generation had so profoundly affected men's thinking. Many lessons were learned, and it requires no explanation that different kinds of citizens learned very different lessons.

For their part laborers learned more decisively than ever before that their future in the American industrial system depended upon the existence of strong national organizations, and that any interest which interfered with this effort (for example, dualisms such as rival unionism, socialism, political action) could only harm laborers in their collective endeavors. It was at this point that many labor leaders began to shun partisan politics, adopting instead a policy of "reward your friends and punish your enemies." Furthermore, depression demonstrated equally clearly that organization to be effective must be permanent. Hastily conceived efforts to combat the consequences of a major business downturn could not serve labor satisfactorily.

What businessmen learned was of an entirely different order. Just before the great railroad strikes the *Commercial and Financial Chronicle* had assured employers that "labor is under control for the first time since the war," and the business press had echoed and re-echoed this assurance. As events had indicated, however, this confidence was misplaced. Instead industrialists discovered that both they and their concerns were confronted with a highly explosive situation. The great need, they concluded, was a larger standing army and more effective legislation. As a result the next few years saw much attention given to the improvement of state militias and the enactment of laws restricting the right to strike.

But no doubt the most important lessons were those learned by the more thoughtful members of the larger community, and unfortunately there were all too few of these. Thus it was apparent that industrialization, important though it is from the standpoint of the economic level a society can attain, creates problems of a vital and intricate character. One of those problems, indeed one of the most vital of them all, is the problem of the unemployed. Plainly a society can not long exist which does not provide its members with a useful function to perform. America had for the first time in her history witnessed a serious uprising of those industrialization had made propertyless. Somehow this leviathan would have to be kept in check, and there were some farseeing citizens who doubted that militias, armories, and antistrike laws constituted an adequate technique.

In Search of a Remedy. Unfortunately, even the most farseeing members of the community were unable to suggest what would constitute an adequate remedy. However, the American way, the way of democracy, is to give large disaffected groups what they want—within reason. And laborers in 1878 knew what they wanted. The great agitation was for more money circulation, and toward achieving this end workers were more willing to join hands with farmers than ever before. Only because of the existence of a set of special circumstances did the earlier cry for greenbacks now become merged with, and in time irrevocably lost in, the movement for "free silver."

It is customary to refer derisively to the economic naïveté which led farmers and workers to press for inflationism in 1878, and few would insist that there was not an important element of naïveté present. Thus labor's insistence on greenbacks as a way of achieving industrial democracy through cooperatives financed by 3 per cent credit was incongruous with American capitalism. In a similar way the farmer's notion that his difficulties could be remedied by changes in the supply of currency was a gross oversimplification. On the other hand, however, it is impossible to understand the evolution of the American labor movement apart from labor's reluctance to accept the transition from independent work to the wage system. And it was only natural that farmers would not quickly adjust to an economic situation in which they could not govern their own money supply.

While all this is true, the fact remains that these considerations actually explain little of the greenback-free silver agitation. On the side of labor the more important emphasis was now the need for a lubricant to set the wheels of industry turning once more. What laborer in 1878 could doubt that a prosperous economy was labor's only real protection? To be sure, economists in this post-Keynes era are by no means agreed upon the virtues or the details of such a purely monetary approach to the problem of depression, but there are few today who would call it sheer nonsense.[1]

From the vantage point of the farmer, the frame of reference was only slightly different. What he wanted was not so much inflation as destruction of the deflationary tendencies he believed to be inherent in the national banking system. A part of this deflationism consisted of the discrimination against agricultural regions in national bank note circulation, but only a part of it. On a seasonal basis, also, credit was always scarce

[1] Because an exchange economy is, from one point of view, a double circular flow of goods and money, thinking about the business cycle tends more and more to emphasize what is called "aggregate purchasing power." Employment means producing the flow of goods, but this stream can be no larger than the volume of spending which keeps it flowing. Although there are complications which must be carefully taken into account, especially from the standpoint of the particular solution suggested here, it is not at all unreasonable to believe that the flow of goods can be strengthened by strengthening the counterpart flow of spending.

just when it was needed most—at crop-moving time. The reason was that in the slack seasons surplus money tended to flow to New York where it might become so committed to speculative or semispeculative ventures as either to be unavailable "back home" or, more likely, available only at an "extortionate" rate of interest.

On a longer range basis, there was a still more deflationary factor at work. As the economy accumulated a larger stock of capital, the rate of interest tended to fall. This trend pushed government bonds progressively higher in price, giving rise to a premium which discouraged the issuance of national bank notes since circulation could only amount to 90 per cent of par value. By the time a 25 per cent reserve was maintained and other special costs and taxes were paid, there was increasingly little profit in this kind of operation. These circumstances were of no particular concern to the urban East because there "checkbook" money was able to make up any

TABLE 47. THE FARMER'S GRIEVANCE

Year	Per Capita Money in Circulation
	(Dollars)
1866	18.99
1868	18.39
1870	17.50
1872	18.19
1874	18.13
1876	16.12
1878	15.32
1880	19.41
1882	22.37

Source: Secretary of the Treasury, *Annual Reports*.

deficit in the money supply, but it was no small matter to farmers that the per capita money in circulation reached its lowest point in 1878.

There was still another way, too, in which farmers and laborers felt the nation's money system had deteriorated. The National Banking Act had been an attempt to replace state control of the money supply with federal government control, and at first the tax on state bank notes accomplished this result fairly well. But with the use of checks as money rather than notes the state bank returned to an important position in the nation's financial structure. Under the circumstances an insistence by the non-industrial classes upon a *national* currency can scarcely be dismissed as naïve.

Given a farmer-labor interest in an increase in the money supply, why did this agitation reach a crest in 1878? There were two reasons. First, depression and a series of disastrous strikes had given labor an almost un-

TABLE 48. A NATIONAL SYSTEM NO LONGER

Year	Number of Banks		Total Assets	
	National	State	National Banks	State Banks
			(Millions of dollars)	
1868	1,640	247	1,572.2	163.5
1878	2,056	1,173	1,750.5	1,330.2
1888	3,120	3,527	2,731.4	2,739.0
1898	3,582	5,918	3,977.7	4,631.3

Source: Bureau of the Census, *Historical Statistics of the United States, 1789-1945*, pp. 264-65.

precedented sense of solidarity and urgency. Second, 1878 was the last year prior to full resumption of specie payments. There were few workers or debtor farmers who did not fear that this process could result only in a further contraction of note circulation.

And why did a movement built around paper money merge with a free silver campaign at this particular moment? Again a number of factors were involved, and again these had deep roots in the past. Ever since gold had been discovered in California much of the romance of the West had centered around rich strikes of precious metals. In fact, the "miner's frontier" during and after the Civil War had been substantially in advance of the agricultural frontier, and had contributed much to the general opening up of the West. Many of these strikes produced no permanent mining industry, going through an entire life cycle from "boom" towns to "ghost" towns in a few years, and the residue of agricultural development left behind was typically of little economic significance. But the silver finds themselves had contributed a great deal to the nation's supply of silver, and some of the strikes had revealed veins which could be profitably worked over a number of years. Almost overnight the United States became one of the world's largest producers of silver, the biggest silver find of the generation (at Nevada City) coinciding exactly with the renewed demand for inflation.

Suddenly the nation's output of silver made that metal far more abundant relative to gold. Moreover, in the world at large similar forces were at work. In fact, not only was new silver output rapidly increasing, but central Europe, finding it impossible to keep both gold and silver circulating together in a bimetallic system, was beginning to abandon bimetallism in favor of a full gold standard. With the supply of silver increasing relative to the supply of gold, and with the demand for gold increasing relative to that for silver, the price of gold naturally began to rise while the price of silver fell. The change in the price of silver taking place within a decade of the ending of the Civil War was greater than that which had taken place in the preceding two centuries. In the United States this had the consequence of overvaluing silver at the mint ratio of sixteen to one, whereas previously the mint had favored gold in the same way.

TABLE 49. THE "CRIME OF '73"

Year	Silver Production	Market Ratio of Silver to Gold
	(Millions of fine ounces)	
1866	7.7	15.43
1871	17.8	15.57
1872	22.2	15.63
1873	27.7	15.93
1874	28.9	16.16
1875	24.5	16.64
1878	51.2	17.92
1890	32.8	19.75

Source: Bureau of the Census, *Historical Statistics of the United States, 1789-1945,* pp. 151 and 277.

Faced with a decline in the price of their product, the silver interests with some logic turned to the United States Treasury. At the legal ratio it would have been much more profitable to sell silver to the government than to place it on the world market. But when silver owners reached Washington they discovered, much to their dismay, that silver dollars were no longer being coined. An act omitting this coin from the Treasury's list had been passed several years before, a purely routine measure since at that time it was more profitable to dispose of silver at the world price. However, whereas when the law was passed no one had raised any question about it, when the world price of silver fell below the mint price a loud outcry was raised. Labeling the "repudiation" of silver a conspiracy by conservatives against the common man, silver interests united with farmers and laborers in the demand for cheap money.

The silver legislation which resulted from this union has been almost uniformly condemned as an ill-disguised "grab" by the silver interests. While no one would question this interpretation as far as it goes, there are two points which should be kept in mind. First, even as a "grab," legislation favoring silver was very much in the spirit of the times. What basis could there be, for example, for discriminating between silver and wool from this standpoint? Second, nothing is more certain than that a silver "grab" would never have been taken seriously if it had not fortuitously coincided with the first post-Civil War peak of cheap money agitation.

The fight for cheap money was intense but brief. First, a bill was presented revoking the power to issue bonds in order to accumulate gold for resumption purposes. Next, Representative Bland of Missouri introduced a bill providing for free coinage of silver at the sixteen-to-one ratio. (Missouri was perhaps the most prominent silver-producing state in the nation at this time, since much of the other production was in areas not yet admitted to statehood.) This proposal also passed the House. The attack on the money position of the conservatives was carried still further when Senator Mathews of Ohio proposed to make government bonds payable in the silver dollars coined under the Bland law. When, in the Senate debate on this measure, questions were raised concerning the foreign investor who had been promised gold, Senator Mathews' retort was: "What have we got to do with abroad?"

Sound money easterners, confronted with this veritable barrage of cheap money proposals, had to be content simply to salvage what they could. The Mathews resolution and the bill repealing resumption bond issues were both lost, and Bland's bill was converted into a limited coinage measure by means of an amendment by Senator Allison of Iowa calling for the purchase of $2 to $4 million worth of silver bullion each month. In this form President Hayes vetoed the bill, but in less than twenty-four hours it had secured the necessary two-thirds majority to become law over the opposition of the President.

The Impact of the Machine. The Bland-Allison Act could scarcely be called a major inflationist victory. Thus, even if the basic problem confronting farmers and workers had been amenable to solution in this way, it would have done little good. More fundamentally, however, the difficulties the various segments of the economy were meeting could not be resolved along these lines; for behind the burden of the farmer's debts, behind the collapse of labor's organizations, there lurked another problem which to a substantial extent was responsible for all the others. That problem was the impact of the machine on the economic life of a nonmechanized economy.

One of the clearest ways in which this impact can be visualized is in the secularly falling price level which marked the thirty years following the Civil War. Almost unbroken by upward price swings, and these of remarkably short duration, this period saw the index of wholesale prices fall 60 per cent. Obviously such a profound change in the economic environment could not take place in so short a time without significantly affecting every important group in the economy.

Few would argue that this downward trend in prices was solely caused by the rapidity with which machine technology was now developing. It is true, however, that price declines over this period seem to have been particularly drastic in a number of areas in which the machine was advancing most rapidly. It is also true, and equally significant, that the fall in the price level greatly accelerated the introduction of mechanization. Im-

TABLE 50. ENTER THE MACHINE

Year	Wholesale Price Index (1926 = 100)
1866	116.3
1871	82.8
1876	72.0
1881	64.4
1886	56.0
1891	55.8
1896	46.5

Source: Bureau of the Census, *Historical Statistics of the United States, 1789-1945,* p. 234.

proved machinery makes possible lower costs, and lower costs enable a producer to meet a lower price level without becoming a casualty. In short, whether as cause or effect (or both), there was a close relationship between falling prices and mechanical innovation. In the thirty years following the Civil War the United States Patent Office issued more than half a million patents as compared with less than fifty thousand in the seventy years preceding.

Stating the matter a little differently, it is even possible to see in the advance of mechanization a basis for the farmer's emphasis upon monetary factors. The advent of the machine was bringing about an unprecedented increase in economic activity—the production and sale of goods and services. In so far as the supply of money (including the checkbook variety) was not keeping pace with this expansion, the inevitable result would have to be a falling price level.[2] The fact that this decline was world-wide in scope was only a detail, for the prices of the western farmer's surpluses were by now largely determined in world markets. The rapid urbanization of western Europe had made that area much more dependent upon agricultural production in this country than before the Civil War, and economic conditions in the Middle West faithfully mirrored the price of wheat in England.

On the other hand, however, it is easy enough to trace out in price level terms the implications of mechanization for farmer well-being. Better machinery, better methods, better seed, better animals, and the like, all made it possible for a given quantity of goods to be turned out with less manpower. But with the trails to the West continuing regularly to fill with

[2] This is a particularly good example of the operation of the "quantity theory of money" $\left(\frac{MV + M'V'}{T} = P\right)$. M (cash money) and its velocity (V) were changing relatively little, while M' (deposit money) was increasing significantly. But T (transactions, or the volume of trade) was increasing so fabulously as "America's industrial revolution" proceeded apace that prices (P) tended persistently to fall.

settlers anxious to take up still more land, there was no necessary connection between the number of farmers actually at work and the number which could be supported at remunerative income levels by the existing population and income distribution. In fact, the more unsatisfactory economic conditions became, the more did farmers feel compelled to utilize science even more intensively and hence increase output still further.

Laborers were caught in an even more vicious circle by increasing mechanization. The introduction of machinery meant first and foremost technological unemployment and hence a period of painful adjustment for many workers. There were several ways in which this deterioration in well-being might come about. One possibility was that the wage level itself might be pushed down by the unemployment created by the machine. Another was that re-employment in another trade or even another concern might involve a loss in seniority status. Still another was the fact that the introduction of machinery was often based on a breaking down of complex skills into operations which could be performed by less trained and less experienced hands. With startling rapidity such activities as watch-making, the manufacture of sewing machines, pianos, and organs, and the making of farm implements were becoming predominantly factory operations. And when the worker faced with this situation sought to organize to protect himself, he frequently found his way blocked by the "reserve army" of the technologically unemployed who could with little difficulty be turned into unwilling "strike-breakers."

It is not to be supposed, either, that this underlying economic transformation posed less serious problems for the nation's business interests. The entrance of the machine introduced a new phenomenon with which management now was forced to cope, a phenomenon making business enterprise more hazardous than ever before. The introduction of specialized equipment implies a heavy fixed capital cost which then becomes a powerful conditioning force in connection with every important business decision.

Expensive machinery cannot be installed in the first place unless a large market is available over which output can be sold. Immediately, therefore, firms over a wide area are brought into active competition with one another. Moreover, expensive machinery cannot be operated efficiently except at or near capacity. Any weakness in the market which threatens capacity operation is apt to result in sharp price cutting as competitors seek to keep costly equipment running at full speed. If price cutting becomes severe enough, a number of firms may cease to take in enough revenue to cover fixed costs. When that happens only those concerns with the lowest operating costs or the largest financial resources can survive. The fear of being one of those businessmen whose concern does not survive is in its way as painful as a worker's fear of unemployment, and by the same token the experience of actual bankruptcy under these circumstances is broadly comparable with the experience of unemployment.

A Study in Contrasts. However, although the machine was not selective in its choice of victims, one fact associated with its coming was apparent. Whereas labor and the farmer were at the moment meeting with virtually no success in coping with their problem, the business interests (apart from the men and firms who fell by the wayside) were working out a highly satisfactory adjustment. For one thing, labor exploitation frequently offered a way to meet this situation, in view of labor's extreme weakness, although it is only fair to emphasize that the thirty years of falling prices after the Civil War saw real wages rise materially. It did not soften the blow for exploited laborers, and it does not now make this period in American economic history any more savory, but it was nonetheless a fact that in many cases businessmen were literally forced to "sweat" their workers in order to stay in the competitive running.

Another way the employer could meet his problem was to increase the size of his establishment. To be sure, this was often at the expense of some erstwhile competitor—unless the total market was increasing rapidly enough for both to improve their position in this way. This process might take the form of buying the rival's property after the latter had succumbed in the competitive struggle, or of buying out or otherwise merging with the competitor before the situation had reached this critical point. Still a third technique was to come to an agreement with the competitor in order to prevent competition from reaching cutthroat proportions, although this method of adjustment was not typically successful until the competitive situation had become more or less stabilized in other ways—until only a handful of competitors was still in the competitive struggle.

The progress being made along these lines can be visualized in Table 51. In manufacturing, where the machine was making particularly rapid progress, the average size of establishments increased over a thirty-year period more than 150 per cent as measured by number of employees, more than 200 per cent as measured by value of the product, and 500 per

TABLE 51. A SUCCESSFUL ADJUSTMENT

Year	Value of Product	Invested Capital	Number of Employees
	(Average for manufacturing establishments)		
1869	$16,780	$ 6,720	8
1879	21,100	10,960	11
1889	28,070	19,020	14
1899	54,969	43,360	21

Source: *Statistical Abstract of the United States, 1939*, p. 772.

cent as measured by invested capital. The role of the machine can be more concretely seen here in the fact that investment per employee increased from less than $1,000 to more than $2,000. These figures are even more impressive when it is remembered that such industries as oil refining, steel making, meat packing, and farm machinery manufacture were increasing in size much more rapidly than the average.

Businessmen did not begin making their adjustment to the new conditions in the 1870's. But it was at this time that responses along these lines became so widespread and everywhere visible as to become of major significance in the minds of important elements in the community. The increase in firm size, including the wholesale swallowing up of competition in the process, became so pronounced that it has been termed a "movement" (the "consolidation" movement), and it was at this time that it became a social problem of the first magnitude.

The problem, of course, was monopoly. Concentration of control in an industry, it was felt by many, was one thing when it arose out of economies of producing on a larger scale, or even out of a desire to avoid ruinous, cutthroat competition. But concentration which extracts monopoly profits from consumers was very much another thing. Put differently, it seemed clear that businessmen were solving their problem by "exploiting" unfortunate fellow-citizens unable to solve theirs. And of course they were. A large business firm had overwhelming bargaining-power advantages as compared with both workers and farmers.

Just what it was that so concerned many people can be excellently illustrated in the railroad field, and it is especially understandable why much public attention was focused upon this industry. As an early solution to the problem of overhead costs and excessive competition, certain railroads had established rate schedules in cooperation with one another, each road agreeing not to undercut the charges thus set. A more advanced stage in this evolution was the "pool," a special variation of the rate agreement designed to give the carriers involved an incentive to maintain rates by taking care of their financial needs. One way this was accomplished was by pooling revenues received. Another technique was to distribute the available traffic. Certain large shippers were designated as "eveners"; in exchange for preferential treatment these shippers would distribute their business to certain railroads on some basis satisfactory to the roads in the pool.

The classic cases of successful attempts to control railroad competition were the famous Chicago-Omaha pool and the Southern Railway and Steamship Association. Of these two organizations, however, the latter represented the highest evolution achieved by institutions created for this purpose. It included a legislative body, an executive committee, a commissioner with broad powers, and a board of arbitrators, and for many years it maintained "order" among transportation companies in the Southeast where for long periods before "chaos" had reigned. Because of its success this organization was a model toward which other such efforts tried to evolve.

Outside the rail field, too, the pool was used as a means of lessening the rigors of competition. Thus manufacturers of cordage formed one of the first nonrailroad agreements for industry stabilization, a share-of-the-business pool in which excess sales were fined and the proceeds given to those who sold less than quota. The Michigan Salt Association was formed in 1878 to protect Michigan producers from the disastrous consequences of repeated rate wars. The following item suggests how complete a control this group was able to establish. In time it destroyed what had once been a very disturbing factor in the salt market—the practice followed by large dealers of buying large quantities of salt in the summer months for sale in the winter when supplies were low and prices high. Under the pool arrangement middlemen received only a small commission for each barrel sold.

However, pools were less than completely effective in bringing about the desired results. For one thing, they violated the common law and therefore could not be legally enforced. In consequence they tended to break down with frustrating regularity as members succumbed to the tendency to undercut. Other bases of control for stabilization purposes were hence continually being explored. The supply of raw materials or a patent or freight-rate arrangements were all reasonably good alternatives, although all were subject to the difficulty that their success depended upon a long chain of favorable circumstances. What was needed was a fully legal and hence enforceable method of achieving the ends so inadequately attained by pooling arrangements.

The First Great Trust. Such a method was found in 1879; the first genuine "trust" in American history, the authentic parent of all succeeding ventures of a similar nature, was created in that year. It is altogether fitting that this device was first used by the man who said, "The American Beauty rose can be produced in its splendor and fragrance only by sacrificing the early buds which grow up around it," and whose business methods precisely reflected this sentiment. John D. Rockefeller was already in his prime. He had achieved much by way of enlarging the scope of his firm's petroleum activities, and he was anxious for greater achievements. For a man of his capacities the times were exactly right. With Rockefeller's rise to industrial pre-eminence the stage was set for the work of the dynamic, aggressive, and ruthless promoter who was to dominate America's economic development for the next thirty years.

During the post-Civil War prosperity many small oil firms had already been forced to capitulate to larger and hence more efficient competitors.

Just prior to the panic, moreover, the first major step toward a fuller industry control had been taken. An organization called the South Improvement Company was formed as a combination of a number of the major producers. By serving as an "evener" in a Pennsylvania, Erie, New York Central pool this combine secured an advantage under the published freight rate of more than 25 per cent, plus a similar rebate on all oil shipped by competitors, plus a copy of all waybills covering shipments by competitors. At the time this agreement was entered into there were twenty-six refiners in Cleveland. Within three months twenty-one of these independents had joined forces with Rockefeller's organization. From this moment the Standard Oil Company was the unquestioned leader of the industry.

Almost immediately, although by error, information about the contracts between the railroads and the South Improvement Company became public property, and the resulting outcry, legal action, and other pressures caused the company's charter to be repealed and its rebate contract annulled. But the damage was already done; Rockefeller's control over oil refining in the nation's most important refining center was almost complete, and his domination extended over one-fifth of the entire nation's refining capacity. Moreover, his close alliance with and success in securing favors from trunk line railroads continued to be an important factor in his achievements. So too did the rigid practice of reinvesting the large earnings his concerns were earning for him. He reduced his costs by such innovations as building his own barrel factories and utilizing all the by-products which were commercially valuable, and maintained and strengthened his hold on the industry by investing heavily in pipeline transportation (a cheaper method of transportation than by rail).

By the middle of the 1870's Rockefeller had already determined that the entire industry was to be "integrated" under his supervision, and every effort was being made toward achieving this end. In one way or another independents were either squeezed out or coerced into the Standard Oil camp. Oil producers were prevented from securing the transportation facilities needed to make the market in which they sold really competitive. Even huge railroads were compelled to give his concern advantages they would rather not have granted. In 1879 a climax was reached in the form of an "alliance" between the Standard and a number of other important producers. The result was the Standard Oil Trust controlling virtually all of the facilities for transporting oil by pipeline and well over 90 per cent of the refining capacity.

As formalized a little later the new organization consisted of a concentration of the majority stock in the corporations involved in the hands of nine trustees. From this fact came the popular name "trust," and since many another consolidation was built on this model over the next few years, the term "trust" has come to refer generally to high concentration of industry control in the hands of a single concern. With the completion of this agreement the extreme flexibility of the corporate form of business organization was demonstrated as never before. And much more was yet to come.

Contrary to popular belief, John D. Rockefeller was highly scrupulous in his observance of the letter of the law. (Is it necessary to add that he employed expensive lawyers to interpret the law closely in his behalf?) The same was broadly true of most other trust promoters, although practices then followed did violate the accepted code of business ethics effective at a later time. Contrary also to popular belief, the Standard Oil Trust (as well as most other trusts) was not at base a scheme to establish monopoly as such or even to achieve power as such. While at some point along the way the motive of monopoly no doubt did often enter in, and while there is some reason for believing that one of the qualities needed by the most successful promoters was ruthlessness, it is still true that the basic economic fact behind the "consolidation movement" was the desire to stabilize a painfully unstable competitive situation. Only in terms of that fundamental background fact can this great development be accurately judged.

It was all very frustrating. To this point the nonindustrial interests had not succeeded in winning a single important victory over their business adversaries—either in politics or out of it. If the struggle were not to be abandoned (and no one seriously suggested this) two courses of action were open. Either the trust would have to be destroyed so that the bargaining power of individual business units would not be as irresistible as it now was, or laborers and farmers would have to achieve a comparable bargaining strength. At the moment it looked very much as though labor were ready to join the farmer in an all-out attack upon the trust; labor's own search for bargaining strength through organization seemed very much thwarted. The same machines, depression, and laws which were protecting and fostering capital combinations were systematically crushing the life out of labor combinations.

QUESTIONS FOR DISCUSSION

1. Why was the farmer's victory over the railroads so short-lived?
2. Did President Hayes do right in 1877 to call out federal troops against striking railroad workers? What other alternatives were there?
3. What were the lessons learned from the labor unrest of the 1870's by the various segments of the community?
4. What kind of labor "discipline" is required in an effectively functioning industrial society? Were the fears of businessmen justified in the 1870's?

5. Why were farmers so anxious to increase the supply of money in 1878? What was labor's principal interest in an inflationist policy at this time?

6. How did the coming of the machine contribute to the economic problems of this period?

7. What was the "consolidation movement," and why did it develop at this time?

8. Why were businessmen able to make a more successful adjustment to the coming of the machine than other major economic groups?

9. What would have been a successful adjustment for laborers? For farmers?

Chapter 23

FRUSTRATION COMPOUNDED

1879 Resumption of specie payments.
1880 John Garfield elected President.
1881 Chester Arthur became President after the assassination of Garfield.
1882 Chinese Exclusion Act.
1883 "Revision of the tariff by its friends."
Pendleton Act reforming Civil Service Administration.
1884 "Railroad Panic."
Resurgence of agrarian discontent.
First Democratic President since the Civil War elected—Grover Cleveland.
1885 Knights of Labor won their great victory over Jay Gould.
1886 Haymarket Square tragedy; Knights began a steep descent from power.
American Federation of Labor organized.

The Resumption of Specie Payments. If the proponents of the Bland-Allison Act intended to embarrass the Treasury's return to specie (and certainly this was one factor involved), they were disappointed. Secretary Sherman set about the task placed upon him with energy and foresight, and well before January 1, 1879, the needed gold reserve had been accumulated by the sale of bonds abroad. While this process was going on, moreover, he took steps to avoid the shock to the domestic money market which such fundamental transactions might have produced. He deposited government funds in the national banks, made an agreement with the banks that they would use paper in interbank payments rather than insist on gold, and secured memberships for the subtreasuries in the important clearinghouses so that the treasury's gold holdings could be kept for reserve purposes. Thus when the time arrived to redeem paper with gold there was barely a ripple of maladjustment in the financial world.

It is worth emphasizing, however, that more than Secretary Sherman's financial ability was required; accumulating gold out of the money markets of the world is more than a financial transaction. Involved also is a nation's entire balance-of-payments position. For a number of years after the Civil War the United States exported almost as much gold as it produced. Had this condition continued it would not have been possible to accumulate the reserve Sherman felt was necessary for resumption. Nothing is taken from the skill the secretary displayed in asserting that he was immeasurably aided by a fundamental change in America's international exchange situation.

A number of factors contributed to this result. The most important of these was the fact that the productive power of the young American economy had so developed that what had been a chronically unfavorable balance of commodity trade now became a permanently favorable balance, a result which appeared as soon as depression had readjusted the American price level more in line with world prices. Part of this change was the result of the rapid building up of the West, with its meat and grain surpluses, and the fact that American foodstuffs had become a regular part of Europe's supply of such goods. In part also it was the result of a rapid improvement in the cotton economy of the South.

Still another important part, however, is to be attributed to the growing power of the manufacturing industries of the country and the consequent growth of America's ability to supply herself with such goods. In the first twenty years following the Civil War manufactured goods as a percentage of total American imports fell from more than one-half to less than one-third. During the depression, in fact, some American manufacturers had even responded to the lash of deflation by promoting sale of their goods abroad for the first time. To be sure, many if not most of these sales had been the result of "dumping"—the sale of goods for a price which does not cover full costs—but even so they did suggest the place America was coming to occupy in the larger world economy. So too did the fact that for the first time America (Philadelphia) was chosen as the site of one of the great world's fairs (the sixth).

However, a favorable balance of trade is not the same thing as a favorable balance of payments, and there were sizable items on the other side of our international balance sheet. Thus reliance on iron and steel in the shipbuilding industry rather than lumber, coupled with America's high labor costs and legislation prohibiting foreign-built ships to register under the American flag, gave the United States a comparative disadvantage in this activity—and in consequence foreigners earned large sums against this country on account of freight charges. When to this drain is added the fact that debt repayment and interest charges were rising relative to new investments, it is evident that the favorable balance of trade was approximately balanced by an unfavorable "invisible items" balance. The change in America's foreign trade position, therefore, lay not in the fact that America had become a consistent net importer of gold. Rather, her average rate of gold export simply became less than her annual production rate.

Even this shift might well have failed to make possible the rapid gold accumulation which Secretary Sherman deemed necessary for resumption. The need was too immediate to be met by the slow process of actual mining. Something more was clearly necessary, and for a time the issue was genuinely in doubt. Finally the break came in the form of a severe crop shortage abroad and bumper crops in this country. Had it not been for this fortuitous development the nation might not have achieved resumption in 1879, and certainly this status would not have been attained so comfortably.

TABLE 52. FOUNDATION FOR RESUMPTION

Year	Excess of Exports Over Imports—Merchandise	Excess of Imports Over Exports—Gold
	(Millions of dollars)	
1878	257.8	1.0
1879	264.7	77.1
1880	167.7	97.5
1881	259.7	1.8

Source: Bureau of the Census, *Historical Statistics of the United States, 1789-1945*, p. 244.

Some Labor Victories. It was not the resumption of specie payments which dispelled the clouds of depression and embarked the nation on another period of prosperity, although conservatives would have liked to convince the public at large that this was the case. But conservatives did reap one benefit from the return of prosperity which more than compensated for this failure to associate resumption and prosperity in the public mind. It separated the laborer from active cooperation with the farmer, and thus the business community could breathe easier on the money question. An active economy meant jobs for workers—a situation in which labor would have to fight against the lag of wages behind prices. Both these things combined meant an opportunity and an incentive to take up a different line of endeavor.

One phase, and at the moment much the more important phase, of this new task was active, militant pressure on the economic front. These endeavors were largely limited to the skilled trades because they were the only groups powerful enough to exert this kind of pressure. A number of new national unions were formed, already existing organizations rapidly expanded their membership, and in 1881 a loose federation of trade unions was formed to give the economic struggle over-all guidance and assistance. This was the Federation of Trades and Labor Unions, an organization which was one day to become the American Federation of Labor. One of the guiding spirits behind this movement was an outstanding American of that day, Samuel Gompers, a leader in the cigar industry in New York.

Because unskilled and semiskilled workers, as always before in American history, had little place in this flourishing trade union movement, and even more because the nation's technological advance was creating such a large group of these workers, an organization in which they played the dominant role also had a vigorous existence during this period. The group which fell heir to this task was the Knights of Labor. Forced to give up its secrecy by the public reaction against labor movement violence in the recent depression, the Order was achieving much more in the way of membership and power than had been possible under depression conditions.

Understandably the Knights accomplished little for workers on the economic front, and it was for this reason that this group was at the moment of less importance than it was soon to become. About all it was yet suited to do well was to press for legislation benefiting labor in both state and national governments. This it did do, often in cooperation with trade union groups, and some substantial gains were achieved. Significantly, however, labor did not utilize its political strength for attacking the trust. Equally significant is the fact that there was nothing utopian about these political endeavors.

The first political victory won by the laborers was in 1882. For a number of years the labor movement in California had been confronted with a unique problem, one which had so occupied its attention and energies that it had done little to support labor's earlier inflationist program. California's gold rush had originally "caused" the problem by attracting to this country a large number of Chinese immigrants. Later, in the building of the Central Pacific Railroad, the west coast labor shortage had been combatted by the importation of a large number of Chinese coolies.

This Asiatic component in their midst created a great deal of difficulty for American workers. In the first place, the Chinese laborer's extremely low standard of living militated against labor's efforts to raise its own economic level. As long as there were "foreigners" willing to work for nominal wages, a strike for higher pay was almost certain to fail. Furthermore, this problem tended to spread from California to the rest of the country as eastern employers brought in Chinese workers as strikebreakers. These conditions aroused intense hostility in labor circles, a hostility at first taking primarily the form of abuse of and discrimination against the Chinese. During the depression feeling in California cities had on occasion run so high as to result in a series of unfortunate race riots. In 1882 opposition became sufficiently powerful that a law was passed forbidding the immigration of Chinese laborers.

The Chinese Exclusion Act, however, was a product of more than labor unrest. Another and in many respects different problem was also involved. Whereas immigrants coming to this country from western Europe had been relatively easy to assimilate into the American way of life, the Chinese were much less so. Western Europeans, after all, came from the same racial stock and cultural origins as Americans. In the case of the Chinese not only was the language of the two peoples totally different, but the entire cultural history and predilections were poles apart. The result was that the Chinese, more than any other foreign group in the United States, tended to isolate themselves in communities of their own and hence to insulate themselves from the American cultural process. It has been said that the 1882 law preventing further Chinese immigration saved this country from another race problem similar to the White-Negro problem.

Closely related to this immigration problem, moreover, was another one differing from it only in degree. With the return of prosperity, as usual, the sea lanes filled once again with European immigrants. In 1882 almost eight hundred thousand arrived, an unprecedented number, while the en-

TABLE 53. INDEX TO PROSPERITY

Year	Immigration
	(Thousands)
1878	138.5
1879	177.8
1880	457.3
1881	669.4
1882	789.0

Source: Bureau of the Census, *Historical Statistics of the United States, 1789-1945*, pp. 33-34.

tire decade saw a total of three million foreigners flock to American shores. Many of these newcomers, of course, conceived the idea of coming to America on their own, but a large number were actively recruited by western states, land companies, land grant railroads, factory owners, and steamship lines.

This situation, of course, was no different from that existing at certain other times in America's history. What was different—and herein lay the problem—was the source of many of these immigrants. For the first time immigrants from southern and eastern Europe were beginning to arrive in the United States in significant numbers. Heretofore the inadequacy of transportation facilities had limited the number from these areas, while the painful beginnings of industrialization in western Europe had encouraged people from those areas to seek higher wages or cheap land in America. With the improvement of transportation facilities and the coming of age of industrialism in England and Germany, the "old immigration" began to taper off and to be replaced by the so-called "new immigration." As yet the problem was not acute in terms of numbers, and even southern and eastern Europeans did not present an assimilation problem as difficult as did the Chinese, but it was soon apparent that this problem would one day have to be resolved in the same way as that of the Chinese.

Tariff Reform Fails. Labor's immigration success could not be said to have been purchased at the farmer's expense. The great victory achieved by the worker in 1883, however, was so purchased. In that year agitation for tariff reform again became intense, and once again staple farmers and laborers stood on opposite sides of this issue.

The farmer's tariff problem was that the government's revenue was once more excessive. Year after year excise duties and customs levies were yielding a surplus above expenses of more than $100 million. To farmers this was doubly disastrous. Not only did it represent a burden of taxation which was clearly unnecessary, but it was rapidly eliminating the government indebtedness on which their already inadequate money circulation was based (although this situation would have been far worse than it was had it not been for the fact that a substantial portion of the surplus was being disposed of by way of the silver purchase program). But while laborers were no more anxious to shoulder an unnecessary tax burden than farmers, they were not willing to reduce taxes at the expense of protection. The worker's attitude toward low-paid foreign labor was precisely the same whether it resided inside America or outside.

The battle against tariff reduction proceeded simultaneously on two fronts. One front consisted of a commission appointed to study the revenue and tariff structures for the purpose of making recommendations to Congress. Headed by the secretary of the Wool Manufacturers Association, and including representation from both sugar- and wool-growing farmers, the commission was frankly protectionist. As expected it proposed no great change in the protective system, although it did recommend a substantial reduction in duty levels—a reduction the chairman publicly referred to as "a reluctant concession to public sentiment."

The second front was in the House Committee on Appropriations. Protectionists reasoned that if the surplus was too great the proper remedy was to increase government spending. The outstanding example was the appropriation for the Pensions Bureau. Whereas this expenditure should by now have been declining year by year, and indeed had been until tariff reform again became a live issue, in a dozen years it increased more than 300 per cent. A rivers and harbors appropriation more than twice as high as any previous measure of this type was presented to the President for signature, and when it received a stern presidential veto it was quickly passed over the veto.

These manipulations of the government's finances to support a higher level of protection brought a storm of public protest, a protest most clearly symbolized by a congressional election in which the Republican majority in the House was turned into a Democratic majority. Thus it was another "lame-duck" Congress which in early 1883 enacted a new tariff law. It is no wonder, under these circumstances, that the earlier attitude favoring a concession to public sentiment, however "reluctant," turned into a stubborn, unshakable hold-the-line stand. And the line was almost held.

As would be expected from its stronger agricultural representation, the Senate prepared a genuine tariff reform measure. The House, on the other hand, insisted on a bill which conceded as little as possible to the reformers. The House approach ultimately won the day, too, as enough Senators (many of them from agricultural states) voted for the higher levies to enact them into law. Once again tariff reform sentiment had been resoundingly defeated. Instead, $25 million was lopped off the internal revenue burden, including a reduction of the tax on tobacco of one-half.

What are we to think of laborers thus decisively approving a protectionist policy? Are workers wise or stupid who so behave? Certainly they can by no stretch of the imagination be called stupid. The worst charge which can be levied against a protective tariff from the standpoint of the worker is that it raises the cost of his level of living. But to a man whose principal asset is his job, what is a small reduction in standard of living compared with unemployment? Besides, it was common knowledge that the American worker received higher real wages than were available in any other industrialized nation—even with the tariff. The worker no doubt exaggerated the connection between the tariff and his job, and the "cheap foreign labor" argument for a tariff is not economically valid as it is usually stated.[1] However, the fact remains that the dynamics of an industrial economy is such that shifts in structure are constantly taking place, shifts requiring painful readjustments for the workers victimized by them. Trade restrictions are unquestionably a way of minimizing or at

[1] This argument is that cheap labor abroad can, simply because it is cheap, produce goods able to undersell the product of more highly paid domestic labor. The fallacy here is twofold. First, the wage rate paid is not a usable measure of labor cost of production. *High wage rates* normally mean *high productivity,* and may therefore be perfectly compatible with *low labor cost.* Second, in international trade goods ultimately exchange against goods—that is, imports are bought with exports. It follows that, speaking generally, the workers not employed to produce imported goods are roughly compensated for in the form of workers employed to produce goods for export.

least crudely managing these dynamic changes. It is perhaps no overstatement to suggest that labor's support of protection during this period was one of the most realistic aspects of an over-all labor program not yet distinguished for its realism. Workers already painfully adjusting to the machine are hardly to be blamed for not cheerfully accepting other such adjustments as well.

Equally important, what are we to think of those farmers' representatives who voted with the majority in 1883? Here is a somewhat more complicated problem, although certain parts of the answer are clear enough. For example, it is a significant fact that the 1883 revision did not reduce the duty at all on such items as beef, pork, hams, bacon, lard, cheese, butter, wheat, corn, and oats. Already the process had begun of convincing the farmer that he could be protected by a tariff even though he exported his output, a process which was to become notoriously successful before the farmer's economic understanding improved on this point. In the second place, the expansion of the West was gradually creating a strong sheep industry in a number of states, an agricultural industry which could intelligently be protectionist since the country was a net importer of wool. And finally, some credit must be given the swarm of lobbyists that filled the hotels in Washington while the tariff bill was under discussion.

Further Frustration. While labor organizations continued to grow throughout the prosperity of the early 1880's, their successes were not long to outweigh their defeats. There was setting in a period of frustration almost as serious as any labor had yet faced.

One phase of this frustration is almost amusing. F. W. Taylor, a very young man forced to give up a brilliant academic career because of weak eyesight, resolved to apply the tools of scientific study to an analysis of business management in the same way that it had already been applied to technology. At the Midvale Steel Company in Philadelphia he completed an investigation which has since become the basis of an important modern profession. The purpose of his studies was to discover wastes in motion or coordination in order that they might be eliminated. Though jeered at in the beginning more often than encouraged, Taylor's findings were little short of electrifying. He was able to demonstrate that intelligence applied to such a question could uncover a multitude of opportunities for greater efficiency.

Of course, there was nothing in all of this that was amusing to workers. They resented the inference that they were to be treated as machines in the sense of working with machinelike singleness of purpose and untiring monotony. Moreover, one of the central cores of organized labor's system of beliefs is the notion that there is a fixed amount of work and that when it has been done unemployment will arise. Greater efficiency thus can only mean more unemployment. To get around this obstacle in the minds of laborers Taylor suggested paying by the piece on the basis of a "standard" day's work, but laborers were too suspicious of employer motives to respond favorably. They feared employers meant to use piece payments as a device to "speed up" the work pace without really increasing wages.

The irony lies rather in this. "Freddie" Taylor was no labor-hater; he was primarily a scientist studying with admirable objectivity a problem in which he was interested. There is no occasion for surprise, therefore, that he found as many faulty practices followed by management as by labor. But when he endeavored to get this message across to the only people who could remedy these situations, he met with almost no success. Employers were willing to force better working habits on employees, but took full advantage of the fact that no one was in a position to force better practices on them. More than a generation was to elapse before "scientific management" as applied to management rather than to labor was to receive a sympathetic hearing in the business community.

However, labor had little to worry about on this front as yet, for few employers were interested in Taylor's work. A much more important phase of labor's frustration took place on the economic pressure front, where organized labor was for the first time meeting in combat one of the new combinations.

The concern involved was the Western Union Telegraph Company. This giant firm had originated in a consolidation of more than fifty different companies, and it had since enjoyed a steady and profitable growth based on extending its own lines, the absorption of competition, and the performance of a generally satisfactory service. By 1883 President Norvin Green was rapidly achieving his ambition of a virtual monopoly of the nation's telegraph business. With a capitalization of more than $80 million and approximately four hundred thousand miles of wire, his concern was one of the greatest in the land. This fact was common knowledge, too, and there was a widespread criticism of the holding as a private monopoly of such an important element in the life of the community. Part of this feeling no doubt grew out of the strong financial interest in Western Union then held by Jay Gould.

Labor shared this unrest against Western Union, especially the telegraph workers themselves. In mid-1883 a strike against the company was called in order to secure for laborers some of the fruits of the position the company had achieved. Specifically, labor demanded an eight-hour day and a 15 per cent increase in wages. Dramatically demonstrating the general antagonism toward the company, this action was widely supported by the public at large, and so intense was this feeling that for several years the threat of government ownership was a substantial one. This endeavor failed, however, and even a serious beginning at regulation was still far in the future. The workers failed, too, and after a month of strike distress the workers who were not blacklisted returned to their jobs.

These difficulties faced by labor were next accentuated by the short depression beginning in 1884. This economic downturn was, even in its own day, dubbed the "railroad panic," although this characterization was misleading in several ways. In the first place, the "panic" element was exceedingly brief and by no means as severe as other such episodes in America's development. In the second place, the railroad industry was by no means the only major segment of the economy involved. The prosperity of the early 1880's was as full as any the nation had as yet enjoyed, and expansion in a number of other areas rivaled at least that in the railroad field.

Still there was a certain logic in referring to a "railroad panic." Perhaps the most dramatic peacetime industrial achievement in any country at any time was the progress made in railroad building during these few years. As shown in Table 54, construction increased almost 400 per cent in five years, reaching the tremendous total of twelve thousand miles in the year preceding the reaction. If no other economic expansion than this had taken place during these years, a readjustment of some magnitude would still have been required.

TABLE 54. KEY TO PROSPERITY

Year	Mileage Built
1878	2,500
1879	5,000
1880	7,000
1881	10,000
1882	12,000

Source: Bureau of the Census, *Historical Statistics of the United States, 1789-1945*, p. 200.

And there were other reasons, too, for identifying the new depression with the railroad. Speculative and often fraudulent practices continued to be an integral part of the progress being made in railroad expansion, and indeed this period perhaps ranks above any other in American history from this standpoint. Furthermore, as a result of a major change in the techniques used in financing railroads, the new depression was the first to witness the bankruptcy of a significant fraction of the nation's railway mileage. This change, in fact, was so marked and so pervasive in its effects that it was to become an important factor in every succeeding economic downturn.

The earliest railroads had been financed primarily by the sale of stock. But with the greater emphasis on construction in undeveloped territory capital had to be secured primarily from "outsiders." Such capital demanded greater security than could be offered in stock contracts, and bonds were therefore increasingly issued. It was this greater security afforded bondholders which made American railways so much more vulnerable to deflation. Bonds carry a fixed return, and if it is not paid the bondholders may legally possess themselves of the property (throw the concern into bankruptcy). The actual result need not have been so pronounced, but for two reasons more bonds were issued than were warranted by the speculative nature of the projects involved. First, unwary bondholders could easily be lulled into a false sense of security by the fact that railroads do have a high proportion of "mortgageable" property. Second, a high bond ratio contributed a great deal to the opportunities of the speculator promoter; with more bonds outstanding a given property could be controlled by a smaller investment and the chance of earning a high return on common stock investments made that much greater.[2]

These financial developments during prosperity and the resulting bankruptcy of many railroads did much to accentuate public antagonism toward the railroads. Sharp financial practices are always suspect to men and women who work with their hands. Furthermore, many a poor man had succumbed to the oily tongue of the promoter and purchased securities which were either worthless at the outset or became worthless as soon as the economy began the painful process of liquidation. The farmer, too, had a special grievance. During this period railroad mastery over inland waterways became almost complete, a fact to which the steady abandonment of canals and canalized rivers bore mute testimony. With the exception of the Great Lakes where special conditions prevailed, traffic was declining markedly on every one of America's once flourishing inland waterway channels. In part this was only a manifestation of economic progress, although there was an element of deliberate "cutthroat competition" engendered by the railroad as well. Indiscriminate as he often was in his economic understanding, the farmer could scarcely have done other than accuse the railroads of the wanton destruction of a transportation medium which had once provided him a measure of protection against the

[2] Thus a concern capitalized 50 per cent in bonds could be controlled by an investment equal to (at a maximum) 25 per cent of total capitalization—instead of 50 per cent for a concern having only common stock outstanding. Similarly, a given dollar profit would yield a higher rate of return on the common stock the more the capitalization was in the form of bonds. Suppose, for example, a $1 million concern, capitalized one-half by 6 per cent bonds and one-half by common stock. If the concern makes a net profit of $100,000, compare the rate of return to the stockholder with that which he would receive if all the capitalization had been in common stock.

railroad. The very fact that the "Panic of 1884" was referred to as the "railroad panic" both resulted from public hostility and added to it.

The Knights of Labor. The economic downturn beginning in 1884 was neither as long nor as severe as its predecessor. Unemployment was not as great and the real wages of the average *employed* worker rose significantly, for wages fell on an average by less than the cost of living. Perhaps its principal consequence was that it created enough unemployment to make possible a renewed employer attack against the trade unions, with the result that the Knights of Labor became by far the most powerful labor organization in the land. And when in consequence the Knights began to recruit skilled workers in substantial numbers there was precipitated a war to the death between the craft unions on the one hand and the Knights of Labor on the other.

It was not, to be sure, merely a battle between organizations. At stake were the principles on which the future of the American labor movement was to be based. On its side, the Knights of Labor was essentially a protest against the power of wealth and its unjust accumulation, and its program emphasized the need to abolish the economic system responsible for "the pauperization and hopeless degradation of the toiling masses." (More specifically many Knights felt that the machine had so destroyed the value of labor skills that there was no effective basis for the building of a labor power within the existing framework.) As an alternative the Knights suggested and worked toward the time-honored principle of producers' cooperation—a mode of economic organization which would assist workers to escape from the capitalistic wage system.

The trades, on the other hand, were hostile to any program for overthrowing the existing order. They preferred rather a type of organization capable of wresting concessions from employers within that system. Since they did in fact under more normal circumstances have the power necessary for this task (since, in other words, these workers were the ones most benefiting from the wage system), they understandably could not go along with an attack such as that contemplated by the Knights.

The difference in approach between these two organizations can most succinctly be illustrated in terms of a victory won by labor shortly after the appearance of a new depression. Ever since the Civil War the legislation permitting immigrants to enter the country bound by labor contracts had remained despite all labor's efforts to have it repealed. Recently, however, many laborers had become particularly incensed at this practice because contract immigrants were coming to be widely used as strikebreakers. Moving to meet this threat at its source, the Knights of Labor pressed hard for repeal—almost unaided by craft leaders. The skilled trades were not threatened as unskilled workers were by the influx of foreign workers, for the "new immigration" contained few skilled workers. (By contrast the trades actively pressed for Chinese exclusion legislation; one-fourth of all United States cigar-makers were Chinese.)

During the next few years this battle within labor was to be fought out on a broad front. Not only was this encounter one of the most interesting and meaningful in all labor's history, but it proceeded in an amazingly paradoxical fashion. In the first place, the Knights of Labor, the antagonist destined to go down in the struggle, was the group which achieved the greatest successes during this decade. In the second place, these successes were in turn won largely by means of strikes and boycotts, weapons the Order disapproved in principle but which were approved by its opponent.

From the beginning strong pressure to use the strike and the boycott had been felt by leaders of the Order. Thus the telegraph strike was largely a Knights undertaking, and perhaps its failure was in part a result of this inconsistency and the consequent ineffectiveness of strike efforts. However, successful or not, the pressure mounted, and the first major response of the organization to the coming of a new depression was a wave of strikes equaling or surpassing anything in the nation's past history. Fought out primarily for recognition or in opposition to wage reductions, this 1884 series of strikes resulted in a succession of decisive failures. Later, as the Order turned more and more to the use of weapons of militancy, failure became less and less the result of inexperience. Moreover, failure was by no means the invariable outcome of these endeavors.

Toward the end of 1884 the repeated failure of strikes brought the boycott into use on a large scale. When this weapon, too, failed, the effort returned to strikes. In this field in 1885 the Knights of Labor achieved its first real victory, a victory made all the sweeter by the fact that its opponent was none other than Jay Gould himself.

The initiating cause was a wage reduction on two of Gould's railroad properties—the Missouri, Kansas, Texas and the Wabash. When the workers on these two roads went out on strike they were at once joined by the workers on Gould's other major railroad, the Missouri Pacific. So complete was the walkout, supported as it was by the railway brotherhoods (engineers, firemen, brakemen, and conductors—the most highly skilled and completely organized workers in the railroad industry) that management soon capitulated. Wages were restored to the old level, and the strikers were re-employed. Six months later another strike took place in which the principal issue was management's failure to live up to the terms of the first agreement. Again management gave in, but not before Gould had himself intervened rather than see the strike prolonged. For the first time in the history of the United States a group of laborers had brought to heel a major industry. More than that, the Knights of

Labor had demonstrated that it could deal with the most powerful capitalist in the nation on equal terms. In this second Wabash strike the Knights were abandoned by the railroad brotherhoods—these groups now beginning to fear competition from this lusty rival.

The effect of this achievement on the minds of workers was immediate and dramatic. Here was a champion of the oppressed masses worthy of full support. Tens of thousands of workers rushed to its banners, and workers all over the country took new hope from the months of pentup discouragement and bitterness—a result much accentuated by exaggerated reports of the power of the Knights of Labor. Some of these accounts, to be sure, were intended to terrify the public into limiting a power thought by many to have grown too great. But to laborers who had long felt the power of an arrogant industrialism there could scarcely be an excessive power in the hands of labor. New members continued to pour in until at the peak of its power in the following year the Order could boast a total of seven hundred thousand members—almost three times as many as the craft unions could claim.

Moreover, not only were laborers winning unprecedented victories but they were also beginning to enjoy a measure of popular good will. For example, Henry George, running on a radical labor-reform ticket, was barely defeated in the 1886 mayoralty race in New York. Even more significant, perhaps, was the fact that George was defeated by Abram S. Hewitt, an industrialist-statesman whose views on labor had almost nothing in common with those of such men as Norvin Green, F. B. Gowen, or Jay Gould. Hewitt believed sincerely in the need for labor organizations, and deplored the antiunion stand of the leading industrialists of the day. It was unfortunate that almost immediately the Knights proceeded to alienate a large portion of this public sympathy.

Flushed with success as no American labor group had ever been before, Knights leaders now began looking about for a cause worthy of their steel. They settled upon the eight-hour day. A nation-wide strike was called for May 1, 1886, a strike in which a total of more than a third of a million workers directly participated.

There were many reasons why this effort failed. One of these was the fact that a "general" strike is no way to achieve labor victories as long as public good will is important. Another reason was the depression; it is difficult to win consistent strike victories in the midst of unemployment. But the most important reason was no doubt the organization and makeup of the Knights of Labor. On the one hand, the order was hierarchically organized in the sense that decisions were centralized at the top. Long since craft unions had discovered that effective strikes require a high degree of localized generalship. On the other hand, the tens of thousands of unskilled, extremely heterogeneous laborers in a powerful organization for the first time were not yet disciplined to the delicate task of fighting employers without appearing to challenge the foundations of society. The resulting episodes of violence and destruction, no part of the plan of Knights leaders, too quickly reminded the community of the "outlawry" which had accompanied the preceding depression and helped it to forget the legitimacy of labor's demands. When an anarchist, belonging to a small splinter group in the labor movement with which the Knights in fact had no sympathy, threw a bomb in Haymarket Square in Chicago killing or wounding some twenty policemen, people were all too willing to attribute the atrocity to the Knights.

The tragic failure of the eight-hour movement was quickly followed by a series of other reverses. A third strike on the Gould lines degenerated into the seizing of property and the sabotaging of locomotives. In Chicago a packers' association led by Armour & Company instituted a memorable lockout to accent their demand that the workers return to a ten-hour day to enable Chicago to compete on more even terms with Cincinnati and Kansas City. So complete was this defeat that unionism in packing plants was virtually destroyed for a period of thirty years. Coal-handlers and longshoremen in New York struck against wage reductions, but although they were supported in one way or another by thousands of other workers in the area these strikes completely collapsed after some weeks of bitterness and hardship.

It was the beginning of the end for the Knights of Labor. A veritable wave of lockouts and employer associations was organized in opposition, these actions being liberally supported by state and local police. Simultaneously the various trade groups and the new American Federation of Labor (a more formal organization established to resist continued aggressions of the Knights of Labor) with Samuel Gompers at its head responded to the return of prosperity by solidifying and expanding their own ranks. These assaults, coupled with its own unwieldiness as an attempt to weld skilled and unskilled, native and foreign workers into "one big union," rapidly proved to be too much for the Knights. As a result the way was opened for a new advance by the skilled trades, and within a short time these groups were taking fullest advantage of their opportunities.

Defeated on the fighting front, the Knights might have been expected to fall back on the cooperatives which had all along been their most important principle of development. Unfortunately, however, this latest attempt to supplant the wage system had already met with disaster. Most of the enterprises established were on a small scale and hence were doomed from the beginning. Some fell victim to the antagonism of more orthodox entrepreneurs. A few, and typically the most successful, were converted into more orthodox concerns as a result of the "freezing out" of outsiders by insiders. But by 1886 there could no longer be any doubt that the principle of producers' cooperation as a solution to labor's problem in an industrial society was once again ending in disillusionment.

No Relief for the Farmer. While laborers were acting out an old drama on a new stage, farmers were similarly occupied. On the national political scene the major efforts were still money and the tariff. Furthermore, with a Democratic President in the White House, there had originally been some room for hope. This was especially true in the case of the tariff, for Grover Cleveland was eager to press for a reduction, and the Democratic party was willing to help. However, the Republican Senate was an insurmountable barrier. In 1886 the best opportunity to reform the tariff in years came to exactly nothing.

On the money question, the situation was much different although the outcome was the same. Here Grover Cleveland was not only not eager, but was stubbornly opposed. Even before his inauguration he had distressed his farmer friends by calling for the cessation of all purchases of silver under the Bland-Allison Act. Of course, Congress paid no attention to this demand, but it was disturbing nonetheless.

In 1886 the money issue arose again in a critical way. The Bland-Allison silver being coined and put into silver was refusing to stay in circulation. As silver piled up in the Treasury while the gold reserve dwindled, the nation was threatened again with leaving a gold payment standard. Silverites and inflationists were jubilant; they at once set about to pass legislation to help this process along. President Cleveland met this crisis—the "Silver Blizzard of 1886"—in the same way he met all other threats to policies he considered indispensable. He vetoed his party's inflationist proposals. Possibly this event more than any other during this period convinced the farmer of the necessity of a separate political organization, one outside the two major parties.

On the local front a new farmers' organization was springing up to replace the rapidly declining Grange. Called by different names in different parts of the country, for it was not possible to unite the northern and southern farmers into the same organization (for example, a running conflict between vegetable and animal oil interests could never be resolved), the most common title was the Farmers' Alliance. Once again the farmer turned to organized cooperation. Cooperative elevators, grain exchanges, and cotton distributing concerns were inaugurated to make another attempt to free the farmer from the tentacles of a growing industrialism and the trust structure into which it was being transformed. Once again, however, it was all to no avail. Apart from a few outstanding exceptions cooperative ventures were uniformly unsuccessful. Farmers were no more able than laborers to find their way out of the slough of frustration by means of institutions running against the grain of the industrial society evolving all about them.

Why was it that farmers' and laborers' cooperatives did not do well despite the earnest efforts put into them? What was there about these endeavors that was incompatible with the rest of the economy? For one thing, both laborers and farmers were often naïve in thinking that the middleman's function could be done away with in an exchange society. Moreover, the cooperative principle of one-man-one-vote can easily make for an unwieldy organization if extreme care is not taken. Then too there were frequently such practical difficulties as inadequate capital, unfair competition from private capitalists, or the sheer failure of group solidarity. Farmers are traditionally individualistic, and one of the most important characteristics of American labor has always been a mobility militating against deep community roots of the sort required for successful cooperation. Still another consideration on the labor side is the fact that producers' cooperatives are opposed to trade unionism to the extent that they destroy employment for workers in private concerns.

But undoubtedly the largest obstacle was this. The secret of successful business enterprise is efficient business management. This is no less true of cooperative than of noncooperative concerns. In the industrial society of the late ninetenth century the personal qualities which made an effective business manager were most highly rewarded in private enterprise. Farmer or labor cooperatives simply could not compete, so great were the opportunities available in the business world.

As far as the farmer's more general grievances were concerned, nothing had happened to abate them. Much had even happened to accentuate them. During the early 1880's the prices of farm products fell one-third, far more than the over-all wholesale price index. In addition, it was not unusual for 50 per cent of the farms in an area to be mortgaged at 8 per cent interest. It seemed clear that the bargaining power of the farmer was growing progressively weaker as consolidations proceeded apace. Small wonder that farmer organizations were beginning to adopt more radical platforms—such as, for example, government ownership of the railroads. For his part, and whether the worker joined in this fight or not, the farmer was about to launch the most concerted drive yet against the Rockefellers, the Greens, and the Goulds.

QUESTIONS FOR DISCUSSION

1. What were the principal economic factors making the resumption of specie payments possible?

2. Was the Chinese Exclusion Act an appropriate step for a "democratic" society to take?

3. Were there differences from the standpoint of labor's economic well-being between a Chinese Exclusion Act and a protective tariff?

4. What were labor's objections to "Taylorism"? How valid was this opposition?

5. Why was the depression beginning in 1884 called the "railroad panic"?

6. What is the connection between methods of railroad financing and the vulnerability of railroad concerns to depression?

7. Many persons during this period were of the opinion that railroad over-capitalization made railroad rates higher than they would otherwise have been. Is this analysis correct?

8. Why was the Knights of Labor as an organization less successful in its day than the Congress of Industrial Organizations in ours?

Chapter 24

ATTEMPTS AT REFORM

1886 Cullom Committee report.
Wabash decision.
1887 Interstate Commerce Act.
Cleveland message to Congress demanding tariff reform.
1888 State action against the trusts.
Benjamin Harrison elected President.
1889 Department of Agriculture raised to Cabinet status.
1890 Sherman Anti-Trust Act.
Sherman Silver Purchase Act.
McKinley Tariff.

It was high time. If anything were going to be done in this field, the time to begin was surely now. While farmers' and workers' organizations were meeting with disaster in almost every quarter, organization in the business community was proceeding apace. The Standard Oil Trust was able to continue its march toward monopoly, although certain of the independents by concentrating in the same way as the Standard were able to form a "counter-trust" which in time became the Pure Oil Company. A bitter rivalry among small concerns in the steel industry was reducing the number of firms in this industry at a prodigious rate, the leader of the giants at the moment being Andrew Carnegie. Andrew Mellon and aluminum were beginning a partnership which was one day to produce the nearest thing to a complete monopoly the economy was ever to know. In the field of communications a truce between Western Union and its major rival, Postal Telegraph, gave Green virtually all he had ever wanted, while F. N. Vail was already beginning the process of exploiting patents, which was in time to make the American Telephone and Telegraph Company undisputed master of the vast business of telephonic communication.

And these organizations were only the most prominent of the new consolidations growing out of another American depression. In addition, other industries were seizing this way out of a situation in which competition was either potentially disastrous or at least painful. A Whisky Trust was formed, the Distillers and Cattle Feeders Trust. The National Cordage Company tightened its grip on the production of twine, rope, and miscellaneous cordage products by securing a virtually complete monopoly of the world's supply of manila hemp. Cottonseed oil producers, makers of linseed oil, the lead industry, and sugar refiners all created a centralization of control over a large fraction of total output.

Preliminary Skirmishes. It was not because the public minimized the rapidity with which industrial trusts were being formed that attention turned first to the railroad problem. This selection of adversaries was rather the result of a set of special circumstances. The role played by the railroad in the making of certain concentrations such as the Standard Oil Company had not escaped public notice, and the wholesale way in which the railroads were continuing to discriminate in favor of large shippers and the politically prominent suggested that a solution to the railroad problem was a prerequisite to any success against the trust problem itself. This connection was no doubt exaggerated in the public mind, for there were forces behind industrial combinations far more fundamental than the accident of railway charges, but the agricultural hostility to the railroads inherited from "Granger" days made such an exaggeration understandable.

More specifically, two events in 1886 precipitated the attention now given to bringing the great railroad corporations into a more responsible relationship to the larger community. A Senate investigating committee charged with making available the facts on which a federal railway policy could be based brought in a most revealing document. Spelling out chapter and verse of the deliberate policy of discrimination being followed, the Cullom Committee asserted that the "paramount evil chargeable against the operation of the transportation system of the United States, as now conducted, is unjust discrimination between places, persons, commodities, or particular descriptions of traffic." A rigorous pattern of regulation was recommended.

The Cullom Committee report was given much point by a Supreme Court decision handed down in the same year. Involved was a case of discrimination charged against the Wabash Railroad. The facts were the following: Between Peoria and New York a certain class of freight was being transported for 15 cents per hundred pounds, whereas between Gilman and New York (a distance shorter by sixty miles than the Peoria-New York haul, trains from Peoria even passing through Gilman on their way to New York) the charge for transporting the same class of freight was 25 cents. Recognizing the injustice of this situation, the Illinois regulatory commission had ordered this discrimination to be removed. This the railroad strenuously sought to avoid; to raise the rate on the long haul would cut the Wabash out of a share of the Peoria-New York traffic because the trunk lines had long since adopted the 15-cent rate, while to lower the rate on the short haul (where competition with other carriers was not a factor) would reduce that rate to less than full costs. Understandably, one step in this resistance campaign was an appeal to the courts.

The issue raised was a momentous one. Relying on Munn v. Illinois, the state maintained that it could regulate in the interstate commerce field until the federal government did. Counsel for the railroad, on the other hand, argued that such a construction of the Constitution virtually took power over interstate commerce out of the hands of the federal government. The Court promptly agreed with the railroad position, and in retrospect it is apparent that the position taken by the state could scarcely have been the final word on this question. Reversing its own stand of ten years earlier, the Supreme Court now asserted that interstate commerce regulation could not be a state function under any circumstances. The implications of this decision were at once obvious. Since the railroad industry was overwhelmingly interstate in character, the only way of controlling it would be through the federal government.

The response of Congress was immediate. On February 4, 1887, the Interstate Commerce Act was passed. Striking at the railroad problem at its roots, the act forbade discrimination, prohibited pooling, required the publication of rates, forbade rate changes on less than ten days' notice, and declared that charges were to be just and reasonable. A regulatory commission, the first such body established by the federal government, was created to see that the various provisions were obeyed. The commissioners selected by President Cleveland, moreover, were all able men, setting about their task with competence and enthusiasm. It was, in short, the fault of neither the law nor its administrators that this work all had to be done over again under very trying conditions. Still, supporters should have suspected that this would be the case. Not only was the victory too easy, but it was an unmistakable fact that nobody seemed to take it very seriously. And in 1887 thirteen thousand miles of railway line were constructed, a new record, assisted by an unprecedented flow of capital from abroad.

The passage of the Interstate Commerce Act was followed almost immediately by a rash of antitrust laws in the states. Conspiracies in restraint of trade had always been opposed to common-law doctrines, and it was partly for this reason that the early pools and other loose forms of combination were gradually being abandoned. But the common law was soon seen to be inadequate for dealing with the problems now arising. While price agreements and pooling arrangements were not enforceable, they were at the same time not illegal—no punishments were stipulated which could operate as preventives. Seeking to remedy this defect by positive legislation, a dozen states passed laws prohibiting various known methods of restricting competition.

Perhaps no one seriously supposed that state action would be adequate in view of the fact that the principal trusts were clearly interstate in character. Thus most proponents of reform still looked forward to federal legislation. However, even now no move was taken against industrial trusts at the national level. Another intermediate step first seemed indicated.

By 1887 the notion that enterprises formed to eliminate competition were at least in part supported by a tariff law whose purpose was to prevent foreign concerns from competing with domestic ones was becoming current. The "invasion" of Washington by business lobbyists whenever a tariff bill was up for discussion seemed evidence enough on this point. This charge made a powerful addition to already existing arguments against the tariff.

TABLE 55. ARGUMENT FOR TARIFF REFORM

Year	Government Surplus
	(Millions of dollars)
1881	100.1
1882	145.5
1883	132.9
1884	104.4
1885	63.5
1886	94.0
1887	103.5
1888	111.3
1889	87.8
1890	85.0

Source: Bureau of the Census, *Historical Statistics of the United States, 1789-1945*, pp. 296-97.

At this point, too, another new argument supporting tariff reduction appeared. By now all the bonds callable by law had been redeemed, and further use of the government surplus in reducing the national debt could only be accomplished by buying bonds in the open market. Because the rate of interest had steadily fallen since these debts were contracted, this meant paying a substantial premium.[1] Retirement of the national debt

[1] The value of capital assets is determined by a process called "capitalization," or dividing the annual income from the asset by the going rate of interest. Stated from a somewhat different standpoint, an individual with money to invest will not pay more for one asset than for any other producing the same money income. A corollary of the capitalization process is that the lower the rate of interest, the higher the price of income-earning assets. Thus a 6 per cent, $1,000 bond will sell at par if the going rate of interest is 6 per cent, and at $200 above par if the interest rate is 5 per cent.

more rapidly than the public interest required was one thing. Taxing the lower income groups, however, in order to put an unearned increment in the hands of wealthy bondholders was a very different matter.

Grover Cleveland was highly indignant. Casting to the four winds the caution urged upon him by his political advisers, he devoted the entirety of his annual address to Congress in 1887 to the tariff. No radical presentation of free-trade ideas, Cleveland's approach was still uncompromising. He refused to countenance a reduction in tobacco and distilled spirits taxes, for he believed that users of such commodities should bear a share of the nation's tax burden regardless of surplus revenue.

This state paper set the stage for both a major tariff battle in Congress in 1888 and the presidential election of that year. The outcome of the Congressional struggle was determined before it began. A tariff reduction measure could not have received favorable action by a Republican Senate. The election contest also turned out badly for reformers. Fought out almost solely on the tariff issue, with Cleveland himself as the Democratic candidate, it resulted in a Republican victory. Still worse, the Republicans interpreted their election victory as a popular demand for an even higher level of duties. There was, in truth, only one bright spot in this entire situation. The agitation against the trusts had become so general and so powerful, along with the charge that "the tariff is the mother of trusts," that the Republicans were forced to put a strong antitrust plank in their platform.

The Battle Opens. At this point, and possibly spurred on by the tariff defeat, the movement against the trusts began in earnest. The first step, it was concluded, was to learn as much as possible about them. In February, 1888, a committee of the senate of the state of New York instituted an investigation of the Standard Oil Company. In July a committee of the United States House of Representatives reported the results of a study it had made of the oil and sugar trusts. The findings were simple enough although startling to many. "This form of combination was obviously devised for the purpose of relieving the trusts and trustees from the charge of any breach of the conspiracy laws of the various states, or of being a combination to regulate or control the price or production of any commodity." Thus bluntly did the House of Representatives committee analyze the situation.

The evidence seemed to support the accusation. Trustees insisted that the several corporations remained separate and distinct, that stockholders had exchanged their stock for trust certificates and hence had no legal title to the property of the corporations involved, and that the trustees only held stock in the corporations and hence did not buy or sell or combine with anyone else for any purpose. The House committee, however, made it plain that it was not deceived by this complex of legal fictions.

In 1889 two states took a further step. New York, declaring that the trust system was spreading "like a disease through the commercial system of this country," brought suit against the North Sugar Refining Company, one of the members of the Sugar Trust. Simultaneously Ohio brought action against the Standard Oil Company of Ohio. In both of these complaints it was asserted that the company involved had violated its charter by tranferring control of its operations to others. The Ohio case promptly turned into a long drawn out court battle, but in New York the North Sugar Refining Company summarily lost its charter. The trust method of industrial combination was clearly under heavy pressure.

While these events were taking place, however, the power of the nation's corporations was continuing to increase. In 1890 the Diamond Match Company was formed, including among its assets virtually all the saw mills and factories on which this industry depended. The same year saw the first steps taken in the formation of what was a few years later to be a combination of most of the concerns in the cracker biscuit industry—the National Biscuit Company. Similarly, tobacco concerns began the process of consolidation which was one day to bring virtually the entire industry under a single management. James B. Duke had just finished a deliberate price war which had convinced most of the firms in the cigarette branch of the industry that independent competition was a too expensive luxury. Ninety per cent of this business was thrown together in a concern called the American Tobacco Company, with Duke as president. In ten more years, through ruthless competition and a monopoly on cigarette-making machines, the rest of the industry was to be whipped into line. Consolidation profits on this merger consisted of $15 million worth of common stock backed by nothing except the future profits of the combine.

By 1890 farmer members of the various branches of the Farmers' Alliance were especially clamoring for action at the national level. (Prairie farmers insisted that when the Plow Trust was formed the price of plows had doubled.) This demand was perhaps strongest in Minnesota where a unique sequence of events caused feeling to rise to an exceedingly high pitch. In April, while the executive committee of the Minnesota Alliance was in session, the Supreme Court handed down another critical decision. Munn v. Illinois had pronounced the doctrine that where a state could legally regulate a public utility, the state legislature is the "court of last resort" as to what constitutes a just as distinguished from a confiscatory rate. Now the justices had decided that such a principle would not do. Instead, they said, the question of rate reasonableness was a judicial and not a legislative matter.

The so-called Minnesota Rate Cases, it was to develop, did not cripple state regulation as much as was at first feared, although it was evident that the Court's decision would have been no different if the Interstate Commerce Commission had been involved rather than a state commission. But, not being clairvoyant and feeling deeply oppressed by the industrial economy, the Minnesota Alliance denounced the outcome of the Minnesota Rate Cases savagely. This decision, it was asserted, meant "the subjection of the people and the states to the unlimited control of the railroad corporations of this country," and a resolution was adopted stating that the Alliance would "appeal from this second Dred Scott decision to the people of the nation . . . with a request that they unite with us in an effort to amend the constitution so as to abolish this new slavery."

Perhaps Minnesota and other farmers took some comfort in the fact that even at that moment their appeal was receiving a public hearing. In Washington the Congress was debating a measure to provide federal legislation relative to the trust problem. But if farmers did take comfort in this fact, their hopes were largely misplaced. For in the nation's capital it was clear that the trust issue was to be scarcely more than a sideshow to the main event. The business interests were determined to increase the tariff and were preparing a legislative program oriented almost exclusively to that objective. Already the wheels were in full motion.

The Tariff Intervenes. The first phase of this program was carried out in the House Committee on Appropriations. Since the tariff controversy revolved primarily around the issue of surplus revenue, one of the most certain approaches was to increase government spending. The new Congress promptly authorized a spending program exceeding by more than $100 million the amount appropriated by the preceding Congress. Most of the increase was in government pensions where an over-enthusiastic administrator disbursed funds so lavishly that he had to be removed from office by President Harrison. And, moreover, this was the same President

TABLE 56. PRECAUTION AGAINST TARIFF REFORM

Year	Veterans' Pensions
	(Millions of dollars)
1871	34.4
1876	28.3
1881	50.1
1886	63.4
1891	124.4
1896	139.4

Source: Bureau of the Census, *Historical Statistics of the United States, 1789-1945*, pp. 299-300.

who was himself so anxious to see the surplus spent that he took the unprecedented step of urging a rivers and harbors bill on Congress.

Meanwhile work on the new tariff measure had commenced. Here the first step was the holding of hearings. It was not that Congress was eager to learn new facts on which a "scientific" tariff policy might be built; the need was rather to find out from the protected interests how high the tariff must be to reserve the American market for the American producer. Against the danger that rates would be demanded which would increase the government's revenue was placed the possibility that some rates could be put at a level so high that revenue would be decreased instead. (Appropriately, the bill was entitled "An act to reduce the revenue . . . .") In the finished bill this hope was in large part fulfilled.

Understandably these maneuverings were accompanied by misgivings in administration circles. For a number of reasons the western wing of the Republican party would have to be dealt with cautiously at this point, and the general agricultural depression was only one of these. Another was the western farmer's insistence that the tariff policy of the nation did not serve his best interests. In the preceding three years the government had spent almost $50 million in premiums alone in the process of buying bonds not subject to call in the open market, while over a somewhat longer period the debt had been scaled down so drastically that the number of bank notes in circulation had fallen almost 50 per cent in eight years. Before Republican leaders dared bring the tariff to the floor of the House it was clear that steps would have to be taken to counteract the antitariff views of many westerners.

Table 57. A Viewpoint on the Tariff

Year	National Bank Notes
	(Millions of dollars)
1882	352.5
1883	347.9
1884	330.7
1885	308.6
1886	307.7
1887	276.9
1888	245.3
1889	207.2
1890	181.6

Source: Bureau of the Census, *Historical Statistics of the United States, 1789-1945*, p. 275.

There were several possibilities, and it is characteristic of the management skill possessed by spokesmen for the business interests that none was missed. One point of attack, thus, was the fact that by 1890 farmers in general and western cattlemen in particular were especially up in arms over the trust problem. The dominant city in the meat packing business was now Chicago and here the Beef Trust (Armour, Swift, Morris, and Hammond) virtually controlled the price of beef to suit themselves—or at least so a Senate investigating committee reported. Not only were these concerns the largest producers, but they exercised considerable control over the stockyards, the stockyards railway companies, banking facilities in the stockyards district, and the refrigerator car business. Still worse, when the cattle farmer had sought to get out from under the power of the trust by, for example, shifting the center of the industry farther to the west, he had found on the one hand that it was almost impossible to overcome Chicago's economic advantages and on the other hand that the trust was also a powerful influence in other locations.

Western cattlemen, moreover, might not have been so anxious for anti-trust action except for the fact that their industry was in the throes of a major readjustment. Ever since the Civil War farmers of the range had, for the most part, been prosperous. Using to a large extent the public domain, which could be had at no cost, the rancher's debt problem was less critical than that of the prairie farmer, although his transportation problem was fully as acute. Since the land in use was public property, however, it could not be fenced for purposes of either scientific breeding of better meat types or limiting the number of cattle in the interest of a more wholesome development. Gradually the range became overstocked—a difficulty made all the more painful by the gradual westward movement of a "farmer's frontier" which, aided by the invention of barbed wire and the windmill (to say nothing of the Homestead Act and the intensive "colonization" work of the railroads), was slowly but surely making contact with the far western "miner's frontier." Squeezed between the homesteader (the bitterly hated "nester") on the one side and the desert on the other, the industry was vulnerable at best. In the middle of the 1880's an unusually severe winter was followed in quick succession by a dry summer and another disastrous winter. Depression in the industry was intense, and in 1890 it was in the middle of an adjustment which can with some accuracy be called the end of the "rancher's frontier." Painfully harassed, livestock farmers were in no mood to be trifled with.

A second group of westerners figured heavily in the preparations being made for passage of the McKinley Tariff. In the preceding two years six western states had been admitted to the Union, several of which were important producers of silver. In addition, certain of the older western states were also closely identified with the silver issue. As the price of silver continued to fall despite purchases under the Bland-Allison Act, these interests could be counted on to support a new silver purchase program. So too could those farmers who felt the need for more money in circulation.

Out of these several ingredients the Republicans painstakingly concocted an antidote for the tariff measure they were anxious to pass. Western cattlemen were offered an act designed to curb the consolidation tendencies so marked throughout the economy, and it was hoped that many other farmers would also bear with the tariff legislation they did not want in exchange for the trust legislation they wanted very badly. Western silver producers were given a law requiring the Treasury to purchase virtually the entire annual output of the nation's silver mines (four and a half million ounces every month) at a price substantially above the market, a measure which it was also hoped would make inflationist debtors feel more kindly toward the new tariff.

Both of these pieces of legislation, in their passage as well as in their content, bore plainly the mark of their origin. The Sherman Anti-Trust Act was given one negative vote in the House, none in the Senate. All during its progress through Congress, moreover, administration spokesmen were twitted about the obvious connection between the antitrust measure and the coming tariff bill. The Sherman Silver Purchase Act, on the other hand, received almost no negative votes from the Republican side of Congress despite the powerful sound money sentiment in the Republican East, while it received almost no affirmative votes from Democrats although the Democratic party was the more inflationist of the two. In addition, whereas the Bland-Allison Act had been an inflationist measure first and a silver subsidy second, the new law was a silver subsidy first and an inflationist measure second. This judgment arises not merely from the way the law worked out in practice. The revised measure greatly increased the amount of silver to be purchased, but it did not call for silver coinage.

And what was the nature of the revenue law thus dearly bought? In the first place, it took another large slice off the tobacco taxes as one way of reducing the revenue. Another surplus reduction provision was the complete abolition of the duty on sugar and its replacement by a government subsidy of 2 cents on every pound of sugar produced domestically. The bounty, incidentally, was not merely for the purpose of draining away more revenue, but also to subsidize the production of beet sugar—a new industry to be found in an infant status in several western states. These two sections of the McKinley Tariff were estimated to have reduced the revenue by more than $75 million annually. To these savings were then added the reduction brought about by putting some duties at so high a level that imports were almost completely choked off.

All along the line, including almost all agricultural products, protection was increased—duties being raised above the Civil War level. One special provision of the tariff sections of the law, however, is especially indicative of its underlying character. It had to do with tin plate. Heretofore almost none of this product had been produced in America. Despite this fact, a substantial duty was levied on tin plate on the condition that the levy would be removed if domestic output did not quickly become greater than imports. In other words, the tin-plate duty was under no circumstances to become merely a tax.

Was the antitrust law farmers were forced to be content with worth this sacrifice? Certainly its terms were sweeping enough. Every combination, contract, or conspiracy in restraint of trade in interstate commerce was declared to be illegal. From this standpoint, perhaps the only fault to be found with it was that the penalties were inadequate. What would a nominal fine amount to for one of these giant concerns, and what jury would put in prison an otherwise respectable corporation executive? In addition, the new law also stood under a legal cloud. The Supreme Court hurdle still had to be passed. Possibly the business interests were only taking a calculated but very narrow risk, confident that they were still secure within the protective arm of the judiciary.

The Shadow of Failure. But defects such as these were minor in comparison with another disability from which the Sherman Anti-Trust Act suffered. When the test came, when it was time for every proponent of trust reform to stand up and be counted, organized labor ignored the call. It is not to be supposed that there was no antagonism toward trusts among laborers as individuals. No doubt such publications as Henry George's *Progress and Poverty*, Edward Bellamy's *Looking Backward*, and Henry D. Lloyd's *Wealth Against Commonwealth* were read in laborers' homes with as much feeling as in the homes of farmers. Yet the fact remains that when the great architect of the American Federation of Labor, Samuel Gompers, was approached on the matter of this legislation while it was still pending, he was unenthusiastic to the point of being opposed. This reaction is easy enough to understand in retrospect, and it sheds additional light on the deepest roots of the ideas which have gone into the modern labor movement. For that reason it can best be understood in the context of the death struggle being fought out between the American Federation of Labor and the Knights of Labor.

The Knights of Labor, speaking primarily for those workers who had made the least successful adjustment to economic society as it then existed, was directing its efforts toward bringing about fundamental changes in that society. But for the very reason that these workers had not yet secured economic power in their own right, they were dependent upon using the power possessed by the skilled trades to achieve the "utopian" ends they had in mind. Thus what was essentially involved here was the use of the strategic position of the skilled worker for the benefit of the unskilled.

Samuel Gompers' organization operated on almost the opposite premise, as would be expected from the fact that it spoke for those workers who had most successfully adjusted to the existing situation. But since the skilled workers had achieved their success by using their strategic power in particular ways, they were not easily convinced that they could be even more successful if they would use their power differently. It exaggerates only a little to assert that the American Federation of Labor was based on the use of the position of the skilled worker at the expense of the unskilled.

The very organizational structure of the Federation makes plain its underlying premises, and its name is also suggestive on this point. Here was no strong central governing agency such as the Knights had developed. Rather, each trade was given almost full autonomy, with the top officials performing only the loosest of "federative" functions (such as protecting every trade against the existence in the Federation of any rival union engaged in the same trade). Thus it was recognized that the labor union was to be an "uplift" movement having a very narrow base, the relatively small trade rather than the mass of laborers. So ingrained was this doctrine in the philosophy of the skilled trades that they did not even concede the need for a strong intertrade organization until the Knights began successfully encroaching upon their domain in ways that isolated trades could not readily combat. Thus the American Federation of Labor early recognized that it was just as basic to protect laborers from other laborers as to protect laborers from employers.

In terms of the Sherman Anti-Trust Law the implications of all this are obvious. A trust is also an economic "uplift" movement with a very narrow base, the members of the combine. Businessmen in forming trusts were doing precisely what the trade unions desired to do. For labor to protest against the right of business to seek economic security in combination was to make their own position in the economy hopelessly vulnerable, and this was no less true even though business combines were at the moment making labor's organization endeavors extremely difficult. Another side to this was the fact that, under prevailing circumstances, an anticombination law might be applied against them and not against their business rivals. Still another facet was that a strong trade union, however much it might achieve against an ordinary business concern, might do even better against a highly profitable trust. Certainly labor had not achieved as much against little employers as it was now achieving against big ones.

These observations can be put in broader perspective, too. America in 1890 was in the middle of a major economic transition, a transition from an agricultural economy of abundance to an industrial economy of scarcity—from an economy in which goods are produced for use to one in which goods are produced primarily for exchange (profit). Such an economy puts a premium on the ability of possessors of goods or factors to withhold their possessions from the market and thus raise their prices.[2] Heretofore neither laborer nor farmer had really accepted the new society, putting a large proportion of their resources instead into the promotion of different sorts of utopias. Business, on the other hand, had long since frankly accepted this situation; the trust was simply the most advanced stage of that recognition.

To be sure, business had not created the new order; the machine had done that. But the new order could not be secure until either labor or agriculture joined the business interests in making it effective. The fight between the utopian Knights of Labor and the nonutopian Federation of Labor was the first clear indication that labor might be the interest that would make the new society "official."

Much more than a struggle between contrary philosophies of the American labor movement was therefore at stake in this contest. At issue also was the entire character of American economic society, the direction which future evolution was to take. Already, it is now safe to say, history had written the outcome. In the short run the success of the Federation over the Knights was written in the fact that the Order's brief moment of power was made possible only by a depression which temporarily weakened many trades. The longer run outcome, the victory of "conservative" trade unionism over "radical" revolutionism, was written in the fact that from the very beginning labor utopianism had invariably disappeared in any economic situation in which collective bargaining could flourish. In short, the significant fact in 1890 was not so much that the American Federation of Labor did not support the Sherman Anti-Trust Act. Rather the significant fact was that the Federation defeated the Knights. The year 1890 saw the trade unions using their energies to launch a major collective bargaining drive to secure the eight-hour day (perhaps the real beginning of the movement which was one day to make eight hours the standard in American industry) instead of supporting antitrust legislation.

The aftermath of the McKinley Tariff is itself of some interest. Only the abolition of sugar duties could be pointed to as a concession to consumers, and by what can only be referred to as an error in tactics this was

[2] Where goods are produced for use, their value is roughly proportional to their volume. Where goods are produced for exchange, on the other hand, their value is determined as much by their unit price as by their volume. Put differently, the total value of a stock of goods may, under certain circumstances, be increased by reducing the number of units of which it is composed. The trick here is to make the demand for one's product *inelastic*, and then govern output in such a way that price times quantity will be a maximum figure.

postponed until the following year. Duty increases, on the other hand, were scheduled to go into effect October 1, 1890. In November, 1890, the nation's citizens went to the polls to vote for Congressmen and Senators. The result was the most disastrous election defeat the Republicans had ever experienced. It would appear that the concessions made were, even so, not adequate.

No one could yet tell what the effect of the antitrust law was to be. But it was soon even more clear that the burden of effective antitrust work was thereafter to fall on the federal government rather than the states. Only one reason, moreover, was the fact that a trust of any consequence operated across state boundaries, and hence was engaged in interstate commerce. The other major reason was more subtle but equally important. In January, 1891, the Sugar Trust abandoned the trust device altogether. A new corporation was formed which issued its own securities, using the proceeds to buy up a controlling interest in the constituent companies. No change in business methods or centralization of control was involved; the only change was in legal structure. Henceforth the American Sugar Refining Company, not a group of trustees, would call the tune in the sugar industry.

Of course, any state had full legal power to deny the incorporation privilege to a corporation whose charter sought the right to hold stock in another corporation, and indeed every state had initially taken this position. However, New Jersey had lately concluded that it was good policy to encourage corporations to reside within her boundaries rather than to frighten them away with restrictive legislation and narrowly written charters. As a consequence New Jersey laws no longer prevented an extension of the trust device by way of the holding company route. Already the American Tobacco Company had made this important discovery. Now the Sugar Trust was able to get out from under its legal difficulties in the same way. A few years later even the Standard Oil Company was to find a safer haven in New Jersey.

Perhaps the most significant thing about the stand taken by New Jersey was this. As a result, laxity in incorporation laws in one state set the pattern for the legislation of other states, not merely because a corporation could obtain a charter in the most lax state and operate under it anywhere else, but also because other states anxious to secure charter fees and annual taxes were tempted to enter into competition with one another to see which could relax its restrictions the most. This in fact is what happened, although not all states made a bid for the prize. There is some doubt among scholars of this period of American history as to whether New Jersey maintained her lead or whether little Delaware overtook her. In any event, the race was a close one and after the middle of the 1890's a corporation could secure a charter in some state almost no matter what it proposed to do. These developments held little comfort for opponents of American trusts.

Reform on the Land Front. One other victory was won by reformers during this period. For years the fire of workers and farmers had been directed at the nation's land laws and their administration. What these laws had theoretically been intended to accomplish was an opportunity for land tenants and oppressed workers to find freedom from dependent relationships on the public domain. Unfortunately, this legislation had operated in almost every conceivable way to defeat the objectives sought by early land reformers.

In the first place, some of their ideals were unrealistic. Many of those most in need of help were workers earning, say, $250 a year. Such people could not easily keep their families from hunger without other members of their families working; still less could they take a half-year's salary to transport their families to the site of free government land, to say nothing of the capital required to make an effective start in agriculture. Furthermore, agriculture was already a highly skilled occupation, especially where the use of the new agricultural machinery was required, and to undertake to make a living at it without prior experience was a quick form of economic suicide. In the absence of legislative provision of assistance to urban workers desiring to relocate themselves, homestead legislation could not be of much aid to the laborer. Actually, and still more fundamentally, a shift of city folk to the farm was in the last half of the nineteenth century much like trying to swim against a strong current. For every worker who left his city employment to make a success at homesteading, probably ten farmers' sons successfully moved from farm to city. Thus perversely had the so-called "safety-valve" theory operated in practice.

In the second place, no care was taken to prevent homestead land from being used for nonhomestead purposes. Thus homestead patents could be commuted to cash purchase after proving settlement or cultivation (and indeed the old Pre-emption Act had continued in force throughout the entire homestead period to date). This provision, coupled with lax requirements as to what constituted proof of settlement or cultivation, opened the door to the accumulation of large tracts by speculators or others, which land could then be sold at the going price. Sometimes this procedure had at least the justification that in some parts of the public domain one hundred and sixty acres was not enough for a farmer to make a satisfactory living on. More often, however, there was not even this excuse for monopoly, and in retrospect it almost seems that abuse was the rule rather than the exception.

In the third place, other land legislation was passed which made possible the compounding of these abuses. In general this other legislation was for the valid purposes of permitting larger holdings where the character of the region made a more extensive utilization necessary and exacting a price for lands which, because they contained timber or mineral resources, were especially valuable. But the price asked in these latter cases was typically so far below the real worth of the resources available as to encourage their wasteful use. Moreover, the larger unit laws were often fraudulently applied to land suitable for homesteading in smaller plots. And finally, it was possible (although almost never legitimate) to secure a large plot of land by taking advantage of the provisions of several laws.

The complication of as well as the abuses brought about by supplementary land laws can be pointedly illustrated. A Timber Culture Act had been passed, allowing homesteaders to apply for an additional one hundred and sixty acres on condition that forty acres be planted to trees within four years. The Desert Land Act made an entire section (six hundred and forty acres) available on payment of a nominal sum on condition that it be irrigated within three years. One hundred and sixty acres "unfit for cultivation" were opened for purchase at appraisal value by the Timber and Stone Act for the exploitation of the timber and stone found thereon. It is easy to see that if the conditions imposed were not enforced, and if the land thus disposed of was not actually land inappropriate for homesteading, the homestead dream could easily fall victim to capitalist greed. In 1890 it was possible for a single settler to secure almost two full sections of land without violating the *letter* of the law.

TABLE 58. DEFEAT FOR AN IDEAL

Years	Homestead Entries [1]	All Other Entries [2]
	(Millions of acres)	
1871-75	6.2	23.1
1876-80	11.5	21.4
1881-85	12.5	78.2
1886-90	16.3	73.7

[1] Final.
[2] Original.
Source: Bureau of the Census, *Historical Statistics of the United States, 1789-1945*, p. 120.

In short, land legislation and administration after the Civil War had been simply another episode in the eagerness for rapid expansion the nation had exhibited from its earliest beginnings. As such, of course, it was only a continuation of the policy of liberalization which had been gradually developing before the Civil War. There was, however, this subtle but basic difference. Before the Civil War, liberalization had been in the interest of western farmers. After the Civil War, although the western farmer was by no means wholly excluded, the principal beneficiary of liberalization was the eastern capitalist. Just as banking policy and railroad legislation made their contribution to the rapid expansion of the nation at whatever cost, so too did land policy contribute to this same end at the cost of making immensely rich resources available for private profit.

Whether such an approach was or was not in the public interest is difficult to say. Certain it is, however, that the "common people" (laborers and farmers) had long resented the policy being followed, and in 1891 this agitation ended in a limited victory for reformers. Cash sales by the government were ended, a limit of three hundred and twenty acres for any one individual was provided, and the Pre-emption Act was repealed. Not all abuses were thereby ended, and in view of the fact that the best lands had already been taken up, much of the damage was already done. But in these days when the nonbusiness interests were winning few victories at best, even this much was gratifying.

Of course, to the farmer a land policy victory of whatever proportions could not rank with the antitrust and railroad victories he thought he had achieved. Under the circumstances, therefore, it is not surprising that farmers were looking forward to even greater victories in the future. When the mirage lifted, they were to find themselves more hopelessly ensnared than ever before.

QUESTIONS FOR DISCUSSION

1. What evils was the Interstate Commerce Act intended to eliminate?
2. How was the tariff related to the nation's money supply?
3. Why was the nation able to pass a law regulating railroads in 1887 but unable to reduce the tariff in 1888?
4. What was the legal problem with which the trusts were confronted?
5. How did the business interests secure the votes required to enact the McKinley Tariff?
6. What were the principal points of difference between the American Federation of Labor and the Knights of Labor?
7. Did organized labor make a "wise" choice on the matter of antitrust policy?
8. Were the innovations introduced into incorporation laws in the latter part of the nineteenth century of benefit to the country or were they injurious?
9. What were the major problems associated with land policy at the end of the century? Was there any advantage in "locking the stable door" at this late date?

Chapter 25

TRIAL BY FIRE

1891	First signs of impending economic difficulties.
1892	Populist party formally organized.
	Homestead strike.
	Cleveland elected President again.
1893	"Panic of 1893."
	Sherman Silver Purchase Act repealed.
1894	Wilson-Gorman Tariff.
	"Coxey's Army."
	Pullman Strike.
1895	Sugar Trust exonerated by the Supreme Court.
	Government's use of an injunction against Debs upheld by the Supreme Court.
	Income tax declared unconstitutional.
1896	William McKinley elected President.

While the agrarian attack on the nation's corporations and its monetary system was going forward, the economy was enjoying the high point of its greatest prosperity and expansion to date. In approximately a dozen

TABLE 59. INDEX TO EXPANSION

Year	Fuel Production: Petroleum	Fuel Production: Coal: Bituminous	Fuel Production: Coal: Anthracite
	(Trillions of B. t. u.)		
1829	–	3	4
1849	–	64	109
1869	25	415	464
1889	211	2,507	1,239
1909	1,099	9,949	2,205
1929	6,044	14,017	2,008

Source: Bureau of the Census, *Historical Statistics of the United States, 1789-1945*, p. 155.

years national wealth had increased by more than $20 billion (50 per cent), railroad mileage had doubled, manufacturing output had increased 40 per cent, steel output had increased from one million to five million tons (and the United States had become the world's leading producer of this product), and for the first time the nation's exports exceeded $1 billion in a single year. During this period, moreover, farm prices increased almost 15 per cent, and real wages rose by about the same amount.

Economic Skies Darken. Of course, there was nothing about the pressure for reform which converted this expansion into the most painful depression yet. Such rapid development could not have gone on indefinitely in any event. Financial resources had been extended to the limit, and in some lines, particularly in railroad building, overexpansion had again been a part of the growth process. Thus the economy was vulnerable, and so interconnected had various parts of the economy become that the resulting deflation was sure to be severe. Moreover, the national banking system could be counted on to magnify rather than absorb such shocks as might be encountered. When to these facts is added the sharp conflict over the nation's money mechanism, it is not surprising that a painful liquidation was in the offing.

The first shock came in the form of the failure of Baring Brothers in London, still a prominent English banking concern and one doing a large business in American securities. The result was a flurry of liquidation abroad that caused a brief but wholesale dumping here of foreign-held stocks and bonds. In the first six months of 1891 some $70 million in gold was exported, and the Treasury's gold reserve fell alarmingly. There were, however, no major consequences of this brief panic, for a huge grain crop in this country coupled with shortages abroad turned the foreign exchanges in our favor in the latter part of the year and thus eased the money market. Some of the most shaky business enterprises in the country were forced to the wall, although too few to make this a genuine readjustment process. Among those concerns narrowly escaping destruction was the George Westinghouse Electric & Manufacturing Company in Pittsburgh.

Even though this event did not significantly alter the economic situation, it did set in motion a train of other events which was to have profound consequences a little later. Prior to 1891 the Treasury had regularly paid its clearinghouse balances in gold and received most of its customs receipts in the same form. However, concerned over the decline in the gold reserve held for the redemption of paper money, the Treasury began settling its balances with paper money. Simultaneously, whether or not as a result of the government's action, banks began increasingly to use paper money in settling their own interbank balances. It was only a short step from this to the remitting of customs receipts to the Treasury in this currency as well. A first step had been taken toward abandonment of the gold standard.

It is not easy to judge the extent to which these moves were caused by the silver legislation of preceding years. The banks could justify their action by insisting that when the government ceased to remit gold they were forced to conserve their supplies for foreign trade purposes, while the government could defend its step by pointing to the unfavorable balance of payments. This approach would exonerate the silver legislation of all blame. But it could also be maintained with some reason that the banks began to pay balances in paper because of the excessive supply of currency, and that the unfavorable balance of payments was primarily the result of foreign hoarding in fear of currency depreciation in America. On this view the whole fault would lie with the attempt to "do something" about silver.

Whichever view is taken, one thing is certain. These developments began to focus attention on the consequences of the silver situation for the gold standard to an extent heretofore unknown. The government was, after all, regularly adding to the currency supply by many millions of dollars each year—without any regard for the currency needs of the nation. If this augmented currency were needed in the carrying on of the nation's business, well and good, except that an increase in the amount of paper money redeemable in gold would necessitate an increase in the gold reserve. On the other hand, if ordinary exchange relationships could not absorb the additional currency, the excess would certainly be used to deplete the gold reserve. In either case the gold standard was steadily being watered down and hence made more vulnerable to fluctuations in public confidence.

Furthermore, there were special aspects of this situation which made the nation's monetary base particularly unstable. Under the law the silver certificates being used to purchase silver could be redeemed in either gold or silver. The Treasury's insistence on gold redemption of course made silverites angry at the discrimination against silver, while the option in the hands of the Secretary might easily become the basis for a belief that silver redemption was to be instituted. Both of these factors contributed greatly to the financial difficulties so soon to threaten the credit of the nation. And underlying both of them was the additional fact that the government's revenue had been reduced below the safety point in the frantic effort to make the McKinley Tariff appear more logical to rank and file citizens.

In 1892 the events of the preceding year were almost exactly repeated. The first six months saw a drain of gold from the United States, and the last half saw this flow again reversed by a heavy export of foodstuffs. During this year, however, the financial problem became especially acute when the Secretary of the Treasury announced that a deficit was pending for the following year. It was at this point that a shaky financial situation began to be complicated still further by the withering away of the industrial boom, and this development was in turn accompanied by one of the most bitter and significant conflicts between labor and capital to date.

Defeat at Homestead. For two years the price of steel had been edging downward, falling to $22 for a ton of steel billets in early 1892. At the Homestead works of the Carnegie Steel Company, an agreement between the skilled workers and management was scheduled to expire June 30. Under this contract wages were to rise and fall with the price of steel, except that a fall in steel prices below $25 a ton would not be reflected in reduced wages. In the circumstances it is understandable why workers wanted to retain favorable contract provisions and why the company wanted to rewrite unfavorable provisions to its advantage.

These factors, however, only partly explain the bitterness of the Homestead conflict. Much of the rest can be understood only in the light of the fact that Henry Clay Frick had recently become chairman of the Carnegie board of directors. A hard-headed, heavy-fisted, highly competent nineteenth-century capitalist (America's "coke king"), Frick yielded to none in his antagonism toward labor unions. To him, thus, winning more favorable contract terms was probably second to his desire to destroy the Amalgamated Association of Iron, Steel, and Tin Workers, no doubt the most powerful trade union in the history of the American labor movement. (Had Andrew Carnegie not been in Europe, this ugly episode would probably not have taken place.) The meeting of such a union in mortal combat with a modern-type manufacturing corporation—the first such encounter in the history of the country—could not have been other than a major event in the nation's economic development.

The company's offer as a basis for renewal was a reduction of the sliding-scale minimum wage to $22, and a termination of the new contract December 31 rather than June 30. This last would give the company the advantage of negotiating the next agreement during the slack season rather than the busiest one. On May 30 the company delivered an ultimatum to the workers saying that if an agreement were not signed by June 29, the company would treat with each laborer as an individual. The last conference was held June 23, at which time the company raised its minimum to $23 and the union lowered its minimum to $24. Thus when on June 29 the strike began it was understood on both sides that the only real issue was the existence of the union.

Even before negotiations ceased, however, Frick had arranged for the employment of three hundred Pinkerton detectives as guards. Whether the workers feared these guards were really intended to function as strikebreakers, or to act as bodyguards to strikebreakers imported from downtown Pittsburgh, is not certain. But when the Pinkerton men arrived the men of Homestead endeavored to keep them away, and a pitched gun battle ensued in which several men were killed and a number more seriously wounded. For almost two weeks open war existed between the population of Homestead and the company in its efforts to gain full control over its property. After the Pinkerton men had been driven off there was no further disorder, but despite that fact units of the state militia were dispatched to Homestead, where they stayed for the duration of the strike. Taking advantage of the restoration of order, the company resumed production as far as possible by hiring nonunion men.

Workers in other Carnegie mills also went out on strike, following the lead of Homestead. Over a period of five months the strike went on, only to be called off November 20 when the union treasury gave out and a hard Pennsylvania winter loomed just ahead. Most of the men who struck returned to work, but not until they had given up their union status. The price of defeat, thus, was the loss of whatever security the union was able to provide. What was true at Homestead, moreover, was true also in other Carnegie mills, and since Carnegie's company was a pace-setter in the entire industry, the same result occurred generally in steel manufacturing concerns. In short, labor made the bitter discovery that even with its newly developed principles and under highly favorable circumstances it was not yet a match for "big" business. It is ironical in retrospect to note that this crushing of organized labor in the steel industry was a preface to the greatest development that industry had yet enjoyed. For example, it was in 1892 that the great expansion based on the fabulous ore deposits in the Lake Superior area began.

The Homestead controversy, together with several smaller labor upsets, furnished an important part of the background for the presidential election of 1892. This was another tariff-oriented contest, although less exclusively so than four years earlier, and once again Grover Cleveland and Benjamin Harrison were the principal contestants. Possibly certain laborers, especially iron and steel workers, felt less unkindly toward Cleveland's tariff views after their recent experience. They had seen all too clearly that tariff protection did not necessarily mean labor protection. Moreover, many other citizens were still outraged by the McKinley Tariff and the Treasury discrimination against silver. Out of these and other ingredients Cleveland achieved a comfortable victory over his Republican opponent, and prepared to accomplish some of the things Democrats had long insisted should be done. No doubt the item highest on this list was tariff reform.

Panic and Depression. Unfortunately ill fortune dogged the footsteps of tariff reform at this point. Approximately one week before Cleveland's inauguration the first signs of approaching panic appeared in the form of the failure of the Philadelphia and Reading Railroad Company, one of the giants of the business world. Put together by the Drexel-Morgan interests, the combine of which the Reading was the center included the New York Central Railroad, the Lehigh Valley Railroad, and numerous road and coal companies. Heavily loaded with fixed charges, the company was unable to withstand the decline in general demand now setting in, and to say that the country was shocked at this turn of events is to put the matter mildly indeed.

The financial world and the nation at large, however, promptly recovered from this disaster. Americans are notoriously hard to convince that a period of economic readjustment is due. A second shock to public confidence soon appeared—in the money field. In March and April the unprecedented amount of $25 million of gold was exported, and the Treasury's gold reserve fell below $100 million (the widely accepted level of minimum safety) for the first time. Precipitated in part, no doubt, by the liquidation of American securities held abroad, the consequence of this threat to the nation's credit was an accelerated tendency to hoard gold. From this point the vicious circle of liquidation could only spread—in all directions.

In May came the greatest blow of all. The National Cordage Company, the Cordage Trust, was taken over by its creditors. This failure produced a complex set of reactions. On the one hand, there was an understandable anxiety in the knowledge that such a concern could be so badly managed and so economically frail. On the other hand, there was a tendency to associate the trusts with the panic and hence for public resentment against consolidations to grow stronger. This last was no doubt a misunderstanding of cause-effect relationships, but it is true that the failure of the Cordage Trust opened the floodgates of deflation. Everywhere one turned, banks, railroads, manufacturing concerns, mortgage companies, and wholesale and retail firms were falling by the wayside. In the year 1893 alone more than fifteen thousand commercial houses, some six hundred banks and other financial institutions, and more than fifty railroads went under. Before the ensuing depression had spent itself, one-fourth of the nation's railway mileage was in bankruptcy, railroad construction had virtually ceased, and 60 per cent of all railroad stocks had ceased to pay dividends.

June saw the financial net inexorably tightening. In that month the British closed the Indian mint to silver coinage, an action resulting in a marked fall in the world price of silver. Silverites, still seizing on every opportunity to advance their cause, were prompted by this turn of events to increase agitation for silver redemption—that is, a bimetallic money standard. This in and of itself was sufficient to start a rumor that the new Democratic Secretary of the Treasury was going to take advantage of the authority written into the Sherman Silver Purchase Act to do just that. Gold hoarding, domestic and foreign, could only increase under such circumstances, and the Treasury's gold reserve continued to fall.

Certainly the new administration did not institute a policy of silver redemption, and apparently never had any intention of so doing. Whether such a policy would have accentuated the panic as many still insist can only be conjectured. Similarly whether Cleveland could have accomplished as much as he did by attacking the revenue problem first rather than the money question is equally uncertain. There was, to be sure, ample reason for turning to the revenue first, because as the government began to run a deficit, gold payments to meet operating expenses became an additional drain on the gold reserve. It was perhaps not generally understood that the Treasury had been able to "hoard" silver in the 1880's while still maintaining the gold standard only because of the persistent surplus. What is certain is that Cleveland's own "sound money" inclinations were too strong to allow him to pass up an opportunity to eradicate the silver heresy. And it is surely not unkind to suggest that the money action taken made no visible contribution to the nation's economic health, whether or not this was due to the fact that the "evil" consequences of the silver policy were already in operation.

TABLE 60. CHALLENGE TO THE GOLD STANDARD

Year	Government Surplus (+) or Deficit (−)	Net Gold Exports
	(Millions of dollars)	
1891	+26.8	68.1
1892	+ 9.9	0.5
1893	+ 2.3	87.5
1894	−61.2	4.5
1895	−31.5	30.1
1896	−14.0	78.9

Source: Bureau of the Census, *Historical Statistics of the United States, 1789-1945*, pp. 244 and 296.

Unwilling to wait until Congress convened for its regular session, Cleveland called a special session for the express purpose of repealing the Sherman Silver Purchase Act. His agrarian supporters were furious—and rebellious—long before they arrived in Washington, and agrarians constituted the bulk of the strength behind the administration. (Was it not obvious, they insisted, that the panic was caused, not by the purchase of silver by the Treasury, but by the impounding of money in the Treasury?) In the House, where the power of the industrial East was most pronounced, repeal was the work of only a few days. But in the Senate, the stronghold of the western farmer's influence, the response to the President's demand was defiant hostility. Not until late October, after Cleveland had exhausted every resource at his disposal, was a favorable vote achieved. The repeal measure as finally passed, although winning for the President the ill will of much of his party, was thereafter claimed by Cleveland as his most valuable service to the country.

Perhaps it was. Many since then have agreed with that judgment. Be that as it may, however, the more immediate consequence was that it was a bruised and battered Democratic party which turned next to the critical problem of the government's finances. At one time the noble intent had been to produce a more equitable tax system, to destroy the structure of special privileges built into the protective tariff system. Now the time had come to translate that high ideal into reality under circumstances which could not have been more unfavorable.

Intraparty discord carried over from the money controversy was probably the smallest difficulty. A more basic one was the fact that only a revenue surplus could offer a favorable opportunity for tax reform, whereas the existing situation was the reverse. Most important of all, however, was the make-up of the Democratic majority in the Senate. The second Democratic Senate since the Civil War contained such a bare majority that no revenue measure could be passed at all without the affirmative votes of forty-three out of forty-four Democratic Senators. Furthermore, Louisiana, still a part of the "solid" Democratic South, had always felt a strong protectionist interest on account of its valuable sugar industry. Other protectionist spots were also to be found in the areas represented by Democratic Senators.

Of course the task was impossible, but the struggle was a memorable one. To the genuine reform measure passed by the House, the Senate added more than six hundred amendments, most of them raising duties above the level in the House bill. Although some reductions were achieved (such as placing wool and lumber on the free list), the completed measure made Cleveland so angry that he let it become law without his signature.

The reasons for this attitude were not far to seek. Once again sugar was taxed. This could not have been avoided, of course, in view of the revenue situation, but it was unfortunate that the major visible achievement of the Democratic tariff was an increase in the price of sugar. Still more unfortunate was the fact that the Sugar Trust had been allowed a differential of one-fourth of a cent a pound on refined sugar.[1] Some comfort could be

[1] By placing a tariff on refined sugar larger than that on raw sugar, an advantage was given to the refining of sugar domestically rather than outside the country. The result was the importation of raw sugar for domestic refinement. Furthermore, because there is so little waste (such as impurities which it would be uneconomical to transport over a long distance) in the refining process, even one-fourth of a cent a pound was significant.

taken in the fact that this differential was smaller than that allowed under McKinley's tariff, but any differential at all was most inappropriate for a party which had vigorously denounced exploitation by trusts.

Only one real accomplishment could be pointed to by tax reform enthusiasts. As one of its key provisions the 1894 tax law provided for an income tax on all incomes in excess of four thousand dollars per year (corporation or personal), the first such tax since the business interests had succeeded in eliminating the one levied during the Civil War. At long last a step, if only a short one, had been taken toward a more even distribution of the tax burden.

The Depths of Despair. As always depression and inadequate relief measures formed an environment within which unrest of various kinds found much to feed upon. Although prices fell, wages often fell more rapidly, and union members especially were maddened at the sight of the wage scales they had worked so hard to develop being shattered before their very eyes. Not only, too, were many employed workers suffering a reduction in real wages, but unemployment rose to levels hitherto unknown. The year 1894 saw unemployment reach the staggering total of four million, and almost one million laborers involved in some kind of industrial warfare.

Moreover, industrial upheaval was not the only channel through which a growing despair was expressed. As men and women all over the nation weighed the economic order the business interests were creating and found it seriously wanting, a contagious unrest led "armies" of the discontented to form for the purpose of personally presenting their grievances to the government in Washington. By far the most famous of these "industrial armies" was that led by Jacob S. Coxey of Ohio. Today the term "Coxey's Army" is little more than an epithet of opprobrium, and certainly there was in these "marches on Washington" little of the kind of wisdom needed for a solution to the social problem they represented. In the context of its times, however, this phenomenon was a dramatic indication of a social failure of the gravest kind. No better evidence could be had of the satisfaction of capitalism with itself in the last decade of the nineteenth century than the contemptuous way these malcontents were treated.

One of the most significant facts about "Coxey's Army" was that Coxey himself was independently wealthy. Thus it was in no sense to redress personal grievances that he trudged the long and weary distance separating Ohio from the nation's capital. (In point of fact, Coxey made the trip mounted on one of the beautiful white horses for the breeding of which he was famous all over the Middle West.) Rather his motivation was a deep concern about society's underlying problems and the men then being crushed by the failure of society to solve them. His ideas as to what the government should do to improve conditions, of course, could only have been termed absurd by the world in which he lived. But in these days, days in which ideas such as those represented by John Maynard Keynes have gained a large measure of respectability, they seem much less ridiculous. His proposal was the employing of the unemployed in the building of highways and other public improvements, the work to be paid for by the use of irredeemable paper money. A cynical view of Coxey's efforts was that he used the despair of the unemployed to win free advertising for a "Good Roads" bill for which he had long been contending and which occasioned much discussion in Washington while the march was in progress.

It perhaps goes without saying that the "industrial armies" were not successful. Coxey reached Washington with some four hundred men, far fewer than he had intended. The "army" was allowed to parade, although not on the Capitol grounds, and several men, including Coxey, were finally arrested for walking on the Capitol grass. With this the "army" disbanded and its members began the difficult task of getting back home. Simultaneously other "armies" were beginning to march only to meet a similar fate. But it is worth emphasizing that at precisely the moment when Coxey and his fellow leaders were being arrested for "trespassing" on the Capitol grounds, the Capitol itself was swarming with the paid agents of industrial interests seeking to defeat the tariff reduction bill then pending. Clearly the sense of social and governmental responsibility which must ultimately develop in an industrial society had not yet progressed very far in America.

There were no long-range consequences of the marching "armies" of 1894, at least of a direct nature. Indirectly, however, a connection can be seen between these events and another one taking place in the same year, and the common link was to have profound ramifications for American history in later years.

Eugene V. Debs had originally been Secretary-Treasurer of the Brotherhood of Locomotive Firemen. In that position he had seen repeated strike failures where only one trade was involved, and he had determined that the only solution was to bring all railway workers into a single union. Putting these views into an action framework, Debs was largely instrumental in establishing a new organization for this purpose—the American Railway Union.

In March, 1894, the employees of the Pullman Palace Car Company, located at Pullman, Illinois, voted to join the new organization, only one example among many of the erosion of the position of the American Federation of Labor in the face of deep depression. Soon thereafter a select committee of Pullman workers met with company officials to request at least a partial restoration of a series of devastating wage reductions.

The company refused, the next day firing three members of the committee, and the workers elected to go out on strike.

No doubt this action was ill-considered, for industrialist George Pullman had every advantage. First, the principal work done at Pullman was car construction, and the depression had already bitten so deeply into that activity that the company's first response to the strike was simply to close down its operation until further notice. Second, Pullman the town was a unique and magnificent experiment in employer-employee paternalism, a city modern, clean, and well kept, but owned and controlled by the company. Within its confines no employee was permitted to own property, and every rental agreement contained a ten-day termination clause. The company's second response to the strike was to begin eviction proceedings against workers who could not pay their rent—a rent which had not been reduced as wages fell.

The workers were helpless. Unless pressure could be brought against Pullman in some other way, the strike was already lost. At a meeting of the American Railway Union in June it was agreed that all other railway employee members of the larger union would cease handling Pullman cars unless the company would consent to arbitration. When the company refused, a sympathy strike (a sort of secondary boycott) was put into effect. Immediately the union found itself pitted against the General Managers' Association, an organization composed of the major railroads operating in and through Chicago. Backed by such powerful allies, the Pullman Company paid its regular 8 per cent dividend and refused to make any concessions.

The issue was joined when the railroads decided to couple Pullman cars in regular trains in such a way that they could not be separated without property destruction. Thus in refusing to handle Pullman cars, railway workers ended up by refusing to handle any train in which Pullman cars were thus included—even mail trains. The result was a general tie-up of railway transportation over a wide area, with many members of the railway brotherhoods joining in even though these organizations were opposed to the strike. Although no part of the plan of the strike, a lawless element in Chicago used the unrest and agitation as an opportunity to plunder, burn, and destroy property in much the same way as twenty years earlier. In all, damage estimated at $80 millions was done. On July 7, the strike already lost, Debs and other officers were indicted and arrested. Six days later they were charged with contempt of court for disobeying an injunction aimed to prevent them from inducing railway employees to strike.

A very special significance attaches to this injunction in American economic history. As the strength of labor organizations had grown, industrial discipline had steadily deteriorated—from the standpoint of employ ers. The practice of *collective* bargaining was less favorable to the capitalist than the *individual* bargaining it was replacing. Yet, since Commonwealth v. Hunt, the old doctrine of conspiracy had become progressively less useful to employers in labor disputes. What was needed was a substitute device, one which would put the shadow of illegality on collective action by workers and thus provide a basis for terminating or preventing strikes by legal action. This would, of course, have the advantage of putting the worker clearly in the wrong in any violence which took place.

Such a device was the injunction, a virtual reincarnation of the conspiracy technique. The theory was that justice required the prevention, before the fact, of strike damage to property where such damage threatened to be irreparable. In a strike situation the property involved was not, of course, physical property, because destruction of physical property was already a criminal offense. Rather the property referred to was the profitable relationship between the producer and his customers. Obviously these are threatened by a strike, and just as obviously such damage might turn out to be irreparable. Logical enough as far as it goes, this legal legerdemain makes the by no means obvious assumption that only capitalists and not laborers have intangible "property" rights in ordinary economic relationships.

An evolution had been taking place in this direction for a number of years. Slowly but surely the necessary legal precedents were being established. In the processes by which the Pullman strike was stopped by the federal government, as well as in their success, the new institution reached a natural fruition.

At first it appeared that this weapon could not be used at all. Governor Altgeld of Illinois stubbornly insisted that federal intervention was not necessary. The pressure on the government mounted, however, as the General Managers' Association complained more and more loudly. Finally Richard Olney, a prominent corporation lawyer and Cleveland's Attorney General, was able to convince Cleveland that the carriage of the mail and interstate commerce gave Washington not only a basis but a responsibility for acting. Already Olney had had much success with injunctions in dealing with the "industrial armies," and the injunctions associated with the Pullman strike grew out of these experiences. Thirty-six hundred deputies were sworn in by the federal marshal in Chicago and alerted for action, many, significantly enough, selected, armed, and paid by the railroads. (It was thought that railroad men could more easily discover who the strike leaders were, and take appropriate action against them.) It was this clumsy and biased action by the government which, as much as anything else, gave rise to the violence in Chicago. Later, on July 6, United States troops arrived. The following day the arrests were made and the strike was over. For the first time a major labor dispute had been terminated almost entirely by means of an injunction. The labor injunction had come of age.

Although, as with many another lesson, overlearning through repetition was necessary, the Pullman dispute and its outcome contained two important lessons for labor. First, most of the workers involved in the Pullman dispute were making no demands on their employers. They were instead striking *in sympathy with* Pullman employees. This kind of pressure, this "ganging up" on a single employer by workers who are not directly involved, is a kind of labor pressure which the American people have never endorsed. Since labor's strength depends to a considerable extent on the support of public opinion, this strike technique has been for the most part abandoned. The same is true of boycotts of the sort promoted by the Knights of Labor. Such actions can only be effective in so far as they are "secondary," engaged in by workers not seeking to profit directly.

The second lesson learned by labor in connection with this event was of less significance at the moment, but its portent for the future was far more ominous. Confirming the worst fears Samuel Gompers had had when the law was being debated, the Sherman Anti-Trust Act was invoked against labor in the Debs case.

Conservatism Rescued. While the machinery of the law was thus working itself out in the labor field, another legal battle was being waged. Shortly after the passage of the Sherman Anti-Trust Act an action had been started against the Sugar Trust. A combine controlling more than 90 per cent of the sugar refining capacity of the country, the American Sugar Refining Company was one of the most obvious candidates for prosecution. Specifically, the ground for the action taken was the purchase by the trust of four refineries in Philadelphia, its only remaining competitors of importance. The government's action, filed against one of the Philadelphia units purchased, charged combination in restraint of trade aiming at monopoly.

There is no basis for doubting that on any reasonable interpretation of the language used in the Sherman Act the Sugar Trust was guilty. Yet, falling back on an exceedingly legalistic view of the issues involved, the Supreme Court in the first antitrust action to reach that tribunal dismissed the charge of the Attorney General. The view of the Court was that the case at hand did not involve interstate commerce. Only manufacturing facilities were at issue, and manufacturing was explicitly said not to be commerce. A strained interpretation, surely, in view of economic realities, but at the same time one closely in accord with the spirit of the early 1890's. While the law was on the one hand devising ways to prevent labor from organizing, it was on the other hand fashioning legal terminology making business combinations easier to arrange. That the holding company form of consolidation would now become even more popular was inevitable. Immediately corporation lawyers began to tell their clients that the Sherman Act was a sheep in wolf's clothing. (It is, in fact, not at all impossible that the government selected its first major case and prepared its brief in such a way as to increase the probability of a favorable precedent from the standpoint of the corporations.)

When the case of Debs's arrest reached the Supreme Court on appeal early in 1895, the discrimination against labor organizations was made "official." Upholding the decision of the lower court, the Supreme Court declared that Debs had violated the law. Thus the use of injunctions as an employer weapon in labor disputes was given the sanction of the nation's highest tribunal, and the way was thus prepared for a long and fruitful use of this device by the nation's employers.

Indirectly, moreover, the Debs case contributed to the defeat of laborers (and farmers) in still another way. While it was being decided, the Court had occasion to pass on the constitutionality of the income tax portion of the Wilson-Gorman Tariff—the lower class version of a more equitable distribution of the tax burden. Although the Supreme Court test was little more than routine, since the income tax question was a constitutional issue and powerful interests were violently opposed, there was little basis for anticipating an adverse verdict. Shortly after the Civil War the wartime income tax had been hailed into court for a similar test. On that occasion there had been no question in the Court's mind that an income tax was constitutional.

Now, however, there was a difference. The business interests had been in control of affairs for a more extended period, and hence their point of view was more dominant. Put another way, the legal profession was rapidly becoming identified with the corporation-capitalist system of values. For this reason especially it was unfortunate for the income tax cause that it came to the attention of the Supreme Court in the emotional environment created by the Debs case. The income tax was, in such an environment, successfully attacked as a radical, revolutionary instrument of the same stripe as the violence associated with the Pullman strike. (There is no doubt that Debs had become a mild revolutionary, although his generalship in the Pullman strike had not reflected this side of his philosophy.) In a five-to-four decision the Court declared the income tax to be a direct tax and therefore unconstitutional unless apportioned to the several states on the basis of population. On such a basis, of course, an effective income tax could not be built. And the irony of this decision was that it probably created far more revolutionary sentiment than had actually been reflected in the income tax law itself.

The depression did not bring defeats only to organized labor, or at least this depression did not leave in its wake the devastation in the ranks of organized labor which had always before accompanied a major deflation. As Gompers later stated when looking back over this period: "It is noteworthy, that while in every previous industrial crisis the trade unions were literally mowed down and swept out of existence, the unions now in existence have manifested, not only the power of resistance, but of stability and permanency." Possibly Gompers overstated the power of resistance which had been achieved, but stability was clearly demonstrated. For this reason this period is often referred to as the beginning of the modern labor movement in America.

Saving the Gold Standard. But if there were present in the deepening depression factors in which labor could take comfort, the same could not be said of the farmer. The failure of tariff, trust, and tax reform coupled with the pinch of mortgage payments and low prices was generating in farm circles a feeling which can only be described as acute frustration.

TABLE 61. THE HEIGHT OF FRUSTRATION

Year	Retail Price Index	Index of Farm Prices
1893	100	100
1896	98	77

Source: Bureau of the Census, *Historical Statistics of the United States, 1789-1945*, pp. 234-35.

Especially was this true in parts of the West where economic skies had cleared in the 1880's just long enough to generate a real estate boom of sizable proportions (the incurring of new mortgage obligations), a boom which had of course disastrously collapsed early in the new depression. As the months went by, moreover, and no action was taken on silver, the one issue the farmer was certain would give him relief, frustration began to give way to sullen desperation. It is not surprising, thus, that the farmer began even more to think in terms of a political instrument not related to either of the major parties. Accordingly the several alliances were rapidly merging with the new and powerful Populist party.

Actually, there did arise any number of occasions on which a silver or a bimetallic standard would have been only the line of least resistance. Indeed a vicious circle developed, putting an ever greater pressure on the gold standard—a phenomenon history has dubbed "the endless chain." Paper money would be presented to the Treasury for redemption in gold. Then, partly because it was against the law to retire greenbacks (although not silver certificates) and partly because the Treasury continued to show a deficit even under the new tariff act, the paper thus redeemed would be paid out again. When this paper returned to the Treasury again and again, the "endless chain" terminology appeared to be most apt. In the short space of two years some $200 million in paper money was redeemed by the Treasury in gold.

The Treasury's response to this state of affairs, given its fixed opposition to a silver or a mixed standard, was repeatedly and almost frantically to sell bonds in order to buy gold. Most of the difficulty inherent in this process was the fact that many purchasers of bonds would withdraw gold from the Treasury in order to buy bonds. Then, when the Treasury arranged for a banking syndicate to market bonds (especially abroad) while simultaneously protecting the government against gold withdrawals, a storm of criticism was raised claiming that Cleveland had "mortgaged the United States" to greedy Shylocks (Belmont and Morgan). There was little if anything to this attack, and the precautions taken did not achieve their purpose, but the incident did add fuel to inflationist wrath.

After four bond issues in a little more than a year had totally failed to place the gold standard on a solid footing, it was evident that something would have to be done. The nation could not go on half gold and half silver. While a convincing case can be made for the proposition that the money controversy did not produce the depression, it was nonetheless true that continued agitation and even more the administration's desperate struggle for gold were deepening the circle of deflation. A depression policy of withdrawing bank reserves from ordinary use in the face of active gold hoarding was perhaps the worst monetary policy which could have been devised.

By mid-1896 certain of the political consequences of the "battle of the standards" had reached an advanced stage. So intense had agricultural distress become that the West and the South had agreed to bury their differences in order to implement certain fundamental policies. As one farmer manifesto described the situation:

> On the one side are allied hosts of monopolies, the money power, great trusts and railroad corporations, who seek the enactment of laws to benefit them and impoverish the people. On the other side are the farmers, laborers, merchants, and all others who produce wealth and bear the burdens of taxation. The one represents the wealthy and powerful classes who want the control of the government to plunder the people. The other represents the people contending for equality before the law, and the rights of man. Between these two there is no middle ground.

Silver, in other words, was only one of the ways (if at the moment the most important one) in which the "people" felt they might regain their lost "rights." Others included the divorce of currency from banking, 2 per cent credit, a progressive income tax, postal savings banks, government ownership of the railroad and communication industries, and certain reforms in government such as the direct election of Senators.

Neither of the major parties wanted to go before the people on the money question. But with the Populist party gathering to itself most of the South and West, there was no alternative. The Republicans, speaking first, met their problem by declaring for gold. The Democrats, on the other hand, repudiated Cleveland and all other gold Democrats, declaring for the free coinage of silver at a ratio of sixteen to one with gold. When William Jennings Bryan ("The Boy Orator of the Platte") delivered a dramatic address against the gold standard the convention literally went mad with emotion. Then, although the Republicans did their best to wage a campaign on the basis of the tariff ("Bill McKinley and the McKinley Bill"), they were in the end forced to do battle on the silver question and on it alone.

It was not the first great battle fought by the farmer against the industrial sector of the economy, and it was not to be the last. In a significant sense, however, it was the greatest. Never before or since has the farmer come so close to winning a major battle of a distinctly "utopian" character. With Democrats and Populists throwing their strength together in both of the nation's vast agricultural regions, Bryan won the electoral votes of all but a half-dozen farm states. Not since before the Civil War had West and South thus stood together on a major political program. Unfortunately, more was necessary. Every one of the industrial, high electoral vote states of the East and North were won by McKinley, who thus won the election by a comfortable margin. Silver had suffered its most decisive defeat to date.

Several factors contributed to this result. First, the last months of the campaign saw a marked rise in the price of wheat, a fact which may well have tipped the balance in favor of McKinley in the states lying between the Mississippi and Missouri Rivers.

Second, the westward movement of industrialization was making industrial several states which had once been solidly agricultural—such states as Minnesota, Illinois, and Ohio. Thus Illinois, a generation earlier the leading representative of the "Granger" movement, was already so urbanized as to exhibit a political behavior differing sharply from states farther west or south.

Table 62 dramatically indicates what had been taking place. Whether measured in terms of working population, income, wealth, or exports, agriculture's contribution to the economy had greatly decreased since the Civil War, and by 1896 agriculture's dominant position had been irretrievably lost. In the years the South and West had been acting to a large extent independently, farmers had lost their power to determine the nation's economic policies.

TABLE 62. DEFEAT FOR THE FARMER

Item	1860	1900
	(Per cent)	
Percentage of population ten years of age and over engaged in agricultural occupations	59	38
Agricultural income as a percentage of total national income	32	21
Crude exports as a percentage of total exports	72	41

Source: Bureau of the Census, *Historical Statistics of the United States, 1789-1945*, pp. 14, 63, and 246.

A third important factor can be seen in the voting behavior of American workers. If these had supported the farmer's cause, the outcome might well have been very different. However, highly protectionist in their thinking, these voters no doubt cast many McKinley votes for the Republican tariff policy. And although many workers were still supporting "utopian" money measures (Bryan's strength in the East was in urban areas; eastern farmers refused to support the candidate of their western competitors), evidently a majority of workers were beginning to see the money issue in a somewhat different light. For workers endeavoring to reform the social order, a cheap money policy has much to commend it. But for workers trying to push their way upward within the capitalist system, the price increases which must inevitably accompany inflation represent a real danger.

Again the farmer and the worker had parted company. Now, on the money issue as well as the tariff, labor was making its stand with the business interests. The embattled farmer was standing virtually alone—defeated on almost every count.

QUESTIONS FOR DISCUSSION

1. Would the silver legislation of the post-Civil War period ultimately have driven the United States off the gold standard? How?
2. What was the issue fought out between labor and capital at Homestead? Why was this battle such an important one?
3. Who was "right" and who "wrong" at Homestead? Would the cause of labor have been furthered if workers had not used force on this occasion?
4. Why were the Democrats unable to reform tax legislation as they had long planned?
5. What were the difficulties associated with the battle between organized labor and the Pullman Palace Car Company?
6. Did the "battle of the standards" bring on the depression of the 1890's or did the depression precipitate the "battle of the standards"?

7. Why were the "common people" treated so differently in the depression of the 1890's by comparison with the way they were treated in the depression of the 1930's?

8. How did the "endless chain" operate? Why did it create such a problem? What did the government do to correct it? Why were these efforts unsuccessful?

9. Why would free coinage of silver at a ratio of sixteen to one with gold have meant a silver standard rather than a bimetallic one?

PART IV

THE NATION MATURE

(1896-1929)

Chapter 26

A NEW ERA OPENS

1897	Beginning of recovery.
	Dingley Tariff.
1897–98	Supreme Court emasculated the Interstate Commerce Act but applied the antitrust laws vigorously to railroad cases.
1898	Erdman Act.
	Spanish-American War.
1899	"Open-door" policy in China declared.

There is rarely sound basis for sharply delineating one epoch in history from another. On the other hand, if ever a basis did exist for making such a demarcation, it was in 1896. With a suddenness that is almost breathtaking the orientation of the American economy and its problems took on a markedly different aspect. To be sure, beneath certain striking differences the historical process was operating as continuously and subtly as ever. But the appearance of new problems and an altered emphasis in the attack on old ones made it unmistakably clear that America's economic relationships had turned a significant corner. Nowhere was this more true than in connection with money. In a few short years this issue, one which had come close to dominating the attention of the nation's leaders for almost two decades, had become a secondary public policy question.

The Money Issue Settled. It has been said that the election of 1896 settled the money question. This is an exaggeration. It is true that the election relieved much of the pressure on the Treasury created by the hoarding of gold and that the larger issue was settled soon thereafter by the rising tide of prosperity. But when it is then insisted that the return of good times was brought about by the election verdict, the argument has been carried too far. On the one hand, there was nothing about the electoral vote count to make farmers who had for thirty years been attacking the country's money mechanisms suddenly feel happy about those institutions. On the other hand, the economic depression which had ravaged most of the Western world was already beginning to lift in Europe.

So interrelated economically had the world become that world prosperity could only mean American prosperity. In other words, the liquidation of the 1890's had run its course.

The most immediate factor in this revival in America was an increased demand in Europe for American goods. A drought in Europe coupled with an excellent crop year here made possible an export of wheat from the United States almost double that of the preceding year. Furthermore, the restoration of prosperity abroad generated a greater demand for the output of American factories. The result of this dual increase in foreign sales was an export business in 1897 again reaching $1 billion, an export surplus over imports of more than $250 million, and a net inflow of gold of $45 million. The following year saw the excess of exports reach $650 million and the gold inflow more than $100 million. Obviously a nation could not continue to have problems with its gold supply under these circumstances.

Naturally, too, the economic impetus of these developments spread to other parts of the economy. Thus the price of American securities rose sufficiently to make them once more attractive to European investors. In conjunction with the liquid capital which had accumulated here as a result of deflation, these funds made it possible to resume railroad construction on a substantial scale and to modernize large sections of line either inadequately built or badly deteriorated. This work in turn brought a new prosperity to the iron and steel industry, as did also the progress of urbanization and the growth of manufacturing generally. From all these points the new prosperity spread in ever widening circles, and before the year was out the glut of money which had piled up in the Treasury was rapidly moving out into the channels of trade.

But all this explains only a portion of the immediate subsidence of the money question. The fact of prosperity makes it clear why "sound money" advocates ceased to fear for the integrity of gold. It does not explain why inflationists became suddenly content with the gold standard. The nation had had prosperities before which had not converted the farmer to a belief in gold. Why on this occasion did the farmer become less extreme in his money views?

TABLE 63. A NEW ERA FOR THE FARMER

Year	Wholesale Price Index (1926 = 100)
1897	46.6
1902	58.9
1907	65.2
1912	69.1

Source: Bureau of the Census, *Historical Statistics of the United States, 1789-1945*, pp. 233-34.

The answer is simple. Agitation for silver had been a result of the persistent decline in the price level after the Civil War plus an unprecedented increase in the world's supply of silver. Now, however, there was setting in a secular price rise no less pronounced than the previous fall, with the result that the farmer was able to share in the nation's prosperity. In the face of this fact the farmer could not continue to feel that a shortage of money was his major problem.

Simultaneously there came a reversal of the world situation as far as the supply of gold and silver was concerned. Whereas in the years preceding 1897 the output of gold had been relatively small while silver production was correspondingly large, world production of gold after 1897 rose sharply while silver output remained relatively smaller. As the world's annual output of gold increased 100 per cent, the value of silver ceased to

TABLE 64. END OF THE MONEY QUESTION

Year	Index of Farm Prices (1926 = 100)	United States Gold Production
		(Millions of dollars)
1896	39.6	53.1
1901	52.8	78.7
1906	57.3	97.2

Source: Bureau of the Census, *Historical Statistics of the United States, 1789-1945,* pp. 151 and 233.

fall in terms of gold and the silver side of the farmer-silver coalition was also to a considerable extent mollified.

Actually, too, it is probable that there was a causal connection between these two developments—a greater gold production and an increase in the price level. Prior to 1897, despite a tremendous increase in the need for money to take care of an unprecedented economic expansion, the supply of gold on which the world's money was coming more and more to be based had remained relatively fixed. The worst deflationary consequences of this fact were mitigated, to be sure, by a rapid expansion in the use of checkbook money; but in view of the fact that much of the world was turning from gold to silver, perhaps this mitigation was insufficient to prevent a secular price fall. After 1897, on the other hand, the shift to gold had already been effected, the use of deposit currency continued to increase, and possibly the expansion of business needs was not so great on a relative basis. Under such circumstances the increasing output of gold might have contributed much to the period of rising prices now setting in. As far as the farmer's own prices were concerned, however, another important factor was the somewhat slower relative expansion of agricultural production in the face of an inelastic demand, or, stated differently, the accelerated tempo of the population movement to the city.

It is not to be supposed that these several factors relegated the money question to a position of political unimportance immediately. Thus when the Republicans first assumed the responsibilities of office they did not turn at once to legislation on the question of money—the issue on which they had been elected to office. Two factors explain this failure. For one thing, Democratic votes would be solidly opposed to gold legislation, and with the Republicans sharply divided on this issue it was doubtful if such legislation could be passed. More important was another fact. For the first time since the Civil War the West had broken away from its Republican moorings, and a little care would now be required to heal this breach. Rather than force an issue which would further antagonize their erstwhile colleagues, the business interests brought forward another issue, one containing almost infinite possibilities for healing political wounds—the tariff.

There were, indeed, several excellent reasons for bringing up the tariff again at this moment. First, the Democratic tariff had never yielded a surplus, partly because of the depression and partly because of the demise of the income tax, and the government's finances were in a state of disorder. A second factor was the necessity for remedying the Democratic "meddling" with the principle of protection. Still a third was the breach in Republican ranks, a rift the Democratic tariff with its free wool and lumber had made especially susceptible to surgery by means of the tariff. The resulting tariff bill clearly reflected these latter two purposes.

On the matter of protection the Dingley Tariff rivals the McKinley Tariff for the distinction of being the highest tariff the nation had yet had. This aspect of the measure was well taken care of in the House. In the Senate, however, where "silver Republicans" held the balance of power, the other major factor shaping the bill did its work. To some extent this took the form of reducing rates approved by the House, rates particularly important to western groups. Moreover, wool, lumber, and hides were taken off the free list where wool and lumber had been put by the Democrats and where hides had been for the past twenty-five years. And finally, the duty on sugar was raised—a corollary of the fact that the Democratic duty on this product was lower than the bounty that had been repealed.

The sequel to these political manipulations for the benefit of the farmer was that they were largely successful. With the appearance of a rising price level and agricultural prosperity, and the consequent disappearance of the money issue, West and South once more parted company. Populism evaporated, western farmers returned to their political alliance with the business interests, and southern farmers became once again staunch Democrats.

West Versus South. Few phenomena in American political history seem more strange at first glance than this continued aloofness of the two great agricultural interests from one another. Yet, when its economic foundations are examined, it becomes readily understandable. And of the several factors contributing to this result, the heritage of the Civil War is perhaps the smallest factor.

For example, attention can in this connection constructively be focused on some of the more important differences between the western farmer and his southern colleague. In the West the farmer was in a significant sense an independent entrepreneur—even when he did not own his farm or was oppressed by other forms of indebtedness. Typically he owned the equipment used (or at least a mortgage on it), and for the most part he made his own decisions about what proportion of his energies to devote to particular kinds of activities such as raising corn, raising wheat, raising livestock, or other enterprises. Furthermore, western farming was a *machine* agriculture and growing more so with every passing year. In short, western farming was an agriculture which was itself, to a high degree, industrialized, entirely apart from the fact that it often felt itself to be in "bondage" to the larger industrial community.

By contrast the southern farmer was typically not an independent entrepreneur—and not alone because farm tenancy in the South was almost twice as great as in the West. More often than not the worker owned neither his equipment nor his mules. His was not ordinarily the judgment determining how much cotton to produce and how much of his effort was to be devoted to other endeavors. Instead the southern farmer had typically fallen under the tyranny of the crop-lien system; credit (often for buying the food necessary to provide the manpower with which the crop was to be produced) would be supplied on the basis of a mortgage on the next crop and with this leverage the creditor frequently made the basic management decisions. Where creditor and the supplier of provisions were the same person, a situation which was not uncommon, the farmer-creditor relationship closely resembled the first step in the breakup of feudalism or the indentured labor farming of two hundred years earlier.

Under these circumstances an "industrialized" agriculture could scarcely have developed in any event. Workers were too ignorant and too poverty-stricken to make even a start in this direction. (There was, be it noted, little difference between the races in this regard, although a larger proportion of Negroes than whites were farmers.) But there was a still more important reason why southern agriculture was neither mechanized nor becoming so to any significant extent. Technologically it was not yet possible to pick cotton by machine, and there was little economic advantage in mechanizing other stages of cotton production as long as labor had to be kept available for the harvest season. Tobacco was almost equally notorious as a labor-using commodity. Had other conditions been different this problem could have been solved on a seasonal labor basis, but without a substantial industrial development and with a share-crop labor system such a solution was not possible. Thus, whereas economic distress in the West was due largely to the effects of a falling price level in the face of an indebtedness incurred in the purchase of land and machinery, the chief difficulty in the South was low productivity due to the absence of capital

TABLE 65. THE FAILURE OF RECONSTRUCTION

	Agricultural Population		Agricultural Wealth		Wealth per Capita of Agricultural Population–1900
	1870	1900	1860	1900	
	(Millions)		(Billions)		
North Atlantic	3.2	2.7	$2.5	$ 2.9	$1,076
South Atlantic	4.2	5.7	1.2	1.5	263
North Central	6.5	9.2	2.5	11.5	1,250
South Central	4.8	8.6	1.7	2.8	325
Western	0.4	1.1	0.1	1.7	1,545
United States	19.1	27.3	8.0	20.4	747

Source: Bureau of the Census, *Twelfth Census.*

with which to work. (Perhaps, however, if labor had not continued to be so cheap in the South, entrepreneurs would have been compelled to solve the problem of picking cotton by machine just as western agriculture had been compelled to solve in that way problems unique to it.)

In turn much of this worker inferiority in agriculture could have been alleviated if the South had developed industrially outside of agriculture in the same way as in the North, and it is true that cotton textile and steel manufacturing had a marked development after the Civil War. On the other hand, however, the South did not gain relative to the rest of the economy in manufacturing and railroad building, and had probably retrogressed a little by the turn of the century. For this failure the neglect of the South by northern capital and the impossibility of protecting southern manufacturing with a tariff must both be given a share of the responsibility. But the fact remains that had the aristocracy found a profitable outlet for its abilities in industrial pursuits, southern agriculture might have been freed for a more wholesome growth, although it is of course also true that an agricultural advance releasing workers from this occupation was a prerequisite to manufacturing development.

Much of this can be summarized by saying that the transition from slavery to free agriculture could not be made in a single leap. More concrete, however, is the fact that while the western farmer's grievances were directed primarily at the structure of America's economic institutions at the national level, the southern farmer's wrath was most immediately focused upon his local oppressors. At best there could be little political cooperation between South and West until the two systems of agriculture became more nearly alike.

This conclusion can be stated in another way, too. Most of the political power in the South was in the hands of the landlord-merchant-banker-capitalist class (a fact which did have a great deal to do with the heritage of Civil War, or at least the race problem out of which the Civil War grew). Thus when the western farmer made his basic political alliance, his choice was to join hands with the eastern business interests or southern capitalists. Faced with this alternative the alliance with the East had much to commend it, not the least of which was the tariff on wool, sugar, hides, and lumber. It is not without interest in this connection that Democratic Louisiana almost invariably voted Republican on the tariff.

On this view the more fundamental question requiring an answer is not why West and South drifted apart after 1897, but how it happened that they were able to get together even for this important effort. The nature of the "Populist Revolt" in the two sections of the country suggests the answer. Whereas in the West the Populist movement was only a normal third-party protest against the nation's economic policies, in the South this movement was essentially a rebellion against sectional leadership by an oppressed group. Put differently, the large group which had not secured representation in the "solid South" was striving desperately to achieve recognition. The western farmer was trying to utilize his political power to accomplish specific ends; the southern farmer was rather trying to secure political power. It was only due to the conjunction of a set of highly unusual circumstances that these two basically different purposes were able to make use of a common political instrument. As soon as these conditions disappeared the West abandoned its "unnatural" allies, while the elite of the South promptly took steps to see that another "revolt" did not occur. In short, the southern farmer could not secure a voice in decision making as long as white farmers along with other white folk drew a rigid line of discrimination against approximately 50 per cent of their farmer neighbors.

In this reversion of South and West to earlier relationships, of course, there was nothing new. But alongside this fact there was beginning to take place a phenomenon which was a departure from the past. Whereas eastern capital had until now avoided the South, concentrating instead on the exploitation of the West, with the end of frontier conditions in the

West in sight northern capital began flowing southward.[1] Thus there was commencing a process of real reconstruction in the South, a reconstruction more fundamental and more permanent than anything that had taken place to date. For the first time it was being generally recognized that the South's problem had always been, not the question of slavery or even of race, but the absence of capital and skilled entrepreneurship. Even now there was to be no miraculous expansion, but at least a beginning was being made.

Disintegration on the Reform Front. Gradual improvement in the money and price situation meant that farmers would now direct their reform energies into other channels. No opponent could have been more logical than the business corporations which were visibly growing greater year by year, and a rising price level naturally focused a disproportionate amount of attention on rising freight costs and hence railroad corporations. Thus, while the western farmer was perhaps somewhat mollified in his renewed relationships with the business community by tariff concessions, he lost no time in serving notice on his colleagues that more would be necessary. In their turn his colleagues lost no time in informing him that more would be hard to get. Stated differently, the farmer was probably unprepared for the developments the year 1897 was to bring in the field of railroad regulation.

For some time it had been apparent that the Interstate Commerce Commission was fighting an uphill battle in its efforts to control these great concerns in the public interest. Some of its difficulties were simply legal, revolving around the problem of integrating the work of a new, nonconstitutional government agency with that of long existing, constitutional agencies. Thus carriers were given unlimited freedom to appeal Commission decisions to the courts, the testimony necessary for effective prosecution of complaints could not be compelled as in a court of law, and the courts even for a time allowed carrier defendants to introduce evidence on appeal which had not been available to the Commission when it had initially made its ruling. The results of these halting, stumbling efforts at commission regulation were long delays in settling cases and frequent reversals of the Commission by the Supreme Court, a situation encouraging an even greater rate of appeals to the courts and an even greater delay in settling cases.

[1] The "principle of opportunity cost" in economics states that factors of production tend to migrate from lower to higher rewards. As the productivity of, and hence the return to, capital began to fall off in the West, investment opportunities in the South began to look more appealing. By the same token, labor in the South (especially Negro labor) was more and more moving from low wage rates in the South to higher rewards in the North, a factor which would have been more influential in accelerating the southward flow of capital than it was if the birth rate in the South had not been so high.

All this, of course, was merely the normal course of institutional evolution, and therefore understandably slow. Moreover, there was good reason for supposing that in the end these obstacles to effective control would be overcome. Even when the Supreme Court reversed the Commission in fifteen of the first sixteen rate cases appealed, not all reformers were pessimistic. But when in 1897 the Supreme Court rendered two decisions which almost completely destroyed the effectiveness of the Commission, there was much gloom in reform circles.

At the time the Interstate Commerce Commission was created, the great evil to be corrected was discrimination; and of all forms of discrimination, the most obnoxious was felt to be discrimination against the short haul in favor of the long as in the Wabash case. By 1897, as a result of hard and patient work, the Commission had gone far toward eliminating this problem. Then, in a decision involving a small Alabama railroad, the Supreme Court reversed the Commission, declaring that long- and short-haul discrimination was lawful if conditions at the points in question were not identical. Since conditions would never be identical, this simply meant that the railroads could violate this part of the law with impunity. The other decision was even more sweeping in its destructive effects. Here the Supreme Court held that the Commission had no power to prescribe reasonable rates no matter how unreasonable the challenged rate was found to be. Almost immediately the practice of discrimination became as widespread as ever before.

There was, to be sure, one bright spot in this picture. In 1897 the Trans-Missouri Freight Association case was decided by the Supreme Court. Involved was one of the most effective of the railroad pools created to bring about a more orderly competition in that industry. The charge was that this organization was a combination in restraint of trade within the meaning of the Sherman Act, and that it should therefore be dissolved. For once the Supreme Court agreed with the Department of Justice, and this association was forthwith outlawed. The following year another such organization, the Joint-Traffic Association, was given the same treatment. For the first time the antitrust legislation had been positively used for purposes closely related to those for which it had been enacted.

Although farmers no doubt appreciated even a little progress along reform lines, there were several facts about this turn of events which gave pause for thought. On the one hand, it did not escape notice that the authority used in breaking up these two railroad rate associations was the Sherman Act rather than the Interstate Commerce Act, despite the fact that the railroad legislation had specifically outlawed pools and that the anticombination law had been specifically designed to combat restraints of trade outside the railway field. On the other hand, it was apparent that a new and vigorous crop of industrial combinations was being formed and that no effective steps were being taken against them. Here, in other words, were further indications of the ineffectiveness of both the Interstate Commerce and Sherman Acts. What it all clearly meant was that the work of reform had not yet really begun, and farmers were grimly resolved that it should begin at once.

A New Problem. However, the problem of controlling the nation's corporations was not destined to be an important issue in 1898—or for several years thereafter. A totally new question was beginning to loom on the horizon, and until it was in some measure resolved, reform would have to wait.

For almost thirty years the countries of western Europe had been pushing outward in what had come to be called the "new imperialism." A more or less direct outgrowth of the Industrial Revolution, this expansion was apparently motivated largely by the capitalist desire to secure new markets, new sources of raw material, and new areas in which to invest "surplus" capital. It was not, of course, that new territory was absolutely necessary for the respective economies involved, or even that new markets, raw material supplies, or investment opportunities were not available on any basis other than an extension of national sovereignties. But profits are, other things equal, higher where the least capital has previously been invested—that is, in undeveloped areas—and the fruits of economic expansion naturally seemed more secure if only a government controlled by the capitalists themselves had to be dealt with. Thus the countries of Europe were rapidly laying off for themselves, in Africa, Asia, and the Near East, territories in which their nationals were to have exclusive exploitation rights.

Economic incentives for expansion, of course, were not the only motivations. Side by side with these factors were others, or at least the rationalization of expansion policies often dwelt on other matters. For example, missionaries were anxious to carry the message of Christianity into distant lands, although there were instances in which missionary activities were used as a poorly disguised "front" for commercial development. There was also earnest belief in the need to carry the advantages of western civilization to the more underprivileged parts of the world. Here again, however, there was notoriously little concern for the welfare of peoples outside the orbit of potential profit. And finally, considerations of national prestige and power were important.

Understandably American businessmen were not confronted with the problem of expansion as soon as European capitalists. When the "new imperialism" began to take root, America was just emerging from the Civil War with much of an entire continent still to exploit. Thirty years of intense domestic development, however, had exhausted the greatest immediate opportunities and by the middle 1890's American capitalists were also beginning to look around for opportunities offering larger margins of profit. It was not that new areas in which to invest capital or from which to purchase imports were a pressing necessity. America was still absorbing large foreign investments, and domestic raw materials were still adequate. What Americans perhaps felt the greatest need for at the moment was a market for "surplus" manufactured goods.

Several facts can be suggested which indicate how real this problem was, how rapidly America had developed as an industrial, manufacturing nation. First, Table 66 shows a forty-year growth in the field of manufactures few would have thought possible. In less than two generations workers in manufacturing industries had become four times as numerous while the value of manufacturing output had increased 600 per cent. Second, although there was, to be sure, a population differential to be taken into account, by the turn of the century the United States was turning out as great a volume of manufactured goods as England and France combined. Third, between the Civil War and the end of the century, the proportion of America's exports constituting manufactured goods increased by more than 100 per cent. Fourth, as soon as the depression of the 1890's began to lift, there arose in Europe an outcry against the "invasion" of the continent by American manufactures.

TABLE 66. TOWARD WORLD LEADERSHIP

Year	Number of Establishments	Number of Wage Earners	Value of Products
	(Thousands)		(Millions of dollars)
1859	140	1,311	1,886
1869	252	2,054	3,386
1879	254	2,733	5,370
1889	355	4,252	9,372
1899	512	5,306	13,000

Source: *Statistical Abstract of the United States, 1939*, p. 772.

Bare facts, however, fail to do justice to this development; only when America's growth as a manufacturing nation is viewed from the standpoint of the causes bringing it about does it take on its fullest significance. One of the most basic of these causes was a low man-land ratio. A great wealth of resources and the relatively few people on hand to exploit them first of all contributed to the ease with which capital could be accumulated from within and attracted from without. Capital does not find its way easily to economies in which the bulk of current output is absorbed in human subsistence. In large part, moreover, another important characteristic of the American economy is attributable to this same factor. Without a persistent scarcity of labor, Americans would not have developed the capacity for invention without which the manufacturing achievement could not have come to pass. It is not to be forgotten, for example, that industrial success was made possible only by a mechanization in agriculture releasing millions of workers for manufacturing employment.

Closely related to this low man-land ratio was the large area over which the United States was spread. This meant not only many different kinds of raw materials but also a wide market over which to distribute manufacturing output. Since modern industry is most effectively carried on on a large scale, it is of the utmost importance that the United States, with a rapid internal population growth fed by a huge stream of immigration, was able to take full advantage of an advancing technology and an increasingly minute division of labor without becoming dependent on the foreign trade policies of other nations.

How important other factors were, or more accurately the extent to which other factors were independent causes of the manufacturing development, is more conjectural. America has always been a land singularly free from tradition. This has resulted in a flexibility of mind and temper and a mobility of labor which have contributed much to the rapidity with which technological advance has gone forward. The way in which the country has given men of outstanding business ability freedom from moral and legal restraints as they experimented with the new for their own profit is also of importance. On the other hand, however, these factors in turn may go back to the low man-land ratio which made it unnecessary to introduce rigidities into the social and economic structure for the purpose of protecting those whom freedom and rapid change might otherwise have destroyed.

American Imperialism. The connection between the pressure of an expanding industrial economy and imperialism was especially evident in America's first adventure in that direction. For some fifteen years Hawaii had been shipping large quantities of sugar to the United States free of duty, sugar much of which was produced with the aid of the $50 million of American capital invested there. Then, under the McKinley Tariff, Hawaii lost her preferred position in the American market. The consequence was an economic crisis out of which a political revolution was instigated with the "unofficial" aid of the American government and the active leadership of American interests in Hawaii, interests which by now virtually dominated the Hawaiian economy. The fixed purpose behind American participation in the revolution was the annexation of Hawaii by the United States. For several years Hawaii was an important political issue, and in mid-1898 under pressure of a dispute with Spain an annexation treaty was approved.

Economic determinists have sought valiantly to find economic causation for the Spanish-American War. In general this effort has not been successful. Unquestionably powerful economic interests were anxious to expand in the Caribbean and Far East. To Cuba alone some $50 million of American capital had already found its way; most of America's sugar imports came from Cuba, while Cuba's trade with America amounted to $100 million annually, and American expansion into the Philippines was widely believed to be an important step toward a greater share in the trade with China. Furthermore, once the die for war had been cast these economic interests supported it enthusiastically, particularly after they defeated a South-West demand that an income tax be levied to finance it. In the beginning, however, the traditional American business pacifism dominated the industrial community. The motivations which did bring the decision to fight seem rather to have been such things as a desire for enhanced national prestige and the idea of the "white man's burden," two subtle and less offensive ways of applying the doctrine of "survival of the fittest" to international affairs, both generously fortified by an extensive newspaper propaganda campaign ("yellow journalism").

This second adventure in imperialism was also closely related to the American tariff. Cuba had prospered greatly under the McKinley Tariff, her sugar being for the first time allowed to enter the American market on even terms with the domestic product. An economy able to sell sugar in America in the face of a substantial tariff could not fail to profit from a reduction in that tariff to zero. When the Wilson-Gorman Tariff took away the privilege granted four years earlier it was Cuba's turn to revolt. And although American interests did not actively foment revolution in the Caribbean, this uprising too was oriented directly toward United States' annexation. Revolutionists deliberately destroyed property with a view to bringing about American intervention.

There was reason enough for an overflow of American idealism in connection with Cuba, for by any test of humanitarian government Spain's rule in Cuba was seriously at fault. Building on this foundation, a large segment of the press made the most of every incident which might lead to conflict with Spain. Behind this endeavor, in addition to America's traditional sympathy for the underdog, was a small but powerful group who viewed war with Spain as an opportunity for this country to fulfill her "manifest destiny" among the other nations of the world. More specifically this group, one of the most important members of which was Theodore Roosevelt, desired to see the United States the dominant power in the western hemisphere and a power able to stand on even terms with any other power in the Pacific and the Far East.

Theodore Roosevelt's "splendid little war" was soon over. At its conclusion Puerto Rico, Guam, and the Philippine Islands were taken over by the United States, and Spain renounced all sovereignty over Cuba. The way in which economic interests and America's sense of world mission became fused in this episode was excellently indicated in a statement by Senator Beveridge of Indiana: "The Philippines are ours forever, 'territory belonging to the United States,' as the Constitution calls them. And just beyond the Philippines are China's illimitable markets. We will not retreat from either. We will not repudiate our duty in the archipelago. We will not abandon our opportunity in the Orient. We will not renounce our part in the mission of our race, trustee, under God, of the civilization of the world."

The winning of the war, however, did not prove to be so definitive a step down the road to empire as had fondly been hoped. In the Senate, where acceptance of the treaty of peace had ultimately to be forged, there broke out a determined opposition. Little objection was raised to the acquisition of Puerto Rico and Guam, for these lands were relatively nearby. But the Philippine Islands were an entirely different matter. Their great distance from the United States and their seven millions of alien people, many of whom were committed to strive for independence from American no less than Spanish rule, made this venture seem a dangerous departure from cherished American traditions. And besides, tobacco and sugar producers were afraid lest this new competition prove injurious to their interests, while men like Samuel Gompers expressed the concern that American labor standards would be menaced by cheap Oriental labor. The strength of this opposition is suggested by the fact that annexation was approved by a margin of only one vote more than the required two-thirds majority.

No sooner had the treaty with Spain been ratified than it became apparent that more than possession of the Philippines would be necessary to permit economic penetration of China by the United States. By 1899 European imperialism was beginning to focus on the Far East, and several European powers were endeavoring to carve out spheres of influence within which they would have more or less exclusive rights. Their appetites now whetted by small achievements, the business interests exerted extreme pressure upon the administration to check this development.

In September, 1899, John Hay sent his celebrated "open-door" communication to the great powers on the other side of the Atlantic. What he requested was nothing less than that these powers give up the attempt to carve out exclusive spheres of influence in China. Understandably the European nations were not enthusiastic, and they promptly told Mr. Hay as much. But Mr. Hay, partly because a bluff was the most powerful weapon at his disposal, replied to each that in view of the favorable reception his proposal had received, the United States would regard the policy outlined as "final and definitive." Considering America's weakness in the Far East, the "open-door" policy met with an astonishing degree of success. Not for thirty years, and then only under the stress of the period between two world wars, did it break down completely.

These beginnings ushered in an imperialist program for the United States destined to be carried much farther before the nation began to retreat from its implications. The Caribbean was to become a veritable "American lake," the United States was to stand astride a magnificent canal in Panama, this country was to become a sort of "big brother" to a number of Latin American nations, and America became in time an important influence in Far Eastern affairs.

On the other hand, however, it must be said in all honesty that from an economic point of view American imperialism was not especially successful. Imperialist ventures, for one thing, were almost invariably financially costly or otherwise troublesome. At the same time neither her possessions in the Pacific nor those in the Atlantic became important markets or investment outlets, and China did not become economically significant to American businessmen. The major achievement, perhaps, was the shortening of the water transportation distance between Washington, D. C., and Los Angeles, an achievement more strategic in the interest of national defense than an aid to American commerce.

Stated differently, the United States continued to expand her influence beyond her own shores, but the principal technique was not imperialist extensions of sovereignty. For example, American investments in Canada and Latin America far overshadowed investments in territorial possessions. The great attractions for American investors have been opportunities to develop sources of raw materials such as bauxite, copper, tin, iron ore, oil, and others, and manufacturing facilities to stimulate foreign sales in the face of foreign import barriers. As far as markets for our own goods were concerned, this country, just as other imperialist nations, discovered that the best customers of industrialized nations are other industrialized nations rather than undeveloped areas.

And there were factors on the other side of American imperialism, too. Thus this country's domination of Cuba and Puerto Rico helped to fix upon those lands a one-crop, absentee-owned economy which has not been advantageous to them, although America's influence has been good in the fields of sanitation and health. Moreover, American imperialism ("dollar diplomacy," as it has been aptly termed) did not make this country a popular "big brother."

It is always challenging to speculate on how history might have developed, although of course no answer can be given with any degree of certainty. But if the American economy was not significantly influenced in a direct way by its adventures in imperialism, one indirect effect can be suggested. If the United States had been unable or unwilling to engage in imperial efforts, it can hardly be doubted that European nations would have carved out spheres of influence for themselves very near America's borders. In numerous ways, economically as well as otherwise, the future of the United States might have been substantially altered if this had happened. Almost without meaning to, and certainly without much real appreciation of what was involved, America had suddenly become a world power.

QUESTIONS FOR DISCUSSION

1. To what extent were changes in the money supply responsible for price level trends after the Civil War? Would the economy have been better off if it had used silver as its standard prior to 1900?
2. What economic developments were responsible for the disappearance of the money issue?
3. Why was new tariff legislation enacted at this time?
4. What were the major economic differences between the agricultural organization of the South and West?
5. How was the slowness of industrialization in the South after the Civil War related to the Negro problem and the aftermath of the abolition of slavery?
6. How did the Supreme Court emasculate the Interstate Commerce Act, and why?
7. What factors were mainly responsible for the rise of the United States as a great industrial nation?
8. How was it possible for the United States to become a heavy exporter of manufactured goods *and* raw materials while still maintaining a high protective tariff?
9. Why was American imperialism less successful than similar efforts by Europeans?

Chapter 27

BACKGROUND FOR REFORM

1900 Gold Standard Act.
1901 United States Steel Corporation organized.
Northern Securities Company formed.
Theodore Roosevelt became President after McKinley's assassination.
1902 Anthracite coal strike.
Reclamation Act.
1903 Department of Commerce and Labor established.
Expediting and Elkins Acts.
"Rich Man's Panic."

By early 1900 the nation's economic condition and its gold position had improved sufficiently to make it possible for the business interests to secure the full gold standard they had been struggling to obtain ever since the Civil War. The legislation achieving this objective met comparatively little opposition, although it did seem expedient to include two special clauses to soften the blow for the still sensitive West. On the one hand, the minimum capital for a national bank was reduced to $25,000 and the smallest city in which such a bank could be located became three thousand. On the other hand, national banks were allowed to issue notes up to the par value of deposited bonds instead of 90 per cent. With these concessions included, the Currency Act of 1900 (often known also as the Gold Standard Act) became law in March.

The farm community, moreover, had no reason to complain that their political colleagues had on this occasion made a gesture only. Within five years national bank note circulation increased more than 50 per cent and by the outbreak of World War I it had more than doubled. At the same time the number of national banks increased markedly, partly because it was now possible for such banks to be organized with a smaller capital and in smaller communities. This last was not all net gain, to be sure, for there was a tendency for banks in smaller communities to go under more readily than those serving a larger population. But the farmer was pleased, and perhaps this was the important consideration.

TABLE 67. EXPANSION IN BANKING

Year	Number of Banks		Total Assets		National Bank Note Circulation
	National	State	National	State	
			(Millions of dollars)		
1900	3,732	6,650	4,944.2	5,841.7	300.1
1905	5,668	10,742	7,327.8	9,590.4	480.0
1910	7,145	15,950	9,896.6	12,553.7	683.7
1915	7,605	19,457	11,795.7	16,008.4	782.1

Source: Bureau of the Census, *Historical Statistics of the United States, 1789-1945,* pp. 264, 265, and 275.

Consolidation Reaches Its Apex. However, from a broader point of view these concessions were no more than a dry bone tossed to a starving dog. Side by side with these developments, developments reflecting underlying economic conditions far more than business good will, there was taking place a combination movement completely dwarfing anything the nation had yet seen. Whereas just before the turn of the century there had been less than one hundred industrial combinations with a total capitalization of less than $1½ billion, after six years of intensive, new consolidation activity these totals had risen to more than two hundred concerns possessing a total capital of more than $10 billion. When this new combination movement came to an end the principal reason was that there was little more combining which could be profitably done.

The major causes underlying the consolidations of earlier years were all present in this new movement. Technical advances, especially improvements in power-generating machinery and an accelerated trend away from hand to machine production, continued to make ever larger operating units more efficient than smaller ones. The result was apt to be an excess of productive capacity which could frequently be relieved only by a process bankrupting some of the less efficient concerns and by mergers among the remaining. Population growth and the steady progress of railroad transportation also made their contribution.

Beyond these factors making for large-scale producing units, too, there were still operating the same forces making for coordinated price and production decisions among establishments making independent management decisions in other areas. Where surplus capacity threatened, each of the concerns involved often had a mutual interest in a defensive alliance. Whether the defense was against the outsider desiring to secure a foothold, or the possibility that one member of the group might be able to overpower the others, or simply the advantage possessed by buyers in a weak market, the gains from joint action were both real and obvious.

Nor did the new consolidation movement have anything basically new to offer in the way of methods. Monopolized raw materials and monopolized patents were still important. Cutthroat and even illegal methods of competition were again indulged. And when all else failed, hold-up prices were paid to secure (if only to destroy) a stubborn competitor's plant. As before it was a winner-take-all, no-holds-barred struggle which could end only in a monopolized or a very narrowly controlled industry.

On the other hand, despite these many similarities between the new process and the old, close examination reveals several fundamental differences. For example, the intensity of the new drive seemed clearly to exceed that of the old. Thus the techniques used by John D. Rockefeller, the prototype of earlier-year trusts, were never as consistently "underhanded" as those used by John H. Patterson in achieving a dominant position for his National Cash Register Company. Here the bribing of competitors' employees to secure trade secrets, the setting up of "bogus" independents for the purpose of making competitors feel more at ease while a campaign against them was launched, the selling of goods at extremely low prices in order to drive competitors to the wall, the encouragement of contract repudiation, the damaging of competitors' machines and the showing of defective models of competitors' machines, patent infringement suits for the purpose of intimidation, and a "graveyard" of defunct competitive registers used to chasten competitor-visitors at the Dayton plant—all these practices were so much a matter of course that salesmen were given formal instruction regarding them. The difference, perhaps, was not the result of a "higher" ethical sense in the earlier period. Rather in the one case combination moves were made cautiously as though in fear of what the law might do; while in the other, steps were taken boldly in the confident certainty that the law would do nothing.

In the second place, the new consolidations were almost exclusively of the holding company type. Here was a development for which the antitrust legislation could properly take credit. It was by now apparent that the law would not approve the looser forms, and hence the tighter control had rapidly become widespread—primarily with the aid of New Jersey charters. But it would scarcely be accurate to term this an antitrust *achievement*. Actually it was a clear-cut antitrust *failure*, because the tighter control was soon recognized as a far superior device from the standpoint of the consolidators.

The development and widespread use of the holding company technique, and even the use of the corporate form of business organization, was moreover giving rise to an important new economic development. When the corporation had been first accepted an immediate consequence had been the separation of ownership from management. Whether this development had been good or bad, there could be no question that industrial evolution had now taken another decisive step. Ownership of a large corporation by many individuals scattered over a wide area meant that a smaller proportion of shares would suffice for control, and that small holders were thereby placed not only outside management but outside control as well. In other words, whereas at an earlier stage of development owners had "controlled" the corporation even though they did not "manage" it, under the new arrangements big business owners neither controlled nor managed their concerns. This result, too, could obviously be achieved more easily and carried further where a few individuals were able to secure control by purchasing a fraction of the outstanding securities of a holding company and using this concern to purchase a fraction of the outstanding securities of one or more producing concerns.

This aspect of holding company consolidations was closely related to still another difference between the old combinations and the new. With the maturing of American capitalism the amount of investible funds had enormously increased. The complexity of modern finance, the large quantities of capital needed, the many sources of capital, and the wide variety of uses to which it was put made it natural that capital specialists would arise. Such concerns by the turn of the century had come to control huge sums of liquid capital, and indeed only such concerns commanded resources adequate to put together one of the larger consolidations and take care of its continuing capital needs. With the holding company device the opportunity for banker-promoted consolidations was superb. The investment bankers could not only retain a controlling interest in the parent concern and thus reap whatever profits combination made available, but they were in a position to award themselves fabulous contracts and fees for providing promotion and banking services. Indicative of this evolution is the fact that the Standard Oil Company was organized by John D. Rockefeller, industrialist, while the United States Steel Corporation was organized by J. P. Morgan, banker.

The rise of financiers to such an important position created in America what historians have termed the era of "finance capitalism"—a period in which the most important business decisions were made by bankers. Such a development is readily understandable in terms of the economic conditions prevailing at this time. Many industries were growing so rapidly as to be almost wholly dependent upon *outside* capital, this fact providing the opportunity for securing control by financiers. The incentive was furnished by the desire for power, and the very American tendency to exploit a situation promising lucrative returns. Trusts arose out of this relationship because outside capital suppliers stood to lose heavily from a destructive price war, and because to this group would accrue the profits resulting from a monopoly position. It is possible (if not probable) that consolidations by financiers were on the whole less "defensive" in their origin than when the architects were the industrialists directly involved, although finance capitalists insisted that their great service was to "stabilize" the economy.

The United States Steel Corporation. The organization of the United States Steel Corporation excellently illustrates the major characteristics of the new combination movement. Behind this consolidation was a threat of competition so frightening as to make even the industrial giants tremble at the prospect. Over the years the making of steel had become an industry of highly fixed costs, and the heavier fixed costs hang over an industry the greater is the anxiety to avoid competitive price wars. At this point Andrew Carnegie was the principal producer of unfinished steel, his market consisting primarily of concerns making a wide variety of finished products. A decision was reached, however, within the circle of Morgan steel interests at the center of which was Federal Steel, to go into the business of making steel. Such a decision had much to commend it from the standpoint of economic efficiency, but in the circumstances it was almost foolhardy. It was commonly acknowledged that Carnegie could make steel cheaper than anyone else.

TABLE 68. A FABULOUS RECORD

Year	Steel Production
	(Thousands of long tons)
1871	73.2
1881	1,588.3
1891	3,904.2
1901	13,473.6
1911	23,676.1
1920	42,132.9
1929	56,433.5
1941	73,963.6

Source: Bureau of the Census, *Historical Statistics of the United States, 1789-1945*, p. 187.

Carnegie's response was only to be expected. His competitor's decision to integrate *backward* was met with a decision to integrate *forward*—to go into the business of producing finished products and to build a railroad from Pittsburgh to the Atlantic Ocean. Knowing that Carnegie's financial strength and industrial efficiency made this no idle threat, Morgan took fright because his Pennsylvania Railroad (as well as his steel interests) was directly in this line of fire. At a cost of almost $500 million Carnegie was bought out and the danger averted.

The United States Steel Corporation was a consolidation of consolidations. Each of the nine constituent concerns was the product of a number of prior consolidations, some being already virtually monopolies in a specialized branch of the industry. The nine concerns combined had an estimated asset value of almost $700 million, on the basis of which this gigantic new corporation issued the following securities:

Common stock	$ 510,000,000
Preferred stock	508,000,000
Bonds	384,000,000
Total	$1,402,000,000

In other words, 50 per cent of the company's capitalization was pure "water"; none of the common stock and only a little more than 50 per cent of the preferred stock had any assets behind it. But so successful was this consolidation that the Morgan syndicate received $62½ million for promotion services, while in only two of the next twenty-eight years did the United States Steel Corporation miss paying dividends on its common stock. With the formation of this, the most outstanding consolidation of them all, the new industrial combination movement reached its climax.

Railroad Consolidation. It is not to be supposed, however, that the new combination movement was limited to the industrial field. There were railway combinations too, and indeed it could be convincingly argued that among the nation's railroads this development was carried to heights even greater than among manufacturing concerns. In part this was because the depression of the 1890's had plunged many roads into bankruptcy, in part because such a large fraction of railroad capitalization is ordinarily in nonvoting bonds and preferred stock, and in part because the railroad industry already consisted of a relatively few concerns. Insisting that combination was necessary to rescue the railroads from an insolvency created by excessive competition, bankers and railroad men proceeded to reduce the number of the country's railroad companies still further. (This stress on the need to "stabilize" the industry had merit, too. The recent depression had generated a new epidemic of rate wars, which had wrung much "water" out of railroad capitalization—another way of saying that investors had lost a great deal of money.[1])

[1] "Water" is squeezed out of a railroad's financial structure in the following way. Unable to pay bond interest, the railroad is thrown into receivership. One of the important tasks of the receivership period is to relate the road's capitalization to the existing situation more realistically. This means to reduce the amount of fixed charges (bond interest), the failure to pay which is the critical fact leading to bankruptcy, and this is accomplished by issuing stock to bondholders in exchange for the surrender of a portion of their bond holdings. But in order to give this new stock a "fair" chance to receive a "reasonable" return, this step is typically accompanied by wiping out some of the claims of existing stockholders on a proportionate basis.

The extreme to which railroad consolidation was carried can readily be described. Before this movement had run its course seven financial interests controlled two-thirds of the railway mileage of the country, mileage generating 85 per cent of the nation's railroad earnings. Moreover, four of these seven interests were so closely related to one another that for all practical purposes the seven groups were reduced to four. Thus a handful of capitalists led by J. P. Morgan dominated the entire Atlantic seaboard area plus the northern transcontinental routes—an association of interests controlling the nation's two greatest railroads, the New York Central and the Pennsylvania, so closely as virtually to throttle all competition in the area served by them.

In railroad consolidations no less than in industrial ones, banker control was the order of the day. Sometimes responsible in their relationships with their charges and sometimes irresponsible, bankers were widely maligned by the public for their role in railroad monopoly. Railroads, after all, were acknowledged by this time to be public service corporations, and the sight of financiers brazenly manipulating railroads to suit their whims and pocketbooks was most disconcerting. As always, of course, examples of poor, unscrupulous management loomed larger in the public eye than efficient, conservative management. But that banker control at its worst was an evil to be combated was unequivocally demonstrated to the satisfaction of anyone possessing even the slightest inclination toward reform by the experience of the Chicago and Alton.

Prior to falling in the hands of the bankers, the Chicago and Alton had been both conservatively financed and prosperous. Within a few years thereafter the bankers had increased its capitalization by 200 per cent, $80 million, of which only $18 million was invested in railroad property. In this way $66,000 for every mile of its road was added to its liabilities without adding a dollar to the value of the road's assets. In the series of "deals" by which this was accomplished insiders netted a cash profit in excess of $20 million and secured almost complete control of the company's now worthless common stock. And so engrossed were they in financial manipulations that the property itself was allowed seriously to deteriorate.

If the Chicago and Alton looting was the most brazen example of "legal robbery" in the railway field, it was still only one of many. Furthermore, this case did less to bring the problem of banker control and monopoly in the railroad field to the public's attention than did another episode which reached its climax in 1901. This was the battle of the giants for control of the Burlington Railroad, a battle in which the prize was control over virtually the entire railway network west of the Mississippi River.

As matters stood before the battle opened, E. H. Harriman, along with Kuhn, Loeb & Co., investment bankers, controlled the Union Pacific and the Southern Pacific, while J. J. Hill together with the "House of Morgan" controlled the Northern Pacific and the Great Northern. Both interests had long eyed covetously the rich territory served by the Chicago, Burlington & Quincy and the Chicago connection it offered, and both set out to secure control.

The first victory went to Morgan and Hill when the Burlington's directors agreed to sell the bulk of its common stock to them. Harriman, undaunted, sought to purchase a controlling interest in the Northern Pacific in order to accomplish indirectly what he was unable to achieve directly. When Hill and Morgan in turn discovered this strategy they frantically endeavored to purchase enough of the outstanding shares to prevent Harriman from cutting himself in. On May 9, 1901, this Wall Street struggle reached its most dramatic point. It was discovered that both interests had secured control; that is, in the excitement and the accompanying short selling, more shares of Northern Pacific stock had been sold than were actually in existence. In a single hour the price per share sky-rocketed from $160 to $1,000, and the giants compromised in order to prevent a general panic. The compromise consisted of the formation of the Northern Securities Company, a holding company controlling both northern transcontinentals and the Burlington, with both Hill and Harriman on the board of directors.

It is easy to understand why farmers faced with rising costs were especially eager to trim these industrial and railroad "frankensteins" more nearly down to size. At the same time the difficulties involved in making any real headway against them must have semed almost insuperable, especially when past defeats were recalled. However, fortune dealt very kindly with the farmer at this point. As a result of a series of paradoxical events he was presented, at almost exactly the right time, with an ally without whose aid he would have been severely handicapped.

Theodore Roosevelt was known by his political supporters as a liberal of the western variety even before he became Vice-President under William McKinley. In fact, it was really because he was such a liberal that he became Vice-President. When as Governor of New York he had sought to give effect to his economic views by curbing the wide latitude of freedom for profit-making which New York businessmen had enjoyed since the Civil War, the business community became thoroughly alarmed. The solution determined upon was to "elevate" Roosevelt to the vice-presidency, where it was felt he would be out of harm's way. As a result when William McKinley was shot to death in September, 1901, the man in the White House as leader of the businessman's party became none other than the man the business interests had tried to render harmless by making him presiding officer in the Senate.

Liberalism and Imperialism. The reform campaign could not get under way immediately. In quick succession two other issues arose which were given precedence. By the time these matters had been brought to some kind of decision Theodore Roosevelt was all the more recognized as a "champion of the people."

In the first place, basic legislation relative to America's new dependencies had to be enacted. As much as any other single issue, the matter of tariff protection occupied the foreground of this debate, and the question raised was essentially whether America's dependent peoples were to be treated as American citizens or given an inferior status. Traditionally protected interests soon indicated that they had no intention of allowing equal treatment where their own well-being was involved.

Puerto Rico was the first test. On the side of equal treatment it was pointed out that these people had given up a preferred position in the markets of Spain and Cuba when they entered the orbit of the United States, and that for this country now to treat them as "foreigners" would be a cruel blow indeed. Fighting desperately against the power of American liberalism, protectionists were able to eke out only the barest victory. Tariff rates were fixed at 15 per cent of the Dingley rates, and even these were to end in two years.

From Puerto Rico the contest shifted to the Philippines, and here the protectionist victory was more substantial. A reduction of only 25 per cent from the regular duties was accorded. Tariff proponents were thus highly confident when the Cuban case came up for decision in 1902.

Cuba's problem was much the most difficult one. The most popular version of the cause of American intervention in Cuba, after all, had been the unsympathetic treatment of Cuba by Spain. For the United States now to adopt an equally unsympathetic policy would scarcely do, and with Hawaiian and Puerto Rican sugar both admitted to the American market duty-free, Cuba would indeed be seriously injured. Yet at the same time Cuba was a more important supplier of sugar to the American market than either of these other sources, while beet sugar interests insisted that the Dingley Tariff had been passed as a pledge to them on the basis of which millions of dollars had been invested. On the other side the Sugar Trust fully supported the idea of free Cuban sugar, while the sugar interests of Cuba were themselves primarily made up of Americans.

The ultimate outcome was a compromise. By means of a reciprocity treaty (made possible in large part by the powerful stand President Roosevelt took on the side of the "liberals") a 20 per cent reduction of duties was provided. However, it was also provided that as long as this treaty was in existence, no other reductions in the sugar duty specified in the Dingley Tariff would be allowed.

In a much broader sense dependency legislation perhaps gave the death blow to American imperialism. Expansionism over the long pull depended on pressure from the business interests, and these interests could hardly be expected to support such a program if they were to be denied its more obvious fruits. Since these fruits could be realized only through legislation according inferior rights to subject peoples, American idealism was a formidable obstacle to be overcome. That it could not readily be overcome is no doubt owing in large part to the fact that one of America's strongest traditions was an expansion based on equal rights for the citizens of new territory. On the other hand, whether American imperialism was unsuccessful because of American liberalism, or whether liberalism was not overcome because the policy with which it conflicted was not successful, is difficult to say. Perhaps the causal relationship worked both ways.

Action and Reaction on the Labor Front. The second matter which intervened before reform could be undertaken was in the field of labor relations, a field in which a number of important things were happening. For one thing union membership was growing rapidly, and most of these membership gains were in the relatively young American Federation of Labor. The remarkable fact about this development, moreover, was not that labor union membership had never before grown so rapidly, for the Knights of Labor at one time had experienced an even more dramatic growth. Rather the new gain was noteworthy primarily because it was permanent. Samuel Gompers' philosophy of "pure unionism" was, at the turn of the century, paying big dividends.

Of course, much more than "philosophy" was involved in labor's new gains. A period of rising prices affects laborers much differently from farmers. Whereas the farmer is benefited by rising prices, especially if he is in debt, the laborer is confronted with a deteriorating standard of

TABLE 69. NEW GAINS FOR LABOR

Year	Labor Union Membership: All Unions	Labor Union Membership: American Federation of Labor	Index of Cost of Living (1913 = 100)
	(Thousands of workers)		
1897	440	265	75
1902	1,335	1,024	84
1907	2,077	1,539	95
1912	2,405	1,770	102

Source: Bureau of the Census, *Historical Statistics of the United States, 1789-1945,* pp. 72 and 235.

living unless by skillful use of bargaining power he can keep money wages moving upward as prices advance. For thirty years after the Civil War workers had enjoyed a progressive improvement in real wages primarily as a result of a falling price level. With a fundamental change in economic conditions it would now be necessary for labor to work hard simply to hold its own. Thus there was good reason for an intense organization drive, and reason enough for such a drive being highly successful.

Several other factors also contributed to a new increase in labor strength. The growth of larger scale enterprises, particularly trusts, made the employer a more formidable opponent. At the same time the progressively greater number of employees working together in a single establishment made worker organization easier even while it was becoming more important. Similarly the new prosperity now pervading the nation made workers that much more in demand and hence improved their bargaining position. Within the short space of ten years the proportion of workers organized doubled, although, as an indication of how weak the labor movement still was, the increase in this percentage was only from three and one-half to seven. Some industries, on the other hand, were organized to a much greater extent.

Despite these impressive victories, from the standpoint of numbers there were perhaps moments when labor had occasion to have misgivings about the decision made with respect to the basis of its own organization, implying as this did a "tolerance" of industrial trusts. One such occasion was a union recognition strike in the steel industry, an effort to retrieve the losses suffered at Homestead. Timed to coincide with the completion of the new consolidation (on the mistaken notion that the industry would be relatively easy to deal with at this critical time), this strike ended so disastrously for labor that unionism in the steel industry was not again a significant force for almost forty years. An important factor in this defeat was especially revealing to workers; the banker dominated combine is apt to feel even less of a bond with its employees than the industrialist dominated concern. Moreover, the worst consequence of this failure was the fact that many other large concerns accepted steel's leadership in the field of labor relations.

Such reverses, however, were not a sufficient ground for retreat. On the one hand, labor already understood the danger of a strong antitrust law applied to themselves. On the other hand, workers were achieving some things much more important than mere numbers and at the same time sufficiently important to outweigh temporary reverses in conflicts with particular employers. By far the most significant of these accomplishments was a rapid expansion in the use and acceptance of the trade agreement as a basic "contract" between employer and employees. The use of this instrument meant that the employer could no longer make decisions affecting conditions of employment without consulting his laborers and thus giving them an opportunity to apply pressure. Perhaps equally important, this device provided a basis for legitimizing job security by means of the "closed shop" (meaning that only union men could be employed) and for preventing the labor movement from splintering off into utopianism and violence in periods of depression. What was involved, in short, was the acceptance of a status of copartnership between labor and capital in the management of industry.

Another vital achievement was an advance in public acceptance. This was especially demonstrated in connection with a dramatic episode in the coal industry, the other event which preceded the new reform program. Coal was better organized than most industries, boasting a union membership of one-fourth of all workers, and in this industry the spirit of the new day dawning in labor relations was exemplified as in few other fields. Shortly before the turn of the century, with a union membership of only ten thousand, the United Mine Workers had called a strike to which more than one hundred thousand workers responded. Ending in an unqualified victory for the union, the strike strategy was set in motion again in the midst of the presidential campaign in which William McKinley was re-elected. Another substantial success was achieved, although one factor in this achievement was pressure put on the operators by Mark Hanna, who as McKinley's campaign manager felt that unless the strike were quickly settled it might detract from the President's chances at the polls.

For the most part these victories were in the bituminous side of the industry where employers were many and scattered and hence not capable of resisting a powerful labor attack. It is not surprising, therefore, that these efforts were only preliminary skirmishes for a much greater test of strength in the anthracite fields. Here production was closely dominated by a few large operators, and in addition workers in the anthracite fields were more typically foreign-born. But in spite of obvious difficulties a decision was reached in 1902 to make a bid for an improvement in working conditions. A series of demands was made (including union recognition), and when these were unequivocally refused, a strike was called. For five months one hundred and fifty thousand anthracite workers stayed out of the mines, completely paralyzing the entire industry. Finances for this encounter were derived from a tax of $1 per week levied on every employed miner, and by this means some $2 million were collected. Other trade unions, too, and certain nontrade union organizations added almost $400,000 to this total.

In October, with the nation facing a serious coal famine, President Roosevelt decided the time had come for the government to take a hand. The action he chose to take, however, was not calling out the troops as Hayes and Cleveland had done before him. Rather, true to the humanitarianism he had already displayed in the dependency legislation, he called a conference of operators and union leaders and asked them to agree to arbitration. The union leaders promptly assented, but the operators refused. When the President continued to make his request, and as public opinion mounted against the operators, they finally capitulated. The appointment of an arbitration commission terminated the strike, the workers receiving in the ensuing award much of what they had requested. And although they did not receive one of their most cherished demands, union recognition, they did accept the commission's recommendations.

Even apart from the elements of failure in this effort, labor had still achieved a great deal. For perhaps the first time public opinion had helped settle a strike in labor's behalf, and that despite the fact that labor had tied up a strategic industry for many weeks and that episodes of violence costing in all some fifty lives had taken place. (In this connection it is worth emphasizing that an especially offensive and widely quoted remark by George F. Baer, president of the Reading Railroad, about the "divine right" of capital and capitalists contributed much to this result.) Heretofore a successful major strike had typically been branded by the general public as a revolutionary attack on the social order. (It was no doubt in large part because of this reaction by the public that President Roosevelt did not send troops to Pennsylvania's anthracite fields. He had certainly not exhibited in his public career to date any particular interest in the well-being of labor.)

The reason for this gratifying turn of events was not far to seek, and the coming of age of labor organizations was perhaps not the most important factor. Anthracite mining was an industry closely monopolized by a handful of eastern railroads, and these in turn were largely controlled by New York financiers. Thus, there was a strong tendency to identify the coal miner's battle with the attack about to be launched against the trust. Fortunately for labor there was at least this much of good in the trust movement; it was providing an excellent propaganda weapon for use in breaking down the traditional social resistance to labor's objectives and methods.

As often before, labor's successes furnished the incentive for a renewed attack by employers against the new unionism. And precisely because labor's efforts were so successful, the employer counteroffensive was more intense than any to which labor had yet been subjected. Since the nation was highly prosperous at the moment, the union-destruction campaign did not now rise to the level it was later to reach, but it did record accomplishments of which antiunion employers could well be proud.

One especially important accomplishment was the increase of state militia forces for use in strike situations. Another was the creation of many employers' associations on a local basis. The functions performed by such organizations are well illustrated by the activities of the one organized in Dayton, Ohio, the home of the National Cash Register Company, perhaps the outstanding group of its kind. A standing strike committee endeavored to break strikes by offering a financial reward to those men who continued working and by giving financial assistance to strike-bound employer-members. In addition, every employee of member concerns was given a card which had to be presented with the old employer's recommendation written on it before he could be employed by another member concern.

Inevitably, with so much at stake, the employers' counteroffensive did not limit itself to work on the local level. Nationally also the fight was carried to the foe. The National Association of Manufacturers offered leadership for local efforts aimed at destroying the closed shop and preventing union recognition. Another organization, calling itself the American Anti-Boycott Association, dedicated itself to defeating trade union boycotts and to securing legislation against them. A typical method was to take selected cases into court with the view of achieving valuable legal precedents. Still more broadly a political battle on the national front was successfully sponsored by the National Association of Manufacturers.

Prelude to Reform. It was in 1902 that the first step was taken which might broadly be classified as reform. For many years it had been observed that the Far West contained many millions of acres of fertile agricultural land requiring only irrigation to be highly productive. A number of techniques had been utilized from time to time to encourage private irrigation work. Thus, the price of such land had been reduced and the several states involved had been authorized to promote private irrigation projects. Now, however, the federal government took the unprecedented step of setting aside proceeds from public land sales as a revolving fund out of which the first cost of irrigation work might be financed. Although, to be sure, the Reclamation Act did not become important as a factor in the development of the West, it has furnished the legal basis for such great projects as Grand Coulee and Hoover Dams.

The next effort at reform was in the railway field. On February 11, 1903, the Expediting Act was passed, an enactment designed to speed up the wheels of "justice" where cases involving the Interstate Commerce Act or the Sherman Anti-Trust Act were concerned. When the United States was the complainant and when the Attorney General certified the case as being of general public importance, the circuit courts were to give precedence to and expedite suits brought under these two laws. Not a big step, certainly, this law was clearly only a beginning; but reformers could take comfort in the fact that it was a *good* beginning.

The next step went at the business at hand more directly, although it was exclusively directed at abuses in the railroad industry. On February 19 the Elkins Act was passed for the purpose of eliminating personal discrimination, an evil which earlier attempts had failed to curb. In large part because of imperfections in this earlier legislation almost no enforcement work had been possible; carriers and their customers had found so many ways of evading the rules previously formulated that they had been of virtually no effect. One of the most ingenious of these, for example, was the "midnight tariff" technique whereby the carrier would publish a new and much lower rate for a single day so that favored shippers could take advantage of it. Rates were often also cleverly quoted in such a way that only a particular shipper could make use of them, or concerns were favored in the distribution of cars in a period of shortage or given substantial allowances for "services rendered" even though no real service was involved.

In view of the fact that concerns such as Standard Oil and International Harvester were prominent among those profiting from railway discrimination, the Elkins Act was viewed by many as a major action against the trust. Certainly the evil was thereby eliminated. Making the carrier as well as its agent punishable, and making the recipient of a rate advantage equally liable with the giver, the new law quickly reduced personal discrimination to a problem of small proportions. And when the Oil Trust, the Beef Trust, and the Sugar Trust were assessed heavy fines in the early years of the act's enforcement, there was even more reason for reformers to be pleased.

Yet, apart from these more or less superficial achievements, it was evident that little *real* progress was being made. For one thing there could be no mistaking that the railroads were the principal beneficiaries of the Elkins Act, discriminations forced on railroads by large shippers amounting to as much as $1 million a year for a single carrier. As a member of the Interstate Commerce Commission took pains to point out, this law was conceived by the railroads and passed largely by them in their own interest. Moreover, as Commissioner Prouty also emphasized, the real railroad problem as far as the public was concerned was the level of rates, a level steadily and visibly rising. The silence of the Elkins Act on the subject of the Interstate Commerce Commission's authority over railroad rates was eloquent.

But there was no opportunity now to do more, for another economic crisis was in the offing. Ever since the Wall Street struggle between Harriman and Hill, the stock market had been a trifle weak. Whether this was because that episode coincided with the climax of an orgy of stock speculation, or whether the episode itself created suspicion in the public mind, is uncertain. In any event the investing public had been almost avidly buying the newly issued shares of the many new combinations being formed. The coming to light of the battle between the giants to secure shares for control rather than profit, however, had made it so plain that many security transactions did not have their customary meaning that the more conservative investors had begun to approach the market more warily.

By 1903 this situation had become marked. A number of underwriting syndicates which had guaranteed the sale of securities for still more new combinations found themselves unable to dispose of their holdings and pressed by their own banks for settlement. Whether J. P. Morgan's term, "undigested securities," or J. J. Hill's expression, "indigestible securities," was the more apt is perhaps beside the point. But with these securities hanging heavily over the market, the country's financial situation was in no position to withstand a substantial shock. When such a shock did come in the form of the passing of dividends by the United States Steel Corporation, a number of business failures, and the collapse of the newly

TABLE 70. ECONOMIC EXPANSION DEFIES EVEN PANIC

Year	Miles of Railroad Built
1900	4,100
1901	3,900
1902	5,200
1903	5,500
1904	5,900

Source: Bureau of the Census, *Historical Statistics of the United States, 1789-1945,* p. 204.

formed (and Morgan backed) United States Shipbuilding Corporation, the retribution was swift and painful.

The "Panic of 1903" is often called also the "Rich Man's Panic" because such a large proportion of the general investing public had by this time withdrawn from the market and because its consequences did not spread significantly beyond the financial sector of the economy. Actually only two results of any importance seem to have been forthcoming, for American prosperity went on virtually unchecked. First, it seriously hampered the combination movement, even though this movement was probably in its final stages for the moment anyway. Second, it contributed to the postponement of the replacement of London by New York as the world's financial center. The year before, with England financially and economically burdened by the Boer War, a number of nations including England herself had begun turning to American bankers for funds.

Jubilance, however, was premature. The ending of the Boer War and the Wall Street panic ended these hopes—although not for long.

QUESTIONS FOR DISCUSSION

1. Could the trust movement have been prevented from reaching a more or less "natural" climax? Under what circumstances?

2. What is the meaning of "finance capitalism"? Did it represent a "wholesome" development in the American economy?

3. For what was the Morgan syndicate paid $62½ million in connection with the formation of the United States Steel Corporation?

4. If J. P. Morgan had not "integrated" the steel industry, would someone else have done so? Is the same true of John D. Rockefeller in the petroleum industry, and other cases?

5. What was the economic basis of the role played by bankers in American economic life around 1900?

6. Did "finance capitalism" intensify the formation of trusts or did the need to "stabilize" fixed cost industries produce America's "finance capitalism"?

7. How true is it that the economic conditions which produce prosperity for the farmer mean hard times for labor, and vice versa? Was the period under consideration here an illustration of this principle?

8. Could labor have continued to make organization gains without using some such device as the "closed shop"?

9. What reforms were accomplished in 1901 and 1902? How significant were these?

10. How does the concept "undigested securities" differ from that of "indigestible securities"? Does the term "Rich Man's Panic" supply any part of the answer to this question?

Chapter 28

THE GREAT BATTLE BEGINS

1903 Beginning of the "muckrake" era.
1904 Northern Securities Company struck down by the Supreme Court.
1905 Lochner v. New York.
1906 Hepburn Act.
Pure Food and Drug Act.
Meat Inspection Act.
1907 "Panic of 1907."
1908 Aldrich-Vreeland Act.
Loewe v. Lawler.

It is ironical that the twentieth century in the "land of opportunity" opened with an intense general unrest, one which was not to be stilled in any fundamental way for a third of a century. The zeal for reform which was abroad has been called by many names, some complimentary and some the reverse, but whatever the terms used it is customary to characterize the opening years of the new century in terms of this spirit. No other single trait is as representative of them.

Frustration in the Land of Opportunity. What lay behind this widespread agitation for economic, political, and social changes? Why were citizens in the "land of opportunity" displeased with the opportunities available to them?

The very asking of these questions points to the obvious answer. At the turn of the century Americans by the millions were inclined to ask with some show of impatient cynicism, "What opportunities?" And an examination of the environment within which these Americans lived made this question not wholly illogical. From the standpoint of farmer, worker, professional person, or small businessman—the overwhelming majority of the population—the fulfillment of the American dream left much to be desired.

For example, how could the average farmer think of his situation with satisfaction? True, prices were now rising, and farmers were better off than they had been. But at the same time it could not be denied that more than one farmer in three operated a farm owned by someone else, a higher proportion than at any previous time and a proportion growing greater with each census. While agriculture had grown fabulously more productive in the last half-century, the level of life enjoyed by the farmer himself was still harsh. Where were the luxuries, the comforts, and even the conveniences which this expanding productivity should have made available?

Farmers had persistently tried to improve their position. To be sure, some of their endeavors had no doubt been naïve, money correctives being a case in point. Furthermore, there were few results to show for such of these efforts as were not naïve. The installation of expensive machinery had apparently had no other effect than to make possible the industrialization of America and Western Europe. In various ways, such as education and research, state and federal governments had assisted the farmer to raise a larger crop from a given plot of land, to get more meat, milk, or work from farm animals, but this labor, too, seemed to have issued in few benefits for the farmer himself. Cooperatives had been formed to take some of the economic pressure off the farmer, and even now a new wave of cooperative formation was in the making (the most successful cooperative period yet). But even here was no fundamental factor in the improvement of the farmer's economic well-being.

Farmers were not, of course, so naïve as to suppose that they would now be better off if they did not have improved machinery, superior farming methods, better seed and animal types, and other improvements. Moreover, farmers did now enjoy a somewhat less back-breaking existence than their grandfathers. What the farmer objected to, what made him somewhat cynical about references to the "land of opportunity," was the fact that so much hard work and complicated planning were required simply to maintain his position.

Laborers had even more reason for cynicism. Although real wages had steadily increased for twenty-five years after the Civil War, they were now little more than holding their own; indeed, workers were often compelled to struggle bitterly against employers tightly organized in opposition to prevent a fall in real wages as the price level rose. Furthermore, except for a relatively small group of skilled, organized workers, few wage earners received an income above the level of subsistence, while many received incomes substantially below that level. For these inadequate returns workers were putting in on an average fifty hours per week, and often more. Working to and frequently beyond the point of fatigue, laborers were more vulnerable than would otherwise have been the case to occupational diseases and the special hazard of working with exposed, high-speed machinery. And when workers attempted to secure legislation designed to correct the most obvious abuses, such as those involving women and child laborers, they found themselves confronted with a society whose leaders were highly conservative—steeped in a tradition made prior to twentieth-century industrialization.

Workers, like farmers, could not claim that their lot was growing visibly worse. Still more could they not maintain that workers in other lands were better off than they. In fact, in no modern nation were wages and working conditions as favorable as in the United States. Here also what rankled was the fact that the actual situation was far from the promise held out by the American dream.

Professional people and small businessmen likewise could not make the reality square with the ideal. For decades the ideal of success had been closely bound up with the concept "captain of industry." However, the farther industrialization advanced, the more it seemed that the most prized business opportunities were being monopolized by the favored few, leaving very little for others. In 1904 twenty-six corporations controlled 80 per cent or more of the output of the industries they represented, while seventy-eight controlled 50 per cent or more. Between the rapid progress of "trustification" and a rising price level, it must have seemed to these groups, too, that they were only maintaining their position.

The Roots of Liberalism. Granted that there were discouraging aspects of the situation surrounding these large groups of people, this fact alone does not explain the widespread feeling of deep unrest. It is no explanation because there was, objectively, no more reason for dissatisfaction at the turn of the century than at any prior time. What if one-eighth of the population did live in abject poverty? So had it always been. What if the most wealthy 1 per cent of the population did possess as much wealth as the other 99 per cent? When had significantly different conditions prevailed? The question calling for an answer is why the "submerged nine-tenths" suddenly began to feel sorry for itself.

There is no single answer, and perhaps no answer could be demonstrated convincingly to be true. It will suffice here, therefore, simply to suggest a factor which many students of this period have emphasized. America's greatest era of reform sentiment followed closely on the heels of the closing of the land frontier to the west.

It is true, of course, that more land was taken up under the Homestead Act after the turn of the century than before. And it is also true that relatively few of the nation's poor had ever taken advantage of the nation's land laws. However, there can be no doubt that virtually all the first-class land had been disposed of by the time the century ended, and there is little room to question the assumption made by many that the existence of the frontier provided a psychological cushion against economic distress for a multitude of people who never thought seriously about going west. Thus a plausible case can be made for the proposition that the American dream of almost unlimited opportunity remained an important force in American history as long as the existence of the frontier could effectively bridge the gap between the fact and the hope. When the bridge collapsed, it is understandable that disillusioned people everywhere simultaneously realized that the dream could only be made real by intensive, active work directed toward that end.

Perhaps another way of expressing this proposition would make it more concrete. As long as men felt that they might one day be able to take advantage of unrestricted capitalism, as long as men felt their well-being to be dependent upon this institutionalized laissez faire, just so long did they not take a stand against it. Only when the rise of obvious irresponsibility, the appearance of monopolies on a wholesale basis, and the failure of the late nineteenth-century efforts at reform convinced men of the naïveté of their reliance on a vanishing frontier, did enthusiasm for reform arise. From this standpoint the challenge thrown down was not so much an attempt to make the American dream come true as a first step in formulating a dream more consistent with existing realities. If the majority could not share directly in the fruits of enterprise, enterprise could at least be prevented from exploiting the majority.

Much of this can be made still more specific, too. One of the names given the first decade of the twentieth century was "the era of the muckrakers," this name referring to the journalists who fanned the flame of rising liberalism by exposing the excesses of unrestrained individualism. It is of more than casual significance that the most effective work of this kind was done by and for such magazines as *McClure's*, *Cosmopolitan*, and *American*, this significance lying in the fact that such periodicals had an overwhelmingly "middle class" circulation.

There are at least three reasons why a more self-conscious middle class group was now rising on the American scene. First, the complex process of distribution required by modern capitalism was creating not only a larger number but a larger proportion of such people—clerks, secretaries,

Table 71. The Intensive Frontier

Year	Total Population	Per Cent Urban
	(Millions)	
1900	76.0	39.7
1910	92.0	45.7
1920	105.7	51.2

Source: Bureau of the Census, *1950 Census of Population.*

bookkeepers, lawyers, and teachers. Second, and even more important, with the disappearance of the *extensive* frontier and especially with the trend toward developing the *intensive* frontier by means of larger firms rather than more firms, a time had been reached when the really "big" opportunities were not expanding as rapidly as the population. Whereas jobs as clerks, secretaries, bookkeepers, and the like had often in the past been only learning opportunities on the way up, this was becoming visibly less true. Just as the urban proletariat was at an earlier date forced to come to terms with the fact that life as a laborer was likely to be permanent, so now did the urban middle class have to face up to a similar reality.

And third, the consequences of big business abuses were much more apparent to the average citizen than they had been earlier. On the one hand, it was not easy to get urban easterners aroused over manipulations involving a railroad out west. On the other hand, this was the time when American cities were beginning to take on their modern character. Streets were being paved, public buildings were being erected, modern sanitation facilities were being installed, and electricity was revolutionizing the lighting of and transportation within cities. Inevitably, thus, the relationship between government and private businesses in these several fields was very close. Equally inevitably a high degree of individualism would result in much graft and corruption. These things, taking place within full view of millions of urban dwellers imbued with the traditions of democracy, could hardly have failed to produce a sharp reaction.

New Successes—New Defeats. Whatever the source of this new sentiment, there can be no mistaking its effectiveness. The term "muckrakers" was first used in this way by President Roosevelt, who apparently intended to soften the attack being launched against laissez faire. He likened these writers to the character in Bunyan's *Pilgrim's Progress* who "could look no way but downwards with a muckrake in his hand." However, when confronted by indignant citizens wanting to know if he condoned the practices the "muckrakers" were uncovering, the President hastened to ally himself with whatever truth these writings contained. But so rigorously truthful (if also sensational) were the leading works in this literature of protest, and so influential was it in keeping public indignation at fever pitch, that the appellation stuck, minus the overtones of opprobrium intended.

No important aspect of the nation's life escaped examination; few escaped a public lashing. The questionable methods by which trusts were formed together with their power over those weaker than they, the ugly scandals associated with control of government by business and the consequent violation of the public's trust by elected or appointed officials, the commercial (sometimes careless but often deliberate) use of poisons to make food more attractive or tasty, the callous use of child workers in the earning of profits by men who needed profits much less than the children needed sunlight and better education, and the sordid interpenetration of religion and the press with economic interests—all these facets of American life were explored and exposed to public view.

The literary phase of the new reform movement reached a climax, although perhaps only one of several, in the year 1904. In that year also a suit long pending against J. P. Morgan's Northern Securities Company reached the Supreme Court. The Court took advantage of this opportunity to make an unprecedentedly strong statement relative to combinations in restraint of trade. "It need not be shown," said the majority opinion in Northern Securities Company v. U. S., "that the combination, in fact, results or will result in a total suppression of trade or in a complete monopoly, but it is only essential to show that by its necessary operation it tends to restrain interstate or international trade or commerce." Furthermore, this was the first time the Court had spoken disapprovingly of a holding company type of combination; indeed, what was even more significant, it was really the first opportunity the Supreme Court had been given to pass on a holding company consolidation. Thus reformers were much encouraged, while in business circles great concern was expressed for the future of other holding company organizations.

The "muckrake" campaign and the Northern Securities Company case furnished much of the background for the presidential campaign of 1904, and the business interests were in something of a quandary. On the one hand the liberal spirit so typified by Roosevelt was decidedly not an appropriate trait for "their" candidate to have. When the Northern Securities suit had first been brought, Morgan had tried to reason with the President. "If we have done anything wrong why can't you just send your man [the Attorney General] to see my man [a Morgan lawyer], and we will work something out." Roosevelt, however, had taken a most "unreasonable" position in refusing this suggestion, and business leaders would have been very happy to drop him if they had dared. But unfortunately the maintenance of power in Washington at this moment demanded that the prevailing reform sentiment be recognized, and there was no better way to do this than to nominate "Teddy" to succeed himself.

This the business interests reluctantly decided to do. They did, however, take the obvious precaution of arriving at an understanding with Roosevelt for the purpose of keeping his reform proclivities within some bounds. Close students of this period suggest that this understanding took approximately the following form. To eastern business interests went Roosevelt's promise not to disturb existing adjustments relating to the tariff and the currency—these issues thus were to be kept outside the orbit of the President's reforming zeal. As a corollary it was understood that "'trust-busting" might go on, and that land reform might also go forward.

(The President had already evinced considerable interest in conservation, a gratifying fact to those citizens who had long deplored the lavish gifts of valuable public resources to private persons and concerns for private profit.)

That Theodore Roosevelt took seriously the antitrust work demanded by public opinion there can be no doubt. In all some forty-four proceedings under the antitrust laws were brought during his term of office, some against important combinations—as, for example, Standard Oil, American Tobacco, and Du Pont (the Powder Trust). It is more than doubtful, however, if Roosevelt deserves his high reputation as a "trust buster." Although he did institute more actions against trusts than all his predecessors combined, there was very little to show for these efforts. Apart from the Northern Securities Company, it would be difficult to demonstrate that Roosevelt actually succeeded in "busting" a single trust. Furthermore, Roosevelt's predecessors had also had a high degree of success in actions against railroads. Illustrative of the gap between trust prosecution and the restoration of competition was the action taken against the Beef Trust.

For some thirty years the major packing companies had practiced some form of pooling arrangement. Gradually these arrangements had become more formal until a high degree of stability had been achieved by means of a market division agreement with quotas for each company. Newspaper and Congressional attacks, however (so obvious was this stifling of competition), moved the Department of Justice to take action, and this case reached the Supreme Court in 1905. Without difficulty a permanent injunction was secured against the anticompetitive practices being followed by the concerns involved. Then, before the year was out, three of the five major producers formed the National Packing Company, a holding corporation, and as directors in the new concern the same persons met regularly to make the same business decisions that had previously been made by these same individuals as members of the old pool. Moreover, a way was soon found to include the other members of the "Big Five" in another price fixing, market dividing agreement. And monopoly went on.

Reverses for Labor. While the war against the trusts was thus meeting another defeat, the struggle for human rights was meeting with reverses in another arena. For many years workers had been persistently endeavoring to enlist legislative support in their battle for improved working conditions. Such matters as health and safety standards, employers' liability, maximum hour laws, and restrictions governing the employment of women and children were understandably included on labor's list of necessary reforms, the first three for the obvious benefits workers would receive directly and the last to prevent the exploitation of women and children from undercutting the jobs and wages of men with families to support.

This legislative program was not ordinarily a major item on labor's agenda because through successful collective bargaining these issues could be resolved more adequately from labor's point of view than was possible by means of the minimum standards which could be written into statutes. But nonetheless labor did feel a high degree of class solidarity on such matters. And the American Federation of Labor was perhaps more active in this field than was its custom, a consequence of heavy pressure by an evolutionary socialist movement currently threatening to undermine worker loyalty to Gompers' organization.

It could not really be said that labor's endeavors in these directions had been especially successful in securing concessions from conservative legislatures, and no doubt primarily for this reason the cause of labor legislation had not as yet been significantly hampered by the courts. With the turn of the century, however, and the appearance of a stronger reform sentiment, the situation changed in both of these respects. On the one hand, labor's efforts were now strongly supplemented by assistance from a number of middle class, liberal groups, groups such as the National Consumer's League, the National Civic Federation (an organization in which a few prominent although hardly representative businessmen such as Mark Hanna exercised considerable leadership), the National Child Labor Committee, and the American Association for Labor Legislation. On the other hand, this drive was soon pushing through legislation which could not be justified by narrow interpretations of the Constitution, and thus for the first time the judicial barrier became a formidable one.

The courts did not interpose objections at all points, and in the period between the turn of the century and World War I the decisive beginning of modern social legislation in all fields and in virtually every state took place. State child labor laws, for example, were not hampered by court decisions. The health and education of the younger generation is always of great importance in any society. Neither were laws designed to protect the worker from the hazards of particularly dangerous occupations. Here again a strong case could be made for intervention on the ground of society's needs rather than the desires of a special class. But where adults were concerned, or where workers were not exposed to especially dangerous conditions, the broad definition of laissez faire with which the nation had been living for some years would not permit legislative restrictions. Either it was argued that the property of the employer was being taken from him without due process of law, or it was insisted that the worker's freedom of contract was being taken away. Wherever, in short, the beneficiary of the legislation seemed to be labor as a class rather than society as a whole, the courts were apt to register a veto.

At the moment the controversy was over the specification by law of maximum hours for men. Recently the Supreme Court had upheld a

Utah statute establishing eight hours as the work day in that state's mines. Partly on the strength of this precedent New York passed a law limiting bakers' hours to ten. Although a majority of these workers had been trying unsuccessfully for a number of years to achieve this goal, and although most industries in the state were already operating with a ten-hour day or less, the Supreme Court saw fit to strike down this law in the first such case in which the federal courts had reversed a state supreme court. The difference, of course, between this law and the one passed in Utah was that there were no characteristics of the baking business justifying special treatment as in the case of Utah's mining industry. In the words of the majority: "This statute reached and passed the limit of the police power."

The majority opinion in Lochner v. New York did not go unchallenged, even in 1905. In a dissenting opinion Justice Holmes took pains to emphasize that the case was decided on the basis of an economic theory in which a large part of the community no longer believed. Put differently, where property is possessed only by a small minority, property rights in the "land of opportunity" could not be allowed to reign supreme. In time Holmes' view of the legal and economic premises required in labor law decisions was to become a fairly consistent majority view. It was to be a long, hard struggle for labor, however, before that time was reached, before the courts were persuaded to believe that legislation protecting labor was not a violation of the ideals of the founding fathers. And, what is more important, there was in 1905 little indication of the achievements which were to be won.

Much more visible at the moment was something else. The fiscal year 1905-06 saw F. W. Taylor serve a term as President of the American Society of Mechanical Engineers. Whereas his theories concerning "scientific management" had spread slowly to this point, they now began to receive the closest attention. Taylor himself was still no proponent of the "labor as a commodity" approach to worker-employer relationships in industry. But unavoidably his theories did lend support to the all too prevalent tendency for capitalists to put human resources on the same plane as raw materials. Beginning with this intensive exploitation of Taylor's ideas, labor developed a powerful opposition to "scientific management" which has to this day not disappeared. The trouble was that managements did in fact often use piece-rate pay systems in exactly the way labor feared—to speed up production for the benefit of stockholders—and that the basic idea underlying this method of payment was a direct challenge to labor's notions about group solidarity.

There was good reason for the appearance at this time of "scientific management" as an important preoccupation in the minds of employers, and for its use in this particular way. By the beginning of the twentieth century capital had become relatively abundant in the American economy, and labor was by now the only really scarce factor. It is thus obvious why managerial attention was being more and more directed to the task of getting a larger return in output from labor expenditures. While it is appropriate enough to mention this development as one of the sources of labor's problem, thus, it is also appropriate to emphasize that employers were having their problems too. A competitive economy imposes certain conditions upon those who work within its framework, and one of these is the need to economize scarce factors. Similarly, while it is just to say that workers have resisted much that has traditionally been implied by "scientific management," it is only fair to add that resistance has most often taken the form of a desire to participate in the management of scientific advance rather than an attempt to prevent it.

Equally visible, too, was another phenomenon. With prosperity had come a new wave of immigration, the largest to date. In the first fourteen years of the twentieth century arrivals averaged almost one million a year and in six of these years they exceeded that number. Hard circumstances abroad and the great improvement in land and sea transportation account for much of this fresh inundation, although as always the correlation with business conditions here was high. Moreover, steamship companies, railroads, landowners, and employers were still assisting in swelling the number of newcomers, while recent immigrants did much to induce friends and relatives to join them.

TABLE 72. THE ALL-TIME PEAK

Year	Immigration
	(Thousands)
1905	1,026.5
1906	1,100.7
1907	1,285.3
1910	1,041.6
1913	1,197.9
1914	1,218.5

Source: Bureau of the Census, *Historical Statistics of the United States, 1789-1945*, p. 33.

So great was this influx it has been estimated that by the time of World War I one-half of all factory workers were of foreign birth, a fact which could not help having profound consequences on labor's efforts to raise the level of its own well-being. For a time, too, it even seemed as though labor might at last be successful in achieving restrictive legislation. The trend toward the "new" immigration (arrivals from eastern and southern

Europe) was more marked than ever, two thirds of all European immigrants now coming from Austria-Hungary, Italy, Russia, and the Balkans. All that could be accomplished, however, was a slight broadening of the definition of "undesirable" immigrants and steps designed to check Japanese immigration (the so-called "Gentlemen's Agreement"). The strength of the groups desiring the flow to continue was still too strong to accomplish more. Even the workers' middle class allies abandoned them in this struggle. The tradition of America as a haven for the oppressed was too powerful; Americans not directly implicated in labor's struggle could not easily distinguish between the downtrodden of America and the downtrodden of Europe.

A Real Achievement. In 1906 the reform campaign began in earnest. The unsuccessful suit against the Beef Trust had not finished the public's business with that industry. Even more important was the problem of the nation's health—more important at least after the publication of Upton Sinclair's *The Jungle.* Here was one of the most brilliant exposés of the entire "muckraking" period. Intended as a portrayal of labor conditions in the Chicago stockyards, its principal effect was to focus attention on the conditions under which the nation's meat was prepared and distributed. No sooner had this book become a standard library item in middle class homes than the Meat Inspection Act was passed. Taking advantage of the fact that most meat was transported in interstate commerce, the federal government assumed responsibility for more wholesome conditions.

Closely related to this enactment was the Pure Food and Drug Act of 1906. Aroused especially by Samuel Hopkins Adams' exposé of patent medicines and fraudulent advertising, the nation with this law sought to protect itself against the poisons which commercial profit saw fit to include in foods and drugs. Neither of these laws could be termed a huge reform success, carefully compromised as they were so as not to impinge seriously on corporate profits. And as would be expected in such circumstances, proponents of stronger measures accused President Roosevelt of "selling out" to the corporations while the business interests in turn accused him of "selling out" to the radicals and revolutionaries.

The nation also had unfinished business with the country's railroads which it went far to complete in 1906, and the struggle of reformers against capitalists on this issue has been called the "Great Battle of 1906." Western farmers, naturally enough, led in this assault. Representative Hepburn of Iowa introduced the new regulatory measure into the House where it was speedily and overwhelmingly approved. In the Senate, however, the strength of business interests generally and railroad interests specifically was much greater and the battle was long and bitter. At first Roosevelt worked actively for a strong bill, even to the point of cooperating directly with the Democratic party. But in this endeavor he was apparently soon given to understand that he was treading dangerously near a violation of his truce with the business community, with the result that he turned his back on this alliance and placed his influence behind a compromise more suitable to the "Old Guard."

Actually the Hepburn Act barely escaped being a completely innocuous measure. Had not several special factors fortuitously intervened, in fact, no measure with "teeth" would have gotten by the Senate. One of these factors was a threatened breakdown in the nation's railroad services; the high prosperity of 1906 almost overloaded America's splendid transportation system. A second was a nationwide scandal over the distribution of coal cars by Pennsylvania railroads, while a third was disclosures of illegal rebates on the Atchison, Topeka & Santa Fe touching the President's Cabinet.

The final factor had to do with a wholly unrelated matter. "Muckraking" attacks on the life insurance industry had been largely responsible for the launching of a full-scale investigation in the state of New York. Revelations from this investigation shocked the nation, and incidentally brought quick fame to the investigating committee's lawyer, Charles Evans Hughes. The illegal use of life insurance funds for investments denied by law to such companies, the use of large sums of money to influence legislators and newspapers, the payment of exorbitant salaries, nepotism, and an amazing indifference on the part of officials to the public trust placed in their hands were among the more sordid of the disclosures made.

One of the consequences of this investigation was a thoroughgoing reform law in New York, a law widely imitated in other states in which large insurance firms were located. Another was the passage of the Hepburn Act—a milestone in the history of the nation's control over its railroads. With the insurance scandal breaking just as the Senate debate on the railroad act was at its highest point, the business interests were forced to retreat from their uncompromising stand. Then, when it was apparent that the bill was to pass, its most relentless opponents voted for it almost to a man. Thus the three votes cast against it in the Senate made it appear that it had met with little opposition. It was not so; while the new law did not accomplish anything with respect to long-and-short-haul discrimination, it is not true that a provision giving the Interstate Commerce Commission power to prescribe "just and reasonable" rates was welcomed by supporters of laissez faire. No more welcome was the so-called "commodities clause" in the new law. This provision specified that railroads were no longer to transport goods which they owned, a provision primarily intended to destroy the anthracite coal monopoly long held by a handful of railroads.[1] And what capitalist in 1906 could look with equanimity upon a law extending the Commission's power over sleeping-car, express, and pipeline companies, switching and terminal facilities, and even the accounting practices of all concerns under its jurisdiction?

It is understandable that capitalists the country over would denounce the Hepburn Act, and when its passage was shortly followed by a financial panic, it was but a short step to place responsibility on the failure of public confidence resulting from the new regulations. The argument, however, proved too much. On the one hand, the Hepburn Act, promising as it did to introduce greater financial stability into the railroad industry by giving the Commission limited power to check destructive rate wars, perhaps even assisted the flow of capital from Europe. On the other hand, panic in the United States was shortly preceded by a similar upset in such far distant and scattered places as Egypt, Japan, Germany, and Chile.

Although the "Panic of 1907" was far from the most severe the nation had ever had, perhaps none created a greater over-all impact. One of the principal reasons for this was the fact that the business community had widely advertised to the public that the economy was now immune to panics. No doubt those who made these assertions so dogmatically were sincere; the new finance capitalism was very conscious of its power, and one of its major objectives was to stabilize conditions for the more effective operation of business. One of the most dramatic episodes of this panic period was an attempt on the part of the financial capitalists under the leadership of J. P. Morgan himself to moderate the effects of the crash. And but for the fact that this particular panic was accompanied by the most irresponsible banking practices the nation had seen in many a year, financial leaders in Wall Street might have been successful in this endeavor.

A second reason for the shock which engulfed the nation was the devastation wrought among the recently organized trust companies. These concerns had been created to perform the functions of executor, administrator, or trustee, and hence held a position relative to the public not unlike that of insurance companies. Basically sound in underlying principle, for this was a kind of specialized economic activity appropriate to the new age, these concerns would not have been seriously disturbed by the panic if they had limited themselves to the function for which they were created. Instead, however, they had invaded the deposit banking field, and the state

[1] The problem to be corrected here was this. Already it was illegal for a railroad to charge one customer more than another—to charge itself less for hauling its own coal than it charged a competitor coal company. This requirement, however, was easily nullified by the simple expedient of charging both an excessively high price. For the railroad this involved only taking money from one pocket and putting it in another, but for the competitor the economic drain was very real. The only preventive seemed to be to prohibit railroads from hauling their own goods.

laws governing their activities had not been written with this in mind. As a consequence, with deposits inadequately protected and portfolios filled with speculative securities, these concerns were highly vulnerable to deflation.

The Knickerbocker Trust Company was the first to feel the impact. With $35 million of deposit liabilities and barely a 10 per cent reserve, it went under on October 22, 1907. Immediately a number of the other trust companies in New York collectively asked the New York banks for aid. Aid from the banks and the federal government did manage to save some of them, although not until the process of liquidation had been carried very far.

TABLE 73. PANIC DEFIES ECONOMIC EXPANSION

Year	Miles of Railroad Constructed	Steel Production
		(Thousands of long tons)
1905	4,200	20,023.9
1906	6,300	23,398.1
1907	5,600	23,362.6
1908	3,500	14,023.2
1909	3,400	23,955.0
1910	3,200	26,094.9

Source: Bureau of the Census, *Historical Statistics of the United States, 1789-1945*, pp. 187 and 202.

The ensuing depression was substantially more severe than that accompanying the "Rich Man's Panic" of four years before. Unemployment mounted until approximately one worker in six was unemployed. Commercial failures for a period of twelve months were more than 100 per cent above normal, including the infant Westinghouse Electric Company and the huge concern responsible for most of the street railway transportation in New York City, while steel production fell almost 50 per cent and freight traffic more than 10 per cent. Fortunately, recovery was swift; within a few months the financial part of the holocaust was over, and within a year economic conditions in general had regained most of the ground lost.

Since the "Panic of 1907" was to a considerable extent a financial phenomenon, it was only logical that the institutional readjustments primarily involved the financial sector of the economy. Thus New York promptly moved to correct the haphazard way her trust companies had been allowed to develop. On the national front an act was passed in 1908 designed to make the nation's financial organization more flexible in the face of economic dislocation. By its terms national banks were authorized to issue emergency currency to tide the economy over short crises. Scheduled to expire after six years, this law more than once served the purpose for which it was passed before it was superseded by more basic monetary legislation.

At the same time, however, no one supposed that the Aldrich-Vreeland Act went to the roots of America's financial difficulties. The new panic was a typical national banking system deflation and by now the pattern was becoming unmistakable. A period of speculation had drawn into the eastern money market funds from abroad and the interior, funds deeply embedded in the financial mechanism by means of the pyramid of bank reserves reaching its apex in New York. When the speculative fever passed its crest, withdrawals from abroad and the interior placed eastern monetary institutions under a cumulative strain, and once the deflation began it was thus dispersed under pressure to every corner of the economy. The business interests, anxious to make "their" system as shock-proof as possible the better to defend it from reformist pressures, and stung into action by two deflationary spirals in four years, now determined that this weakness in the economy would have to be overcome. Accordingly the Aldrich-Vreeland Act also provided for the appointment of a National Monetary Commission to make a comprehensive study of the changes needed in the nation's money and banking mechanism.

More Reverses for Labor. Another outgrowth of panic and depression was a substantial setback for labor in its struggle for organization. The depression in and of itself, moreover, would have been serious enough. Unfortunately for labor, the distress engendered by unemployment was made the occasion for a strengthening of the employers' counteroffensive against labor. While prices did fall in 1908 with many employed workers consequently enjoying higher real wages, and while unemployment did not plague the economy for long, still the loss in union membership and prestige could not be denied. More and more as the American labor movement matured, workers had become certain that labor's *first* need was organization. Given this, such things as higher wages and improved working conditions would follow; without this, labor was simply at the mercy of the employer. It was for this reason that the basic conflict between employers and employees was coming more and more to center around the "open" versus the "closed" shop.

Labor suffered other reverses in 1908, too, although for the most part they were not related to the depression. For example, in that year the Supreme Court delivered two important decisions indicating still more clearly what labor's standing before the law now was. One had to do with management-labor relations in the railroad industry; the other fastened the

Sherman Anti-Trust Act on labor union activity to a degree hitherto undreamed of.

Because labor organizations were able to secure a more strategic power position in the railroad industry than almost anywhere else, skilled workers here had long been powerful. So successful had they been, in fact, that they had carefully avoided an allegiance even with the American Federation of Labor. Conversely, because a railroad strike could quickly damage the economy, the public was early led to experiment with legislation designed to help maintain labor-capital harmony in this industry. Just before the turn of the century one such law had been passed, the principal provision of which was the setting up of an arbitration machinery.

The place of the Erdman Act in American history has nothing to do with the law's success, for it performed well in no major test. However, a somewhat less important provision had prohibited employer discrimination against workers on account of union membership, a prohibition felt by laborers at the time to be a significant victory. In 1908 the Supreme Court declared this part of the Erdman Act to be unconstitutional. Arbitration machinery to protect the nonlabor public was legal enough; an antidiscrimination clause to protect the labor part of the public was apparently going too far.

Several years prior to 1908 the United Hatters of North America had called a strike against D. E. Loewe and Company of Danbury, Connecticut, for the purpose of securing a closed shop. Additional pressure was brought to bear against this bitterly antiunion employer by means of a nationwide boycott. A suit against the union (financed by the Anti-Boycott Association) charging violation of the antitrust laws was carried to the Supreme Court, a suit demanding triple damages and asking that union members as well as officers be held financially responsible.

The Court's decision was rendered only a few days after the decision on the Erdman Act. It consisted first and foremost of another comprehensive indictment of the secondary boycott. Even more important, however, it placed labor unions squarely within the prohibitions of the Sherman Act. Prior to this the Court's decisions on this point had been peripheral to the main issues involved. Most important of all, the Court agreed that union members should be held financially liable. Damages of almost $250,000 were assessed, the greater part of which was ultimately paid by the workers.

Added to these difficulties, the postpanic years saw an intensified use of the injunction as well. A boycott against the Buck's Stove and Range Company of St. Louis, invoked in part because the company had violated a collective bargaining agreement, was met by a federal court injunction demanded by the Anti-Boycott Association. Written by the plaintiff's lawyers and signed by the judge without significant change in wording, this document has been characterized as one of the most sweeping orders in the history of American law. An injunction granted at the request of the Hitchman Coal and Coke Company forbade union organizers to attempt to organize employees who signed agreements not to join the United Mine Workers while in the company's employ ("yellow-dog" contracts).

Labor's efforts were, of course, not all in vain—even in the courts. Thus it was in 1908 that the Supreme Court in a unanimous decision established the constitutionality of maximum-hour legislation for women in an Oregon case. Within a dozen years most of the states had responded to this new freedom by passing laws which had previously not been able to withstand legal attack. To this extent the roadblock interposed by Lochner v. New York was surmounted.

It was not enough. Defeats at the hands of the judiciary far more than made up for successes. As a result American Federation of Labor leaders felt compelled to make a fundamental decision. Whereas they had earlier resolved to restrict their activities largely to the bringing of economic pressure against employers, mixing in politics only as a secondary activity, they now decided it would be necessary to compete more actively with employers for control over the government. Put more concretely, labor was now coming to the conclusion that it could not leave the government alone for the simple reason that the government would not leave it alone. From this point forward labor thought and worked to an important extent in terms of a positive political program. High on the list of items included therein were an anti-injunction law and the exemption of labor from the antitrust laws.

QUESTIONS FOR DISCUSSION

1. Why was there unrest in the "land of opportunity" as the century opened?
2. What were the bases for a middle class "revolt" at this time?
3. This period in American history has been called "the end of laissez faire." How accurate is this description?
4. Why was there so much resistance in the United States to placing non-property rights on a par with "property rights"?
5. What were the major innovations in the Hepburn Act? Why were they so powerfully resisted?
6. Was it just a coincidence that effective railroad regulation and the end of rapid railroad expansion came at almost exactly the same time?
7. Why were the new trust companies so vulnerable to a change in economic climate?
8. How did the national banking system contribute to the onset of deflation in 1907?
9. Why did the nation delay so long before it took seriously the defects of the national banking system?

Chapter 29

SUCCESS—AND FAILURE

1908	General Motors Corporation formed.
	William Howard Taft elected President.
1909	Republican insurgency.
	Payne-Aldrich Tariff.
1910	Ballinger-Pinchot controversy.
	Mann-Elkins Act.
1911	Standard Oil and American Tobacco Companies broken up by order of the Supreme Court.
	Social legislation in the states.

Consolidation Goes Forward. The story of reform in the early years of the twentieth century was not entirely a situation of moving ahead one step and slipping back two. But while labor was reeling from a succession of blows delivered by depression, employers, and the courts, the combination movement and the advance of finance capitalism were growing rapidly. With Wall Street and the nation still in the grip of panic, J. P. Morgan took charge of the acquisition of the Tennessee Coal, Iron, and Railroad Company, the principal steel-producing concern in the Birmingham area, for the United States Steel Corporation. The avowed and no doubt the sincere purpose of this transaction was to prevent the panic from widening as the result of the bankruptcy of an important financial concern holding a large block of stock in this firm, and thus when it was "cleared" in advance with the administration in Washington to make certain it would not become the basis for an antitrust action, the President of course agreed. (What else could he do? On the other hand, one wonders if there were not ways of saving the financial situation while still leaving the Birmingham concern independent.)

No sooner had panic begun to give way to depression, furthermore, than Elbert Gary, Chairman of the U. S. Steel board, called the leaders of that industry together in the first of the famous "Gary Dinners." Here it was announced that there was no reason why the price of steel should fluctuate with business conditions, going up in good times and down in bad. In consequence, it was emphasized that the price of steel would not fall in this depression. And it did not, even though steel output fell by almost half. (It is only fair to add that the corporation did not reduce wages either.) The point of this maneuver was to stabilize business conditions, or at least this was the basis on which it was put. And perhaps it did contribute to that end. At the same time, however, it is not without significance that the demand for steel is what economists call inelastic. This means that within broad limits profits will be higher or losses smaller if prices are kept higher rather than allowed to fall. The "Gary Dinners" were to be a regular feature of the economic situation for a number of years thereafter, and industry leadership by the giant combine did not cease even when these dinners were no longer held.

That the consolidation movement (apart from banker control and price leadership) was not yet dead was also demonstrated in 1908. To this point America had never succeeded in solving in any very real sense her short distance transportation problem. A faster and more convenient way to get from one community to another was almost desperately needed. It followed that immense rewards would accrue to those who could make this possible. For twenty years a number of keen, ambitious inventors had been seeking to resolve the many technical problems.

By 1908 the period of commercial development of the automobile was clearly at hand. Some sixty producers were in the field, all of them operating under the pressure of limited capital and intense competition. To a degree capital was limited because competition was intense, but the more important factor was the highly speculative nature of the industry. Technology was advancing rapidly, the product itself was changing frequently, and there were present all the other difficulties of a new industry, including the difficulty of predicting demand. As a result the industry persistently tended toward overproduction and the mortality rate for concerns was very high.

These conditions in the infant automobile industry provided all the ingredients which had gone into earlier combinations. Heavy fixed costs created pressure for increased output so that unit prices could be reduced and the market expanded as a basis for still further price reductions, and an "excessive" number of concerns trying to increase output constantly threatened chaos. Besides, William C. Durant, without doubt the most colorful figure in the early history of this industry, had visions of a greatly expanded industry with a very large place in it reserved for himself.

In 1908 Durant took the first major step toward making his dream come true. He combined Buick, Cadillac, and Oldsmobile, together with a number of lesser firms, into a concern which he called General Motors. (Henry Ford's company was almost swallowed up in this combine, although not because the Ford concern was in financial difficulties.) From such small beginnings this concern went on to become the largest firm in America's greatest industry, turning out even after the automobile reached maturity 40 to 50 per cent of the industry's output. The beginning of consolidation, plus the simultaneous discovery of vast petroleum resources in the Southwest, set the stage for the prodigious growth this industry was to enjoy over the next few years.

Meanwhile the bankers were busily extending their power. Gradually over the years life insurance companies had become "big business" from the standpoint of control over capital, and control over capital was the key factor during this period. As an illustration of the rapidity of the growth taking place in this field, the insurance investigation in New York revealed that within a forty-year period after the Civil War two insurance companies (the Mutual Life Insurance Company and the Equitable Life Assurance Society) increased their combined assets from less than $3 million to $750 million. Tens of millions of dollars flowed into these concerns each year in premiums, an amount increasing every year, and these funds had to find prompt outlets in investments or the concerns could not operate profitably.

It is no wonder that control of these concerns was an important objective of such men as Thomas Fortune Ryan and J. P. Morgan. Here was reason enough for Morgan's paying $3 million for insurance stock having a par value of $51,000. Furthermore, the bond connecting insurance companies with banks could easily be strengthened once the initial point of control had been established, because state insurance laws often permitted these concerns to buy bank stock. The Hughes investigation had revealed how far this relationship had already been carried as insurance companies sought to participate indirectly in speculations forbidden to them by law.

By 1908 the time had arrived for binding the various financial institutions in the economy still more tightly. As yet commercial and investment banking were largely independent of each other, at least more so than was considered desirable by the financial leaders of the day. The principal reason was state regulation. New York, for example, would not permit her banks to sell securities to the general public. Always, however, banks had purchased securities from the brokers most closely associated with them, and loans to brokers and individual traders had become an important part of the business of commercial banks. Thus it was only another violation of the spirit of a law already violated in spirit many times when in 1908 J. P. Morgan decided to do away with the fiction. The First National Bank, the heart and center of Morgan's banking interests, organized an affiliated investment banking company. This precedent was shortly followed by others.

An interesting and significant irony developed out of this closing circle of financial interests. After the Hughes investigation, New York had moved to destroy the connection between banking and insurance by compelling insurance companies to dispose of their holdings of bank and trust company stock. Later it was discovered that disposition had taken the form of sales to investment bankers closely associated with the insurance companies. The new union between commercial and investment banks, therefore, meant that no real diminution of centralized financial control had been achieved.

The progressive advance of finance capitalism was almost fatal to Will Durant's dream. He was essentially a promoter, not a manager or a technician. Starting his combine with too little capital and expanding more rapidly than his resources warranted, he was soon in financial difficulty. From this difficulty he was able to extricate himself only at the price of turning control of his company over to the bankers for a period of five years. Securing control again at the end of this period, he was once more virtually replaced by his financial rivals. This time he was rescued, however, by the fact that Du Pont had at the moment more funds than it could profitably reinvest. Enough of these surplus funds were put into General Motors to secure for Du Pont a controlling interest in the company, and Durant was kept out of the clutches of the bankers.

Defeat and Victory on the Tax Front. As Theodore Roosevelt's presidency came to an end the problem of a successor created much difficulty. Reformers, of course, wanted a man of Roosevelt's own stripe, although businessmen were understandably weary of the constant attacks emanating from the nonbusiness sectors of the community. So powerful still was reform sentiment, and so strategically situated is an American president to dictate his party's presidential nominee, that a compromise was inevitable. The mantle fell on William Howard Taft, known in labor circles as "the father of injunctions" and a man whose reform proclivities and personality were both weaker than those of his predecessor. When, for example, Roosevelt was asked how strongly his successor would fight for reform policies, he answered in all kindness and respect for his good friend that "they" (the conservatives) would push against him a little. By this Roosevelt did not mean that conservatives had done no pushing against him; he meant simply that Taft would do less resisting. He was right.

The principal concessions to reformers made by the Republican platform in 1908 were a promise of tariff revision, a pledge to carry railroad regulation still further, and a declaration in favor of stronger antitrust laws. Taft campaigned actively on these issues, and on the question of the tariff he made it unmistakably clear that his idea of revision meant reduction. So everyone else interpreted the term, at least outwardly. It was not until the convening of a special session of Congress to "revise" the tariff that rank and file party members realized that their leaders had no such idea.

They meant instead to fight against reduction, and even to promote some upward revisions.

Immediately there broke out, in both House and Senate, a legislative battle even more bitter than that over the Hepburn Act. Opposing eastern manufacturers were midwest farmers and a large group of middle class urban residents up in arms over the increase in the price level. At stake, thus, was an issue of the utmost importance to several groups. As the battle developed during the long, hot summer of 1909, it was evident that the American economy, and with it the tariff controversy, had reached a somewhat more advanced stage.

During the latter years of the nineteenth century, midwesterners and easterners, although they had had differences over the tariff, had never been unable to find a basis for compromise. By 1909, however, prairie farmers were beginning to conclude that a tariff level satisfactory to manufacturers was too great a price to pay for the little protection received by producers of export commodities. The midwest was learning, in short, the lesson John C. Calhoun had taught the South long before the Civil War; tariff taxation falls with particular force upon exporters of agricultural staples.

The leader of the party "Regulars," Nelson W. Aldrich of Rhode Island (father-in-law of John D. Rockefeller, Jr.) did not question the validity of the farmers' complaint. Unfortunately, however, manufacturers had come to feel about agricultural tariffs much as farmers felt about manufacturers' tariffs, for many agricultural products were now important industrial raw materials. And so the problem in 1909 was less a question of finding a suitable compromise than of testing which side could command the most votes.

It was the easterners, laborers included, although the votes of western sugar, wool, and hides producers were also helpful. The tariff bill passed in 1909 was not a general increase in duties, but it did carefully avoid such decreases as might produce discomfort for American manufacturers.

This struggle saw introduced into the tariff controversy a new spirit, a spirit also appearing in the battle between labor and capital. At one point it could have been convincingly argued that protection and labor "discipline" were necessities in the business adjustment to the machine and the national and international competition implied by the machine. But so far had the adjustment been carried and so well established was the American economy in the world economy that what had once been a necessity had clearly become a convenience—at times even a luxury. Just as there seemed to be a trend away from "defensiveness" in trust formation as "finance capitalism" reached its apex, so did there seem to be a trend away from "defensiveness" in both the the tariff and labor relations fields.

Defeated on the tariff, "Insurgent" Republicans endeavored next to achieve a readjustment in the nation's tax structure. A small beginning had been made in the tariff bill in the House by the inclusion of a moderate inheritance tax. When the Senate promptly deleted this provision, a graduated income tax was proposed as an amendment. As the debate on this measure proceeded it became apparent that a large group of agricultural and labor spokesmen were willing to vote for it.

There were numerous reasons why the business interests objected to an income tax. First, as the nation's more affluent members they would be directly injured. Second, although the tariff was not as important in the government's revenue system as it had once been, it was still so large an item that another important revenue source might generate an increased pressure for lower duties. Third, it was widely feared that if an income tax measure were again passed and again invalidated by the Supreme Court, that institution might lose so much prestige as to be less effective in protecting business interests in other ways.

The strategy followed to defeat the income tax (after denunciations of it as socialist legislation had failed) was to split its supporters. This was done by submitting instead a corporation tax limited in duration to two years. As events were in time to work themselves out, the cure was almost worse than the disease. Taft insisted that the two-year limitation be deleted before he would support it as a substitution. Then, on the floor of Congress, the "Regulars" were forced to agree to the submission of the income tax to the states as a constitutional amendment. Much to their dismay it was supported by the states, and instead of having only an income tax the business interests were burdened with both a corporation tax and an income tax.[1]

Conservation of the nation's resources was the next focus of attention in this phase of the battle for reform. It had of late become standard practice for presidents to withdraw from private entry valuable resources which had been made available so generously when few were concerned about conservation. This policy Roosevelt had carried especially far, despite the bitter opposition of western lumbermen, sheepmen, cattle ranchers, and owners of water sites. When Taft's administration endeavored to continue this policy opposition became even stronger, and the struggle between "Insurgents" and "Regulars" broke out anew.

The focal point for this new controversy was the so-called Ballinger-Pinchot dispute. Ballinger as Secretary of the Interior set about restoring

[1] It is obvious that personal income taxes cannot be passed on to those lower down in the income hierarchy. Less obvious is the conclusion generally agreed to by economists that taxes on business income cannot be "shifted," for example, to the consumer. Prices, so this argument goes, are broadly related to costs of production at "the margin"; that is, the prices must be high enough to cover the production cost of those producers who have no net income to be taxed. Where a monopolistic situation prevails, furthermore, it is presumed that the concerns involved are charging about "what the market will bear" and that therefore prices cannot be raised significantly as a result of heavier taxes of the income variety.

to private entry lands which had been withdrawn under Roosevelt. Pinchot as Chief of the Forest Service protested this reversal of policy, and at once conservation became a political storm center. The dismissal of Pinchot was the immediate outcome, and prairie farmers and many others could never thereafter be convinced that Taft did not betray his predecessor. Actually, however, the policy and practice of conservation did not suffer under Taft's administration, even though it did proceed at a somewhat slower pace. For example, by the end of his term the President's statutory power to withdraw resources was virtually complete. The real trouble was still that it was too late for even a liberal conservation policy to salvage very much.

Success on the Transportation Front. One other reform battle was fought in 1910, the most important in this series as far as results were concerned. Nothing had as yet been done to solve the long-and-short-haul discrimination problem on the nation's railways, nor to remedy certain other regulatory defects. Farmers faced with rising costs were understandably eager to see these matters attended to. Especially were they anxious to provide the Interstate Commerce Commission with power to suspend railroad rate increases until an investigation could be made to determine the necessity for them. In fact, this new regulatory measure was debated against the background of general rate increases either instituted or promised, and as soon as the new law was passed these increases were disallowed.

Once again regulation could only be strengthened over the bitter opposition of the business interests, but with this step the Commission was restored to something approximating the status it was originally intended to have. In addition to the power to suspend rates, power to prescribe minimum rates was also included. With this authority the Commission could fully protect the carriers from destructive competition as well as the public from excessive, discriminatory charges. The Commission was even given authority over telephone, telegraph, and cable companies, but, partly because the problems of railroad control were so time-consuming, little was done with this power or with that over pipelines conferred by the Hepburn Act. Only one important power did the Commission not now have; it had no authority over capitalization, a matter which was in fact crucial to regulatory effectiveness. Unfortunately, however, it was almost too late to accomplish much in this way; capital structures were already greatly unbalanced in the direction of excessive fixed charges. But despite this failure of the Mann-Elkins Act of 1910, it was one of the most basic of all the railroad regulatory laws.

After the passage of this act the nation's railroad policy was all the more attacked by conservatives. It was charged that the reformers had destroyed a great industry by making it unattractive to private enterprise. A certain superficial plausibility was given to this charge by the fact that railroad mileage in the country did not increase significantly after the law was passed. On the other hand, however, there was now ushered in an *intensive* railroad development just as vital in its way as the extensive growth prior to this time. Second, third, and fourth tracks were added. Terminal facilities were expanded. Both track and equipment were greatly improved. In all, while miles of road did not continue to increase as they had in the past, over a twenty-year period the book value of investment in this industry

TABLE 74. A SHIFT IN EMPHASIS

Year	Railway Mileage	Book Value of Investment
	(Thousands)	(Billions of dollars)
1910	240.3	14.6
1930	249.1	26.1

Source: Bureau of the Census, *Historical Statistics of the United States, 1789-1945*, pp. 202 and 204.

increased by eighty per cent. The Mann-Elkins Act did not destroy the extensive railroad frontier; it simply coincided with the disappearance of that frontier.

Along with this new attempt to control the economy's transportation system in the public interest, reformers also made progress toward a closely related objective. Years before, the canals and rivers of the nation had ceased to be important arteries of commerce. In part this was because these waterways could not effectively compete with railroads, and in part it was because railroads had often set about systematically to destroy their water rivals. Although not explained wholly by the zeal for reform (even business interests in communities along waterways were anxious for revival), this period was marked by an earnest effort to restore these once important transportation routes to their old vigor. The Ohio River was canalized, much money was spent improving navigation on the Missouri, eventually a "deep waterway" from the Great Lakes to the Gulf of Mexico was achieved, as was also an intracoastal waterway system from Maine to Florida and from Florida to Texas. Simultaneously, the Erie Canal was restored to usefulness and the Panama Canal built. (Once again Erie Canal expenditures were undertaken by the state of New York.)

It is ironical that the success of these efforts to create additional competition for the railroads was almost inversely proportional to the cost of the facilities provided. Put differently, the more "artificial" a waterway was to be in finished form, the greater its cost and the less it added to the nation's transportation network. Conversely, the less "artificial" it was to be when completed, the less the outlay required and the more important it was likely to be. Thus where a small effort could make available a long water transport haul—as between the Atlantic and the Pacific, and between Lakes Superior, Huron, and Erie—the results were good. But where, as in the case of most of these, the entire waterway was virtually useless without artificial channeling, little was gained. It is in part for this reason that legislation in this field is popularly referred to as the "pork barrel."

Because these efforts did fail, the Great Lakes System was virtually all that remained of the great water-transport system which had once meant so much to the nation. Its strategic location between the Atlantic and the great grain producing region of North America, between the tremendously rich Michigan deposits of iron ore and the principal steel centers, and between eastern coal producing regions and western coal consumers made it able to compete with the railroads on even terms. In fact, so superior were these waterways in the transportation of iron ore that it even proved profitable to build storage facilities at lower lake ports to avoid the necessity of using the railroads when the Lakes were frozen.

While most of this legislation did not achieve the desired results, another kind of legislation achieved much more. Two years after the Mann-Elkins Act was passed, in the so-called Panama Canal Act, rigorous steps were taken to prevent railroads from continuing to take unfair advantage of competitors by water—for example, by lowering rates long enough to bankrupt a water competitor and then raising them to monopoly levels. What little competition water carriers were able to provide was thereby protected, and a little later the internal combustion engine (in automobiles, trucks, and airplanes) was to supply a competition to railroads that water facilities were never able to provide.

Failure on the Antitrust Front. The year 1911 was a big year in the antitrust field, too. Suits against the great Oil and Tobacco Trusts reached the Supreme Court. Both of these cases had been started on their way under President Roosevelt, but his successor's administration had prosecuted them vigorously. Now, for the first time, the Court was being asked to rule on the holding company device in connection with an industrial trust. The contention of the government was no less than that the Sherman Anti-Trust Act declared *all* combinations in restraint of trade illegal regardless of results or methods.

As to methods, the Court agreed with the government; the holding company form of organization was declared in the Standard Oil decision to be no assurance against prosecution. On the question of results, however, the Court refused to accept the government's contention. Unless the judiciary is allowed to exercise discretion on the matter of what is or is not an unreasonable restraint it would be impossible to avoid violating the "protection of property" provisions of the Constitution. In short, the Court felt it must either have discretion or it must declare the Sherman law unconstitutional. Faced with this alternative, the Justices concluded they had no choice but to exercise their own judgment.

Having built up a logic which might just as readily have been used to exonerate the Standard Oil Company, the Court proceeded to declare it a combination in restraint of trade. (The catalog of abuses of what was then considered good business ethics practiced by the Standard Oil Company in achieving its position was too extensive to be ignored.) Accordingly, an order was issued demanding dissolution. Here, however, new difficulties arose. And whether the final dissolution order was ineffective because the Court honestly did not know what to do or because the Justices really did not intend it to be effective will never be known for certain. In any event, what the Court asked was that the parent company dispose of its stock holdings by distributing them to its own stockholders. In this way a "community of interest" trust was created to replace the holding company being dissolved. Careful studies made a few years later concluded that little if anything had been accomplished by way of restoring competition to the oil industry.

The American Tobacco Company decision followed directly from the Standard Oil decision. This concern was also declared to be engaged in restraint of trade, and ordered to be dissolved. A method of dissolution, however, even one acceptable to the Court, was in this case much less easy to devise. Several of the units making up the combine were themselves dominant in the particular branch of the industry they represented; for example, the American Snuff Company, even if separated from the American Tobacco Company, would still violate the antitrust laws in the snuff business. Although a real attempt seems to have been made to deal seriously with this problem, the resultant decree permitted a highly concentrated industry to remain—one in which "community of interest" relationships could easily be (and probably were) built. Using snuff again as the representative situation, three major companies were created, each with about 30 per cent of the industry's capacity. Only some 7 per cent of the industry remained in the hands of independents.

The following year several other antitrust actions were taken, all instituted by Taft's Attorney General. Results were no more substantial than they had been in earlier years, and, as often before, the law fell most heavily on railroads. The Aluminum Company of America was enjoined against certain anticompetitive practices it was following; the Southern Pacific and Union Pacific were separated from each other; a step was taken toward breaking up the combination of the major anthracite railroads; and the Terminal Railroad Association of St. Louis was told it could not exclude from membership any railroad wishing to join its organization. In addition to these results, the principal significance of these cases is the indication they afford of the antitrust activity of Taft's administration. Against the widely accepted notion that Roosevelt was active in this field while Taft was not, it is to be said in rebuttal that with half as much time at his disposal Taft instituted more suits than did the famous "trust buster." And certainly few would claim that Roosevelt's activities were more successful in altering the structure of American industry than were Taft's.

The fact is that the efforts of neither produced substantial changes in the underlying economy. Therein lies a most significant paradox. After almost a quarter of a century the antitrust laws had accomplished virtually nothing, and that despite the continuous and widespread existence of an intense antitrust sentiment. And not only had these laws achieved little of a positive nature, but the period in which they had been on the books included the years of most extensive trust formation, a combination movement which had tapered off only because the principal consolidation opportunities had been exploited.

Even these facts do not indicate how great this paradox was. Two other points need also to be suggested to round out the picture. First, the antitrust laws had actually functioned perversely. By their operation firms had been progressively driven from less formal combinations to more formal ones. Thus when the courts began to frown upon pooling and other crude agreements between competitors, the holding company device had been perfected. Later, as the courts began to disapprove of holding company combinations, the trend was for a time at least in the direction of outright merger of the properties being combined. In short, far from bringing the problem of monopoly under control the law was actually forcing it into forms in which it was virtually uncontrollable.

A second point is even more striking. By contrast with the law's failure to deal successfully with industrial monopoly, the public was easily able to fasten controls on the nation's railroads. On no less than a dozen occasions, some six or so of them major, the people had acted to bring these concerns into a more responsible relationship with the underlying community. When the laws had been seen to be inadequate, they had been extended. When judicial interpretation had emasculated their plain intent, they had been rewritten in such a way as to make that intent inescapably clear. When enforcement had seemed to be weak, steps had been taken to strengthen it. At no point, although the process had taken time, had the public been forced to concede defeat. In short, during the same period of time in which the antitrust laws had been demonstrated to be a virtual fiasco, comprehensive railroad regulation had become an accomplished fact.

An Interpretation. Why this difference? Why was it that the spirit of reform was equal to the one task but quite unable to cope with the other? It is no answer to say that the administration in power was often unwilling to strengthen the antitrust laws, for the administration in power had often enough been reluctant to strengthen the railroad laws. Nor is it any answer that the funds appropriated were insufficient; the nation was not so short on funds that more could not have been made available. It is not even an effective answer that the Supreme Court was primarily at fault, or that legislators were unable to frame laws that would demand "correct" judicial interpretation. These were precisely the same problems which had been successfully met by the same legislators in the railroad field. No, it seems only reasonable to insist that, with respect to the antitrust problem as well as the railroad problem, if the will had been present, a way would have been found. It is well to remember, in this connection, that the antitrust laws were in fact rigorously applied in railroad cases.

Why, then, was the will not present? At least three factors at once suggest themselves. In the first place, it is highly significant that nothing accomplished in the railway field, not even the successful antitrust actions, really altered significantly the evolving structure of that industry—the high degree of concentration and the limited nature of the competition remaining. Rather the assumption was that the high fixed cost character of railroad transportation made the industry to a considerable extent inherently noncompetitive. Yet the explicit assumption behind the antitrust program was essentially that other fixed cost industries could be so altered in structure by legislative fiat as to be made competitive in the nineteenth-century, small-scale, many-firm tradition. Furthermore, every other reform *achievement* (for example, the Food and Drug Act and the Meat Inspection Act) had taken for granted the existing industry structure, and had sought instead only to limit abuses within that framework. These facts are well worth contemplating by those made unhappy by the failure of the reform movement to alter the structure of manufacturing industry.

In the second place, it is worth noting that long before effective railroad regulation became a reality the ground had been thoroughly prepared. In the "Granger" cases the Supreme Court had pronounced the railroad industry to be a public utility, as distinguished from a purely private enterprise, and from this position the nation had never retreated. Thus, by the beginning of the new century the country was fully accustomed to thinking of the railroads as belonging in this special category. In the absence of this background it would no doubt have been impossible to subject railroads to the thoroughgoing regulation which had in fact evolved. Until the public had become similarly prepared to think in such terms with respect to industrial monopolies, there would perhaps be little hope of enacting the kind of legislation required by the situation. Put differently, the public utility concept had been deliberately framed in such a way as to make it apply to a segment of the economy. Thus to an important extent the prerequisite to thinking of the railroad as a public utility was continuing to apply the private enterprise ideal in the industrial field.

The extent to which this factor must have been involved can almost be documented. Not only during this period did railway regulation come of age, but a regulation victory of equal significance was simultaneously being won. It was at this time that electricity was decisively establishing itself and in the process revolutionizing not only American industry but urban life as well. Classified almost immediately in the public mind as a public utility within the meaning of Munn v. Illinois (if for no other reason than because of the vital importance of the new power for urban transportation), steps were taken by various states to subject power-generating and distribut-

TABLE 75. REVOLUTION IN POWER

Year	Electric Power Production
	(Billions of kilowatt-hours)
1902	6.0
1912	24.8
1922	61.2
1932	99.4
1942	233.1

Source: Bureau of the Census, *Historical Statistics of the United States, 1789-1945*, p. 156.

ing concerns to thoroughgoing regulation on the railroad model. Although many states already had railroad or public service commissions of a sort, the modern public utility commission with comprehensive regulatory powers unquestionably dates from this period—the period during which antitrust legislation was being resoundingly defeated. What is most significant of all, despite the fact that state after state over a seven-year period created a "strong" regulatory commission, is that the Supreme Court did not in any way intervene.

In the third place, there seems to be good reason for supposing that the failure of antitrust legislation owes much to the unwillingness of labor to take a strong stand in favor of such a policy. Only reforms receiving substantial support from farmers, laborers, and the middle class could apparently be passed. When the Sherman Act was originally enacted, labor's attitude had been that both labor and capital should be left clear of the law to work out their destinies unhampered. Twenty-one years later this attitude, though still prevalent, was no doubt powerfully supplemented by another one. Intelligent labor leaders could scarcely press for more restrictive antitrust measures while the ones in force were being used with much greater vigor against labor than against capital. Put differently, labor could work actively to implement legislation under the public utility concept without endangering its own position, whereas this was by no means certain in the antitrust area.

Clouds on the Labor Front. Whatever the reason or reasons for the failure of the antitrust laws, it is certain that labor was still putting most of its emphasis elsewhere. Equally certain is it that these efforts were crowned with sufficient success to justify the emphases actually selected, and, with the return of prosperity, it was possible to resume the forward advance of organization and collective bargaining disrupted by depression and employer resistance. Interrupted only by a decline in business brought about by the outbreak of war in Europe, the American Federation of Labor regained the membership it had lost and gained 40 per cent more members in addition. Throughout this expansion, moreover, the Federation retained its dominant position in the labor movement; approximately three-fourths of all organized workers continued to be Federation members.

One of the great achievements of this period was on the social legislation front, and especially in connection with what is called employer's liability laws. Prior to 1911 little progress had been made toward relieving workers of the full burden of injuries received while at work, although the feeling had been growing that these burdens should rather be considered as a cost of doing business—that at best workers are apt to bear more than their fair share of such costs. In part the slowness of this evolution had been due to judicial conservatism, although principally it had resulted from general community conservatism, and as yet little had been accomplished by way of breaking down this resistance. The year 1911, however, was a turning point. Although legislation shifting a part of this burden from the worker was of doubtful constitutional status, veritable avalanches of workmen's compensation laws were passed. Ten states enacted such legislation in 1911 alone, and twelve other states appointed investigative commissions. In the next few years the principle of distributing a large part of the burden of industrial accidents to society at large (by way of the employer) was accepted almost everywhere. In other words, and most appropriately, this problem was attacked by making worker disabilities expensive to profit-seeking employers—by making safety profitable.

This and other legislative victories made labor acutely aware of the importance of maintaining the public good will so tardily won. Hence it was unfortunate for the immediate future of the labor movement that the year 1912 saw the climax (although not the end) of a development which threatened to wrest from labor much of the middle class support it was now enjoying.

The threat came in several different forms. A part of it appeared in the form of one of the most active periods of socialist activity the nation had ever known. Significantly, Eugene V. Debs was a leader of this agitation, and before the year was out he was to poll almost one million votes as a candidate for president. Another part took the form of uprisings by western workers against powerful absentee employers. Because miners and lumbermen are apt in any event to be dominated in their behavior less by the refinements of "civilization" than many other groups, and because westerners were still highly imbued with the pioneer spirit, these struggles more nearly resembled civil war than any preceding episodes in American labor's history.

But if these were the ingredients which most immediately resulted in a new "radical" labor movement, the deeper cause was the failure of the craft type of organization to satisfy some of the most basic needs of workers. A strategically placed craft union could easily tie up an entire plant at the expense of the unskilled, achieving gains if the strike was successful only for its own group. Thus, in the Homestead strike the workers who actually stood to gain from success constituted only a small minority of the workers actually employed. Conversely, a strike by the mass of unskilled workers had virtually no chance of success unless the craft groups cooperated. There was reason enough in this period for the song sung by many an unskilled laborer:

> Ain't it hell in the A. F. of L.
> All you get is sympathy.

Given these ingredients—socialism, revolutionism, and industrial unionism—it is not surprising that a rival labor organization appeared and that it unequivocally declared war on Samuel Gompers' American Federation of Labor. Calling itself the Industrial Workers of the World, thus including the idea of industrial unionism directly in its title, this organization set as its goal the creation of an entirely new society. Its code of principles and its propaganda, moreover, went out of their way to suggest to the community at large that it would not stop short of violence in attaining its ends. This was as misleading as it was unfortunate. It was misleading because the new organization was never particularly violent either in underlying attitudes or actual techniques, and unfortunate because any violence which occurred was immediately laid to its door, no matter what the source. (Often, for example, violence could be traced most directly to specific actions of employers or to their completely unyielding attitude in dealing with workers.)

The history of the Industrial Workers of the World can be quickly told. Because it was not composed of homogeneous elements, it was plagued by factional struggles from the very beginning. For this reason, because it repelled conservative unionism of whatever kind by the implicit threat to the existing order which it contained, and because it was not successful at quiet, routine, union management, it was never an important factor in the labor movement. As time went on factional difficulties were progressively resolved by the withdrawal of the more conservative groups (withdrawal usually into the Federation), leaving a hard core of genuinely revolutionist members able to wield even less influence. When during World War I this remnant denounced America's participation, it began a steep descent into oblivion.

However, this group has a significance in American economic development much greater than this history would suggest. First, it is indicative of the strength of the industrial union movement, a movement which had not disappeared when the Knights of Labor fell from power. Second, it is indicative of the extreme conservatism of the American Federation of Labor. This group was not, to be sure, entirely negative on the subject of industrial unionism; its acceptance of miners and textile workers is evidence enough on this point. But if the Federation had openly rather than begrudgingly accepted this extension of its own economic principles it is doubtful if the "Wobblies" would have gained any momentum at all. Neither, in all probability, would socialism have grown as it did. Of course, this reluctance was fully understandable. Industrial unionism ran sharply counter to the basis of the Federation's success, and occasional attempts to use craft strength for the benefit of unskilled workers served only to strengthen its exclusiveness. Furthermore, this organization was at the moment steeped more than ever in conservatism because of the intensity and success of the employer counteroffensive.

Third, even more important than these considerations were the consequences of the rise and fall of the Industrial Workers of the World for the future of the labor movement. Appearing as it now was in company with a full dress revolutionism, industrial unionism could all the more not be accepted by the Federation. Unavoidably, thus, a vicious circle was set up which could not readily be broken. The more radical rival organizations became, the more was the craft organization bound to remain closed to them; the more unwelcome they were in the Federation, the more radical they necessarily became. It is, in short, easily possible that the success of industrial unionism was postponed by two decades as a result of the developments now taking place.

Fortunately, however, there was already some evidence that this problem would one day be solved. One of the outstanding advances made by labor occurred in this period in the form of a successful, permanent organization in the clothing industry. Here, in an industry whose workers were principally women or immigrants, a union based largely on the industrial principle emerged as one of the most powerful in the nation. For the first time, thus, women and immigrants figured importantly in the American labor movement. Understandably, in view of their long history of orientation in that direction, the clothing workers' unions retained a trace of radicalism for many years. But, on the other hand, their success was largely proportional to the relinquishment of these elements in their origin, an evolution paving the way for ultimate acceptance in the Federation. In turn this success provided a foundation for building on other than radical grounds.

One other important development was taking place on the labor front. For years the railroad brotherhoods had been extremely conservative organizations. In part because their members were skilled workers occupying the strategic position in America's most strategic industry, they had been so fortunate as to be able to win recognition and many demands with a minimum of striking. The railroads in their turn had been able to grant labor's demands because they were in a position to pass on to the consumer cost increases so induced. Instead of strikes, the brotherhoods had concentrated their energies on self-insurance because private concerns were reluctant to insure men in so hazardous an occupation.

The perfection of railroad regulation changed all this. No longer able easily to pass cost increases on to the consumer, railroads began to resist cost-increasing demands by labor. When, soon after the passage of the Mann-Elkins Act, the Interstate Commerce Commission refused to allow a rate increase, the railroads declined to grant labor demands then pending—demands motivated by the steady rise of the cost of living. The result was a railroad-labor dispute in 1912 which, although settled without a strike by mediation machinery already provided by earlier legislation, turned out very unfavorably for the workers. Out of this and later similar experiences railroad labor forged a somewhat altered philosophy of its need for organization, becoming steadily more militant in its outlook. This transformation has been matched over the years by increasingly comprehensive attempts to frame legislation enabling labor controversies in the railroad industry to be resolved without work stoppages tying up this vital segment of the transportation system of the country.

Possibly the experience of railroad workers with the regulated railroad industry was one of the reasons laborers in general did not press for more stringent controls designed to alleviate the trust problem. It is also possible, however, that they, in common with many other Americans, were not yet convinced that the approach then being taken toward this problem could not be successful. In any event, the time had almost arrived when a fresh, new attempt was to be made to solve this problem along traditional lines. And there is no doubt that much of this new program was framed with labor's needs and desires specifically in mind.

QUESTIONS FOR DISCUSSION

1. Are relationships such as those implicit in institutions such as the "Gary Dinners" in the best interest of society as a whole?
2. What was the objection prior to 1908 to commercial and investment banking functions being carried on by the same concern? Why was it so important to financiers to alter this situation?
3. What are the economic consequences of a shift from excises to a greater reliance on progressive income taxes in financing the government? Was such a shift injurious to the economy at this time?
4. What was the connection between the building of artificial waterways and reform sentiment? Was this approach logically justifiable, entirely apart from the soundness of many of the projects themselves?
5. Of what significance was the "rule of reason" promulgated by the Supreme Court in 1911?
6. Why were court cases more fruitful when the defendants were railroad companies rather than industrial trusts?
7. Why was regulatory legislation so successful in railroad matters and so unsuccessful where industrial concerns were involved?
8. Why did the American Federation of Labor become so unreceptive to industrial unionism?
9. To what extent can workers alter the distribution of a society's real income through organization?

Chapter 30

THE "NEW FREEDOM"

1912 Woodrow Wilson elected President.
1913 Income tax amendment (16th) declared ratified.
 Underwood Tariff.
 Pujo Committee report.
 Federal Reserve Act.
 Popular election of U. S. Senators provided in the 17th amendment.
1914 Federal Trade Commission Act.
 Clayton Anti-Trust Act.
 Beginning of war in Europe.
1915 La Follette Seamen's Act.
1916 Federal Farm Loan Act.
1917 United States entered the war; mass of war legislation.

There was in 1912 a widespread feeling that the reform movement was not meeting with high success, that the attempt to loosen the hold of laissez faire on the nation was being seriously frustrated. Roosevelt supporters charged that Taft had abandoned his predecessor's liberal policies, and Roosevelt himself vigorously echoed these sentiments when he returned from his hunting trip in Africa. As a result Roosevelt did his best to unseat his friend in the White House from the leadership of the Republican party. Failing in this, he ran for the presidency under the banner of a third party—the "Bull Moosers." Meanwhile the Democrats had discovered Woodrow Wilson, a candidate eminently qualified to lead agrarian reformers and to weld together the reform interests of farmers, laborers, and the urban middle class.

How strong reform sentiment still was in 1912 is indicated by the fact that Roosevelt and Wilson overwhelmingly swept the country, Taft receiving only eight electoral votes. But the consequence of the split in the Republican party was that Wilson was elected, although it is possible that Wilson would have won in a straight-out battle against Taft. In any event, the significant fact about the 1912 election was that Republican conservatives such as N. W. Aldrich no longer held the reins of power. For the first time, in other words, reform forces were a real majority group in the nation's capital. Perhaps now the reform campaign could proceed more smoothly. Perhaps now a successful campaign against extreme laissez-faire principles could be launched.

An Unprecedented Accomplishment. The push began immediately. At a special session of Congress called for this specific purpose, the new administration made short work of passing a downward revision of the tariff. And whereas Grover Cleveland's tariff reduction had been scarcely more than token, the Underwood Tariff turned back the hands of the tariff clock two-thirds of a century; the level of duties enacted closely approximated that of the Walker Tariff of fifteen years before the Civil War.

Short work was similarly made of another issue long high on the list of reformers. By early 1913 enough states had ratified the proposed income tax amendment to make it a part of the Constitution. Justifying income tax legislation in part by the reduction in revenue resulting from tariff revision, reformers proceeded to enact the first permanent personal income

TABLE 76. A NEW TAX STRUCTURE

	Percentage of Federal Government Revenue From			
Year	Customs Levies	Income and Profits Taxes	Other Internal Taxes	Other Revenue
1909	50	–	40	10
1919	4	60	25	11
1929	13	60	14	13
1939	6	40	50	4

Source: Bureau of the Census, *Historical Statistics of the United States, 1789-1945,* pp. 295-96.

tax in the nation's history. Never again was America's tax structure to be as regressive as it had always before been. Never again was the customs revenue to be an important source of government tax receipts.

Moreover, these enactments were only the beginning. From the tariff and taxation the administration turned to another question which had long been a matter of controversy between the major economic groups. In the resulting revision of the nation's money and banking system, although they did manage to secure some of the things they wanted, the business interests were to experience an even more basic frustration.

It had long been recognized that the old National Banking Act had not accomplished the purposes for which it was created. Thus, with the growth of deposit or "checkbook" currency, national banks had progressively declined in importance, giving way to the more rapid growth of state banks and the truly phenomenal rise of trust companies. A uniform currency had been created over the years, to be sure, but national bank notes by now represented only one-fifth of total circulation. Nor was the currency now in use as elastic as was desired. During prosperous times, when additional circulation was needed, banks could use their resources more profitably than in the purchase of government bonds on which to base a larger note issue, while in depressed times the reverse was true. Furthermore, the relationship between government bonds and note circulation, established to provide a market for government bonds, had worked perversely. Because of the country's need for currency, the government had been forced to forego debt retirement and hence to give up its freedom in fiscal matters. And finally, the old legislation had done little to protect the community against bank failures, even though national banks were safer than state banks.

Besides these failures of the existing system, certain other banking and monetary objectives had become important in the preceding fifty years. It was recognized that the American system suffered from a decentralization not found in any modern nation, a product of the early years of banking evolution in this country. The result was that the reserves on which the entire banking system rested were widely dispersed, with the financial stability of the nation thus resting on the uncoordinated decisions of thousands of different individuals. This defect, in fact, was even accentuated by the operation of the National Banking System. Since the deposits of the banks in the nation's great financial centers were in large part the reserves of other banks all over the country, a financial shock at any point in the system was apt to be magnified rather than absorbed.

On the general outlines of the defects of the existing banking organization there was well-nigh universal agreement. Much controversy arose, however, when it came to the nature of the changes necessary to make the system function more adequately. On one side were the business interests, who would have preferred to see a genuinely central bank managed by private bankers. On the other side were the nation's farmers, who feared a central bank only slightly less than such a bank controlled by the banking community. Their preference would have been a minimum of centralization but with control lodged in the Treasury Department.

In one sense businessmen and bankers had only themselves to blame that they had not taken advantage of their control over the government to enact their preferences into law. However, their reasons for not doing so are reasonable enough in retrospect, although in 1913 they did perhaps regret their inaction. In the first place, prior to the two twentieth-century panics, the business community had felt that the system was functioning reasonably well. After all, the principal nineteenth-century complaints had come from farmers. In the second place, and perhaps even more important, conservatives had feared that if the subject were opened up for debate and legislation, the farmer interest might succeed in creating an instrument far worse than the one already in existence. Not until economic conditions had made business very uneasy about the monetary system had highly placed Republicans been willing to assume positive leadership.

But be that as it may, it was a misfortune of the worst kind, as far as conservatives were concerned, that the National Monetary Commission made its report, embodying to the full the ideas of Aldrich and his colleagues, on the eve of the election of a reform, Democratic administration. And it was no less than a tragedy from this same point of view that positive legislative action on the money question was begun against the background of the report of the Pujo Committee.

This committee had been launched by the House of Representatives to investigate the "money trust," to find out the facts regarding America's new finance capitalism. The ensuing report did much to excite agrarian tempers even more against centralization and banker control. It showed, for example, how a great concentration of money and credit had developed by consolidations of competitive banks and trust companies, interlocking directorates and stock ownership, powerful investment houses, and huge insurance companies. It demonstrated that this concentration of control over money and credit put a few persons in a position to grant or withhold capital, and that with this power these men had secured control over much of American industry. Four closely related financial institutions, the report asserted, held three hundred and forty-one directorships in one hundred and twelve banks and in transportation, public utility, and insurance companies having an aggregate capital in excess of $22 billion.

From the standpoint of its effect on a public opinion already zealous for reform, the Pujo report could not have come at a more critical time. Ten years before a similar report would at least have shown that some competition existed in the top levels of this financial hierarchy. The Standard Oil Company, with almost more funds than it knew what to do with, had turned some of its wealth and energies into financial avenues. Although never the equal of the Morgan circle, the Rockefeller ring of interests had contested the field with the Morgan group quite sharply—as in the Harriman-Hill battle over the Northern Pacific. By 1913 Rockefeller's group had largely withdrawn, leaving Morgan in undisputed leadership of American capitalism and at the pinnacle of his influence. Only the Mellon interests in Pittsburgh could be compared with those of Morgan, and they were careful not to clash with their New York superiors. And, as damaging as any other single fact, the Interstate Commerce Commission was at that moment preparing a report on the New York, New Haven and Hartford Railroad Company which was outspokenly to charge Morgan's management of that line with recklessness, illegality, deception, and with virtually ruining a great railroad. What Morgan had attempted (and almost succeeded in doing) was to use his control over the New Haven to establish a complete transportation monopoly throughout New England.

Public agitation over the Pujo report was quieted not at all by Morgan's death in 1913. J. P. Morgan and Company still stood intact, as did the circle of interests it coordinated. Probably this excitement was at its highest point in the latter part of the year when the money issue began to be debated. As a result little time was spent with the suggestions contained in the Aldrich Committee report; that is, the ideas of complete centralization and banker control. The battle waged, thus, was essentially fought out within the Democratic party with extreme agrarian inflationists opposed to more orthodox men such as Carter Glass and Woodrow Wilson. The careful and patient work of these leaders succeeded in keeping most of the inflationist measures out of the final law, a fact which was some consolation to disgruntled conservatives.

The Federal Reserve Act as finally passed bears unmistakably the marks of the conflicting interests out of which it was created. Instead of a central bank with branches it created twelve regional banks, although a central board was established to exercise supervisory functions. The members of the Federal Reserve Board were to be the Secretary of the Treasury, the Comptroller of the Currency, and five members appointed by the President. On the other hand, however, two of these five must have had previous banking experience, while one-third of the directors of each regional bank were to be bankers. One-third was also to represent business at large, including agriculture, while another one-third was to represent the public. The first two groups of regional directors, moreover, were to be elected by the member banks which would be composed of all national banks and such state banks or trust companies as would care to join the system. And while membership by state institutions had to be left on a voluntary basis, it was not long before the new system had become overwhelmingly dominant.

TABLE 77. A NEW BANKING SYSTEM

Year	Number of Banks		Deposits	
	Federal Reserve Members	Nonmembers	Federal Reserve Members	Nonmembers
			(Billions of dollars)	
1915	7,615	18,260	8.9	9.1
1925	9,538	18,320	32.5	12.1
1935	6,410	9,068	34.9	6.4
1945	6,840	7,163	118.4	18.2

Source: Bureau of the Census, *Historical Statistics of the United States, 1789-1945*, pp. 266-67.

From the standpoint of the defects of the legislation it was replacing, the new act was well conceived. Extreme decentralization was corrected by requiring all the legal reserves of member banks to be deposited with the Federal Reserve banks. Pyramiding of reserves was prevented by forbidding the Federal Reserve banks to have dealings with anyone other than member banks and the government. Elasticity was provided for by the creation of a new currency, the federal reserve note, which was to be backed by gold and short-term commercial paper—although with the widespread use of "checkbook" money, note elasticity was not as important as it had been when Louisiana first inaugurated this innovation some seventy years before. All these provisions combined added up to a banking system in which financial shocks at any point could be quickly absorbed rather than communicated to other parts of the system, and one in which circulation (including "checkbook" money) could be depended upon to expand approximately in proportion to need.

Reasonably content with its achievements thus far, the administration turned next to the trust problem. In 1914, with the same air of knowing exactly what the country needed that had been displayed in the fiscal and financial reforms, two laws were passed supplementing the Sherman Anti-Trust Act. In view of the experience of the preceding few years this was indeed a display of high self-confidence. For this there was excellent reason. The campaign platform on which Woodrow Wilson had run had been popularly referred to as the "New Freedom." Many reforms had been encompassed in this term, referring as it did to releasing the majority of the American people from their bondage to business corporations, but perhaps none had been so specifically implied as antitrust legislation. Perhaps on no other subject, furthermore, did President Wilson have such strong and definite views.

The first measure was the Federal Trade Commission Act. Because the Sherman Act made no attempt to prevent the creation of monopoly, and because it had thus far been impossible to destroy monopoly once it had been created, this law was aimed primarily at prevention. A new commission was created to prevent concerns in interstate commerce from engaging in unfair methods of competition, it having been noted that many trusts had used such methods in their formative years. For this purpose it was given the power to make investigations, order concerns to abandon unfair practices, and to apply to the federal courts to enforce its orders.

The companion measure was also aimed at a specific shortcoming of the earlier legislation. Many people had long contended that the Sherman Act was too vague and general, that a law making more clear exactly what was forbidden would have better results. Accordingly the Clayton Act enumerated price discrimination, exclusive contracts, interlocking directorates, and holding company relationships as practices which must cease if they threatened competition in any way, and charged the Federal Trade Commission with the task of enforcing its provisions. And, in order that no misunderstanding on the point might again arise, labor unions and farmer cooperatives were specifically exempted from the operation of the antitrust laws. Taken all in all it would seem that reformers were fully justified in viewing these measures as the "New Freedom's" most basic achievement. It was too easy in 1914 to forget that the subtle shift in emphasis from cure to prevention was already an implied confession of defeat.

War Intervenes. While work was still going forward on these enactments, the outbreak of war in Europe brought a temporary halt to reform activities. Late in July, 1914, hostilities began in earnest, the first major economic consequence being the closing of the London Stock Exchange on July 31 for the first time in history. Apprised of this fact by cable, the board of governors of the New York Stock Exchange declared their purpose of opening on schedule that day. By opening time, however, this decision had been reversed, the doors of the Exchange to be closed "until further notice." As an indication of how severe the shock of war was to the financial community, the New York market was not again opened to unrestricted trading for a full eight months. Never before in its history had the New York Stock Exchange been closed for longer than ten consecutive days.

No doubt a wise decision was made. With the onset of an expensive world war all the major nations in Europe would immediately have sought to shift their resources into war activities. This would have meant selling for cash as many outside investments as possible, and all this selling converging on the one market remaining open to general trading might have been disastrous.[1]

But if the immediate financial crisis was quickly met, the same was not true of the first impact of war on the underlying economy. In the preceding twelve months America had exported $1½ billion worth of goods to Europe, three-fourths of which went to England and Germany. As German and British warships began policing the ocean to prevent outside goods from reaching their respective enemies, America's export trade came virtually to a standstill. The fear that 1914's unprecedentedly large wheat crop could not be marketed caused a decline in the price of wheat of

1 Actually it was not cash that was wanted, but rather imports which could be used in strengthening the war effort at home. The United States was in a reasonably good position to furnish the goods needed, as later events were to demonstrate vividly. But time was needed to make the adjustments required—to direct the productive mechanism into the necessary channels. Closing down the exchange was a precaution against a rapid conversion of claims into cash which would create financial and other dislocations here, but which would not speed up the process of making available the goods foreign nations actually wanted.

more than 10 per cent in three days. Similarly the cessation of cotton exports in the face of the largest crop ever produced brought about a fall in its price of 40 per cent before the end of the year. So great was the consternation gripping the business world that steel output fell to 30 per cent of capacity. It speaks volumes for the thoroughness of the recent monetary reforms that this upheaval was not accompanied by financial panic.

It was in the midst of the most hectic phase of this initial shock that America was called upon to make a momentous decision. When war came, gold reserves in the United States amounted to less than double the amount of immediately maturing foreign obligations, and with every other important nation already off the gold standard there was much apprehension lest foreign withdrawals endanger our own gold holdings. Indeed, the issue arose because the liquidation of foreign-held American securities and the shock to America's export business were actually resulting in a substantial outflow of gold. Many, perhaps even a majority, of the banker group opposed continuing gold payments. Against the arguments made by these bankers, however, other bankers insisted that to remain on gold would add immeasurably to America's future prestige in the international money market. Eventually these contentions won the day, no doubt because they were presented by some of the most powerful bankers in the country, and the decision was made to bend every effort to continue gold payments.

The decision made proved to be a good one. Foreigners did indeed liquidate many American securities and in the process "raided" the American gold market to the tune of $750 million. But so tremendous were United States exports as compared with imports over the next few years that gold losses were far more than counterbalanced by the importation of $1½ billion in gold. As a result the nation was able to stay on gold with all that this meant in international prestige without experiencing any financial inconvenience.

By mid-1915 the economy had recovered from the first disruptions of the conflict and was partaking of some of the advantages of being the major neutral nation in a world at war. At this point some two years remained to the United States before she too was drawn into the conflict. Some part of the energies of the nation was devoted to continuing the task of reforming American capitalism. Already, however, the force of this movement was beginning to diminish; as the war abroad became more and more real to Americans, the sentiment of idealism began visibly to give way before a realistic appraisal of America's position in the world conflict and to shift its emphasis from domestic reform to what was later termed "saving the world for democracy." Nevertheless in the time remaining several solid accomplishments were recorded, accomplishments which have successfully weathered the test imposed by the passage of time.

One of these achievements was the passage of the La Follette Seamen's Act in 1915. So hard pressed was the American merchant marine in its hopeless struggle against the economic advantages possessed by other nations in this area that working conditions had become extremely bad, even by the relatively low standards then prevailing in this country. Motivated in part by a feeling that an American industry should not be allowed to meet foreign competition at labor's expense, in part by the realization that the American merchant marine was losing the competitive battle anyway, in part by the fact that working conditions for sailors are almost synonymous with living conditions while the ship is at sea, and in part by the fact that the control over seamen by ship captains was so medieval in its comprehensiveness that sailors were actually only second class citizens when on duty—a law was passed limiting work hours, requiring up to 50 per cent payment of wages while the ship was in a port other than its base port, abolishing wage allotments to creditors, and specifying certain minimum working and living conditions.

In 1916 a number of innovations long demanded by the farmer were introduced. Thus two acts were passed (one for grains and one for cotton) providing for the establishment of standards of quality and forbidding the movement of the products involved in interstate commerce without prior grading and marking by a licensed inspector. A closely related law required warehouses to meet certain requirements as a condition of receiving a license to ship goods in interstate commerce. All these measures were intended to make the individual farmer less at the mercy of the large-scale buyer with superior bargaining power—to make available to the farmer a warehouse receipt on which a bank loan could be based and thus to lessen his need to sell his product when the market was at its seasonal low point.

More important than this legislation, however, was the creation of government financed institutions to ease the farmer's credit problem. The Federal Reserve Act had taken a short step in this direction by allowing national banks to loan money on real estate to a limited extent, and by making commercial paper based on agriculture eligible for rediscount by Federal Reserve banks. Further steps were necessary partly because national banks were relatively few in number in rural areas and partly because the Federal Reserve Act permitted real estate loans to be extended for a maximum period of five years. The new legislation set up twelve regional Federal Land banks authorized to make capital available to farmers for a period of more than five years. This was to be accomplished either through the medium of farm loan associations organized by farmers or joint stock land banks organized by private corporations.

The latter part of 1916 saw an end to domestic reform in an event which owes at least as much to the wartime economic situation as to reform sentiment, thus excellently illustrating the way in which these two elements were becoming intermingled. Acting jointly, with the full realization that no such action would be possible if the United States became a belligerent, the major railway brotherhoods demanded an eight-hour day. When their request was refused and mediation had failed to bring the parties together, a strike date was set at which time every railroad in the country was to be closed down. Spurred to action by this threat to our own defense preparations, Congress enacted an eight-hour day for railway workers. Never had such a sweeping labor victory been achieved at virtually no cost in wages lost or loss of public good will. Such a victory would have been impossible even under existing circumstances had it not been for the lingering reform idealism. Later, moreover, as other worker groups sought to achieve the eight-hour day, the Adamson Act served as an important precedent supporting their endeavors.

War Comes to America. If the intervention of world war could have simply postponed the reform campaign "for the duration," America's later history would no doubt read differently. Nothing of the sort happened, however. Reform was postponed, to be sure, but not merely for the war period. As peace gave way to neutrality and neutrality to war, and as war in turn gave way to the aftermath of war, the prestige of the reform administration steadily deteriorated until ultimately it stood before the people almost wholly discredited. The story of how and why this came about is one of the most important chapters in the economic development of the United States.

There were several factors involved. The first in point of time was the fact that, through necessity far more than choice, the "New Freedom" was converted into a war administration, responsible for a general regimentation of economic life which could not help but rankle a people accustomed to an unusually high degree of freedom from government interference. Thus one of the tragedies befalling the reform movement was its later identification in the popular mind with the frustrations and inconveniences of the program of controls accompanying a modern industrial war—an identification which administration war propaganda ("war to end wars," "war to make the world safe for democracy," and the like) probably did much to accentuate.

This is not meant to suggest that Americans did not approve the war declaration when it was made, or that they did not respond magnificently to the plain demands of the situation. They did both of these things, despite the fact that much of Wilson's re-election campaign had been built around the slogan, "He kept us out of war." And it is not to be supposed either that the administration imposed a degree of regulation in excess of that required for the effective prosecution of the war. If anything, the restrictions invoked were inadequate rather than overly stringent. But the creation of five thousand different government agencies to carry on aspects of the war effort was a transformation Americans could not take in stride so early in the twentieth century.

The difficulty arose because the American economy was heavily taxed by the demands made upon it by war. Long before the United States entered the conflict, this country had become a vital supply center for the Allies. For example, exports of American wheat to Allied nations increased seven times in value, wheat flour two times, meat two and a half times, sugar four times, and zinc thirty-seven times. This large and sudden drain on America's productive capacity would have taxed the economy in any event. When to these demands were added those of a people made highly prosperous by foreign war and an economy beginning war preparations on its own account, the result was a severe strain.

TABLE 78. THE IMPACT OF WAR

Year	Energy Consumption	Steel Production	Freight Ton Miles	Merchandise Exports	Merchandise Imports	Federal Government Debt
	(Trillions of B.t.u.)	(Millions of long tons)	(Billions)	(Millions of dollars)		
1913	17,831	31.3	301.7	2,428.5	1,813.0	1,193.0
1918	21,842	44.5	408.8	6,047.9	3,031.2	25,482.0 [1]

[1] June 30, 1919.

Source: Bureau of the Census, *Historical Statistics of the United States, 1789-1945,* pp. 155, 187, 203, 244, and 305.

As foreign governments, the American government, and the domestic economy all made simultaneous claims on the same stock of scarce resources, the situation soon threatened to get out of hand. In the absence of coordination it was virtually impossible to put first things first, and the consequences of failure would have been such basic things as inflation, which would in turn increase the financial cost of the war and stimulate labor unrest; an overloading of the nation's transportation system as railway and port facilities were suddenly called upon to handle an unprecedented flow of goods converging on the eastern seaboard; an ineffective manufacturing economy in which concerns were able to secure some of the materials needed to produce vital war goods but not all, and in which some firms continued to produce goods having little significance for the war economy while producers of badly needed goods were slowing down for want of materials or labor; and an ineffective military program brought about by the failure of the nation to supply itself with adequate shipping facilities or to produce war goods in proper balance with one another.

Obviously such consequences had to be avoided. But it is at the same time understandable that Americans refused to abandon long standing traditions until the underlying situation had reached a point that precluded all other alternatives. No one voluntarily relinquishes treasured values to a greater extent than is necessary to protect other treasured values. Thus almost nothing was done by way of centrally coordinating the economy prior to the actual entry of the United States into the war. Both England and France had urged certain minimum steps in this direction, steps they had found indispensable in their own experience, and they had even imposed a little integration by designating J. P. Morgan and Company as their sole purchasing agent in this country. However, this was a trifling measure relative to what was required, and Americans were perhaps made even more stubborn by the well intentioned efforts of "foreigners" to tell them how to manage their own affairs.

This reluctance to embark upon a program of government control in turn led to a series of half-hearted efforts just sufficient to prevent disaster but not adequate to prevent the situation from continuing to deteriorate. Voluntary programs were outlined, to be replaced by compulsory ones only when they threatened to break down completely. Controls were established at one level of the production-distribution process and ignored at another. The vitally important War Industries Board endeavored to exercise a degree of coordinative responsibility over several aspects of economic life with no real authority other than a superior knowledge of the over-all economic situation, while the War Food Administration attempted to control prices with no legal powers at the retail level at all. And as important as preventing inflation was thought to be, no efforts were made to control wages.

All this is not for the purpose of demonstrating that the nation would have been better off if social inertia had been less pronounced. Such a conclusion could properly be reached only after a very careful weighing of plus and minus factors. On the one hand, because the war ended soon after America's entry and hence never became a "total" effort here, the hesitation to impose stringent controls at first often had the result that such controls were never imposed at all. To this extent the policy followed represented a net gain. On the other hand, it is also possible that this timidity just as frequently resulted either in the need to exercise more rigorous controls than would otherwise have been required or in a greater frustration with the incidence of controls than would otherwise have been felt.

Whatever the decision on this question, however, the important fact is that the war period did see a progressive tightening of controls and an increasing public awareness of and reaction against controls. The manner in which restrictions irked and distracted Americans in all walks of life can be abundantly illustrated, and it is at the same time easy to see the processes by which the inconveniences of wartime regimentation were transformed into hostility toward the ruling administration in Washington.

For example, in the early months of the war, priorities were issued in excess of the capacity of the manufacturing concern or railroad involved, an administrative failure largely the result of too many agencies authorized to issue priorities. The inevitable result was the inability to fill promptly all priority orders, while the goods really needed first were often delayed and those which could more appropriately have been delayed were often rushed to delivery. Where the goods in question were component parts, it was not unusual for them to arrive at the point of need before the finishing plant was ready to receive them, and so limited was storage space that goods were frequently left on railroad cars because they could not be unloaded. When the priority agencies then began despatching "expediters" to hurry along priority shipments, mere confusion often gave way to sheer chaos.

On the price control front equally great difficulties were confronted and equally acute animosities were created. Businessmen were not impressed with price fixing and hence profit controlling activities resting on shadowy legal foundations, while the government hesitated to strengthen legal foundations lest the American free enterprise system be destroyed in the process. The only alternative was to solicit cooperation from industry leaders on the basis of appeals to patriotism and close examination of profit ratios. When price control efforts of this kind were not especially successful, partly because the price structure was already badly out of balance when they were begun and partly because government officials were either unable or reluctant to drive a hard bargain, consumers faced with a higher cost of living were highly critical. The government leaders responsible for this work took some comfort in the fact that price control failures would be largely compensated by the operation of the new excess profits tax, and indeed corporate profits after taxes were smaller in 1918 than in either of the preceding two years. But even here there was bitter criticism because an excess profits tax by definition discriminates against young, expanding concerns in favor of old, established ones.

In time, too, the government came to exercise controls over the nation's food and fuel supply, the very heart and center of the economy of every individual. Moreover, several substantial accomplishments were recorded on this front. Thus by making allotments of wheat to flour mills, and by concluding price guarantee agreements with more than twenty thousand grain elevators, a more stable flow of wheat into the channels of distribution was induced; the farmer's incentive to withhold his product in expectation of a higher price was thereby removed. As another aid to the consumer, the government assumed virtually all responsibility for the distribution of sugar. Here was a commodity produced under widely varying cost conditions, and to a considerable extent imported. Government control made it possible for the nation to secure enough sugar without paying for it all a price covering the costs incurred in the highest cost area.

Even though efforts such as these imposed burdens directly on producers for the benefit of consumers, it is not to be supposed that consumers and taxpayers exhibited only sentiments of gratitude. On the contrary, these consumer protecting measures required some sort of agreement between the government and producers as to profit margins, and consumers already frustrated by price rises would scarcely have been made enthusiastic about any such agreement so made. Furthermore, the government was indeed generous. For example, the food administrator, Mr. Hoover, allowed the meat packers 9 per cent on the capital employed in the food end of their business (including borrowed capital), even though prices of packer products not related to the food supply were not controlled at all. Consumer dissatisfaction was further enhanced by the inauguration of "wheatless," "meatless," and "heatless" days, even though these sacrifices were to a considerable extent voluntary. With respect to fuel, moreover, "heatless Mondays" had to be endured despite an increase in coal prices sufficient to make normally unprofitable mines productive.

The impossibility of satisfying in the over-all a single group can be excellently illustrated by the case of the farmer. In an attempt to keep the so-called corn-hog ratio (the price of corn relative to that of pork) at a point which would not discourage pork production, the government allowed the farmer a pork price 43 per cent higher relative to the price of corn than that ordinarily considered profitable. Yet in other ways the food administration was successful enough in limiting price increases as to subject it to a storm of criticism from the farmer group. This criticism was easily enough countered with the assertion that the needs of war demanded keeping prices from rising above that level necessary to assure the needed production. But it was always too easy to insist (and often all too true) that the profit margins allowed some other groups were in fact larger for this argument to be very effective.

Few phases of the economy escaped untouched. There were the inevitable conscription controversies over who was to stay and who to go. Consumers were asked to save resources by carrying packages instead of having them delivered, and in various other ways. Efforts were made to limit speculation in the interest of more stable prices and hence the more orderly marketing of essential goods. Certain industries, such as the building industry and automobile production, were limited in their output by the withholding of materials. Various measures were taken to eliminate waste by standardizing products—that is, reducing the number of sizes and styles produced. A government agency was created to seize, hold, and administer patents formerly owned by German nationals. The United States Shipping Board was organized to provide the nation with a more nearly adequate merchant fleet.

It is not to be thought that war controls, even price controls, were an unmitigated failure. On the contrary enough order was introduced into the war effort to make possible an American contribution far exceeding anything believed possible by either Europeans or Americans, while at the same time the flow of needed civilian goods was fully maintained. Productivity and total national product, despite the building of an army of some four million men and the largest navy in the world, increased markedly, in part because of the government's success in bringing about economies impossible on a purely individual decision basis. And although prices did rise considerably, the margin between wholesale and retail prices was actually reduced during the control period. The trouble with the control program from the standpoint of the people's reaction to it (especially after the war) was thus not its failure looking at it as a whole, but rather the inability of most persons to view it in that perspective. Instead they were prone to think of it in terms of their own small corner of the economy. Put differently, the unpleasantness of controls was all too apt to be remembered after the need for them had been forgotten.

The way in which a successful control program could be and was vilified in the process of turning public opinion against the government is most easily seen in the field of railroad transportation. Long strained to the limit at peak times, the railroads early in the control period showed unmistakable signs of complete breakdown. The reason was in large part the lack of coordination between domestic transport and offshore shipping accentuated by the unrestrained issuance of rail transport priorities and the presence of too many "expediters." Hundreds of loaded cars were consigned to east coast ports at times when they could not possibly be unloaded on arrival. When the backing up of freight cars at the ports became so serious that essential traffic could hardly move at all, drastic measures clearly had to be taken.

The most important step was a cessation of independent, competitive action by the railroads, a move making possible their integration into a single operating unit. A first attempt to achieve this result, voluntary cooperation by the railroads themselves, wholly failed to bring about the desired improvement. The second and more extreme measure of government operation was more successful. For twenty-six months the government managed virtually the entire rail network of the nation, and the threatened disruption of essential railway traffic not only did not occur but the tie-up of cars at the ports and the use of railroad cars as warehouses were gradually but steadily eliminated.

Only one thing was left to be desired by this performance. Unquestionably the government lost money; that is, the revenue received for the service rendered was not sufficient to pay the earnings guarantee without supplementation from the Treasury. Depending upon what is included in the calculation, this deficit amounted to something in the neighborhood of $1½ billion. This fact, interpreted in the form of the proposition that government management was inefficient, has from that day to this been used by business (especially railroad) interests as propaganda against any and all government intervention in the business world.

Now, to be sure, the government may have been inefficient, and it may have been more inefficient than private management. If so, however, and this would be almost impossible to judge in view of the highly abnormal conditions prevailing, the deficit does not necessarily have anything whatever to do with the matter. Financial results are not alone the function of efficiency in the technical sense; they are also a function of the price charged. A concern, for example, which gives away its product is not inefficient because it makes no profit. In the case of the railroads during World War I the government raised wages perhaps to a greater extent than private managements would have done, while raising rates to a smaller extent than could have been justified by advances in costs. The first of these things was done as an insurance against work stoppages; the second was motivated by a desire not to add more fuel to the fire of inflation. Both were part and parcel of the attempt by the government to perform its overall, wartime functions, and neither had anything to do with efficiency as such.

The misleading nature of this propaganda is not its most significant aspect, however. What is important is that this facet of the war experience, along with others, was effectively used later to support a violent reaction against the administration in power during the war, a reaction which was profoundly to affect the American economy in the postwar years. Stated more broadly, this phase of the tragedy of the "New Freedom" was not that it failed, but that its very successes were turned against it.

QUESTIONS FOR DISCUSSION

1. What were the major accomplishments of the "New Freedom"?
2. How did the views of businessmen and agrarians differ on the subject of bank legislation?
3. In what ways was the Federal Reserve Act intended to make the economy more stable and less subject to panics?

4. How was the nation's monetary mechanism affected by the outbreak of war? Why was this country able to stay on gold whereas all other important world powers were not?

5. What is there about a modern industrial economy that makes necessary such an elaborate network of controls in wartime?

6. Why is it important to coordinate government purchasing during a war? Why is it so difficult?

7. What are the principal problems associated with price controls during a war?

8. Would the economy have been better off if the government had not operated the railroads at a loss during World War I?

Chapter 31

A PAINFUL REACTION

1918 End of the war; domestic controversy over the League of Nations.
Webb-Pomerene Act.
1919 Postwar inflation; labor unrest.
Versailles Treaty and Senate opposition.
Volstead Act.
1920 "Rule of reason" applied to U. S. Steel.
Transportation Act of 1920.
Merchant Marine Act.
End of the postwar boom.
Warren G. Harding elected President in a "solemn referendum" on Wilson's foreign policy.

Another factor contributing to the disaster soon to overtake Woodrow Wilson and reform was also associated with the war effort, although relating to the economic burden of war rather than the impact of controls. Thus it had to do essentially with financing the war and the price level, and the web of relationships in which these two things are closely intertwined.

The Burden of War. Although unemployment in an economy is no happy thing in and of itself, that economy can almost count itself fortunate which begins a major war effort with unemployed resources. Under such circumstances war production can be achieved without encroaching on the prewar standard of living. The United States was not in this happy situation in 1917. The over-all level of output had increased steadily prior to American participation, but after that time it showed little change. Thus when production for war came by 1918 to absorb almost one-fourth of the national output, there was no alternative but for the level of living to suffer. Fortunately this reduction was from a consumer economy already made highly prosperous by the years of neutrality. Still, however, a fall in real income is not a pleasant experience, and the government in power when such occurs will invariably suffer.

TABLE 79. THE WAR BOOM LEVELS OFF

Year	Gross National Product
1914	100
1915	108
1916	114
1917	120
1918	115

Source: By permission from *National Product in Wartime*, by Simon Kuznets, p. 148. Copyright, 1945, The National Bureau of Economic Research, Inc., New York.

The way the government diverted resources from the civilian to the war economy was partly bound up with the control programs. More important, however, were the techniques used in financing the conflict. In an exchange economy the production even of war goods implies making money payments to the factors producing them. These money payments in turn give their recipients claims to goods they cannot have if the war effort is to go forward. Thus the government must either take a large amount of this money away again or it must "manufacture" money for its own use more rapidly than new income is being placed in the hands of spenders.

One way money can be obtained from citizens is through taxation, and in World War I this device was extensively used. For example, the income tax was made much more steeply progressive, in addition to the imposition of an excess profits tax. In all some $10 billion of war costs was met in this way. Even so, on the other hand, this was somewhat less than one-third of the total cost of the war. To this extent, therefore, recourse had to be had to other means.

TABLE 80. WAR WITHOUT TAXATION

Year [1]	Total Expenditures	Total Receipts	Deficits
		(Billions of dollars)	
1917	2.0	1.1	0.9
1918	12.7	3.7	9.0
1919	18.5	5.1	13.4

[1] Fiscal year ended June 30.
Source: Bureau of the Census, *Historical Statistics of the United States, 1789-1945*, pp. 296 and 299.

Another way in which purchasing power can be secured is by means of government borrowing. In World War I the entire remaining two-thirds of the war's cost was financed through government bonds. In view of the fact that in every previous important war effort in the country's history a considerable part of the financing had been done by means of paper money, this record represented a great change.

From a somewhat broader standpoint, however, this was a change in theory only. The major difference, economically speaking, between borrowing and printing paper money is that new currency creates an upward pressure on prices, while the transfer of purchasing power from an individual or a business concern by means of a loan does not. The financing of World War I was an innovation in America's history, not because new purchasing power was not created, but because a way was found to create new purchasing power without printing paper money. Put differently, a way was found in which the government could borrow money from its citizens without reducing their purchasing power.

The key to this development was the system of "checkbook" or credit currency which had by now to a considerable extent replaced paper money. Since banks were permitted to loan money with government bonds as collateral, an individual or a business concern might subscribe to a bond issue and still retain his own purchasing power by the simple expedient of negotiating a bank loan and pledging bond holdings as security. Furthermore, banks could themselves buy bonds without reducing the purchasing power of individuals and business firms. In all approximately $1 billion worth of bonds was sold under the "borrow and buy" program, and approximately $4 billion worth was sold directly to the banking system.

There were several special aspects of the Amercian economy during World War I which contributed to these results, too. In the first place, the net inflow of $750 million in gold in the settlement of an unprecedented export trade balance increased bank reserves, which could then be multiplied through the manufacture of bank credit. In the second place, although the new Federal Reserve banks had not been created with this in mind, the new centralization of reserves made it possible to carry credit expansion to almost any length. Thus the Federal Reserve banks were authorized to encourage the "borrow and buy" policy by offering a lower rediscount rate on loans backed by government bonds than on other loans, and these banks purchased on their own account several hundred millions of dollars' worth of government bonds. In all, federal reserve notes in circulation increased fivefold. Indeed it has been widely asserted that without the new banking system the nation's financial mechanism would have broken down early in the war period.

With money incomes increasing as a result of the creation of purchasing power, goods could only be transferred from the civilian to the war economy by means of a rising price level. That is, since consumer incomes rose more rapidly than did production, only higher prices could prevent individuals from maintaining or even raising their standard of living (as was the practice in the case of most individuals whose incomes rose as rapidly as the price level or more rapidly). The first year of American participation saw an increase in retail prices of almost 20 per cent, while the second saw an advance of approximately 18 per cent more. Over all, the increase from the beginning of the outbreak of war in Europe to the Armistice was 50 per cent.

Not every consumer group suffered a loss in real purchasing power. One of the groups able to protect its real income was organized labor. Wartime labor demands, particularly the need to shift workers from industries which were decreasing their output to expanding industries, gave labor an excellent opportunity to bargain for pay increases. High profits and high prices, furthermore, provided a strong motivation for using the available bargaining power, while long hours and the generally accentuated tempo of economic life further increased labor unrest. The consequence was that income and working conditions were improved or at least maintained to a greater extent than had been the case in any preceding war in the nation's history.

TABLE 81. THE CHALLENGE OF INFLATION

Year	Index of Average Hourly Earnings	Consumer Price Index
1914	100	100
1916	110	109
1918	150	149
1920	218	200

Source: Bureau of the Census, *Historical Statistics of the United States, 1789-1945,* pp. 67 and 236.

Labor made other gains during the war period, too. The number of workers belonging to trade unions increased more than one-fourth, and labor was recognized by the war administration to the extent of representation on war agencies having responsibilities in the area of industrial disputes. These two facts were closely related, too; the government's general principles where labor relationships were concerned included recognition of the right to organize and bargain collectively, the right of women to equal pay for equal work, the right of labor to minimum living standards, and the basic principle of the eight-hour day. No doubt the government's labor policy contributed in turn to the war effort. The American Federation of Labor maintained an official no-strike policy, and although during the war months there were many strikes, the majority were by nonunion workers and were inconsequential in terms of man-hours lost.

It is difficult to state in figure terms the effect of the war period on the well-being of labor, for data on incomes are inextricably intermingled with the wartime reduction in the length of the working day. Thus in a number of industries labor achieved the eight-hour day (often a forty-four-hour week), but continued to work longer hours at time-and-a-half for overtime. This much can be said. Statistically, workers maintained their real income status on the average, which means roughly that as many workers achieved gains as suffered losses.

Farmers were also economically benefited by the war. An inelastic demand and the failure of agricultural output to increase as demand increased resulted in price increases for the farmer's goods far exceeding those

TABLE 82. BONANZA FOR FARMERS

Year	Index of Farm Prices (1926 = 100)
1915	71.5
1917	129.0
1919	157.6

Source: Bureau of the Census, *Historical Statistics of the United States, 1789-1945*, p. 233.

registered in any other major segment of the economy. Only the cotton farmer failed to share in this gain; many British cotton mills lost their foreign markets when the war disrupted ocean trade.

Many business concerns, too, registered gains in income, especially those most strategically situated from the standpoint of government contracts. Not only does this fact show up in profit statistics, but it was widely understood that good business management in a period of high taxes required the concealing of as many profits as possible by inflating costs. The largest share of these increased profits, to be sure, did not directly benefit the majority of business owners—being retained instead as undistributed surpluses. But the gains were nonetheless real for this disposition of them, and wartime tax increases by no means succeeded in absorbing them.

From this analysis it is easy to determine where the burden largely fell. In addition to the cotton farmer the principal disadvantaged group was the rapidly growing urban middle class, the group whose money income proved least flexible in the face of war conditions. Government employees, for example, are estimated to have lost approximately one-third of their real income, while salaried workers in private industry lost about one-fourth. A large number of people who ordinarily received much of their income from property also suffered. These results are in sharp contrast to the country's Civil War experience when the principal burden fell on the wage-earner, a contrast roughly measuring labor's success in improving its position in the intervening years.

These experiences of the various segments of the economy during the war years point unmistakably to a second set of reasons why reform and

Woodrow Wilson were soon to stand discredited before the country. One of the important factors in the public's acceptance of labor's rise to power had been support from a large part of the urban middle class. When, however, labor was able to maintain and even improve its economic position at the expense of this large group of supporters, it was only to be expected that much of this good will would turn into hostility.

Since so much of the prewar reform program had represented labor demands, labor's loss of support was only the other side of loss of enthusiasm for the reform movement. When this loss of enthusiasm was next transformed into distrust of the reform administration, the circle was complete. Nor was such a transformation illogical. The "New Freedom" was after all the first national administration genuinely friendly to labor.

The loss of prestige by the reform administration and by labor thus reinforced one another in a complex but singularly vicious way. Enemies of labor were apt by a very natural process to become thereby enemies of Woodrow Wilson's government, while opponents of the ruling administration could scarcely avoid being drawn into opposition to labor. With this net of circumstances drawing tighter and tighter, Wilson's enjoyment of wide popular acclaim was vanishing even before the war ended.

The Postwar Boom. After a war financed by highly inflationary methods there is almost no avoiding a period of liquidation soon thereafter. Even without inflationary financing, in fact, a postwar economy is faced with such a large problem of readjustment as virtually to assure this result. It is, moreover, uncertain whether the governmental policies adopted during reconversion have much to do with the severity or timing of the ensuing reckoning. But if government policies are a significant factor, there can be no doubt that the policies adopted after World War I were excellently calculated to make the postwar recession both soon and sharp.

The signing of the Armistice on November 11, 1918, was the signal for beginning with almost feverish haste the process of withdrawing the government from its wartime economic responsibilities. Two days after the Armistice the War Industries Board began to end price controls. Within four weeks more than one-half of all outstanding and uncompleted government contracts had been cancelled, typically allowing no more protection to the concerns involved than arranging for one month's production at the current rate. Virtually the entire armed force was demobilized in a twelve-month period, these discharges taking the form of release by military units without regard to employment possibilities. Feeble efforts were made to bring about an orderly restoration of military personnel to civilian life, but nothing effective was accomplished. Congress, for example, refused to appropriate funds for an emergency public works program.

The nation might easily have had its postwar recession then and there; in fact, in the early part of 1919 business activity did turn sharply down. Then, without anyone taking steps to bring about such a favorable turn of events, business moved upward again in a postwar boom which was to last for approximately a year.

Was this outcome sheer luck, or did it demonstrate the powerful recuperative capacity of a private enterprise economy freed from hampering restrictions? The answer is, neither. There were at work a number of specific economic forces powerful enough to delay depression for a time. Whether this was a boon or a misfortune, however, is open to question. Before the boom had worn itself out the price level had risen more than 30 per cent above the wartime high.

One of the economic forces involved was continuance of the wartime shipbuilding program. Many Americans sincerely wished to see this country regain its earlier position on the world's seas, and the recent war experience provided an excellent argument. Another was the withdrawal from the labor force of several million persons who had entered it only under pressure of war conditions. A rapid rate of automobile manufacturing and general construction activity was resumed as soon as wartime restrictions began to be removed. American exports continued at a very high level under the impetus of large governmental loans to the Allies and the need for relief and rehabilitation goods in Europe. The government continued for a year after the war to spend substantially in excess of its income, and partially because of this fact and partially as a result of the cycle of inflation itself, bank credit continued to expand.

During the inflation interlude between war and depression the most dramatic developments were naturally in the labor field. Union membership had reached new highs, union treasuries were full, employment was high, labor had been guaranteed a number of rights during the war which it was now anxious to retain, wartime no-strike restraints could now be lifted, and the price level was rapidly rising. Out of these ingredients there developed in 1919 a wave of strikes and labor unrest unprecedented in Amer-

TABLE 83. A TIME OF STRESS

Year	Workers Involved in Work Stoppages	
	Number (Thousands)	Per Cent of Employed Wage Earners
1905	302	2.1
1916	1,600	8.4
1919	4,160	20.8

Source: Bureau of the Census, *Historical Statistics of the United States, 1789-1945*, p. 73.

ican history. In that year also labor began to reap the harvest of the antagonism built up against it in the war years—all the while another field was being planted with the same crop. Organized labor did, however, add to its membership by another one-third in the postwar inflation period.

It was unfortunate for labor's cause that one of the first uprisings to attract the attention of the entire nation was a semirevolutionary one. A general strike was called in the highly unionized city of Seattle, an attempt being made to tie up the entire city. At base this walkout was a wage increase demand by metal workers in the large shipbuilding industry in Seattle, and the "sympathetic" aspect grew naturally out of the importance of ship-worker prosperity to the economic health of the entire city. Immediately the public was aroused from one end of the land to the other, and every organ of public opinion turned to the attack. In the end the strike failed, but not before Seattle's mayor had won national acclaim for the ruthless way he dealt with the strikers and for his choice of words condemning them.

It was unfortunate, too, that this episode was soon followed by a policeman's strike in Boston. There were reasons enough for grievance against the city administration, to be sure, but ironically it was not for improvements in wages and working conditions that the strike was called. Rather the cause was refusal by the city to recognize the American Federation of Labor as the policemen's bargaining agent. The work stoppage itself was orthodox and orderly in the best tradition of American labor, and little notice would have been taken of it if the withdrawal of the forces of law and order had not resulted in an orgy of pillage and destruction. Again the public became aroused, and this time it was the Governor of Massachusetts who became the nation's hero. He called out the National Guard to keep the peace while an entirely new police force was employed, and when Samuel Gompers protested these roughshod tactics, the governor made the classic statement which endeared him to all conservatives. "There is no right to strike against the public safety by anybody, anytime, anywhere." This was Calvin Coolidge, and but for this incident he would probably never have become President.

These episodes, however, might both have been minor occurrences except for the fact that labor was already agitating, especially against the rising cost of living, on a broad front. The Amalgamated Clothing Workers under the leadership of Sidney Hillman, threatened with unemployment because of the sudden cancellation of government contracts, struck successfully for a reduction in hours to forty-four per week despite the imposition of a lockout in many New York shops. A dispute involving a quarter of a million shopworkers on the nation's railroads was settled when the government, still in control of the rail network, signed national agreements with these workers similar to those long in force between the railroads and the "Big Four" Brotherhoods.

In 1919 also the first serious attempt in a decade was made to organize the vast and vital steel industry. Indicative of the need for organization was the fact that blast-furnace employees worked a twelve-hour day, a seven-day week, and had either an eighteen- or a twenty-four-hour shift once every two weeks. When the industry's leaders refused to meet with labor representatives, a strike was called. With the press generally hostile and management using its tremendous resources in opposition (for example, by means of wholesale discharges of union leaders located through a vast spy system), the strike was a dismal failure. Never had the craft form of organization been more of a handicap; Chairman Gary was undoubtedly sincere when he emphasized that the company could not permit the leaders of 15 per cent of the workers to speak for the entire labor force. However, a few years later the eight-hour day was established, partly as a result of the public education achieved through the strike (much of this being the result of tireless activity by the Federal Council of Churches), although another important factor was Elbert Gary's long held belief in this step.

Simultaneously with the steel dispute, the other great strike of this period was taking place. The bituminous coal industry had emerged from World War I a "sick" industry.[1] The result largely of the rapid increase in the amount of energy derived from one unit of coal, a development in turn

TABLE 84. A NEW FUEL REVOLUTION

Year	Pounds of Coal per Kilowatt-Hour of Electricity
1900	7.00
1913	4.00
1920	3.00
1925	2.00
1930	1.60
1935	1.44
1940	1.34
1945	1.30
1950	1.19

Source: Federal Power Commission.

[1] A "sick" industry is one which employs more of the economy's resources than can be rewarded remuneratively and is apt to remain in this condition for a long time unless conditions are extremely favorable. The trouble is that the principle of opportunity cost often does not function as effectively "backward" as it does "forward"; that is, factors of production are frequently less mobile in response to decreases in demand than in response to increases in demand. Labor and capital both are so specialized or otherwise tied to traditional employments that they often prefer to remain less remuneratively employed rather than to take the costly step of transferring elsewhere.

resulting in the main from the rapid advance in the use of electric power, this industry now found itself in an overexpanded position. This condition, moreover, had been greatly accentuated by the wartime expansion, and in the postwar period it was not easily corrected because the industry had heavy fixed costs which often made operation at a loss preferable to cessation of operation at a greater loss. The impact of this situation on workers can easily be imagined. And to make matters worse, the nonunion, low wage fields in West Virginia and Alabama persisted in expanding at the expense of the union fields.

The coal strike was intended to achieve a 60 per cent wage increase and a thirty-hour week. Little was actually achieved, however, the workers receiving only a 14 per cent wage increase and a government commission to adjudicate their demands. Actually, thus, the principal consequence of the strike was a sharp alienation between the Wilson administration and labor, an alienation already begun as a result of the administration's failure to halt inflation. Unfortunately, in other words, both the administration and labor lost in a very real sense their "last friend."

No one is to be particularly blamed for what happened. Employers were also often injured by readjustment difficulties, and wages were the largest single item in the cost of producing coal. The administration was of course deeply harassed by inflation and the other problems of postwar adjustment. But when the workers were told that, although the Fuel Administration had lifted price controls on coal, a strike would be construed as a strike against the war effort, they were understandably angered. How could it be, they wanted to know, that the war was over for employers but not for them? When the strike did take place anyway, the government responded with an injunction restraining union leaders from having anything to do with its promotion. Even the extremely conservative Executive Committee of the American Federation of Labor denounced the government's stand. It is a remarkable fact, however, that for a number of weeks four hundred thousand miners were not mining coal. Another pressure was thus added to the forces of inflation and to the sources of public antagonism to labor.

With the issuance of this sweeping labor injunction, only one thing remained to be done to restore labor to its prewar legal status. In 1919 that step too was taken. A federal court upheld a judgment against a union for triple damages under the Sherman Act for calling a strike. Already the Clayton Act exemption had been breached and the last tie between labor and Woodrow Wilson irreparably broken.

Perhaps laborers would not have minded the return of the *status quo ante* so much if they had not soon thereafter been forcefully reminded that this status quo had other undesirable features. The law was still grossly discriminating against workers on the antitrust front. Twice during the war Congress had specifically relaxed these laws for business concerns. One such action legalized pooling by American ship companies, while the other permitted agreements among concerns engaged in the export trade. During the war also the Supreme Court had refused to dissolve the Shoe Trust, rescuing it by means of the famous "rule of reason" enunciated in the Oil and Tobacco cases. Now, in 1920, the Supreme Court was ready to go still further in using the "rule" to deal liberally with industrial combinations. The subject before it could hardly have been a more appropriate one. It was the United States Steel Corporation.

The important points made by the Court were two. First, the Steel Trust had long since abandoned the predatory tactics by means of which it had originally achieved its position, following now a "live and let live" policy. Not the possession of power, said the Court, but the way it is used is the test of "unreasonableness" in trade restraints. Second, although it was granted that there had once existed an intent to monopolize, the Court asserted that this object had never been achieved. At the time of the consolidation the concern's percentage of control had been in the neighorhood of three-fourths, whereas it had since fallen to one-half. Thus the Supreme Court exonerated the Steel Trust of wrongdoing under the antitrust laws even though it was common knowledge that this giant concern had dictated prices for the entire industry for the past fifteen years. From legislation intended to apply to large industrial concerns and not to labor, the antitrust laws had been converted into legislation applying to labor and not to large industrial concerns.

There were other evidences in early 1920 that the reform campaign was being overwhelmed all along the line by the reaction now setting in. The time for legislation relative to the postwar status of the railroads arrived, and a spirited debate took place as to what form such a measure should take. Legislation could simply have been passed returning the lines to their erstwhile owners, but the law actually passed went much further.

Three major innovations were included in the Transportation Act of 1920. First, railroad capitalization was made one of the responsibilities of the Interstate Commerce Commission. This provision might almost be interpreted as "liberal," except for the fact that its principal supporters were the holders of existing railroad securities. Notably the Commission was given no authority over holding companies. Second, an elaborate machinery was established for settling rail labor disputes. Here too was a provision with some of the earmarks of the earlier reform zeal, but laborers soon discovered that the new approach to labor-management problems was of little benefit to them.

Finally, and most important of all, the new legislation recognized more clearly than ever before that the railroad industry could not function effectively on a competitive basis. On the one hand, the thirty-three-year-old prohibition against pooling was repealed. On the other hand, railroads were urged to consolidate into a relatively small number of large units where this would not "unduly" restrain competition. The consolidations thus urged have never been a significant factor in America's economic development, the principal reason being that most of the consolidating which could profitably be done had already been accomplished. Indeed, this result was practically guaranteed by the legislation itself; strong railroads were specifically expected to consolidate with weak ones. But the law is nonetheless an excellent landmark along the road of changes in public thinking about the nature of the American economy.

In ocean transportation also 1920 saw an attempt to make a major adjustment to peacetime conditions. Here, too, no spirit of reform was involved. Behind this sentiment was primarily the desire of business generally and shipping interests in particular to get the government out of the shipping industry—and on terms favorable to ship operators and builders. Accordingly provision was made for the sale as quickly as possible of government-owned ships to private concerns, and for limited ship construction subsidies. This battle was to be fought all over again during the next few years before anything significant was accomplished; it was to develop that this country could not compete with foreign shipping without subsidies far greater than the majority was prepared to approve in 1920.

Reaction Begins in Earnest. If by the middle of 1920 the tide of reaction was still running relatively slowly, the reason was that tempers seldom rise to fever pitch in periods of prosperity. In the second half of the year, however, this saving force disappeared as postwar inflation gave way to recession. Over the next twelve months the index of wholesale

TABLE 85. THE PRICE OF PEACE

Month and Year	Pig Iron Production	Railway Freight Revenue	Exports	Prices: Retail Food	Prices: Farm Crop	Prices: Farm Livestock	Payrolls in New York State Factories
August, 1920	100	100	100	100	100	100	100
July, 1921	28	85	55	71	40	63	66

Source: Department of Commerce, *Survey of Current Business.*

prices fell more than one-third, industrial production declined more than one-fourth, unemployment rose to almost five million, one hundred thousand businesses were plunged into bankruptcy, and in the next few years more than four hundred and fifty thousand farmers lost their farms. No previous downturn in American history had wrought such devastation in so short a time.

The factors behind this new phase of postwar economic activity are easily distinguishable and in the main were little more than the converse of the factors generating the preceding prosperity. Thus in the first half of 1920 the government's large deficit turned into a surplus, partly because domestic spending was declining, partly because government loans abroad were tapering off, and partly because taxes were increased in an effort to end the rise of the national debt. This factor was in turn supplemented by a sharp drop in American export prices. The United States had greatly expanded agricultural acreage during the war to satisfy demands previously supplied from sources such as Australia and Argentina, partially cut off from the world market by the wartime shortage of shipping space. These other sources were now not only able to re-enter the market but had war-accumulated surpluses needing to be disposed of. When to these factors was added the collapse of a speculative accumulation of inventories, the postwar boom was simply unable to withstand the pressure. Because many long-term investors were fearful of deflation, and because mortgage money was difficult to get with so much money tied up in stock market speculation, the war-created deficit in building could not take up the slack.

There is controversy still over the role played by the Federal Reserve System in bringing on this downturn. The Federal Reserve Act had not contemplated that the new organization would play an *active* role in providing economic stability. Faith in the gold standard was still too strong for national leaders to suppose that assistance at this point by mere men could be helpful. At the same time the power placed in men's hands by the Act weighed heavily on the consciences of those possessing it as the postwar boom mounted higher and higher. It is, moreover, a fact that as soon as the government's needs made it possible for the Treasury to get along without Federal Reserve support in the bond market (a support which had contributed a share to the "easy money" situation underlying the postwar inflation), the several Federal Reserve banks generally followed New York's lead in restricting credit by raising the rediscount rate.[2] It is for this reason that some insist on laying the downturn at the door of the banking system. However, since a postwar adjustment was clearly due it seems more realistic to absolve the system of this charge while giving it credit for the fact that

[2] Federal Reserve "support" of the government bond market means buying enough bonds to prevent them from falling below par (or some other predetermined figure). This process of putting into circulation whatever "money" is needed for this purpose has the effect of keeping interest rates relatively lower than they would otherwise be (the higher the price of fixed-return securities, the lower the rate of interest). In turn low interest rates stimulate investment and hence contributed in the case at hand to the inflationary boom. Not until the government bond market could get along without support (broadly speaking, when the federal government was no longer running a substantial deficit) could the Federal Reserve System take steps to *raise* the interest rate to *discourage* investment and thus help prevent the boom from running away with itself.

1920 saw the beginning of the first American depression which did not open with a financial panic.

All segments of the economy suffered as deflation became the order of the day. Industry suffered decreased profits, although out of surpluses built up in the preceding years dividends were kept almost at prosperity levels. Labor's income cost came essentially in the form of unemployment, for the index of consumer prices fell on the average more than wages. For manufacturers deflation meant sharply curtailed output for a time, but it also meant a great improvement in raw materials prices relative to the prices of finished goods. Thus it was on the farmer that the greatest burden fell. Wheat and wool fell in price by 60 per cent while corn fell even more. Only agricultural prices fell during the depression to prewar levels. To be sure, this experience was in a way only the reverse of the farmer's special war prosperity. Unfortunately, however, many farmers had taken their wartime gains in the form of a down payment on a plot of land at inflated prices, just as many farmers had done during the Civil War. When deflation resulted in tens of thousands of mortgage foreclosures, it became apparent that farmers were actually being deprived of their current real income and their wartime gains at the same time.

It was in the midst of the first dark days of deflation that another election campaign opened in the United States. The Democrats naturally stood on their record, which no doubt looked better to them than to many other people. Republicans, on the other hand, had the task of mobilizing all the elements of discontent which had been steadily accumulating. The crowning misfortune of the "New Freedom" was that its "day of reckoning" coincided so exactly with a painful postwar recession (although it is also significant that the Democrats had already lost control over Congress).

The general historian tells this part of the Wilson story somewhat differently, or at least he typically places the emphasis on other factors. He lays stress, for example, on the fact that Woodrow Wilson was currently expending all his energies in a highly idealistic attempt to commit the United States to an organization which would put an end to war. This, he says, was why the Democrats were overwhelmingly defeated at the polls. The American people had lived an isolated existence for so long that they resisted the idea of a more permanent involvement.

Certainly this is a part of the story deserving of emphasis. At the same time, however, it is also worth stressing that such an emphasis does not contradict the picture painted here. Few Americans in 1920 were merely visionary in their rejection of internationalism in favor of "Americanism." Rather there were concrete and practical interests to be protected by the stand taken. One explanation—one in all probability going far toward explaining the election results—is that countless thousands of people interpreted Wilsonian idealism as an attempt to fix permanently on the nation the wartime restrictions, frustrations, and inconveniences. The result was that the last vestiges of the reform movement were swept away, and the business interests were restored to the position of dominance from which they had been toppled by the "New Freedom."

Warren Harding himself best stated the keynote of the era now opening. "America's first need is not heroics, but healing; not nostrums, but normalcy; not revolution, but restoration; not surgery, but serenity." Of these characterizations it was "normalcy" that most caught the imagination of the people. "Return to normalcy" became one of the watchwords of the day, a standard in terms of which policies and decisions could be adjudged good or bad.

Understandably one of the first things "normalcy" was interpreted to mean was the rooting out of the American scene all traces of the foreign ideologies many felt had crept into the country during the war. With the success of the Communists in Russia, left-wing groups all over the world had taken heart, endeavoring to duplicate the socialist achievement in their own lands. In the United States antagonism to such endeavors was perhaps stronger and more violent than in any other major nation. Businessmen were firmly in control of affairs, men who had more to lose from the advance of socialism than anyone else. Other groups, however, such as the urban middle class, the farmer, and even organized labor were quick to lend a hand.

One of the major consequences of this "antiforeignism" was an entirely new departure in immigration legislation. Labor had long sought restrictive legislation, but the opposition of the business interests had consistently made such action impossible. Now, amid the enthusiasm of postwar "Americanism," a drastic step was taken. Not only was the flow of immigrants reduced to a mere trickle as compared with the prewar rate, but the flow of immigrants from eastern and southern Europe (the "new" immigration) was for all practical purposes shut off completely. For the first time and from that point forward the "land of opportunity" was to be reserved for the use of those already here, and with this step an important barrier to the achievement by labor of job control was destroyed.

Although a restrictive immigration policy had long been desired by labor, it was not for that reason that it was finally successful. Labor was soon to discover that "normalcy" had a very special connotation as far as its own activities were concerned. For a conservative business leader to draw a distinction between anticapitalist activities of the radical socialist type and the anticapitalist activities of labor unions seeking to limit managerial prerogatives through collective bargaining would have been difficult enough at best. Even in ordinary times labor had almost never secured recognition except by coercion. With the power of society concentrated in the hands of businessmen, and with genuinely revolutionary groups active (if not successful) on every hand, there was all the more reason not to expect "liberal" labor attitudes to prevail. Labor itself, in fact, was partly responsible for its loss of position. This was hardly the time for a "sympathy strike" immobilizing the entire economy of a great American city, or a strike by the entire police force of an even greater American city. Furthermore, it could not be denied that many postwar strikes were by "outlaw" groups not supported by the more acceptable organizations such as the American Federation of Labor or the railway brotherhoods, and that some of these "outlaw" groups were obviously led by revolutionaries. And finally, labor's prestige was not enhanced when both coal and railroad workers openly advocated nationalization for their industries.

However, no amount of caution in all probability would have saved labor from the fate about to descend upon it. Many employers had long been awaiting an opportunity to wage a war of extermination against organized labor, especially the war-created infant unions. The beginning of deflation and the postwar reaction against all things liberal provided an opportunity which could scarcely have been improved upon. As soon as economic liquidation began in earnest the drive opened, its short-range objective being substantial wage reductions. At a meeting in Chicago in January, 1921, the National Conference of State Manufacturers Associations declared that workers "have the right to work when they please, for whom they please, and on whatever terms are mutually agreed upon between employee and employer and without interference or discrimination on the part of others." The sting here was in the word "employee," carefully stated in the singular. Under the guise of protecting laborers from their "enemies"—labor organizations, labor leaders, and foreign ideologies—the new approach was to be "the American Plan" built around the open shop.

The methods used were as various as they were ingenious, a result only to be expected in view of the fact that the campaign was led by employers' associations with a long record of opposition to organized labor. Many companies engaged in extensive espionage activities; nationwide advertising and publicity were employed; national organizations such as the National Association of Manufacturers lent assistance to numerous local employers' groups; the National Open Shop Association was formed for the same purpose; the Bethlehem Steel Corporation announced it would not sell steel to builders or contractors operating on a union shop basis; labor intimidation and organized strike-breaking were inaugurated on a large scale. In all millions of dollars were spent in this attempt to restore to America the "good old days" when private property could be managed by and for its owners without let or hindrance.

In this activity, furthermore, employers were not forced to work alone. Legislatures throughout the country busied themselves erecting statutory barriers to the formation of unions with radical aims, and the distinction between such unions and those with a long tradition of "orthodoxy" behind them was not always carefully drawn. The most extreme legislation was no doubt that passed in Kansas. Strikes were forbidden in industries "affected with a public interest," and an industrial court was established to regulate wages, hours, and working conditions. And the most extreme aspect of this legislation was that the industries characterized as being "affected with a public interest" included economic activities extending far beyond those the Supreme Court had been willing to place in this category. (How like the 1920's that extreme orthodoxy would thus find a way to use a tool of liberalism, the public utility concept, for reactionary purposes.)

Of course, too, the nation's courts, long an ally of employers in their antiunion battle, were not idle. A federal law regulating child labor was declared unconstitutional, as was a law establishing minimum wages for women in the District of Columbia. A consequence of these decisions was that similar laws in one-third of the states had to be repealed, modified, or retained in virtual defiance of the Supreme Court. Machinists were declared in violation of the antitrust laws because of a boycott designed to force unionization in a concern manufacturing printing presses. The Supreme Court even upheld a judgment maintaining that the courts could limit picketing to "peaceful" picketing, which in the case at hand meant no more than one picket stationed at the entrance of each plant. No stone was left unturned in this feverish attempt to define "normalcy" in the field of labor-management relations in terms of mid-nineteenth-century concepts.

While the longer-range success of this antiunion movement could not so soon be assessed, it immediately became apparent that its short-run objective was being achieved. Wages were pushed down all along the line. Significantly, however, so sharp was the recession and so strenuously did labor resist reductions that wages did not decline as rapidly as prices. In consequence, real wages for those remaining employed did not fall. Under the circumstances this outcome must surely be counted as a signal victory for labor, although it is also to be remembered that employers trying to destroy unions were naturally hesitant about using their power too ruthlessly. At the same time both employers and employees well understood that the real test was to come later, in the fate of the unions themselves.

QUESTIONS FOR DISCUSSION

1. Upon what groups did the economic burden of World War I fall? Can any part of the burden of a war effort be "postponed" by internal borrowing?

2. Why do modern governments prefer to inflate the money supply by selling bonds to banks rather than by printing paper money? How does this process work?

3. What developments were primarily responsible for breaking the bond between labor and Woodrow Wilson?

4. How did the continuance of the wartime government deficit contribute to postwar inflation? What was the relationship between this deficit and the expansion of bank credit?

5. What developments were primarily responsible for breaking the bond between labor and the urban middle class?

6. Was Calvin Coolidge "right" in the stand he took in 1919? Does his statement apply equally to other kinds of strikes against the government?

7. Was the Supreme Court's decision in the steel case in 1920 a statesmanlike one? Did the Court have any alternative?

8. What "caused" the economic downturn in 1920? To what extent was the central banking system responsible?

9. What did "normalcy" mean in the labor field after World War I?

10. Why are farmers better off than most during war periods, and worse off than most during periods of postwar adjustment?

Chapter 32

BACK TO "NORMALCY"

1921 Business depression.
Historic immigration policy reversed.
Birth of the "Farm Bloc."
Emergency Tariff.
Packers and Stockyards Act.
1922 Capper-Volstead Act.
Fordney-McCumber Tariff.
Coal miners and shopmen strike.
1923 Intermediate Credit Act.
Calvin Coolidge became President at Harding's death.
Presidential support pledged to Mellon's tax program.
1924 Harding Administration scandals.
"Dawes Plan" for German reparations.

It is not to be supposed that a new approach to labor-management relations was the only or even the most important meaning of "normalcy" to the business interests now taking full advantage of their return to power. There were other dimensions of the "new era" as well. One of these, and perhaps the one providing the key to an understanding of the others, was a special relationship between business and government.

Rebirth of Laissez Faire. The term *laissez faire* is frequently used in this connection, and there is no objection to its use if it is clearly understood what is meant. Freedom from government interference is certainly not all that is implied, although this is the aspect of laissez faire usually emphasized. The most unblushing laissez faire proponents had no difficulty in the 1920's in justifying to their own satisfaction such things as subsidies for the high-cost shipping industry or for the rapidly developing aviation industry. Because there was this other side to what is frequently referred to as laissez faire, however, it is more accurate to think of it as a government-society relationship in which the government uses its power to resolve conflicts of interest in favor of business. In this sense the return to laissez faire was the most important part of what was meant by returning to "normalcy."

This being the case, it is understandable that one of the first items on the agenda was new tariff legislation, the eradication of the reform "meddling" known as the Underwood Tariff. To be sure, this law had never actually been operative because the coming of war had more than replaced the protection thus taken away. However, it would soon become operative and all haste was needed to prevent such a contingency. There were other reasons for haste, too. American business, as a consequence of hostilities against Germany, had fallen heir to many German patents for chemicals and dyestuffs, and a lusty new infant was arising on this basis—an industry soon to be one of the pillars of modern industrial America. Since Germany's development in these areas was substantially in advance of our own, a barrier clearly needed to be erected to protect this infant from world competition. Furthermore, the best time to overcome the American farmer's resistance to high industrial tariffs was while the Midwest was reeling from the devastation of a depression falling with particular force upon it.

The strategy followed was completely successful. In exchange for increased tariffs on agricultural products and reduced tariffs on a number of industrial products used largely by farmers (for example, agricultural machinery), debt-ridden farmers reluctantly supported an industrial tariff pushed to unprecedented levels. During the course of this struggle, however, an entirely new element entered the tariff controversy—one which was never again to be separated from it.

The United States had entered World War I as a debtor nation, owing debts to foreigners far greater than those owed to her by foreigners. In the early stages of the war many foreign investments in this country had been liquidated in order to secure goods and services to be used in the war effort. A little later extensive borrowing in this country commenced, and by the end of the war some $7 billions were owed the United States by

TABLE 86. FROM A DEBTOR TO A CREDITOR NATION

(In billions of dollars)

	United States Investments Abroad				Foreign Investments in the United States			
Year	Total	Direct	Portfolio	Short-Term	Total	Direct	Portfolio	Short-Term
1914	3.5	2.6	0.9	–	7.2	1.3	5.4	0.5
1919	7.0	3.9	2.6	0.5	3.3	0.9	1.6	0.8

Source: Bureau of the Census, *Historical Statistics of the United States, 1789-1945*, p. 242.

foreign nations. Even apart from debts contracted by governments in connection with the war, the United States was now a creditor nation.

Debts owing citizens of one country by citizens of another can ultimately be paid only in goods and services; the creditor must accept imports in excess of its own exports. Already the United States had adopted the policy of subsidizing an economically inefficient merchant marine, thus reducing one source of payments to this country by foreigners. Many were afraid lest a high tariff still further restrict the opportunity of foreigners to discharge their obligations. This would be injurious, not only to American creditors (including the government) but to important international relationships as well.

Such fears were freely voiced during the postwar tariff debates by such men as Woodrow Wilson and Cordell Hull. Despite this new challenge, however, the Fordney-McCumber Tariff of 1922 was in no way modified. Nicholas Longworth of industrial Ohio (Speaker of the House of Representatives), for instance, defiantly asserted it would be better to abandon the entire debt than to open the American market to foreign producers. American manufacturers were not yet as concerned about foreign markets for their own output as they were one day to become. And besides, this issue did not turn out to be as important during the 1920's as had been feared because the United States imported large quantities of gold and continued loaning abroad at the rate of almost $1 billion per year. An export trade balance is appropriate for an *immature* creditor.[1] The day of reckoning, in other words, lay in the future.

Concessions for the Farmer. Relatively few staple-producing farmers still felt by 1922 that relief for agriculture could be achieved by means of a tariff. No great economic understanding was required to demonstrate that import duties on products customarily exported can not benefit their producers. And even a casual reading of the provisions of the industrial tariff revealed that the reductions made were chiefly in commodities the United States could produce more cheaply than the outside world. Understandably, therefore, agricultural leaders pressed actively for measures which would be of assistance to farmers. These efforts were in a few short years to chalk up an impressive record of victories.

While the tariff issue was still pending, a special antitrust law was passed governing the packing industry. The Packers and Stockyards Act made it

[1] An "immature debtor" is a nation borrowing capital from outside its own borders. A "mature debtor" is a nation that is paying interest and principal on past foreign borrowings more rapidly than it is incurring new external debts. An "immature creditor" is a nation whose capital account shows net loans to other countries. A "mature creditor" is a nation receiving more interest and principal remittances than it is sending out in the form of new loans. An "immature debtor" and a "mature creditor" must necessarily have an import trade balance; a "mature debtor" and an "immature creditor" must have an export balance.

unlawful for these concerns to engage in unfair practices, to combine for the purpose of controlling prices, to agree on market divisions, to create a monopoly, or to charge unreasonable or discriminatory prices. It is of significance that after only seven years—and most of them very abnormal years in the bargain—the farmer had already given up hope of effective protection by means of the reform legislation of Wilson's administration.

Shortly after this act was passed, President Harding signed the so-called Capper-Volstead Act. Here was another evidence that the farmer distrusted the general antitrust legislation. This act again specifically exempted farmers' associations and agricultural cooperatives from the operation of the antitrust laws, in addition to exempting them from federal taxation. Spurred on by deflation, farmers had launched a new drive to improve their position by way of the cooperative route, and they could therefore not afford to leave anything to chance. Besides, they had seen what the Supreme Court had done to the exemption written into the Clayton Act for labor organizations.

A little later still a third measure of importance to farmers was approved. The Federal Reserve Act had gone far toward solving the farmer's short-term (sixty to ninety days) credit needs. His long-term (five years or more) needs had been in large part provided for by the Federal Land Bank Act. Still, however, his need for credit from the planting season to harvest time had not been met. An Intermediate Credit Act now created a Federal Intermediate Credit Bank in each of the twelve land bank districts to serve this need in two ways. First, these banks were to assist with the discounting of agricultural paper. Second, they were to make agricultural loans (through agricultural associations and private banks) for periods of from six months to three years.

All this was in one sense not at all in the laissez faire spirit. Yet, from a more fundamental standpoint, this legislation could readily be made to qualify. If the interests of business were to be served, government action would frequently be necessary. At such times votes were of the utmost importance, and votes controlled by nonbusiness interests might be unavailable if concessions were not made. Fundamental to an understanding of this legislation for agriculture is the fact that there had just been created in Washington a group known as the "Farm Bloc"—Senators and Representatives with farm constituencies regardless of party affiliation. Once again, and again under the pressure of economic deflation, South and West were uniting for concerted action. Bowing gracefully to the facts of political life, the business interests made the necessary concessions.

Laissez Faire Achievements. The first fruit of these concessions was the Fordney-McCumber Tariff. A second was a basic revision of the nation's tax structure. To accomplish this task Andrew Mellon, one of the richest men in the country and one of its great business leaders, was appointed Secretary of the Treasury. His idea of the tax policy now needed was to remove the excess profits tax, reduce income taxes generally (although especially in the upper brackets), and to make up for these reductions sufficiently to maintain a substantial annual surplus by means of consumption taxes. It was an excellent tax program for a rapidly expanding economy such as America's was during this period, at least if little thought was to be given to the matter of distributing the national dividend. Certainly this is what Mellon had in mind; that is, he wished to see the nation's investment needs taken care of and he was not especially concerned with distribution problems. There was a little difficulty getting the new tax program under way, agricultural resistance delaying it somewhat, but in the end it was put into operation almost exactly as originally outlined. It is worth noting that Mellon was Secretary of the Treasury under three consecutive presidents (or, as it was pointedly remarked at the time, three presidents served under Mellon).

Another area in which government was called upon to assist business was in connection with labor disputes. A business having a powerful union to deal with often needed a strong ally. Thus in the coal dispute of 1922, another in the series of controversies between union and operators which was virtually to destroy unionism in that industry before the decade was over, President Harding offered full federal assistance to state governments endeavoring to protect property or workers desiring to work. This dispute was more noteworthy in the perspective of history, however, for other reasons. On the one hand, it was accompanied by the so-called "Herrin massacre," the killing of some twenty officers of the law by strikers after two of their own group had been shot down without cause. On the other hand, this controversy marked the emergence of John L. Lewis as one of the nation's outstanding labor leaders. No doubt the appearance of such a leader, rugged and ruthless where the interests of mineworkers were concerned, was one consequence of the no-holds-barred character of the battle between employers and employees in 1922. A basis for this character, in turn, was the readiness of the government to join forces with the employer.

A clearer example of what government assistance could mean was given in the 1922 shopmen's strike. The recently created Railroad Labor Board had, just before the onset of depression, awarded a 22 per cent wage increase to the shop workers on the nation's railroads. Immediately thereafter the railroads began attacking these gains, pointing to the drastic decline in the general price level as evidence that a downward adjustment was indicated. When President Harding appointed to serve on the Board a slate of public representatives more inclined toward the railroad point of view, the way was opened for just such an adjustment.

The first step was to abrogate the national agreement, leaving each railroad free to deal with its own workers. Aided by widespread unemployment, a number of railroads were able to eradicate the new unionism. Then in quick succession the Railroad Labor Board ordered two wage decreases which would have completely wiped out the previous advance. The resulting strike was widely attacked in the press as a revolt against legally established machinery for adjustment, and hence was perhaps doomed from the outset. At the same time it is now clear that the cards were hardly dealt fairly, and that workers justly complained that they had been the last group to receive an inflation increase in wages and were now commanded by the government to be among the first to accept a deflation decrease.

The workers at one point could have secured most of their demands—at the price of giving up their union. This they refused to do, and the strike went on. At this point the government unleashed its most powerful weapon. Basing his action on both the government's power over interstate commerce and the antitrust laws, the Attorney General requested an injunction prohibiting unions from supporting the strike. Faced with this blow and already running short of funds, the strikers capitulated. On most of the nation's railroad lines the nonunion shop was to prevail for a number of years thereafter.

The open shop campaign and the assistance of employers by the government in labor disputes made 1922 a record year in the American labor movement. Never before had labor unions lost so many members in so short a time, and this despite a rapid increase in the proportion of the

TABLE 87. "NORMALCY" AND THE WORKER

	Labor Union Membership (Thousands of Workers)	
Year	All Unions	American Federation of Labor
1915	2,560	1,946
1920	5,034	4,079
1921	4,722	3,907
1922	3,950	3,196
1930	3,632	2,961

Source: Bureau of the Census, *Historical Statistics of the United States, 1789-1945*, p. 72.

population included in the urban laborer group. As could have been anticipated, many of these losses were in the war-created unions which had not yet established themselves on a permanent basis. Others were in the "sick" industries, such as bituminous coal, and in industries in which machines were eliminating workers. But there can be no doubt that these losses were intensified by an antiunion drive powerfully reinforced by the authority of the government.

"Normalcy" and the Trust Movement. Closely akin to the special relationship between government and business during the "new era" (indeed highly dependent upon it), and in contrast to the status of labor organizations, was still another dimension of "normalcy." A new wave of business consolidation was inaugurated, carrying concentration of control to heights undreamed-of when the ill-fated antitrust movement had gotten under way a generation before. This new surge, however, differed in one significant respect from its predecessors. Whereas earlier periods of combination had taken place in the teeth of a government in Washington which at least pretended to be hostile, consolidation in the 1920's was carried on under the watchful eye of a national government eager to see that no obstacles were placed in the way.

The methods of encouragement used by the government were numerous. A first, and the most obvious, technique was simply not bringing suits under the antitrust laws. Moreover, aggressive actions almost invariably took the form of suits against labor unions or building material rings or food racketeers, actions which would receive popular support but would not affect the structure of industry. And where cases were started which did reflect the spirit of the antitrust laws, they were typically settled by means of consent decrees. This is a device by means of which a defendant is given the opportunity to mend his ways in exchange for dropping the suit. Unquestionably there are legitimate uses for the consent decree, but there is wide agreement that its use in antitrust cases during this decade led to extremely lax enforcement while still enabling the administration to build up a fairly impressive *paper* record of accomplishment.

Another technique followed was the careful selection of appointees for Supreme Court and Federal Trade Commission vacancies. During the entire decade not a single "liberal" was appointed to the Supreme Court, and not a single Wilson appointee to the Federal Trade Commission was kept on beyond the expiration of his initial term. The result of these shifts in personnel was that the Commission sought significant changes in the structure of industry only rarely, and even when this did happen the Court would often reverse the Commission. It is noteworthy, moreover, that the Commission and the Supreme Court were most likely to see eye to eye when the methods of competition involved were those which the common law would have outlawed if there had been no antitrust legislation.

Even the legislation so confidently written by the "New Freedom" seemed to contribute to rather than deter the new consolidation movement.

On the one hand, Clayton Act prohibitions gave concerns a powerful incentive to continue the abandonment of holding companies in favor of an even tighter kind of control—outright merger—just as the Sherman Act had earlier driven them to abandon loose pooling arrangements in favor of a tighter control through the holding company. And even where holding companies were involved, the recent decision in the steel case (the "rule of reason") did much to nullify Clayton Act intentions. On the other hand, the Federal Trade Commission Act's attempt at prevention was likewise quickly swept aside. Unfortunately the law had not defined "unfair methods of competition." This fact made the work of the Commission vulnerable to Supreme Court intervention, and the Court did not hesitate to announce that the working out of such a definition was a judicial function. With "New Freedom" legislation thus rendered as impotent as preceding attempts to solve this problem, there were indeed no barriers to industry concentration. By the end of the decade the Federal Trade Commission was even participating actively in the organization of "trade practice conferences" of industry representatives—and helping to enforce the rules of "fair competition" thus derived.

A case involving the Aluminum Company of America illustrates especially well the ineffectiveness of the new agency. Findings of the Commission, highly adverse to the company, were brought to the attention of the Attorney General. When, however, the Attorney General requested a full report of this investigation, he was informed that it could not be made available without the written permission of the Aluminum Company because the information had been supplied voluntarily. Apparently permission was not granted, for legal proceedings were never brought. Perhaps, on the other hand, permission was never requested. Andrew Mellon was one of the largest owners in this concern. Ironically but not surprisingly, furthermore, these developments were taking place simultaneously with the generous use of governmental power to uphold by force the Mellon policy of antiunion paternalism in the aluminum industry in an episode in labor relations as ugly as any witnessed by this decade.

In an environment such as this, combinations could scarcely help flourishing. Over a ten-year period some fifteen thousand different concerns disappeared as a result of being acquired by or combined with another company. By the end of the decade the chain store—a relative newcomer in the field of concentration—was selling at retail approximately one-fourth of all the economy's food, drugs, tobacco, apparel, and general merchandise, while independents in these fields were beginning to form cooperative chains of their own. At the end of the decade, too, ten groups of holding companies controlled almost three-fourths of the nation's electric power. It was estimated that the two hundred largest nonbanking corporations possessed nearly half of the corporate wealth of the country,

40 per cent of the business wealth, and one-fifth of the total national wealth.

Not only was combination invading the retail sales field, but it was beginning to penetrate America's traditionally decentralized banking industry. Although national banks were forbidden to establish branches until late in the decade (and then only within the confines of a single city), many state banks could and rapidly did in the 1920's set up branches. Where state laws permitted branch banking earliest, in California, the huge Bank of America with its five hundred units became the outstanding example of what could be done in this field. Bank mergers also characterized this period, the number of mergers in a single year rising to a peak of almost three hundred and fifty. By the end of the decade, taking into account failures as well as consolidations, the number of banking concerns in the country had fallen 20 per cent. Not enough of a reduction took place, to be sure, to introduce a centralization such as characterized the banking systems of other nations, but a long step was taken away from the complete absence of coordination which had long governed American practice.

Striking as these developments were, three aspects of the new movement stand out. The first was consolidation in the relatively young electric utility industry. Here several factors especially invited combination. Individual electric plants are by their very nature monopolistic, and hence concentration ran into virtually no danger from the antitrust laws. Because these concerns have a high percentage of mortgageable property and because their earnings are relatively stable, they particularly lent themselves to holding company control. A high bond ratio supported by mortgageable property and stable earnings meant that control could be secured with a smaller investment than would otherwise be required. Thus the formation of utility holding companies became the way to make promotion (and other) profits par excellence.

So profitable, in fact, were transactions of this kind that holding company was even pyramided on top of holding company until three layers of holding companies above an operating company was not at all unusual. The extreme case of Samuel Insull's empire saw as many as eight holding companies pyramided on top of one another, creating a financial empire controlling $2½ billion worth of wealth and responsible for the production of one-eighth of the electric power generated in the country. In the railroad field, where similar conditions also favored the holding company device, a $1 million initial investment was built into control of a dozen Class I railroads with assets of approximately $1 billion.

A second striking development was the extension of the concentration idea into the international economy. American firms were not the leaders here, primarily because of the antitrust laws; German industrialists must be accorded this distinction. But to the limit permitted by law, and laws were conveniently flexible in the 1920's as far as such activities were concerned, Americans did actively participate. The two sulphur producing companies in the United States made an agreement with an Italian cartel controlling the other major source of the world's supply of sulphur. Du Pont entered into an arrangement with German chemical and dye manufacturers whereby patents were shared but monopolized. General Electric made an agreement with the Krupp interests in Germany which raised the price of tungsten carbide from $50 to $450 per pound. These and a dozen other international "consolidations" were joined by American firms during this period.

A third important aspect of concentration during the "new era" was the trade association. During the war numerous industry committees had been formed to work with the War Industries Board in connection with industry related problems. Out of this practice had grown a realization of how many useful functions such organizations could perform, one of these being to bring about a level of cooperation somewhat greater than that permissible under the antitrust laws. After the war, under a succession of conservative administrations and the active encouragement of Secretary of Commerce Herbert Hoover, this method of cooperation grew rapidly. Even a conservative-minded Federal Trade Commission gradually adopted the practice of dealing with organized groups of concerns rather than with individual concerns. In the early phases of this growth the Supreme Court did declare illegal the more crude attempts at direct price fixing, but organizations which avoided such obvious tactics were safe.

The Climax Reached. Just as the consolidation movement in its origins had been related most fundamentally to the economies of large-scale production, so was the advance during this period. In the utility industry and retail trade, for example, there were numerous ways in which concentration could reduce costs. One of the most important of these was management economies; the services of outstandingly capable men could be more effectively utilized. There were also economies in buying and selling, to say nothing of a greater bargaining power in dealing with other giants. In the automobile industry the basic factor was technological. A machine-oriented industry, the making of automobiles required vast quantities of capital which in turn necessitated large-scale output. For a variety of reasons this industry continued to be highly competitive, although the emergence of Ford, Chrysler, and General Motors as the industry's leaders went far toward "stabilizing" this industry.

However, just as other phases of the consolidation movement had been motivated in part by other than efficiency factors, so too was this one. Promotion profits played their part as before, as did the sheer desire for power. But that these factors alone would never have produced the consolidation phenomenon was amply demonstrated by the fact that the movement did not include all industries, and the fact that the new chain stores so quickly established themselves despite bitter opposition from their smaller-scale rivals. Thus bituminous coal, textile manufacturing, agriculture, and the boot and shoe industry—to mention only a few conspicuous examples—were passed almost completely by, while in the retailing field consolidation fell far short of the proportions reached in other industries.

With this new wave of concentration the structure of the American economy became approximately what it has since been, and, as far as fixed dates can be assigned to the beginning of historical "eras," this period marks the end of a determined effort on the part of a large segment of the population to "bust" the trusts. Never again was this project to be an important characteristic of American economic life.

In part the abandonment of this struggle reflected public recognition of the impossibility of accomplishing significant results. Even more, however, it grew out of the fact that the emerging industrial structure seemed to be less dangerous than had once been supposed. For example, with the disappearance of the conditions responsible for its development, "finance capitalism" disappeared from the American scene and Wall Street ceased to be so dominant a factor in the economy. On the one hand many concerns became able to finance more of their own capital needs, and on the other hand many cities began to challenge New York's preeminence in their own areas. In many of the basic industries, furthermore, the earlier extreme geographical concentration was disappearing in favor of more decentralization. Partially as a result of these developments almost every one of the great trusts of former years now directly controlled a much smaller proportion of its industry's business than had once been the case. And finally, it was by now apparent that large segments of the economy would remain available to the individual entrepreneur. When it is remembered that much of the earlier reform agitation had come from the smaller businessman, it is easy to see why this transformation dulled the edge of pressure for industrial reconstruction.

For another reason, too, consolidations now seemed less dangerous. The ruthless, predatory practices which had once characterized trust behavior were also disappearing. Several factors help explain this evolution. For one thing, the threat of the antitrust laws no doubt contributed to that development. Too much emphasis should not be given to this pressure, of course; it was all too apparent to industrialists that they had little to fear from antitrust legislation. But the persistence of this matter in the public mind might well have suggested that community tolerance did have limits.

A second factor was probably more important. Once "rationalization" (a high degree of centralized control) had been achieved in an industry, the few firms remaining did not provide an environment favorable to the practices to which the greatest objection had been raised. Thus behavior which did not take account of competitors' reactions was foolish, and once competitor reactions were taken into account "offensive" tactics became simply suicidal. Furthermore, it was now evident that the methods once used in building combinations, including the ruthlessness of many of those involved, had determined only who won the contest rather than whether the industry would or would not be consolidated. "Live and let live" now seemed to be the more intelligent policy. In fact even the making of "moderate" profits seemed to be the better part of wisdom because "high" profits might make "outsiders" more anxious to force their way "inside." It is significant that in enunciating the "rule of reason," the Supreme Court was not so much telling "big business" what to do to escape the toils of the law as it was expressing a viewpoint on industrial ethics which the community had already largely accepted.

Much of this can be summarized by saying that a new generation of business leaders had emerged. Whereas much consolidation and ruthlessness had been at base an attempt to escape the tyranny of overhead costs by avoiding cutthroat competition, the new leadership had developed other ways of resolving this difficulty. With only a few concerns in the major fixed-cost industries, a more subtle collaboration was available in the form of price leadership, interlocking directorates, and gentlemen's agreements—thus obviating the necessity for either a higher degree of concentration or destructive ("suicidal") practices. Beyond this possibility, moreover, price competition can be permitted but still kept within bounds by such devices as basing-point pricing, a technique of limiting price reductions to the amount of freight competitors are willing to absorb.[2] And such competitive inclinations as are not satisfied in this way can be worked off in the form of product differentiation (advertising) and service competition.

There are many, it must be emphasized, who remain hostile to the "new competition." One accusation against it is that it is not competition at all; it is rather the studied *absence* of competition. This charge is largely false, for while competition has changed its form, it has not disappeared. Another charge is that the "old competition" operated by reducing prices, while the "new competition" operates by increasing costs (and hence prices). For example, the "new competition" often operates by adding

[2] "Basing-point pricing" refers to a price system in which the customer pays a base price plus freight from a certain location to the point of consumption. Where more than one firm use the same base price and the same basing points, the result is the quotation of identical prices by all the firms using the system. A firm located some distance from a basing point may compete for customers located near a basing point against competitors who are more favorably situated. However, success here means that the seller must "absorb" the freight differential—the actual cost of shipping the goods over and above the cost of shipping them from the nearest basing point. This device has been especially prominent in industries such as steel and cement where transportation costs are a substantial item.

luxury features to utilitarian items to such an extent that the added characteristics are more expensive than the basic qualities desired. This charge contains a large element of truth, although it is an extremely complicated question whether this development is desirable or undesirable.

Still a third accusation is the most basic of all from the standpoint of the functioning of the economy. Wherever the "new competition" came to prevail, there developed an area of price inflexibility. Thus by the 1920's it was becoming clearly observable that "rationalized" industries tended to reduce output rather than prices when a decline in demand threatened. Equally observable was the superiority of the "new competition" from the standpoint of making profits and avoiding losses. In agriculture, the mining of bituminous coal, the manufacture of boots and shoes, and textile manufacturing—industries still characterized by the price flexibility of the "old competition"—the consequences of downward swings in the cycle were obviously much more severe. Whether this was simply because these fields were not "rationalized," or whether "rationalized" industries are also able as a result of their price inflexibility to shift the burden of recession onto their less fortunate colleagues, is still a matter of debate.

"Perpetual Prosperity." There was one other important dimension of the "normalcy" toward which the business interests were endeavoring to move the American economy. This was prosperity, and so completely was it achieved that men and women all over the nation began referring with unassailable confidence to the "perpetual prosperity" achieved by the "new era." Quite naturally businessmen took full credit for this achievement, insisting that it demonstrated the correctness of the policies being followed, and the nation was not inclined to dispute this assumption of credit in the face of such convincing evidence.

TABLE 88. "PERPETUAL PROSPERITY"

Year	Industrial Production *	Prices † Wholesale	Prices † Consumer	Factory Hourly Earnings †	Federal Government Debt ‡ (Billions)	Industrial Stock Prices * (1923–1925 = 100)
	(1947–1949 = 100)					
1924	44	63.8	60.8	$0.55	$21.3	91.9
1925	49	67.9	65.8	0.54	20.5	122.0
1926	51	65.0	68.0	0.55	19.6	132.4
1927	51	62.0	65.5	0.55	18.5	171.4
1928	53	62.9	64.8	0.56	17.6	214.8
1929	59	61.9	65.6	0.57	16.9	292.6

* Federal Reserve Board.
† Department of Labor.
‡ Department of Commerce.

Economists, at least with the advantage of the hindsight provided by history, are not inclined to be so generous. There seems to be nothing in particular about a successful antilabor drive, a protective tariff, a federal budget surplus (especially in view of the fact that state and local government deficits were more than compensating for Washington's surplus), and business consolidation, which would in theory produce and maintain a period of prosperity. On the other hand, economists can identify several other factors which they feel had a great deal more to do with what actually took place.

For one thing, a highly depressing force all through the preceding deflation had been the fact that producers had been caught with large stocks of goods on hand purchased at high prices. During the ensuing process of selling this inventory at lower prices and/or adjusting its "book" value downward, these concerns appeared to be operating at a loss even though goods purchased at current prices could still be sold at a profit. When this burden had been lifted by the painful process of liquidation, businessmen could once again focus their attention on the current margin between raw materials prices and the prices of finished goods—a margin made even wider by the low level of agricultural prices during this decade. At this point the employment of idle resources could begin, and prosperity ushered in in earnest.

Once the upward turn commenced, it was supported by a number of additional factors. First, consumer purchasing soared to record proportions. Not only did the price level fall during deflation by more than wages, but it continued lower during this entire decade. Thus when employment began to replace unemployment, purchases of consumer goods swiftly recovered. By 1923 these expenditures were already some 15 per cent in excess of the peak of the war boom, even as measured in constant dollars.

Consumer expenditures would no doubt have contributed much support to a new prosperity in any event. This result was doubly assured, however, by an almost new development in the field of finance—consumer credit, or as it was more popularly named, installment buying. Consumer credit could never have become a significant economic factor as long as consumer purchases were overwhelmingly of the perishable variety. But when a substantial proportion of these goods became durable, the way was opened for their purchase on credit. Financial concerns could not only demand and get a high rate of interest, justified in part by the risk involved, but they could take a lien on the property being financed and so arrange payments that the creditor's equity was normally in excess of the resale value of the merchandise. Probably no other development so well illustrates the advance of the American economy in its ability to care for its people. No other nation in the world was able to furnish so many of its people with a radio, a refrigerator, and an automobile.

An equally pervasive factor was a favorable technological situation as America launched what has often been called her "second industrial revolution." One important basis for this development was the increase in manufacturing capacity brought about by the war. Another was the decisive flowering of the modern age of steel chemistry—the perfection of processes for making an enormously wide variety of special-purpose steels at relatively low cost. Slight differences in this metal, it was found, differences which could be easily brought about by alloying other metals with it in small proportions, could adapt it to almost any task. And while not yet as important as it was to become, chemistry was already beginning to invade other fields on a large scale. Rayon, for example, began a long career of warfare against "king cotton" in the 1920's.

A third important supporting factor was a boom in residential construction. The wartime deficit (consisting in part of the normal progress of urbanization accelerated by war conditions) had still to be made up, rents were in consequence high enough to offer an incentive to investment, mortgage money had been made plentiful by the deflation, materials prices had fallen, and labor was abundant. As an indication of the force with which this factor supported a high rate of business activity, the index of the value of construction contracts awarded increased 150 per cent while the index of residential construction rose almost 200 per cent. (And how typical of this period that the housing need was converted into a public antagonism toward union activity by building workers!)

One other factor made a major contribution to recovery and prosperity. Led by the automobile industry, the economy made giant strides toward the creation of a mass production economy. The dominant figure in this development, one of America's greatest contributors to the modern industrial economy, was undoubtedly Henry Ford. Based on a high degree of product standardization (as Ford expressed it the customer might have his car any color he liked as long as it was black), "scientific management" in its best sense, the dependable and flexible industrial power made avail-

TABLE 89. KEY TO PROSPERITY

Year	Automobile Production	Automobile Registrations
	(Thousands of Vehicles)	
1900	4.2	8.0
1910	181.0	458.4
1920	1,905.6	8,131.2
1929	4,587.4	23,060.4

Source: Bureau of the Census, *Historical Statistics of the United States, 1789-1945*, p. 223.

able by electricity, and a minute division of labor—mass production makes possible the creation of goods at extremely low cost. When low costs are in turn translated into low prices, the way is opened for a vast industrial expansion.

Not alone because it symbolized the development of mass production, the automobile industry itself played a dominant role in the new prosperity. With the price of automobiles pushed low enough that millions of people could afford to buy one on the installment plan, the people of the nation gave vent to their propensity to travel as they had never before been able to do. During this decade the number of automobiles produced in a single year reached the fabulous total of almost five million while total registrations increased to more than twenty-three million, and without a doubt by the end of the decade this industry was, next to agriculture, America's largest. It employed 7 per cent of the nation's wage earners, produced 13 per cent of all manufactured goods by value, paid 9 per cent of manufacturing wages, purchased 15 per cent of the output of the steel industry, and was the largest purchaser of such other products as plate glass, nickel, and lead.

And even this summary of the importance of the automobile industry does not do it full justice. It powerfully reinforced the demand for better roads, and indeed it was largely expenditures for roads that brought about the state government deficits during the period which counterbalanced the fiscal surplus of the national government. The automobile industry also facilitated the growth of metropolitan regions through the building of suburbs, and in this way related itself closely to the boom in residential construction. It brought about an increased demand for the output of the petroleum industry, as well as a large number of filling stations and various other kinds of roadside constructions. To refer to the new prosperity as the "Model-T prosperity" would be to exaggerate only a little.

No Prosperity for the Farmer. One major group did not share in the new upsurge. The farmer's income remained low, especially the producer of cotton and grain. In fact it was largely the distress of the farmer which

TABLE 90. INDEX TO DISTRESS

Year	The Farmer's Parity Ratio
1913	100
1918	118
1921	75
1925	92
1929	89

Source: Bureau of the Census, *Historical Statistics of the United States, 1789-1945,* p. 99.

made it possible for labor to enjoy the "new era" to some extent; only the persistent low price of agricultural raw materials made it possible for real wages to remain at a high level. At no time during the 1920's was the ratio of the prices farmers paid to the prices received as favorable as it had been just prior to the war.

There were a number of reasons for the distress of farmers. Overproduction during the war was one factor, coupled with the fact that agriculture is slow to adjust to fluctuations in demand. Because of his high fixed costs (agriculture is the only important industry in which labor is essentially a fixed cost), the farmer is virtually compelled to produce all that he can regardless of price expectations.

But agricultural depression in the 1920's was not merely the result of postwar recession. More fundamental factors were also at work. One of the most important of these was the fact that the emergence of the United

TABLE 91. ONE CAUSE OF FARMER DISTRESS

Period	Percentage of United States Exports Consisting of	
	Crude Foodstuffs	Finished Manufactures
1896-1900	18.9	21.3
1926-1930	6.4	45.4

Source: Bureau of the Census, *Statistical Abstract of the United States, 1941*, p. 533.

States as a manufacturing nation meant that her greatest comparative advantage in international trade was now in the manufacturing field rather than in agriculture. The nation's relative gain in exporting the one type of good was to a degree at the expense of agricultural export markets as other areas of the world began to sell in these markets in order to secure purchasing power with which to buy American manufactures. This painful evolution was accentuated, moreover, by the birth of a "Balkanized" Europe characterized by self-sufficient nationalism. Significantly, this period saw the first decrease in the acreage under cultivation in the country's history.

Thrown more and more on the domestic market, the farmer found himself at an additional disadvantage. Because the demand for his product is inelastic, an increasing per capita income in the United States did not result in a proportional increase in the consumption of agricultural staples. This fact in the face of the technological revolution being wrought in American agriculture by the gasoline engine and the continued application of science to farming could only have been adverse to farm income in the absence of a more rapid decline in farm population than in fact took place.

TABLE 92. TRANSFORMATION IN AGRICULTURE

Year	Total Population	Agricultural Employment	Tractors on Farms	Production Indexes: Productivity per Worker	Production Indexes: Production
	(Millions of persons)		(Thousands)	(1935-39 = 100)	
1910	92.4	11.6	1	77	85
1925	115.8	10.7	549	94	99

Source: Bureau of the Census, *Historical Statistics of the United States, 1789-1945*, pp. 26, 65, 97, 98, and 100.

Not only did the tractor and the truck make possible an increased output which would have been difficult to sell in any event, but the rapid replacement of manual and animal labor by mechanical labor even reduced the need for agricultural products formerly consumed by men and animals. To some extent an expansion in the dairy industry and the raising of meat animals provided an offset, although an inadequate one. And while the great cotton producing area had the advantage that its product is not eaten, even here there was the difficulty that the domestic textile industry was not expanding—in part because of the mushroom growth of competition from producers of rayon.

A few figures can readily make plain the plight of the farmer. His share of the national income declined from 23 per cent at the wartime high to 13 per cent at the peak of the postwar industrial prosperity, while his share of the consumer's dollar declined from 51 per cent to 39 per cent. Farm tenancy increased significantly, and a smaller proportion of the nation's tenants than ever before were men realistically expecting in the not distant future to own their own farms. It is a striking paradox that during one of the strongest prosperities the nation had ever experienced per capita farm income averaged less than one-half that enjoyed by the nonfarm population.

While the majority of Americans were eager to praise the business interests for the new prosperity, the farmer was only too anxious to condemn them for a painful depression. It is therefore not surprising that farmers everywhere increasingly clamored for still further concessions. And when the nature of these new concessions became known it is not surprising either that the business interests refused to grant them. In the ensuing battle between depressed farmers and an economy highly prosperous and content a vitally important chapter in America's economic development was written.

QUESTIONS FOR DISCUSSION

1. What is the meaning of the concept "laissez faire" as applied to the period under consideration here?
2. How essential to the development of the nation was the new laissez faire?
3. Did the farmer receive any concessions during this period that might appropriately be termed *substantial*?
4. Why did Andrew Mellon believe the tax program he proposed would contribute to the well-being of the nation? How correct was he?
5. To what extent was the combination movement of the 1920's brought about by the laissez faire spirit which prevailed?
6. Could John D. Rockefeller have followed a "live and let live" policy? What would have been the consequences if the United States Steel Corporation had followed in the 1920's the business policies followed by Rockefeller in the 1880's?
7. Why did concentration of control flourish so vigorously in the electric power industry? Why was its success so limited in retail trade lines?
8. What is the justification for the term "Model-T prosperity"?
9. Why did the agricultural segment of the economy remain depressed after the postwar deflation?

Chapter 33

DESCENT FROM "NORMALCY"

1924 First McNary-Haugen Bill presented to Congress.
La Follette bid for the presidency.
1926 McNary-Haugen Bill defeated in both Houses of Congress.
Revenue Act implementing the Coolidge-Mellon fiscal program.
1927 Coolidge vetoed the first McNary-Haugen Bill.
1928 Coolidge vetoed the second McNary-Haugen Bill.
Merchant Marine (Jones-White) Act.
"Young Plan" for German reparations.
Herbert Hoover elected President.
1929 Agricultural Marketing Act.
Stock market crash.

Distress for the Worker. As farmers, nursing their depression inflicted wounds, began to entertain thoughts of rebellion against "normalcy," there were several reasons why labor might have been tempted to join them. The open shop drive plus the end of the war boom and the improved relationship between wages and prices had brought about a decline in union membership of almost one-third, and this despite the fact that labor was enjoying for the first time in its history a prosperity period in which the movement to organize was not seriously hampered by a flood of immigrants.

In the second place, this weakening of labor organization came hand in hand with a particularly acute labor need for unified action. The 1920's were notable for extraordinarily rapid advance in productivity, an advance largely attributable to technological progress. Mass production methods were extended to more areas of the economy, parts and processes were further standardized, mechanical power continued to replace animal power as central stations rendered obsolete the generation of electricity in small quantities by individual firms, "scientific management" became influential enough to reduce costs, and mechanical techniques were devised as a substitute for the unskilled labor no longer available through immigration. Taking all segments of the economy into account, the quantity of labor

TABLE 93. PRESSURE ON THE WORKER

Year	Output per Man-Hour in Manufacturing Industries
1909	39.4
1919	45.3
1929	78.1
1939	100.0

Source: Bureau of the Census, *Historical Statistics of the United States, 1789-1945,* pp. 71-72.

required for each unit of output declined more than one-fifth in this ten-year period.

An economic transformation of such magnitude, concentrated as it was in a relatively few basic industries, could not have failed to generate disturbing consequences for laborers. To be sure, as economists properly insist, industry can theoretically and in the past has always been able to absorb workers displaced by technical advance—or at least the equivalent of those displaced. Thus technological unemployment can scarcely be an important problem for the economy as a whole. But it cannot at the same time be doubted that this problem was during this period a serious one for the workers directly involved. A study made covering three industrial cities revealed that of every one hundred workers who became unemployed during the preceding year, forty-five were still unemployed. Especially for workers at the peak of their social responsibilities, and for those so far along in years that reemployment opportunities were few, is technological unemployment a disaster of the first magnitude. In another study, covering only workers displaced by technological advance, almost two-thirds of those who had found new jobs were receiving wages one year later lower than those paid in the job lost.

There is, of course, a limit to what labor unions can accomplish for their members with regard to this problem. However, a few things can be done to minimize the shock. For example, seniority can be insisted upon in dismissals, a procedure which if it does not in all cases assure that the workers retained are those to whom readjustment would be the most painful experience, does introduce a crude sort of equity into the process. A strong union can also force the acceptance of rules which slow down the innovation enough to allow more time for adjustment. While there is something about "featherbedding" which arouses distrust and anger in the average American, success in minimizing the personal crises accompanying "progress" does serve the useful function of distributing its cost more equitably.

A third factor in favor of a farmer-labor coalition against "normalcy" was the fact that labor was itself receiving few of the gains from increased productivity even though forced to bear most of the burden. Despite an increase in man-hour output in manufacturing approaching 70 per cent, real wages rose less than one-fourth. By contrast corporate profits rose by almost two-thirds. These developments were easily seen even while they were taking place in the form of greater inequality in income distribution. During the prosperous 1920's the proportion of national income received by those having incomes of $5,000 or above increased by approximately 10 per cent while the proportion received by those lower down on the income scale suffered a corresponding decrease.

Within the limits of its strength labor did try to combat this growing discrepancy. However, the fact that real wages were rising was a serious obstacle to the aggressive activity which would have been necessary to alter the flow of the income stream. So too was the fact that mass production industries such as metallurgy, automobiles, and rubber manufacture were almost wholly unorganized, while economic depression in shoe manufacturing, shipbuilding, coal mining, and textile manufacturing was a handicap to workers employed in these industries. In the absence of enough force to make its wishes known through "power" channels, labor elected to follow the next best alternative. By means of an extensive educational campaign an attempt was made to convince influential persons (meaning primarily businessmen) that unless wage increases kept pace with the advance in productivity, the time would soon come when wages would no longer be adequate to permit workers to buy all the goods being produced, at which time the economy would experience a severe depression.

It cannot be said that these endeavors were without influence. Such arguments took firm root in the popular mind, and many highly placed business executives verbally espoused this cause—although there is little reason for believing that many businessmen ever took it so seriously as to permit it to interfere with the flow of profits. (In other words, this doctrine as espoused by industrialists was essentially an after the fact rationalization—the fact being that real wages were rising.) The truth was that the business world was too enthusiastic about another theory of economic relationships to give much credence to a rival interpretation. In business circles it was insisted that prosperity permeates the economy from the top (income brackets) down (to the lower income brackets) rather than from the bottom up, and emphasis upon maintaining purchasing power through high wages simply could not be reconciled with that thesis. (It is obvious, incidentally, that Andrew Mellon's tax policy was the clearest single embodiment of the business position on this point.) The later history of business-labor relationships suggests that labor's educational campaign relating high wages to prosperity in the popular mind bore fruit in the following decade rather than in the 1920's.

So convincing were the reasons for joining with a disgruntled agriculture that such a union came close to developing. In 1924 La Follette of Wisconsin endeavored to lead a farmer-labor coalition to victory in the presidential campaign of that year. Revealing clearly that the basis for union was not convincing enough, this third-party movement came to nothing. Not only did La Follette make few inroads on the position of the major parties, but he so failed to attract large numbers of labor voters that the president of the American Federation of Labor asserted shortly after the campaign that labor's support had been an erroneous departure from its traditional nonpartisan political policy. (Gompers himself, it should be noted, had never had his whole heart in this endeavor.) And the limited assistance the new party received from farmers perhaps indicated how little farmers relished such an alliance at the moment. American farmers have been notoriously slow to concede the validity of the nonproperty rights workers have insisted on establishing.

The fact of the matter was that if labor had reasons for joining forces with the farmer, it had even stronger reasons for not doing so. One of these was the fact that the status quo was at least generating a high level of employment, the first and most important requirement for labor prosperity. An active alliance with agriculture would put the laborer on the antiprotection side of the tariff controversy, and would thus tend to create even more "technological" unemployment. Furthermore, most of the increase in real wages laborers were enjoying resulted directly from the farmer's distress—the low prices currently being received for agricultural products. Whatever measures were adopted for the benefit of farmers would almost certainly injure these foundations of labor's own prosperity.

"Welfare Capitalism." Beyond these considerations, however, the important factor was undoubtedly the dramatic new relationship now growing up between capital and labor. As a result of a number of interlocking forces, labor and business leaders were visibly losing the spirit of irreconcilable conflict which had in the past characterized their relationships with one another.

On the side of management the most important motive behind this new departure was probably the intense desire to curb unionism. Having accomplished about all that was to be expected from such activities as the "American Plan," a new strategy now seemed indicated. Put differently, having carried the attack *à la* vinegar to its logical conclusion, a swift transition was being made to the attack *à la* honey.

From labor's standpoint the most important consideration was no doubt the underlying temper of the times. With militant action of almost any kind apt to be interpreted by the general public as revolutionary, a less vulnerable pattern of activities seemed highly desirable. Such an alternative, moreover, seemed particularly indicated in view of the fact that strikes in the post-World War I period had had a tendency to fall into the hands of semirevolutionaries. The search for a new type of adjustment was also motivated by the fact that full employment and rising real wages imposed their own limit on what could be achieved through the traditional type of labor organization. For obvious reasons no course of action which did not to a large extent abandon orthodox aggressiveness could fulfill either of these requirements.

The forces behind the "new era" in labor relations were not, of course, limited to considerations as narrowly selfish as those suggested here. Labor and capital are to a significant extent dependent upon each other, and it is most appropriate that this interdependence receive its due share of recognition and emphasis. Among capitalists as well as laborers it is understandable that there should have developed a certain amount of revulsion against the idea of an indefinite future filled with unrelieved conflict. These motives, however, do not appear in the perspective of history to have been especially dominant, and even if they had been this fact would not have altered the importance of what was happening. Beneath the surface of prosperity and expansion there was growing up a pattern of behavior which, if it had persisted, would have had major consequences for later economic growth.

One outlet for the energies of labor unions was labor banking. Many labor leaders sincerely believed that through the medium of "finance capitalism" industry might be directed along lines more congenial to worker needs. Thus the savings of the worker could be withheld from the antiunion employer—and used instead to relieve the friendly employer from intimidation by open shop associations or similar organizations. Sparked by the activity of the railway brotherhoods, labor banks were organized in the 1920's having a paid-in capital of several million dollars. One such bank alone, in fact, the Brotherhood Investment Company with a home office in Cleveland, Ohio, had an authorized capital of $10 million, although by no means all this amount was actually paid in. At the peak of this movement there were some thirty-six labor banks boasting a total of more than $100 million in deposits.

Another expedient adopted by labor was labor-management cooperation. If, it was argued, labor could convince capital that it was interested in efficiency rather than restriction, conflict might be minimized and labor's position improved in proportion. On the Baltimore and Ohio Railroad the most noteworthy example of this approach was built. Shopmen agreed, in exchange for the carrier's promise to recognize the union and not to contract out any work which could be done in its own shops, to reciprocate by making shop work as inexpensive and as high in quality as possible. From the Baltimore and Ohio this program spread to other railroads, and before the decade was over similar agreements were to be found in a number of industries. Had this development gone on for another decade it is not improbable that much of the orientation of labor unionism in America might have been rechanneled in these directions.

While workers were thus actively transforming their approach to the labor-capital problem, employers were similarly occupied. Under their auspices many devices were promoted to cement the bond between themselves and their "colleagues." One of the more important of these was employee stock ownership. Here the leaders were such companies as United States Steel, the Pennsylvania and New York Central Railroads, and the Standard Oil Company. Spreading ultimately to more than a million workers, this innovation was heralded as conclusive evidence of an economic revolution in which the country's wealth was passing into the hands of wage earners.

A second employer sponsored program was group insurance, providing coverage over and above the workmen's compensation now compulsory in almost every state. By the end of this decade more than five million workers were covered by group insurance plans with policies having a face value of $10 billion. Side by side with group insurance, pension agreements also experienced a rapid development. In this program too some five million workers were enrolled. And before the "new era" came to an end, health, safety, and recreation programs were inaugurated in scores of companies covering a large but unknown number of laborers.

The most successful of all the employer devices for building solidarity with workers was the company union. Originating just prior to the war, and given a great impetus during the war in the "work councils" promoted by the government to minimize work stoppages, this device enjoyed a great favor in employer circles during the twenties. These plans ("industrial democracy" as they were popularly called) were at first broadly accepted by workers, and so dispirited and weak had labor become that company unions continued to grow in number and size even after labor discovered that all too often they were designed primarily to prevent workers from joining bona fide labor unions. At one point such plans were in operation in more than three hundred concerns covering a million and a quarter employees.

Much of the employer's effort in these directions can be summarized under the heading of "personnel administration," the generic name given to employer programs for dealing with worker needs less directly related to the worker's performance on the job than such things as wages and supervision. During the war labor scarcity plus a high labor turnover had prompted employers to investigate ways of raising employee morale and hence efficiency. The major discovery had been that workers reacted very favorably to any evidence that the employer was responding to them as human beings rather than machines. It was even found that "welfare" devices were of great assistance in securing worker acceptance of scientific management. In the 1920's the short-run consequences of these discoveries were worked out primarily in terms of the employer battle against the unions, and indeed more than a few traces of this approach still linger on. However, the idea of achieving greater productivity as well as other less material ends by the use of a wide variety of institutionalized devices was destined to make an indispensable contribution to industrial society long after the emphasis of this period had passed away.

Both labor and capital registered gains under the new "welfare capitalism," as this search for worker-management harmony has been termed. Capital achieved a more "disciplined" working force, while workers found the new relationship preferable to unremitting warfare as long as they were operating at a substantial disadvantage. Even company unions, organized to divert workers' attention from their own unions, could not avoid giving workers some reason for allegiance. The installation of the eight-hour day in the steel industry, for example, was in large part a product of the new philosophy. So too was the Railway Labor Act of 1926, still another unsuccessful attempt to create a machinery for settling disputes in this industry. Furthermore, it was during this period that important matters such as lunch rooms, recreation facilities, pensions, and insurance programs found a permanent place in the industrial order. Indeed, it speaks highly of the foundation organized labor had already built that employers found it necessary to substitute "honey" for "vinegar."

At the same time, however, "welfare capitalism" turned out to be no real solution to the labor-management problem. Labor banks failed from mismanagement, overenthusiasm, and the fact that workers could not put enough money in them to accomplish the objectives sought. Cooperation oriented toward efficiency failed because there repeatedly arose situations in which it defeated labor's short-range purposes by destroying jobs. Employee stock ownership shortly ran into the difficulty that laborers could not secure enough corporate ownership to become "capitalist" in their thinking. As far as insurance and pensions were concerned, labor ultimately decided it would have to advance this cause through collective bargaining rather than employer-dominated programs. Understandably, too, workers became more and more bitterly opposed to the *company* union.

But these are essentially superficial reasons for the failure of the "new era's" search for industrial solidarity. Beneath them was a much more fundamental fact. With the inexorable advance of the machine, and with progress in mass production techniques utilizing mainly unskilled and semi-skilled workers, time was beginning to run out on the dominance of craft unionism in the American labor movement. Although there is basis enough for sympathizing with the plight in which organized labor found itself, it is still one of the principal measures of the extent to which the existing mode of organization had reached the limit of its leadership that it fell in so readily with plans to maintain the status quo in the face of the almost complete helplessness of laborers in the steel, rubber, automobile, coal, and textile industries. It is small wonder the labor movement of this period was strongly tinged with radicalism; "respectable" labor groups had virtually turned their backs on the workers now most in need of help. The important fact, therefore, from the standpoint of America's economic development, was not so much that "welfare capitalism" failed as that craft unionism, in "welfare capitalism," turned up what has since been demonstrated to be a blind alley.

The Farmer Squelched. If the close relationship developing between organized labor and the nation's corporations helped laborers decide not to desert the business interests in favor of an alliance with farmers, they were soon confirmed in the stand thus taken. The year 1927 made it unmistakably clear what the farmer wanted, and the goal thus sought was one which labor was not yet willing to support.

Farmers were, to be sure, no longer insistent upon tariff reductions. They had decided this battle was futile. Instead agriculture was determined to "make the tariff effective for the farmer"—to "secure equality for agriculture in the benefits of the protective tariff."

There was no lack of realism in the farmer's new thinking. He had once and for all given up the utopianism which had characterized his struggle against industrialism ever since the Civil War. Unable to organize to improve directly the bargaining power which is the essential prerequisite to well-being in an exchange society (as laborers and businessmen had done), the farmer had come to the conclusion that he would have to seek his objective indirectly. In short, the only way he could secure united strength was through government; the geographical barrier to organization could apparently be overcome in no other way.

Neither was there any lack of enthusiasm for the task at hand; all the intellectual resources of the "Farm Bloc" were devoted to this problem—a problem now centering on a surplus production in agriculture which could not find sufficiently remunerative foreign markets. Stripped to essentials the solution proposed was absurdly simple. The obvious need was to subsidize exports.

No charge against the taxpayer was suggested. Wheat or cotton producers would instead be charged an "equalization fee" on all units produced, the proceeds to be used to subsidize exports and hence reduce the quantities to be marketed domestically. The domestic price would, under such a program, be higher than otherwise, or at least it would if farmers did not increase production and drive it down again. But, apart from this possibility, the subsidies demanded by the farmer did have the merit of being a financial burden only to farmers—especially foreign ones.

Despite this saving fact, nonagricultural interests found a number of reasons for resisting this proposal. To laborers it meant the threat of higher living costs, and while workers were willing to support such an increase in exchange for job protection by means of the tariff, they were not willing to see food and clothing prices increased at no gain in job security. Furthermore, although many workers would no doubt willingly have made sacrifices to gain an improvement in the legal status of unions (their principal objective in the La Follette campaign), they felt that the cost of living threat was too great a concession.

Business interests also detected a threat to their well-being. Not only did the export subsidy promise higher raw material costs at home, but it seemed likely to lead as well to an undermining of the tariff through reductions in the cost of living and raw material costs abroad. And who could be sure that foreign nations would not retaliate against American manufactures for this undermining of their own international purchasing power, or that increased agricultural exports would not reduce exports of manufactured goods? [1] Thus it was that the farmer was forced to fight his battle almost alone.

It was a magnificent fight, too. Twice farm representatives succeeded in getting their measure (the first and second McNary-Haugen bills) passed in both Houses of Congress. Each time, once in 1927 and once in 1928, Calvin Coolidge returned it with a thumping veto. (The measure embodied the principle of price fixing, said the President, and, what was far worse, it was legislation favoring a particular class rather than society as a whole.) Let it be remembered that it was Calvin Coolidge who endeared himself to the corporate East by declaring that "the business of the United States is business." It was also Coolidge who at one point confided to a political colleague that farmers had always been poor, that nothing could really be done about it, but that it was important for the government to appear to be trying to do something about it.

The failure of the "debenture" legislation, coupled with the still chronic depression in agriculture, furnished much of the background for the presidential campaign of 1928. Both major parties were explicit about what they were willing to appear to be trying to do for agriculture—and the McNary-Haugen proposal was not included. What was included, and all that was included, was a "Federal Farm Board" to assist in the "more orderly marketing" of farm products. The idea was to create an administra-

[1] The natural course of events in an industrializing economy is for exports to become increasingly manufactured products while imports are becoming increasingly of the raw material variety. This follows from the fact that industrialization implies a progressive cheapening of the factors of production most essential to factory production, and a progressive increase in the cost of those factors most needed in raw material producing industries. Artificially to stimulate agricultural exports would unquestionably be tantamount to slowing down this evolution.

tive body which would either directly support the market for "excess" farm products by itself buying in times of "surplus," or would loan money to producer cooperatives to enable them to hold crops off the market until the price improved. In either case the underlying assumption was that the farmer's difficulty was the financial necessity which forced the farmer to sell his products at harvest season when prices were lowest.

The farmer by now knew better, and he therefore did not propose to give up his export subsidy in exchange for anything so trivial. During the campaign this determination was greatly complicated by the Republican candidate's (Herbert Hoover) repeated reference to the need for relief for the farmer *and* limited revision of the tariff. This was promising, or threatening, depending on the point of view. If it meant only such revision as would help the farmer, well and good. But if it meant an increase in the industrial schedule, the farmer could already see the little good done by a "Federal Farm Board" promptly destroyed by an enhanced tax burden.

Prepared for either eventuality farmers attempted to attach an export subsidy amendment to the Federal Farm Board measure, the first order of business when Congress convened in special session early in 1929. Failing in this they renewed their demand in connection with the tariff controversy later in the session. When it developed that the business interests actually intended a general upward revision, the farmer's worst fears were confirmed. Immediately it was recognized to be of the utmost importance to secure the debenture program along with the tariff.

The battle was as bitter as it was futile. Repeatedly the Senate, where agriculture's strength was greatest, asked the House to accept the proposed amendment. Just as repeatedly the House, in which body labor's greatest power lay, refused. Ultimately the Senate was forced to give in and the cherished export subsidy proposal had to be abandoned for the moment. The result was that the Smoot-Hawley Tariff, the highest tariff in America's protectionist history, contained a full line of protection for business and labor but virtually none for agriculture. Moreover, adding insult to injury, President Hoover in the course of the debate communicated to Congress his disapproval of export subsidies in terms which could just as easily have been used to destroy the arguments for a protective tariff.

It is not correct, as many still believe, that the Smoot-Hawley Tariff was a Republican response to the depression. Neither is it correct that this legislation had anything to do with the onset of the crash of 1929. The new tariff was conceived in high prosperity, despite the fact that it did not reach President Hoover's desk until the nation was already undergoing the first discomfort of a major liquidation. True Republicans did not alter their course when depression struck, and many a businessman was certain that smoke would begin pouring out of the chimneys of idle factories as soon as the tariff bill became law. But the year-long controversy between farmers and their political opponents over the debenture program absolves America's highest tariff from the charges either of causing or being caused by the "Great Depression."

Prosperity at Its Crest. On the other hand, however, if one is asked to explain what did bring about this disastrous collapse, the problem is much more difficult. It is tempting to suggest that the crisis might have been postponed, or at the least moderated, if the economy had taken more seriously the purchasing power theory of wages advanced by labor. Indeed a good case can be made for the proposition that the progressive concentration of income in the upper income brackets did ultimately bring about a situation in which the rate of capital formation out of high income savings was greater than could be supported by the purchasing power in the hands of the majority of the people. Unfortunately, this case would be much more convincing were it not for the fact that in such important areas of the economy as construction and automobiles, demand had reached something like a point of temporary saturation which seems to have borne little relation to the structure of income distribution. Perhaps the most appropriate way of viewing the collapse is simply to say that in 1929 another intense American expansion came to an end.

More important than the causes of this decline (since economists are not agreed on what "causes" depressions) is a description of the major elements out of which depression came in 1929—the factors which gave to this depression its unique characteristics. One such characteristic, of course, and in many respects the most important one, was its length; no preceding American downturn had lasted so long. For this fact economists have two explanations. In the first place, an industrial economy is said to be subject to "long waves" of growth and relative stagnation in addition to what is ordinarily thought of as the business cycle. "Long wave" upswings are said to be brought about by the exploitation of some great new series of inventions, while downswings are thought to consist of adjustments to the new structure of production and prices before another series of innovations

TABLE 94. AMERICAN "LONG WAVES"

Period of		
Trough	Peak	General Description
1785-95	1810-17	Iron and textiles
1844-51	1870-75	Steam and steel
1890-96	1914-20	Electric power Automobiles Chemistry

Source: Schumpeter, *Business Cycles.*

starts the economy off on another round of rapid development. During "long wave" upswings, depressions are usually short and mild while downswings tend to produce longer and more severe depressions. As can be seen in Table 94, America's "Great Depression" coincided with the downward portion of a "long wave" movement.

However, on two other occasions (in the 1840's and the 1890's) the American economy had had a similar experience. Why was the depression of the 1930's of longer duration than these liquidations? Here economists point out that there is a building cycle which proceeds in large part independently of "long waves" or the business cycle itself. Moreover, the consequences of fluctuations in construction have been becoming progressively more important as urbanization and industrialization have become dominant features of our economic life. In 1929, for example, construction made up almost 8 per cent of total national output, and hence a dip in this activity could not help having significant repercussions. As Table 95 shows, this activity began to move lower long before the economy itself became depressed. The "Great Depression," in other words, not only coincided with "a long wave" downswing, but it coincided also with a downward movement of the building cycle.

TABLE 95. GENESIS OF DEPRESSION

Year	Construction Expenditures
	(Billions of dollars)
1921	8.2
1922	9.8
1923	11.6
1924	12.8
1925	13.9
1926	14.7
1927	14.8
1928	14.6
1929	13.9
1930	11.7

Source: Bureau of the Census, *Historical Statistics of the United States, 1789-1945*, p. 168.

Another unique characteristic of the depression of the '30's is the extent to which it is remembered in terms of the stock market crash which ushered it in. To be sure, this downturn was not unique in the way in which the preceding prosperity had been accentuated by speculation, but it was the first occasion on which speculation in securities had been the dominant factor. (Earlier in the decade a real estate boom had shared the speculation stage, but this fever had subsided well before the securities boom reached its peak.) Indeed, almost every important aspect of the spirit of the "new era" was accurately mirrored in the securities markets as the 1920's drew to a close.

There was reason enough in the high and ever higher profits being earned for speculative confidence; security prices would have risen in any event. But one of the most important facts about speculation is that it can itself push the market higher. If enough people expect prices to rise, and buy on the basis of that expectation, the very increase in buying will generate the higher prices anticipated. When it has thus been demonstrated, even in so circular a way, that the expectations held were justified, buying will be given another impetus and the price rise carried still further.

It is plain that security prices may in this way reach levels which bear little relation to the profits and dividends which are their *objective* basis. Even this does not necessarily check the boom as long as *subjective* expectations are high. However, it is also part of a general speculation that it provides out of its own momentum some of the objective basis on which it rests. As speculators sell at a profit they have an increased income with which to buy houses, automobiles, fur coats, and the like, in addition to still more securities. Thus the whole process is cumulative and self-reinforcing—until something happens to prick the flimsy bubble of exaggerated expectations.

The speculative boom of the late 1920's, just as all other such phenomena, had to rest at base upon an abundant supply of money. This was provided in the first instance by the expansion of commercial bank credit, and more remotely by the ease with which the Federal Reserve System made its credit available. Abundant credit was used in part to expand industry's productive capacity, in part to finance installment sales of the goods produced with this expanded capacity, and in part to finance the purchase on credit of securities whose values were increased by these sales. As the boom progressed, moreover, and especially as business concerns began to supply more and more of their own capital needs, banks began to invest a larger and larger proportion of their resources in long-term and hence less liquid assets such as securities and real estate rather than more liquid, short-term commercial loans. And as real capital formation reached a saturation point, retained business profits found their way increasingly into the stock market.

So readily available was money and so excited was the speculative fever that corporate securities became of interest to a far wider group of people than even before. For one thing this development was well suited to the emphasis of "welfare capitalism" on employee stock ownership. Large numbers of the urban middle class were also drawn into the "market." As the boom went on, the fever became contagious. With so many people involved who understood little of what was going on, it was possible to sell almost any securities. The close relationship now existing between commercial banks and investment companies also assisted in foisting off on an unsuspecting public securities a more sophisticated group of purchasers would not have accepted. One of the important consequences of this fact was its contribution toward the creation of the vast, unwieldy utility empires which grew up during this period.

So eager were small investors to participate in Wall Street's riches that a fundamentally new financial institution grew up to exploit this demand. The so-called investment trust would sell its securities to the general public—catering especially to those with little capital—and use the proceeds to enter the market at whatever points seemed most profitable. Small investors entering the market directly have the difficult problem of "diversification," of avoiding "putting all their eggs in one basket." The investment trust solved this problem. Each holder of an investment trust share is automatically as diversified as the company's over-all holdings. There were abuses, of course; almost everything financial was overdone during the 1920's. Many trust funds were used more speculatively than was desirable with the life savings of middle class citizens. And when the crash came, investment trusts contributed their share to the decline in security values by abruptly withdrawing funds from the call-loan market in order to buy securities at reduced values. But the new device did succeed in channeling small investor funds into Wall Street.

From the standpoint of the domestic economy a speculative boom can not go on indefinitely apart from expansion in the underlying economy. Eventually, in the absence of such expansion, expectations must depart radically from economic realities. When that happens it is only a matter of time until people begin having doubts, and a fever of speculation can not exist after doubt arises. In the American economy of "The Roaring Twenties" expansion meant essentially automobile production and construction. When, some months before the actual crash, both of these areas of the economy began to contract, it was all too apparent that the boom was about to recede. Unfortunately, there were too few who recognized the symptoms.

Perhaps one reason why so few did diagnose the situation correctly was that the domestic economic picture was in turn complicated by developments in the international economy. Here was still another major characteristic of the nation's greatest depression; not since early in the nineteenth century had international factors played such an important role in American economic life.

Ever since the World War the financial heritage of that conflict had lingered on, presenting problems which had never been quite resolved. For example, the United States had continued to insist that the funds loaned to the Allies must be repaid (as Calvin Coolidge expressed the American position, "They hired the money, didn't they?"), while the Allies insisted they could not pay these debts unless Germany were required to pay an equivalent in war reparations. The United States refused to acknowledge any connection between the two kinds of obligations, not recognizing loans to the Allies as a part of America's war effort in lieu of more American lives lost, or other sacrifices. But the nation's leadership in Washington did not quibble about European logic as long as debt payments kept coming in, despite the fact that the reparations burden placed on Germany was too heavy for her to bear.

As long as Germany continued to make her payments, Europe made regular remittances to the United States. In turn Germany could keep up her end of this process as long as the United States continued to loan

TABLE 96. MORE OF A CREDITOR THAN EVER

	U. S. Investments Abroad				Foreign Investments in the U. S.			
Year	Total	Direct	Port-folio	Short Term	Total	Direct	Port-folio	Short Term
	(Billions of dollars)							
1919	7.0	3.9	2.6	0.5	3.3	0.9	1.6	0.8
1930	17.2	8.0	7.2	2.0	8.4	1.4	4.3	2.7

Source: Bureau of the Census, *Historical Statistics of the United States, 1789-1945*, p. 242.

freely abroad. This we were willing to do, for a time, our long term capital investments abroad rising to a peak of more than $1½ billion in a single year. In short, the level of American exports and a large part of the structure of international indebtedness rested in the last analysis on a high level of American investment abroad.

Simultaneously with the first contractions in construction and automobile output in the United States, the international economy also began to weaken. The speculative boom in Wall Street had reached such proportions that funds could be more profitably invested in the stock market than abroad. It would be a gross exaggeration to assert that depression abroad was "caused" by this fact and hence by the tapering off of American foreign investments; European economies by 1929 contained much the same sorts of maladjustments as the American economy, if not in quite so pronounced a form. But there can be no doubt that this sequence of events in the international economy did much to make the crisis when it came more severe. Put differently, this was the first world depression in which the influence of the United States was the most important single factor.

The intricate interrelationship between the international and domestic economies is especially clearly seen in Federal Reserve policy. After the wartime interval off the gold standard, most of Europe struggled back to gold. However, America's critical position in the international economy tended to set up a flow of gold in this direction which threatened so to unbalance the world distribution of gold as to make an effective gold standard impossible. Partly because the business interests preferred such a policy, and partly to dampen the tendency for gold to flow to this country, the Federal Reserve System held to an "easy money," low interest policy. This was accomplished primarily by the other banks following New York's lead in maintaining a low rediscount rate, and by means of a cooperative, extralegal organization of open market operations (the purchase of government securities by the Federal Reserve banks). Perhaps something was achieved for the international gold standard in this way, although the United States was a net importer of gold in the 1920's to the extent of more than $2 billion and the decade ended with more gold concentrated in France and the United States than was good for international economic stability. Domestically, however, this policy had the effect of raising speculation to even greater heights and thus indirectly at a later point of striking an almost fatal blow at the international economy.[2] Then, ironically, when the Federal Reserve System endeavored to use its powers to curb the boom through a tighter credit policy, it was too late. By that time so much nonbanking money was available to the stock market that little was accomplished through central bank restrictions. Clearly the new banking system was more effective in preventing panics than in curbing overexpansion.

The Descent Begins. The factors which precipitated panic on the stock market cannot be isolated with certainty any more than can the causes of depression. In a highly speculative situation many things can affect confidence sufficiently to bring about a wave of selling. But once the dike springs even a small leak, the angry waters cannot long be held back. So it was in October, 1929.

On October 15 an outstanding economist asserted that stock prices had reached a permanently high plateau and would go higher over the coming months. The chairman of New York's National City Bank echoed these sentiments. On that day and the day following the market broke on an average of ten points a share. Economist Irving Fisher's analysis of the

[2] The perversity of these results was almost complete. Deposit credit ("checkbook" money) was "manufactured" by the central bank (by way of the rediscount rate and open market operations) in order to keep interest rates at home from appearing more attractive than the pattern of rates abroad. The low cost of money, however, stimulated investment (less productive investment opportunities could profitably be exploited), thus contributing to the objective foundation on which speculation was primarily built in its early stages. The "easy money" policy followed also made readily available funds with which to carry on active speculation when the popular mood became so inclined. At that point the subjective aspects of the speculative process made Wall Street so attractive that overseas money markets were practically abandoned.

TABLE 97. THE DESCENT BEGINS

Month	Index of Automobile Production	Index of Industrial Stock Prices
	(1923-25 = 100)	
January	121.3	275.0
April	188.1	285.8
September	125.8	358.5
October	114.9	316.3
November	65.8	219.4
December	36.3	229.3

Source: Federal Reserve Board.

break was that the "lunatic fringe" (speculators who did not understand how sound the economy really was) had been shaken out of the market. On October 22, his ally in optimism, Charles E. Mitchell, repeated his earlier assertion of confidence. The next day the market plunged an average of fifty points per share, the total loss of security values exceeding $4 billion. This break was followed within twenty-four hours by "Black Thursday" (October 24) when the stock exchange became completely demoralized. Almost thirteen million shares of stock changed hands, and the price drop was the greatest in the history of Wall Street. At one o'clock in the afternoon the ticker was still recording transactions which had taken place at eleven-thirty. On October 29 an even larger number of shares was dumped on the market, this day representing the peak of the 1929 financial crisis.

Naturally people in high places tried to reassure the fearful. Large capitalists were deeply involved in the financial edifice so disastrously crumbling, and they could see the peril of insolvency if liquidation continued at such a violent pace. Politically, the business interests had even more at stake. They had broadly justified their policies on the ground that "perpetual" prosperity had thereby been created. Moreover, when doubts had been expressed about the height of the speculative boom no less a public personage than Secretary of the Treasury Mellon (as well as other high officials) had opined that there were no evidences of an unhealthy condition developing. The political prestige of the business community, therefore, and the privilege of continuing to formulate the nation's economic policies were clearly hanging in the balance.

To the credit of the capitalist group, an attempt was made to hold back the gathering storm. As nonbanking concerns withdrew funds they had made available to the stock market in order to avoid further losses, bankers put up more than $1 billion to fill the gap thus created. Sincere, although obvious and in the end futile, efforts were made to support the market directly. On the political front the country's leaders lost no opportunity to inform the people that the nation was still sound and prosperous.

It was not so. Not only could the panic itself not be prevented from deepening, but, what was of far greater import, it could not be prevented from spreading its depressing influence to the general economy. Those who lost money in the debacle were forced to curtail purchases of industry's output. Particularly affected, perhaps, were automobile and other durable goods sales, postponable purchases already being bought to a large extent on credit by people confident about their indebtedness in part because of the exuberance emanating from Wall Street. This shrinkage in demand, added to the contraction in durable goods output which had commenced during the boom itself and to the downward spiral of foreign trade, created an unemployment which rapidly became the familiar vicious circle of deflation. In short, as it was made abundantly clear with the passing years, the financial debacle was an episode of the depression, not its cause.

Even after these things became more or less clear, the nation's leadership did not abandon the struggle. Although the "new era" was threatened, as all could plainly see, its admirers understandably sought to salvage what they could. They could not know it then, but the grim fact was that comparatively little was actually salvageable. Woodrow Wilson with his "new freedom" had endeavored to challenge the organization of the economy on a laissez faire foundation. Perhaps in part because the time was not yet ripe and in part because war rudely intervened, this effort had largely failed. Now, however, what an earlier generation had definitively begun a gigantic depression was to carry to a successful conclusion. The days of governing the nation primarily in the interest of the business community were almost over; the end of the "new era" signalled the death knell of laissez faire.

QUESTIONS FOR DISCUSSION

1. What problems was labor confronted with in the 1920's?
2. Is it socially desirable to slow down technological progress in order to give those who are injured by it a better opportunity to make a satisfactory adjustment?
3. How was the businessman's conception of the way an economy operates related to labor's difficulties?
4. Why has American labor always bitterly resented employer paternalism? Why did this attitude almost break down in the 1920's?
5. What were the important features of "welfare capitalism"? Why did this approach fail?
6. Why was the farmer no longer pinning his hopes on a protective tariff? How did he propose to solve his problem?

7. Was the farmer's solution to his economic problem as ridiculous as his political opponents insisted? Would this have been superior to the Federal Farm Board experiment?

8. Why did businessmen object to the farmer's proposal? Why did laborers object?

9. To what extent would it be correct to say that the "Great Depression" was "caused" by speculation? What "causes" speculation?

10. How does speculation feed upon itself? After a period of speculation, why is the decline so sharp?

11. Why was the "Great Depression" so severe?

PART V

THE NATION IN CRISIS

(1929-1954)

Chapter 34

ENTER THE "FIRST NEW DEAL"

1930 Smoot-Hawley Tariff.
1931 Moratorium on interallied debts.
1932 Reconstruction Finance Corporation created.
"Bonus Army" episode.
Glass-Steagall Act.
Relief and Construction Act.
Federal Home Loan Bank Act.
Norris-LaGuardia Act.
1933 "First New Deal" launched.
Enactment of a mass of emergency (relief and reform) measures.

The Ways of Orthodoxy. President Hoover's stature as a statesman has unjustly suffered from the misfortune which made the greatest depression in the country's history coincide with his four years in the White House. This injustice does not arise, however, from the fact that popular opinion has it that Hoover sat idly by doing nothing while millions of his countrymen were suffering cold, hunger, homelessness, and the despair of unemployment. Popular opinion, to be sure, does exaggerate the Hoover inactivity; his administration anticipated in embryo much of the program of his successor. But there is enough truth in the usual assertion that repeating it is not unfair.

Rather Herbert Hoover's prestige has suffered for two other reasons. On the one hand, he entered the presidency with a world-wide reputation as a great humanitarian, earned as relief administrator in war-torn Europe after World War I. Yet, faced with the suffering of fellow Americans, he seemed to many callous and indifferent. That President Hoover was never either of these things seems unquestionable. At the same time a man with a different reputation might have suffered less in public good will from the events following 1929.

On the other hand, it was Hoover's fate to be placed at the critical point in a process of fundamental social change. Such changes are usually gradual, growing out of deep roots in the past and never fully freeing themselves from the institutions which preceded them. The period of the early 1930's, however, was one of those rare occasions on which transformations were demanded almost more rapidly than human beings could adjust to them.

TABLE 98. THE GREAT COLLAPSE

Year	Industrial Production *	Prices ‡ Wholesale Farm	Other †	Consumer	Factory Weekly Earnings ‡	Unemployment ‡ (000's)
		(1947 – 1949 = 100)				
1929	59	58.6	65.5	73.3	$25.03	1,550
1930	49	49.3	60.9	71.4	23.25	4,340
1931	40	36.2	53.6	65.0	20.87	8,020
1932	31	26.9	50.2	58.4	17.05	12,060

* Federal Reserve Board.
† Other than farm products and foods.
‡ Department of Labor.

It was not only, either, that this new depression was more severe than any of its predecessors. After all, the depression was at least two and perhaps three years old before it was recognized for what it really was; the term "Great Depression" has been given to this period by history's perspective rather than the perspective of Herbert Hoover's administration. Very nearly and possibly fully as large a proportion of the urban labor force had been unemployed in previous depressions. The important fact, however, and one not recognized in the highest official circles until matters had drifted from bad to worse, was that in the past forty years the labor group had grown to be a much larger proportion of the total population. This fact provided much of the social force which eventually erupted, unseating the men least able to free their thinking from the dead hand of the past.

The powerful hold of the past on Hoover and the men around him was visible on every hand. Businessmen had always preferred to "let nature take her course" in depressions, at least where the alternative was government interference in "private" matters. On November 21, 1929, having decided that the crisis was more than a stock market readjustment, the President called a conference of leading industrialists. A solemn promise was elicited from business not to initiate wage reductions or to try to maintain profits by creating additional unemployment. Of course, such promises proved to be empty. Private entrepreneurs are simply unable to operate at capacity paying full wages when deflation is going on all around them. The best indication of this failure in the present instance was the fact that real wages began immediately to fall, even for those employed, despite a steady decline in the cost of living. Distributions to stockholders on the other hand were, for the most part, maintained for nearly two years.

Another long-held doctrine of businessmen was that if government assistance did become necessary, action by state and local governments was

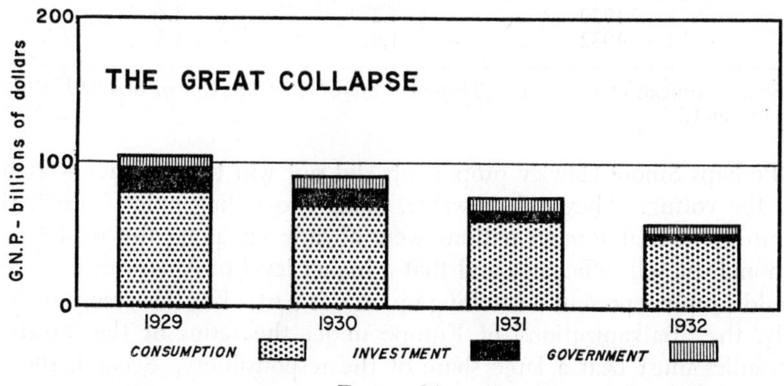

FIGURE 14.

preferable to interference by the federal government. On November 23, 1929, President Hoover wired governors and mayors requesting them to cooperate in a program of public works expansion. Here, too, no results were forthcoming. The depression was a *national* phenomenon, and could effectively be dealt with only on a *national* basis. A really helpful program of public works would have required heavy support from the federal government, a support which would have threatened the budget surplus businessmen considered such an important part of fiscal policy.

Still a third step taken by the Hoover administration maintained direct contact with more than one hundred years of American history. This was the Smoot-Hawley Tariff which became law on June 18, 1930. Although its origin some fifteen months before had had no connection with the depression, it is understandable that against the backdrop of deflation and deteriorating international economic relationships the concluding stages of debate on this measure saw the issues it represented broadened considerably. Businessmen, thus, were inclined to argue that this tried-and-true remedy for so many business ills was just what the economy needed. This was countered by the assertion that higher American duties would cause foreign nations to retaliate by erecting barriers against United States exports. Much point was given to this contention by the fact that no less than twenty-three foreign nations sent formal protests to Congress, and there is now no doubt that much retaliation did result. Similarly a petition signed by more than one thousand American economists was transmited to Congress insisting that the proposed new tariff would damage both the domestic and the international economies.

TABLE 99. IMPACT ON FOREIGN TRADE

Year	Exports	Imports
	(Billions of dollars)	
1929	5.2	4.4
1932	1.6	1.3

Source: Bureau of the Census, *Historical Statistics of the United States, 1789-1945*, pp. 180 and 246.

Perhaps Smoot-Hawley proponents did not win the argument—as they did the voting. They did, however, make two telling points. First, they pointed out that foreign nations were already far along the road toward nationalistic self-sufficiency and that a higher level of American protection would simply represent a catching up on our part. For this result, incidentally, the "Balkanization" of Europe under the terms of the Treaty of Versailles must bear a large share of the responsibility. Second, they insisted that the loss in employment resulting from a decline in exports would be offset by a decline in imports. In vain did tariff opponents assert that self-sufficiency abroad was in part caused by the earlier Fordney-McCumber Tariff, and that changes in foreign trade levels would in all probability create maladjustments which in a deflationary situation could not be kept from spreading.

Amid these manifestations of orthodoxy, only two steps were taken which bore traces of a different approach. First, the federal government's own construction program (for buildings to house various government activities) was increased from a maximum of $35 million per year to $65 million, and federal grants to states for highway construction were likewise doubled.

Second, the Federal Reserve System sought to relieve the business situation by making money "easier." Unfortunately, the existence of large excess reserves in commercial banks made a reduction in the rediscount rate an ineffective tool for accomplishing this purpose, and when an unprecedented series of open market operations was launched it developed that businessmen could not be induced to expand their operations by money manipulations.[1]

[1] It has been said of monetary policy used for the purpose of stabilization that "one can pull but not push with a string," meaning that these control techniques can inhibit economic activity but cannot in and of themselves simulate business. Thus the rediscount rate is useful for this purpose only when commercial banks are operating so close to the limit of the funds available to them that they are forced to borrow from the Federal Reserve System. Likewise if open market operations only increase the *excess reserves* in commercial banks, this device is of little benefit. In short, business expansion in the last analysis depends upon the willingness of businessmen to go into debt in order to expand their operations.

Deepening Depression. Despite these well-intentioned efforts, the depression continued to deepen. Twelve months of deflation saw stock prices fall 40 per cent and industrial production almost 20 per cent, while unemployment increased to more than four million persons. And although the farmer does not in a depression suffer from unemployment, liquidation was dealing especially hard with him. Whereas the index of consumer prices had fallen less than 10 per cent, prices of farm products had fallen more than 15 per cent. Wheat and cotton prices, especially, had sunk virtually to the destitution level for a large number of farmers, the decline being 25 and 33 per cent, respectively.

If the farmer's situation had not been so serious, he could with much justice have said "I told you so" to his industrial colleagues. Although the Federal Farm Board spent during its first year of life some $150 million trying to hold up farm prices, particularly wheat and cotton prices, it was overwhelmed, with no prospect of any greater success for the future. Again, as in the downturn following World War I, nonagricultural producers were taking advantage of their greater concentration to let output rather than prices be the principal equilibrating factor. The first year of deflation saw the prices of manufactured goods fall 7 per cent while the index of industrial production was falling 18 per cent, whereas in agriculture the price of farm products dipped 16 per cent and production slightly increased. Farm spokesmen were quick to point out that the farmer's distress was intensified by this fact, a position widely supported by academic economists.

It might be thought that by this time the administration would have been ready to launch unorthodox programs in order that more tangible results might be achieved. Scarcely anything, however, was farther from the minds of the nation's leaders. The thinking in Washington was if anything narrowing as a federal budget deficit loomed on the horizon for the first time in a dozen years. Still relying on local action, the President did organize in October, 1930, the so-called President's Emergency Relief Organization for the purpose of coordinating local, private relief. Through the governors of the several states some three thousand relief committees were created to relieve the distress of mass unemployment. Already, however, private and even nonfederal government resources were so nearly exhausted that there was an unfortunately small amount of aid to be "coordinated."

By 1931 the emphasis of the administration had turned to a crude form of work relief. A campaign was promoted (the "Give-a-Job" campaign) to induce private citizens to employ members of the growing army of unemployed for yard work or other miscellaneous odd jobs. With unemployment now at seven million and most Americans feeling the pinch in some way, this appeal was perhaps the most absurd step of all in a series of measures history has branded as ludicrously inadequate. The very triviality of this approach to impending social disaster was reason enough for the appearance in 1931 of the first loud outcry against Washington "indifference," an outcry which grew visibly louder with the passage of a bill authorizing government aid in the purchase of feed for the livestock of drought-stricken farmers (on the ground that farmers were businessmen in need of credit) but which would not put the government's resources at the disposal of farmers whose greatest need was food for their families. A major aspect of this mounting unrest was the passage in February of a special loan program for veterans—over President Hoover's veto.

In sharp contrast with the President's tenacious orthodoxy in connection with the crisis at home was his statesmanlike grappling with an international crisis which first became acute in mid-1931. Slowly but surely depression had stretched to the breaking point the fine threads holding the complex international economy together. On May 11, 1931, the weakest link snapped when the largest bank in Austria declared itself unable to meet its obligations. Germany's financial structure followed almost immediately, and within six months half of the world including England had gone off the gold standard.

Hoover's first response, on June 21, was to declare a one-year moratorium on intergovernmental debts, a moratorium which ultimately became complete forgiveness. The second, a logical supplement to the first, was a detailed program for maintaining private credits to a Germany overburdened with short-term credits—mainly from this country. Both of these steps exhibited courage and statesmanship of a high order, for America's business leaders placed the sanctity of European debts to the United States second only to a balanced budget in their list of orthodoxies to be held at almost any cost.

The history of America and the "Great Depression" records few ironies more profound than the fact that Herbert Hoover took his major positive step toward relieving the economic situation in an area in which probably little could have been accomplished anyway. It is, in other words, easy to exaggerate the importance of the moratorium, coming as it did in the face of almost certain default. Furthermore, as events were soon to demonstrate, disintegration in Germany had already proceeded too far to be arrested. Even more broadly, small islands of internationalism could not have stood for long against the angry waters of the frantic nationalism by now sweeping over the western world. Because it could be plausibly argued that devaluation, exchange controls, and import restrictions were useful in "exporting" unemployment to other countries, a competitive race to "beggar-my-neighbor" was developing which mere internationalist gestures could not check. And besides, the nation responsible for the Smoot-Hawley Tariff was scarcely qualified to lead the world back to the "higher" road of international statesmanship.

Orthodoxy Under Pressure. Early in 1932 the administration was ready to take its most positive step to date on the domestic front. Since the financial crisis the banking situation had steadily deteriorated. Although bank failures had not reached alarming proportions, and although they had been limited largely to banks not belonging to the Federal Reserve System and to banks serving small, rural communities, they had been numerous, and it was now evident that even a sound central banking organization could not save the domestic financial structure from the consequences of a *general* liquidation. By this time, with securities and real estate far lower in value than when originally acquired, many banks could not achieve the liquidity needed to meet withdrawals except at heavy losses. It was thus clear that beneath the surface the nation's banking structure was highly vulnerable. A significant drop in public confidence might set in motion a demand for liquidity which would be disastrous.

As a precaution against such a contingency the Reconstruction Finance Corporation was created, authorized to make loans to banks (including agricultural credit agencies), insurance companies, and railroads. There was, of course, much opposition to this step. The President was accused of setting up a "bread line" for business while refusing aid to the unemployed. He denied the charge, basing his refutation on the long-standing, businessman's doctrine that economic well-being can only reach the masses by filtering down from the hierarchy above. And in a mature capitalism such as the United States now had there was a great deal more to this thesis than administration opponents were willing to concede publicly. The failure of a bank, an insurance company, or even a substantial industrial concern did mean disaster to folk all the way down the income scale. However, use of this argument in the face of widespread suffering no doubt did deepen resentment against Hoover and those around him. Especially when later in the year the government drove the "bonus army" of veterans out of Washington, using all the weapons of modern warfare, did many people feel that the administration was not sincere in its expression of concern for the majority of citizens.

Shortly after the Reconstruction Finance Corporation Act was passed, a near-crisis arose in connection with the money supply. Federal reserve notes were required by law to be backed by gold in a ratio of at least 40 per cent. Unfortunately, the decline in business activity had reduced the amount of commercial paper held by the Federal Reserve Banks, the other element in the legal backing for the country's principal circulating medium, and by February, 1932, the gold backing had risen to 63 per cent. Now, with international liquidation beginning to gather momentum, sales of foreign-held American securities were generating an outflow of gold amounting to $50 million a month. The time could be seen approaching, thus, when the supply of circulating notes might have to be contracted.

This had to be prevented, and promptly; currency contraction added to general deflation would have been intolerable. The remedy proposed and speedily enacted into law was the first Glass-Steagall Act authorizing the use of government obligations as backing for the note circulation over and above the 40 per cent gold requirement.

TABLE 100. PRESSURE ON MONEY

Year	Gold	
	Exports	Imports
	(Millions of dollars)	
1930	–	280.1
1931	–	145.3
1932	446.2	–

Source: Bureau of the Census, *Historical Statistics of the United States, 1789-1945*, p. 243.

It was at approximately this point that the administration's underlying philosophy of the government's relation to its people in time of depression was first effectively challenged. The Reconstruction Finance Corporation had perhaps foreshadowed a break in this doctrine; agricultural credit was to be made available to individual farmers, although only through already existing or specially formed credit agencies. In July a similar step was taken in the home finance field. Twelve regional Home Loan Banks were established with authority to rediscount first mortgages for home-lending institutions. To be sure, both of these enactments were so hedged about with the restrictions necessitated by a rigid insistence on "sound" financial principles (that is, the requirement of full and adequate security) that the "little fellow" benefited scarcely at all. But the climate was visibly softening, nonetheless.

This change did not come with a rush. The President fought a stubborn 1932 battle, and a successful one, against a number of proposals offered for inflating the currency. Mid-1932 also saw the passage of the largest peacetime tax increase in the nation's history, a last desperate attempt to restore the nation to economic health by balancing the budget. This measure, however, was not wholly an administration victory. Taking advantage of the President's desire to raise taxes, administration opponents made a direct assault on the "Mellon Plan" of concentrating the tax burden on the shoulders of those in the lower income brackets. It was at least fortunate that at a time when one of the great needs was to force more of the resources of higher income citizens out of hoarding and into circulation that new taxes came to rest primarily on this group.

But administration successes were now almost a thing of the past. Not only was the budget not balanced despite the tax increase, but the balanced budget doctrine was itself under serious attack. Led by British economist John Maynard Keynes, a small but growing group of economists was beginning to question the analogy between government and private finance on which this philosophy rested. Popularized by a much more influential group of social commentators, as, for example, Stuart Chase, the new approach asserted that only the federal government could command the financial resources needed to get the wheels of industry turning again, and that the federal government should shoulder this responsibility. More specifically, it was urged that the government should spend more, not less; reduce taxes rather than increase them.

July 21, 1932, saw the first real dent made in established fiscal policy. In the Emergency Relief and Construction Act the Reconstruction Finance Corporation was authorized to help finance both relief programs and public works, and the Federal Reserve Banks were authorized to make loans to individuals in emergency situations. Furthermore, this act even relaxed the rigidity with which self-liquidating public works projects were insisted upon, and created even more flexibility by permitting some use of grants-in-aid rather than loans. Of course this measure met with presidential opposition, the sentiment being voiced that "though the people support the government, the government should not support the people." But with unemployment now at the staggering total of twelve million, the President really had no choice but to retreat as gracefully as he could. It is a striking commentary on how far underlying attitudes had evolved in a few short years that the last full year of Herbert Hoover's term in office saw the national debt increased more than $2½ billion.

TABLE 101. ANOTHER DEPRESSION CASUALTY

Year *	Federal Government: Surplus	Deficit
	(Billions of dollars)	
1927	1.2	–
1930	0.7	–
1931	–	0.4
1932	–	2.5

* Fiscal year.
Source: Bureau of the Census, *Historical Statistics of the United States, 1789-1945*, pp. 295-96.

In one other important way the philosophy of the businessman was forced to give way even before the nation's leadership was entrusted to other hands. Under the impact of depression organized labor was disintegrating in cohesion and power so rapidly, and the plight of the workingman was so widely recognized, that a law was passed limiting the power of federal courts to issue injunctions in labor disputes. Labor groups were no longer to be restrained from financially supporting a strike or presenting to the public facts relating to a strike, federal injunctions could no longer be issued without a hearing or opportunity for cross-examination, and "yellow-dog" contracts were prohibited. No one, of course, supposed that the Norris-LaGuardia Act was solving an immediate problem for laborers; strikes were not popular in the early 1930's, for obvious reasons. Much more important was it at the moment as an indication of the trend in popular thinking as America prepared to elect another president.

Orthodoxy in New Hands. Words are not effective instruments for conveying deep human emotions, and perhaps this is especially true of the dark despair which accompanies a modern industrial depression. The life of a society consists essentially of the work and play of citizens—work to provide the material means for subsistence, mingled with enough play to relieve the harsh monotony of mere existence. Because this is true, because civilization rests at base upon the scarcity of economic goods, there is no more fundamental test of a society's effectiveness than its ability to keep its members usefully occupied. The society that fails at this point makes itself vulnerable to a disorganization which can be damaging in the extreme.

This was the problem confronting the United States in late 1932. Men who had spent hundreds of hours walking the streets looking for work (and walking by dozens of idle factories in the process), families that had been forced to pawn or sell most of the remnants of better days (and had even then been forced to move to a poorer section of town and "go on relief"), veterans who had offered their lives in the service of their country in World War I and were now threatened with being put out into the street with their families, men who were unable to buy nourishing food for children whose growth and health demanded this above all—such people were correspondingly less willing to be governed by society's normal rules of conduct. They were rather becoming steadily more like the hungry dogs with which many actively competed for the contents of the best stocked garbage cans.

In such a context and against the background of a painfully slow evolution in the direction of positive federal action, it is easy to understand the campaign emphasis on the "forgotten man." The Democrats, if elected, proposed to remember such "forgotten" groups as the farmer and the laborer, to give them a "new deal." Against this same background it is easy to understand why so many people considered themselves to have been "forgotten." By an overwhelming popular majority Franklin Delano

Roosevelt was given a mandate to right the "wrongs" perpetrated by the preceding administrations.

In one sense the opportunity to do this could not have come under more unfavorable circumstances. By almost every measure this was the lowest point in the entire depression period; the steel industry, for example, was operating at less than one-fifth of its capacity. Moreover, the greatest single crisis of the entire depression period lay just ahead. All during the last half of 1932 the vulnerability of the country's banking system had been accentuating—despite the fact that the Reconstruction Finance Corporation had authorized $2 billion of loans (banks and trust companies being by far the major recipients) and that many banks had been kept open by this assistance. Regrettably, too, as a result of politics and a misunderstanding on the part of the Clerk of the House, the names of banks in difficulty had been made public. Thus the influence of the Reconstruction Finance Corporation was not all good.

Whether this publicity was what broke the back of the banking structure will long continue to be debated. An equally likely factor was the publicity flowing from Congressional committees inevstigating the practices of banks during the prosperous 1920's. Here were revealed notorious cases of speculation and banking unwisdom (bordering on fraud in numerous instances) which might also have unsettled the mind of the public regarding the safety of its liquid capital. Understandably, Republicans charged that the cause was the public's fear that the party of William Jennings Bryan would now "tinker" with the currency, while Democrats attributed the crisis to Republican neglect and incompetence.

Probably none of these factors was more than incidental to the dramatic developments now beginning to unfold. The most important consideration was surely the fact that the network of financial relationships tying the nations of the world together had been weakening for a number of years, and that the chain of events commenced by the fall of the Kredit-anstalt in Austria was only now reaching this country in full force. But whatever the cause or causes, a national and international "run" on the American banking system began early in February, 1933. In a three-week period member banks withdrew almost $2 billion in currency from the Federal Reserve Banks, out-of-town banks withdrew $750 million dollars from New York banks, and foreign financial concerns liquidated assets held in this country even more rapidly. On March 3 alone, the day before Roosevelt's inauguration, New York banks lost to citizens and foreigners approximately $300 million. As one indication, however, that the public was concerned less about currency manipulations than about the soundness of the banks, only a small proportion of the withdrawals was in gold. As the drive for liquidity gathered momentum, every bank became liable to a "run" by its depositors, and no bank, however sound, could withstand a concerted onslaught of this kind.

One by one the governors of a number of states put a temporary halt to the destruction within their jurisdictions by declaring banking "holidays." Well before the inauguration the banks in half of the states had already been closed. On inauguration day the banks in the remaining states closed their doors. Thus when Franklin Roosevelt took the oath of office as President of the United States, the nation's economic heart had, for the moment, ceased to beat. The new President's position was definitely an unenviable one.

TABLE 102. PRESSURE ON THE BANKING SYSTEM

Year	Bank Suspensions by	
	Federal Reserve Members	Nonmembers
1928	73	426
1929	81	578
1930	188	1,164
1931	516	1,778
1932	331	1,125
1933	1,275	2,729
1934	1	56

Source: Bureau of the Census, *Historical Statistics of the United States, 1789-1945*, p. 273.

From another point of view, however, the very desperateness of the economic situation may have been a boon to the incoming administration. If nothing else, it provided an opportunity to make a dramatic entrance onto the scene of national affairs, and Franklin Roosevelt was most adept at taking advantage of fortuitous circumstances. In his inaugural address he made a significant beginning. Asserting that "the only thing we have to fear is fear itself," he promised "action, and action now."

These words were promptly followed by reassuring deeds. Before bank opening time on Monday, March 6, a presidential proclamation was issued completing the banking "holiday" by closing the Federal Reserve Banks. This same proclamation prohibited the export of gold and the redemption of currency in gold, with the result that the United States was in fact if not in theory no longer on the gold standard. On March 9 a special session of Congress passed the Emergency Banking Act, the principal purpose of which was to set forth procedures by which sound banks would be allowed to reopen. Two days later the Economy Act was passed. Here the emphasis was upon balancing the budget, an emphasis especially comforting to a business world grown impatient with Hoover deficits.

The effect of these swift, bold moves was electric. As soon as banks began reopening, hoarded currency returned to circulation. Within three weeks more than $1 billion had been disgorged, and economic life was rapidly returning to normal. One of the great gains to the "New Deal," thus, was the enthusiastic support it was now granted. The banking crisis, tragic though it might have been, served this important purpose. A sharp, clean break was thereby made between the old philosophy of minimum government interference and a new philosophy calling for positive government action to restore economic health and relieve suffering. If the nation had been uncertain before, supporting Roosevelt because he stood against Hoover, it was now ready to follow where he led.

Not only, either, was the "forgotten man" now an ardent administration supporter, but even businessmen were reassured. This, indeed, is one of the most significant facts about the "First New Deal." A basic Roosevelt objective was relief and recovery, and he well understood that business confidence was necessary to the attainment of these goals. In order, therefore, to give the self-healing forces within the economy full opportunity to function, the new President bent every effort to keep the business interests on his side. The best evidence of this is the fact that in a situation in which he could readily have found sufficient popular support to nationalize the banking industry as a reform measure (had not the chairman of the great National City Bank just resigned against the backdrop of the revelations of Congressional investigating committees?), he chose rather to adopt the most conservative possible methods for assuring its continued operation in private hands. Similarly the vast rail network might easily have been nationalized as tens of thousands of miles of road fell into bankruptcy. Instead the Emergency Transportation Act was passed—and another tottering industry was saved for private operators.

A More Vigorous Relief Program. Unfortunately for its purposes, perhaps, the administration could not limit itself to measures wholly acceptable to the business community. The wounds of depression were too deep and the clamor for long denied relief too strong. As soon as the most pressing demands of the banking crisis had been taken care of, the administration began to devote a part of its energies to the great army of the unemployed—now one-third of the urban labor force.

Three kinds of legislation were developed. One was a program of unemployment relief for young workers. The depression had fallen on this group with particular severity since it possessed the smallest amount of job seniority. To provide relief at the source for this problem, and also to remove many young workers from job competition with older workers, the Civilian Conservation Corps was created. Over a period of seven years two and one-quarter million young men in fifteen hundred camps in every state in the union were put to work on such useful public projects as erosion and flood control, recreation facilities, forest fire prevention, conservation of wild life, and landing fields. One of the earliest "New Deal" relief measures, this was at the same time one of the most successful. The major problem associated with this program was its inadequacy relative to the number of applicants.

A second relief measure consisted of making available to the states the financial resources of the federal government by means of the Federal Emergency Relief Administration. This was no more than had already been done by the preceding administration, the primary difference being that still more of the funds so transferred were to be gifts (grants-in-aid) rather than loans. The third type of relief was a public works program closely resembling that developed, if somewhat grudgingly, under Herbert Hoover, although on an expanded scale.

So little different was this pattern of relief expenditures from that sponsored by the preceding administration that there was little reason for conservative apprehension; the greater sums required and a lesser emphasis on self-liquidation seemed only details by comparison with the relief felt that the departure from the past was not greater. In fact, this program differed so strikingly both in scope and philosophy from the one later supported by the "New Deal" as to make even more certain that it was framed for the specific purpose of allaying conservative fears. This conclusion is still further supported by another fact. Because Roosevelt had made much of his respect for a balanced budget, because business leadership was relying heavily on that attitude, and because the relief program meant that the balanced-budget idea would be an immediate casualty, the President endeavored to hide the actual deficit behind the fiction of a separation of "ordinary" from emergency or "extraordinary" expenditures. This attempt was not especially successful and the fact of a steadily increasing deficit soon had to be acknowledged, but no doubt it did serve some purpose in convincing conservatives that the administration "had its heart in the right place."

Simultaneously with work on unemployment relief, the nation's leaders were busily engaged in ironing out details for a second major emphasis of the "First New Deal." By 1933 the plight of the farmer was pathetic. Cash farm income had plunged from $7 billion to $2 billion, a decline more than twice as great as the fall in consumer prices. Supporting more than one-third of the nation's population, farmers were currently receiving only 5 per cent of the national income, and mortgage foreclosures were proceeding at a prodigious rate. The $500 million appropriated to the Federal Farm Board as a "revolving fund" had been expended almost in its entirety in the attempt to support agricultural prices, and millions of bushels of wheat and hundreds of thousands of bales of cotton in the hands of the government were the only tangible fruit of these activities. The Republican attempt to "do something for the farmer" was a total wreck.

As attention was directed anew to this problem, immense difficulties arose. On the one hand, the large, staple producers did not agree with the smaller, diversified farmers on the kind of program that would be most effective. The former wanted an export subsidy, while the latter most felt the need for credit inflation. On the other hand, farmers as a group were opposed to any program which would subject the farmer to government regimentation, while the administration was convinced that any workable plan would have to include limiting the surplus by government. The Federal Farm Board experience seemed to indicate the impossibility of a program to raise prices that was not accompanied by measures reducing output, and indeed the Board had repeatedly made just such an interpretation of its experience.[2]

On the inflation issue, the President was faced with a cruel dilemma. To give in to this ancient, agricultural panacea for low prices might destroy the confidence he was trying to build up in the business world, while to deny it might be to forfeit an almost equally important farm support. Furthermore, both Grover Cleveland and William Jennings Bryan before him had faced a similar dilemma, and each had been crushed by it. Cleveland had chosen "sound" money and destroyed his own political future; Bryan had chosen "cheap" money and almost destroyed his party's political future. F. D. Roosevelt, cherishing both his own and his party's future, could obviously follow in the footsteps of neither of these predecessors.

Ultimately the pressure for inflationary legislation became irresistible. In the corn belt especially farm tempers had risen to revolutionary proportions. Farmers banded together to prevent foreclosure sales at ruinous prices. Produce trucks were overturned to prevent goods from being taken to market at giveaway prices. At LeMars, Iowa, a judge who refused to promise not to sign any more foreclosures was hanged by the neck until nearly dead—then smeared with axle grease and let loose.

While these things were happening out in the country, Congress was debating farm legislation. Although numerous states were passing mortgage moratoria, it was well understood that Washington would have to act, and soon. During the Congressional delay farmers were even invited

[2] In a free enterprise society it is, after all, the level of prices (and through prices the level of profits) which furnishes producers with the basic cues as to how much to produce. To whatever extent this process operates effectively it is only reasonable to suppose that the fixing of an arbitrary price level above that which would prevail in a "free" market would result in a greater output than would be brought forth by the "free" price. Since this method of bringing the farmer's income up to the desired level requires the government to purchase whatever is produced in excess of the amount consumers will buy at the "fixed" price, the more that is produced the greater will be the cost of the program to the general taxpayer.

to wire the White House collect for mortgage relief. (This program was not limited to agriculture, either; a Home Owners Loan Corporation was created to perform a similar service for distressed urban homeowners.) Thus when President Roosevelt was presented with the inflationary Thomas Amendment, he simply could not have stood against it. What he did do was a master stroke. He used his influence to make these powers (for example, to issue $3 billion worth of fiat money, to coin silver at a ratio of sixteen to one with gold, to devalue the dollar, and to sell $3 billion worth of securities direct to the Federal Reserve Banks) permissive rather than mandatory, and then let most of them lie idle. In other words, he chose neither "sound" money nor "cheap" money, but both. By so doing he avoided the fate of both Cleveland and Bryan, and, much more important at the moment, he kept the antagonism of conservatives to a minimum. Currency inflation as outlined in the Thomas Amendment would probably not have meant the "end of western civilization" as was suggested by some, but this assertion accurately depicts the sentiment of many business leaders.

With inflation approved, the way was opened for the completion of the farm relief program. In addition to inflation, it provided for reducing and refinancing mortgages at lower interest rates. On the matter of prices the new legislation committed itself to no less a task than to raise their level to the point at which the purchasing power of farm commodities would be as great as in the five highly prosperous years just preceding World War I; that is, the price of one unit of each of the seven "basic commodities" (wheat, cotton, corn, hogs, rice, tobacco, and dairy products) was to be made high enough to enable its seller to buy as many other goods with the proceeds as he could have purchased in the earlier period. (Later nine lesser agricultural products were declared to be "basic" from the standpoint of this legislation.) Thus in one measure the farmer was given everything he had been demanding for more than half a century: inflation, cheap credit, and price guarantees.

The act of May 12, however, was not all the farmer might have wanted. Price guarantees were not in the form of export subsidies, and provision was made in the law for production controls. In this fact, moreover, there may well be another evidence of the President's concern about business attitudes. Industrialists could at least congratulate themselves that the new program did not undercut the American tariff by subsidizing foreign workers as an export subsidy would have done.

The Beginnings of Reform. If the "First New Deal" did endeavor at every possible point to minimize the shock of new leadership to established interests, it did not wholly repress the reforming zeal which was perhaps its most important contribution to American history. On May 18 the

President signed a bill creating the Tennessee Valley Authority. Although it could be justified in part in relief terms in view of the desperate poverty of the residents of the Tennessee River Valley area, there was no denying or disguising the broad social purpose behind this enactment. In addition to a miscellany of specific objectives (flood control, navigation, power generation and resale, proper use of marginal lands, reforestation), themselves indicative of the reform sentiment of its sponsors, the Authority was to make and carry out plans "for the general purpose of fostering an orderly . . . physical, economic, and social development" of the region. Furthermore, as a part of the public reaction to the fantastic rise of utility empires in the 1920's and their disastrous crash in the early years of the depression, the rates charged by private utility companies were to be tested as to reasonableness by the "yardstick" of costs at the government-operated plants in the valley of the Tennessee. It was even specifically provided, to the great satisfaction of advocates of "public" power, that the Authority might compete directly with private utilities in order to supply power to residents of the area not already enjoying electric service at "reasonable" rates.

Understandably, the beginnings of reform did not neglect the financial institutions which had played an important part in the stock market crash. In part because large segments of the public were still smarting from the way in which they had been "taken in" during the years of prosperity and speculation, and in part because it was now recognized that to an unrealized extent certain private institutions (Wall Street, in the popular mind) were "affected with a public interest," the nation now acted to place restrictions where none had been before in an effort to correct some of the more obvious deficiencies.

For example, it was a sharp blow to the prestige as well as the freedom of private enterprise when on May 27 the so-called "Truth-in-Securities" Act was passed. Its object was to prevent misrepresentation in securities by requiring issuers to make available to the buyer an accurate picture of the company's financial situation. No attempt was written into the law, as much popular opinion now vaguely believes, to prevent sellers from selling or buyers from buying worthless securities. All the "Truth-in-Securities" Act required was that the seller furnish the buyer the information needed to determine that they were worthless.

Also oriented to the recent financial crisis was another major denial of the thesis, "business knows best." This was the second Glass-Steagall Act, signed June 16. The most discussed innovation in this new banking legislation was the creation of a Federal Deposit Insurance Corporation guaranteeing bank deposits of not more than $5,000. Not intended simply as a protection of the "little fellow," this step was also and perhaps primarily intended to destroy the motivation behind bank "runs" which can so easily bring the entire system crashing down.

Equally important was another provision separating investment from commercial banking. The intent here was to prevent commercial banks from engaging thus indirectly in transactions prohibited by law, from speculating in their own stocks, and from unloading "sour" securities from their own portfolios upon unsuspecting investors. Similarly motivated were provisions prohibiting member banks from making loans as agents for nonbanking corporations, and from paying interest on demand deposits. Bank executives were forbidden to borrow money from their own banks and were required to report loans from other banks, and bank holding companies were placed under stricter control.

Most important of all, however, were the sections of this act designed to centralize banking decisions, particularly in the Federal Reserve System. First, the minimum capital required for a national bank was raised from $25,000 to $50,000. Second, state-wide branch banking was permitted for national banks. Third, the Federal Reserve Board was empowered to limit loans made by member banks on securities. Fourth, the informal arrangements for cooperation among the Federal Reserve Banks on open market policy were made legal. Since the Federal Reserve System had apparently been unable to prevent the excesses of the late 1920's and the ensuing crash, perhaps steps could be taken which would make this possible for the future.

These attacks on the free enterprise system as it had been in its heyday no doubt did make many conservatives unhappy. But that it did not do serious damage to business confidence is probably due in large part to the fact that all this time work was rapidly progressing on a recovery measure which was virtually a businessman's dream come true. Even the most conservative easterner could not get very angry with the administration that, on the same day the new Glass-Steagall Act became law, also put on the books the National Industrial Recovery Act.

QUESTIONS FOR DISCUSSION

1. Why during the downturn after 1929 did farm prices fall more drastically than other prices even though agriculture was already depressed?

2. Can private enterprise do anything substantial to check a major liquidation once it gets under way? Can the federal government?

3. What were the principal elements in the depression program of the Hoover administration?

4. Why does "orthodoxy" secure such a powerful hold on men's minds? Why was this especially true of Republicans at this time?

5. How did the Smoot-Hawley Tariff fit into the economic situation as it existed in mid-1930?

6. To what extent is a modern money and banking system based upon "confidence"? What is the meaning of "confidence" in this context?

7. Why was the American banking system vulnerable to a general liquidation? Could a banking system be devised which would not be vulnerable in this way?

8. How did the new administration resolve the banking crisis? Why did these techniques work?

9. What changes did the "New Deal" introduce into the handling of the general problems growing out of the depression?

10. How did the farm program of the 1930's differ from that proposed by farmers in the preceding decade? How were they alike?

Chapter 35

ENTER THE "SECOND NEW DEAL"

1933 National Industrial Recovery Act.
London Economic Conference.
The United States abandoned the gold standard.
Prohibition amendment repealed.

1934 Year of transition to the "Second New Deal"; legislation less oriented to the emergency as such or to relief as distinguished from reform.
Formal default on World War I debts to the United States (except Finland).
Johnson Debt Default Act.
Nye Munitions Investigation.

1935 "Second New Deal" launched; emphasis now openly on reforming the economic and social system.
Italy's attack on Ethiopia.
Neutrality Act of 1935.
NRA declared unconstitutional.

A Frontal Assault on Depression. The National Industrial Recovery Act has with justice been called the capstone of the "First New Deal." Almost everything which preceded it had been frankly recognized as "salvage" operations—measures designed to shore up the weakest areas of the stalled economic mechanism by providing relief for those in deep distress. What was now required if the economy were to be gotten off dead center, it was felt, was a program which would attack the problem at its source.

But what was its source? Here was an important preliminary question, and one to which there were numerous answers. However, with an administration in Washington earnestly endeavoring to maintain good relationships with the business community, it should occasion no surprise that the definition of the problem accepted was that of industrial leaders.

For a long time American industry had been organizing itself into a great variety of business associations for the purpose of introducing more stability into business operations. Success to date had been limited by the fact that price and production "coordination," clearly the essence of any attempt to achieve industrial integration, were under the ban of the anti-trust laws, and by the further fact that these agreements were voluntary and hence unenforceable. With the coming of depression and a sharply reduced demand for industrial products, the consequences of these facts became painfully evident. A devastating wave of price and wage competition developed as firms attempted to secure enough volume to cover fixed costs by reducing prices and a lower break-even point by reducing wages. The result had been a steady deterioration in real wages and a succession of bankruptcies, consequences which no doubt did contribute to the vicious spiral of deflation. What business leaders were urging as the government's principal attack on depression was the legalization of price and production agreements—a broadened "self-government" in industry.

This proposal that the government not only legalize but enforce the "new competition," summarily reversing forty years of history, sounded much less startling in 1933 than would a similar proposal today. Under the circumstances a most persuasive case could be made. In a free enterprise system production and hence employment depend upon profits, and a savage competition persistently threatening profits is thus injurious in the extreme. On the other hand, however, this case was not compelling—at least without qualification. Labor was by now a confirmed believer in the importance of purchasing power for high level economic activity, insisting that profit and production arrangements which did not also stress wage maintenance were bound to fail. These two approaches, to be sure, are not as antagonistic as they appear on face to be. Wages are a cost as well as purchasing power, and excessive costs can stall the economic machinery as quickly as inadequate purchasing power. So complex is this balance, in fact, that economists are not yet agreed on the limits within which it is best in a depression to maintain wages rather than reduce them. Furthermore, because of the spiral process by means of which deflation grows and deepens, wage maintenance is a safeguard against price cutting and price maintenance is a safeguard against wage cutting.

The measure finally framed, written to give industrial leaders virtually everything they wanted, made concessions to labor in a number of ways. Child labor in firms engaged in interstate commerce was prohibited, the most sweeping forward step in this field ever taken and one destined to be permanent. The objective here was to make more work available to unemployed heads of families. An enlarged program of public works (the Public Works Administration) was authorized to relieve unemployment in another way and to create purchasing power. The "codes of fair competition" to be instituted were to include a limitation on the number of hours workers were to work as still another device for distributing the available jobs. To prevent employers from lowering wages as hours were reduced, minimum wages were to be included in the various "codes." And finally, in order to make certain that minimum wage levels did not become also the maximum, the famous Section 7(a) was included guaranteeing labor the right to organize and bargain collectively with employers.

At first glance it would seem that workers also were given much of what they had always wanted, particularly the guarantee of collective bargaining, and indeed from these beginnings great things were one day to flow. For the moment, however, this first look was misleading. Even in the face of the existing emergency, employers were not willing to abandon the "American Plan"—except under a heavy pressure which an administration concerned with courting the business community was not willing to bring to bear. Thus it was circulated about that the law did not prohibit the formation of *company unions*, and with this issue resolved in favor of employers the National Industrial Recovery Act became law June 16, 1933. The administration which had been swept into power because it had expressed deep concern for the "forgotten man" had placed its seal of approval upon a measure which almost re-created the relationship between the government and big business Andrew Mellon and Calvin Coolidge had worked so hard to promote.

While the National Industrial Recovery Act was still in the legislative mill, another international crisis arose. A number of nations had sent representatives to a meeting called the London Economic Conference to discuss plans for combating the worldwide depression on a cooperative basis. Two of the important items on the agenda were stabilization of national currencies (for the purpose of ending competitive, "beggar-my-neighbor" policies) and reduced trade barriers. As this gathering, with hopeful eyes all over the world watching its every move, solemnly debated the great questions before it, a tragicomedy developed in which the United States played a leading role.

For several reasons America was not yet ready to be internationalist minded. Both the industrial and the agricultural legislation were intended to raise American prices as the major challenge to depression on the domestic front. If successful, one result might be to invite foreign goods into this country. To prevent such a contingency both enactments had included authority to raise tariffs whenever required to protect the domestic programs. Obviously this was no time to be talking with other nations about reducing import barriers.

Similar considerations prevented American cooperation in the field of monetary stabilization. Since an increase in tariff rates might reduce foreign purchasing power for American goods, another method of achieving the necessary protection was also kept in readiness. This was devaluation of the American dollar in terms of gold. In the months since the United States had cut itself loose from gold the dollar had fallen in international exchange and the outward flow of gold had consequently ceased, but the administration evidently felt that our money had not yet depreciated enough to counterbalance the depreciation of other currencies—to offset the advantage currently enjoyed by those nations which had already gone off gold.[1] Until America's leaders were convinced on this point, they felt they could not afford to jeopardize the internal recovery process by agreeing to stabilize.

The tragedy of the London Economic Conference was the unreadiness of the United States to join in an attempt to attack the depression on a world-wide basis. But behind the tragedy there is another side to the story, one humorous to the point of being almost ludicrous. The American representatives had not been informed that their nation could not enter into the London negotiations in good faith. On July 3, in the very midst of deliberations, the President sent his famous "bombshell" message to the Conference informing the world that this country still had some adjustments to make in its currency. From that moment the meeting had little serious purpose, and soon thereafter it adjourned.

The Honeymoon Comes to an End. To the extent that they thought about such things at all, most Americans probably applauded Roosevelt's action. Under the circumstances this emphasis on taking care of our own recovery first had a wide appeal. But if Americans did not criticize this action, the same could not be said of other aspects of the administration's program. On every hand there was accumulating evidence that the "honeymoon" of the "First New Deal" was over.

One such indication developed in connection with the farm program. The price support legislation had not been completed in time to introduce acreage restrictions into 1933 planting plans. However, Washington leaders reasoned that if restriction is logical before a crop is in the ground, there could be nothing illogical about a similar restriction after planting. Accordingly a campaign to destroy agricultural commodities for the purpose of raising their prices was launched. Some ten million acres of growing cotton, twelve thousand acres of tobacco, ten million acres of corn, six million swine (a corollary of the action taken with respect to corn), and

[1] A fall in the price of a nation's monetary unit in the international economy is only another way of saying that that nation's exports have become cheaper and that its imports have become more expensive. This means that a passive trade balance is becoming less so, or even active; in the case at hand the change was sufficiently marked to restore the United States to approximately the situation that existed before the "flight" from gold began. Because this country was one of the last to take this step, it was at least not open to the charge of trying to "export" unemployment ("beggar-my-neighbor") by inducing a more "favorable" trade balance than prevailed before the crisis.

twelve thousand acres of peaches were destroyed. Destruction of wheat was avoided only because a drought had already accomplished what man would otherwise have done.

Immediate and bitter was the public outcry against this destruction of food in the face of widespread want. And perhaps this sort of thing is a sad commentary on modern economic society. The fact is, however, that, many years after businessmen and workers had made this same discovery, the farmer was at last learning that an economy based on abundance does not pay. For many years, in other words, the American economy had been moving toward a wider and wider recognition of scarcity as one of the foundations of private well-being in an exchange economy. It is unfortunate that the farmer first learned this lesson while the nation was suffering from a severe depression. Equally unfortunate is the fact that the first methods used were so crude by comparison with the more subtle techniques used by other groups (such as strikes, patents, layoffs, and tariffs). But there was then and there is now little logical basis for preventing the farmer from fitting himself in with the system in which he finds himself. Certainly there was no group then, as there is none now, powerful enough to try with any real hope of success.

It is probable that this outcry was only partially motivated by humanitarian instincts. By the time this destruction began in earnest the capstone of the "First New Deal" was also under powerful pressure from a number of quarters, and no doubt many people were availing themselves of any opportunity to criticize. In the first place, no provision had been made for protecting the consumer, and businessmen resisted virtually every suggestion that they reap their benefits through greater volume rather than higher prices. Second, "industrial self-government" had originally been intended to coincide with a considerable public works program so that price recovery would be accompanied by employment expansion. But when the public works part of this endeavor proceeded at a veritable snail's pace, price advances seemed grossly unfair.

A third difficulty was still more basic. It had also been anticipated originally that industry agreements ("codes of fair competition," as they were called) would be promptly completed so that wages would be protected simultaneously with prices. But so complex was the task of completing hundreds of codes that progress on this front was frustratingly slow. While the recovery program in the abstract was pushing prices steadily upward, the delay in completing recovery codes in the concrete was working a distinct hardship on many workers.

With respect to this part of the problem the administration did take one important step. In late July the President's Re-employment Agreement set forth a "Blanket Code" to be placed in operation pending the completion of specific industry codes, a document establishing minimum wages of thirty cents per hour and a maximum of thirty-five hours per week for factory workers. Moreover, this "Blue Eagle" campaign (the "Blue Eagle" being a symbol by means of which a concern could inform the public that it was conforming to the recovery law) was only one of the ways the government sought to keep purchasing power adequate. However, the rapid increase in the number of workers enrolled in company unions and the tendency of codes to discriminate against small producers made these endeavors far from successful. It is now conceded that throughout the entire period covered by this experiment large employers as a group held the whip hand. The government bureaucracy was simply incapable of expanding and acquiring the requisite skills rapidly enough to maintain the needed balance between the various segments of the economy.

To these complaints was next added the most crushing accusation of all. For a time it had appeared that emergency expedients were to be highly successful. Industrial production, prices, and even stock values had staged a truly remarkable comeback in the weeks following the inauguration, and on the surface it seemed that the recovery program was proceeding along exactly the right lines. By the last quarter of the year, however, it was evident that the boom was fading. What had been hopefully mistaken for the beginning of recovery was apparently only a speculative, inventory boom based on the expectation of rising prices resulting from the National Industrial Recovery Act. When it became apparent that expectations were feeding only on themselves, the upswing collapsed.

Table 103. A False Hope

1933 Month	Industrial Production *	Prices ‡ Wholesale Farm	Prices ‡ Wholesale Other †	Prices ‡ Consumer	Factory Weekly Earnings ‡	Factory Employment ‡
March	60	70	91	96	75	80
July	100	100	100	100	100	100
November	73	93	107	104	97	103

* Federal Reserve Board.
† Other than farm products and foods.
‡ Department of Labor.

As production steadily fell throughout the latter months of 1933, with industrial prices continuing to hold their mid-year gains, protests against the onesidedness of the recovery program mounted.

Closely related to these criticisms of the industrial side of the administration's efforts were attacks against the agricultural legislation. On the one hand, consumers were no more protected in this program than in the industrial legislation. On the other hand, many farmers soon found themselves worse off than before the law was passed. As often as not sharecroppers and tenants were in one way or another deprived of government checks (for checks were sent to owners rather than operators), and frequently they found themselves off the land in the bargain as acreage restrictions went into effect and as landlords used relief payments to buy tractors. Furthermore, as harvest time approached farm prices began to decline until, with the tendency for industrial prices to maintain earlier gains, it began to appear to many that the farmer too was being sacrificed to the industrial sector of the economy. And the very fact that production controls had been instituted in the first place was enough to antagonize many farmers. By late fall the "Corn Belt" was once more on the verge of systematic violence.

Redoubled Efforts. With the hopeful signs of recovery fast fading, the nation was faced with still another winter of growing unemployment—a development the new administration could not tolerate. To keep this from happening the President inaugurated a second round of recovery measures, the first of which was a forced devaluation of the dollar on October 22.

This late-1933 currency action was admittedly based on academic theory—a typical "brain trust" performance in keeping with the experimental character of the "New Deal." Some economists sincerely believed that the relationship between the value of gold and the price level was such that a rise in the former would automatically result in a proportionate rise in the other. Roosevelt, prompted in part by a situation now almost desperate, resolved to test the theory. The Reconstruction Finance Corporation was directed to buy large quantities of gold in order to boost its price. Unfortunately, for the economy as well as the theory, the outcome was not as expected. Although it proved relatively easy to raise the value of gold, the price level did not follow. By 1933 there was a great deal of difference between increasing the "quantity" of *gold* and increasing the quantity of *money*. This difference, indeed, was essentially why these years witnessed the disappearance of the much revered gold standard throughout virtually the entire world.

A second expedient was an action designed to improve the position of small businesses and laborers within the framework of the industrial codes. On October 22 businessmen in small towns were exempted from the "Blanket Code," and a more effective machinery was established for investigating price increases and handling complaints against unfair business practices. A little later regulations governing employer-employee relationships within the codes were considerably tightened in favor of workers. These changes did not produce either quick or substantial results, but they did go far toward quieting the storm of criticism beginning to envelop the entire code philosophy.

Still a third device (and by far the most important one) for promoting recovery anew was a wholesale expansion of the work relief program. A Civil Works Administration was created on November 8 which, with the expenditure of almost $1 billion in a six-month period and employing at its mid-winter peak more than four million persons, did much to sustain the economy during the fifth winter of depression. The most successful of all the new modes of improving the existing situation, this organization was a significant departure from the Public Works Administration approach. The need was too great and too immediate to permit limitation to conventional type public works projects; the new program was clearly of the "make work" variety. Many projects were not even particularly useful, to say nothing of being self-liquidating. Here, in short, was the definitive beginning of the much discussed and bitterly reviled public works program developed on a much broader scale a little later.

A fourth action came to nothing, but it is nonetheless significant as an indication of the way the mind of the administration was now functioning. Again with the idea of broadening the work relief program, the Public Works Emergency Housing Corporation was created on November 29. The intention was slum clearance and low-rent housing projects, but it was ruled by the Comptroller General that no legislative authority existed for such a program. Although an approach to recovery by way of better housing for Americans had to be abandoned for the time being, the idea did not die.

By the end of 1933 these "second thoughts" of the administration in Washington were beginning to form a rather definite pattern, and to the discerning eye it was clear that the "First New Deal" was already beginning to pass out of the picture. Currency devaluation, an increasing concern for small businessmen and laborers even at the expense of big business, "make work" public works not even pretending to be necessary projects, and government invasion of such a basic field for private enterprise as housing were certainly not the work of an administration striving to retain the confidence of business leaders. A most unwelcome truth was thus slowly dawning on the business world: President Roosevelt's concern really was the "forgotten man," while his apparent concern for business had been based on the recognition that recovery could only be built on business confidence. And as successive steps revealed a more and more basic conflict between these two allegiances, there was no longer any room to doubt which one would be chosen. Put differently, now that the first shock of transition from one administration to another was over, the "New Deal" could afford to show its true colors.

New Directions. If it was evident that the "First New Deal" was disappearing, it was much less evident what the "Second New Deal" would be like. However, as the months went by, a more accurate picture began to form. As it formed, moreover, the emerging pattern of policies was far from reassuring to the major business interests.

In the first place, it was soon learned that the "Second New Deal" was to be oriented more toward internationalism than was its predecessor. On January 30, 1934, the Gold Reserve Act was passed. This measure in effect announced that America's currency adjustment was complete, and on the basis of its authority the President declared that the dollar was now to be stabilized at a value of thirty-five per ounce of gold. That this country was not only willing but anxious to stabilize the international value of the dollar was also advertised by the fact that a large part of the Treasury's "profit" from devaluation ($2 billion) was to be set aside for the purpose of maintaining the value of the dollar in the international economy.

A little later the United States created the Export-Import Bank, a government corporation authorized to extend credits if American exports could be facilitated thereby (especially export trade)—private bankers having become unwilling to extend such credits because of the ever widening circle of restrictions on exchange relationships. Steps were also taken to end so-called "dollar diplomacy" and in various other ways the United States began trying to demonstrate to Latin America that she earnestly desired to be a "good neighbor." This phase of America's internationalism met with particular success, despite the fact that the United States had admittedly not been an especially good neighbor.

In June an even more impressive internationalist step was taken. The Reciprocal Trade Agreements Act was passed giving the President authority to raise or lower duties by as much as 50 per cent in exchange for equivalent concessions from other nations. After leading the movement toward higher trade barriers ever since World War I, this country was now ready to launch a historic reversal of policy and role. It was not, of course, known in 1934 how seriously this legislation would be taken by the administration, but it did not escape notice that its machinery was placed in the State Department and that Secretary of State Cordell Hull had been an ardent free trader all his public life.

America's conversion to the cause of internationalism, however, was by no means as unqualified as it appeared on the surface to be. The $35 per ounce price for gold, whether deliberately or otherwise, proved to be so high that other nations had to act swiftly and decisively to keep their own monetary gold stocks from flowing to this country, and in consequence there was no rush on the part of others to accept such a low value for the dollar as a basis for stabilization. In fact, it turned out that the dollar was "pegged" at too low a level for the long-range integrity of the gold standard, especially in view of the fact that the United States was still the world's largest creditor. On the other hand, however, the high price of gold did have its good side. Since domestic prices did not rise in proportion to the increase in the value of gold, foreigners selling gold to the Treasury and using the proceeds to buy American goods made an excellent

TABLE 104. MALDISTRIBUTION OF GOLD

Year	Net Gold Imports
	(Billions of dollars)
1931	0.1
1934	1.1
1935	1.7
1936	1.1
1937	1.6

Source: Bureau of the Census, *Historical Statistics of the United States, 1789-1945*, p. 243.

bargain. In other words, tariff reductions under the Reciprocal Trade Agreements Act were made possible in part by the high price this country paid for gold.

What the United States had decided to do with gold, moreover, it decided in June, 1934, to do also with silver—although for different reasons. (Particularly was this action not to be classed as "internationalist" in its orientation.) As a result of pressure from debtor-farmers and depressed silver producers, the Treasury was commanded artificially to raise the price of silver by large-scale purchases. The administration tried to avoid this mandatory inflation, and its consequences were in one quarter of the world disastrous. Poor China discovered she could not remain on a silver standard in competition with the enormous purchasing power of this country and as a result found her economy disrupted by a most chaotic financial situation. This fact was no asset when shortly thereafter she was called upon to wage a major war against Japan.

The year 1934 saw still another dimension of the "Second New Deal" spelled out in some detail. Emphasizing once again the impact made on the public mind by the stock market crash, the Securities Exchange Act was passed subjecting security markets and security brokers to extensive regulation. (Already the New York Stock Exchange—the "Big Board"—had taken the hint by tightening its own self-discipline.) Included in the new law were measures preventing "market rigging" and in general limiting the advantage of "insiders" over "outsiders," and giving the Federal Reserve System power to determine what proportion of a stock purchase must be paid in cash.

It is no exaggeration to say that security markets were in 1934 transferred from the status of private concerns to the status of "public utilities." That same year a similar determination was made in other fields. A Federal Communications Commission was created to exercise supervision over radio broadcasting based on the need to allocate frequencies in order to prevent wave length chaos. The same body was given wide powers over telephonic and telegraphic communications. An Air Mail Act was passed, the most definitive step to date in the direction of extending common carrier regulation to the young commercial aviation industry.

There were even other evidences in 1934 of where F. D. Roosevelt's administration stood on the matter of free enterprise laissez faire. A Railroad Retirement Act was passed setting up a pension fund for railroad employees, a fund into which employers as well as workers were to contribute. Also in the railroad industry there was created the first government agency in the nation's history designed to help settle labor disputes but weighted on the side of the employee (the National Railroad Adjustment Board). The Frazier-Lemke Farm Bankruptcy Act was passed to help farmers reacquire farms lost through bankruptcy or to suspend such proceedings for five years if creditors refused to agree to "reasonable" terms. An amendment was added to the internal revenue laws to stop up loopholes which had permitted the wealthy to avoid payment of income taxes in the lush 1920's. And finally the Federal Housing Administration was created putting the federal government into the housing finance business on an immense scale—and not merely the low cost, slum clearance end of it either—and for the first time the financing of homes was placed on a basis that put home ownership within reach of a large fraction of the population.

Even more revealing than these long-term reforms, although reflecting the same general philosophy, were the 1934 developments on the National Recovery Administration front. Responding to charges that the codes fostered monopoly (attempts to enforce "fair competition" have always tended to become the destruction or limiting of competition), the President announced it to be the intention of the administration to prevent such practices from being written into code agreements. A special investigation launched to explore the truth of the charges and make recommendations abundantly documented several ways in which this legislation was operating badly for labor, small business, and the consuming public.

On October 22, for example, the various antagonisms having reached a distinct climax, it was announced that no longer would code provisions limiting production be enforced. A similar ban on price fixing had already been promulgated. By now, too, the government was making it unmistakably clear that it was becoming less and less sympathetic with the use of company unions to frustrate the exercise of independent choice of bargaining agents by workers. As the President himself expressed it: "I ask that the letter and the spirit of free choice be accorded to its workers by every corporation in the United States." A greatly increased number of strikes in 1934, almost half for the purpose of securing recognition for independent unions, also suggested that labor was taking the government's new attitude seriously.

Business leaders must have wondered as 1934 drew to a close what had happened to "their" America, the society they had virtually ruled since the Civil War. It may not be true, as General Smedley D. Butler reported to a House Committee, that during 1934 a group of Wall Street brokers urged him to lead a fascist march on Washington to overthrow the new "anti-business" government. On the other hand, if it is true, it is understandable; men do not easily give up the world they believe in, and there was reason enough for businessmen to feel that the world they believed in was being rapidly and deliberately hacked to pieces. When in November, 1934, the Democrats accomplished the almost impossible feat of winning even larger margins in both the House and the Senate in a nonpresidential election year, the outlook was dark indeed.

Accent on Reform. To this point the evidence as to what the "new" America was to be like was largely piecemeal and circumstantial. No sooner had Congress assembled after the elections, however, than the nation was given a fairly complete description by the new society's chief architect. In his annual message on January 4, 1935, President Roosevelt explained in the most direct words possible just what the "Second New Deal" proposed to accomplish.

According to the President the "First New Deal" had failed to achieve recovery because it had accepted the existing capitalist system. Unfortunately, this system as inherited possessed grave defects which would have to be eradicated before it would again operate effectively. Reform, in other words, was now held to be inseparable from recovery. Having failed in the attempt to achieve recovery without reform, the nation must now endeavor to achieve recovery by means of reform. From a program in which reform was an important though incidental element, the administration was shifting to a program the very essence of which was reform.

Nor did the President leave his audience in doubt as to what was implied by the term "reform." Speaking very generally, social justice was what was meant; the "overprivileged" would have to be weeded out and the "underprivileged" lifted up. More narrowly, reform meant providing citizens of a modern exchange economy with the security taken from them by the impersonal operation of supply and demand. The tragedies of ordinary economic living which the great masses of people are powerless to avert must become group responsibilities rather than fall disproportionately and arbitrarily on individual members. In short, modern economic society must give the average individual enough guarantees so that he will feel he is participating in a worth-while enterprise.

Custodians of the faith of private enterprise were justifiably upset by these utterances. It seemed eminently clear to them that this was an outright repudiation of the principles that had made America great. For three fundamental reasons, however, such judgments were overly harsh. In the first place, the security President Roosevelt was now claiming for the average citizen was not essentially different from that earlier achieved by industrialists when they destroyed or united with their competitors in order to make business life more endurable. The President was simply insisting that security is not for the Rockefellers and the Morgans alone. In the second place, the doctrine that economic well-being filters from the top of the social hierarchy down to the mass of more lowly members had certainly been given an excellent chance. It was singularly appropriate, especially in a democratic society, that the opposite view should now have a few innings. And finally, American "reforms" of the 1930's did no more than help this country "catch up" with actions which had long since been taken in every other important industrialized nation, and many of these steps corresponded closely with measures which had been appearing with increasing frequency on the statute books of various states.

Only the historian of the future can tell whether President Roosevelt evolved to his 1935 position or had all along been eagerly awaiting the right opportunity to express it, whether he genuinely believed reform to be essential to recovery or was simply taking advantage of emergency conditions to implement a "liberal" policy, whether he was the guiding spirit of his reform program or was rather responding to political pressures. For present purposes, however, all this is unimportant. What is primarily of interest here is the meaning of the "Second New Deal" as worked out in specific policies.

For example, what did it mean in the field of agriculture? It might have been thought that by 1935 nothing of consequence could be done for the farmer. Already the federal government had been instrumental in refinancing a fifth of all the farm mortgages in the nation, reducing by an average of one-fourth the mortgage debt of forty thousand farmers, giving every farmer a five-year moratorium on his debt with the right to buy his farm back at a price set by district court, and establishing procedures under which farmers who had already lost their farms could get them back more easily. All this, plus the price support program and participation in direct and work relief, plus the fact that state governments had also been active in some of these same ways, added up to a "rescue" campaign for farmers far exceeding any before undertaken in the history of the country.

Nonetheless in 1935 a way was found to carry this campaign even farther. Feeling that the farm program did not help, and in some instances positively injured, certain classes of farm people—small, diversified producers, tenants, sharecroppers, and migrants—Congress and the President established the Resettlement Administration. The major work of this agency was to transfer farm families from submarginal land to land on which a more adequate living could be earned, to rehabilitate land capable of supporting a family with a greater investment and proper care, and in general to get farmers off relief where possible. While it cannot be said that a great deal was accomplished in these areas, it cannot be doubted that government activities had reached a new high in paternalism.

The Resettlement Administration was created in April. In May a less extreme program was launched in the form of the Rural Electrification Administration. Here the problem to be corrected was not so much destitution as the fact that farmers had not yet received their fair share of the comforts and conveniences a modern economy is capable of producing—that is, that private utility companies had been reluctant to extend lines into low population density areas. By means of loans at low rates of interest and labor provided by the work relief program, power lines were to be extended into rural areas not found profitable by private companies. Justified most directly in terms of work relief and an expected increase in the sale of appliances, the Rural Electrification Administration still met with powerful resistance. Private utilities especially charged that the government was invading the proper field of private enterprise, a charge supported at least in part by the fact that this program was to give preference to projects distributing power generated by publicly owned plants. Moreover, the unit of organization and administration at the local level was to be a rural electrification "cooperative." Apparently a part of what was involved in the new reform-security approach to recovery was a redefinition of the "proper" field for private enterprise.

The Heart of the New Program. These innovations on the agricultural front, however, turned out to be minor affairs by comparison with the next item on the agenda. In May also the Works Progress Administration (the famous-notorious WPA) was created, an organization to do on a more permanent basis what the Civil Works Administration had done temporarily. Almost $5 billion was made available with which to transfer as many of the unemployed as possible from direct relief to work relief. Behind this major shift in public policy was the idea that direct relief should be handled at the state and local levels, and the belief that employment, as distinguished from the dole, would preserve self-respect, conserve skills, and utilize vast, idle resources in the creation of new wealth. Before this agency finally wound up its affairs it had given employment to more than eight million different individuals, one-fifth of all the workers in the country. Although forced by law to avoid work conflicting with private employment, one-fourth of a million projects were undertaken dealing with an unbelievably wide range of economic and social activities.

No part of the entire "New Deal" program was more controversial than this, and even today it is almost impossible to offer a definitive judgment of its work. There are too many angles from which it can be viewed, as well as conflicting criteria that can appropriately be used in judging it. Perhaps the most to be said in its favor is that every major principle governing its work can be explained in such a way as to save its proponents from the charge of being either stupid or "radical." In other words, there is much room for legitimate difference of opinion.

TABLE 105. CHALLENGE TO DESTITUTION

Year	Federal Government Expenditures for: Relief and Work Relief	Public Works	Aid to Agriculture	Total Expenditures	Surplus (+) or Deficit (−)
	(In millions of dollars)				
1925	–	204	54	3,063	+ 717
1929	–	242	71	3,299	+ 738
1933	80	442	73	3,864	−1,784
1937	2,548	803	922	8,177	−3,149

Source: Secretary of the Treasury, *Annual Reports*.

A glance at a few of the difficulties encountered by this program will abundantly demonstrate why this is so. First, one of the principles invoked was haste; the depression was already more than five years old with more than ten million workers still unemployed. To put into full operation a gigantic program such as this in a minimum period of time could not help making this agency extremely vulnerable to charges of poor management (merging with incompetence and even corruption in the extreme cases).

Second, the necessity of avoiding projects employing workers who might otherwise be taken on by private enterprise automatically opened the way to the charge of engaging in "useless" work. They were indeed "useless" when measured from the standpoint of profit possibilities; however, that is not the only criterion of worthwhileness. But where the critical need is to make "useful citizens" out of millions of unemployed citizens, too much stress can be placed on the usefulness of the work done, although it seems reasonably certain in retrospect that relatively little real "leaf raking" was deliberately countenanced.

Third, the accusation that work-relief projects were inefficiently carried out is readily supportable from a certain point of view. But where men are employed to do work customarily done by machines while usable machines are idle just around the corner, it at least makes sense rather than nonsense to argue that the purpose of the program was, after all, to provide employment for men rather than machines.

Fourth, the Works Progress Administration could not possibly have escaped the charge of "ruining" good workers for private employment. Wages for work were naturally higher than relief payments. But how much higher should they have been? To pay wages lower than the average prevailing wage would be to discriminate against the worker in public employment and hence to defeat much of the purpose of helping workers retain their self-respect. On the other hand, the payment of prevailing scales invariably meant paying more than some private employers. In any community private employment wages vary all the way down to just above the "relief" level. And even in the less extreme cases, private employers could not help resenting work relief which prevented them from lowering the prevailing wage scale.

Fortunately, it is not necessary here to evaluate the Works Progress Administration from any of these standpoints. Its position in history must primarily be determined, not on the basis of how well or how badly it did what it set out to do, but on the validity of the task it set itself to accomplish. While Herbert Hoover was still President the federal government at long last agreed that it must bear some of the responsibility for the burden of depression. The philosophy behind this decision, however, was that a society cannot afford to risk the upheaval apt to result from widespread suffering, and that the resources of state and local governments were inadequate. By 1935 the philosophy of the federal government's responsibility had evolved a long step further. In a modern economy based on work, wages, and exchange, an economy in which all sorts of values are intimately bound up with regular employment, society must not only help its citizens keep body and soul together but it must in addition strive to maintain these other values. In short, the "New Deal" faced squarely, for the first time in this country, the implications of depression in an industrial society.

More than this question of philosophy was involved, too. Also at issue was a very practical consideration of basic economic relationships. By 1935, behind the moral and intellectual leadership of John M. Keynes, many people were insisting that a large stream of purchasing power "created" by the government was a prerequisite to recovery. Thus, it was argued, money received by relief workers would be quickly disbursed to private enterprise concerns, which firms would thereby be induced to expand their own employment. But since tax money could not be effectively used to "prime the pump," tax receipts so frequently being money individuals would otherwise have spent themselves, it was insisted that only deficit spending by the federal government could achieve the desired result.[2] To be sure, it was already recognized that this approach was beset by major difficulties, not the least of these being the danger that businessmen would reduce their spending as a result of a fear of government deficits and other "anticapitalist" activity. But this way of thinking had a solid scientific basis, and since 1935 it has come to be accepted by a large proportion of academic economists and other leaders.

Such a profound change in approach naturally met with powerful resistance; social institutions are by definition highly conservative, and the individualistic notion that the unemployed are either lazy or incompetent had deep roots. More specifically, it is understandable that, at a time when this aspect of "New Deal" thinking was not as widely accepted as it is today, businessmen accustomed to holding economic activities to the standard of prices and profit margins were profoundly disturbed. There is little doubt, too, that their despair would have been even greater if they had not suddenly (if not unexpectedly) acquired a major ally.

The First Challenge. On May 6, the same day the Executive Order establishing the Works Progress Administration was issued, the Supreme Court of the United States declared the Railroad Retirement Act unconstitutional. The use of contributions from younger employees to pay pensions for older employees (the insurance principle on which any retirement program must be based) was declared to be a taking of private property without due process of law from those who contributed the most. Moreover, the Supreme Court asserted that it could see no connection whatever between pensions and the interstate commerce clause of the Constitution on which the act had been based.

Three weeks later the Supreme Court made another onslaught on the "New Deal." The President was bluntly informed that he could not remove a member of one of the independent regulatory commissions (in this case the Federal Trade Commission) on the ground that the Commissioner's views did not accord with the presidential program. Mr. Humphrey, a conservative Hoover appointee, was now dead, replaced by a more liberal man of Roosevelt's own choosing, but the decision was nonetheless

[2] This is the historic "multiplier" that is such an important part of economic thinking today. According to multiplier analysis, new expenditures, money which would not otherwise be spent, will be "multiplied" as they are transformed into income in the intricate exchange process characteristic of modern society. Such money will be spent over and over again, adding to national income each time it changes owners. On each occasion, unfortunately, a portion will be saved rather than spent, and therefore the "multiplier" has definite limits. In technical terms the "multiplier" will be 100 per cent divided by the proportion of new income which is saved rather than spent. Thus if 10 per cent only is saved, new expenditures will generate national income equal to ten times their own amount. If 20 per cent is saved, the "multiplier" will be reduced by one-half.

a jarring one for the administration. Simultaneously, the Court held the Frazier-Lemke Farm Bankruptcy Act to be unconstitutional. Here, too, the indictment was the taking of property without due process of law, and the Court specifically refused to give weight to emergency conditions. Conservatives could take much comfort from the fact that the new administration was not to have a completely free hand to destroy long-standing and vital American institutions.

But, alack and alas, the Supreme Court is too judicial a body to make a really good ally. On May 27, the Court also declared the National Industrial Recovery Act unconstitutional. To businessmen this loss of their last important link with the "First New Deal" was a bitter blow. The administration, for its part, no doubt breathed a sigh of relief to have this burden painlessly rolled off its back. But even the "Second New Deal" could derive little real satisfaction from this decision, for it was based upon such a narrow view of the interstate commerce clause (much narrower, for example, than the Court had frequently invoked in labor injunction cases) as to place in jeopardy several of the pillars of the reform program now beginning to gain momentum.

Certainly, as of May, 1935, the larger decision could have gone either way. Conservatives, speaking primarily for the business interests, had not at all given up the fight and they had important advantages on their side. In turn the "New Deal," now thinking in terms of the nation's laborers more than any other group, had, in the vernacular, only begun to fight. As the issue, thus squarely and sharply joined, settled down to open warfare within the framework of the American Constitution, virtually all adult Americans watched developments with avid interest.

QUESTIONS FOR DISCUSSION

1. What were the purposes of the National Industrial Recovery Act, and how was the Act supposed to accomplish these purposes?
2. When an economic decline is in process, should the cost or purchasing-power aspect of wages be more important for public policy?
3. How were labor's interests provided for in the National Industrial Recovery Act? How well were these interests served?
4. Why did the United States "scuttle" the London Economic Conference? Can this action be convincingly defended?
5. Must a modern industrial economy be based upon scarcity? Under what circumstances could an industrial society be based upon a different principle?
6. What was the economic basis of the upswing in mid-1933? Why did this "boom" collapse?

7. Why did the price level not rise as the price of gold fell? What did the United States gain from devaluation?

8. Could the National Industrial Recovery Act "experiment" have been made to work better than it did? How?

9. How could America's silver legislation force far-off China to abandon the silver standard? How could this process injure China's economy?

10. What was the underlying philosophy of the "Second New Deal?" How did this differ from the tenets of the "First New Deal?"

One of my books
LITHO
IN
U.S.A.

Chapter 36

LABOR ON THE MARCH

1935 National Labor Relations Act.
Social Security Act.
Birth of the Committee for Industrial Organization.
1936 Vigorous growth of industrial unionism.
German reoccupation of the Rhineland.
Anti-Comintern Pact signed by Germany, Italy, and Japan.
Neutrality Act of 1936.
1937 The sit-down strike.
Victory won by industrial unionists.
Roosevelt's Supreme Court battle.
Wagner and Social Security Acts upheld by the Supreme Court.

Reform Goes Forward. During the remainder of 1935 the "New Deal" seemed to have everything its own way. In June another unorthodox relief program was inaugurated—the National Youth Administration. This was a further method of removing younger workers from the labor market and compensating them for the disproportionate burden of unemployment borne by them. At the same time it was a program designed to help the nation's educational institutions and make the democratic slogan "equality of opportunity" ring less hollowly. By this legislation needy and deserving young men and women were given financial assistance in order that they might go on with their education.

July saw passed the most "anticapitalist" measure to date. Section 7(a) of the National Industrial Recovery Act had been a tongue-in-cheek concession to workers by the "First New Deal" in order to get the more important industrial code principle enacted into law. On July 5, 1935, however, less than six weeks after Section 7(a) had been invalidated along with the "codes," the National Labor Relations Act (the so-called Wagner Act) was passed re-enacting several of the essential features of 7(a). This "Labor Magna Carta" was to prove one of the most fundamental consequences of the entire "New Deal" program.

The emphases and wording of this measure demonstrated how anxious the "Second New Deal" was not to be misunderstood. Five specific activities were declared to be "unfair labor practices" if engaged in by employers: (1) interfering with employees in the exercise of guaranteed rights, (2) supporting a company union, (3) firing or hiring workers for union activity, (4) discriminating against workers for invoking the provisions of the new law, and (5) refusing to bargain collectively with properly elected employee representatives. A National Labor Relations Board was created to assist in interpretation and in identifying the appropriate bargaining agency. And on the whole, employers did not misunderstand; they promptly set about expediting the act's invalidation by the courts, advised one another to disregard it, and engaged in numerous obstructive tactics to thwart its operation.

August, 1935, might aptly have been dubbed "Black August" by believers in individualistic laissez faire. Interstate motor carriers were subjected to thoroughgoing regulation under the Interstate Commerce Commission, although, interestingly enough, a major pressure behind this regulation was the railroad industry. A good case could be made at this point for the proposition that the railroad industry's current "sickness" was a result of competition from unregulated motor carriers. The Social Security Act was passed providing federal government assistance for state unemployment insurance and old-age pension programs by means of a payroll tax on both employers and employees. Here a motivating factor was the strong public support given the "Townsend Plan" ($200 a month for every person over sixty) and Huey Long's even more formidable "Share-Our-Wealth" movement.

The same month also saw the passage of another bank regulation act—the Banking Act of 1935. Earlier "New Deal" legislation in this field had admittedly been temporary, and hence the banking lessons learned in the 1920's still needed to be embodied in permanent form. Equally important, however, with the abandonment of gold as the regulator of domestic monetary affairs it was essential that some other mechanism be substituted in its place. For both of these reasons this legislation went much further toward centralizing money and banking control than had ever been possible before. And not only was more power concentrated in the Federal Reserve System, but the System's power was also much more highly concentrated at the expense of the power until then wielded by the regional banks.

Specifically a new Board of Governors was created to replace the old Federal Reserve Board. Perhaps the principal purpose behind this change was to get rid of conservative Republican appointees, although another factor was the desire to remove the Secretary of the Treasury and the Comptroller of the Currency as ex officio members in order to protect the Board's independence. To this new group was given the power of approving the president of each Federal Reserve Bank, the authority to control credit by raising or lowering the rediscount rate, and the power to approve the rediscount rate established by each district bank. A new open-market committee was established consisting of the Board of Governors and five representatives of the Reserve Banks. Finally, all state banks having deposits of $1 million or more were required to become members of the System.

In August still another piece of financial legislation was placed on the books, this one also taking its point of departure from the excesses of the "roaring twenties." The victims were the fantastic and often near fraudulent utility empires. Amid a powerful barrage of criticism made possible by the spending of millions of dollars by the public utility lobby, the Public Utility Holding Company Act of 1935 was passed with enough "teeth" to bring a high degree of orderliness into what had been a veritable "crazy quilt" structure. The pyramiding of holding companies atop one another was limited to two tiers, public utility systems were required to be geographically integrated, and the Securities and Exchange Commission was given wide authority over utility financial practices. In addition the Federal Power Commission was given extensive powers over other phases of interstate electric utility operations.

These challenges to private enterprise, moreover, did not end the inroads made against laissez-faire principles in August, 1935. A new farm mortgage law was passed, carefully rewritten to avoid constitutional objections and thus a little less favorable for debtors. On the same day a carefully revised Railroad Retirement Act became law. The next day, in the Bituminous Coal Stabilization Act, the "code" earlier established for the bituminous coal industry was in substance re-enacted in order to prevent cutthroat competition in this industry from destroying labor standards. New enactments in the petroleum and alcohol industries were added evidence that the administration might have successfully rewritten most of the now defunct codes if it had been so inclined. It was indeed most exasperating the way legislation favoring other groups was being rescued while that favoring business was simply left to lie where the Supreme Court destroyed it.

And even these measures did not complete the reforms enacted in that awful month. On August 30 there was passed the so-called Wealth-Tax Act, a new tax measure built more specifically than ever before on the principle of "ability to pay." Distinguishing in tax rates between large and small corporations, graduating rates sharply upward in the highest brackets of individual income, and even taxing excess profits, the new law was referred to in conservative circles as one for "revenge" rather than revenue. To President Roosevelt, however, it was nothing of the sort; its purpose was "to create a broader range of opportunity, to restrain the growth of unwholesome and sterile accumulations and to lay the burdens of Government where they can best be carried." Put differently, the Wealth-Tax Act was an essential part of the declared intention of the "Second New Deal"—the weeding out of the "overprivileged." (It is worth noting in passing that this measure also owed much to the vigor of Huey Long's "Share-Our-Wealth" movement as the "New Deal" began to make plans for another presidential campaign.)

So sweeping were these threats to free enterprise that it is no wonder businessmen were genuinely alarmed. One prominent industrialist gave voice to this insecurity in an open letter to the President in which he pleaded for a "breathing spell." The President's reply, intended to be reassuring, indicated that he was fully aware of the mood of the business community. "This administration came into power pledged to a very considerable legislative program. . . . This basic program has now reached substantial completion and the 'breathing spell' of which you speak is here—very decidedly so." This assertion was emphasized by the fact that the legislative activity of the following year consisted essentially of measures building on laws which had long been on the statute books—measures such as a broadening of the merchant marine subsidy program and a strengthening of the regulations governing the nation's commodity exchanges.

Industrial Unionism Emerges. However, it is understandable that businessmen were not especially comforted. Just as the dog is not spared in its suffering because its tail is cut off a little at a time, so industrialists were not relieved to learn that the administration's legislative program was basically completed. The next trial, the next inch to be cut off the tail, was the matter of living with the consequences of the legislation already enacted. And of all these consequences, the one most dreaded was the acceptance by labor of the invitation to form *independent* unions.

A preview of what was in store was offered alert and anxious business leaders by the annual convention of the American Federation of Labor in Atlantic City in November. Of all the "forgotten" men, those most completely ignored to date were workers in the mass production industries—automobiles, steel, oil, cement, chemicals, aluminum, electrical appliances, and textiles. At intervals the Federation had continued efforts to organize these workers on a craft basis, but such efforts had never met with success, for workers in these industries felt more of a bond with each other despite skill differences than with unknown workers in other industries. For some years labor leaders in these industries had urged the granting of rights permitting organization on an *industrial* basis, but so hard had the institutional crust of the Federation become that such requests had invariably met with refusal.

The 1935 convention proceeded true to form. A resolution asking for an all-out organizational drive to enroll mass production workers in industrial unions was roundly defeated. But for all its sameness, the 1935 repetition did reveal one subtle difference; the industrial point of view, though still in the minority, was visibly more intense than in the past. No sooner had the convention gotten well started than William Hutcheson, conservative boss of the carpenters, and John L. Lewis, the coal miners' dramatic champion, engaged in fisticuffs on the convention floor. (It was broadly prophetic of the next few years in labor's history that Lewis came off best in this encounter.) Before the convention adjourned the representatives of eight would-be industrial unions, led by such men as Lewis and Philip Murray of the miners and Sidney Hillman of the textile workers, walked out in protest against their colleagues' stand. Labor had been given a veritable "charter of liberties," and these men meant to see that it was well used.

The Committee for Industrial Organization was not originally conceived for the purpose of bringing about a major breach in labor's ranks. The "insurgents" planned rather to work inside the Federation. But when Federation leaders refused to yield, and when labor's leaders in the mass production industries refused to return without concessions, the specter of dual unionism which Samuel Gompers had taught the labor movement to fear over almost every other evil became a living reality. Both America and labor have paid a price in jurisdictional strife for competition between these two great labor organizations, but competition in labor just as in business has brought compensating advantages. The labor movement today would

TABLE 106. A "MAGNA CARTA" FOR LABOR

	Number of American Workers Enrolled in			
Year	All Labor Unions	The American Federation of Labor	The Congress of Industrial Organizations	Independent Unions
		(Millions of workers)		
1929	3.6	2.9	–	0.7
1936	4.2	3.4	–	0.8
1937	7.2	2.9	3.7	0.6
1940	8.9	4.2	3.6	1.1
1945	14.8	6.9	6.0	1.9

Source: Bureau of the Census, *Historical Statistics of the United States, 1789-1945*, p. 72.

not be the robust and vigorous institution it is had craft unionism continued to dominate labor's world, and it is a striking fact that a huge new labor union sprang up almost overnight without seriously affecting the total membership of the Federation. As of November, 1935, industrial leaders were given due notice that a new, aggressive unionism was on the march.

The onslaught did not come immediately. Time was required to organize the industries involved, especially with industrial leaders using every device learned in one hundred years of antilabor history to obstruct labor's efforts. But evidences of its beginning were all too apparent.

Another Judicial Challenge. Early in 1936 the "New Deal" was again visited by judicial troubles. The price support program enacted for the farmer was at the moment being financed by processing taxes imposed at the level of the manufacturer. When a test case in which the plaintiff charged unconstitutionality on the ground that the tax had been levied for other than revenue purposes reached the Supreme Court, the Court agreed. The processing tax was declared not to be a true tax but an expropriation of one group for the benefit of another, and Congress could not use its legitimate powers to accomplish purposes outside its constitutional authority.

Quite apart from the Court's mandate to repay to manufacturers a tax already passed on to consumers, and an obligation to pay to farmers money which had to be returned to taxpayers (actually this dilemma was resolved by levying a special "unjust enrichment" tax on those receiving refunds), the administration was placed in an unpleasant position. To be sure, there were other ways of boosting farm prices. "Surpluses" were regularly being distributed through relief channels, exports were being subsidized on a small scale, and "surplus" commodities were being diverted from usual into lower value uses. But there were important drawbacks to each of these alternatives. Relief distribution on anything other than a minimum basis ran into opposition from businessmen afraid the government was invading normal distribution channels. Subsidization of exports ran sharply counter to the reciprocal trade agreements program. Disposition by way of lower value uses was a none-too-subtle technique of waste that had no long-term future in the face of American public opinion. And besides, all these methods, even when taken together, were inadequate and too uncertain to be the government's sole reliance for such an important program.

Clearly what was needed was substitute legislation accomplishing the same things as the law invalidated by the Court. So urgent was this need felt to be that in less than two months a solution had been readied, presented to Congress, passed, and signed by the President. The key to the new approach was soil conservation. For generations American farmers had neglected their soil, allowing wind and rain to have their way with it almost unmolested. At the moment, moreover, the nation was experiencing a series of severe droughts giving point to the seriousness to the nation of this neglect of an indispensable and nonreplaceable resource. The pathetic, westward trek of the "Okies" furnished the most dramatic part of the background for this new agricultural legislation.

Already a Soil Conservation Act had been passed in order to make a beginning at combating this evil. What was more logical than to combine soil conservation with price supports, thereby strengthening the former and making the latter constitutional? The Soil Conservation and Allotment Act of February, 1936, undertook to do precisely this. It was designed to make soil conservation "profitable" for the individual farmer by paying him for diverting land from soil-depleting to soil-building crops (such as pastures and legumes), for increasing the area planted to soil-building crops, and for adopting soil-building practices (such as the use of fertilizer, and contour farming). Conversely, the farmer was to find it "unprofitable" not to practice conservation because only by so doing could he receive payments under the price support program; the list of soil-depleting crops, in other words, read strangely like the earlier list of crops produced in "surplus." While this legal "dodge" was not permanently necessary as far as the Supreme Court was concerned, it is safe to say that this relationship between policies not inherently connected was of much assistance from the standpoint of the long-range development of the soil conservation program, another of the great achievements of the "New Deal" period.

Aside from Court damage to the agricultural program, a damage relatively easily remedied, the administration fared reasonably well at the hands of the Supreme Court in 1936. In February the Justices gave a solid constitutional foundation to a Tennessee Valley Authority long harassed by litigation. The Authority, said the Court, could legitimately sell to the consuming public the power generated at Wilson Dam. For the first time the Authority could begin to breathe easily—and push ahead a little more rapidly with its plans for developing the resources of the valley of the Tennessee.

Simultaneously with this development, it should be observed, the Tennessee Valley Authority was rapidly losing another battle, the only real defeat it suffered in these early years. Because it was a government corporation—built by government funds, not subject to taxation by states and municipalities, and established for other purposes in addition to power generation and distribution—no allocation of costs could be devised commanding enough general support to permit this operation to be used as a "yardstick" against which to judge private utility rates. But perhaps this did not really matter much after all. The very existence of the Authority had a most chastening effect on private companies in the Tennessee River area. And in the process of adjusting their rates downward to meet Tennessee Valley Authority competition, private utility companies were rewarded by an increase in volume and hence lower costs they had not anticipated.

TABLE 107. NOT A "YARDSTICK," BUT . . .

Unit	Average Residential Rate 1933	1937
	(Cents per kilowatt-hour)	
United States average	5.49	4.39
Tenn. Elec. Power Co.	5.77	2.86
Georgia Power Co.	5.16	3.04
Alabama Power Co.	4.62	2.97
Tenn. Valley Authority	–	2.41

Source: Senate Document No. 56, 76th Congress, First Session, Part I, p. 151.

In May the Supreme Court laid unsympathetic hands on the Bituminous Coal Stabilization Act. The ground was the same one used in invalidating the original agricultural legislation. A tax had been levied on all coal producers, and then refunded to those who complied with the provisions of the law. The Court maintained—with perfect justice—that this levy was not a true tax at all but a coercive device to assure submission to "code" regulations governing such matters as wages, hours, working conditions, and the guarantee of collective bargaining. Since the federal government could not legitimately regulate these matters under any power accorded it by the Constitution, roundabout control through the taxing power could not be approved.

Although this decision was highly adverse to the administration's program, it would in and of itself have troubled Washington leaders very little. It was a relatively simple matter to revise the coal law to meet the Court's objections, and in less than a year this had been accomplished. In another way, however, this decision was a grave threat to administration plans; it seemed to cast a legal shadow over the Wagner Act where the "New Deal" was endeavoring to bring about a better environment for workers in a more direct way. As if to give point to these misgivings, the Court two weeks later invalidated a New York statute regulating minimum wages for women and children. So much comfort was in fact taken in this turn of events by conservatives that the lawyer's committee of the Liberty League (a group organized in the early days of the "New Deal" to uphold the rights of property against other rights) assured employers that the Wagner Act might be violated with impunity.

Here was without question the greatest crisis the "Second New Deal" was called upon to meet, roughly comparable with the banking crisis of the "First New Deal." If the Wagner Act were destroyed, the Social Security Act would be certain to go soon thereafter. The loss of these measures would mean no less than the complete disintegration of the broad principles on which the administration was now standing. The President might have made an issue of Supreme Court interference then and there but for one consideration. His first re-election campaign was now in progress, and wisdom dictated waiting until the people had ratified the "Second New Deal" before raising a new controversy.

The "Second New Deal" Validated. Meanwhile, however, organized labor was proceeding on the assumption that the Wagner Act was fully valid. Not yet outcasts from the parent organization, the industrial unionists decided to launch an all-out attack on the open shop citadel of American business—the steel industry. Since this would mean trampling under foot the impotent craft organizations already possessing organizational "rights" in that industry, the Federation had no choice other than to brand the "radicals" as traitors.

A warning was issued first. The answer of the Committee for Industrial Organization was the creation of the Steel Workers' Organizing Committee on June 16. Soon thereafter a new, revitalized United Automobile Workers was formed and taken into the new group. In September the suspension of the seceding unions became official. Almost simultaneously the United Mine Workers moved its headquarters from Indianapolis to Washington, D. C. While this move was probably not motivated entirely by political considerations, it was not wholly a coincidence that it preceded by only a few weeks the donation of $500,000 of United Mine Workers' funds to the campaign of the President who had given organized labor the finest opportunity for growth in its history. Other labor groups were of the same mind. Through the medium of Labor's Non-Partisan League, millions of workers participated more directly in a presidential campaign than they had ever done before.

The importance of his re-election to labor was only one reason why F. D. Roosevelt won such a decisive victory in November, 1936, an even more sweeping one than four years earlier. Another was the concern he had expressed for depression casualties in all corners of the economy, and the vigor with which he had challenged the "plutocrats" on behalf of society's less fortunate citizens. It is true, of course, that he had fallen heir to a particularly favorable opportunity to challenge the existing order—the near collapse of the entire economic system. But Roosevelt supporters were no less enthusiastic for this extenuating circumstance.

Still another factor in the President's 1936 popularity was the steps the administration was taking to woo small businessmen to its side. The Wealth-Tax Act had reduced taxes on the majority of the nation's corporations, the large number of smaller ones, and a new 1936 tax law carried this purpose even further. The new device was an undistributed profits tax designed to force corporations to pay out their earnings in dividends rather than reinvesting them. At issue, in addition to the assistance smaller businesses might receive from this innovation, were two major questions of public policy. First, is it in the public interest for the corporation rather than the investor to decide whether or not to reinvest his earnings? Second, is it in the public interest for the corporation to withhold income from the stream of purchasing power when there is a strong probability that the investor would keep it in that stream if he had the opportunity? Answering both of these questions in the negative, the administration took the logical step of taxing undistributed corporate profits.[1]

In a second important way the "Second New Deal" served the interests of the small businessman; it helped him in his chronic struggle against "big" business. One aspect of this was the administration's acceptance of the Supreme Court's decision destroying a National Recovery Administration widely felt to favor the larger concern. A move similarly interpreted and applauded was the 1936 Robinson-Patman Act. By its terms business concerns were forbidden to charge different prices to different customers, unless costs were different. Intended as a "roadblock" in the way of the rapid depression growth of chain stores at the retail level (such concerns were large enough to coerce manufacturers into quoting them more favorable prices than their smaller rivals), this enactment powerfully supplemented a rash of state measures imposing special taxes on these concerns. It was only because the chains were sufficiently solidly grounded in operating economies that they were able to hold their own and continue to advance against these artificial barriers.

Although passed too late to influence the 1936 election, and although it was much less of an administration measure than the Robinson-Patman Act, the passage of the Miller-Tydings Act was another important episode in the battle of little business against big. At the same time this act was by far the more successful of the two. What it did was to repeal a portion of the Sherman Anti-Trust Act by enforcing among concerns engaged in interstate commerce state laws authorizing manufacturers under certain circumstances to fix minimum resale prices for their products at the retail level in order to protect retailers from "cut-rate" competitors. (Ironically, it is now acknowledged that the principal beneficiaries of such laws are manufacturers rather than retailers.) The most controversial aspect of this legislation was the fact that every distributor of a "fair trade" item was bound to observe the "fair trade" price set in a contract between the manu-

[1] The reasoning here was again closely related to "Keynesianism" or the "new economics," as it was already coming to be called. Unless there is a flow of money to keep the exchange process in good working order, the flow of goods (and consequently the level of employment) upon which citizens are so dependent must be correspondingly low. It seemed appropriate in 1936, therefore, to concentrate a particularly stern attention upon those individuals (or institutions) who withheld this life-giving fluid from the stream. Put differently, at a time when business concerns could not be induced to invest, corporate saving was no doubt an economic depressant.

facturer and *any* distributor. Many were to be the legal and other battles fought out over the issue of holding firms to the terms of a contract they had not signed.

Undoubtedly, however, the most important factor in the return of the "Second New Deal" to power for another four years was the sound recovery to which the President could point. While progress was still painfully slow and full employment a long way in the future, the movement upward had been hearteningly steady. Moreover, recovery had been most spectacular precisely where the most people were involved. Unemployment had fallen almost 30 per cent, factory weekly earnings had risen fully 30 per cent as compared with a much smaller increase in consumer prices, and farmer purchasing power had gone up 50 per cent.

TABLE 108. PARTIAL RECOVERY

Year	Industrial Production *	Prices ‡ Wholesale Farm (1947 – 1949 = 100)	Wholesale Other †	Consumer	Factory Weekly Earnings ‡	Unemployment ‡ (000's)
1933	37	28.7	50.9	55.3	$16.73	12,830
1934	40	36.5	56.0	57.2	18.40	11,340
1935	47	44.0	55.7	58.7	20.13	10,610
1936	56	45.2	56.9	59.3	21.78	9,030
1937	61	48.3	61.0	61.4	24.05	7,700

* Federal Reserve Board.
† Other than farm products and foods.
‡ Department of Labor.

No doubt too much credit was given the administration for these results; at least administration critics loudly proclaimed this to be the case. It was insisted, for example, that after four years of deepening depression the economy had been "shaken out" so thoroughly that an upturn would have developed in any event. On the other hand, it could be plausibly argued that recovery policies had had a great deal to do with the progress made—and administration enthusiasts were of course not slow to come forward with innumerable variations on this theme. Moreover, both sides could point to statistics with which to bolster their claims. It could be plainly seen that private investment had achieved a remarkable comeback from the virtual eclipse it had suffered at the depths of depression, and that in dollar terms consumer expenditures had risen even more rapidly. Administration supporters were certainly within the bounds of reason to suggest that business investment, undoubtedly a crucial aspect of depression-prosperity dynamics, had been given a fundamental boost by the purchasing

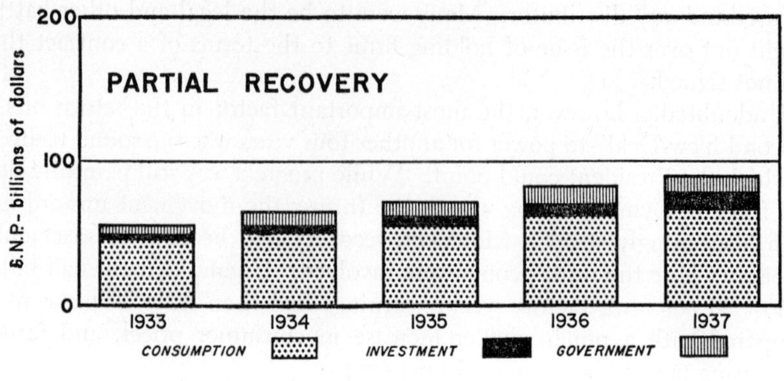

FIGURE 15.

power the government had poured into consumer hands. And, at the same time, it was not in the least ridiculous for administration opponents to argue that the preceding deflation had improved profit prospects sufficiently that investment would have expanded anyway. Unfortunately, however, so complex are the inner workings of an industrial economy that it is difficult to be certain which factors are cause and which effect. Even more unfortunately, it is never possible to re-enact the play using the alternative setting.

Industrial Unionism Succeeds. No sooner was the election out of the way than labor's new drive to improve itself began with a rush. It did not, however, begin in exactly the way Committee for Industrial Organization leaders had planned. With high courage they had organized a campaign to break open the steel industry, and so great was this challenge and so limited their resources that one such battle at a time seemed to be the wisest course. Their discomfiture can be imagined when on December 28, 1936, the nation was electrified to learn that the workers in the Fisher Body Division of General Motors had refused to leave the plant until the United Automobile Workers was recognized by the company. Within a month most of General Motors' operations were closed down in a similar way. As the dramatic use of the "sit-down strike" began to spread, both within and outside the automobile industry, the Committee for Industrial Organization and the nation as a whole were each confronted with a major problem.

The problem for the infant labor organization was what its own role should be. Its resources were already committed to the steel campaign, and the temptation was thus great not to dilute precious strength by dissipating it over too wide a front. But the abandonment of the automobile workers might well damage the new industrial organization by convincing workers it was no more interested in their well-being than the Federation had been. This consideration clinched the matter, and Committee leaders forthwith made the automobile workers' cause their own. It turned out to be an excellent decision; nothing was so effective in securing support among steel workers as the successes achieved in the mass production automobile industry.

The nation's problem was very different. Immediately it became a burning issue whether the "sit-down strike" was a revolutionary technique or not. Certainly it did transgress property rights as these were then understood by most Americans. At the same time there was a widespread and growing feeling that in a modern society there must be important rights other than property rights—rights for propertyless wage earners being a conspicuous example—and that at least property was not being destroyed or permanently alienated. Never far in the background, too, was the fact that the nation's employers had widely agreed to ignore the Wagner Act, an action surely as revolutionary as that now being taken by workers. For weeks the question was passionately discussed from every type of forum and in all quarters of the country.

Actually the question was highly academic. What determines whether an activity is revolutionary or not is, in the last analysis, the attitudes of people in high places. Ten years earlier the "sit-down" technique would without question have been so classified. Not so in 1937, however. Such men as President Roosevelt in Washington, D. C., and Frank Murphy, governor of the state long known as the capitol of the automobile industry, owed too much to labor votes to call out the militia against the "sit-down" workers. (Besides, who wanted to take the responsibility for ordering troops to evict workers from their factory strongholds?) Partly for this reason and partly because they could not come into court "with clean hands," employers made only a half-hearted attempt to utilize the law in securing control of their property. General Motors did secure an injunction ordering the workers out, but there was no serious attempt at enforcement after it was discovered that the issuing judge was a large holder of General Motors stock. Later, this question was resolved legally in favor of plant owners; the "sit-down strike" is not today on the list of "acceptable" labor weapons. But by that time the beginning of real labor organization in the mass production industries was an accomplished fact.

The Supreme Court Challenged. While this battle was in progress another battalion of prolabor forces was being moved into battle array on a different front. Franklin D. Roosevelt was now such a confirmed supporter of labor's cause (in substantial part, it must be admitted, because he had found it politically so rewarding) that he was determined to help industrial unionism succeed. But for this success it was of the utmost importance that the Wagner Act be declared valid by the Supreme Court, and the Social Security Act was almost equally vital to the program of the "Second

New Deal." The President's role in the labor drama now being acted out was thus clearly indicated. His responsibility was to see to it that nothing went wrong on the judicial front. That he intended taking this responsibility seriously was evident as early as January 6, 1937, when in a message to Congress he asked the Supreme Court to "do its part in making democracy successful."

This step was followed less than a month later by the transmission to Democratic leaders in Congress of a plan for reforming the federal judicial system. Included were ideas long advanced by competent authorities for speeding up and in general streamlining the judicial process. Tucked away in another part of the recommendation, however, was the suggestion that the number of Supreme Court justices be increased to not more than fifteen. (Specifically, what the President suggested was that he be authorized to appoint one new justice for every present justice over the age of seventy.) This meant that President Roosevelt would be authorized to appoint *six* additional justices, that, in the words of the man in the street when the proposal was made public, he might "pack the court" to make certain it rendered decisions to his liking.

The time was to come, and soon, when virtually the entire nation became violently partisan on one side or the other of the court issue. For the moment, however, the President did not press the matter; the Reciprocal Trade Agreements Act was coming up for renewal shortly and it seemed wiser to wait until that had been attended to before raising the issue of "dictatorship." Furthermore, the attention of the nation was still focused on the labor front where in the automobile and steel industries labor and capital were locked in decisive combat.

After March 1, everything began to happen at once. On March 2 without a strike "Big Steel" (the large steel firms following the lead of the United States Steel Corporation) signed a contract with Philip Murray's new organization granting a wage increase, an eight-hour day, a forty-hour week, vacations with pay, and seniority rights. This almost unbelievable achievement was followed in less than a month by the capitulation of General Motors, and in less than two months by the negotiation of a contract with Walter Chrysler. Similarly striking accomplishments were taking place in the rubber and textile industries. Still less than two years old, and less than one year after being formally disavowed by the American Federation of Labor, the Committee for Industrial Organization had carried the labor movement to its most important successes of the century.

On March 9, with reciprocal trade legislation renewed for another three years and with labor's astounding achievements still hanging in the balance of a judicial decision expected at almost any moment, the President carried his court appeal to the people in one of his famous "fireside chats." Instantly there was touched off one of the greatest battles in the history of parliamentary democracy. All over the nation men and women rose to the defense of the Court and the constitutional tradition for which it stood, and many of these were people who agreed that the Court was threatening the country's economic and social future. In other words, it was possible in 1937 to recognize the paradox of a judicial branch of the government out of sympathy with the program of the elected representatives of the people without subscribing to Roosevelt's drastic solution.

How near America came on this occasion to a major constitutional change is difficult to say. Possibly the bitter rebellion which broke out within the Democratic party over this issue would have prevented approval of the President's program in any case. What is clear is that a series of events now transpired which made it easy for party members to withhold support. On March 29 the Supreme Court flatly reversed itself by upholding the right of a state to pass minimum wage legislation, a decision foreshadowing a more liberal interpretation of the due process clause of the Constitution in other areas. Two weeks later, wonder of wonders, the Court unequivocally upheld the Wagner Act. With this much pressure off the administration, Congress shelved the "packing" proposal and substituted in its place a bill providing for voluntary retirement from the Supreme Court with full pay at the age of seventy. This move in turn paved the way for the retirement of archconservative Van Devanter on May 18, and on May 24 the Social Security Act was upheld. The administration was now safe from immediate crisis, and in the next four years President Roosevelt had the opportunity of appointing seven Supreme Court justices. The battle, in short, was lost even while the campaign was being decisively won. In terms of causal relationships it seems reasonable to suggest that the battle was lost in large part because the campaign was won; perhaps also the campaign was won because the battle was fought—at least in part.

Industrial Unionism Meets Reverses. Labor's lot was not all victory in 1937. Only two of the "Big Three" in the automobile industry were signed up. The Ford Motor Company was another matter. At the River Rouge plant near Detroit, union organizers were severely beaten for endeavoring to distribute leaflets just outside the plant gates. The Ford publicity department told the world that the beatings were administered by "loyal workers" who did not want the union to come between the company and its laborers. A picture distributed to the world along with this analysis, however, seemed to tell a different story. In the hip pocket of one of the "loyal workers" a pair of handcuffs was showing, the kind of equipment more logically associated with a company guard than a "loyal worker." But, for the moment, this was as near as the new union came to completing negotiations with Henry Ford.

TABLE 109. LABOR ON THE MARCH

	Work Stoppages		
		Workers Involved	
Year	Number	Number	Per Cent of Employed Wage Earners
		(Thousands)	
1930	637	183	0.8
1931	810	342	1.6
1932	841	324	1.8
1933	1,695	1,170	6.3
1934	1,856	1,470	7.2
1935	2,014	1,120	5.2
1936	2,172	789	3.1
1937	4,740	1,860	7.2

Source: Bureau of the Census, *Historical Statistics of the United States, 1789-1945*, p. 73.

In "Little Steel" another defeat was suffered. Led by the unforgettable Tom Girdler, and assisted by the fact that these plants were often the dominant employer in their communities, these companies refused to accept the example set by their larger colleagues. In May, the same month that brought defeat at River Rouge, a strike was called in these concerns by a steel union now highly confident of its newly found strength. The result was a total defeat for the union and one of the ugliest episodes in the history of the American labor movement. Intimidation and brutality on the part of employers culminated in the "Memorial Day Massacre" in South Chicago, the killing of ten workmen. But so stubborn and uncompromising were leaders on both sides that one of the best friends organized labor had ever had (President Roosevelt) was at one point moved to make a public statement which included the phrase "a plague on both your houses."

Despite these defeats, however, the emergence of industrial unionism marks an important milestone in the advance of organized labor. For the first time workers without or with little skill had achieved a position of influence within the American economy. Significantly this position was not achieved by means of the cooperative utopianism of the Knights of Labor nor yet through the "radical" unionism of the Industrial Workers of the World. Still more significantly the successful route was found to be virtually identical with the one long traveled by the American Federation of Labor. Paradoxically, the success of the Committee (later Congress) for Industrial Organization demonstrated that the real secret of the Federation's success was not the craft basis of organization as Federation leaders had insisted. Rather it was the achievement of strategic power within industry. What the new advance now made plain was that such power can be secured in more than one way—that the Federation principle of *exclusive jurisdiction* can be adequately achieved on an industrial basis as well as through craft organizations. Stated differently, the judgment of history must be that a point was reached where this vital principle, stubbornly limited to the craft as the basic labor unit, became a barrier to labor progress rather than an aid.

A number of candidates have been suggested for the distinction of being the most enduring consequence of the "New Deal" period in American history. One of these, and one fully deserving of inclusion in such a list, is the emergence of industrial unionism. On the other hand, however, almost all the enduring consequences of this period can be fitted into a broader framework. What the "New Deal" was endeavoring to do, and what it did do to an extent which dismayed and frightened conservatives, was to modify the predominant position held in American society by property rights, the modification consisting of an elevation in the social system of certain "human" rights not identifiable and often in conflict with property ownership. The emergence of industrial unionism and the assault it made on the "prerogatives of management" in areas where property rights had long reigned supreme only illustrated the evolution taking place.

QUESTIONS FOR DISCUSSION

1. Why were the National Labor Relations Act and the Social Security Act such important milestones in the nation's economic development?
2. How much of the "New Deal" program would have been enacted in the succeeding twenty-five years even if there had been no depression?
3. Would industrial unionism have become an important factor in the American economy if the way had not been paved by legislation?
4. What were the principal features of the banking legislation of 1933 and 1935? How did this legislation grow out of the experience of the 1920's?
5. Why was legislation in the public utility field considered necessary at this time? What did this new legislation attempt to do, and how were these things to be accomplished?
6. How did the Tennessee Valley Authority manage to force lower utility rates without bankrupting the private utility concerns in its area?
7. What benefits did small businesses expect to receive from the Robinson-Patman and Miller-Tydings Acts?
8. Who was "right" and who "wrong" in the Supreme Court controversy? Who won and who lost?
9. Are strong labor unions essential to the operation of an industrial society? If so, does this mean that the "prerogatives" of management must be weakened?

Chapter 37

DRIFTING INTO WAR

1937	Outbreak of fighting between China and Japan.
	Two more neutrality acts passed.
	Roosevelt's "quarantine the aggressors" speech.
	Sharp business recession.
1938	Ludlow Amendment narrowly defeated.
	German annexation of Austria.
	Munich "appeasement" of Hitler.
	Congress' approval of a billion dollar naval building program.
1939	Outbreak of war in Europe.
	"Cash and carry" neutrality proclaimed.
1940-41	Evolution of an active, all-around defense program.
	Japan extended her sphere of influence in Asia.
	Economic recovery.
1941	Pearl Harbor.

Reform Grinds to a Halt. The validation of the "Second New Deal" is of course not to be minimized. But it is nonetheless a significant fact that little reform legislation was passed in 1937. On July 22 the Farm Security Administration was created, an organization designed to take over and expand the work being done by the Resettlement Administration in rehabilitating farmers at the lowest end of the economic well-being scale. Early in September a similar program was instituted for urban folk by a measure authorizing the government on a larger scale than before to provide low rent, "decent" housing for slum dwellers. In view of the fact that the administration had just been returned to power by the greatest margin in the country's history, this was not a rich harvest.

There were, to be sure, reasons why a program of reform sweepingly approved was so timidly continued. One was the loss of party harmony in the battle over the Supreme Court. As a result of that bitter contest many liberals became fearful lest the President, under the guise of humanitarian reforms, make a concerted drive on the American Constitution in favor of expanding his own power. Thus many erstwhile administration supporters, though still enthusiastic about the cause of reform, no longer had the old confidence in the leader espousing it.

In the second place, further progress was visibly retarded by the fact that the President was surrounded by a large number of people who were eager to continue the program of reform as long as it seemed to be demanded in the interest of recovery, but who were quick to register opposition when the question became the pursuit of reform for its own sake. Thus many southerners lashed out against a Farm Security Administration which gave a long exploited group economic opportunities more attractive than exploitation, and "moderates" all over the country became alarmed at the President's proposal to establish seven more "Tennessee Valley Authorities" in various parts of the country. And so certain were most people that recovery was no longer an issue that the administration even took steps to prevent a runaway boom—steps such as reducing the number of people on Works Progress Administration projects and in general deserting "pump priming" in favor of a balanced budget. The Federal Reserve System abandoned its "easy money" policy by raising reserve requirements to the maximum level permitted by law, and by "sterilizing" much of the gold now flowing into the United States from Europe in a veritable torrent.

These obstacles to reform, however, might in time and with patience have been surmounted. But the prestige of the administration was shattered almost beyond repair when in the third quarter the recovery on which the President's re-election had been in large part based gave way to a sharp

TABLE 110. A BITTER DISAPPOINTMENT

Month and Year	Industrial Production *	Prices ‡			Factory Weekly Earnings ‡	Factory Employment ‡
		Wholesale				
		Farm	Other †	Consumer		
July, 1937	100	100	100	100	100	100
June, 1938	68	77	94	98	85	74

* Federal Reserve Board.
† Other than farm products and foods.
‡ Department of Labor.

recession. Measured in terms of industrial production the decline in less than a year was 32 per cent, while farm prices fell 23 per cent, factory weekly earnings 15 per cent, and factory employment 26 per cent. Men who had argued that recovery had been the result of the reforms which had been inaugurated were understandably reluctant to press for more of the kind of policies now ending so disastrously.

This is not to say that the policies followed did generate the recession, although administration opponents lost no opportunity to insist that "anti-capitalist" activity had so destroyed business optimism as to prevent the natural resilience of the economy from asserting itself. Thus it was argued that restrictions placed on security issuance and security markets materially slowed down the flow of investment with borrowed funds, that the undistributed profits tax penalized investment in the form of reinvested earnings, and that the attack by labor on management's domain interfered with decision-making oriented to business profits.

Administration arguments designed to counter these charges were no more (and no less) valid than the charges themselves. It was maintained, for example, that the slow rate of investment was caused by a deliberate "capital strike" on the part of the business community designed to discredit the "New Deal," and that the virtual cessation of new security issues was the consequence of the extent to which business was in fact reinvesting earnings. For obvious reasons, furthermore, the administration was inclined to blame the recession on the fact that large-scale deficit spending had begun to taper off. As the administration acted on this belief, a major response to the economic downturn was the reversal of the "tight money" policy recently inaugurated and the abandonment once again of the goal of a balanced budget. Thus powerful had labor's "purchasing-power" doctrine and J. M. Keynes' "new economics" become.

Perhaps the only thing actually involved in this economic relapse was the normal operation of the cycle itself—with no significant political or policy factors entering in at all. Many economists are convinced that the modern economy does, for some reason, move in up-and-down swings of six or seven years' duration. If this is the case, a 1937 recession was only to be expected. Suffice it to say here that, whatever the cause, a sharp downturn coming so soon after the struggle over the judiciary bill could not have helped adding greatly to the political difficulties in which the administration now found itself. Moreover, a recession period was no time to launch still other "anticapitalist" measures.

One other major obstacle stood in the way of active reform work. This was a double split within the Democratic party over foreign and domestic policy. By the latter part of 1937 Adolf Hitler was already far advanced in his campaign for warless expansion. Mussolini was likewise taking Italy into an aggressive imperialism, and Japan was engaged in an ambitious warfare against China. So treacherous had international relationships become that the President and many others were beginning to feel the need for a more adequate defense program and even a mutual security program in alliance with such European nations as England and France. But the taking of a strong stand on this matter ran squarely into the powerful opposition of "isolationist" midwesterners, folk whose roots were still deep enough in Central Europe to make them resentful of implied and expressed criticism of Germany, and of conservatives who did not want to see government spending on the scale this would have necessitated. Of similar persuasion were those who had experienced a severe revulsion at the disclosures of the Nye Committee, and others to whom the spectacle of communism and fascism fighting one another in Spain had been highly disillusioning.

In the country as a whole, the President's support was so extensive that he need not have been deterred by the opposition of western Democrats from taking whatever stand seemed necessary (provided he did not move too rapidly). Unfortunately, however, this cleavage cut sharply across another split developing within the party. The "New Deal's" concern for human rights was beginning to come dangerously close to an attack on the race adjustment worked out between whites and blacks in the South. Generally speaking, southern Democrats had to this point an excellent record of support for liberal-reform measures, but few southerners could support reforms denying the legitimacy of one of the most fundamental institutions of southern culture.

The President's dilemma was this. A coalition of East with South could readily pass legislation in the defense and mutual security areas, while a coalition of East with West could easily pass reform measures. But a course of action based on "whipsawing" the party in such a way was bound ultimately to fail. The time would surely come when southerners would revolt against a vigorous foreign policy or westerners would revolt against reform, at which time the President would find himself unable to secure the legislation he considered essential in either field.

Early in 1938 the unavoidable necessity of choosing between foreign and domestic policy was emphatically demonstrated. The Ludlow Amendment, a bill intended to prohibit the declaration of war by the United States without a popular referendum, was narrowly defeated in the House by the votes of eastern and southern Democrats. Simultaneously an anti-lynching bill supported in the Senate by eastern and western liberals was prevented from being passed only by a filibuster by southern Senators. No warning of dangerous shoals ahead could have been plainer.

A choice was not made at once, or, perhaps more accurately, a first choice was made to pursue domestic policy for at least a little while longer. Government supervision over the nation's transportation system was extended through a control of air transportation similar to that already imposed on rail and motor carriage. The Federal Power Commission was given extensive authority over interstate gas utilities. A new Food and Drug Act was passed bringing up to date the law enacted under another Roosevelt thirty-two years before. And the nation's new agricultural policy was enacted in "permanent" form, although no really basic changes were made. Soil conservation was continued, but it was henceforth to be less directly connected with the price support program; thus acreage controls were no longer tied to the practice of conservation measures, but only farmers practicing such measures could qualify for "parity" payments. This meant, in other words, that the price control program could now stand on its own feet without being camouflaged for the benefit of the Supreme Court. Much to the discomfiture of the farmer, the "permanent" agricultural adjustment seemed to involve an increasing degree of restriction (production control) by the government.

All these measures were closely continuous with the past, involving no genuine reform innovations. However, on June 28 a basically new departure became the law of the land. By the Fair Labor Standards Act the federal government undertook to establish minimum wages (twenty-five cents per hour at first but gradually rising to forty cents) and maximum hours (forty per week, although here also a transition period was allowed) for workers employed by firms engaged in or affecting interstate commerce. In addition child labor, long a target of organized labor and a reproach to the nation, was outlawed in such concerns. When this law was in time upheld by the Supreme Court, the long struggle of labor to persuade society to exercise some responsibility over these matters was at last successful. Organized labor must by now have felt amply repaid for the effort it had expended in assisting President Roosevelt's re-election campaign, even though the principal direct beneficiaries of the new law were undoubtedly those workers not yet protected within a union.

Big Business Under Fire. From the standpoint of historical consequences it is fair to say that the "Second New Deal" came to an end with the passage of the federal "antisweatshop" law. From the standpoint of the administration's efforts, however, and possibly its intentions as well, this is not entirely true. Due attention must also be given to an amazing interlude in which the administration embarked upon one of the most dramatic antitrust campaigns the nation had yet seen.

The reason the word "amazing" is not too strong is that prior to this point the "New Deal" had made no effort to alter the structure of industry in this way, and had in fact begun its attack on the depression by openly encouraging businessmen to collaborate with one another. Even more significant is the fact that while avoiding a method of altering the economic structure which had by now an unbroken record of failure, the "New Deal" had been instrumental in bringing about a profound change in that structure in a very different way. This was by helping labor organize the mass production industries—perhaps the only basic change in the power structure of a modern industrial society which it is possible to achieve apart from direct government control. Now, turning its back on this realistic and successful approach, the administration made a complete about face. And it adopted its new policy without publicly acknowledging that a change in policy was involved or that the previous policy had been a mistaken one.

The new campaign proceeded simultaneously on two fronts. In one quarter Thurman Arnold set out to take away from Theodore Roosevelt the (scarcely deserved) reputation of being the nation's greatest "trust buster." Appropriations for the Anti-Trust Division of the Department of Justice were increased and that body became aggressive on a scale never before witnessed. Suits were brought against a large number and wide variety of "big" businesses—so much so that businessmen charged that "bigness" itself was being considered a "crime"—and several successes were ultimately achieved. Among these were the establishment of restrictions on the use of the practice of "block-booking" in distributing moving pictures to theaters, separating the operation of pullman cars from their manufacture, broadening the practice of patent-sharing among competitors, and forcing the major cigarette companies to be more subtle in their collaboration on prices. Taken all in all, however, it can legitimately be said that there were no more long-range consequences of this new attack on the "trusts" than had been achieved on similar occasions in the past.

The other front consisted of the work of the Temporary National Economic Committee (consisting of Senators, Congressmen, and representatives from several key executive departments), whose principal activity was the so-called "Investigation of Concentration of Economic Power." The results of this inquiry, an inquiry extending over a period of approximately eighteen months, were published in the form of thirty-one large volumes and forty-two smaller monographs. It is generally agreed that these studies contained by far the best description of the structure of the American economy then available, and that if new legislation had been developed in this field the "Investigation of Concentration of Economic Power" would have furnished a solid informational foundation. But it is a matter of historical record that these efforts were no more productive of important achievements than were those for which Mr. Arnold was responsible.

Why did the administration reverse its field on this question? And why, once the new policy was decided upon, were no greater results obtained? On the one hand, there is no doubt that the men now standing closest to the President leaned frankly in the direction of "trust busting" whereas the President's advisers had earlier had a different outlook. On the other hand, the intervention of war must perhaps bear some share of the responsibility for the fact that few permanent consequences resulted. However, it is now reasonably certain that these were not the principal factors involved. Although much of the popular fervor behind the new antitrust drive was continuous with that which had produced the "Granger movement" and "Teddy" Roosevelt's "big stick," there was here an antitrust orientation utterly foreign to anything to which the nation had ever before been subjected. In high administration circles this new attack on "big business" was apparently thought of first and foremost as a weapon against the perverse behavior of the economy. In turn the failure of this campaign may well have been due in large part to the strange mixture of purposes it represented—or, more specifically, to the dubiousness of the assumption on which it rested.

This assumption grew directly out of the "new economics." What administration leaders now professed to believe was that the concentration of profits in a relatively few large concerns whose owners had little control over what was done with them, and the fact that income was concentrated in the hands of a relatively small number of people, had brought about the inadequacy of purchasing power responsible for both the "Great Depression" and the more recent recession. (No doubt some administration supporters did sincerely believe these things to be true, although there is a widely accepted view that this endeavor was a tongue-in-cheek search by the administration for a scapegoat behind which it might escape the penalty for its failure to resolve the economic deadlock.) The thesis was dubious in part because many large concerns had gone out of their way to maintain dividends with little regard for profits, and in part because there is actually so little connection between business concentration and income concentration.

A Period of Stagnation. Because of the difficulties with which it was confronted at the outset, the Temporary National Economic Committee might easily have faded into historical oblivion without leaving a trace. It was saved from this fate, however, by the fact that there now set in a period which has since been something of a paradox in our economic history. Toward the middle of 1938 the economic downturn ceased, but instead of resuming the recovery so drastically interrupted, the economy

TABLE 111. "STAGNATION"

Year	Industrial Production *	Prices ‡			Factory Weekly Earnings ‡	Unemployment ‡ (000's)
		Wholesale				
		Farm	Other †	Consumer		
		(1947 – 1949 = 100)				
1937	61	48.3	61.0	61.4	$24.05	7,700
1938	48	38.3	58.4	60.3	22.30	10,390
1939	58	36.5	58.1	59.4	23.86	9,480

* Federal Reserve Board.
† Other than farm products and foods.
‡ Department of Labor.

seemed to hover around a level of activity far below what could theoretically have been achieved. Whereas the index of industrial production had reached sixty-five at its prerecession high, it was almost three years before it rose consistently above that level. Industrial production, prices, and factory earnings were all lower in 1939 than they had been two years previously, while unemployment was almost two million greater. After ten full years of depression the economy had still not regained the level of performance from which it had fallen.

In the face of this situation the anticoncentration drive became one of the focal points for a long-drawn-out discussion of the state of the economy, a discussion which raged as heatedly in academic as in political circles. Indeed the "Investigation of Concentration of Economic Power" was often referred to as "the battle of the Ph.D.'s" and the profession did not add to its prestige by its failure to agree on the reasons for the perverse behavior of the American economy—why this country was slower to regain economic health than any other major nation. In fact, throughout the entire controversy the world of scholars was divided against itself along a line broadly identifiable as the "liberal-conservative" line of political debate.

The "liberal" point of view, following the thinking of J. M. Keynes, was roughly the following. As an economy becomes more wealthy in terms of per capita output, its people tend to save more of their income. That is, as more of their immediate, material wants are satisfied, they place a higher value on future goods. Saving in an industrial economy, however, can become effective only if capital is thereby accumulated. But since the point of capital accumulation is the sale at a profit of the goods it is capable of producing, the fact that people are saving rather than spending prevents savings from being transformed into capital. The result is that money income is simply hoarded rather than being returned to the income stream, and a portion of the labor force is put out of work.[1]

One of the major "conservative" retorts to this line of reasoning was that if a large number of people are involuntarily unemployed, the reason is because labor as a group insists on wages that are too high. Were it not for the recently developed labor organizations with their powerful resistance to wage reductions, there would not be this difficulty of employing those desiring to work. Furthermore, capital accumulation is essentially related to the advance of technology; as innovations in production

[1] Saving, investment, and consumption are indeed intricately interrelated in an industrial society. Neither saving nor investment can take place in the absence of the other, but neither can investment increase without an increase in consumption. Furthermore, an increase in investment directly contributes to an increase in consumption (by means of the "multiplier"), and an increase in consumption directly contributes to an increase in investment (by means of what is known as "the acceleration principle"). The more important fact, however, from the standpoint of the economic problem of these years, is that all these processes work just as effectively in reverse.

are introduced costs of production and hence prices are reduced, and in this way capital accumulation creates the purchasing power with which an increased output of goods can be bought.

Not at all, replied the "liberals." In the first place, while it is true that wage reductions would reduce costs and to this extent improve the business outlook, it is also true that wages are the purchasing power without which the output of industry can not be sold. In other words, it is impossible to reduce costs and not at the same time defeat this action by reducing purchasing power. In the second place, whereas it might work out that technology, falling costs, and price reductions would create a self-equilibrating system of relationships, the fact is that with business as highly concentrated as it is, competition is not strong enough to push prices down as rapidly as the needs of equilibration would require. And as evidence on this point, it was insisted that the economy's experience in the 1920's should be conclusive.

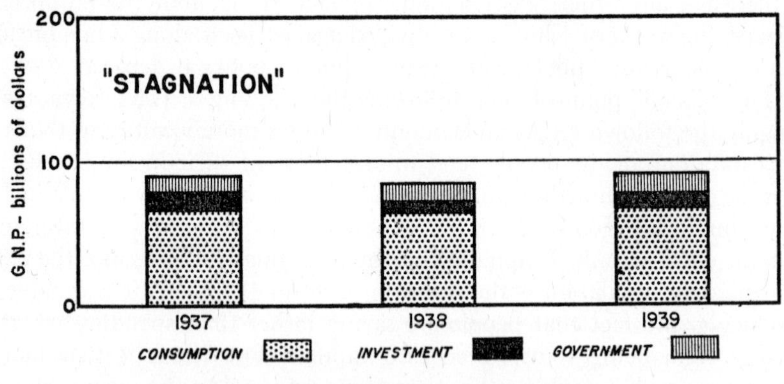

FIGURE 16.

Even so, these arguments relative to the economic principles involved were less intense than academic discussions about the kind of economic policy the government should follow. Here, too, the economists' main tenets closely resembled those somewhat more crudely being advanced on the political front. The most "liberal" position was that the government must take the responsibility for creating enough purchasing power to employ its citizens as long as the private economy does not; if, in short, the American economy was in a "stagnant" condition, short-term "pump priming" must logically give way to "pump priming" on a longer-term basis. Along with this approach, it was suggested, a government program designed to redistribute income in the economy in favor of those who spend rather than save would minimize the need for long-range "pump priming." Other "liberals," not wishing to concede so much of a role to government, insisted that the essential first step should be to restore competition to the

TABLE 112. DEPRESSION AND URBANIZATION

Year	Total Population	Per Cent Urban
	(Millions)	
1920	105.7	51.2
1930	122.8	56.2
1940	131.7	56.5
1950	149.9	59.0

Source: Bureau of the Census, *1950 Census of Population.*

economy. In all probability, so this view went, nothing more would be needed, but certainly nothing more drastic should be attempted until the healing force of "old-fashioned competition" had been allowed to work itself out. Here, of course, was the economist's version of the justification of the Temporary National Economic Committee and its work.

To "conservative" economists both of these approaches were not only error but heresy. Private enterprise operates on the basis of profit expectations. Employment in such an economy depends on the production and installation of fixed capital, capital which must be intensively used over a long period if it is to return a satisfactory rate of profit. However, the willingness of investors to "sink" capital into long-lived investments hinges to a large extent on an underlying confidence that the "rules of the game" will not be changed. The policies insisted on by "liberals," no less than the growth of powerful labor unions, were a major source of changes in the "rules of the game," uncertainties generating an unwillingness on the part of business leaders to expand and hence to employ society's citizens. The economy's difficulties, in short, were not to be remedied by more "pump priming"; what was needed was for someone to fix the "pump" which the "New Deal" had so badly broken.

Long and inconclusively did this debate go on. The resulting stalemate was almost exactly reflected by the simultaneous passage of a measure repealing Roosevelt's much cherished undistributed profits tax and another subjecting investment trusts to rigorous regulation. There is still disagreement on where the truth lies, and essentially the same arguments are still advanced. With respect to the economic doldrums into which the nation had fallen in the 1930's, however, one vital fact did emerge. Whether "anticapitalist" activities had been undertaken only after the system had broken down (as "liberals" believed), or whether the system did not break down until "anticapitalist" activity entered the scene (the point of view of "conservatives"), it was plain that "New Deal" reforms might contribute to a vicious circle of persistent "stagnation." Thus the greater the responsibility assumed by government, the poorer the economy's performance; and the poorer this performance, the greater the responsibility to be assumed by government.

War Comes to Europe. The administration must soon have come to serious grips with this dilemma if international affairs had not dramatically intervened. By the latter part of 1939 a choice in favor of domestic reform as against a strong foreign policy ceased to be realistic, and the attention of the nation's leadership became more and more centered on foreign policy and correspondingly less insistent on changing the "rules of the game" at home. As a result the best means of settling the debate over the causes of "stagnation" was to be lost, unless it could be argued that the war experience proved that if only enough money had been spent recovery would have continued.

August, 1939, saw Adolf Hitler ready to take one more step in his program of expansion without war. He had been only scolded when he reoccupied the Rhineland, tolerated when he moved into Austria, and "appeased" when he sought to secure the Sudetenland in Czechoslovakia. Perhaps he was therefore justified in assuming that a major encroachment upon Poland would provoke no serious repercussions. On September 1 Poland was invaded by German arms. Two days later both France and England declared war against Germany. World War II had begun.

It might have been thought that the appearance of actual war in Europe would quickly have made a vigorous defense and mutual security program generally acceptable. If anything, however, the result was exactly the opposite. For this several reasons may be suggested. First, the traditional opposition of American businessmen to this country's involvement in war now asserted itself more strongly than ever. This did not, of course, prevent business from preparing to take advantage of large orders from Europe's belligerents. Industrial production rose above the predepression level as producers at all stages sought to protect themselves from an anticipated shortage of goods, and the stock market skyrocketed. When the expected orders from Europe did not appear in the huge volume for which preparations had been made, the boom collapsed and the economy sank once more into its "stagnant" condition.

Only agriculture did not participate in this false war prosperity. The farmer's prices were enjoying a steady rise as the depths of recession gave way and this improvement did continue, but a pattern of events closely related to the war situation prevented this rise from taking on boom proportions. For some years wheat and cotton had been subsidized in the world market. However, with the outbreak of war in Europe and Asia it became apparent that export subsidies were an outright gift to both Germany (in the case of wheat) and Japan (in the case of cotton) amounting to millions of dollars a year. When, consequently, export subsidies were hastily discontinued, the resultant collapse of agricultural exports prevented any very significant rise in farm prices.

In the second place, it was still possible to feel that the conflict abroad was a "stupid European war that is none of our business," and that Roosevelt was trying to involve the United States in it to enhance his own power and prestige. These thoughts, too, were given a certain amount of support by the progress of the war during its first winter. Although hostilities had been resoundingly declared on both sides, there was little fighting. Thus it was widely insisted here that it was a "phony war," that no real belligerency was intended.

The curiously ambivalent attitude of the United States was clearly indicated by the neutrality legislation now governing the conduct of America relative to conflicts abroad. By its terms America was to remain neutral, this term meaning, among other things, that we would sell our goods only to those nations who would pay cash and carry them away in their own ships. But since this approach placed Germany at a disadvantage relative to England and France (although greatly favoring Japan as compared with China), it was obvious that the term "neutrality" was being used more to pacify an unthinking public than as an honest description of policy. As one radio commentator expressed it, "We're neutral; we don't care who whips Hitler." "Cash and carry" neutrality, incidentally, was no doubt one reason why foreign orders in America did not rapidly appear.

Not for long could unrealism of so extreme a variety continue. When on April 9, 1940, the Germans invaded Denmark and Norway, and when on May 10 the German "Blitzkrieg" struck at Belgium, Holland, and Luxembourg on its way to France, public opinion in this country began rapidly to change. On May 16 the President took advantage of this shift in attitude to ask Congress to implement a program of national defense appropriate to such "ominous days."

TABLE 113. ACCENT ON DEFENSE

Year	Federal Government Expenditures for	
	Defense	Relief
	(Billions of dollars)	
1940	1.7	4.7
1941	6.3	4.1

Source: Secretary of the Treasury, *Annual Reports*.

Congress was not slow to act. Within two months appropriations amounting to $12 billion had been authorized; within a year this figure had risen to $35 billion, more than the entire cost of World War I to this country. (In other words, it was to be domestic and not foreign arms orders which really lifted the nation out of its economic listlessness.) Almost immediately, moreover, the President began the creation of an administrative organization to coordinate the efforts of the various parts of the economy as it girded for its new task. But even as the defense program went forward with such speed and energy, events were taking place which were eventually to bring America into an all-out, shooting war in every corner of the globe.

On June 10, with France already in grave peril from German thrusts, Italy entered the war on Hitler's side and attacked her neighbor to the north. Less than two weeks later France fell and the grand-but-tragic evacuation of British troops at Dunkirk began. Then, for a little while, Hitler rested, but only to consolidate his gains and prepare for a vast air assault on Great Britain—to soften these islands for invasion. As England stood alone against the Axis powers, and especially as Hitler mounted an air offensive across the English Channel in which night after night hundreds of bombers set about systematically to destroy the great industrial cities of England, Americans began to assess their position in the world even more critically.

Thousands of miles away from these dramatic events, other forces were being set in motion which were in time to be equally significant in American history. Under cover of the war in Europe, Japan began to extend her sphere of influence in the Far East. As Japanese statesmen expressed it, Japan's mission was to "ensure the permanent stability of East Asia." June, 1940, saw Japan moving into Indo China and threatening Hong Kong. On July 2 the United States expressed her disapproval of these moves by embargoing exports to Japan of aviation gasoline and machine tools. As the months went by, and despite protests and threats from Japanese spokesmen, the list of embargoed items was extended to include iron and steel scrap, implements of war, lead, copper, zinc, aluminum, petroleum, and other strategic materials. (It is worth emphasizing, however, that this policy, especially for example in the case of iron and steel scrap, was in part dictated by the needs of America's own rapidly growing defense economy.) Not until some time later did most Americans first begin to realize how serious a matter this embargo policy was to a nation as painfully dependent as Japan upon foreign trade. Her industrial expansion, her very ability to feed her people, to say nothing of her capacity for making war, was in this way gravely threatened.

In the face of these developments American complacency continued to evaporate. By the end of the year a majority of Americans were ready to support the President in his plea that the United States become "The Arsenal of Democracy," the next step beyond a defense program geared to our own needs. The next twelve months were largely spent making good this promise, and in the process an economy which for eleven years had been unable to find itself now began to bustle with an almost forgotten activity. As war orders created consumer purchasing power, and as an increased flow of purchasing power made still greater demands upon industry, the depression rapidly became a thing of the past.

Table 114 clearly indicates how suddenly and how completely this change took place. In a twelve-month period, beginning roughly with the tragedy of Dunkirk, industrial production rose 30 per cent to a level far higher than the predepression peak, unemployment fell by three million to the lowest point in ten years, weekly earnings of factory workers rose to the highest level in the nation's history, and farm prices rose more than 20 per cent. From a situation in which the nation's principal economic

TABLE 114. WAR BRINGS PROSPERITY

Month and Year	Industrial Production *	Prices ‡			Factory Weekly Earnings ‡	Factory Employment ‡
		Wholesale				
		Farm	Other †	Consumer		
July, 1940	100	100	100	100	100	100
June, 1941	130	124	108	104	126	121

* Federal Reserve Board.
† Other than farm products and foods.
‡ Department of Labor.

problem had been that of finding a pretext, however flimsy, for using surplus productive capacity for useful purposes, America had moved to a situation in which her tremendous capacity was beginning to seem pitifully inadequate. It was a most exhilarating experience.

The American Economy Transformed. Perhaps it was fortunate that most Americans did not yet realize what the grim sequel of war production prosperity was to be. If they had, they would have enjoyed it less thoroughly than was actually the case, and surely after eleven years of depression a brief period of economic recovery before the outbreak of war was not undeserved. To be sure, the progress of war preparations was a little slower than it would otherwise have been, but on the other hand virtually everything of importance that transpired in the American economy in 1941 was a helpful if not a necessary preparation for the great conflict now only a few months away. A certain amount of time is required to convert a complex, industrial economy from peace to war activities, and in retrospect it can hardly be said that time was grossly wasted.

For example, it was recognized at the outset that government controls would be required to coordinate the defense effort. In World War II as in World War I, priority and allocation controls were the basis of this regulative mechanism, and by early 1941 the administrative organization having this and related responsibilities had already passed through several stages of development. Thus, whereas in the first stages of war production the technique had been to assign to a single agency limited powers and a great variety of functions, there was a steady evolution in the direction of more extensive powers and a specialization of administrative functions by creating other agencies. In January, 1941, this process can be seen especially clearly; in that month the basic control functions—over production and over prices—were separated from one another. Production controls were centered in the Office of Production Management, while the control of prices was given to the Office of Price Administration.

This evolutionary process in the administrative field has been subjected to a great deal of criticism. Why, it is asked, did this country not profit from its experience in World War I instead of learning most of these same lessons all over again? The answer is a simple one, emphasizing that human being are very human. Men do not give up accustomed modes of living, especially accustomed freedoms, until their experience has convinced them it is absolutely essential. If men really could experience the life lived by prior generations, perhaps history would not have to repeat itself so monotonously. Unfortunately, they cannot; experiences vivid enough to influence behavior must typically be met directly rather than vicariously. (Besides, who knew in 1941 how severe a trial the economy was soon to undergo?) As a result men had to live through the difficulties of inadequate controls before they would consent to more stringent ones. So had it been in World War I, so was it now in World War II. Because this is true it is especially fortunate that the United States was given a little breathing-space before total war enveloped the economy.

In other ways also the year 1941 was well used. At first businessmen were reluctant to expand their facilities. They were concerned lest costly facilities be erected which would be useless after a limited period of operation. This problem was solved in a number of ways. On the one hand, several government bodies (including especially the Reconstruction Finance Corporation) were authorized to make money available for the building of plants at government expense and to loan funds to private enterprise for this purpose. On the other hand, private concerns were given permission to depreciate such expansion on a five-year basis for income tax purposes rather than the usual twenty. This not only furnished protection against losses in case the new facilities were not income productive at the end of five years, but it also gave the companies involved a cushion against high wartime tax rates.

Much was made at the time of this "capital strike" against the nation's security program. Two facts, however, kept this criticism to a minimum.

One was an excess profits tax designed to keep private concerns from profiting from the emergency. The second was the advantage taken of the new prosperity by automobile and steel workers to take care of unfinished business with the Ford Motor Company and "Little Steel." At River Rouge the victory was won by means of a strike, the company agreeing to the closed shop, the checkoff, retroactive wage increases, seniority, and a grievance machinery. In "Little Steel" the victory was at the moment largely legal; the companies simply accepted a National Labor Relations Board decision as to who the bargaining agent was to be. But with this foothold of solid recognition the steel workers soon greatly extended their victory. Had these labor advances not come when they did, they would certainly have come a year or two later, at which time they might have created more difficult problems. As it was, labor and capital went into the war on fairly even terms from the standpoint of bargaining strength.

Similarly, in working out relationships between ourselves and our allies, 1941 saw a great deal accomplished. The most noteworthy aspect of this development was the innovation of "Lend-Lease." Reversing our neutrality policy of "cash and carry," and setting the stage for a reversal of our World War I policy of "putting a price" on the aid extended to our allies, Congress authorized the President to "loan" billions of dollars' worth of war materials to countries vital to the nation's defense. Throughout the entire war period no other basic legislation in this area was required. Thus when Hitler invaded Russia in June, it was a simple matter to add that nation to the list of "Lend-Lease" countries. It perhaps goes without saying that this reversal of "cash and carry" was one of the principal factors making for the now rapid revival of America's exports, although by this time such a revival was of little importance as far as American recovery was concerned.

The economy surmounted one other major hurdle in 1941. The intense reforming zeal which had initially gone into the "Investigation of Concentration of Economic Power" was soon found to be incompatible with an effective defense effort. It was not only easier and cheaper to deal with a few large companies than with hundreds of small ones—problems of priorities and allocations being more effectively handled on this basis, for example—but the product turned out by the leading firms in concentrated industries was more often than not of better quality and less expensive. Although the war administration did make feeble gestures in the direction of small businesses, although "trust buster" Arnold was given a free hand as long as his antitrust campaign was limited largely to the use of verbal weapons, and although the war itself brought high prosperity to little business as well as big in the form of an accentuated demand and subcontracts from larger firms, the excellent studies of economic concentration soon began gathering dust in libraries throughout the country. This phase of the "Second New Deal" was abandoned as nimbly and as quietly as earlier the National Recovery Administration phase of the "First New Deal" had been abandoned. Thus the stage was set for a wartime *increase* in economic concentration rather than the decrease earlier demanded, but at least the country did not have to learn this lesson while Japan's sharply pointed dagger was at its throat.

It is often asserted that World War II came to an unprepared America. In terms of the ultimate demands of this great conflict, this assertion is true enough. But by comparison with the preparedness of America when war came to Europe, or even by comparison with the preparedness of either England or France when war first came to Europe, America at the time of Pearl Harbor was in excellent condition. The two years of time allowed this country by contrast with the suddenness of war's eruption abroad was a kind fortune indeed. Put differently, December 7, 1941, did not find the American economy unprepared in the same way it found the nation's military leaders at Pearl Harbor unprepared.

QUESTIONS FOR DISCUSSION

1. Why did reform activity begin to taper off at this point—apart from the fact that so much had already been accomplished in this field?
2. How could "anticapitalist" activity have contributed to the onset of a new recession? What arguments did the administration use to counter these charges?
3. In what ways might minimum-wage legislation alter an industrial economy? Are such changes desirable?
4. What were the economic foundations of the new antitrust movement? Why was this new drive so unsuccessful?
5. How might income concentration have contributed to "stagnation"? Why is there not a close connection between business concentration and income concentration?
6. Looking back on this period in retrospect, to what extent did the "New Deal" threaten the free enterprise system?
7. Who was "right" and who "wrong" in the argument about the cause of the economy's poor performance after 1937?
8. Why did America's policy of economic sanctions against Japan work such a hardship on the Japanese economy?
9. Why did the American economy begin to suffer from shortages while there were still seven or eight million people unemployed?
10. What steps were taken before Pearl Harbor to prepare the economy for a major war effort?

Chapter 38

CRUSADE FOR FREEDOM

1941 Beginning of all-out war effort.
1942 Comprehensive economic controls instituted.
Submarine menace in the Atlantic.
Japanese victories in the Pacific.
1943 Peak of war production.
Price control program tightened.
Smith-Connally War Labor Disputes Act.
Situation stabilized in the Pacific.
Turning of the tide in Europe.
1944 Bretton Woods Conference.
Dumbarton Oaks Conference.
Turning of the tide in Asia.
1945 End of the war.

Conversion Difficulties. It is not to be supposed that by the time of Pearl Harbor the American economy had completed the transition from peace to war, or even that the defense effort had received full support from all segments of the economy. Most notably in this connection the coming of war found the United States in the middle of a major adjustment and a major controversy having to do with the role of the automobile industry in the defense economy. Just as in World War I this industry had been reluctant to turn its back on peacetime pursuits, so was it in World War II.

Because of the need for large quantities of steel in armament production, running the automobile industry at capacity was unthinkable. Accordingly, car output had already been cut back 20 per cent, and for weeks pressure had been mounting for another reduction. Industry spokesmen, on the other hand, argued that a further limitation would mean operation below the break-even point, and hence at a loss. When the suggestion was made that this great industry retool for the purpose of producing tanks, and especially when this point of view was loudly agitated by a dynamic, young labor leader in Detroit named Walter Reuther, the response was that a modern automobile factory can be effectively used only for producing automobiles.

It is not at all surprising that the issue was an intense one, and even less surprising that a leader in the auto workers' union raised it most forcefully. If this were true, if automobile factories could only produce automobiles, the defense effort would be compelled at great expense to erect vast new tank factories—and the workers who fell victim to automobile cutbacks would have had to seek employment elsewhere. Furthermore, if this principle were generalized for the entire economy, the same procedure would be required at (who knew how many) other points. A more costly way to become the "arsenal of democracy" could scarcely be imagined.

The resolution of this issue provides an excellent example of the way in which the outbreak of shooting war galvanized America into an all-out war effort. Some time before that day a meeting between industry leaders and government officials had been scheduled for Monday, December 8, 1941, at which time the industry had hopes of quieting once and for all the pressure for further reduction. When the group gathered, virtually at the moment the President was delivering his war message to Congress, Paul Hoffman of Studebaker asked if he might make a preliminary statement. It was, "I think the country expects an announcement of a cut in automobile production from us this morning." Almost before it had begun the meeting was over, and immediately there was commenced instead the vast planning which was soon to make the American automobile industry one of the principal producers of war goods in the entire world.

This episode was a symbol of the transition from a "guns *and* butter" approach to the world situation to a "guns *before* butter" attitude. Prior to this time defense contracts for and additional employment in some industries had created a certain amount of unemployment in other industries as an inadequate supply of key materials had to be sparingly rationed where it would do the most good. Stated differently, the conversion of the economy was still proceeding so slowly that unemployment continued to be a factor in the over-all picture. After Pearl Harbor, as government expenditures for war literally exploded throughout the economy, little more was heard about "priorities unemployment."

TABLE 115. THE END OF UNEMPLOYMENT

Year	Armed Services	Civilian Employment	Unemployment
		(Millions)	
1940	0.4	47.5	8.1
1941	1.5	50.4	5.6
1942	3.8	53.8	2.7
1943	8.9	54.5	1.1
1944	11.3	54.0	0.7

Source: Department of Commerce.

War and the Price Mechanism. The unloosing of a rapidly swelling flood of purchasing power, however, created other problems. Increased purchasing power meant that individuals could now increase consumption expenditures, and that it would be profitable for enterprisers to expand production for this market. But since the requirements of modern war are so great, it was essential that such expansion be carefully controlled. Two methods were available by means of which this could be done. The first was to use the government's financial resources in making war production so profitable that private concerns would voluntarily neglect the consumer market. The second was to intervene with direct governmental controls as a substitute for price and profit adjustments.

For two major reasons sole reliance on the price mechanism was not seriously considered. In the first place, this mechanism operates best when economic changes are taking place slowly, poorest when dynamics is proceeding at a more rapid pace. Thus to have permitted the price of housing to rise without limit in a situation in which demand was rising much more rapidly than supply could possibly have followed would have served no useful purpose—a consideration especially although not solely applicable to a long line of consumer durables the general availability of which was reduced to negligible proportions during the war period. The most important aspect of the process of transforming the economy to a war basis was the speed with which it needed to be achieved.

In the second place, reliance on competitive controls runs into the difficulty of maintaining a high level of citizen incentives (morale). It may, for example, be politically impossible to impose tax rates high enough to avoid a level of inflation (that is, drastic changes in the distribution of real income) great enough to make the war effort extremely painful. So high a level of taxation, furthermore, might discourage the expenditure of marginal productive efforts (such as overtime work), and at a time when the nation needed every bit of output it could muster this risk did not seem to be one which should be deliberately taken. Reliance on competition, too, might still not have prevented some individuals from bidding critical materials or finished goods away from more important military uses.[1]

There were equally compelling reasons for not abandoning the price mechanism altogether. First, an unfamiliar economic system can only be

[1] Inflation would not result in changes in the distribution of real income if all prices (including incomes) increased equally. This does not happen, however, with the result that some profit and some suffer. The political difficulty referred to is the fact that those who are most likely to profit from inflation are most apt to be sufficiently powerful politically to block anti-inflation taxation. Competition between consumers (including firms) and the government for the available goods could only be prevented from injuring the war effort by an extremely rigid tax program oriented to current income, supplemented by the "freezing" of liquid or semiliquid assets accumulated out of past income.

imposed upon a society by force, and it is the essence of intelligent government not to undertake a program of coercion if a feasible alternative is available. Second, complete abandonment of prices and price relationships would not have been possible. The modern economy is so complex, and at the same time so delicate, that hastily improvised substitutes could hardly have failed to clog the machinery. Illustrative of the difficulties involved is the fact that an adequate control system was achieved only after many months of experimentation and frustration. A system which allocates to a bus manufacturing company enough metal for nine hundred bus bodies but only five hundred sets of wheels—and this was only one of dozens of similar cases in the early months of the war effort—is obviously not one which can dispense wholly with prices and profits as determinants.

But if the war economy consisted of a mixture of "natural" and "artificial" controls, it is fair to say that the benefit of the doubt was given to the "natural" variety, at least until the war was far advanced. One factor in this, of course, was the need to minimize coercion. Another was the need to evolve an effective control system before abandoning customary relationships. More fundamental was the fact that there was little to fear from inflation as long as unemployment and unused capacity existed on a large scale—as long as the war and civilian segments of the economy could both expand. And finally, a good case can even be made for the proposition that a certain amount of inflation at the beginning of a war is helpful. There is no stimulus as effective as a deteriorating standard of living for pushing normally idle people into the labor force. Similarly, the higher wages paid by defense plants was an indispensable method of diverting a larger proportion of the labor force into those areas.

TABLE 116. THE PRICE PROBLEM

Year	Wholesale Price Indexes	
	Farm	Other Than Farm and Food
	(1947-1949 = 100)	
1940	37.8	59.4
1941	46.0	63.7
1942	59.2	68.3
1943	68.5	69.3
1944	68.9	70.4

Source: Department of Labor.

Administering the War Effort. Because an important reliance was to be placed on man-made controls, the administrative machinery by means of which these were to be set in motion was rapidly expanded. In January,

1942, the War Production Board was created, the successor agency to the Office of Production Management, and charged with the task of concentrating the nation's productive energies upon those projects most important to the creation of the sinews of war. January also saw the creation of the National War Labor Board with the function of preventing labor disputes which would interfere with the war effort. Labor and capital had already given a no-strike, no-lockout pledge, but it was still felt that extra insurance would not be amiss.

Closely related to both of these steps was the passage of an Emergency Price Control Act on January 30, a measure giving the Office of Price Administration extensive power to keep the wartime price level within bounds. The work of the War Production Board, in so far as it was successful, would reduce or at least prevent substantial increases in the supplies of many consumer goods—such as, for example, automobiles, new houses, refrigerators, radios, washing machines, and the like. It seemed only logical that controls limiting supply in the face of a rapidly mounting demand should be supplemented by holding prices to a reasonable level. Perhaps even more important, inflation tends to encourage hoarding and the violation of controls, both of which would be highly adverse to a wartime economy. And as far as the War Labor Board was concerned, no one had any illusions about the consequences of a rising price level on labor peace.

It was a grossly defective price control law, so its critics loudly insisted. No authority was included for controlling wages, and farm prices were not to be checked until they were 10 per cent above parity. These concessions were granted as a result of pressures applied to the legislative process, hence conforming reasonably well to the demands of parliamentary democracy. But it was apparent that there could be no realistic expectation of holding the price line with a formula omitting both wages and farm prices.

At the same time, however, there is a logic in what was done, although one somewhat more easily seen in retrospect than in the early days of 1942. From the standpoint of wages, there were still more than four million persons unemployed. With the need not only to get these into the active labor force but in addition to bring about other necessary employment adjustments, the case for tight wage controls was not compelling. Furthermore, it was clear that wage controls could not be successful unless broadly supported. The pressure which developed for excluding wages from the price control formula at this point was indication enough that such support was not yet available.

Farm prices presented a different situation, but the justification here was no less convincing. These prices had just broken the parity line, on an average, for the first time since World War I (although, to be sure, the farmer had achieved a substantial gain in man-hour productivity in the interim). To tell the farmer he must be content with parity after suffering from chronic depression for twenty-odd years was scarcely an obvious move. In the second place, because agricultural output does not respond as readily as industrial output to demand increases, farm prices are placed under the most intense inflationary pressure with the outbreak of war. Again the wisest course seemed to be to let more of this pressure spend itself before clamping the price lid on tightly. And finally, the argument that higher than parity prices would be necessary was not at all beside the point. War had thus quickly, in other words, transformed agricultural "surpluses" into threatened shortages.

TABLE 117. PROSPERITY FOR THE FARMER

Year	Parity Ratio (1910-1914 = 100)
1910	106
1918	118
1921	75
1929	89
1933	60
1937	92
1940	80
1941	94
1942	106
1943	119
1944	116

Source: Bureau of the Census, *Historical Statistics of the United States, 1789-1945*, p. 99.

Whether the government responded to the pressure or the logic of existing circumstances, or whether the pressure roughly reflected the logic, the fact remains that the January law did achieve little by way of controlling prices. No doubt the most effective feature of this measure was a provision whereby the government could pay a subsidy to high-cost producers of such strategic materials as copper, lead, and zinc. In this way it was possible to secure the output of mines which could not ordinarily be worked at a profit without at the same time paying for all output a price high enough to make submarginal operations profitable.

Stress and Strain on the Economy. If the underlying feeling in January was that effective price control could be postponed, the same was not true of certain other aspects of the war effort. Already it was apparent how great a strain a two-front, modern war thousands of miles away would be on the American economy, and swift action was necessary to meet this challenge.

One major difficulty, for example, was the inadequacy of the nation's aluminum supply. A young industry at best, and controlled in this country solely by the Aluminum Company of America, this segment of the economy was totally unprepared for the demands made upon it by an unprecedented airplane production program. A number of steps were taken to assure enough of the metal for the most urgent uses. Scrap drives were inaugurated to increase the supply of raw material, the use of aluminum in the making of such things as kitchen utensils was forbidden, and concerns with large inventories of aluminum were forced to reduce them. It was even necessary to build at government expense several plants for the manufacture of aluminum.

In the creation of aluminum manufacturing capacity another wartime shortage rapidly emerged. This industry is a huge consumer of electric power and hence the new plants had to be located with this need in the foreground. Interestingly enough, much of the electric power available for such a purpose was to be found near government projects such as the Tennessee Valley Authority and those in the Pacific Northwest, projects which the private power industry had fought bitterly at their inception. Equally interesting is the fact that the location of aluminum capacity in the Northwest contributed to the only major labor shortage the nation suffered throughout the war period. This was true, not because aluminum production is a heavy user of labor, but because the decision to construct new aluminum facilities carried with it the decision to build homes, etc. for construction workers and plant laborers.

A second major problem of economic adjustment was the critical shortage of shipping. Between the wars the American merchant marine had dwindled to insignificance because, despite larger and larger subsidies, the United States could not compete favorably with other nations in shipbuilding and ship operation. With the coming of war, however, and the need to supply millions of troops over ocean distances of thousands of miles, there was no alternative but to supply ourselves at whatever cost with as much shipping as possible. Meanwhile, the greatest care had to be taken not to use shipping space for any but the most urgent needs. Thus coffee and sugar frequently had to give way in the face of the need for imported raw materials (such as bauxite, for example), and bananas and coconuts became almost unheard-of luxuries in many places. To coordinate shipping in order that the maximum benefit could be derived from the limited supply, a special agency known as the War Shipping Administration was created.

In the shipping field the great achievement was unquestionably that of Henry Kaiser. Prior to this the period required for turning out a standard cargo ship was almost twelve months, and the principal concerns in the business insisted that this time could not be significantly reduced. Kaiser thought it could. When the government decided to gamble on Kaiser's ability and good faith, the time required to produce a cargo ship was trimmed to less than two months. The secret was prefabricating large sections of the vessel while the steel foundation was being put into place. Before this success was achieved Kaiser had experienced so much difficulty securing his allocations of steel from the United States Steel Corporation and Bethlehem Steel Corporation (both important operators in the West Coast shipbuilding industry) that the Reconstruction Finance Corporation loaned him funds with which to go into the steel business himself. It was, incidentally, the tremendous expansion of West Coast shipbuilding, together with the fact that a large part of the expansion in airplane production took place there, that primarily brought about the West's labor shortage.

TABLE 118. THE ECONOMY OUT OF JOINT

Year	Ships Constructed	Automobile Production	Aircraft Production
		(Millions)	(Thousands)
1940	319	3.7	12.8
1941	703	3.8	26.3
1942	1,108	0.2	47.8
1943	1,901	–	85.9
1944	1,723	–	96.3

Source: Bureau of the Census, *Historical Statistics of the United States, 1789-1945*, pp. 211, 223, and 224.

Another difficult problem, especially in the first part of the war period, was created by the success of Germany's submarine campaign. Customarily huge quantities of crude oil are carried by sea from the Southwest to Atlantic seaboard refineries. When, however, the Germans began to sink some two out of every three of these tankers, different arrangements had to be made. World War II was a motorized war as had no war ever been before, and in the existing state of technology motors meant essentially petroleum-using motors. So vital was this product that some of the measures adopted in its behalf were very drastic.

For example, gas rationing in the eastern states was first inaugurated to conserve this precious liquid. Millions of barrels of oil were hauled by the far more expensive medium of rail transportation, the government making up the difference in transport cost to keep the price level from being affected. A little later, after an intense battle over whether or not scarce steel should be used for this purpose, two large pipelines were constructed (the "Big Inch" and the "Little Big Inch") to carry petroleum and its products from the Southwest to coastal consumption points. In order to supervise the over-all program relative to this important product, moreover, a special government agency was created—the Petroleum Administration for War.

All these problems, however, basic though they were to a successful war effort on the home front, were of less significance than still another difficulty. Japan's expansion in the Far East cut this country off from its only supply of natural rubber, and synthetic rubber was not yet a commercial product. Here the most drastic steps of all were taken. Long before gasoline rationing in the East could have been eased on account of improvement in the transportation situation, it was imposed on the entire country as a way of conserving rubber. New automobiles (the few still being produced) and trucks were distributed without spares. Tires and tubes were rigorously rationed, although at first many more ration tickets were issued than there were tires and tubes to be bought. (Ration tickets were jocularly as well as bitterly referred to during this early period as "hunting licenses.") Milk and other deliveries in cities were to a large extent "rationalized," eliminating much of the use of rubber for competitive business purposes with respect to these services. The largest part of the work of the Office of Defense Transportation, a special agency established to expedite the transportation aspect of the war effort, was work made necessary by the shortage of rubber.

Far more important than conservation measures, as well as far more expensive, was the unbelievably rapid expansion of synthetic rubber production in government-owned plants. So vital was this program in fact that another special agency—the Office of Rubber Administrator—was created to see that nothing interfered with it. Even at the war's end the cost of production of the synthetic product was not yet competitive with natural rubber, despite tremendous technological progress; but what was of greater significance, the annual output of the substitute was equal to prewar consumption. Sacrifices had to be made for this tremendous achievement, to be sure. No doubt the most widely discussed burden was a cutback in the manufacture of whiskey. Unfortunately for this industry, one of its principal raw materials was also needed for synthetic rubber production.

The Fight Against Inflation. While work was going forward with respect to these problems, the cost of living was steadily rising. Between the passage of the price control law and the last of April the over-all index rose more than 2 per cent a month. Calling for a more concerted effort at this point, the President on April 27 outlined a seven-point anti-inflation program consisting of heavier taxation, ceilings on retail prices and rents, wage controls, control of agricultural prices, individual savings, rationing of scarce consumer goods, and credit controls.

The first (and for a time the only) response to the President's appeal came from the Office of Price Administration, a response no doubt deliberately coordinated with the President's statement. Although prior to this, retail prices had been controlled scarcely at all, that situation was abruptly ended for the duration with the issuance on April 28 of the famous General Maximum Price Regulation. By its terms the highest price charged during the preceding month was made the legal maximum price for nearly everything purchased by ultimate consumers. Simultaneously more than three hundred defense areas were designated as critical from the standpoint of housing (later extended to include the entire nation), and rentals charged therein frozen. The reason for coordinating such moves with a presidential appeal is obvious. Because it touched the lives of millions of people directly and drastically, the Office of Price Administration had a greater problem of public relations and hence public support than any other agency. Thus White House backing was especially helpful.

It would be hard to say whether the multitude of tasks related to price fixing (that is, making calculations and adjustments relating to costs, cost differentials from firm to firm and from product to product within a firm, and profit margins) was more or less burdensome than the task of rationing those goods which became especially scarce. Suffice it to say that the decision to fix prices carries with it the need to ration. The alternative is to distribute scarce goods on a first-come-first-served basis, and a surer way to injure civilian morale in the case of items like coffee and sugar or the war effort directly in the case of tires could scarcely be devised. Put differently, where price controls break the "natural" connection between supply and

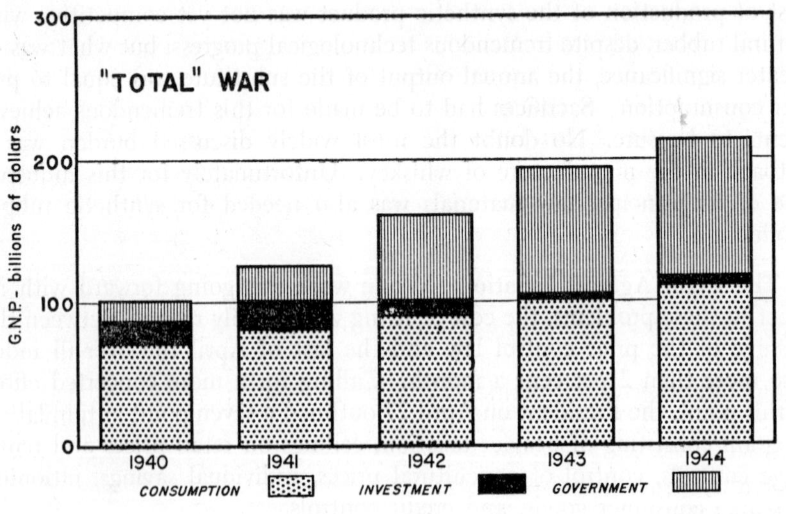

FIGURE 17.

demand, the gap must be bridged by some form of "artificial" allocation. Before this part of the control ordeal was over, the Office of Price Administration had established an administrative framework for rationing which consisted of district boards, state boards, and eight thousand local boards.

The setting of retail price ceilings (with the exception of those prices tied closely to uncontrolled farm prices) was only one part of the program demanded by the President, and to those who lived through this period day by day it must have seemed a long time before the other parts fell into place. Yet, taking into account the nature of parliamentary democracy and the simultaneous existence of other problems requiring attention, it seems in retrospect that progress was rapid from this point forward. On May 6 consumer credit controls were tightened by the Board of Governors of the Federal Reserve System, a step which would have been somewhat more effective than it was if the rise in individual incomes had not been so rapid that there continued to be too many people able to pay cash for consumer durables.

Two months later, on July 16, the War Labor Board took its first major step toward inflation control. By now there could be no doubting that rising prices would quickly be reflected in higher wages and that higher wages would almost as quickly find their way into the price level. Thus when the Board promulgated the famous "Little Steel Formula," it was to a considerable extent out of deference to itself (in the form of easing long-range problems in the field of labor disputes) that it acted. This formula set a limit on hourly wage rate increases to those raises necessary to match the rise in the cost of living in the preceding eighteen months—an action marking a genuine turning point in the battle against inflation.

Although the "Little Steel Formula" was broadly successful in accomplishing its purpose, an incident which occurred in the fall of 1942 excellently illustrates the complexities implicit in any attempt to control wage rates. The War Labor Board permitted exceptions to the "Formula" in cases where wage "inequities" needed to be eradicated. Basing their claim on this principle Studebaker employees in South Bend, Indiana, petitioned for an increase of four cents per hour; General Motors in Detroit had been granted an increase of this amount, and it was claimed that for ten years wage changes by General Motors had been accepted by Studebaker. The petition was granted. Unfortunately, however, Studebaker was already the high wage plant in South Bend. As a result the Board had to deal with an unending stream of petitions from other South Bend workers requesting an adjustment based on the Studebaker increase. And, a situation far worse for the war effort, the Board's refusal to grant all these petitions resulted in many skilled workers leaving other defense jobs in order to work for Studebaker.

TABLE 119. PROSPERITY FOR THE WORKER

Year	Manufacturing			Consumer Price Index (1947-49 = 100)
	Weekly Hours	Hourly Earnings	Weekly Earnings	
1940	38.1	$0.661	$25.20	47.8
1941	40.6	0.729	29.58	52.2
1942	42.9	0.853	36.65	61.3
1943	44.9	0.961	43.14	68.3
1944	45.2	1.019	46.08	67.4

Source: Department of Labor.

In September the President acted again. In a message worded sufficiently sharply to arouse much ire on Capitol Hill, Roosevelt informed Congress that if it did not take steps to halt inflation through legislation he would assume responsibility himself without additional legislation. The result was the Stabilization Act of October 2. At long last the power to control farm prices was granted, and the power over wages which the War Labor Board had already assumed was made official. The rigor of this enactment is indicated, moreover, by the fact that in the case of wages as well as farm prices the ceilings now imposed were somewhat less favorable than previous commitments. In both cases the highest prices to date, with exceptions, were made the maximum. Farmers thus were denied the 110 per cent of parity guarantee, while laborers were denied the right to increases in hourly rates to compensate for prior increases in the cost of living. At the same time, however, the majority of farmers were in fact receiving at least as much as the earlier guarantee, and labor's weekly earnings had in most instances more than kept pace with living costs.

In practice, to be sure, this step did not work out as rigorously as was intended. Important responsibilities in connection with farm prices were lodged with the "farmer's friend," the Department of Agriculture (later the War Food Administration), and higher agriculture prices were to be permitted where necessary to increase production vitally needed for the war effort. In addition, the War Labor Board continued its policy of permitting wage increases needed to correct inequities in the wage structure or aid in the prosecution of the war. To prevent interagency squabbles which might threaten the inflation control program, the President created the Office of Economic Stabilization, and this agency did add something to the program by way of over-all supervision. But the "freeze" was made flexible (probably not unduly flexible, in view of the underlying situation) and the cost of living continued to inch upward. If, indeed, account is taken of the fall in the quality of many goods and the shift by firms to "low end" lines, the rise in the price level was materially greater than Department of Labor statistics suggested.

Only one more step remained to be taken on the price-control front. If a large enough bite could have been taken out of incomes in the form of taxation, holding the price line would have been much easier. Here, also, the President urged vigorous measures. The result was what has often been called "the greatest tax bill in history." However, large though it was from a historical standpoint, it was framed to yield only half as much revenue as Roosevelt had specifically requested. In view of the large amount of income to be left in the hands of spenders relative to the volume of goods available at ceiling prices—the "inflationary gap," as it was called—it is unfortunate that the passage of this measure coincided so closely in time with the Congressional elections of that year. Perhaps partly because it was an election year this tax measure included steeply progressive individual income tax rates in addition to a broadening of the individual income tax base far beyond anything the nation had ever seen, and these were to be important features of the tax structure from that point forward.

Not all the so-called "inflationary gap" was really inflationary, of course. Voluntary savings are as much an anti-inflation device as taxes, although less dependable. During World War II the public cooperated magnificently from this standpoint. Because consumer durable goods were not available, because people were convinced that buying war bonds was an evidence of patriotic assistance to the country, and because the price line was held sufficiently well that citizens did not feel impelled to spend their money before it depreciated, an unprecedented amount of saving was made available to the government. Put differently, holding the price line contributed to the voluntary saving done by the economy, while voluntary saving helped greatly in the matter of holding the price line.

TABLE 120. AGAIN INADEQUATE TAXATION

Year	Gross Private Saving	Federal Government Deficit	Per Capita Disposable Income at 1952 Prices
	(Billions of dollars)		
1940	16.0	1.4	$1,117
1941	23.0	4.9	1,271
1942	41.8	32.9	1,417
1943	47.4	46.4	1,451
1944	57.0	54.0	1,517

Source: Department of Commerce.

These steps taken in 1942 essentially set the pattern for the wartime fight against inflation. Its success, though marked, was limited by three major facts. First, too many loopholes were left for allowing farm prices to rise. Second, wage controls were oriented exclusively toward straight-time hourly rates rather than weekly earnings. Third, the wartime increase in the federal debt was "monetized" by the sale of bonds to the banking system in the amount of almost $90 billion. Admittedly a tight price-control program was not possible in the face of these limitations. On the other hand, when all phases of the problem of organizing the economy for war are taken into account and not the problem of inflation alone, it is possible that about all was done that could be done in the price field.

Victory on the Home Front. While these actions were being taken, the problem of over-all war production had reached a major crisis. Because the control system then in use was breaking down, it was apparent that production goals could not be achieved. The difficulty was that scarce materials were being allocated to producers on the basis of project planning which had not been carefully coordinated from the standpoint of the feasibility of the goals set forth. As a result, preference ratings were being heavily overissued in some critical lines, and when holders endeavored to translate their "paper" materials into "real" materials they were unable to do so. In addition, producers would often find themselves with a high enough rating on some materials to satisfy their basic needs, but with so low a rating on other items that they either could not effectively use the goods they had or had to slow down their production lines for a time. The inevitable consequence of these inadequacies in the control mechanism was a powerful tendency toward inventory-hoarding, a procedure which obviously would soon have been fatal to the war effort.

By November, 1942, a solution had been found, one which marked out the path to be followed by production control for the rest of the war period. Called the Controlled Materials Plan, it was based upon the assumption that the key materials in the domestic economy were steel, copper, and aluminum, and that consequently the other raw materials needed for war production could be made to go as far as these items would go. Starting from this assumption the plan called for the stating of all output needs in terms of these three products, which plans were then screened within the War Production Board to assure that the over-all demands did not require the use of more controlled materials than were available. After this "feasibility" tailoring had been completed, allocations of other materials were fitted into the total goals to see that producers had available everything needed to turn out the finished products wanted. In an amazingly short time this new system of control had basically remedied the defects of its predecessor, and war production was moving rapidly toward the unbelievable heights reached the following year.

TABLE 121. THE PRODUCTION ACHIEVEMENT

Year	Industrial Production (1947-1949 = 100)	Agricultural Production (1935-1939 = 100)
1940	67	110
1944	125	130

Source: Federal Reserve Board and Department of Agriculture.

It is not too much to say that after 1942 no major decisions or changes in policy were made. Rather what took place was essentially a working out of the implications of decisions already made. Early in 1943 the rationing responsibilities of the Office of Price Administration were greatly expanded. To coffee, sugar, tires, and gasoline were added canned and packaged foods and meat. The need for rationing in these areas was in part because the armed services' demand for them was so great, but in the case of meat it was also a result of the fact that with the improvement in individual incomes brought about by the war many more people could now afford to buy meat. (It speaks worlds for the American economy that it was able adequately to supply a major two-front war without a decrease in over-all civilian consumption of nondurable goods.) With the later addition of shoes to the list of rationed items, this activity reached approximately its wartime peak.

April, 1943, saw labor growing restive as the cost of living edged upward, and it was determined in Washington that a further step should be taken in that area. On April 8 the President issued his "Hold-the-Line" order, requesting all price control agencies virtually to abandon the use of discretion in approving price increases. This administration boost to the price-control program was shortly followed by two other steps closely related to it. For the first time the General Maximum Price Regulation was translated into dollars-and-cents ceilings, and in this form it was much more easily enforced. Simultaneously a subsidy program was inaugurated under which processors of meat, milk, bread, coffee, butter, sugar, and other food items received government checks in exchange for not passing along certain costs to consumers. By this device the price of food was actually "rolled back" several months.

Between the "Hold-the-Line" order and the end of the war, roughly a two-year period, the cost of living in the United States rose only 2 per cent. By almost any standard this was a remarkable accomplishment, especially in view of the fact that in the same period factory weekly earnings rose more than 10 per cent. That it was so successful is no doubt due to the fact that every major group in the economy—business, agriculture, and labor—was enjoying high prosperity, that, in other words, the great pressure groups were approximately in equilibrium one with another. It was, of

TABLE 122. PROSPERITY FOR BUSINESS

Year	Corporate Profits
	(Billions of dollars)
1940	2.9
1941	7.8
1942	11.7
1943	14.4
1944	13.5

Source: Department of Commerce.

course, assisted by the fact that the parity ratio actually trended slightly downward from this point forward, by the fact that the civilian economy was well supplied throughout the war, and by the fact that the level of patriotic fervor remained high. And it is equally clear in retrospect that the subsidy program was an important factor in this achievement in that it reduced greatly the wage-price tension which would otherwise have been engendered. But, with all these factors, it is still a tribute to the statesmanship of Franklin Delano Roosevelt that he was able to abandon "New Deal" partisanship sufficiently to achieve this kind of balance between normally antagonistic forces.

The record, it must be added, was by no means perfect. In mid-1943 the coal miners sought to break the price control line in so far as their wages were concerned. Demands were made which could not even remotely be justified under existing regulations, and both the operators and the government stood firm against them. The President even made a personal appeal to the workers not to obey John L. Lewis' strike call, encouraged no doubt by the fact that three years earlier the miners had ignored Lewis' plea that they support Wendell Willkie rather than Roosevelt in the presidential election of that year. The President was to learn, however, that while workers do not always take the advice of their leaders on political matters, the situation is far different where the economic struggle with employers is directly involved. In outright defiance of the government, the workers did strike until a large proportion of their demands was granted.

The nation was in no mood for this sort of thing. Labor had achieved great gains in both status and economic well-being during the war period. Real wages had risen substantially, unemployment had fallen to a negligible amount, union membership had increased, labor leaders had been given recognition in administering the war effort, and scientific management was rapidly being transformed from its emphasis on the exploitation of human machines to a "human relations" approach oriented more than ever to the worker as an individual. Furthermore, perhaps at no other point in the economy had labor made such dramatic gains as in the coal industry.

From its prewar status as a "sick" industry, coal had suddenly become very scarce and coal miners had profited correspondingly. When these workers began to "sabotage" the war effort while "our boys are dying on foreign battlefields," the wrath of the majority of Americans was aroused.

The nation's response was the Smith-Connally War Labor Disputes Act passed in June, a measure intended sharply to curtail labor's right to strike in time of war. Apparently feeling that all labor should not be penalized for the misdeeds of a few, Roosevelt interposed an emphatic veto. But, so intense was sentiment throughout the country, it was promptly enacted into law despite the President's objections. Ironically, of course, it was other labor groups rather than the miners who reaped this whirlwind, for workers in the coal pits had already received a pay increase large enough materially to "bend" the price control line. At the same time, however, other labor groups were able to reap some profit from this shift in the line of battle in the struggle against inflation.

It was a sobering event in the history of organized labor, although in the heat of war emotions it was not fully appreciated for what it was. The Smith-Connally Act served notice on labor that the right to strike would not be tolerated without limit. To be sure, limits established in anger in the middle of a major war effort could scarcely be a permanent solution, and there were as yet few indications as to what such a solution would be like. But at a later date labor would look back to 1943 and see the decisive beginning of a trend it could not view without alarm.

The crest of the war production effort came in 1943; the industrial production index reached its peak in October. In that year just over 41 per cent of the nation's output was devoted to war purposes. This rate of war-related production was only slightly lower in 1944, the year in which the shooting war reached its climax. A premature reconversion campaign got under way late in 1944, only to be hastily put aside with the opening of the "Battle of the Bulge" in December. By mid-1945, however, especially after the war in Europe ended, reconversion again became an important matter. When quite unexpectedly Japanese capitulation followed close on the heels of the German surrender (thanks to the devastating and perhaps unnecessary use of the atomic bomb), the American economy was faced with by far the largest task of orienting itself from war to peace it had ever confronted.

QUESTIONS FOR DISCUSSION

1. What were the economic foundations of the controversy between the automobile industry and the government?

2. Why does the price system operate most poorly when dynamics is proceeding at a rapid pace? Is this why the price system has come under man-made controls at more and more points in recent years?

3. Was the 1942 price control law "defective" as its critics claimed? Why could the inflation controls imposed in 1943 not have been brought into use earlier?

4. Why do solutions to problems in one area of the economy often create problems in other areas?

5. Does an increase in real per capita disposable income mean that the average individual is consuming more economic goods?

6. What was the so-called "inflationary gap," and why was it so significant?

7. With gross private saving running consistently higher than the federal deficit, why did the government have to sell nearly $100 billion worth of bonds to the banking system?

8. To what extent was World War II financed by inflationary methods? Why were these methods used?

9. How was it possible to control prices so effectively after mid-1943 despite the existence of a number of highly inflationary factors?

Chapter 39

THE WAR BLOWS COLD

1945 Harry Truman became President at Roosevelt's death.
United Nations Organization created.
Beginning of reconversion.
Lend-lease terminated and British Loan negotiated.

1946 Battle over price control; record number of strikes, primarily for higher wages.
Full Employment Act.
Price control ended.
Administration victory over John L. Lewis.
First disagreements between Russia and the West.

Internationalism Comes to America. In one important respect it was a very different America that turned from war to peace in 1945. With the exception of the reciprocal trade agreements program inaugurated under the stress of deep depression, the United States had always been aggressively isolationist. In fact, under circumstances in some ways similar to those prevailing in 1945, World War I had ended in a revulsion against the internationalist fervor which had led to American participation. Now, with a suddenness and a completeness that is even at present difficult to grasp, the nation committed itself to a vigorous and almost unqualified internationalism.

Long before the war ended there had been created a solid basis for international cooperation. First in point of time was the United Nations Relief and Rehabilitation Administration. The task of this organization was to take a preliminary step toward relieving the worst hardships resulting from the war by making available food, clothing, temporary shelter, medical care, and welfare services to devastated regions.

While this effort was being launched to attack more immediate needs, other endeavors were going forward looking to the longer range problem of reconstruction. One such endeavor was the Food and Agriculture Organization. Because agricultural production and consumption are geared to worldwide markets, it was recognized that an international body might be of much assistance in this area in a research and advisory capacity. Thus it was felt that only an international group could grapple with the problem raised by restrictionism in producing nations despite inadequate food supplies elsewhere. What would be required in situations of this kind would be a "pool" into which national "surpluses" could be placed for use as needed; a little later the International Wheat Agreement began operation as an application of this technique to the world's most basic food. In particular, however, the Food and Agriculture Organization in its early years stressed the need to maintain food production at the highest possible level for a few years if serious nutritional deficiencies were to be avoided during the reconstruction period.

Somewhat more tangible from the standpoint of immediate consequences were two organizations designed to deal with the financial problems of the postwar world. One of these was the International Monetary Fund, a device for keeping international exchange relationships stable. A "fund" of national currencies was created on which a nation suffering from a temporary disequilibrium in its balance of payments might draw. Similarly, necessary adjustments in exchange rates could be effected cooperatively without the "beggar-my-neighbor" policies which inevitably develop where such changes are made on a purely unilateral basis. Stated more broadly, the International Monetary Fund was intended to make possible the necessary flexibility in international economic relationships without the painful deflation which often accompanies "unassisted" dynamics.

The Fund was not intended as a supplier of long-range capital, although balance-of-payments problems do clearly merge with capital needs. Particularly was this expected to be the case in the immediate postwar years, for maladjustments would be closely related to capital destruction as well as fundamental economic evolution. To help take care of the needs in this area, an International Bank for Reconstruction and Development was created, a "pool" of liquid capital to be put to use where it was most needed in helping restore the world economy to a more normal functioning. Not an attempt to freeze private banks out of the international lending field, the International Bank was organized on the (undoubtedly correct) assumption that there would be many capital needs which would not carry with them enough certainty of profit to be attractive to private lenders.

Simultaneously with the creation of these and other international agencies, steps were being taken to integrate them into an over-all body which would assume even broader responsibility for problems transcending national boundaries. Thus was the United Nations Organization conceived—an ambitious attempt to achieve objectives long since abandoned by the League of Nations. On the very eve of the ending of the war, in San Francisco, the charter for the United Nations Organization was approved by representatives of most of the nations of the world. The enthusiasm of the people of this and many other countries at the signing of this document was dimmed only by the sudden death of President Roosevelt and the fact that the war was not yet over.

Not only did the United States take the lead in establishing these foundations for a cooperative world order, but just as the war ended she took a unilateral step no less significant in demonstrating her eagerness to cooperate in the postwar world. Against less opposition than in any extension thus far, the Reciprocal Trade Agreements Act was so liberalized that the President was given even more power to negotiate tariff reductions. Thus while the reciprocal trade program had not yet achieved a great deal by way of reducing trade barriers—depression, the threat of war, and war all intervening—notice was served on the rest of the world that it was our intention to pursue this policy more vigorously than ever.

Whence came this internationalism so unfamiliar to the American scene? Several factors were undoubtedly at work, not the least of these being a widespread feeling that only through international cooperation could a lasting peace be achieved. Twice in little more than a generation Americans had been forced to take a leading part in a gigantic world war. It is understandable that new and strange devices would now be acceptable as men and women weary of war resolved that this should not happen again. And it is even understandable that men believed a smoothly functioning international economy to be one of the important roads to peace. (Unfortunately, this causal relationship is probably more correctly stated the other way around.)

Much more than an intense desire for peace, however, was responsible for America's new internationalism. Even business interests, one of the traditional strongholds of this country's trade restriction isolationism, now wanted to see the world economy rebuilt on the basis of a high level of interregional exchange. For these interests there were other issues at stake.

It must be emphasized in this connection that the American economy emerging from the war was much expanded and improved by comparison with its prewar counterpart. In addition, the natural evolution of this nation's economic system (an evolution greatly accelerated by the war) was toward the production of more and more industrial goods; in the field of large-scale production—areas requiring huge capital outlays and using a large amount of horsepower per worker—it was by now commonly acknowledged that this nation had no equal. Put more pointedly, the nation which had never had to concern itself especially about whether or not its export level was high enough now found it necessary to give serious and continuous thought to this question. Remembering the deadly drying up of international trade before and during the "Great Depression," and taking account of the fact that at best most other nations of the world were not in a position to carry on trading relationships on a normal basis, business

TABLE 123. INDUSTRIAL GIANT OF THE WORLD

Average Total Assets per Employee of the One Hundred Largest Manufacturing Corporations in 1949

Number of Companies	Type of Industry	Average Investment
4	Tires, rubber products	$ 5,600
4	Autos and trucks	6,900
4	Electrical equipment	7,100
9	Food products	8,700
9	Iron and steel	10,700
14	Machinery and equipment	10,800
3	Pulp and paper	13,000
7	Nonferrous metals	15,300
6	Chemical products	15,400
4	Distilling	28,800
20	Petroleum products	32,200
4	Tobacco products	41,200
12	Other manufacturing	11,800
100		12,200

Source: By permission of National City Bank of New York.

leaders as well as producers of agricultural staples had good reason for bending every effort to the task of reversing the prewar, worldwide trend toward national self-sufficiency.

Reconversion Gets Under Way. It goes without saying, however, that not all America's attention was devoted to international economic problems. There was also the need to guide the gigantic war economy smoothly back to a peacetime basis. Here, moreover, could be seen the old America at its impatient best. No sooner had the war in Germany ended than the rapid release of soldiers from the armed services began, along with the wholesale cutting back of war contracts. Then, when the atomic bomb brought a sudden end to the Pacific struggle, the eagerness of Americans to return to "normalcy" once more was given virtually free rein. As an indication of the speed with which the economy was "cut loose" from its wartime orientation, in a single week in August, 1945, one million eight hundred thousand workers were released on the basis of cuts in program. In a single month before the year was out more than one and one-half million men were released from the armed services, and plants in the metals and chemicals industries employing some eight million workers at war's end lost in a painfully short period of time well over three-fourths of the orders on their books.

In view of the fact that virtually all the "experts" were predicting a sharp reconversion recession, all this seems in retrospect almost foolhardy. For several reasons, however, it was not as reckless as it can easily be made to sound. First, the accusation at one point that demobilization was being delayed out of concern for the capacity of the economy to absorb released service men aroused such a storm of protest that the administration concluded that such a course would be politically inexpedient—whether or not the accusation was true, and whether or not the transition would thereby have been made more smooth. Second, there was also danger in delay, and this hazard had to be carefully weighed against the consequences of haste. So starved had the economy been for several years for consumer durable goods (including housing), and so much "liquid" purchasing power had consumers accumulated during the war, that the postwar price structure was recognized to be closely related to the speed with which production in these fields could be resumed on a large scale.

Fortunately, too, there were a number of factors at work in the economy which were able to absorb much of the shock of rapid reconversion. A vast veteran education program was developed which kept hundreds of thousands of veterans off the labor market until reconversion was well advanced. Similarly, hundreds of thousands of people who had entered the laboı market only because of the war emergency now withdrew, becoming "voluntarily unemployed." Unemployment insurance for both industrial workers and veterans did much to prevent purchasing power from falling and dragging the entire economy down in the familiar deflationary cycle. Indeed many a worker and many a veteran even used up some of his war accumulated purchasing power to make his personal transition from war to peace as much a "vacation" as a period of idleness spent looking for work. The wartime excess profits tax, by allowing concerns to "carry back" reconversion losses against the excess profits taxes paid during the war, helped firms to avoid contributing to a downward spiral by taking extremely deflationary measures to protect themselves. In the process of renegotiating war contracts (a device designed to "recapture" the excessive profits from contracts drawn up too hastily or with inadequate information) additional care was taken to make sure that businesses were not unduly injured by the speed of reconversion. And finally a $6 billion tax reduction—including the elimination of excess profits taxation entirely—was of assistance in minimizing the discomforts of reorienting the economy to peacetime activities.

Against this background of intense reconversion-readjustment activity, the nation endeavored to restore as nearly as possible the life so rudely interrupted by war (all of it, that is, except the depression). Unavoidably, therefore, behind every decision made there lurked a vital issue. Was the "New Deal" dead? Was the responsibility of government to be extended still further in the guaranteeing of security and minimum living standards? It was the war, after all, that had put an end to the advance of the "New Deal" program, and thus many quite naturally expected that the new "return to normalcy" would include picking up these threads where they had been dropped. Others, men who preferred to think along different lines, insisted that the death of President Roosevelt and his succession by an "old line" politician could only mean a sharp reversal of underlying philosophy in government circles.

President Truman did not leave his own position long in doubt. As he himself explained this action privately, he wanted to let diehard conservatives ("the Hearsts and the McCormicks") know that he was not in their camp. On September 6, 1945, the new President sent to Congress his agenda for postwar legislation. Distinctly "New Dealish" in tenor, this document called for an increase in the minimum wage to sixty-five cents, an expanded social security program, national health insurance, a national housing and slum clearance project of wide scope, and a federal program looking toward the abolition of discrimination against the Negro. Dubbed "Harry Truman's Fair Deal," this agenda for legislative action was a forthright warning that the new administration believed its mission to be to carry on the program commenced by its predecessor. For many years thereafter one of the focal points of controversy in both political and economic debate was to be the "welfare state" and the "drift toward socialism."

Even as Harry Truman's message was being read to a Congress already burdened with the problems of reconversion, it was evident that he would not have everything his own way. No longer was the pain of deep depression a goad to the acceptance of measures more and more to the left of center, and even before the war there had been developing a sentiment to the effect that government responsibilities had expanded far enough. Especially was this the case with southern legislators who took particular offense at the new President's stand on the race question. When to these considerations was added the fact that Truman had inherited a group of highly conservative executives from the war administration, it was not to be expected that the "Fair Deal" would soon become the law of the land. Perhaps even Harry Truman did not expect it, although he clung tenaciously to his program in the face of a series of reverses that would have overcome a man less firm of purpose (or one less sure of the sources of his political support).

The way in which reconversion decisions typically took reference from this issue can be conveniently illustrated by the problem of surplus property disposal. When the war ended, the government had in its possession vast quantities of goods of various kinds which it no longer needed, and war plants and other facilities valued at more than $20 billion. So specialized and exclusively war-oriented had much plant expansion been that two-thirds of it had been financed directly by the government, and it was estimated that the Defense Plant Corporation held title to 10 per cent of the nation's entire plant capacity. Everyone agreed that the government should realize as much as possible from these assets as quickly as possible.

From the standpoint of the goods involved haste was dictated by the need to dispose of government holdings at a time when, because of high consumer demand and relatively low peacetime production capacity, their sale would not take business from private enterprise. Prompt government relinquishment of productive facilities was motivated by a desire to take the government out of competition with private enterprise on a longer range basis.

Thus far there was agreement. Beyond this point, however, there developed a series of bitter controversies centering primarily on the disposition of facilities. For example, should disposal policies include an attempt to implement the antitrust laws by favoring new and small concerns at the expense of large, established ones? The President's inclination, and that of the group of liberals growing up around him, was to use the disposal opportunity in this way, and the basic legislation governing this activity even demanded this procedure. But so strong were the forces of conservatism that government plants were in the end more often than not turned over to concerns already active and prominent in the industry involved, the major exception being the creation of two additional companies to compete with the Aluminum Company of America.

Foundation for Inflation. An even better opportunity for the President to give effect to liberal tendencies was in the field of economic stabilization. As soon as reconversion began in earnest, it was realized that, in so far as purchasing power was maintained, the lag in redirecting productive energies to peacetime output might easily disturb the delicate balance of forces which had kept inflation under control during the latter part of the war effort. Accordingly, plans were made to retain the Office of Price Administration during the reconversion period. As that agency began to take these new responsibilities seriously, a torrent of criticism was directed against what was publicized as the administration's desire to make wartime regimentation permanent.

No sooner had the nation begun to accommodate its thinking to the idea of peace, however, than it was seen that this precaution was not at all absurd. The inflationary pressures visibly building up were taking on formidable proportions. Not only did war-created shortages and war-accumulated purchasing power offer an excellent environment for price increases, but labor was growing restive after several years of patriotic acquiescence and hence anxious to take advantage of its freedom from the wartime no-strike pledge. At the same time many of the country's laborers had a ready-made issue on which to test their strength—a strength now greatly enhanced as a result of accrued organization gains and war-filled union treasuries (sometimes called war chests). The rapid decline in overtime hours, and hence overtime wage rates, threatened workers with a substantial reduction in take-home pay. Here was a battle worth fighting, and the major unions began preparing to demand increases in hourly wage rates sufficient to compensate for the decline in hours worked.

The war experience should have told the new administration how to respond to this situation, that only as *all* price lines are held can *any* price line be maintained. But the administration was caught in a dilemma from which there was no easy escape. With highly trained economists—private as well as public—freely predicting a recession (unemployment reaching six to eight million at its peak), it seemed reasonable to insist that the maintenance of a high level of purchasing power was of the utmost importance. On the other hand, a stabilization policy oriented to this expectation would obviously not be effective if the real danger was inflation. A choice had to be made, and one that had an excellent chance of being completely wrong. Partly because it was anxious to woo the support of organized labor, and partly because the long prewar depression was still vividly in everyone's mind, the decision in Washington was to fight recession rather than inflation.

Given the underlying assumption, the course followed is readily understandable. It is, in fact, understandable that an administration which had so chosen would try to carry water on both shoulders as soon as it became apparent that it had put its money on the wrong horse! In any event, President Truman and his official family took the amazing position that most industries could afford substantial wage increases without raising prices.

Actually the administration was no doubt correct from the standpoint of objective fact. Most companies could have increased wages without raising prices. What was less clear, however, was why they should do so. America's private enterprise system had always been based upon a policy of selling for what the traffic would bear, and there was no reason for believing that the old basis had been abandoned—that decisions of this sort were not still to be made by businessmen on the basis of profit considerations. Thus, when business leaders were bluntly told that profit opportunities were to be deliberately foregone in order that labor might receive a larger share of the national dividend, they were all the more convinced that the "Fair Deal's" major tendencies were in the direction of "un-American," socialistic planning.

In the end it was not possible for the government to have it both ways. After a round of strikes more widespread than any the nation had ever experienced, workers did win substantial pay increases—and probably in the bargain concluded that the President was on their side. For their part, employers put heavy pressure on the stabilization agencies to allow price increases. Faced with this double pressure the government was ultimately forced to give way, adopting a strategy of delay in the hope that inflationary

TABLE 124. PRELUDE TO INFLATION

Month and Year	Man-Days Idle	Per Cent of Working Time
	(Millions)	
January, 1945	0.2	0.03
May, 1945	2.2	0.29
September, 1945	4.3	0.73
October, 1945	8.6	1.39
November, 1945	6.9	1.20
December, 1945	7.7	1.39
January, 1946	19.7	3.13
February, 1946	22.9	4.19
March, 1946	13.8	2.28
April, 1946	14.3	2.19
May, 1946	13.7	2.06
October, 1946	6.2	0.85
December, 1946	3.1	0.46

Source: Department of Labor.

pressures would soon be countered by the recession still expected at any moment.

The Beginning of Foreign Aid. While this problem was coming to a head, another postwar issue was being forthrightly met. By contrast, however, it occasioned comparatively little controversy because it could readily be disposed of along lines already blocked out by America's new internationalist foreign policy.

Scarcely had the war in the Pacific ended than the United States abruptly terminated lend-lease shipments, in a "rough and harsh manner," to use the words of Winston Churchill. Obviously the economic impact of the war was not yet ended, and hence its cost was not at this point fully incurred. To this extent the nation did repeat the error made after World War I. There was, however, this important difference. On the earlier occasion America had expected repayment for assistance rendered her allies during as well as after the war; this time it was to be only the assistance rendered after the shooting ceased. Furthermore, the error was not this time to persist for so long.

Few doubted that dollar credits of some sort would be needed after lend-lease transfers ceased. Thus, until productive capacity in Europe was to a considerable extent restored, outside help was virtually indispensable. Some of these credits, it was assumed, could be taken care of by the International Bank, the Monetary Fund, and the Export-Import Bank—and indeed these media were heavily used for this purpose. But it was also understood that direct intergovernmental credits would also be required; therefore, it did not come as a surprise to the nation when representatives of Great Britain met in Washington with government leaders in this country to work out the details of a loan agreement.

In December, 1945, the details of this agreement were made public. Superficially it was only a business transaction between two nations. In all $3¾ billion were to be made available, repayable over a fifty-year period at 2 per cent interest. These clauses, however, were perhaps largely the "window dressing" needed to secure Congressional approval. Other provisions clearly indicated the deeper purpose of this country—to replace bilateral trading relationships with multilateral ones. Thus no payments were to be due for five years, the time assumed to be necessary to rebuild the British economy, and even then payments were to be waived or scaled down in years during which England suffered from balance-of-payments difficulties. Still more fundamentally, it was provided that England's war accumulated debts to sterling area countries were to be scaled down to realistic figures, and that one year after the loan was approved by Congress the British would make sterling (pound) credits freely exchangeable with (convertible into) any other currency. With both pounds and dollars on a basis of full convertibility multilateral world trading would indeed have been given a substantial impetus.[1]

A Stand for Full Employment. The next major battle between liberals and conservatives involved another issue taking reference from the expectation of a sharp postwar recession—and hence indirectly from the nation's experiences in the "Great Depression." Liberals felt that these tragedies should be prepared for in advance through the assumption by government of the responsibility of making jobs available for men who are willing to work, and, in accordance with this philosophy, the Murray-Wagner Full Employment Bill was presented to Congress. In its original form this measure would have provided for the appointment of economist-specialists who would draw up at intervals a national production and employment budget showing the amount of government spending required to achieve the desired goal, and for a Congressional commitment to appropriate the necessary funds.

Conservatives took vigorous exception to these proposals. Such a blanket approval of the philosophy of deficit spending and the language of economic planning was anathema to them. (Besides, the bill assumed an advance in the science of economic prediction which the facts scarcely war-

[1] A high level of international trade can only be built on a multilateral basis, meaning that an export surplus in country *A*'s trade with country *B* can be offset against an import surplus in *A*'s trade with *C* and an export surplus in *B*'s trade with *D*, and so on. In other words, accounts between pairs of countries can not be forced artificially into balance if maximum trade is to be achieved. But multilateral trade in turn is impossible without currency convertibility, that is, *A*'s receipts from its export surplus with *B* must be acceptable purchasing power in settling for its import surplus with *C*, and so on.

ranted.) Since, however, they did not care to stand openly against the measure's avowed purpose, their attack consisted of watering down its provisions by amendment. The act finally passed on February 20, 1946, substituted an "economic report" for the more operational "budget," eliminated all references to the right to work, and committed the federal government only "to coordinate and utilize all its plans, functions, and resources for the purpose of creating and maintaining, in a manner calculated to promote free competitive enterprise and the general welfare, conditions under which there will be afforded useful employment, for those able, willing, and seeking to work, and to promote maximum employment, production, and purchasing power." It was a highly accurate observation, whether uttered by jubilant conservatives or disgruntled liberals, which later characterized this measure as a "New Year's Resolution."

More was involved in this turn of events, however, than a conservative victory over postwar liberalism. Deeper down, the Full Employment Act of 1946 fell victim to the fact that a serious reconversion recession did not develop. Whereas the expectation had been that unemployment would exceed six million, actually it did not reach three million. If this downturn

TABLE 125. FRUIT BASKET UPSET

Month and Year	Industrial Production *	Prices ‡			Factory Weekly Earnings ‡	Unemployment **
		Wholesale		Consumer		
		Farm	Other †			
July, 1945	100	100	100	100	100	100
June, 1946	80	109	106	103	95	270

* Federal Reserve Board.
† Other than farm products and foods.
‡ Department of Labor.
** Department of Commerce.

had been more severe, it is probable that full employment commitments would have been correspondingly greater. And no doubt the measure enacted provided a foundation on which to build if circumstances at some point in the future dictated that a stronger stand be taken. To this extent liberals could be content with even this meager outcome of their labors.

Trouble on the Labor Front. By the end of the first quarter of 1946 it was conceded even in Washington that the dragon most needing to be slain was inflation. At this point the wage-price policy to which the administration was so deeply committed became a liability rather than an asset from the standpoint of stabilization—whatever its value in labor good will. Of course the administration continued its delaying tactics (with good reason called by many a "jawbone" attack on inflation), but in the longer perspective it was already clear what the outcome was to be. A few more months remained before the nation's flimsy inflation defenses completely collapsed, months which could probably not have been used to strengthen the anti-inflation bulwark in any event. But it is ironical that President Truman was forced by a set of dramatic circumstances to use much of this painful interlude in such a way as to jeopardize his labor support by taking a firm stand with conservatives against labor.

It was in the coal and railroad industries that new labor difficulties now arose, industries which with all of the superprosperity of the war period still bore traces of the "sickness" which had characterized them in the interwar years. For example, who could doubt that coal would have just as difficult a time adjusting to the decline in demand after the expansion during World War II as it had had in a similar situation after World War I? And, while railroads had taken advantage of war conditions to put their financial structures on a sounder basis, it was obvious that the return of more normal times would seriously erode their position in the economy. Not only was prewar expansion in the trucking field beginning to blossom out anew, but the war had given a tremendous impetus to air transportation. Travel by air was beginning to compete for passengers on shorter hops between smaller cities; contract carriers were challenging the supremacy of the so-called commercial operators; and air transport was launching out into what appeared to be a promising future in the freight traffic field. By war's end, in fact, the four largest carriers were no longer receiving a government subsidy for carrying the mail. Burdened with heavy fixed costs, railroads were especially vulnerable to these long-range adjustments.

TABLE 126. TOO MUCH COMPETITION

Type of Carrier	Per Cent of Inland Intercity Transportation Service					
	Freight ton-miles			Passenger miles		
	1916	1939	1949	1916	1939	1949
Railways	77.2	62.6	61.0	98.0	8.6	8.0
Inland waterways	18.4	17.9	14.6	2.0	0.5	–
Pipe lines	4.4	9.5	13.1	–	–	–
Highways	–	10.0	11.1	–	90.7	90.2
Airways	–	–	0.2	–	0.2	1.8
	100	100	100	100	100	100

Source: Interstate Commerce Commission.

To be sure, it was not because these industries were still "sick" that acute labor troubles now developed in them. Rather, the problem was that labor in the coal and railroad (as well as steel) industries had developed a pattern of collective bargaining based on industry-wide negotiations rather than negotiations with one employer at a time. Apparently they felt that in this way they could more effectively exert the pressure needed to secure concessions. Even this fact, however, would not have been decisive if these industries had not at the same time been absolutely indispensable to the operation of a modern economy. A few weeks of idleness in one of these areas and hundreds of thousands of innocent bystanders would be adversely affected. Just such a situation now threatened a nation in need of all its faculties for the task of reconverting its industry and fighting inflation.

The first threat came in the coal fields. On April 1 the country's bituminous coal miners went out on strike. The principal issue was the creation by means of a royalty on each ton of coal mined of a huge health and welfare fund to be used for providing better medical service, rehabilitation and retirement benefits, lower cost insurance, and safety education—or rather the issue was not so much the creation of the fund as its administration. Whereas John L. Lewis wanted complete union control, the operators insisted on a share in decisions relating to the fund. Lewis' position, no doubt, was a natural reaction to the experiences of an earlier period in which institutions such as this were largely created on a paternalistic basis and often for the purpose of destroying unions.

In the middle of May, the economy threatened with a complete breakdown and the public's temper rising in proportion, Lewis sent the miners back into the pits for a twelve-day truce. Meanwhile, and this fact pointedly demonstrated the shrewdness of this Lewis maneuver, public indignation against labor was rapidly mounting in another quarter. Trainmen and engineers on the nation's railroads, refusing to accept a wage compromise agreed to by other rail workers, were threatening to close down the rail network. On May 17 government seizure of the railroads was ordered. Still the dissident brotherhoods would not call off their strike, scheduled for May 23. On the evening of May 24 Truman appealed to the people over the radio, and incidentally requested the striking workers to return to work the following day.

There was an implied threat in this appeal; it was suggested that if the strike did not end the President might be required to take drastic steps. The steps contemplated (in other words, the threat was not an idle one) were twofold. First, the army was to see to it that trains began to run. Second, the President on May 25 asked Congress to pass emergency legislation dealing with such crises—the refusal of workers to respond to a work appeal by the President when such workers were on strike against plants in government hands under wartime powers. Involved were such things as an injunction, loss of seniority rights, criminal penalties, and the draft. Faced with a situation visibly worsening from their standpoint, the strikers went back to work at the wages earlier refused. The drastic legislation requested by the President was accordingly never passed.

Meanwhile, the government had taken the precaution of seizing the coal mines. This action, taken just prior to the ending of Lewis' truce, prevented a second coal walkout—for the moment. Here, too, moreover, the union sustained a substantial defeat. Lewis did not secure exclusive union control over the new health and welfare fund. An operator representative and an impartial outsider also had to be included.

This May, 1946, labor crisis was not significant because laborers were roundly defeated, nor yet because the President felt compelled to side against labor. It was primarily significant because it so clearly indicated how close labor now was to pressing its advantage further than public opinion would countenance. During the war the Smith-Connally Act had made it plain that there were limits to public tolerance during wartime. In May of 1946 it was made plain that there were peacetime limits also. On May 29 Congress sent to the President the so-called Case Mediation Bill, a measure designed essentially to write the Smith-Connally type of safeguards (limits on the right to strike where the public interest was threatened) into permanent legislation. On June 11 the President, no doubt wishing to hold his loss of labor support to a minimum, returned the bill with a firm veto. But it was nonetheless obvious that the time was not far distant when the right to strike would be limited in the public interest.

Trouble on the Price Control Front. It was immediately after this episode that the price control debacle moved into its last phase. For some time evidence had been piling up that businessmen were withholding goods from the market in anticipation of the complete ending of controls. Even more apparent, and more painful, was the fact that a large fraction of the nation's meat supply was finding its way into the black market rather than ordinary channels in order to take advantage of the higher-than-ceiling prices people were willing to pay. It is no exaggeration to say that it was the meat situation which finally broke the back of price control.

Unfortunately, moreover, Congress was meanwhile following a procedure which could only have aggravated the process of control erosion. Almost persuaded by business pressures and the general economic situation, Congress refused to commit itself to a strong control measure to replace the one expiring. On June 29, one day before controls were scheduled to end, Congress sent President Truman a renewal measure, a proposal which would have resulted in substantial price increases in a number of critical areas. Refusing to be coerced by the calendar or publicly to concede that price control had become a hopeless cause, he sent back a stinging veto, calling the new law "a sure formula for inflation." Not until July 25 was a stronger control measure ready for White House approval, but in the ensuing twenty-six days the index of prices for twenty-eight basic commodities at wholesale rose almost 25 per cent as compared with only 13 per cent

TABLE 127. GENESIS OF INFLATION

Month and Year	Prices	
	Wholesale	Consumer
June, 1943	92	93
June, 1944	93	94
June, 1945	95	97
June, 1946	100	100
July, 1946	110	106
December, 1946	124	115

Source: Department of Labor.

during the preceding three years. Although a new control law was passed and an attempt made to roll back prices to the June 30 level, and although a pretense of inflation control was kept up until about the end of the year, this episode marked the definitive end of the entire structure of price controls with the exception of rent.

Of course there were recriminations; everyone wished to blame everyone else for the inflation now given almost free rein. Business leaders insisted it was labor's postwar pay increases that had opened the door, while workers urged that their success on the pay front had in fact made it possible for the economy to avoid a painful postwar recession and that it was unrestrained profit seeking by "greedy" capitalists which had brought on inflation. Equally vigorous was a controversy over whether the ending of price controls was a good thing. Most businessmen felt that the best interests of the nation had been served because high prices would encourage production and only greater production could defeat inflation. (For purposes of this argument it was conveniently overlooked that the economy was already at virtually full employment and suffering from a long list of materials shortages.) Many others took the position that inflation would wrest purchasing power away from lower income receivers and thus in time precipitate a severe economic downturn. (Here the crucial fact conveniently ignored was that, at the moment at least, the crux of the problem was an "excess" of purchasing power.)

Actually most of this *post mortem* analysis was quite beside the point. In all probability the nation never really had a choice as to whether it would or would not have a postwar inflation. During the war individuals and firms had saved unprecedented amounts of money, partly because patriotism dictated this policy but perhaps more because of the wartime scarcity of consumer durable and investment goods. As a result individuals and businesses had not only accumulated vast purchasing power resources but they had also carried over from the war years a large "backlog" of unfulfilled demands. In fact, on the side of business demand and home construction there were even demand "backlogs" carried over from the depression years. Thus inflation in the United States in the immediate postwar period to a considerable extent took the form of a competition between business firms and individuals for a limited supply of goods. An impressive documentation of this contest were the facts that large, well established business firms complained that the public would not buy new securities, that the majority of business concerns (perhaps partly because they could not sell stock) adopted the "rule of thumb" of paying out in dividends fifty cents of every dollar of after-taxes-profits and reinvesting the other half-dollar, and that consumer credit almost doubled in a twelve-month period following V-J Day.

TABLE 128. BACKBONE OF INFLATION

Year	Private Investment	Personal Saving
	(Billions of dollars)	
1944	7.7	35.4
1946	29.5	10.3

Source: Department of Commerce.

Of course the inflation environment was somewhat more complex than these items would suggest. Thus the government also figured heavily in the scramble for goods. The veteran program required heavy outlays for a number of purposes. Veteran needs (and especially government commitments to veterans), the accelerated urbanization of the war years, and the war increase in the birth rate forced the government into the home construction field to an unprecedented extent. The federal government was almost desperately buying food for use in feeding a hungry, postwar world. There was even talk, some of it in disturbingly official circles, of steel plant expansion at government expense to relieve the serious shortage of that product. Given, in short, such a vigorous three-way tug of war for goods the wonder is not why the United States had inflation, but why there was no more inflation than there was.

More Trouble. The price battle lost, the administration turned almost immediately to another grim struggle in the labor field. Ever since the crisis earlier in the year the government had retained nominal control over the nation's bituminous coal mines. In November Lewis sought concessions for his men, and was turned down. On November 21 the expected walkout began, and Harry Truman, determined on a fight to the finish with John L. Lewis, secured an injunction against the union. When Lewis defied this action contempt proceedings were brought, with the result that the union was fined $3½ million and Lewis himself was fined $10,000.

Again it is worth emphasizing that these actions were taken, not by men who were traditional "labor-haters" but by labor's acknowledged friends. Thus Judge Alan T. Goldsborough, the jurist who dealt so harshly with the miners on this occasion, was an ex-member of the House of Representatives, where he had often voted for "New Deal" measures. In other words, this event was simply another step in the evolution toward a method of protecting the public against an undisciplined use of labor's strike weapon. Few supposed that the answer had yet been found, and labor leaders were understandably furious at the thought that a new national labor policy might include the hated injunction. But without question millions of people throughout the country secured an immense amount of satisfaction in Lewis' humiliating defeat. And, still more ominous from labor's standpoint, it was common knowledge that the newly elected (Republican) Eightieth Congress was already determined to take prompt action on this problem.

It was evident, as 1946 passed into history, that nothing had yet been accomplished by way of implementing "Fair Deal" programs. Illustrative of the fate which had been accorded Harry Truman's version of his mandate was the cold shoulder Congress had given the President's health insurance idea, a project for which he had worked as vigorously as any other. Now, furthermore, the prospect of "reforming" American capitalism was even dimmer. The new Congress was conservative to the core, and hence even more determined that the ghost of the "New Deal" was to be forever laid to rest. No doubt the "man from Missouri" had already given up accomplishing very much along these lines—during his *first* term in the White House.

Much of this indifference to reform, of course, must be put down to the urgency of other matters as the nation endeavored to get its bearings after the most intensive war effort it had ever been called upon to make. But if there were those who thought postwar problems would soon recede far enough into the background to permit an advance on the reform front, they were doomed to disappointment. For just as the United States had gotten itself squared away to tackle its own longer range problems, there appeared on the horizon an entirely new postwar problem—one so difficult and absorbing and expensive that little margin would have been left for reforming zeal even if those in the seats of power had been so inclined. All of a sudden, or so it seemed at the time, Americans learned that allies in time of war are not necessarily allies in time of peace.

The first evidence of this new state of affairs appeared in preliminary discussions between Russia, the United States, England, and France over what to do with Germany. In order that each power might have a voice in the affairs of this erstwhile enemy nation, four separate occupation zones had been created. This arrangement, it had been supposed by the Western

Powers, was only a makeshift until a peace treaty for Germany could be agreed upon, and meanwhile the existence of separate occupation zones was not to be allowed to militate against a high degree of economic unity for Germany. It was therefore most disconcerting to learn that Russia apparently had no intention either of giving up her foothold in Germany or of integrating her occupation zone with the rest of Germany (that is, allowing Russia-occupied agricultural Germany to trade freely with Western-occupied industrial Germany).

This stubborn fact produced a rapid change of view in the West on German policy. Originally it had been anticipated that Germany would be allowed to retain only a minimum of her industrial capacity, a policy dictated in part by the desire to keep her war potential at a low level and in part by the desire of Russia, France, and England for direct reparations. But with the industrial and agricultural sections of Germany artificially separated, these plans underwent a drastic alteration. Thus it was recognized that Germany would have to make a more substantial use of her industrial capacity than had been planned, or she would be unable to export enough goods to enable her to buy indispensable imports. Furthermore, with trade between eastern and western Europe reduced to a trickle, it seemed certain that European reconstruction also required a high level of trade for West Germany—both imports and exports. As a consequence of these discoveries, the Western Powers began to revise upward their calculations as to how much manufacturing was to be done in Germany. With equal dispatch steps were taken to introduce a maximum amount of economic integration into the administration of the three western occupation zones.

Germany was not the only sore point between East and West. By the beginning of 1947, however, a number of such difficulties were beginning to fit together into a meaningful, if somewhat exasperating, pattern. The disappearance of Germany and Japan as strong nations had created a power vacuum which Russia was strenuously endeavoring to fill. World War II had ended, in other words, not in the "peace and good will" many had hoped to find, but in "cold war." Although this terminology had not yet come into general use, it was widely being acknowledged that international tension on a large scale was to prevail for at least the immediate future. The "return to normalcy," in short, was to be in the direction desired by neither liberals nor conservatives; indeed it seemed apparent by the beginning of 1947 that any thought of "normalcy" must, for the moment at least, be put aside.

QUESTIONS FOR DISCUSSION

1. What steps were taken by the United States to cooperate with other nations in meeting the problems of the postwar period? How was each supposed to help?

2. Why with capital so abundant in this country and the need for capital so great elsewhere could private investment not be relied upon to rebuild Europe?

3. Was the speed with which the United States abandoned its wartime orientation wise or unwise? What might have been gained by delay? What might have been lost?

4. In what ways does an anti-inflation policy conflict with the public policy required to combat deflation? Did the administration consistently follow either policy?

5. Why was America so eager to terminate the lend-lease program but so willing to embark upon a multibillion dollar foreign-aid program almost immediately thereafter?

6. Was anything of consequence accomplished in the Full Employment Act of 1946?

7. Is industry-wide collective bargaining contrary to the public interest? Is it a violation of the antitrust laws?

8. Who or what was responsible for the breakdown of price control so soon after the war?

9. Why did inflation remain partially suppressed for a time after the war and then erupt with such suddenness?

Chapter 40

"COLD WAR" AND INFLATION

1947	"Truman Doctrine" announced.
	"Marshall Plan" launched.
	Taft-Hartley Act.
	Reconversion complicated by inflation.
1948	Sharp break in farm prices.
	Foreign Assistance Act.
	"Atlantic Pact."
1949	"Point Four" announced.
	Inflation gave way to recession.
	Several "Fair Deal" reforms enacted.
	"Brannan Plan" defeated.
1950	Outbreak of war in Korea.

The Enemy Challenged. Actually the existence of a "cold war" between East and West would have been a much less serious problem if all the western allies had been capable of shouldering their share of the economic burden thus entailed. Unfortunately, however, 1947 had scarcely gotten under way than it became evident that postwar recovery in Europe had broken down. Having proceeded in a highly satisfactory manner to this point, progress virtually ceased in the second full postwar year—because, many said, these economies had undertaken capital development programs more ambitious than they could support. The obvious corollary of this situation was that the United States would not only have to bear most of the cost of the "cold war" but that she would also have to assist Europe even more than she had yet done if the other Western Powers were ever to be able to share this load.

The full implications of this development were brought home to Americans in two dramatic ways. On the one hand, Russia was openly endeavoring to bring Greece and Turkey into her sphere of influence, and England suddenly announced that she could no longer maintain the status quo in the Mediterranean. On the other hand, communist political organizations were showing a frightening amount of strength in both Italy and France, capitalizing to the fullest extent on the failure of postwar recovery to restore prewar standards of living.

Russia's threat to Greece and Turkey was boldly and quickly met. On March 12 President Truman promulgated the famous "Truman Doctrine," a declaration to the effect that this country would stand firmly against the involuntary expansion of communism in the Near East. (If nothing else had been involved, this step would have been indicated by America's immense oil interests in that part of the world.) Within two months almost $500 million worth of military and economic aid had been approved by Congress for this cause.

The problem of recovery in Europe could not be attacked either so quickly or so directly. What was required here was rather a long-range program which would so restore the European economy to health that it would be less vulnerable to communism's penchant for feeding on its neighbors' weaknesses. So well understood was this need, moreover, that there was little tendency to minimize the extent of the burden being assumed by this country. Thus it was recognized that the job would have to be done thoroughly or it could easily turn out to be "operation rathole" (as opponents persisted in calling it from the very beginning). Similarly it was understood that the maladjustment in Europe's economy was not simply the aftermath of World War II. Two world wars, a crippling world depression, the rise of the United States as a towering industrial giant, and the efforts of much of the undeveloped part of the world to industrialize had produced major structural changes in the world's economy, changes to which the various nations were being forced to adjust themselves even while recovering from the devastation of war. Important among these were the loss by Europe of a large part of her overseas investment, a steady increase in population, and the progressive throttling of an East-West trade which had historically been of great importance. The task of the United States was no less than that of helping Europe make the necessary adjustments without an inconvenience so painful as to invite the "cure" of communism.

Although American statesmen began at once the difficult task of devising a workable program on this front, another project was simultaneously placed high on the agenda of United States' foreign policy. Its nature clearly indicated that this country's interest in Europe was not merely a desire to frustrate the expansion of communism. At the center of our foreign policy was still the almost unqualified determination to restore the world to a multilateral, nondiscriminatory trading basis. Beginning April 10, and with the United States the acknowledged leader of the group, twenty-three nations sent representatives to Geneva, Switzerland, to negotiate wholesale reductions in international tariff barriers.

The Geneva Conference almost came to grief before it had gotten fairly under way. In May the Eightieth Congress, concerned over the large stock of wool in this country, created by what might appropriately be called wartime stockpiling, and eager to take advantage of such an excellent opportunity to cripple the anti-Republican reciprocity program, legislated special tariff protection for the nation's sheep growers. So damaging would this have been to America's Geneva aims that Will Clayton, Undersecretary of State and our chief negotiator in Geneva, flew home to assist the administration in this domestic crisis. Australia, New Zealand, and South Africa (all represented at Geneva) were vitally concerned with wool exports to the United States, and the passage of this legislation would have served notice on every nation that America could not be depended upon to follow through on her expressed intention of moderating barriers to world trade.

It would be juggling with the truth to assert that even with Clayton's assistance the crisis was averted. Actually the protective measure passed both Houses of Congress, the situation in Geneva being rescued only by a presidential veto. As a result of this rescue the Geneva Conference was able to secure the greatest array of tariff reductions ever achieved; at one stroke America's reciprocal trade agreements program accomplished more than during the entire period between its passage and the end of the war. Moreover, the various nations involved went much further than this network of mutual concessions by agreeing that in the years ahead tariff cuts would have to go deeper still and that other nations would have to be included. At the same time, however, despite this huge success, the wool incident did give our European allies food for thought as they contemplated their longer term relationships with the United States. Unfortunately, in other words, America could not compete on even terms with other parts of the world in the production of wool—and there were a number of other industries in this country in the same category.

While the discussions at Geneva were still going on, the first steps were taken in the direction of a long-range European policy. On June 5 Secretary of State Marshall in a commencement address at Harvard gave expression to an approach to this problem which has since been popularly referred to as the "Marshall Plan." Its keynote was that work toward a more rapid and complete European recovery necessitated cooperation between America and Europe rather than the continuance of unilateral assistance. "The role of this country should consist of friendly aid in the drafting of a European program and of later support of such a program so far as it may be practical for us to do so." Thus inauspiciously was launched a plan of action which was to be one of the most dominant economic forces in the entire world for several years.

Three facts about the "Marshall Plan" are particularly worthy of note at the outset. In the first place, it is immediately apparent how close a corollary it was to a foreign policy geared to the restoration of freer trading relationships. In the second place, although for obvious reasons little was made of this point at the time, the new program was far less an abandonment of unilateral assistance than a belated recognition of the fact that sights had originally been set too low on the amount of unilateral aid required. Secretary Marshall's emphasis was no doubt helpful from the standpoint of moderating political resistance to a stepped-up program, but there was clearly no "official" confusion as to what was involved. In the third place, the reference to cooperation seems to have been in part a subtle way of saying that further unilateral aid should be geared to the needs of Europe as a whole rather than to individual country needs.

No sooner had the air cleared in the United States after the Secretary's address sufficiently to note that public opinion was favorable than implementation began—on both sides of the Atlantic. In Europe a commmittee of representatives from various European nations met in Paris to make a detailed analysis of the aid that would be required to finish the task of reconstructing Europe, while in the United States an effort was made to determine how much additional aid this country could afford.

The Wagner Act Challenged. Against the background of these developments on the international economic scene, a historic struggle was taking place over a vital issue on the domestic front. As one of its major projects the Eightieth Congress had resolved to enact legislation which would more nearly harness organized labor to the public interest and restore "equality" to collective bargaining relationships in which it was felt labor was securing the upper hand. The result was the Labor-Management Relations Act of 1947 (popularly referred to as the Taft-Hartley Act), a measure amending the Wagner Act in a number of significant ways.

Superficially at least it is correct to say that the new labor law did not abrogate the basic guarantees of the Wagner Act—the right of labor to organize and bargain collectively. Moreover, it apparently did not in practice result in a serious erosion of Wagner Act premises. At the same time, however, this legislation in one major respect marked a sharp break with the past. Whereas the Wagner Act had dealt only with prebargaining employer-employee relationships, Taft-Hartley undertook to write rules and regulations governing the bargaining process itself. Largely because of this change in approach the complaint was to be increasingly heard that the government was coming to assume too large a role in labor-capital relationships. To this extent the program of the conservatives boomeranged. A project designed to limit the effectiveness of labor's side at the bargaining table was in fact accompanied by a government intervention that was probably neither expected nor desired. Thus, interpreted as a precedent, Taft-Hartley served notice on both workers and management that voluntary collective bargaining processes must steadily improve or they would be even further supplanted by government action.

The new orientation in labor relations can be seen at a number of points. Under Taft-Hartley, first, the closed shop (a plant in which union membership is a prerequisite to employment) was made illegal, although the union shop (a plant in which union membership is made compulsory after employment) was still permitted. A more subtle way of undermining job control by unions was also included; it was expressly provided that state "right to work" laws were to take precedence over federal legislation in this field. (State legislatures often underrepresent urban laborers as compared with their political power in Washington, D. C.) Second, no union security provision (such as the union shop) could be written into a contract if the union was not "democratic" in the sense of charging "reasonable" fees and following nondiscriminatory admission policies. Never before had federal legislation endeavored to regulate the internal affairs of labor unions. Third, the new law encouraged small craft groups to break away from industrial unions which had in the past been their bargaining representatives. Fourth, foremen's unions were denied the protection of the Wagner Act, although these workers were not forbidden to organize. Fifth, collective bargaining in pursuit of "featherbedding" contract provisions was outlawed, and collective bargaining for "health and welfare" provisions was considerably narrowed in scope.

These modifications of collective bargaining would have been substantial enough from labor's point of view even if there had been included no limitations on the right to strike. In all collective bargaining it is of the utmost importance that labor be able to reinforce its demands by means of a threat to strike; paradoxically, the secret of *peaceful* labor relations is the residual availability of a weapon closely associated with *violence*. Thus it was with particular dismay that laborers noted the several provisions in the Taft-Hartley Act restricting this right.

Of least importance in this connection were prohibitions against sympathy strikes (and secondary boycotts), jurisdictional strikes, and strikes by federal government employees. Far more significant was a requirement that a sixty-day notice had to be given by a union of intention to terminate or modify a contract (called a "cooling-off" period), with the proviso that a strike could not be called during this period. Equally important were the fact that striking workers who had been replaced were not eligible to vote in a National Labor Relations Board representation election, and a clause lifting the Wagner Act ban against employers telling workers their views on the subject of labor unions. And most basic of all was the authority given the government to secure an eighty-day injunction (another "cooling-off" period) against any strike threatening the public's health or safety.

Although Taft-Hartley contained several provisions directed at problems which had long troubled liberals (for example, the closed shop, jurisdictional strikes, majority tyranny over labor union minorities, and strikes injuring the larger public), and although labor's position in society remained much improved over what it had been prior to the enactment of the Wagner Act, there was reason for questioning how much real progress had been made. For one thing it was doubtful if delicate relationships such as those involved in collective bargaining could become closely intertwined with government and not be damaged in their effectiveness as a result. It was likewise doubtful if standards could actually be established for defining "equality" in relationships between parties whose situations were totally different. Many people, in fact, were not even sure how successful would be the provisions protecting the public from "crisis" strikes. As so often in such cases, however, only time could determine how much of permanence had been achieved.

Of course Truman vetoed the Taft-Hartley Act—not because it was a "slave-labor law" as labor leaders widely insisted, but because it was a reversal of "the basic direction of our national labor policy." Of course also it was precisely this retreat from "New Deal" philosophies which endeared this measure to those who passed it, and hence there was no difficulty in securing enough votes to override. In this way was the President bluntly reminded, if indeed a reminder was necessary, that the country was still far from ready to embrace his "Fair Deal" version of prewar reform.

Foreign Aid and Inflation. After the issue of labor legislation had been settled, the number one economic problem of the nation was unquestionably postwar inflation. June, 1947, saw the index of consumers' prices some 20 per cent higher than a year earlier and still rising. Furthermore, the postwar scramble for inventory had in large part spent itself, exports had unmistakably leveled off, and business investments had sagged considerably—all without any indication that the underlying boom had significantly been weakened thereby. Encouraged by this impressive show of economic strength, the economy resumed its optimistic advance. Capital investment shortly attained even greater heights, inventory accumulation again became the order of the day, exports remained at abnormally high levels by comparison with prewar standards, and private individuals also continued and even enlarged their own spending programs.

It was most appropriate that next to inflation the most important economic problem confronting the nation was the "Marshall Plan." In the first place, the foreign-aid program was one of the factors contributing to

TABLE 129. INFLATION UNRESTRAINED

Year	Industrial Production *	Prices ‡ Wholesale Farm	Other †	Consumer	Factory Weekly Earnings ‡	Unemployment ** (000's)
	(1947-1949 = 100)					
1945	107	71.6	71.3	76.9	$44.39	1,040
1946	90	83.2	78.3	83.4	43.82	2,270
1947	100	100.0	95.3	95.5	49.97	2,142
1948	104	107.3	103.4	102.8	54.14	2,064

* Federal Reserve Board.
† Other than farm products and food.
‡ Department of Labor.
** Department of Commerce.

inflation. It was as much as anything, for example, talk of price controls and allocation powers to make available foreign-aid goods that set off the new wave of inventory accumulation. Moreover, although no "Marshall Plan" aid as such was made available in that year, 1947 exports were nonetheless greatly aided by the knowledge that it was to be forthcoming. Gold and dollar credits in this country could be used more freely when it became known that these assets were not all that stood between their owners and complete financial collapse. In all more than $4½ billion worth of American exports were financed by means of these funds in 1947.

TABLE 130. STOREHOUSE FOR DEMOCRACY

Item	1946	1947	1948
	(Billions of dollars)		
Total exports	15.0	19.7	16.8
Total imports	7.2	8.4	10.5
Export surplus	7.8	11.5	6.7
Means of financing:			
Foreign aid programs	5.1	5.8	5.1
Liquidation of foreign-held assets	2.0	4.5	0.9
Other	0.7	1.2	0.7

Source: Department of Commerce.

In the second place, it was in substantial part because of inflation in the United States that the need for aid to Europe was so acute. This was especially evident when it proved to be impossible to make the pound convertible in mid-1947 as stipulated in the British Loan Agreement. Thanks partially to rising prices in this country the loan was already approximately 50 per cent expended, and on the basis of full convertibility it would have been completely gone before the end of the year. This same factor, too, had diluted the purchasing power of other postwar aids such as Export-Import Bank and International Bank loans, while gold and dollar credits had suffered most seriously of all. The largest portion of these funds had been accumulated during the war when one of America's great needs was imported raw materials. Having persuaded other nations to sell their goods on credit at a time when we could not spare the exports with which to pay for them, the United States was now making export goods available at prices greatly in excess of those prevailing during the war.

Finally, there was the question whether "Marshall Plan" aid would overburden the American economy. Since there was no objective measure

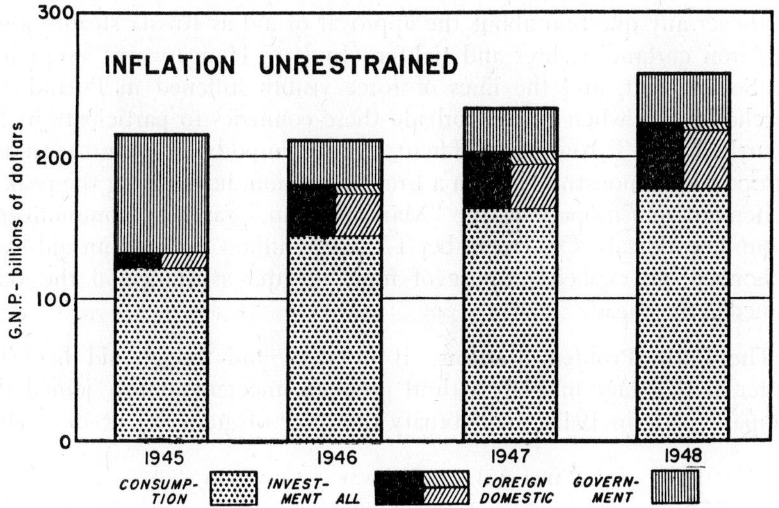

FIGURE 18.

which could be used to resolve this issue, and since much of the debate concerning it was politically oriented, this controversy became essentially whether the foreign-aid program would or would not add to the burden of inflation. On the one side it was argued that it mattered little whether purchasing power was expended for American goods by Americans or foreigners. On the other side it was insisted that foreign-aid funds would otherwise be used for debt reduction, which would act as a brake on inflation. The truth probably would have required emphasis upon both of these ideas; certainly some part of the nation's foreign-aid expenditures would otherwise have found their way into tax reductions.

Actually, however, as events worked themselves out this issue was highly academic. In two ways the Eightieth Congress indicated that inflation was not to be treated as a matter of great importance. On the one hand, twice in 1947 Congress passed a tax reduction measure which would have been most inflationary in the circumstances. On both occasions the country was spared this additional support for inflationary pressures by a presidential veto (although the more important ground for these vetoes was probably the fact that the reductions enacted were of greater benefit to large income receivers relative to smaller ones than seemed appropriate to zealous "Fair Dealers"), but the efforts made by Congress in that direction demonstrated convincingly that stabilization as such was not a fundamental consideration on Capitol Hill.[1] On the other hand, Congress refused to give the President authority to cope directly with the economy's growing inflation.

Although there was no strong sentiment favoring controls designed to minimize the economic dislocation from an expanded aid program, there was never any question about the approval of aid as Russia steadily drew the "iron curtain" tighter and tighter. In 1947 Hungary was swept into the Soviet orbit, and the lines of force visibly stiffened in Poland and Czechoslovakia when Russia forbade these countries to participate in the "Marshall Plan." And in a different way the importance of further aid in Europe was demonstrated when a French election, held during the peak of excitement in Europe over the "Marshall Plan," gave the communists a resounding defeat. On December 17, $500 million in "interim aid" was authorized, an explicit promise of much greater assistance in the years immediately ahead.

The Farm Problem Returns. If inflation and foreign aid held the center of the stage in 1947, a third problem unceremoniously joined this company early in 1948. In February the price of grain fell by more than

TABLE 131. A POSTWAR ADJUSTMENT

Year and Month	Grain Prices	Parity Ratio
1948		
January	100	100
February	80	92
June	79	97
October	70	91

Source: Department of Agriculture.

[1] To the extent that fiscal policy is used for stabilization purposes, it is best in periods of inflation to keep taxes as high as possible (regardless of budget needs), especially on consumption. Although the taxes in question here were income taxes, at the lower income levels tax reductions would unquestionably have been reflected in consumption expenditures. And while almost any tax reduction would have had some of these same consequences, it is interesting to note that a reduction advantaging large income receivers more than those in the lower brackets would have been the least inflationary kind of tax reduction which could have been enacted.

20 per cent and continued to fall throughout the entire year. The South's cotton did not participate in this break because this commodity had undergone its basic postwar "shakedown" some months earlier. In this dramatic way the nation's leaders were brought face to face with a tremendous unsolved problem which had been almost ignored in the superprosperity of war and its aftermath.

The problem was this. During the depression the "parity" price support program had been inaugurated as a purchasing power prop under a sagging economy. Even with this as a motive, however, guarantees had rarely risen above 75 per cent of parity (despite bold political talk about "full parity"), and normally they had been lower. During the war the purpose of government guarantees had shifted to the provision of an incentive for greater output, and this fact plus the generally high prices prevailing had resulted in a substantial increase in production. Moreover, the application of science to agriculture and the continued rapid increase of farm mechanization—accelerated, especially in the South, by the wartime labor shortage—had greatly increased man-hour output and hence American agriculture's capacity to produce "surpluses."

TABLE 132. INDUSTRIAL REVOLUTION ON THE FARM

Item	1930	1945
Number of farm workers per 1,000 acres of crop land	25	21
Number of tractors per 100 farm workers	9	29
Number of motor trucks per 100 farm workers	9	18

Source: Bureau of the Census, *1945 Census of Agriculture.*

To make matters still more difficult (although who is to say that this step was either unnecessary or inappropriate?), Congress had expressly guaranteed the farmer 90 per cent of parity for two years after the war in order to prevent the disaster which had overtaken agriculture after World War I. Since the war, furthermore, it had been possible to temporize with this issue because exports had remained fairly high. To be sure, the February break did not bring many farm prices below the 90 per cent level, but the government was threatened with "surpluses" in some commodities—most notably potatoes and eggs. Not far in the future, also, could be seen a similar "surplus" of butter. The high price of butter and inflation-based legislation removing special taxes and other restrictions of oleomargarine sales were promising to force the government soon to begin "stockpiling" butter in large quantities. All in all it seemed evident that the nation would soon have to contend again with agricultural "overproduction."

Actually the situation was not critical. The biggest immediate question was whether this dulling of the edge of farm prosperity would precipitate a scaling down of the level of general business activity. This fear did not prevail for long, however. By March, 1948, the certainty of quick passage of a substantial foreign-aid measure made it evident that government expenditures would be underwriting prosperity for some time to come. Inventories resumed their advance, investment continued to expand, and the automobile and construction industries continued to set new production records.

Even when the farmer's plight was considered by itself, the problem was not desperate. A significant amount of short-term relief for farmers would be a direct outgrowth of foreign-aid expansion. After all, the farm price break was closely related to the dissipation of foreign purchasing power in this country. Moreover, an alert and energetic "Farm Bloc" could write specific guarantees for the farmer directly into the aid bill. Thus the Foreign Assistance Act provided that goods declared "surplus" by the Secretary of Agriculture were to be purchased only in this country if bought with "Marshall Plan" funds, the Secretary of Agriculture was authorized to pay export subsidies up to 50 per cent of the sale price of such products, and the amount of farm machinery to be included in the program was limited to $75 million worth in a single year. (Despite "surpluses" it was insisted that the trend toward mechanization at home continue at a rapid pace.) The following year it was even possible to convert the International Wheat Agreement into what amounted virtually to a program for subsidizing exports of American wheat.

Parenthetically, it must also be said that the farmer was not the only group that made a good thing out of foreign aid. As it moved steadily through Congress, provisions were added benefiting other interests. Twenty-five per cent of all wheat shipped under the European Recovery Program had to be in the form of flour. Millers in the United States were suffering from a persistent trend away from starches in America's eating habits. Fifty per cent of all "Marshall Plan" goods had to be transported in American ships. Here, in other words, was an excellent opportunity to subsidize the American merchant marine at the expense of foreigners. It was almost provided that all goods purchased by "Marshall Plan" funds would have to be purchased in the United States, although ultimately Senator Paul Douglas of Illinois (onetime President of the American Economic Association) succeeded in convincing enough legislators that all aid made available in the form of dollars must in the final analysis be spent in this country and that it might cripple European reconstruction if it was insisted that these dollars be spent in the United States *in the first instance*.

A Republican Congress in 1948 would have been only too happy to take advantage of these saving factors by not enacting agricultural legislation in the face of declining farmer incomes. This was not merely because 1948 was an election year, either, although that was an important factor. The difficulty was rather that a serious attempt to work out a more satisfactory long-range farm program would inevitably require a lowering of the support level, and no politician could be expected to welcome such an operation on a patient already suffering from income "malnutrition." It was therefore unfortunate for the Republicans that the postwar guarantees expired in 1948, and that a decision on this issue could not be avoided. Speaking figuratively, Congress gritted its teeth and set to work.

Simultaneously with the development of this legislation another step was being taken toward the American ideal of multilateral trade. For some months representatives from fifty-seven nations had been meeting in Havana, Cuba, to work out a set of principles for the conduct of world trade. The United States made excellent use of the Havana Conference to push for a "liberal" document, although in the give and take of negotiation a number of concessions had to be granted (some, indeed, for the benefit of American agriculture). Thus many nations refused to give up their right to regulate their own trade by fiat in the event this seemed necessary to maintain full employment, and some insisted on the right to impose barriers to assist in the development of infant industries. (This latter reservation especially was one to which the United States could hardly take exception in view of her own history.) As a result of such limitations the projected International Trade Organization was not hailed as the broad advance many had hoped it would be, although the principles on which it was founded did promise much improvement over the extreme nationalism which had characterized trade policy in the interwar years. Furthermore, the "defeat" suffered by the United States in Havana in March was soon put into its proper perspective when Congress made it unmistakably clear that its thinking was much less "liberal" than that emanating from the State Department. The American Congress, be it remembered, would ultimately have to approve the charter of the International Trade Organization if it were to become a reality.

No doubt the farm problem in the background accounted for much of this nation's reluctance to accept the full implications of freer trading relationships. A policy of inviting imports while the government was artificially raising domestic prices above the world price level was not an intelligent procedure. At that moment, in fact, the country was witnessing the simultaneous destruction of "surplus" American potatoes and the importation of Canadian potatoes. But, whatever the reason, the occasion for an adverse pronouncement by Congress at this time was the 1948 renewal of the Reciprocal Trade Agreements Act. Although the renewal measure was passed, there were written into it two provisions which greatly dulled its effectiveness. The first was the so-called "escape clause" which had to be included in all future trade agreements. Under its terms each party would reserve the right to withdraw tariff concessions if they became unduly burdensome to domestic industry. The second was the "peril-point" provision whereby the Tariff Commission was requested to tell the President the level below which particular tariffs could not be lowered without placing domestic operators in "peril." To be sure the President was not required to give heed to "peril-point" advice, but it was generally understood that he could not persistently ignore the Commission without inviting major Congressional limitations on his tariff-making power. No doubt other nations felt justified in the stand they had taken in Havana after this action by the American Congress.

From Inflation to Recession. By mid-1948 the "cold war" was taking on a most ominous character. On April 3, debate on this measure coinciding closely with excitement over a major communist coup in Czechoslovakia, the Foreign Assistance Act was signed by President Truman. Approximately two weeks later noncommunist forces in Italy delivered a smashing defeat to their communist opponents in a general election. June 11 saw the Senate approve the principle of collective defense within the United Nations (the "Atlantic Pact"). Then, on June 24, Russia took what was perhaps the most decisive overt step she had yet taken—the "blockade" of Berlin designed to force the Western Powers out of their sector of that city. Russia was able to do this because, unfortunately, the capital of Germany was located wholly within the Russian zone. The price the allies were forced to pay to stay in Berlin, a vital key to the economic and political situation in central Europe, was the supplying of the essential economic needs of more than two million people by air for a period of eleven months while a Western blockade against "iron curtain" territory was making its influence felt. On June 24 also a new Selective Service Act became law in this country.

As international tensions grew apace, and as the "Marshall Plan" offensive gathered momentum, America went through the throes of one of the most interesting presidential campaigns in many years. Superficially what was involved was the quest for a mandate on the issues raised by Truman's "Fair Deal." Democrats sought a vindication of their policy of pushing for such reforms; Republicans sought a validation of their policy of resisting them. From this standpoint the key issue was perhaps the Taft-Hartley Act which a Republican Congress had passed over the veto of a Democratic President.

Viewing the election in this way it is understandable that virtually every "expert" confidently expected Harry Truman to be counted out in 1948.

Again using Taft-Hartley as a symbol, Truman "deserved" to lose; the test of time was to confirm the judgment of the Republican Congress and not that of the Democratic President, and the entire "Fair Deal" program had been blessed with no more success. But when the election result was a decisive Republican-Dewey defeat, and when the "experts" began to probe into the causes of this upset, it developed that the issue posed by the election had not been the "Fair Deal" as much as several other factors which reversed midwestern voting trends now sixteen years old.

Of course, one of these factors was the 1948 decline in farm income. Another was Congress' refusal to vote funds for expanding storage capacity for Commodity Credit Corporation goods, thus threatening farmers with being forced to sell their product at prices below the loan level. Still a third was a long-drawn-out Congressional investigation of whether the Capper-Volstead income tax exemption for farm cooperatives should or should not be repealed. No legislation ensued from this investigation, but even the raising of this issue was not a good campaign plank in middlewestern states—the citadel of agricultural cooperation.

However, the most important factor influencing western farm votes was unquestionably the agricultural legislation passed in 1948. Its key element was the concept of "flexible" price supports; between a "floor" of 50 per cent of parity and a "ceiling" of 90 per cent, actual support levels were to vary inversely with the size of the "surplus." Logical enough as a long-range program looking toward the restoration of an economy without farm price supports, this enactment was much less appropriate as a short-range solution to farmer distress. What it meant was that the farmer most in need of help would in fact receive the least assistance. Put differently, the medicine may have been accurately prescribed but it was hardly reasonable to expect the patient to take it except under the strongest kind of pressure.

Perhaps one other factor, one having less to do with the farm problem and a somewhat closer connection with the "Fair Deal" program, was also important in determining the election results of November, 1948. When Congress repeatedly refused to give the President controls with which to fight inflation (apparently too many people were enjoying it), Truman had elected to fight inflation with tools already at hand. One of these was antitrust prosecutions directed against concerns whose products loomed large in the cost of living. The idea for a new antimonopoly campaign was probably first suggested by the successful termination of several antitrust actions which had grown out of Temporary National Economic Committee days. Furthermore, the inflation argument was certainly used in part to bolster a new attack on "big business" desired on other grounds (as witness, for example, the suit against A & P—probably the lowest price grocery distributor in the country). At any rate the President did "fight" inflation by means of a device which can always be counted upon to arouse a great deal of popular support, and this combination of forces brought about the most intense antitrust campaign ever waged in the United States—as well as helping to elect Harry Truman to a four-year term as President in his own right.

These interrelationships between inflation, antitrust prosecutions, and a presidential campaign appear highly ironical in historical perspective. In the first place, a long-range antitrust program is scarcely an appropriate weapon against a short-range problem such as inflation. In the second place, the history of antitrust movements in this country did not portend success for the new assault, and the mixture of an anti-inflation motive with the usual purposes added nothing to its effectiveness. (For example, the suit against A & P ended more than four years later in what can only be described as a humiliating defeat for the government.) In the third place, statistics now show conclusively that when the election was held in November, 1948, inflation had already run its course. And most ironical of all, it is probable that a Republican tax reduction measure passed over Truman's third veto was a greater contribution to economic stability than Democratic anti-inflation actions. Thus Truman's popular vote consisted in part of expressions of public approval of an antitrust endeavor which neither checked inflation nor altered the structure of industry, and of a tax stand which if not overridden would have made more difficult the nation's transition from inflation to deflation.

A Fresh Look at Basic Issues. The recession now setting in was not severe, unemployment at no point reaching the five million mark. For this several factors were responsible, in addition to the 1948 tax reduction.

TABLE 133. AN ABRUPT REVERSAL

Month and Year	Industrial Production *	Prices ‡ Wholesale Farm	Prices ‡ Wholesale Other †	Prices ‡ Consumer	Factory Weekly Earnings ‡	Unemployment **
November, 1948	100	100	100	100	100	100
October, 1949	80	82	94	98	99	195

* Federal Reserve Board.
† Other than farm products and foods.
‡ Department of Labor.
** Department of Commerce.

First, the government's postwar budget surplus turned into a deficit, one item helping to account for this change being the expansion of aid to Europe. Thus it turned out that, far from being inflationary, the European Recovery Program except for its first few months of life was actually antideflationary. Second, the wartime backlog of demand was as yet far from satisfied in such important areas as housing and automobiles.

However, although the recession was not sharp, it did provide for a time a very different environment within which to carve out policy decisions. In the field of foreign economic relations, for example, early 1949 was not a propitious time to launch a "bold, new program" (President Truman's famous "Point Four") designed to make America's industrial "know-how" available to underdeveloped areas so that backward people could raise their standard of living. Although it was sound enough to argue that such a program might make these areas less susceptible to communist propaganda, and at the same time broaden the foundation beneath the multilateralism this nation was seeking to build, businessmen and workers in the throes of the first economic discomfort in a decade were understandably not enthusiastic.

In another way, too, recession was a threat to the dream of multilateral trade. Imports which had been broadly tolerated when demand exceeded supply became frustrating in the extreme as business activity began to recede from postwar peaks. Manufacturers by the score sought to take advantage of the "escape" and "peril-point" provisions of the reciprocal trade renewal passed the year before. Still worse, by mid-1949 another international conference was under way in Annecy, France, to broaden the trade barrier reductions agreed to at Geneva. New agreements were to be made between nations already a party to the agreement, and in addition ten more nations were to participate for the first time. If "escape" and "peril-point" pressures here had been taken seriously, America's influence at Annecy would have been virtually destroyed, a development which would in turn have ended for the foreseeable future the struggle for multilateralism.

The administration in Washington moved to meet this crisis with great vigor. By means of a new reciprocal trade extension measure, the most restrictive features of the earlier law were repealed and the negotiations at Annecy brought to a satisfactory conclusion. Congress was in the process of approving a Mutual Defense Assistance Act formalizing this country's

Table 134. Reconstructing Europe

Year	Export Surplus	Foreign-Aid Programs	"Marshall Plan" Aid
		(Billions of dollars)	
1947	11.5	5.8	–
1948	6.7	5.1	1.9
1949	6.4	6.0	4.2
1950	2.3	4.3	2.9

Source: Department of Commerce.

participation in "Atlantic Community" defense preparations under the terms of the "Atlantic Pact." To approve this relationship while simultaneously scuttling the Annecy Conference did not seem appropriate. Nor did it seem appropriate to reverse postwar trade policies just as "Marshall Plan" expenditures were reaching their peak—even though some of the imports now threatening the American economy were produced in plants built with "Marshall Plan" funds.

The recession also altered the environment within which domestic decisions were made in 1949. But while deflation was making foreign policy more difficult, it was making possible the first real progress on the "Fair Deal" front. The minimum wage was raised from forty to seventy-five cents per hour, ten million people were added to those already covered by social security legislation, and provision was made for a substantial expansion of government activity in the fields of low rent housing and slum clearance. Outside the field of government, moreover, 1949 was the peak of a similar process taking place around dozens of collective bargaining tables. Organized labor had long since assumed responsibility for on-the-job social security, as, for example, the miners' health and welfare fund. Increasingly as higher wages had become harder to get in the postwar period workers had turned their attention to "fringe benefits," including especially pensions of one sort or another. One of the outstanding events of this first postwar recession year was a dramatic steel strike fought out almost exclusively over a pension program for steel workers. With these developments—legislative and otherwise—there was confirmed a principle of American historical evolution which the "Fair Deal" had persistently ignored: reform, particularly of the sort requiring government intervention, is most apt to be popular in periods of business decline.

Even with the support of recession, however, President Truman did not have everything his own way. On two issues he was forced to accept arrangements far different from those he would have preferred. One of these involved farm policy; the other was most directly associated with John L. Lewis and bituminous coal.

By 1949 there was considerable sentiment, especially in farm circles, in favor of scrapping the flexible price supports enacted the previous summer. However, a policy of high-level supports together with government storage of "surplus" commodities was no political asset to an administration strongly supporting internationalism and in turn strongly supported by labor. From the standpoint of international relationships America's farm program was vulnerable both because it made protectionists out of otherwise free trade farmers by pegging the price of their product above the world price, and because it resulted in a scandalous spoilage or destruction of perishable foods for which there was inadequate domestic demand in the face of a need to make political allies out of peoples much less well off.

From the standpoint of the working classes it was an elementary economic fact that the burden of present policy fell most heavily on consumer-laborers.

To remedy these difficulties the Secretary of Agriculture presented to Congress the famous "Brannan Plan." This proposal suggested that farm products (particularly those which were perishable) be placed on the market to bring whatever they would, instead of being bought at a higher price to be put in storage at government expense, and that the farmer be paid the difference between the market price and whatever percentage of "parity" was decided upon. In this way consumer prices—labor's cost of living—would be lowered (at the expense of the general taxpayer), some farmers might be made more content with the reciprocal trade agreements program, and the United States would be less vulnerable internationally for wasting food in a hungry world.

Mr. Brannan's proposal came to almost nothing in 1949. Resistance from organized agriculture was too powerful. The basis on which this opposition ostensibly rested was the charge that the new plan would regiment the farmer to a somewhat greater extent, and there was an element of truth in this contention; a government paying farmers a direct subsidy rather than an indirect one by way of nonrecourse loans on actual goods might have to be more careful to make sure production was kept within bounds. However, it is easily possible that farmer resistance was at least in large part motivated by a different factor. The "Brannan Plan" proposed to limit the amount of money which could be received by any one farmer, with the result that the larger operators would be to a considerable extent cut off from the "public trough." By 1949 it was widely recognized that more than one-half of the government's agricultural expenditures went to less than 20 per cent of the nation's farmers.

It is interesting to speculate what might have happened to Brannan's suggestion if this proposal had not been included. Certainly it is true that the measure itself was not amended by dropping this provision and then passed. But perhaps the most interesting aspect of the "Brannan Plan's" legislative history was the lineup of agricultural forces with respect to it. The Farm Bureau, an organization speaking frankly for the larger operators, spearheaded the opposition, while the Farmer's Union, a group representing tenants, sharecroppers, and small farmers generally, supported the proposal. And while the immediate issue was whether a serious attempt was to be made to reduce the cost of this program and shift the incidence of its burden, there was also a more fundamental issue at stake. Large-scale agriculture was now visibly winning out in economic competition with small farmers, and there is surely no long-range future in a solution to the farm problem which rewards the inefficient farmer at the expense of his more efficient colleague.

With the failure of this new approach, Congress set about to enact a more orthodox measure. The law which was passed substantially weakened the flexible price-support policy promulgated the year before—and then postponed its effective date for wheat, cotton, corn, peanuts, and rice. At the same time this law also contained a forward looking step, a "modernized" parity formula based on the most recent ten years rather than the period prior to World War I, but here also the progress thus made was largely undone by postponing its application to wheat, cotton, corn, and peanuts (commodities disadvantaged by the new formula). As a result very little was actually achieved in 1949 relative to the nation's agricultural problem, except a drastic retrenchment of government support activity with respect to commodities such as potatoes and eggs where the program had become virtually a national scandal. Furthermore, the application of the new formula gave promise of bringing about in time a price support structure more consistent with consumer preferences, export demand, and production costs.

The problem in bituminous coal grew most directly out of that industry's "sickness." Production expansion during the war, including a marked advance in coal mining technology, was now being compelled to come to terms with the much smaller demand available under more normal circumstances. To cope with this problem, greatly accentuated by recession, Lewis had put his men on a three-day week during much of 1949 in order to distribute the available work more equitably. A laudable purpose in some respects, this policy had the great drawback of taking away much of the economic advantage of more efficient mines, thus complicating the long-run adjustment of the industry as it sought to maintain its position against oil and gas competitors.

TABLE 135. "SICKNESS" IN THE COAL INDUSTRY

	Bituminous coal				
Year	Production (Millions of tons)	Per Cent of Total Fuel Used (B.t.u. basis)	Tons per Man-Day	Employment (000's)	Hourly Earnings
1920	569	67.0	4.0	640	N. A.
1925	520	61.3	4.5	588	N. A.
1930	468	53.9	5.1	493	N. A.
1935	372	48.3	4.5	462	$0.75
1940	461	47.2	5.2	439	0.88
1945	578	45.9	5.8	383	1.24
1950	516	36.5	7.0	370	2.01

N.A. Not available.
Source: Bureau of Mines.

Early in 1950 this share-the-work program merged with an all-out coal strike. Taking advantage of the fact that the country's coal inventories had been kept low by the three-day week (and of course Lewis had had this in mind when the three-day policy was inaugurated), the miners acted to take advantage for perhaps the last time of the position they had won during the war. Once again economic strangulation was threatened, and once again prompt and decisive action by government seemed required. Herein lies the significance of this episode in American economic evolution. For when it was over, the President who had vetoed the Taft-Hartley Act had done more than any other single individual to assure that legislation a permanent place among the economy's basic institutions.

Immediately after the war President Truman had won a resounding victory over John L. Lewis by using an injunction, and indeed the success of this effort had no doubt contributed much to the writing of the "emergency" provisions of Taft-Hartley. Since then, however, Truman had called this law "bad, wrong-headed, vicious, and ineffective," and had done everything in his power to get it repealed. It was with much reluctance, therefore, that the President deemed it essential to stop this strike also by means of an injunction, that is, by invoking Taft-Hartley. Unfortunately for the stand he had consistently taken, the law did work. Early in March the miners went back to work, and the Taft-Hartley Act gained greatly in prestige in the process.

By early 1950 the economy had regained the prosperity which had faded away the year before. One factor in the promptness with which deflation disappeared was the overhanging international tension. Communist forces in China at long last succeeded in driving the Chinese Nationalists from power, and Russia had in this way gained a major ally in the "cold war." Here was even more reason for the nation to give its earnest attention to implementing the "Atlantic Pact." It was in a mood of utmost seriousness that the President called for billions for defense, and in this same mood the nation accepted the challenge thus thrown down. Even responsible talk about defense orders of this magnitude was enough to give the economy some lift.

There was, to be sure, no dramatic increase in arms output during the first half of 1950. But such expansion as there was could scarcely have been better timed. On June 25 the country was electrified by the grim news that North Korea had made war against South Korea. Acting quickly (if not impulsively) on the assumption that Russia was primarily responsible, the United States (in the name of the United Nations) went to the aid of South Korea.

QUESTIONS FOR DISCUSSION

1. What were the economic ramifications of the outbreak of "cold war"? What is the meaning of this term?
2. Why was more foreign aid necessary in the case of England than for any other country, even though England's prewar standard of living was the highest in all Europe?
3. Could a policy on wool have been worked out which would have satisfied producers in this country as well as foreign producers?
4. How did inflation in America contribute to the need for aid abroad?
5. Did the Taft-Hartley Act represent an advance in the nation's evolution toward a more satisfactory relationship between capital and labor?
6. Why did agriculture experience its primary postwar adjustment before the industrial segments of the economy?
7. If the farmer's problem is at base overproduction, would not this problem be improved if agricultural mechanization did not proceed so rapidly?
8. How was the "Marshall Plan" used to bolster sagging points in the economy? Was this its principal purpose?
9. What were the most important economic factors in Truman's re-election in 1948?
10. Would the "Brannan Plan" have been a desirable shift in agricultural policy? Were the policy declarations actually made in 1948 and 1949 sound?
11. In what ways do the "sicknesses" of the railroad, bituminous coal, and agricultural industries differ from one another?

Chapter 41

ANOTHER SEARCH FOR "NORMALCY"

1950 New burst of inflation.
"Red" China entered the war on the side of North Korea.
1951 "Great Debate" on foreign policy.
General MacArthur relieved.
Corruption and crime investigations.
Tension among the Western allies.
1952 Steel strike.
Dwight D. Eisenhower elected President.
1953 Conservative reaction in Washington.
End of the war in Korea.
Republicans chastised in end-of-year election contests.

A New War Effort. The Korean crisis (a "police action," as it was officially called) was never a very big affair, as wars go. No large number of men was required to do the actual fighting, and the government at no point took more than 15 per cent of the nation's output for war and defense purposes—as compared with more than double that percentage in the "Crusade for Freedom." It would have seemed that the powerful American economy could have taken an effort of this size in its stride without undue concern over the question of controls.

In actual fact the economic problem was by no means so easily resolved. For one thing the intensity of the effort required is much better understood in retrospect than when the enemy was pouring across the thirty-eighth parallel in Korea. Looking ahead to the situation as it might develop, American leaders had to think of the possibility that the war might spread; there were few in 1950 who were certain that World War III had not begun. Furthermore, this outbreak of actual fighting convinced the country that its defenses had been allowed to deteriorate far below the safety point—that our foreign policy had been made too exclusively dependent upon *economic* programs. As a result, defense output was stimulated far beyond what would have been dictated by consideration of the Korean crisis alone.

Nor was this the only reason the new war posed economic problems out of proportion with its own intensity. A sudden, sharp increase in the government's military spending—from an annual rate of $17 billion to $35 billion in less than twelve months—would have promptly communicated itself to the underlying economy in any event. Furthermore, there was on this occasion no large pool of idle factories and unemployed men to draw upon in meeting these expanding military needs. This meant at the very least that real income for citizens could not increase as in World War II; increased production would be limited essentially to gains in productivity, new additions to the supply of workers, and increases in the number of hours worked. It speaks volumes for the power of America's productive mechanism that with only a small increase in the labor force and only a slight increase in weekly hours per employee, the needed expansion in military production was accomplished without a *decline* in real disposable income per person.

TABLE 136. GUNS AND BUTTER

Year	Per Capita Disposable Income in 1952 Dollars
1929	$1,045
1939	1,055
1944	1,517
1947	1,375
1949	1,407
1950	1,484
1951	1,486
1952	1,497

Source: Department of Commerce.

It was against the background of this economic tug of war between the civilian and the defense economies (a contest made more acute by a consumer rush to convert liquid assets into goods war might make scarce—for example, sugar, tires, nylon hose, food freezers, and the like) that the nation was compelled to make basic decisions concerning wartime controls. As always there was the problem of keeping the materials needed for defense out of nonessential uses. Likewise, changes in the price level threatened the usual wartime maladjustments in the distribution of goods.

If logic had dictated the decisions made, the underlying uncertainty of the over-all international situation would have suggested the prompt enactment of comprehensive controls. Indeed, by late August powers had been placed in the President's hands which could have been converted into an effective control program—if the will had been present. But the public acceptance needed for the implementation of such a program was not forthcoming. Korea was far away, and the limited character of the conflict as it dragged inconclusively on for a period of three years made it less real to the average citizen. In the dynamics of the actual situation, however, the process was the familiar one of legislating price ceilings but failing to manage farmer, labor, and business pressures sufficiently to make these ceilings operative. The result was that the only real accomplishments were an increase in taxes, a stiffening of monetary and credit controls, and an administrative organization which effectively regulated the flow of defense materials.

No doubt if the crisis had lasted longer than it did, or if the war itself had spread (as indeed it threatened to do when "Red" China entered the war late in 1950), the nation would have risen to the occasion. Such had been the history of previous American war efforts. Moreover, it cannot be said that the "decision" *not* to control inflation was a particularly unfortunate one. Although wages and prices did edge upward throughout the

TABLE 137. INFLATION RETURNS WITH A RUSH

Month and Year	Industrial Production *	Prices ‡			Factory Weekly Earnings ‡	Unemployment **
		Wholesale				
		Farm	Other †	Consumer		
June, 1950	100	100	100	100	100	100
March, 1951	112	125	115	108	118	63

* Federal Reserve Board.
† Other than farm products and foods.
‡ Department of Labor.
** Department of Commerce.

entire period of fighting, the worst of the inflationary threat was clearly over in less than a year. By that time the military situation was stabilized, the nation's defenses were more nearly equal to the needs of a world neither at war nor at peace, and a series of long-drawn-out truce negotiations had begun. With these developments pressure for more serious control programs rapidly dwindled away.

Internationalism Challenged. If the Korean crisis was relatively minor from a purely economic standpoint, the same cannot be said of other aspects of its impact on the nation. Without exaggeration it can be suggested that this event marked the beginning of the end of the America which had emerged from World War II desirous of rebuilding the world along democratic, internationalist lines. Disappointed and disillusioned after five years of heavy expense and high frustration, Americans were visibly turning away from these earlier dreams. It was as if the marching of soldier feet in Korea had pulled down the curtain on a scene now almost played out.

The new note was first prominently sounded on December 20, 1950, when former President Herbert Hoover delivered a major address on United States' foreign policy. Most directly at issue was the question of whether this nation should send troops to Europe as a part of its own collective security program. In a determined and challenging way Hoover asserted that the military interests of the United States did not extend beyond the western hemisphere. While we had made a mistake, he maintained, in committing troops to Asia, we should not compound this error by committing more men to Europe.

Such sentiments expressed a year or two earlier might have been dismissed as the reactionary view of an elder statesman who had outlived his usefulness. There had been other protests against postwar internationalism, but always they had been overwhelmed by the rising tide of newly found idealism. On this occasion, however, there were significant differences. In the first place, Hoover's speech aroused a great deal of enthusiastic response; these views, coinciding as they did with the entry of China into the war and thus involving us in what might easily have become a fight to the finish within the vast borders of Asia, could scarcely help being popular. In the second place, these views were soon echoed by Senator Robert A. Taft of Ohio—the acknowledged leader of Washington Republicans. Going so far as to say that the President had usurped legislative authority by deciding on his own that America (the United Nations) should make a stand in Korea, he asserted that the country's first need was to defend America—not Asia or Europe. It was symbolic of the change taking place in America that a Republican Congress under Senator Taft's leadership had passed the basic "Marshall Plan" legislation, and that Hoover himself as head of a special presidential commission had taken a strong stand on the importance to the United States of an economically strong Germany and Europe.

President Truman vigorously answered these criticisms in his State of the Union message on January 8, 1951. Defiantly branding opponents of the administration's foreign policy as "appeasers," he insisted that the defense of Europe *was* the defense of the United States just as intervention in Korea was required in the best interest of this country. With this rejoinder the "Great Debate on Foreign Policy" began, a debate which was to be a fixed feature of the American scene for some time.

Other evidences of this new sentiment also appeared as 1951 advanced. When President Truman requested Congress to appropriate funds to send wheat to an India ravaged by famine, Congress delayed action for six weeks—for no other reason than that political differences were arising between India and the United States. Likewise, the indecisiveness of the situation in Korea was so frustrating to an America preferring to finish unpleasant military encounters quickly that General Douglas MacArthur, commander of United Nations forces in Korea, was able to secure a considerable backing when he recommended striking at the source of China's war-making strength on the mainland—although a majority of Americans, and especially America's European allies, opposed this move on the ground that it might convert a limited conflict into a general war.

To be sure, American foreign policy did not change abruptly. In fact little came of this rebellion in 1951. Congress approved the sending of troops to Europe, wheat was sent to India, and public opinion strongly supported the President when he relieved General MacArthur of his command. But there was no mistaking what was happening; general agreement on foreign policy (bipartisanship, as it was termed) was rapidly disintegrating.

The "Fair Deal" Challenged. The most important corollary of American disillusionment in international affairs was a mounting pressure on the administration in Washington. And since the war made it necessary to

TABLE 138. "POLICE ACTION" IN KOREA

Year	Industrial Production *	Prices ‡ Wholesale Farm (1947-1949 = 100)	Prices ‡ Wholesale Other †	Prices ‡ Consumer	Factory Weekly Earnings ‡	Unemployment ** (000's)
1949	97	92.8	101.3	101.8	$54.92	3,395
1950	112	97.5	105.0	102.8	59.33	3,142
1951	120	113.4	115.9	111.0	64.71	1,879
1952	124	107.0	113.2	113.5	67.97	1,673
1953	134	97.0	114.0	114.4	70.57	1,523

* Federal Reserve Board.
† Other than farm products and foods.
‡ Department of Labor.
** Department of Commerce.

deal gently with foreign policy, this pressure primarily took the form of attacks on the domestic front. Especially as the war news improved and the fear of Russian intervention diminished was criticism heaped upon the administration. There was of course exaggeration in the charges made, and much of the antagonism expressed was not motivated by the specific grievances complained of. Furthermore, the President went out of his way to invite a "politics as usual" attitude despite the war; for example, he utilized the occasion of his 1951 budget message to request again a national health insurance program, and to press once more for federal legislation abolishing discrimination against Negroes in employment.

One of the focal points of the pressure on the "Fair Deal" in early 1951, and one of the most significant developments of the entire year, was the discovery of and the publicity given to corruption in government by a (Democratic) Congressional investigating committee. The attention of the public concentrated primarily upon the Reconstruction Finance Corporation and its loan policies (together with irregularities in the Bureau of Internal Revenue), the most dramatic fact reported being the possession of a mink coat by the White House secretary-wife of one of the Corporation's young lawyers. As a result of this inquiry the five-man board governing this agency was replaced by a single administrator, although neither this step nor any other tangible outcome of the corruption investigation could be considered fundamental.

Along with this development, organized labor staged a major revolt against the government agencies in charge of the defense program. Although wages were roughly keeping pace with cost-of-living increases, and

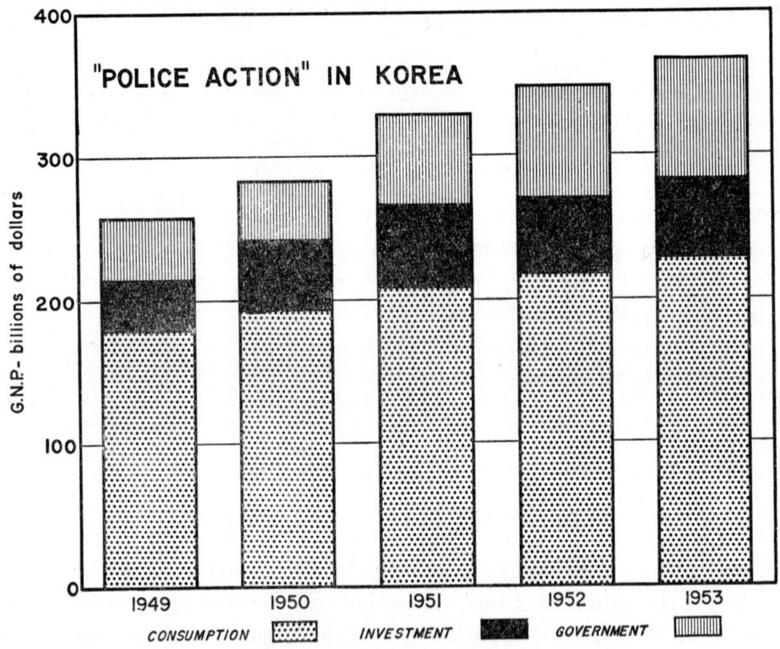

FIGURE 19. National Income Data.

although the President at no time stood firmly against an important labor demand, the worker group felt that its prestige had been slighted by the small voice labor leaders were given in mobilization decisions. For approximately two months labor representatives boycotted these agencies. Little was gained by labor from this action; Mobilization Director Charles

E. Wilson had spent a long, successful life as a business executive (resigning as head of General Electric to take on the defense administration responsibility), and he was determined to keep the basic decisions in his own hands—to run the war effort in a "business-like" way despite the political environment in Washington. Whether this episode was prejudicial to the defense economy as labor's opponents claimed, or whether labor's position was enhanced as labor proponents preferred to believe, can only be conjectured. It is certain, however, that this action in the midst of a serious war effort, together with the fact that even with presidential support labor achieved so little, clearly evidenced the changing climate of public opinion inside the United States.

Still a third domestic issue shared with the war the spotlight of attention during the first half of 1951, and it too demonstrated the rising tide of internal dissatisfaction. For some time a central consideration in Treasury policy had been keeping the rate of interest on the nation's huge debt as low as possible. Following such a policy, however, had required the close cooperation of the central bank; the banking system had to make the supply of money "easy." In other words, the Treasury approach demanded that the Federal Reserve System "surrender" much of its legal power to "tighten" the money market when in its judgment such action was called for. No serious question had been raised about this relationship during World War II, for a money market "easy" enough to allow the government to borrow needed funds was then an unquestioned necessity. Since the war, on the other hand, there had been a steady and visible growth of opinion favoring a return by the Federal Reserve System to something approaching its earlier independence.

Those holding to this view presented themselves to the public as believers in "honest" money—as proponents of tighter inflation control for the benefit of consumers. More fundamentally, however, certain other factors were involved. With the exception of the brief recession period, the rate of interest had steadily risen since the end of the war. The Treasury—the nation's most prominent debtor—while perhaps not happy about this development, had at least bowed to the necessities of the situation sufficiently to permit it. Creditors throughout the country, people with money to invest, of course encouraged this increase in rates. Invested funds would thereby earn higher dollar returns, and if inflation were to some extent checked at the same time, these dollars would even be more valuable.

In short, this issue was essentially the problem of creditors versus debtors which has been a fixed feature of American economic relationships for three centuries, although in a strikingly modern form. As always before, moreover, this new struggle was a sharp one—so sharp in fact that it was commonly referred to as a "feud" between Treasury and Federal

TABLE 139. THE LOW COST OF MONEY

Year	Yield on Corporate Aaa Bonds
	(Per cent per annum)
1929	4.73
1939	3.01
1946	2.53
1947	2.61
1948	2.82
1949	2.66
1950	2.62
1951	2.86
1952	2.96
1953	3.20

Source: *Moody's Investor's Service.*

Reserve officials. The victory, such as it was, went to the Federal Reserve System; the "Fed" stopped supporting government bonds *above* par, and it was understood that gradually Federal Reserve supports would be entirely withdrawn.

Internationalism Threatened. While tempers were rising over domestic issues, and while numerous interests were taking advantage of the situation to snipe at the administration, events were moving with uncomfortable swiftness on the international front. In line with a policy which by now had become firmly entrenched, the United States was currently taking a leading role in yet a third great international effort to reduce trade barriers. Several nations participated in these deliberations (at Torquay, England) for the first time, the most notable being West Germany, and once again tariffs were reciprocally reduced on a wide scale. As an indication of the enthusiasm with which the United States entered into the spirit of this series of conferences, it is estimated that between Smoot-Hawley and the period following Torquay the average level of tariffs imposed by this country fell from almost 50 per cent to less than 15.[1]

Within the context of this new achievement and the deterioration of internationalist sentiment in America, the reciprocal trade agreements program came up for renewal once more. The resulting legislation served

[1] There is no satisfactory measure of the level of a nation's tariff barriers. The figures given here are those usually quoted—based on the number of dollars paid in duty relative to the dollar value of all dutiable goods imported. But because the higher the duty the fewer are the imports which can afford to pay it, this measure is apt to contain a large and unknown statistical error. (In addition, rising prices reduce the *rates* of duty where specific rather than *ad valorem* levies are used.) Since, however, this error can be assumed to be smaller where rates are lower, it is obvious that the change in this country's tariff policy under the "New" and "Fair Deals" was substantial.

decisive notice on our foreign friends that the tariff reduction phase of this country's postwar foreign policy was about over. Although there was no way to hold Republicans responsible for this new outbreak of protectionism, the renewal measure enacted was very nearly identical with the crippling extension voted by the Eightieth Congress three years before. And, as if to accent this lesson, it was by now understood that the United States would *not* join the International Trade Organization which had earlier been considered one of the pillars on which our foreign policy was to rest.

This suggestion of a changing economic relationship between the United States and her allies was given additional point even before 1951 was over. American trade liberalization would have been less important to Europe if the shortage of dollars had not continued to be so serious. This situation, to be sure, had improved considerably with the outbreak of a new war as this country's defense production program got under way. American exports were reduced while import needs greatly increased, and to such an extent were trade balances affected that gold and dollar credits in the hands of foreigners increased by some $4 billion. For a time there was even talk of revaluing certain foreign currencies upward to take fuller advantage of this development.

TABLE 140. THE DOLLAR SHORTAGE CONTINUES

Item	1949	1950	1951
		(Billions of dollars)	
Total exports	16.0	14.4	20.2
Total imports	9.6	12.1	15.1
Export surplus	6.4	2.3	5.2
Foreign aid programs	6.0	4.3	4.7
Accumulation (+) or loss (−) of dollar assets by foreign nations	− 0.1	+ 3.6	+ 0.4

Source: Department of Commerce.

Unfortunately, this phase of the mobilization effort was short-lived. As the edge wore off the struggle by this country to make up for the years during which our defenses had been neglected, and as the American wholesale price level rose by 15 per cent, the dollar shortage returned with a vengeance. In 1951 American exports reached the highest level ever attained.

If the crippling of this country's reciprocal trade program was a blow to European colleagues, the return to chronic maladjustment in payments balances was no less than a tragedy. By this time the United States had expended more than $26 billion trying to correct this imbalance—trying to build a world in which multilateral trade would once again become general. The apparent failure of this enterprise, particularly after so great a sacrifice, was reason enough for the view of an increasing number of Americans that "operation rathole" should be brought to an end. In other words, because the securing of additional dollar credits might now be more difficult, the dollar shortage was to that extent more serious than it had yet been.

It is not surprising in these circumstances that Britain's Labour party was torn apart in 1951 over this question. Superficially the issue was the administration's budget—the fact that too many resources were being set aside for defense and too few for the expansion of social services. Behind this issue, however, there lurked a deep rift in foreign policy and a source of much future tension between the United States and England. The dissident wing of the party in power in Britain accused the United States of embarking on her own defense program more rapidly than necessary, with the result that inflation and defense expenditures were crowding too many social services out of the British budget. Whether or not these accusations are affirmed by the perspective of history, however, there was a great deal more than mere politics in them. On the one hand, the United States implicitly conceded that they contained much truth by deciding on two different occasions to "stretch out" her defense program—to extend it over a longer period of time. On the other hand, a nation like England which lives by importing crude goods and exporting processed ones is especially disadvantaged by inflation because crude goods invariably rise in price more rapidly than finished goods.

Not only were Europeans accumulating complaints against the United States, but a reverse process was also taking place. Here, too, the focal point was trade relationships. If Europe could not balance her payments with this country, and if the United States ceased to finance the imbalance, Europe would be forced to take her trade elsewhere. Of course, there was no other place to take this trade except behind the "iron curtain," and of course a United States to whom international trade was much less important than to Europe would not be happy to see her allies "trading with the enemy." This problem, to be sure, was not yet acute. But to the discerning eye it was apparent that one day soon it might be. When that time came, economic tension between the western allies could become a grave liability to the harmony needed to wage "cold war" effectively with an implacable and "united" East.

The "Fair Deal" Replaced. In trouble both at home and abroad, it was a bruised and battered administration that turned in 1952 to the task of recapturing the public good will so rapidly evaporating. It was thus most discouraging that the new year was ushered in by one of the most tangled labor crises in the country's history. Steel workers were anxious to secure an increase in wages, and when it seemed doubtful that they would receive as large an increase as they desired they threatened to strike—the Korean conflict notwithstanding.

To a degree the administration was responsible for the fact that this situation became as difficult as it did. The steel industry appeared willing enough to concede labor's demands. But the government was still fighting a rearguard action against inflation, and to allow these companies to increase prices sufficiently to compensate for the wage increase would have meant an abrogation of the "formula" for price determination then in use. Since the companies refused to award the full wage increase without full price compensation, a shutdown of the industry seemed inevitable.

The strike was originally scheduled to start on New Year's Day. Yielding to a presidential plea, however, labor postponed the walkout in order that negotiations might continue a little longer. Taking advantage of this breathing spell, the government sought to induce the industry to accept a smaller price increase than industry leaders felt to be justified, while appearing to sanction without question a wage increase which was undoubtedly as inflationary as the price demand. The government carried this phase of its campaign even to the point of a nationwide speech by the President denouncing the steel companies for their unpatriotic, selfish stubbornness, and so heated did the controversy become that Mobilization Director Wilson resigned in protest against the administration's stand.

By April 8 negotiations had broken down and an industry-wide walkout began. The President could have gained an eighty-day stay under the Taft-Hartley Act, but this procedure would have given this "wrong-headed" measure even more prestige and Mr. Truman was reluctant to be responsible for such a result. In answer to those who urged him to invoke the law he argued that the initial postponement was the equivalent of a Taft-Hartley injunction, and that therefore a legal injunction in addition would be unfair. Instead the President shocked the nation by seizing the steel industry in the name of the government.

Never before had a president taken such a step without specific legislative sanction. The authority claimed for the action was a general reference to the American Constitution, although few people possessed imagination enough to stretch the meaning of that document so far. Of course the steel companies challenged the President, and the courts upheld the companies' view that the President had gone too far. By early June the legal battle was concluded in the Supreme Court Building in Washington, and the steelworkers once more left their jobs. Fifty-five days later (after the longest strike in the industry's history), a settlement was reached—on what were virtually the industry's original terms.

When the Supreme Court in June concurred in the judgment of many that the President had assumed powers not rightfully his, another presidential campaign was just getting under way, and the entire affair was a most unfortunate prelude to a request for a vote of confidence. Equally unfortunate was the fact that the farmer's parity ratio was again moving downward. And this time there was no Republican Congress to which responsibility could be shrewdly shifted.

Again there was nothing strange in what was happening to farm prices. Invariably during inflation the farmer's share of the consumer's dollar increases, and just as invariably postinflation readjustments bring this proportion to a lower level. Both processes are a simple function of the inelasticities of demand for and supply of agricultural products. Thus it was that during the recent inflation farmers had fared especially well, and thus it was also that they were again the first major group to feel the pain of readjustment. Small wonder that the farm economy was a matter of grave concern to the administration as it embarked upon a major political test.

TABLE 141. FEAST AND FAMINE

Period	Parity Ratio (1910-1914 = 100)
June, 1950	97
February, 1951	113
June, 1951	107
January, 1952	105
June, 1952	102
November, 1952	99

Source: Department of Agriculture.

It was unthinkable, of course, that farm prices would be guaranteed at wartime levels. Some informed people argued that even 90 per cent guarantees were preventing farmers as a group from making the occupational shifts essential to a long-range solution to America's farm problem. Others doubted that this was an important factor, arguing that the necessary shifts were inhibited rather by the fixed-cost nature of the industry, the difficulty of making the change in "way of life" involved in moving from farm to city, the farmer's poor training for other kinds of work together with his lack of the capital and alternative job information prerequisite to making such a move, and the high rural birth rate. Wherever the truth lay in this debate, it was certain that supports *above parity* would interfere with fundamental adjustments.

The administration's answer to the unwelcome recurrence of this chronic problem was an only-to-be-expected compromise. Once more the effective date for applying flexible price supports to wheat, cotton, corn, peanuts, and rice was postponed, and once more the effective date for beginning the use of "modernized" parity for cotton, wheat, corn, and peanuts was put off. Whether this step did in fact help a discredited administration retrieve its fortunes cannot be determined. Certainly, however, as the sequel was to show a few months later, it did not help enough.

Neither did the two most important assets the Democrats were able to exploit. The first of these was general business conditions ("you never had it so good"). Industrial production had wavered a little in the second quarter of the year, and the spreading strangulation of the steel strike had pushed the index down still further. However, the rebound from this artificial depression then carried output to the highest level since World War II just as the campaign was reaching its most intense stage. The second asset was the official endorsement of the Democratic candidate by both of the major labor organizations, although when the chips were down on election day many individual workers did not follow through.

TABLE 142. THE CREST OF THE BOOM

Period	Industrial Production (1947-1949 = 100)
June, 1950	113
April, 1951	123
October, 1951	119
February, 1952	121
May, 1952	119
July, 1952	115
November, 1952	133

Source: Federal Reserve Board.

The election when it came was in its way as surprising as the one four years before. It was widely expected, of course, that the Republicans would win, although if the victory had gone to the Democrats the nation would not have been as astonished as on the earlier occasion. By repudiating Mr. Truman and projecting onto the national scene a new, vigorous, and appealing personality, Adlai Stevenson of Illinois, the ruling party regained much lost status. The fact was, however, that the Democrats lost while the Republicans did not win. General Dwight D. Eisenhower, a national hero from World War II days, won a tremendous electoral victory as the Republican candidate for the presidency. But in both Houses of Congress, where the nation's basic decisions for the next few years would be made, the two parties were virtually stalemated. At the same time, though, there could be no mistaking the essential fact that the "Fair Deal" was no more.

New Directions. What did it mean? What were the people saying, through the medium of their democracy, in these paradoxical election results? This was the question Republicans pondered as they prepared to present their program of action. The reason for the difficulty was that the outcome was capable of two quite different interpretations.

On one side it could be argued that the United States had taken the wrong turning twenty years before—that the American people had come to look upon the earlier decision in favor of the trend toward big government (the "welfare state" or "creeping socialism," as it was called by political orators) as a mistake. Thus, talk of cutting government expenditures, reducing taxes, stopping the rise of the national debt, and the like, had seemed to strike a responsive note during the campaign. Moreover, the people had repeatedly turned thumbs down on "Fair Deal" proposals to expand the government's responsibilities. All in all it seemed reasonable to conclude that Americans now wanted the role of the federal government in the nation's life to be materially restricted.

On the other side, however, it could be argued that no such meaning was to be found in what had happened. An industrial society, so this view insisted, more and more creates situations in which individuals and groups feel that government action is desirable. It follows that there can be no reversal of history with respect to this evolution, and indeed a glance at other industrialized areas throughout the world would seem to provide abundant evidence on this point. Therefore what the people were saying might well have been some combination of three other things: First, we no longer have confidence in our leaders in Washington; second, while we do not wish to reverse history as far as the role of the federal government is concerned, neither do we want to accelerate it; third, the "Fair Deal" has become too exclusive a spokesman for labor interests. On this interpretation the historical trend was to continue—under different management.

Only time could tell which of these interpretations was correct, but it was apparent at once which one was to be accepted by the Republicans. They set about without delay to trim "big government" down to size—to restore the balance supposed to have been lost because security had been emphasized at the expense of freedom—and to make the United States once again a haven for free enterprise and individual initiative. At the same time it was also evident that the steps to be taken would not be philanthropically motivated. The tip-off here was an unguarded statement by General Motors president Wilson when he was being interviewed by a Congressional committee on the question of whether or not he should dispose of some $2½ million worth of General Motors stock before being sworn in as Defense Secretary. Said he, "I have always operated under the assumption that what was good for General Motors was good for the country." (In fairness it must be added that Mr. Wilson also acknowledged the converse of this statement to be true.)

Of course, miracles were not expected, and certainly none were performed. At the same time, however, the list of accomplishments during the first six months of the new administration was impressive. Most of the price controls imposed during the defense build-up were summarily abandoned—although the majority of these items were already moving out of a seller's market anyway. The federal government's ownership of oil lands off the coast of the United States (off Texas, Louisiana, and California) was transferred to the states. Plans were advanced to dispose of the wartime synthetic rubber plants to private operators, and to transfer the government-owned Inland Waterways Corporation (a water and railroad transportation operation on the Mississippi and Warrior Rivers inherited from World War I days) to private hands. After yeoman service in depression and war, the great Reconstruction Finance Corporation was abolished; to fill the vacuum thus created there was authorized a Small Business Administration to loan money to and generally promote small business operations. Federal government activity in the home building field was sharply curtailed. The Director of the National Bureau of Standards was fired (later reinstated) because the Bureau insisted on holding to its findings that a certain chemical compound added to a battery would not increase its service life. (The implication here was apparently that if the customer bought the product, the findings of science with respect to its usefulness were irrelevant.) In the power field the government reduced appropriations for federal power projects, limited the operations of the Rural Electrification Administration and the Tennessee Valley Authority, and set about reversing the government policy of by-passing private utility companies by selling power direct to large users. Appointments to government agencies dealing with business were made with a view to applying a greatly broadened "rule of reason."

Matters such as these were attended to quickly and with a minimum of public reaction. Other issues were more fundamental in character, and hence the going was more difficult. For example, no real progress in the direction of limiting big government could be claimed until the budget was reduced and the sprawling bureaucracy whittled down. But budget cuts and reductions in personnel typically meant eliminating services on which citizens had come to depend, and such economies invariably met with resistance. Still worse, the administration had promised tax reductions. Inevitably under these circumstances controversies arose among the leaders themselves as to how this conflict of objectives was to be reconciled.

The most intense of these was the President's determined fight to extend the excess profits tax for six months beyond its June 30 expiration date, not because it was thought to be a good tax (virtually everyone in fact conceded that its discrimination against young concerns and industries made it a bad one) but solely because the government could ill afford to give up the revenue. The problem even then was not merely that in six months this levy would bring in $800 million. In addition it would probably have been politically impossible to allow this tax to die without simultaneously reducing individual income taxes. Of lesser importance was a Congressional move to eliminate the excise tax on theater admissions to provide relief for this industry against the devastating competition of television. In both of

TABLE 143. ECONOMIC REVOLUTION IN THE HOME

Year	Television Sets	Air Conditioning Units	Clothes Dryers	Food Freezers
	(Production in thousands of units)			
1946	6	30	58	210
1950	7,464	195	319	890
1953	7,250	1,075	684	1,150

Source: Council of Economic Advisers, *Economic Report of the President*, January, 1954, p. 12.

these instances the President successfully stood against the lower tax level, but despite these precautions an embarrassed Washington leadership was by mid-year asking Congress to raise the debt limit.

An even more difficult task was that of restoring the nation to an "honest money" basis ("hard money" as it was called until this terminology became so associated in the public mind with "hard-to-get-money" as to become a political liability). At first progress was amazingly rapid. In quick succession the rediscount rate was increased, reserve requirements were raised, and the Treasury floated a long-term bond issue carrying the highest rate in many years. Unfortunately, however, this "sound money" policy ran into the roughest sort of weather—partly because it coincided with and partly because it helped bring about the tightest money market in more than twenty years. The large group of debtors vigorously protested, and this group included a substantial segment of the business community. Even more decisive was the close relationship still existing between the Treasury and Federal Reserve despite the "full accord" reached two years earlier and intended to presage Federal Reserve independence. Thus as the money supply grew tighter the Treasury was first forced to refund $5 billion on a short-term basis rather than the long-term basis it would have preferred, and then the Federal Reserve Board was forced to lower reserve requirements and broaden its open market operations in order that refinancing could proceed at all. A complex government bond market, it seemed, could not suddenly support itself on legs atrophied from years of being sheltered by the banking system. Moreover, it remained to be seen whether so huge a government debt structure could be carried by the private market even after the atrophy had been corrected—especially as long as a sizable fraction of the debt was scheduled to mature over the next twelve months. Perhaps a modern central bank cannot really be "independent."

Aid Versus Trade. In spite of the difficulties associated with taxation and money, if the new administration had encountered no problems more troublesome than these it would have been happy indeed. Unfortunately, however, it was forced to give much attention to three other issues, each of which created controversies so acute that no definitive action on them was possible in 1953. Nor does this failure to act imply criticism of the country's new leaders. All these issues had long been chronic trouble spots, and it was therefore not to be expected that they would be readily resolved.

One of these problems was the question of international economic affairs where interallied relationships were deteriorating in an alarming fashion. Quite in conformity with what foreign nations had lately come to expect, President Eisenhower reduced his predecessor's foreign-aid budget—only to find himself fighting unsuccessfully to prevent further reductions by Congress. At the same time, too, Congress began seriously to discuss the possibility of terminating the entire mutual security program in the very near future, while the President on his own shut off further Export-Import Bank loans—purely as an economy measure. Surely there could be no mistaking these announcements to the effect that American aid was not limitless either in time or in amount.

TABLE 144. "OPERATION RATHOLE"?

Year	Per Cent of Exports Paid for with Foreign Aid
1946	56
1947	41
1948	45
1949	51
1950	46
1951	33

Source: Department of Commerce.

As these developments put their inevitable strain on the bonds holding the Western world together, Europeans began approaching their economic relationships with this country somewhat differently. Challenging America to be a "good creditor," they invented the slogan of "trade not aid," the idea being that a lowering of trade barriers here would make it possible for other countries to *earn* dollars instead of receiving them as gifts. "Liberals" in America, including an Eisenhower-Dewey wing within the Republican party, promptly made a battle cry out of this slogan in the fight against an increasingly powerful American protectionism—increasingly powerful despite the fact that many business leaders (those representing "heavy" industries such as automobiles in which America's comparative advantage in foreign trade was greatest) were now standing with the "liberals" on this issue.

What were the results? Did the United States elect to help others earn the dollars they needed? Hardly. Two protectionists were added to the Tariff Commission, and a measure was narrowly defeated which would have destroyed the bipartisan makeup of this agency. The Reciprocal Trade Agreements Act was renewed for one year, although this was achieved only after the Administration had promised not to use the law as a basis for negotiating tariff reductions in that period. "Point Four" funds were cut to the point where for the moment nothing at all could be accomplished toward helping backward regions industrialize. With private investment abroad severely limited by disturbed political conditions, this was an especially disastrous blow to the country's postwar foreign policy. Preference continued to be given to domestic producers in government procurement even at a substantial cost to the Treasury, and import quotas on and export subsidies for agricultural products continued to be utilized. The only step taken which could be classified as a concession to trade liberalization was a measure to simplify customs procedures.

It would be a mistake to suppose that this response to "trade not aid" is to be explained solely in terms of American protectionism. In addition, scholars were beginning to agree that even completely free trade would not eliminate the dollar shortage—some even insisting that this country's high-capital economy based upon intensive research and rapid technological change would create a chronic trade maladjustment for the foreseeable future. After all, ever since the beginning of the 1920's the United States had been supplying foreigners with dollars which were never repaid (or buying their gold at fancy prices for storage at Fort Knox, which amounted to much the same thing). Men are certainly not to be blamed for being unenthusiastic about a trade policy program which would injure American businesses and labor without solving the problem at which it was aimed. No more were men to be censured for remembering that this country already had lower tariff barriers than any other major nation. The multilateral ideal for which this country had been working so intensively was simply not being achieved.

But, whatever the cause or causes, it was apparent that America's new policy was to be "neither trade nor aid," and that it was to have far-reaching consequences. In these circumstances the matter of East-West trade could not help rising to major proportions (and indeed in 1953 it was a bitter issue—especially between Clement Attlee of England and Senator McCarthy of Wisconsin). By now, in fact, this same issue was arising between a trade-hungry, overpopulated Japan and her erstwhile conqueror. Here was an excellent opportunity for a Russia endeavoring to make the difficult adjustments necessitated by Stalin's death; how welcome was this bickering between her enemies while she was resolving her own internal struggle for power. It was most unfortunate that interallied conflict became critical just as the West was achieving its greatest success to date in the "cold war." On September 6 West Germany voted overwhelmingly against candidates standing for German unity behind the "iron curtain." Unfortunately, these two developments were closely related; the future of a reconstructed Western Germany was another bone of contention between the United States and her European allies—especially France.

The Challenge of Farm Policy. Giving in to protectionist sentiment was scarcely a way to implement a philosophy of government retrenchment. At the same time, however, it was not trade policy that put the Republican program under the greatest pressure. This distinction must be awarded rather to the farm price support issue—the second great problem to which the new government was forced to give close attention.

Agricultural prices took their sharpest post-Korea dip shortly after inauguration day, and in this important political sense the problem was accentuated. Even more important, however, the continuing dollar shortage meant that a much more fundamental readjustment would also soon be involved. Although comparative advantage had been steadily moving against the United States in the field of agriculture as this country achieved pre-eminence as an industrial nation, war and foreign aid had for some years operated to minimize the burden of this transition. Now, with agricultural exports at levels far above those which could be sustained in the absence of extensive dollar aid abroad, the tapering off of aid foreshadowed another painful pressure on farm prices.

The situation was ironical to say the least. With some $3 billion worth of "surplus" farm products in government hands and no end in sight, it was plain that the administration would have to place this problem high on the agenda. But so deeply rooted were price supports as a solution that it

TABLE 145. AN "ARTIFICIAL" PROP CRUMBLES

	Agricultural Products (1924-1929 = 100)			
	Exported			Imported
Year *	Total	Cotton	Wheat and Flour	Total
1940	63	77	29	102
1941	25	15	22	128
1947	100	46	201	102
1948	90	24	266	100
1949	109	56	278	102
1950	97	68	172	104
1951	93	50	204	119
1952	111	66	262	108
1953	82	35	177	111

* Twelve-month period ending in June.
Source: Department of Agriculture.

seemed certain the government could not develop an alternative approach, despite the fact that a good case could be made for the proposition that this solution was an important part of the underlying problem. Although declining exports were expected to be one factor in the lean years ahead for agriculture, who could doubt that the price supports designed to protect the farmer were also helping to dry up exports?

General legislation was not required at the moment. Existing laws guaranteed 90 per cent of parity on basic crops for two more years, and Washington officials were only too happy to honor this commitment. This fact allowed a little time for "experimentation" with solutions more in keeping with Republican proclivities. And what were these proclivities? President Eisenhower had campaigned vigorously on a platform calling for 100 per cent of parity "in the market place," a terminology vaguely reminiscent of the wording of Calvin Coolidge's vetoes of the McNary-Haugen measures.

The first opportunity to try for something different arose early in the year in connection with butter. By now, in part because of butter price supports, oleomargarine production was greater than that of butter, and for this reason butter could logically be taken as an excellent example of the need for an altered policy. When asked by dairymen to use his discretion to continue supports at 90 per cent of parity, Secretary of Agriculture Benson agreed but bluntly served notice on these producers that he would expect them to take the initiative (and soon) in working out a more satisfactory solution to their problem—meaning presumably one which would permit butter to get its support from "the market place." A similar approach was implicit in his refusal six months later to support the price of beef despite an especially sharp drop in these prices.

If this approach was based upon an assumed desire on the part of farmers for less government intervention, the administration was soon disappointed. In the face of large carryovers from previous crops and an abundant harvest in the offing, wheat and cotton farmers were asked to choose between no production controls with price supports at 50 per cent of parity and acreage quotas with price supports at 90 per cent of parity. By margins so great as to leave no doubt about their preference, farmers voted for high-level supports. (The joker, of course, was that Congress could often be counted on to modify the crop restrictions imposed by the Secretary of Agriculture.) At an uncomfortably early date, thus, the new government found itself being swept along by the current of the status quo, and a "new look" in farm policy seemed as far away as ever.

Repercussions from Taft-Hartley. The third chronic problem the new administration was compelled to face was the issue of labor-management relations. Many Republicans, of course, would have been delighted to rest content with existing labor laws, or even to make their antilabor provisions more stringent. But a strong appeal had been made to labor in the campaign, looking toward a softening of some of the harshest provisions of the Taft-Hartley Act, and there seemed to be no alternative but to follow through. Matters in which labor was especially interested included the legal status of economic strikers in representation elections, what had come to be referred to as the "hair-trigger" use of federal injunctions, the greater freedom employers now had to work against union organizations, and the special preference Taft-Hartley had given state "right to work" laws over its own union-security clauses. Indeed this last item was rapidly becoming the most critical one on the list—for both sides. No less than a dozen states had passed legislation outlawing the union shop, and several more were in the process. Thus the strategy behind this provision in the Taft-Hartley Act was amply vindicated, and for this reason labor was training its heaviest artillery upon it.

The first step in this process of following through was the appointment of Martin Durkin, international president of the plumbers' union, as Secretary of Labor. (It was at this point that the much exaggerated quip arose that the Cabinet consisted of "nine millionaires and one plumber.") This gave labor a useful vantage point from which to press its demands, although it did represent a shift from the more radical Congress of Industrial Organizations to the sedate American Federation of Labor in the inner government circle. However, the question still remained whether the voice of the "plumber" could make itself heard in a council dominated by "millionaires."

From the beginning drama marked developments in this area. First, a document containing several provisions favorable to labor and apparently enjoying White House support was circulated on Capitol Hill. But as soon as Congressional leaders began to get the drift of its emphasis, the reaction was so intense that the paper was withdrawn by the White House with the explanation that it was only a "rough working paper." When months later it became apparent that Congressional resistance would be too strong to enact legislation of the sort labor was insisting upon, the Secretary of Labor resigned after aiming a parting blast at the President for "breaking his word." So bitter did this turn of events make labor that when shortly thereafter Vice-President Nixon delivered a conciliatory address at the annual convention of the American Federation of Labor for President Eisenhower, he was met with boos and hisses.

Temporarily denied access to the center of power, organized labor was left to its own resources. There was, to be sure, much work to be done quite apart from amending the Taft-Hartley Act—or perhaps in part because of the failure of the movement to amend. For example, labor's own disunity continued to be frustrating and debilitating. No longer was the original distinction between the two great labor organizations realistic; both now included craft unions and both likewise included industrial unions. Even in 1953 genuine unity was still far in the future, awaiting (among other things) a more satisfactory settlement of power relationships within an all-inclusive labor body. However, during that year an event did take place which suggested future possibilities as well as highlighting a major obstacle. A "no-raiding" pact was agreed to by the two organizations —although the powerful teamsters' group in the American Federation of Labor refused to accept this effort at integration.

Steps were also taken in 1953 to remove another cancerous growth which had long plagued labor. That was the problem of "crime on the waterfront," the racketeering which had over the years come to be associated with dockworkers and their unions. Taking an unusually strong stand, the American Federation of Labor voted to expel the affiliate then representing East Coast dockworkers and to sponsor another organization. The battle centered, logically enough, in New York, and before it was over the government of the state of New York had sided actively with the Federation and John L. Lewis had joined forces with the union being purged. The ensuing struggle could scarcely be said to have been "won" by either group. Although the old union managed to eke out a bare majority in a bitter representation election, the fight itself seemed to have dramatically reformed its character and to that extent resolved the problem over which the battle was fought. For the time being at least the "shape-up," a system in which the jobs available that day were literally auctioned off every morning to the highest bidder, was a thing of the past.

Perhaps 1953 was not a fair test for a new administration seeking to reverse twenty epoch-making years of American history. There were too many difficult problems arising all at once, and one year was too short a time at best for the new philosophy really to take root. But, whether fair or not, American democracy rolls inexorably onward; elections are timed according to the calendar and not according to what might from certain other standpoints be considered "reasonable." In a series of critical tests—in Wisconsin, in New Jersey, and in New York—the Republicans in October and November were forced to ask the people to pass judgment. Overwhelmingly, in every case, that judgment was adverse.

Here again it was appropriate to ask, What did it mean? Republicans can be pardoned for easily accepting the rationalization that in view of the difficulties they faced they had not been given enough time. But here also there was an alternative explanation—one which seemed somewhat more convincing as 1953 drew to a close. Perhaps it meant that Americans did not really want the trend toward security by way of big government reversed after all. As they began to ponder whether this was or was not the correct interpretation, many people now recalled a fact which had almost dropped from sight—that the winner in the voting the year before had been a national war hero and not Republicanism. Besides, was it not unmistakably plain that even Republicans were less interested in reducing the government's power than in altering its beneficiaries?

QUESTIONS FOR DISCUSSION

1. What were the major differences between the economic problems posed by World War II and those created by the war in Korea?
2. Who was "right" and who "wrong" in the controversy between the Treasury and the Federal Reserve System? Was this an appropriate time for this question to be raised?
3. What were the economic foundations of the shift in foreign policy away from "internationalism" at this time? Was this change in emphasis a desirable one?
4. What was the international trade problem in 1952-53? What steps might have been taken to resolve it, and why were these steps not taken?
5. What is meant by the term "dollar shortage," and why was the United States so concerned about it? How is the "dollar shortage" related to American tariff policy? To the problem of currency convertibility?
6. Which side of the "trade not aid" controversy had the better argument?
7. Were the issues involved in the steel strike basic or trivial? Was there a more effective way of dealing with this situation?
8. What was the meaning of the 1952 election from the standpoint of economic policy?
9. How fundamental were the first steps taken by the Republicans from the standpoint of reversing the advance of "creeping socialism"?
10. Along what lines might a superior approach to the farm problem have been developed?

Chapter 42

NEW DIRECTIONS?

Republicanism in a New Key. Republicans thus chastised by the people might appropriately have echoed the adage, "It never rains but it pours," as they began their second year in control of the government. For no sooner had the excitement aroused by the 1953 elections begun to wane than it became evident that the nation was in the midst of an economic downturn. The index of industrial production had inched downward for six consecutive months until in January it stood more than 8 per cent below the post-Korea peak. An administration already in difficulty, therefore, was now threatened with the greatest scourge known to industrial society—involuntary unemployment.

Of course in January, 1954, no one could tell how serious the new decline was to be, and in part because of this uncertainty much of the attention devoted to the problem focused on the matter of prediction. Was the nation to be devastated by a catastrophe of the magnitude of the "Great Depression," or was this only an inventory adjustment complicated by the tapering off of defense expenditures?

A virtually unanimous opinion (whatever it was worth, considering the primitive state of economic science in this field) quickly emerged. It was that the economy was experiencing only another stage in the return to more "normal" conditions after well over a decade of superprosperity. Furthermore it was emphasized that, although the interim period would no doubt be painful for some groups, the economy would shortly achieve a more restrained prosperity that would be a welcome relief from the forced-draft conditions associated with hot and cold wars.

There was more than a suggestion that these expectations were often based on nothing more substantial than optimism, a refusal to believe that the powerful American economy could again be stricken by a severe depression. But behind this wishful thinking there was a solid basis for doubting that a repetition of the 1930's was in the offing. Just as the earlier period had coincided with the downward portion of a "long-wave" cycle, so the middle 1950's was coinciding with the upswing of such a cycle. Built on a broad foundation of atomic energy (where investment outlays were running in the vicinity of $1 billion per year), new synthetic textiles such as nylon, orlon, dacron, and others, and a great new plastics industry, the current upward dynamism did indeed seem vigorous. Moreover, with research and development activities by private industry and the government absorbing the unprecedented sum of $4 billion per year and utilizing the services of almost two hundred thousand scientists and engineers, it seemed that the economy could not soon lack for innovation opportunities. In any event there was a striking absence of the debate over "secular stagnation" with which the last years of the "Great Depression" had been marked, and the General Motors Corporation dramatically symbolized business defiance of "the attempt to talk the United States into a depression" by announcing a $1 billion expansion program.

All of this, however, was sheer guesswork, and while the administration promptly joined those who were hoping for the best (belittling the change in economic weather in order "to talk the United States out of a depression"), it simultaneously began to prepare for the worst. In striking contrast with the "let-nature-take-her-course" policy followed by Mellon-Coolidge-Hoover Republicanism, President Eisenhower announced that vigorous steps would be taken to prevent a "rolling adjustment" from widening into an "unnecessary recession." Tax reductions scheduled to take effect January 1 were pointed to as an important antideflation measure, although Congress did let a previously scheduled social security tax increase from 1½ to 2 per cent on both employers and employees go into effect. The Federal Reserve System, furthermore, supplemented this move by adopting a "very easy" money policy. And of course the depression-created unemployment insurance program and farm price supports provided a built-in cushion of great value.

Even these developments do not fully indicate the lengths to which the ruling administration was prepared to go. In the *Economic Report of the President* prepared by the Council of Economic Advisers, for example, considerable emphasis was placed upon the possibility of timing public works expenditures for economic stability purposes. Never, it was observed, had so many opportunities been available in this field. Thus fifty-five million motor vehicles (many of them heavy trucks) were creating a need for highway, street, and parking facilities almost more rapidly than they could be provided even in high prosperity. In addition, the nation's continued urbanization plus a postwar increase in the birth rate so great as to confound the experts promised to keep the nation's need for schools, recreation facilities, slum-clearance housing, and the like in a deficiency status for many years. The Council did go out of its way to stress the role in public works projects which should be played by states and municipalities rather than the federal government, and also the importance of avoiding competition with private enterprise. But far from suggesting that public works activities were a necessary evil, it was observed that the "failure to augment our public assets may check the growth of private wealth."

Less closely related to depression but no less significant as indicative of attitudes not customarily associated with the Republican party were several aspects of the President's *State of The Union Message*. In the President's own words: "This Administration recognizes a third great purpose of government: concern for the human problems of our citizens. In a modern economic society, banishment of destitution and cushioning the shock of personal disaster on the individual are proper concerns of all levels of government, including the Federal Government. This is especially true where remedy and prevention alike are beyond the individual's capacity." Specific proposals to implement these sentiments included extending social security to ten million additional persons, expanding programs for rehabilitating disabled citizens, increased government expenditures in the health field (as a preventive measure against "socialized medicine"), and government support in the fields of education and public housing. To be sure, there is often a wide gap between presidential utterances and completed legislative programs, but there was ample justification here for the widespread feeling that there was more than a touch of the "New Deal-Fair Deal" in President Eisenhower's views.

It would be an exaggeration to suppose that the "New Republicanism" was solely a reaction to the recent elections, although this was certainly not a negligible factor. There were other reasons why the party of conservatism, in control of the government for the first time in twenty years, could not afford to follow in the footsteps of Mr. Hoover's administration.

For one thing, in the preceding two decades the country had learned that prosperity cannot be taken for granted—that the assistance of human planning is often helpful, and that the wrath of an aroused citizenry will promptly be visited upon the administration that does not govern itself accordingly. Even more important, America's position in world affairs made a high level of economic activity the most important single component of an effective foreign policy. On the one hand, for this country to drag valuable allies into the pit of a painful deflation (and no responsible person was so naïve as not to understand that deflation in the United States would spread like wildfire) would strain these relationships to the limit. On the other hand, the appearance of a serious depression would go far toward "proving" Russia's thesis that capitalism must ultimately destroy itself in just this way. And finally, a significant downturn in economic activity could easily destroy for a number of years whatever hope remained for building a more wholesome foundation under farm policy and in general reducing the role of government in the economy. In short, a business-dominated government had virtually everything to gain from continued prosperity, however induced, particularly in view of the fact that the public mind still associated the Republican party with economic disaster.

Whatever the factors bringing about this unfamiliar spectacle, however, it is only fair to add that by and large the nation enthusiastically applauded. Indeed, although partisan politics required that the administration be pilloried for moving too slowly, at only two points did a really serious economic controversy arise. The first had to do primarily with the South, while the second was the familiar friction between low and high income groups in one of its most ancient forms.

Economic Reorganization in the South. The South took its stand against the President's program when he announced that government contracts would be used in so far as possible to relieve unemployment. Actually, this proposal was reasonable enough—interpreted from the standpoint of business conditions in the short run. Unfortunately, much more than this was involved in the eyes of many southern leaders. In that section of the country there was taking place a vast economic evolution of great significance not only for the South but for the entire nation as well. After more than fifty years of frustrating half-achievements, industrialization in the South was at last making real strides, and southerners jealously guarding the progress being made saw in the President's attack on unemployment a threat to these successes.

This long overdue adjustment had first commenced in earnest during the 1920's. To be sure, steel production in the Birmingham area had been an important pillar of the southern economy, and textile manufacturing had been steadily if slowly growing for an equally long time. However, the first prerequisite of an industrialized South was a basic reorganization of southern agriculture, a development which first became substantial with the intense pace of agricultural mechanization following World War I. But this favorable beginning had been painfully interrupted by the "Great Depression," and in the middle of that catastrophe the Southeast could still be referred to with accuracy as "The Nation's Number One Economic Problem." Then, with the coming of war, inflation, and war again, the forward march had been resumed, and by mid-century the iron grip of cotton on the South's economy was being visibly loosened. In a twenty-year period cotton acreage had fallen by 65 per cent, although the concentration of production on the best acres and more efficient farming methods had made it possible to produce almost as many pounds of cotton on the reduced number of acres.

But if the first requisite for a more healthy economy in the South was to lessen her stubborn dependence upon cotton, an indispensable corollary was to employ the resources thus freed more advantageously. One way of achieving this objective was through greater diversification in agriculture.

Each part of the region found new opportunities for specialization in its own way—climatic conditions, soil types, and other natural factors determining the details of these adjustments. Florida became a dominant factor in the growing of citrus and developed a thriving truck-farming business, Georgia found an important new opportunity in the raising of chickens and

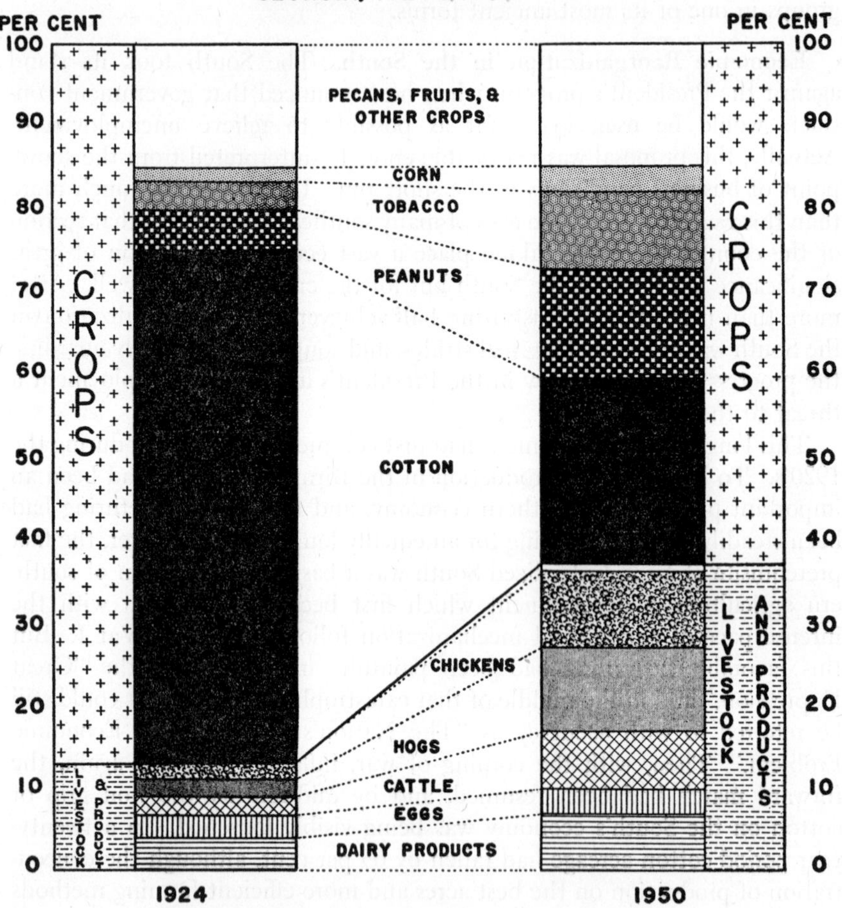

FIGURE 20. Economic Transformation in Georgia.

Source: By permission from University of Georgia Bureau of Business Research.

became in a few short years a major center of broiler production in the nation, and several states rapidly increased the number and quality of their dairy herds and meat producing animals. Whatever the specialty in particular cases, however, there was a close correlation between the progress made in these directions and improvement in per capita incomes.

Although much progress was possible through agricultural diversification, this outlet for released resources would not alone have made possible the economic improvement the South was enjoying, for agriculture in America was a *relatively* declining industry. The rest of this impetus, therefore, had to come from an expansion of secondary and tertiary industries—most notably manufacturing. By mid-century the Southeast was producing almost one-sixth of the total manufactures of the nation, the largest single industry being textile mill products where the Southeast's share of national output was almost 50 per cent.

TABLE 146. ONE VIEW OF THE NEW SOUTH

	Manufacturing Production					
	Workers		Value Added per Worker		Annual Wages per Worker	
Item	1939	1947	1939	1947	1939	1947
Southeast, total *	1,196	1,736	$2,152	$5,008	$760	$1,908
Southeast, textile *	468	545	$2,975	$4,905	$704	$1,922
Southeast, per cent of United States	15.3	14.6	68.6	80.2	66.0	75.2

* Workers in thousands.
Source: Department of Commerce.

Diversification of agriculture and the growth of manufacturing were in their turn supplemented by still a third factor making for an improvement in per capita income. Although this region had the highest net birth rate in the nation, it also had the highest rate of out-migration. Thus while low wage rates along with the availability of important industrial raw materials were drawing capital into the South, higher income levels elsewhere were withdrawing labor. These two forces combined were steadily creating a labor-capital ratio more nearly comparable with that prevailing in other parts of the nation. In the short period of twenty years the Southeast had increased its share of total national income from 10½ to almost 14 per cent, and its per capita income from one-half to two-thirds of the national average.

In the circumstances it is not surprising that southerners were jealous of the progress they were making, particularly when President Eisenhower's program seemed to favor their principal rival in textile manufacturing—New England. Furthermore, the South's newly achieved affluence was at the moment hanging by a slender thread for a number of entirely different reasons. First, southern agricultural income was still closely bound up with

TABLE 147. ANOTHER VIEW OF THE NEW SOUTH

	Income Payments to Individuals					
			Per Capita			
	Total as a Per Cent of United States		Average		Per Cent of United States	
Region	1929	1949	1929	1949	1929	1949
United States	100	100	$680	$1,330	100	100
Southeast	10.51	13.71	344	882	51	66
New England	8.22	6.71	838	1,395	123	105
Middle East	33.70	27.99	926	1,565	136	118
Southwest	5.03	6.61	464	1,166	68	88
Central	29.32	28.40	720	1,414	106	106
Northwest	4.75	4.98	534	1,273	78	96
Far West	8.47	11.60	865	1,610	127	121

Source: Department of Commerce.

cotton, a product currently threatened by a falling-off of foreign demand and in serious competition with synthetic textiles at home. Second, the floor under agricultural income was the price-support program, a program the administration was under considerable pressure to modify. Third, in the South's cotton fields thousands of workers were facing a competition with the machine which in the end would probably drive them from the land. Fourth, work opportunities for most of these displaced agricultural workers would have to be found in manufacturing, especially textile manufacturing, and expansion in this area would bring the South more and more into competition with the Japanese as well as with virtually every young industrial region in the world. And finally, taking the world economy as a whole, textile manufacturing facilities were at the moment overbuilt, with the result that depression haunted the industry in every corner of the globe.

The Challenge of Economic Policy. Little came of the South's protest early in 1954, although it is possible that the President's unemployment policy was not carried out as rigorously as it would have been if no protest had been raised. Perhaps also this issue receded into the background because a much more fundamental one arose almost immediately—an issue likewise taking reference from the inclement economic weather the nation was experiencing.

Almost everyone agreed that the time had come to revise the tax structure that had grown up in the preceding quarter of a century. There were, however, a number of ideas as to the best way to accomplish this task, and not alone because the problem of the government's revenue was still complicated by the felt need in some quarters to balance the budget. As just one illustration of the wide variety of approaches suggested, the National Association of Manufacturers proposed a federal sales tax to (among other things) broaden the tax base and shift more of the Treasury's revenue reliance away from an income foundation highly vulnerable to recession. This proposal was promptly shoved to one side; leaders in both political parties agreed that such an approach was not politically feasible in the face of one of the most difficult and important elections in a number of years.

Partly because 1954 was an election year, and partly because the administration was deeply committed to an antideflationary policy, it was decided early in the debate that taxes were to be reduced and that compensating increases would not be imposed—that, in other words, all hope of fully balancing the budget was to be abandoned for the time being. There was early agreement also that the first step in tax revision should be to modify (if not repeal) many of the special "luxury" excises which had been imposed for war purposes.

Having reached agreement on these points, the several parties at interest settled down to the really fundamental question. Where should the tax burden fall? Should tax savings for consumers (the excise adjustment) be matched by reductions favoring the business community, or should reductions benefiting consumers be further expanded? Around this issue was to rage the most basic controversy to which the appearance of a new recession gave rise.

As was to be expected the administration took the side of tax savings for businessmen. The argument here was that the existing tax structure had grown up when long-term growth in the economy was a secondary matter—when the nation was too preoccupied first with depression and then with security to give serious thought to whether taxes facilitated or inhibited economic progress. Now, however, this matter could no longer be treated as secondary; especially against the background of "cold war" was the performance of the American economy of crucial importance. Only an economy in which business was not "fettered" by antibusiness policies could produce the goods needed for defense in addition to providing a rising standard of living for a rapidly growing population.

Democrats just as quickly took the other side. Business, they insisted, will produce and expand as long as goods can be sold at a profit—as long, that is, as consumers have adequate purchasing power. This being the case it seemed obvious that the appropriate tax policy was to reduce the consumer's tax burden still further. Besides, so this argument went, these relationships are especially important in a business recession; only by bolstering consumer purchasing power could high level economic activity be restored. And against the Republican observation that investment goods industries were more seriously depressed than consumer goods industries,

Democrats retorted that this was because investment was adjusting to drastic inventory reductions, that small shifts in consumer purchasing are apt to result in large inventory adjustments, and that so much investment had recently been added to the economy that an increased rate of consumption expenditures would be required to support it.

There was merit on both sides of this controversy, and by the same token there was merit in the alternative proposals made by both sides. The Democratic suggestion was to raise the personal exemption provided in the individual income tax from $600 to $700. Republicans, on the other hand, argued for two changes in the taxation of corporate profits. First, businessmen were to be given more flexibility in the depreciation rates used in determining costs for income tax purposes. This would, it was asserted, encourage income-generating investment. Second, in order to reduce an "evil" long abhorred by businessmen, the taxation of dividends in the hands of dividend receivers after the corporation had already paid taxes on this same income (popularly called "double taxation") was to be relaxed somewhat.[1] The first $50 of dividends were to be tax free with lesser reductions for incomes containing more than $50 in dividends.

Changes in depreciation-tax policy occasioned relatively little discussion. After all, in perhaps a majority of instances this change would allow a concern to postpone tax payments but would not reduce the amount of total taxes paid. But when Republicans suggested that the personal exemption be raised for dividend receivers but not for anyone else, they were vigorously challenged. In this connection the opposition was quick to publicize data recently made available by the Federal Reserve Board. According to this study only 8 per cent of all American families owned any corporate stock at all, and of this four million families less than 10 per cent (0.6 per cent of all families) owned 80 per cent of all publicly held stock.

What the outcome of this controversy would have been had other circumstances prevailed can of course not be known. By mid-year, however, it seemed apparent that the recession was not to be severe. Although business activity had dipped too far for the term "inventory adjustment" to be fully descriptive (in part because the middle of the recession coincided with a seasonal budget surplus—March 15), by the first weeks in April the index of industrial production was clearly leveling off. Before the tax bill was

[1] The connection between "double taxation" and the long-range performance of the economy is usually explained along the following lines. If a concern and its dividend receivers are both in the 50 per cent income tax bracket, new investment by the firm must bring in 24 per cent net *before* taxes in order to yield 6 per cent *after* taxes to the individual investor. By contrast, if this income were taxed only once, the necessary net before taxes would be reduced to 12 per cent. It would seem to follow that investments in which capital will have a marginal productivity of 24 per cent will be fewer than those in which marginal productivity is 12 per cent, although this conclusion must be qualified in practice by a number of considerations—especially the fact that the corporation income tax laws permit past losses to be averaged in with present profits.

TABLE 148. A "ROLLING ADJUSTMENT"

Month and Year	Industrial Production *	Prices †					
		Wholesale		Consumer	Factory Weekly Earnings †	Unem-ployment **
		Farm	Others ‡			
July, 1953	100	100	100	100	100	100
March, 1954	90	100	100	100	99	300

* Federal Reserve Board.
† Department of Labor.
‡ Other than farm products and foods.
** Department of Commerce.

finally acted upon, thus, it was understood that the economic dip need not be a major consideration. As a result it was the Republican rather than the Democratic proposal which was finally enacted, although the administration's request had to be modified in order to secure acceptance.

This is not to say, of course, that the recession was over before it had had any effect upon legislation. A substantial public housing project (one closely resembling the proposal abruptly shelved the year before) was approved, and once again the social security program was broadened. Other legislation was passed, too, looking toward the critical November elections. After repeated failures over the preceding thirty years, a deep waterway to the mouth of the St. Lawrence was authorized. Also for the benefit of western farmers (among others) the administration's foreign aid recommendation was sharply reduced, and the President was prevailed upon to withdraw a request for additional tariff reduction authority.

On two issues only was the spirit of compromise wholly absent. With regard to the question of farm price supports the Department of Agriculture thoroughly enraged many midwesterners by drastically lowering the support level for dairy products, and on the very heels of this move the administration used its power to the utmost in preventing the postponement of flexible price supports and modernized parity for a third time. (The pressure of the accumulation of agricultural "surpluses"—currently in the vicinity of $7 billion—had finally grown too great to be longer resisted.) In the field of labor legislation a bill containing a number of amendments to the Taft-Hartley Act—amendments desired by organized labor and supported by President Eisenhower—was threatened with so much "conservative" modification that labor leaders joined with Democrats in defeating it.

As it turned out the "new" Republicanism had calculated very closely indeed in deciding where to give way and where to stand fast. When election returns began coming in on the evening of November 2, it was soon apparent that the victor would win by the narrowest of margins. Ultimately it was the Democratic party that won the right to organize both House and Senate, and President Eisenhower promptly scheduled a legislative conference with Democratic leaders. But even this result was no doubt primarily a reaction to the persistence of an unemployment total of 3,000,000 and the continued decline in the farmer's parity ratio rather than an adverse judgment on Republican policy. Ironically, what it all seemed clearly to mean was that the Republican party would have to compromise sharply with its antiwelfare-state principles to hold its own in election contests.

QUESTIONS FOR DISCUSSION

1. Why did it seem reasonable to doubt in early 1954 that another deep depression was on the way?
2. What were the ruling administration's major reasons for fearing a severe decline?
3. Was the South's protest against the President's unemployment relief program justified? Could there have been long-range consequences of such a policy?
4. In what ways did the "new" South differ from the "old"? Why was the South's adjustment precarious at this time?
5. What would have been the consequences of enacting the Democratic tax program into law?
6. In the final analysis, what differences were there between the "new" and the "old" Republicanism? How can these differences be explained, and why were there so few?

SUGGESTIONS FOR READING

(Arranged in approximate chronological sequence)

PART I

For a general approach to economic history, see EAST, GORDON, *The Geography Behind History* (1938), and SELIGMAN, E. R. A., *The Economic Interpretation of History* (1924).

The European context within which American history began can be found in CHEYNEY, E. P., *The Dawn of a New Era* (1936).

PACKARD, L. B., *The Commercial Revolution* (1927) describes some of the more general consequences of European expansion in the sixteenth century, while the price revolution is treated especially pointedly by HAMILTON, E. J., *American Treasure and the Price Revolution in Spain* (1934).

A variety of points of view with respect to the relationship between religion and economic development is presented in WEBER, MAX, *The Protestant Ethic and the Spirit of Capitalism* (1930), ROBERTSON, H. M., *The Rise of Economic Individualism* (1933), and TAWNEY, R. H., *Religion and the Rise of Capitalism* (1926).

The difficulties, progress, and personalities of early European explorers of the New World are detailed in BREBNER, JOHN B., *The Explorers of North America, 1492-1806* (1933).

On England's rapid outward expansion, especially some of the more dramatic aspects, see WILLIAMSON, J. A., in his *Sir John Hawkins, the Time and the Man* (1927) and his *The Age of Drake* (1938).

Details of the early development of several of England's American colonies are related in CRAVEN, W. F., *Dissolution of the Virginia Company* (1932), HULL, WILLIAM I., *William Penn and the Dutch Quaker Migration* (1935), and MORISON, S. E., *Builders of the Bay Colony* (1930).

SMITH, A. E., *Colonists in Bondage, White Servitude and Convict Labor in America, 1607-1776* (1947) describes the processes and problems involved in the institution of indentured labor, while the history of feudal remnants in the matter of land control is treated in BOND, B. W., *The Quit-Rent System in the American Colonies* (1919). The unique land system developed in New England is described in AKAGI, R. H., *The Town Proprietors of the New England Colonies* (1924).

Comprehensive treatments of early colonial America can be found in ANDREWS, C. M., *The Colonial Period in American History* (1934-38), and OSGOOD, H. L., *The American Colonies in the Seventeenth Century* (1904-07).

In BRUCE, PHILIP A., *Economic History of Virginia in the Seventeenth Century* (1935), and CRAVEN, W. F., *The Southern Colonies in The Seventeenth Century* (1949) the focus of attention is on the colonies to the south.

WEEDEN, WILLIAM B., *Economic and Social History of New England* (1890) presents a detailed picture of the problems encountered in, and the growth of, New England.

HACKER, L. M., *The Triumph of American Capitalism* (1940) gives an account of the origins of capitalism in colonial America.

The nature and implications of British mercantilism as applied to New World colonies are analyzed by BEER, G. L., *The Old Colonial System* (1912), HARPER, L. A.,

The English Navigation Laws (1939), and NETTELS, C. P., *The Roots of American Civilization* (1938).

Treatments of specialized aspects of colonial economic life are available in CLARK, V. S., *History of Manufactures in the United States* (1929), DEWEY, D. R., *Financial History of the United States* (1924), JOHNSON, E. R., and ASSOCIATES, *History of Foreign and Domestic Commerce of the United States* (1915), and SCHAFER, JOSEPH, *The Social History of American Agriculture* (1936).

For a description of colonial growth, problems, and relationships in the later colonial period, see OSGOOD, H. L., *The American Colonies in the Eighteenth Century* (1924-28).

A detailed picture of business in Boston in the eighteenth century is contained in BAXTER, W. T., *The House of Hancock* (1945).

Special attention is given to the events leading up to the "War for Independence" by BEER, G. L., *British Colonial Policy, 1754-1765* (1907), and VAN TYNE, C. H., *The Causes of the War of Independence* (1922).

The story of the role played by businessmen during the revolutionary crisis is told by HARRINGTON, V. D., *The New York Merchant on the Eve of the Revolution* (1935), and SCHLESINGER, A. M., *The Colonial Merchants and the American Revolution* (1918).

Economic aspects of the Revolution itself are analyzed by DEWEY, D. R., *Financial History of the United States* (1924), EAST, R. A., *Business Enterprise in the American Revolutionary Era* (1938), NEVINS, ALLAN, *The American States During and After the Revolution, 1775-1789* (1924), VAN TYNE, C. H., *The Loyalists in the American Revolution* (1929), and WINSOR, JUSTIN, *The Westward Movement, 1763-1798* (1897).

Debate on the "criticalness" of "the critical period" is joined by FISKE, JOHN, *The Critical Period in American History* (1888), and MCLAUGHLIN, A. C., *The Confederation and the Constitution* (1905) on one side, and JENSEN, MERRILL, *The Articles of Confederation* (1948) and *The New Nation* (1950) on the other.

The economic background of the making and ratification of the Constitution is dealt with in BEARD, C. A., *An Economic Interpretation of the Constitution of the United States* (1914).

BASSETT, J. S., *The Federalist System* (1906), and BEARD, C. A., *The Economic Origins of Jeffersonian Democracy* (1915) discuss the development of the Hamiltonian program and the difficulties encountered in its enactment.

The transition from Federalism to Anti-Federalism is recounted in CHANNING, EDWARD, *The Jeffersonian System* (1906), and MAI, CHIEN TSENG, *Fiscal Policies of Albert Gallatin* (1930).

PRATT, J. W., *Expansionists of 1812* (1925) gives a concise account of the factors which generated the War of 1812, while the all-important financial aspects of that conflict are presented by DEWEY, D. R., *Financial History of the United States* (1924).

A glimpse of business and one of the nation's outstanding businessmen during this period is available in PORTER, KENNETH W., *John Jacob Astor* (1931).

The industrial revolution in England, together with a description of its overflow into the rest of Western Europe and the United States, is discussed by BOWDEN, WITT, *The Industrial Revolution* (1928), MANTOUX, PAUL, *The Industrial Revolution in the Eighteenth Century* (1928), and USHER, A. P., *A History of Mechanical Inventions* (1954).

The emergence of the tariff as a vital political and economic issue in the United States is discussed by STANWOOD, EDWARD, *Tariff Controversies in the Nineteenth Century* (1903).

An analysis of the new nation, with particular emphasis on this aspect of post-War of 1812 development, is KROUT, JOHN A., and FOX, DIXON R., *The Completion of Independence, 1790-1830* (1930).

PART II

The financial dimension of the prosperity after the War of 1812 is discussed by CATTERALL, C. H., *The Second Bank of the United States* (1903), and SMITH, W. B., *Economic Aspects of the Second Bank of the United States* (1953).

DICK, EVERETT, *The Dixie Frontier* (1948) describes the expansion of the cotton economy during this period.

The revolution of transportation brought about by the introduction of steam is the subject of HATCHER, HARLAN, *The Great Lakes* (1944), HUNTER, LOUIS C., *Steamboats on the Western Rivers* (1949), and LANE, WHEATON J., *Commodore Vanderbilt: An Epic of the Steam Age* (1942).

Tariff history after the War of 1812 is treated in STANWOOD, EDWARD, *Tariff Controversies in the Nineteenth Century* (1903), and TAUSSIG, F. W., *Tariff History of the United States* (1931). A detailed and intimate view written from the standpoint of Calhoun's role in the tariff controversy is WILTSE, C. M., *John C. Calhoun* (1944).

Various aspects of manufacturing and the rise of the factory system are dealt with in BATHE, GREVILLE and DOROTHY, *Oliver Evans: A Chronicle of Early American Engineering* (1935), CLARK, V. S., *History of Manufactures in the United States* (1929), GIBB, GEORGE S., *The Whitesmiths of Taunton* and *The Sacco-Lowell Shops* (1946 and 1950, respectively), GREEN, CONSTANCE M., *Holyoke, Massachusetts: A Case History of the Industrial Revolution in America* (1941), HAZARD, BLANCHE, *The Organization of the Boot and Shoe Industry in Massachusetts Before 1875* (1921), MOORE, CHARLES W., *Timing a Century: History of the Waltham Watch Company* (1945), and WARE, CAROLINE, *The Early New England Cotton Manufacture* (1931).

Special attention is given to commercial relations between the United States and England by BENNS, F. LEE, *The American Struggle for the British West India Carrying-Trade, 1774-1829* (1923), while DANGERFIELD, GEORGE, *The Era of Good Feelings* (1952), has narrowed his presentation essentially to the period of the 1820's. Specialized aspects of these relationships are examined by JENKS, LELAND H., *The Migration of British Capital to 1875* (1927).

For developments on the money and banking fronts prior to the Civil War, see CALDWELL, S. A., *A Banking History of Louisiana* (1935), CHADDOCK, ROBERT E., *The Safety Fund Banking System in New York* (1910), DEWEY, D. R., *State Banking Before the Civil War* (1910), and MILLER, HARRY E., *Theories of Banking in the United States Before 1860* (1927).

ALBION, R. G., has described the rise of New York to a position of dominance, with special emphasis on trade and commerce. See his *The Rise of New York Port* (1939). The story of the Erie Canal is told in another way by BOBBÉ, DOROTHIE, in her *DeWitt Clinton* (1933).

The changing fortunes of the merchant marine and international trade are recounted in HUTCHINS, J. G. B., *American Maritime Industries and Public Policy, 1789-1914* (1941).

An intimate view of the unrest of the late 1820's and early 1830's can be found in FISH, CARL R., *The Rise of the Common Man, 1830-1850* (1937), and SCHLESINGER, A. M., Jr., *The Age of Jackson* (1945). More detailed analyses of this period from the standpoint of the evolution of the labor movement are KUCZYNSKI, JÜRGEN, *A Short History of Labour Conditions Under Industrial Capitalism* (1943), PERLMAN, SELIG, *History of Trade Unionism in the United States* (1922), and SHLAKMAN, VERA, *Economic History of a Factory Town* (1935).

For a thorough analysis of the public school movement in its beginnings, see CREMIN, LAWRENCE, *The American Common School: An Historic Conception* (1951).

The Jacksons and the Lees (1937) by PORTER, KENNETH W., contains much information on the transition during this period from merchant capitalism to specialization.

The trials and tribulations of agriculture during the first decades of rapid industrialization are told by CARRIER, LYMAN, *The Beginnings of Agriculture in America* (1923), and SCHAFER, JOSEPH, *The Social History of American Agriculture* (1936).

Some of the complexities of the public land question as it related itself to every other major issue are presented by STEPHENSON, G. M., *The Political History of the Public Lands from 1840 to 1862* (1917), and WELLINGTON, R. G., *The Political and Sectional Influence of the Public Lands* (1914).

The westward movement which undergirded the question of land policy is discussed by CHITTENDEN, H. M., *The American Fur Trade of the Far West* (1902), SAKOLSKI,

A. M., *The Great American Land Bubble* (1932), TURNER, F. J., *Rise of the New West* (1906), and WHITE, S. E., *The Forty-Niners* (1920).

General transportation development as first the canal and then the railroad captured men's imaginations is chronicled in KIRKLAND, E. C., *Men, Cities, and Transportation* (1948), LANE, WHEATON J., *From Indian Trail to Iron Horse* (1929), MAGILL, C. E., and ASSOCIATES, *History of Transportation in the United States Before 1860* (1917), PHILLIPS, U. B., *A History of Transportation in the Eastern Cotton Belt to 1860* (1908), and TAYLOR, G. R., *The Transportation Revolution* (1951).

The pattern of events leading to and flowing from the "Panic of 1837" is analyzed by BOURNE, E. G., *The History of the Surplus Revenue of 1837* (1909), MCGRANE, R. C., *The Panic of 1837* (1924), and SMITH, W. B., and COLE, A. H., *Fluctuations in American Business, 1790-1860* (1935).

The fascinating if somewhat disgraceful story of state debts during this period is set forth in MCGRANE, R. C., *Foreign Bondholders and American State Debts* (1935).

Why and how the independent treasury system came into existence, together with some aspects of its aftermath, are examined by KINLEY, DAVID, *The Independent Treasury of the United States and Its Relations to the Banks of the Country* (1910). See also TAUS, ESTHER R., *Central Banking Functions of the United States Treasury, 1789-1941* (1943).

DAVIS, J. S., in his *Essays in the Early History of American Corporations* (1917) has portrayed the difficulties and first successes of the corporate form of business enterprise in this country. Also helpful in this connection are BLANDI, J. G., *Maryland Business Corporations* (1934), CADMAN, JOHN W., *The Corporation in New Jersey* (1949), and HARTZ, LOUIS, *Economic Policy and Democratic Thought: Pennsylvania, 1776-1860* (1948).

Much of the romance and significance of railroad development are captured in the numerous studies of individual roads. Included in this list are BOGEN, JULES I., *The Anthracite Railroads* (1927), GATES, PAUL W., *The Illinois Central Railroad and Its Colonization Work* (1934), HUNGERFORD, EDWARD, *The Story of the Baltimore and Ohio Railroad, 1827-1927* (1928), MOTT, E. H., *Between the Ocean and the Lakes: The Story of the Erie* (1902), OVERTON, RICHARD C., *Burlington West: A Colonization History of the Burlington Railroad* (1941), STEVENS, F. W., *The Beginnings of the New York Central Railroad* (1926), and WILSON, WILLIAM B., *History of the Pennsylvania Railroad Company* (1899).

Various aspects of the deepening intersectional crisis are treated in COLE, ARTHUR C., *The Irrepressible Conflict, 1850-1865* (1934), FONER, P. S., *Business and Slavery: The New York Merchants and the Irrepressible Conflict* (1941), HACKER, L. M., *The Triumph of American Capitalism* (1940), NEVINS, ALLAN, *Ordeal of the Union* (1947), RUSSEL, R. B., *Economic Aspects of Southern Sectionalism* (1923), SCHERER, JAMES A. B., *Cotton as a World Power* (1916), TURNER, F. J., *The United States, 1830-1850* (1935), and VAN DEUSEN, J. G., *Economic Bases of Disunion in South Carolina* (1928).

For detailed analyses of the different systems of agriculture growing up in the several parts of the country, see BIDWELL, P. W., and FALCONER, J. I., *History of Agriculture in the Northern United States, 1620-1860* (1925), and GRAY, L. C., *History of Agriculture in the Southern United States to 1860* (1933).

Glimpses of agricultural mechanization can be found in CLARK, NEIL M., *John Deere: He Gave to the World the Steel Plow* (1937) and HUTCHINSON, WILLIAM T., *Cyrus Hall McCormick* (1930 and 1935).

Labor problems and programs in the years preceding the Civil War are discussed in general terms by JOSEPHSON, HANNAH, *The Golden Threads: New England Mill Girls and Magnates* (1949), WARE, N. J., *The Industrial Worker, 1840-1860* (1924), and ZAHLER, HELEN S., *Eastern Workingmen and National Land Policy, 1829-1862* (1941).

Closer attention is given to reform movements as such by BESTOR, ARTHUR E., *Backwoods Utopias* (1950), and TYLER, ALICE F., *Freedom's Ferment: Phases of American Social History to 1860* (1944).

An account of the rise and fall of the clipper ship is given by CLARK, ARTHUR H., *The Clipper Ship Era* (1910).

For the story of immigration during this period, together with its impact on the immigrant and the American environment, see ERNST, ROBERT, *Immigrant Life in New York City, 1825-1863* (1949), HANDLIN, OSCAR, *Boston's Immigrants, 1790-1865* (1941), and HANSEN, M. L., *The Atlantic Migration, 1607-1860* (1940).

Material on the "Panic of 1857" can be found in GIBBONS, J. S., *The Banks of New York and the Panic of 1857* (1858), SMITH, W. B., and COLE, A. H., *Fluctuations in American Business, 1790-1860* (1935), and VAN VLECK, G. W., *The Panic of 1857* (1943).

PART III

FITE, E. D., *Social and Industrial Conditions in the North During the Civil War* (1910) is a study of the northern economy during the war, while SCHWAB, JOHN C., *The Confederate States of America* (1901) is a similar analysis of the southern economy.

Somewhat more general discussions of economic developments during this period are COLE, A. C., *The Irrepressible Conflict* (1934), and RANDALL, J. G., *The Civil War and Reconstruction* (1937).

The spotlight is turned on the financial aspects of the war by DEWEY, D. R., *Financial History of the United States* (1924), and DAVIS, A. M., *The Origin of the National Banking System* (1910).

An intimate account of the role played by Jay Cooke in securing funds for the federal government is given by OBERHOLTZER, E. P., *Jay Cooke: Financier of the Civil War* (1907).

Europe's attitude toward the war in America is developed by JORDAN, D., and PRATT, E. S., *Europe and the American Civil War* (1931).

GROSSMAN, JONATHAN, *William Sylvis: Pioneer of American Labor* (1945) includes a close-up of labor conditions during this era and labor's struggle for self-improvement.

For general discussions of the problems and progress of reconstruction, see BEALE, H. K., *The Critical Year* (1930), and RANDALL, J. G., *The Civil War and Reconstruction* (1937).

More specific analysis of the financial problems associated with the aftermath of the Civil War can be found in MITCHELL, W. C., *History of the Greenbacks* (1903).

Some of the drama as well as the problems associated with the continued westward expansion are related in BILLINGTON, R. A., *Westward Expansion* (1949), GOODRICH, CARTER, and ASSOCIATES, *Migration and Economic Opportunity* (1936), ISE, JOHN, *The United States Forest Policy* (1920), ROBBINS, R. M., *Our Landed Heritage—The Public Domain, 1776-1936* (1942), and TURNER, F. J., *The Frontier in American History* (1920).

Among the many helpful discussions of the rapid industrial and technological advance after the Civil War are CLARK, V. S., *History of Manufactures in the United States* (1929), CRESSY, EDWARD, *One Hundred Years of Mechanical Engineering* (1937), EAVENSON, H. N., *The First Century and a Quarter of the American Coal Industry* (1942), GIDDENS, PAUL H., *The Birth of the Oil Industry* (1938), HACKER, L. M., *The Triumph of American Capitalism* (1940), and NATIONAL INDUSTRIAL CONFERENCE BOARD, *A Graphic Analysis of the Census of Manufactures, 1849-1919* (1923).

The more general aspects of railroad development in the last half of the nineteenth century are treated in BAKER, G. P., *The Formation of the New England Railroad Systems* (1937), BOGEN, J. I., *The Anthracite Railroads* (1927), CLEVELAND, F. A., and POWELL, F. W., *Railroad Promotion and Capitalization in the United States* (1909), GRODINSKY, JULIUS, *Railroad Consolidation* (1930), and RIEGEL, R. E., *The Story of the Western Railroads* (1926).

Again the details of this prodigious development can best be seen in studies of individual railroads. In this connection, see especially GATES, PAUL W., *The Illinois Central Railroad and its Colonization Work* (1934), HUNGERFORD, EDWARD, *The Story of the Baltimore and Ohio Railroad, 1827-1927* (1928), MOTT, E. H., *Between the Ocean and the Lakes: The Story of the Erie* (1902), OVERTON, RICHARD C., *Burlington West: A Colonization History of the Burlington Railroad* (1941), STEVENS, F. W.,

The Beginnings of the New York Central Railroad (1926), and WILSON, WILLIAM B., *History of the Pennsylvania Railroad Company* (1899).

Personal glimpses of a few of the men who made this period what it was are offered in ALLEN, F. L., *The Great Pierpont Morgan* (1949), HEDGES, J. B., *Henry Villard and the Northwest Railroads* (1930), HARVEY, GEORGE, *Henry Clay Frick: The Man* (1928), HENDRICK, B. J., *Life of Andrew Carnegie* (1932), LARSON, HENRIETTA M., *Jay Cooke: Private Banker* (1936), NEVINS, ALLAN, *Abram Hewitt, with Some Account of Peter Cooper* (1935) and *Study in Power: John D. Rockefeller* (1953), and O'CONNOR, HARVEY, *The Guggenheims: The Making of an American Dynasty* (1937).

Agrarian expansion and the agrarian revolution after the Civil War are examined by BUCK, S. J., *The Granger Movement* (1913), ELIOT, CLARA, *The Farmer's Campaign for Credit* (1927), HIBBARD, B. H., *Marketing Agricultural Products* (1921), SANFORD, A. H., *The Story of Agriculture in the United States* (1916), SCHAFER, JOSEPH, *The Social History of American Agriculture* (1936), and SHANNON, F. A., *The Farmer's Last Frontier* (1945).

General treatments of the technological progress in agriculture during these years are available in ARDREY, R. L., *American Agricultural Implements* (1894), and ROGIN, LEO, *The Introduction of Farm Machinery in Its Relation to the Productivity of Labor in the Agriculture of the United States During the Nineteenth Century* (1931).

The special agricultural problems of the nonprairie West are analyzed by CRAIG, JOHN A., *Sheep Farming in North America* (1920), DALE, E. E., *The Range Cattle Industry* (1930), DICK, EVERETT, *The Sod-House Frontier* (1937), OSGOOD, E. S., *The Day of the Cattleman* (1929), and WEBB, W. P., *The Great Plains* (1931).

General tariff history after the Civil War is recounted in STANWOOD, EDWARD, *Tariff Controversies in the Nineteenth Century* (1903), TARBELL, IDA M., *The Tariff in Our Times* (1911), and TAUSSIG, F. W., *Tariff History of the United States* (1931). Tariff history as related to the government's finances is treated in NOYES, A. J., *Forty Years of American Finance* (1909).

Labor's painful struggle to find itself in a rapidly industrializing economy is discussed by BEARD, MARY R., *A Short History of The American Labor Movement* (1924), PERLMAN, SELIG, *History of Trade Unionism in the United States* (1922), and WARE, N. J., *The Labor Movement in the United States, 1860-1895* (1929).

Two of the high points of the labor movement of these years are discussed at length in BIMBA, ANTHONY, *The Molly Maguires* (1932), and DAVID, HENRY, *The History of the Haymarket Affair* (1936).

The "Panic of 1873" is discussed in BURTON, THEODORE E., *Financial Crises* (1931), COLLMAN, CHARLES A., *Our Mysterious Panics, 1830-1930* (1931), and SPRAGUE, O. M. W., *History of Crises Under the National Banking System* (1910).

Monetary and financial difficulties associated with the "Panic of 1873" and its aftermath are treated by BARRETT, DON C., *The Greenbacks and the Resumption of Specie Payments* (1931), LARSON, HENRIETTA M., *Jay Cooke: Private Banker* (1936), MITCHELL, W. C., *History of the Greenbacks* (1903), and NOYES, A. J., *Forty Years of American Finance* (1909).

Stirrings of social unrest in the literature of the day can be found in BELLAMY, EDWARD, *Looking Backward* (1888), GEORGE, HENRY, *Progress and Poverty* (1879), and LLOYD, HENRY C., *Wealth Against Commonwealth* (1894).

The first stages of the trust movement are examined at length in JONES, ELIOT, *The Anthracite Coal Combination* (1914), NEVINS, ALLAN, *Sudy in Power: John D. Rockefeller* (1953), RIPLEY, W. Z., *Trusts, Pools, and Corporations* (1905), and TARBELL, IDA M., *The History of the Standard Oil Company* (1904).

For discussions of the immigration problem during this period, see ABBOTT, GRACE, *The Immigrant and the Community* (1917), HANSEN, MARCUS L., *The Immigrant in American History* (1940), HANDLIN, OSCAR, *The Uprooted* (1951), and HOURVICH, I. A., *Immigration and Labor* (1912).

Analyses of railroad problems against the background of the agitation for regulation during these years are available in CLEVELAND, F. A., and POWELL, F. W., *Railroad Promotion and Capitalization in the United States* (1909), DAGGETT, STUART, *Railroad*

Reorganization (1908), HADLEY, A. T., *Railroad Transportation* (1885), RIPLEY, W. Z., *Railroads: Rates and Regulation* (1912), and TARBELL, IDA M., *The Nationalizing of Business* (1936).

Special attention is given to the crisis in the labor movement of the 1880's and the origin of the American Federation of Labor in GOMPERS, SAMUEL, *Seventy Years of Life and Labor: An Autobiography* (1925), LORWIN, L. L., *The American Federation of Labor* (1933), PERLMAN, SELIG, *History of Trade Unionism in the United States* (1922), and POWDERLY, T. V., *Thirty Years of Labor, 1859-1889* (1890).

Various aspects of the "Panic of 1893" and the ensuing depression are examined in KUZNETS, SIMON, *National Product Since 1869* (1946), LINDSEY, ALMONT, *The Pullman Strike* (1942), MCMURRY, D. L., *Coxey's Army* (1929), SPRAGUE, O. M. W., *History of Crises Under the National Banking System* (1910), and WEBERG, FRANK, *The Background of the Panic of 1893* (1929).

The end of the century push by farmers to bring about important modifications of the economic and social system is the subject of HICKS, J. D., *The Populist Revolt* (1931).

PART IV

General tariff history for this period is available primarily in TAUSSIG, F. W., *Tariff History of the United States* (1931).

The major factors involved in the war with Spain are the subject of PRATT, J. W., *Expansionists of 1898* (1930), and MILLIS, WALTER, *The Martial Spirit: A Study of Our War with Spain* (1931).

Various aspects of American imperialism are developed by JENKS, LELAND H., *Our Cuban Colony: A Study in Sugar* (1928), GAYER, A. D., HOMAN, P. T., and JAMES, E. K., *The Sugar Economy of Puerto Rico* (1938), KNIGHT, M. M., *The Americans in Santo Domingo* (1928), MCCAIN, W. L., *The United States and the Republic of Panama* (1937), RIPPY, F. J., *The United States and Mexico* (1926), HAYDEN, J. R., *The Philippines: A Study in National Development* (1942), and GRISWOLD, A. W., *The Far Eastern Policy of the United States* (1938).

Discussions of the trust movement and the problems it was felt to be creating are contained in JONES, ELIOT, *The Anthracite Coal Combination* (1914), MOODY, JOHN, *The Truth About the Trusts* (1904), RIPLEY, W. Z., *Trusts, Pools, and Corporations* (1905), and SEAGER, H. R., and GULICK, C. A., *Trust and Corporation Problems* (1929).

For a full-length treatment of finance capitalism, see EDWARDS, GEORGE W., *The Evolution of Finance Capitalism* (1938).

General studies of the literature of protest characterizing the "muckrake" era are REGIER, C. C., *The Era of the Muckrakers* (1932), and FILLER, LOUIS, *Crusaders for American Liberalism* (1939). More intimate glimpses are offered in STEFFENS, LINCOLN, *Autobiography of Lincoln Steffens* (1931), and RUSSELL, CHARLES E., *Bare Hands and Stone Walls* (1933).

The successes and failures of the reform movement early in the century are analyzed in CHAMBERLAIN, JOHN, *Farewell to Reform* (1932), and FAULKNER, H. U., *The Decline of Laissez Faire* (1951).

The "Panic of 1907" and its aftermath are examined in ALLEN, F. L., *Lords of Creation* (1935), NOYES, A. J., *The War Period of American Finance* (1926), and SPRAGUE, O. M. W., *History of Crises Under the National Banking System* (1910).

Close-ups of some of the better known industrialists of the early nineteenth century are provided by ALLEN, F. L., *The Great Pierpont Morgan* (1949), GLASSCOCK, C. B., *The War of the Copper Kings* (1939), HOLBROOK, STEWART W., *The Age of the Moguls* (1953), JENKINS, J. W., *James B. Duke: Master Builder* (1927), NEVINS, ALLAN, *Ford: The Times, the Man, and the Company* (1954), O'CONNOR, HARVEY, *Mellon's Millions* (1933), and TARBELL, IDA M., *The Life of Elbert H. Gary* (1925).

Labor's special trials and tribulations during the "reform era" are presented in WOLMAN, LEO, *The Growth of American Trade Unions, 1880-1923* (1924), HARVEY, R. H., *Samuel Gompers: Champion of the Toiling Masses* (1935), FRANKFURTER,

Felix, and Greene, N., *The Labor Injunction* (1930), Berman, Edward, *Labor and the Sherman Act* (1930), and Wolman, Leo, *The Boycott in American Trade Unions* (1916).

Valuable insights into the causes and consequences of radical developments in the field of labor are presented in Brissenden, P. F., *The I. W. W.: A Study of American Syndicalism* (1919), Fitch, J. A., *The Causes of Industrial Unrest* (1924), Hunter, Robert, *Violence and the Labor Movement* (1919), and Perlman, Selig, *A Theory of the Labor Movement* (1926).

Monetary reform and the economic and social background which led to it are analyzed by Brandeis, Louis D., *Other People's Money and How the Bankers Use It* (1914), and Noyes, A. J., *The War Period of American Finance* (1926).

The economic background of America's entry into World War I is the subject of Gratton, C. Hartley, *Why We Fought* (1929), and Tansill, C. C., *America Goes to War* (1938).

Generalized discussions of America in the war are Ayers, Leonard P., *The War with Germany* (1919), Paxson, F. L., *American Democracy and the World War* (1939), and Slosson, Preston, *The Great Crusade and After, 1914-1928* (1930).

Specialized aspects of the war economy itself are taken up in Bogart, E. L., *War Costs and Their Financing* (1921), Clarkson, G. B., *Industrial America in the World War* (1923), Hines, W. D., *War History of American Railroads* (1928), Mullendore, W. C., *History of the United States Food Administration* (1941), and Salter, I. A., *Allied Shipping Control* (1922).

For valuable analyses of the cost of a great modern war, see Bogart, E. L., *Direct and Indirect Cost of the Great World War* (1919), and Clark, J. M., *The Cost of the World War to the American People* (1931).

General studies of the postwar adjustments and the prosperous 1920's can be found in National Housing Agency, *Housing After World War I* (1945), Paxson, F. L., *The Postwar Years* (1939), Samuelson, P. A., and Hagen, E. E., *After the War—1918-1920* (1943), and Soule, George, *Prosperity Decade* (1947).

The "big business" dimension of the "return to normalcy" is subjected to close scrutiny in Allen, F. L., *Lords of Creation* (1935), Burns, A. R., *The Decline of Competition* (1936), and Watkins, Myron W., *Industrial Combinations and Public Policy* (1927).

The spotlight is turned more specifically on the Federal Trade Commission by Henderson, G. C., *The Federal Trade Commission* (1925), and National Industrial Conference Board, *Public Regulation of Competitive Practices* (1928).

For the corporate background of this dazzling era, see Berle, A. A., and Means, G. C., *The Modern Corporation and Private Property* (1934).

Technology and mass production as basic characteristics of this decade are discussed in Barclay, H. W., *Ford Production Methods* (1936), Borth, Christy, *Masters of Mass Production* (1945), Burlingame, Roger, *Backgrounds of Power* (1949), Gideion, S., *Mechanization Takes Command* (1948), Jerome, Harry, *Mechanization in Industry* (1934), Kennedy, Edward E., *The Automobile Industry* (1941), Mumford, Lewis, *Technics and Civilization* (1934), and Polakov, W. N., *The Power Age* (1933).

Special topics relating to labor during the 1920's are analyzed in Douglas, P. H., *Real Wages in the United States, 1890-1926* (1930), Dunn, R. W., *The Americanization of Labor* (1927), Lescohier, D. D., and Brandeis, Elizabeth, *History of Labor in the United States, 1896-1932: Labor Conditions and Employer Policies* (1935), Perlman, Selig, and Taft, Philip, *History of Labor in the United States, 1896-1932: Labor Movements* (1935), Lorwin, L. L., *The American Federation of Labor* (1933), and Witte, Edwin E., *The Government in Labor Disputes* (1932).

Economic progress and its consequences for labor are specifically analyzed in Baker, E. F., *Displacement of Men by Machines* (1933), Douglas, Paul H., and Director, Aaron, *The Problem of Unemployment* (1934), Taylor, F. W., *Principles of Scientific Management* (1911), and Veblen, Thorstein, *The Engineers and the Price System* (1921).

The international economy after the war and America's role in it are discussed by KEYNES, J. M., *The Economic Consequences of the Peace* (1920), LARY, HAL B., *The United States in the World Economy* (1943), LEWIS, CLEONA, *America's Stake in International Investment* (1938), and MOULTON, H. G., and PASVOLSKY, LEO, *World War Debt Settlements* (1926).

The economic burden borne by agriculture is discussed in BLACK, J. D., *Agricultural Reform in the United States* (1929), DEPARTMENT OF AGRICULTURE, *Net Farm Income and Parity Report* (1944), ELIOT, CLARA, *The Farmer's Campaign for Credit* (1927), NOURSE, E. G., *American Agriculture and the European Market* (1929), and SELIGMAN, E. R. A., *The Economics of Farm Relief* (1929).

Explanations of business cycles in general and the 1929 downturn in particular are available in CLARK, J. M., *Strategic Factors in Business Cycles* (1934), MITCHELL, F. C., *Business Cycles: The Problem and Its Setting* (1937), and SCHUMPETER, J. A., *Business Cycles* (1929).

On the crash itself, see ALLEN, F. L., *Lords of Creation* (1935), ANGLY, EDWARD, *Oh Yeah* (1931), FISHER, IRVING, *The Stock Market Crash—and After* (1930), HIRST, F. W., *Wall Street and Lombard Street* (1931), and PECORA, FERDINAND, *Wall Street Under Oath* (1939).

PART V

President Hoover's economic policies are presented more or less objectively by SELDES, GILBERT, *The Years of the Locust: America, 1929-1932* (1933). A sympathetic account may be found in MYERS, WILLIAM STARR, and NEWTON, WALTER H., *The Hoover Administration: A Documented Narrative* (1936). A critical but useful campaign analysis is TUGWELL, REXFORD G., *Mr. Hoover's Economic Policy* (1932). The President's own account is available in HOOVER, HERBERT, *The Challenge to Liberty* (1934).

Interrelationships between prosperity, depression, and international economic relationships are discussed in LEAGUE OF NATIONS, *Report on an Inquiry into the Course and Phases of the Present Economic Depression* (1931), and ROBBINS, LIONEL, *The Great Depression* (1934).

For analyses pointed more specifically at the debtor-creditor position of the United States, see LEWIS, CLEONA, *The United States and Foreign Investment Problems* (1948), MADDEN, J. T., NADLER, MARCUS, and SAUVAIN, H. C., *America's Experience as a Creditor Nation* (1937), and WILLIAMS, B. H., *Economic Foreign Policy of the United States* (1929).

For a study of the Smoot-Hawley Tariff and its consequences, see JONES, JOSEPH M., *Tariff Retaliation: Repercussions of the Hawley-Smoot Bill* (1934).

The role of the Reconstruction Finance Corporation in this depression decade is presented in JONES, JESSE H., *RFC: Seven-Year Report to the President and the Congress* (1939).

A voluminous literature is available on the "New Deal." Among the more general economic works on this subject are MITCHELL, BROADUS, *Depression Decade* (1947), and SNYDER, CARL, *Capitalism the Creator* (1940). For a discussion anticipating much of the social and economic program of the next few years, see CHASE, STUART, *A New Deal* (1932).

Studies oriented more to historical developments than economic analysis are BEARD, CHARLES A., and SMITH, GEORGE H., *The Old Deal and the New* (1940), BROOKINGS INSTITUTION, *The Recovery Problem in the United States* (1936), and RAUCH, BASIL, *The History of the New Deal* (1944).

Less detached in viewpoint and somewhat critical are New Republic, *Balance Sheet of the New Deal* (1936), and Editors of the ECONOMIST, *An Analysis and Appraisal of the New Deal* (1937).

Problems and policies relative to unemployment and relief are discussed in NATIONAL RESOURCES PLANNING BOARD, *Security, Work, and Relief Policies* (1942), WORKS PROJECTS ADMINISTRATION, *Five Years of Rural Relief* (1938), HOPKINS, HARRY, *The*

Realities of Unemployment (1937), and LINDLEY, BETTY, and LINDLEY, E. K., *A New Deal for Youth: The Story of the National Youth Administration* (1938).

Housing problems and policies are reviewed in NATIONAL RESOURCES PLANNING BOARD, *Housing: The Continuing Problem* (1940).

Analyses of and some account of the controversies over government spending are available in BURNS, ARTHUR E., and WATSON, DONALD E., *Government Spending and Economic Expansion* (1940), and MOULTON, HAROLD G., *The New Philosophy of the Public Debt* (1938).

Developments in the fields of banking and currency are recounted in WHIPPLE, A. W., *Monetary Management Under the New Deal* (1940), and PARIS, JAMES D., *Monetary Policies of the United States, 1932-1938* (1938).

For the formula for recovery by devaluation see WARREN, GEORGE A., and PEARSON, FRANK A., *Gold and Prices* (1935). A more objective analysis after the formula had failed to produce the expected results is HARDY, C. O., *The Warren-Pearson Price Theory* (1935).

GESELL, GERHARD A., *Protecting Your Dollars: An Account of the Work of the Securities and Exchange Commission* (1940) is a discussion of the background for and early achievements in the fields of security and security exchange regulations.

The plight of the farmer and efforts in his behalf are the subject of DAVIS, JOSEPH S., *On Agricultural Policy, 1926-1938* (1939), DEPARTMENT OF AGRICULTURE, *Agricultural Adjustment: A Report on the Administration of the Agricultural Adjustment Act* (1933-1941), and NOURSE, E. G., *Government in Relation to Agriculture* (1940).

More specific attention is given to the tenant farmer and the share-cropper by JOHNSON, CHARLES S., EMBREE, EDWIN R., and ALEXANDER, W. W., *The Collapse of Farm Tenancy* (1935), and RAPER, ARTHUR F., *Preface to Peasantry* (1936).

The story of the "Okies" and the background of this phenomenon of the period is told in novel form in STEINBECK, JOHN, *The Grapes of Wrath* (1939).

The "capstone of the First New Deal" is analyzed by LYON, L. S., and ASSOCIATES, *The National Recovery Administration: An Analysis and Appraisal* (1935), and JOHNSON, H. S., *The Blue Eagle from Egg to Earth* (1935).

For studies of the foreign economic policies of the "New Deal," together with the context within which they were framed, see TAYLOR, ALONZO E., *The New Deal and Foreign Trade* (1935).

More detailed analyses of the reciprocal trade agreements program are available in DEPARTMENT OF STATE, *The Reciprocal Trade Agreements Program in War and Peace* (1943), and TASCA, H. J., *The Reciprocal Trade Policy of the United States* (1938).

The Tennessee Valley Authority has been a favorite subject for students of social problems. Samples are DUFFUS, R. L., *The Valley and Its People: A Portrait of TVA* (1944), LILIENTHAL, DAVID E., *TVA: Democracy on the March* (1944), and WHITMAN, WILSON, *God's Valley: People and Power Along the Tennessee River* (1939).

Labor's problems and progress under NRA are discussed by MARSHALL, LEON C., *Hours and Wages Provisions in NRA Codes* (1935), and NRA RESEARCH AND PLANNING DIVISION, *Hours, Wages, and Employment Under the Codes* (1935). Also valuable in this connection is HUBERMAN, LEO, *The Labor Spy Racket* (1937), a study of the union-fighting techniques used by employers.

On the rise of the Committee for Industrial Organization, see HARRIS, HERBERT, *Labor's Civil War* (1940), STOLBERG, BENJAMIN, *Tailor's Progress: The Story of a Famous Union and the Men Who Made It* (1944), and WOLMAN, LEO, *Ebb and Flow in Trade Unionism* (1936).

Appraisals of the operations of the Wagner Act during its first years of life can be found in BROOKS, R. R. R., *Unions of Their Own Choosing* (1939), ROSENFARB, JOSEPH, *The National Labor Policy and How It Works* (1940), and SILVERBERG, LOUIS G., *The Wagner Act: After Ten Years* (1945).

Minimum wages–maximum hours and social security legislation are discussed by PHELPS, ORIE W., *The Legislative Background of the Fair Labor Standards Act* (1939), and EPSTEIN, ABRAHAM, *Insecurity: Challenge to America* (1941).

The Temporary National Economic Committee episode is described at length in LYNCH, DAVID, *The Concentration of Economic Power* (1946). See also in this connection ARNOLD, THURMAN, *The Bottlenecks of Business* (1940), and the TNEC monographs themselves.

For the pros and cons of the "Battle of the Ph.D.'s" over stagnation see, on the "liberal" side, HANSEN, A. W., *Full Recovery or Stagnation?* (1938), and BEVERIDGE, W. H., *Full Employment in a Free Society* (1945). On the "conservative" side, see SWANSON, E. W., and SCHMIDT, E. P., *Economic Stagnation or Progress* (1946), and TERBORG, GEORGE, *The Bogey of Economic Maturity* (1945).

A recent and perhaps less biased examination of the "stagnation" episode is ROOSE, KENNETH D., *The Economics of Recession and Revival: An Interpretation of 1937-38* (1954).

The problems associated with the coming of war are discussed in WAR PRODUCTION BOARD, *Converting Industry: Turning a Nation's Production to War* (1942).

War production itself is treated by Bureau of the Budget, *The United States at War* (1947), KUZNETS, SIMON, S., *National Production, War and Prewar* (1944), and NELSON, DONALD M., *Arsenal of Democracy* (1946).

The processes of and the problems associated with inflation, war and postwar, are the subject of CHANDLER, LESTER V., *Inflation in the United States: 1940-1948* (1951).

A wide variety of materials is available dealing with the postwar period, and other items are being added to this list in a steady stream. Particularly helpful as well as readily available are a number of periodicals. Statistical data along with competent technical analyses are presented especially in *Federal Resrve Bulletin, Monthly Labor Review,* and *Survey of Current Business.* More popular in orientation are *Business Week, Fortune, News Week, United States News and World Report,* and *Wall Street Journal.*

A helpful introduction to the problem of America's commanding position in the world economy, oriented especially to the immediate postwar period, is HANSEN, A. W., *America's Role in the World Economy* (1945).

The dollar shortage, causes and cures, is the subject of KINDLEBERGER, C. P., *The Dollar Shortage* (1950), while PIQUET, HOWARD, *Aid, Trade, and the Tariff* (1953) gives a thorough analysis of the American tariff against the background of the dollar shortage.

The economic implications of the "Marshall Plan" are examined in HARRIS, SEYMOUR, *The European Recovery Program* (1948).

General problems confronting international trade relationships at this juncture in world history are presented in BUCHANAN, N. S., and LUTZ, F. A., *Rebuilding the World Economy* (1947), and LEWIS, CLEONA, *The United States and Foreign Investment Problems* (1948).

WILCOX, CLAIR, *A Charter for World Trade* (1949), subjects the proposed International Trade Organization to intensive analysis.

The performance of the economy is analyzed at regular intervals by the COUNCIL OF ECONOMIC ADVISERS, *The Economic Report of the President* (Annual). In this connection see also MOULTON, H. G., *Controlling Factors in Economic Development* (1949), and SLICHTER, S. H., *The American Economy: Its Problems and Prospects* (1948).

Aspects of the continuing labor problem are examined by BAKKE, E. W., and KERR, CLARK, *Unions, Management, and the Public* (1948), DRUCKER, PETER, *The New Society* (1950), GREGORY, C. O., *Labor and the Law* (1949), SEIDMAN, HAROLD, *Union Rights and Union Duties* (1943), and SLICHTER, S. H., *The Challenge of Industrial Relations* (1947).

Industrial evolution and some of its more important implications are the subject of ADAMS, WALTER (Editor), *The Structure of American Industry* (1950), BRADY, ROBERT A., *Business as a System of Power* (1943), GALBRAITH, J. K., *American Capitalism: The Concept of Countervailing Power* (1952), GORDON, R. A., *Business Leadership in the Large Corporation* (1946), KAPLAN, A. D. H., *Big Business in a Competitive Society* (1954), LILIENTHAL, DAVID, *Big Business: A New Era* (1953), POLANYI, KARL, *The Great Transformation* (1944), SCHUMPETER, J. A., *Capitalism,*

Socialism, and Democracy (1950), and Wright, D. M. *Democracy and Progress* (1948).

Financial developments since World War II are treated in Abbott, C. C., *The Federal Debt* (1953), and Studenski, Paul, and Kroos, H. E., *Financial History of the United States* (1952).

Geographical shifts in the pattern of productive activity, especially toward the South, are investigated by Hoover, E. M., *The Location of Economic Activity* (1948), McLaughlin, G. E., and Robock, S., *Why Industry Moves South* (1949), and Mitchell, Broadus, *The Rise of Cotton Mills in the South* (1921).

INDEX